Joseph Payne

Studies in English Poetry

With Short Biographical Sketches and Notes. Seventh Edition

Joseph Payne

Studies in English Poetry
With Short Biographical Sketches and Notes. Seventh Edition

ISBN/EAN: 9783337014841

Printed in Europe, USA, Canada, Australia, Japan

Cover: Foto ©Thomas Meinert / pixelio.de

More available books at **www.hansebooks.com**

STUDIES IN

ENGLISH POETRY

WITH SHORT BIOGRAPHICAL SKETCHES AND NOTES

Intended as a Text-Book for the Higher Classes in Schools

By JOSEPH PAYNE

EDITOR OF "SELECT POETRY FOR CHILDREN"

SEVENTH EDITION, REVISED AND CORRECTED

LONDON
LOCKWOOD & CO., 7 STATIONERS'-HALL COURT
LUDGATE HILL
1874

LONDON: PRINTED BY
SPOTTISWOODE AND CO., NEW-STREET SQUARE
AND PARLIAMENT STREET

PREFACE.

In compiling "Select Poetry for Children," the Editor's aim was to assist in laying the foundation of a pure and just taste, by interesting the mind, at an early age, in poetry of a superior order —high-toned, beautiful, simple, but not childish. The success which that little volume has met with induces him to believe that the object was, in some degree, appreciated. The present work is intended to supply materials, in the specimens themselves, for the higher cultivation of the youthful taste; and by brief explanatory and critical annotations on particular passages, to develop their spirit and beauty, and to make the learning of poetry in schools— what it has hitherto but rarely been—a valuable auxiliary to the study of our mother tongue. Such a study as is here indicated involves, however, not merely an acquaintance with the general meaning of words and their grammatical relations, but a nice investigation into their origin and history—the vicissitudes they have undergone, and their present significance and power. Inquiries of this kind cannot, of course, be extensively pursued at school, but it is well to arouse the pupil to a sense of their importance, and thus prepare his mind for that sympathy with noble thoughts displayed in exquisite language, which is productive of some of our purest enjoyments. The more general diffusion, moreover, of good taste by means of early cultivation, would probably so elevate the public standard as to suppress entirely such offences as are now frequently committed against it.

The work now offered to the candid consideration of parents and teachers is divided into two parts:—the first consisting of miscellaneous poems and extracts; the second, of poems and extracts from the highest class of English poets, chronologically arranged from Chaucer to Burns, showing the progress of the language, and accompanied by short biographical notices and remarks on the spirit and style of each author.

The specimens given in the second part will be found ample and characteristic. Those from Chaucer and Spenser occupy nearly forty pages, and are printed in the original spelling, in order to give a genuine impression of their style. The appended notes will remove every difficulty arising from the obsoleteness of much of the diction.

It is only necessary to add, that the extracts from the works of Campbell, Shelley, and Wordsworth, are inserted by the obliging permission of the proprietors of the respective copyrights.

THE MANSION GRAMMAR SCHOOL,
 Letherhead, Surrey.
  JAN. 30TH, 1845.

ADVERTISEMENT TO THE THIRD EDITION.

The present Edition has been carefully revised and corrected. A few pieces have been withdrawn, and others of a superior character substituted.

                 J. P.

DEC. 1858.

INDEX.

		PAGE
Adam and Eve in Paradise	Milton	335
Address to an Egyptian Mummy	Horace Smith	19
Address to the Sun, Satan's	Milton	330
Address to Winter	Cowper	455
Advantages of a Cultivated Taste	Akenside	418
Alexander Selkirk's Soliloquy	Cowper	68
Alps at Daybreak, the	Rogers	22
Ancient Britain	Cowper	208
Antony's Funeral Oration	Shakspere	278
Athens	Milton	350
Banquet, the, in Paradise Regained	id.	345
Bard, the	Gray	429
Bees	Shakspere	276
Bees		98
Bells, the	Edgar Poe	192
Boadicea	Cowper	2
Bower of Bliss, the	Spenser	262
Burial of Sir John Moore, the	Wolfe	90
Butterfly, to the	Rogers	73
Butterfly, the	Spenser	265
Calendar of Flora, the	Charlotte Smith	23
Calm Winter's Night, a	Shelley	119
Cataract, on a	Coleridge	178
Cataract and the Streamlet, the	Barton	103
Castle of Indolence, the	Thomson	391
Changes	Southwell	164
Character of Shaftesbury, the	Dryden	356
Character of a Good Parson, the	id.	360
Chevy Chace		39
Christmas	Walter Scott	135
Cloud, the	Shelley	143
Cloudland	Coleridge	157
Common Lot, the	Montgomery	10
Comparison, a	Cowper	80
Conclusion of Paradise Lost	Milton	343
Cottager, the	Cowper	111
Cotter's Saturday Night, the	Burns	461
Cruelty to Animals, against	Cowper	179
Crusade, the	T. Warton	73
Cuckoo, to the	Wordsworth	18
Daffodils, the	id.	118

		PAGE
Death-bed, the	Hood	160
Death of an Infant	Mrs. Sigourney	162
Death's Final Conquest	Shirley	57
Dirge over Fidele's Tomb	Collins	224
Dover Cliffs	Shakspere	278
Dying Boy, the	Mrs. Sigourney	175
Dying Gladiator, the	Byron	206
Dying Mother and her Babe, the	Pollok	33
Early Rising and Prayer	Vaughan	162
Elegy written in a Country Churchyard	Gray	60
Emigrants, the	Marvell	169
End of all Earthly Glories	Shakspere	284
England, to	Coleridge	215
English Rivers	Milton	146
Epistle to Joseph Hill, Esq.	Cowper	166
Epitaphs:—		
1. On a Young Lady	B. Jonson	168
2. On the Countess of Pembroke	id.	168
3. Intended for Sir Isaac Newton	Pope	168
4. For the Tomb of Mr. Hamilton	Cowper	168
Evening in Paradise	Milton	337
Eve of the Battle, the	Byron	132
Excelsior	Longfellow	52
Exordium of Paradise Lost, the	Milton	316
Faculties of Man, the	Pope	378
Female Names	Lamb	48
Firmament, the	Habington	98
Flight of Xerxes	Miss Jewsbury	188
Flowers of the Field, the	Keble	182
Friend, to a	Hartley Coleridge	159
Friends	Montgomery	214
Gathering, the	Chaucer	236
Ginevra	Rogers	201
Glory	Milton	346
Glory of God in Creation, the	Addison	5
God's Watchful Care	Cunningham	104
God, the only Comforter	Moore	214
God, the Source of Excellence	Akenside	414
Good Counsail	Chaucer	251
Greece	Byron	100
Grongar Hill	Dyer	138
Happiness	Pope	380
Happy Man, the	Sir H. Wotton	69
Haunted House, the	Hood	92
Helvellyn	Walter Scott	58
Hermit, the	Beattie	112
Hohenlinden	Campbell	85
Holy Scriptures, the	Dryden	357
Home	Montgomery	147
Homeric Hexameter exemplified	Coleridge	178
Horologe of Flora, the		25
Hour of Death, the	Mrs. Hemans	189

INDEX.

		PAGE
Human Frailty	Cowper	56
Hymn before Sunrise	Coleridge	149
Hymn of the Seasons	Thomson	387
Hymn on the Nativity	Milton	294
Hymn to Adversity	Gray	422
Idea of a State, the	Sir W. Jones	164
Il Penseroso	Milton	310
Imagination	Shakspere	288
Impediments to the attainment of Just Taste	Pope	371
Inscriptions:—		
1. For the Entrance to a Wood	Bryant	127
2. For a Column at Truxillo	Southey	129
3. For a Column at Runnimede	Akenside	129
4. For a Fountain on a Heath	Coleridge	130
5. For a Statue of Chaucer at Woodstock	Akenside	130
6. For a Natural Grotto		131
7. For a Natural Spring	T. Warton	131
Isaac Ashford	Crabbe	155
Ivry, the Battle of	Macaulay	116
Jerusalem before the Siege	Milman	221
King's College Chapel, Cambridge	Wordsworth	185
Knight, the	Chaucer	238
L'Allegro	Milton	304
Lady with a Rose, to a	Waller	115
Landscape, a	Cowper	452
Late Massacre in Piedmont, on the	Milton	159
Lavinia	Thomson	96
Life and Death	Shakspere	276
Lion Hunt, the	Pringle	12
Lodore, the Cataract of	Southey	211
Lord Bacon	Cowley	131
Lucy	Wordsworth	109
Lycidas	Milton	299
Lyrics from the Older Writers:—		
1. The Songs of Birds	Lyly	170
2. The Fairy's Song	Shakspere	170
3. Winter	id.	171
4. Ingratitude	id.	171
5. The Reveillé	id.	172
6. Ariel's Song	id.	172
7. Amiens' Song	id.	172
8. Hymn to Diana	B. Jonson	173
9. To Fancy, at Night	id.	173
10. To Blossoms	Herrick	174
11. To Daffodils	id.	174
Man of Ross, the	Pope	216
Man the Care of Angels	Spenser	262
Man's Ignorance	Pope	376
Man whose Thoughts are not of this World, the	Young	411

		PAGE
March	Cornelius Webbe	119
Martyrs, the	Cowper	203
Masque of the Seasons	Spenser	264
May, to	Wordsworth	225
May Morning	Milton	95
Medal, the	Pope	220
Memory of the Brave, to the	Collins	85
Memory of Thomson, to the	Burns	154
Mercy	Shakspere	286
Messiah, the	Pope	80
Metrical Feet	Coleridge	177
Millennium, the	Cowper	457
Mitherless Bairn, the	Thom	145
Monarch of Dulness, the	Dryden	358
Moonlight Night, a	Southey	181
Moral Beauty	Akenside	417
Moral Maxims, Epigrams, &c.		228
Morning Hymn in Paradise	Milton	338
Mother's Sacrifice, the	Mrs. Sigourney	88
Mountain Daisy, to a	Burns	76
Mouse, to a	id.	78
Music	Shakspere	287
Music on the Waters		99
Nature the Basis of Art	Pope	367
New Moon, the	Bryant	165
Night	Montgomery	161
Nightingale, to the	Drummond	223
Ocean, the	Byron	54
Ode on a distant Prospect of Eton College	Gray	123
Ode on the Spring	id.	70
Ode to Evening	Collins	152
Ode to Fear	id.	397
Old Age	Waller	90
Omnipresence of God, the	Moore	137
On the Poetical Character	Collins	400
"On the Receipt of my Mother's Picture"	Cowper	120
One Friend upbraiding Another	Shakspere	286
Othello's Courtship	id.	281
Ovidian Elegiac Metre exemplified	Coleridge	178
Palace of Ice, the	Cowper	191
Pandemonium	Milton	324
Paradise	id.	331
Passions, the	Collins	402
Past, to the	Bryant	195
Patriotism	Walter Scott	213
Persone, the	Chaucer	241
Picture of a Village Life	Goldsmith	446
Pleasure arising from Vicissitude, the	Gray	204
Pleasures of Retirement, the	Drummond	224
Poet, the	Cowper	227

INDEX.

xi

		PAGE
Poet, on his Blindness, the	Milton	204
Poet's Plea, the	id.	114
Poplars	Cowper	35
Power of Steam, the	Darwin	207
Prayer for Divine Aid	Merrick	1
Pride and Humility	Cowper	111
Prioresse, the	Chaucer	240
Procession of Rivers, the	Spenser	209
Procrastination	Young	410
Progress of Poetry, the	Gray	424
Providence	From Filicaja	149
Psalm of Life, a	Longfellow	51
Queen Mab	Shakspere	285
Rainbow, to the	Campbell	7
Rival Statesmen, the	Walter Scott	156
Rome	Milton	348
Rome, the Ruins of	Spenser	268
Rule Britannia	Thomson	190
Rural Sounds	Cowper	453
Samson's Lament	Milton	218
Satan mustering the Rebel Angels	id.	317
Satan's Meeting with Uriel	id.	328
School Days	Cowper	15
Sennacherib's Army, the Destruction of	Byron	113
Sentence of Expulsion from Paradise	Milton	340
Seven Ages of Man, the	Shakspere	283
Skylark, to a	Wordsworth	102
Slavery	Cowper	454
Sleep, the House of	Spenser	259
Sleep, to	Shakspere	186
Sleeping Babe, the	Hinds	6
Solemn Music, at a	Milton	158
Solitude	Byron	181
Solitude	Mrs. Sigourney	13
Solitude and Adversity	Shakspere	284
Song for the Wandering Jew	Wordsworth	89
Sonnet on Chapman's Homer	Keats	84
Soul's Sympathy with Greatness	Akenside	415
South African Desert, the	Pringle	180
Spanish Armada, the	Macaulay	183
Spanish Bull-fight, a	Byron	27
Spanish Champion, the	Mrs. Hemans	16
Spring	T. Warton	30
Squier, the	Chaucer	239
Star of Bethlehem, the	Kirke White	177
Startled Stag, the	Walter Scott	3
Stonehenge	T. Warton	97
Summer Morning, the	Thomson	383
Swimming	id.	49
Tale of the Enchanted Steed	Chaucer	243
Tear, on a	Rogers	50
Thames, the	Denham	9

		PAGE
Thames and its Tributaries, the	Pope	147
Thermopylæ	Byron	102
Thunderstorm, the	Milton	352
Time's Song		207
Toilet, the	Pope	375
Tranquillity of Nature, the	Wordsworth	222
Traveller, the	Goldsmith	436
Traveller lost in the Snow	Thomson	385
Traveller's Hymn, the	Addison	217
Twilight	Wordsworth	223
Una and the Red Cross Knight	Spenser	256
Una and the Lion	id.	260
Vanity of Human Wishes, the	Dr. Johnson	105
Veni Creator	Dryden	34
Verses left at a Friend's House	Burns	465
Victoria's Tears	Elizabeth Browning	198
War	Porteus	199
Waterfowl, to a	Bryant	66
Weathercock, to the	Greene	36
Winter Walk at Noon	Cowper	456
Wolsey's Fall	Shakspere	273
Wolsey's Death	id.	274
Wolsey's Character	id.	275
Woman	Mrs. Barbauld	55
Woman	Wordsworth	197
Wondrous Nature of Man	Young	408
Ye Mariners of England	Campbell	86
APPENDIX		467

STUDIES IN ENGLISH POETRY.

PART I.

Miscellaneous Poems and Extracts.

PRAYER FOR DIVINE AID.

AUTHOR of Good! to thee I turn:
  Thy ever-wakeful eye
Alone can all my wants discern,
  Thy hand alone supply.

Oh let **thy fear within** me dwell,
  Thy love[1] my footsteps guide!
That love shall meaner loves expel,
  That fear all fears beside.[2]

And oh! by Error's force subdued,
  Since oft my stubborn will,[3]
Preposterous, **shuns the latent good,**
  And **grasps the specious ill**;[4]

Not to my wish, but to my want,
  Do thou thy gifts **apply**;
Unasked, what good **thou knowest, grant**;
  What ill, though **asked, deny.**   *Merrick.*

---

(1) *Thy love, &c.*—let my love towards thee (*not* thy love towards me) guide my footsteps, *i. e.* influence **my actions**.

(2) The line in Racine's "Athalie" in which Joad says, "Je crains Dieu, cher Abner, et n'ai point d'autre crainte," has been deservedly admired, but the above expression conveys the **same** sentiment with **at least** equal force.

(3) **And** *oh! &c.*—*i. e.* and oh! since my stubborn will, subdued by the force of error, often preposterously shuns, &c.

(4) *Specious*—from the Latin *species*, an appearance; hence specious ill is evil which has the **appearance of** good.

BOADICEA.

When the British warrior queen,
    Bleeding from the Roman rods,
Sought, with an indignant mien,
    Counsel of her country's gods;

Sage, beneath the spreading oak,
    Sat the Druid, hoary chief!
Every burning word he spoke
    Full of rage, and full of grief:—

"Princess! if our aged eyes
    Weep upon thy matchless wrongs,
'Tis because resentment ties
    All the terrors of our tongues.[1]

"Rome shall perish—write that word
    In the blood that she has spilt;[2]
Perish, hopeless and abhorred,
    Deep in ruin as in guilt.

"Rome, for empire far renowned,
    Tramples on a thousand states;
Soon her pride shall kiss the ground—
    Hark! the Gaul[3] is at her gates!

"Other Romans shall arise,
    Heedless of a soldier's name;

---

(1) This passage is somewhat obscure. The Druid's "burning words" which follow seem inconsistent with the assertion that the "terrors of his tongue" were "tied" or restrained. The meaning may perhaps be thus represented:—Princess, if you find us weeping over your wrongs in private, instead of denouncing the perpetrators in public, blame us not, for our silence hitherto has arisen from the very intensity of our indignation.—Your personal appeal, however, demands that we should now give utterance to it:—Rome shall perish, &c.—This interpretation is based on the conjecture that "ties" is used for "has hitherto tied." Another explanation may be found in the Appendix, Note A.

(2) *In the blood*—that is, with the blood, as we say, to write in ink.

(3) *Gaul*—It does not appear that the Gauls were among the nations that swept over the Roman empire in the fifth century.—Perhaps "Goth" should be read for "Gaul."

Sounds, not arms, shall win the prize;
  Harmony the path to fame.[1]

"Then the progeny that springs
  From the forests of our land,[2]
Armed with thunder, clad with wings,
  Shall a wider world command.

"Regions Cæsar never knew
  Thy posterity shall sway;
Where his eagles never flew—
  None invincible as they."[3]

Such the bard's prophetic words,
  Pregnant with celestial fire,
Bending, as he swept the chords
  Of his sweet but awful lyre.

She, with all a monarch's pride,
  Felt them in her bosom glow;
Rushed to battle, fought, and died;[4]
  Dying, hurled them at the foe:—

"Ruffians! pitiless as proud,
  Heaven awards the vengeance due;
Empire is on us bestowed,
  Shame and ruin wait for you."   *Cowper.*

THE STARTLED STAG.

The stag at eve had drunk his fill,
Where danced the moon on Monan's[5] rill,

---

(1) In allusion to the love of the Italians for music. As a striking indication of the change in character above referred to, it may be mentioned that the word *virtus*, which among the ancient Romans meant "active courage," is used by the modern Romans in the softened form of *virtù*, to signify "a taste for the fine arts."

(2) *Progeny, &c.*—the ships of England.
(3) *They*—the British, not the Romans.
(4) According to Tacitus, Boadicea poisoned herself.
(5) *Monan*—a spring in the district of Menteith, Perthshire, Scotland.

And deep his midnight lair[1] had made
In lone Glenartney's[2] hazel shade;
But, when the sun his beacon[3] red
Had kindled on Benvoirlich's[4] head,
The deep-mouthed bloodhound's heavy bay
Resounded up the rocky way,
And faint, from farther distance borne,
Were heard the clanging hoof and horn.

As chief,[5] who hears his warder call,
"To arms! the foemen storm the wall!"
The antlered monarch of the waste
Sprang from his heathery couch in haste.
But, ere his fleet career he took,
The dewdrops from his flanks he shook;
Like crested leader, proud and high,
Tossed his beamed frontlet to the sky;
A moment gazed adown the dale,
A moment snuffed the tainted gale,
A moment listened to the cry
That thickened as the chase drew nigh;
Then, as the headmost foes appeared,
With one brave bound the copse he cleared,
And, stretching forward free and far,
Sought the wild heaths of Uam-Var.[6]

Yelled on the view the opening pack,
Rock, glen, and cavern, paid them back;[7]

---

(1) *Lair*—derived from *lay* or *lie*—the place where any one (deer or other animal) is *laid*. Cowper (see p. 69) uses the word in the well-known lines:—

"But the sea-fowl is gone to her nest,
The beast is *laid* down in his *lair*."

(2) *Glenartney*—a vale in Menteith.
(3) *Beacon*—from Anglo-Saxon *bien-ian*, or *been-ian*, to beck or beckon, to call by signs—anything so placed as to give a signal or warning. The use of the word in the above passage is highly picturesque.
(4) *Benvoirlich*—one of the Grampian mountains.
(5) *As chief, &c.*—This description is full of animation. The stag awakening at the summons of his pursuers—his proud survey of the scene—his decisive action—his escape;—the entrance of the hunting party—the shouts and halloos which give "Benvoirlich's echoes no rest"—and the deep silence which succeeds—are all touched with the hand of a master.
(6) *Uam-Var*—a mountain in Menteith.
(7) *Paid them back*—echoed back the sound.

To many a mingled sound at once
The awakened mountain gave response.
A hundred dogs bayed deep and strong,
Clattered a hundred steeds along,
Their peal the merry horns rang out
A hundred voices joined the shout;
With hark, and whoop, and wild halloo,
No rest Benvoirlich's echoes knew.
Far from the tumult fled the roe,
Close in her covert cowered the doe,
The falcon, from her cairn[1] on high,
Cast on the rout a wondering eye,
Till far beyond her piercing ken
The hurricane had swept the glen.
Faint, and more faint, its failing din
Returned from cavern, cliff, and linn,[2]
And silence settled wide and still,
On the lone wood and mighty hill.

Walter Scott.

THE GLORY OF GOD IN CREATION.[3]

THE spacious firmament on high,
With all the blue ethereal sky,
And spangled heavens, a shining frame,
Their great Original proclaim.[4]

---

(1) *Cairn*—a heap of stones—here, a crag or cliff.

(2) *Linn*—a waterfall, precipice.

(3) This beautiful poem is a paraphrase of the first four verses of the 19th Psalm, with which it should be compared.

(4) For some variations in the commencement, see Appendix, Note B.

The words *firmament, sky*, and *heaven*, may be thus distinguished: *Firmament* (from *firmare*, to strengthen), that which is strong, and therefore solid;—the arch or vault of heaven. The old astronomers believed the sky to be a sort of solid frame, in which the stars were set. *Sky* (Greek σκία, a shadow; Swed. *sky*, a cloud; Anglo-Saxon, *scua*, the same), in old English, a cloud or shadow; afterwards the region of clouds—cloudland. Chaucer speaks of "not a *skie*" being left " in all the welkin." *Heaven*—that which is heaved or *heaven* up (according to Horne Tooke), comprehending the upper regions, as opposed to the earth.

In accordance with these distinctions we may correctly speak of the *spacious* firmament—the *blue* sky—the *spangled* heavens, but scarcely of the firmament *with* the sky *and* the heavens, as above.

The unwearied sun from day to day
Does his Creator's power display,
And publishes to every land
The work of an almighty hand.

Soon as the evening shades prevail,
The moon takes up the wondrous tale,[1]
And nightly to the listening earth
Repeats the story of her birth;
While all the stars that round her burn,
And all the planets in their turn,
Confirm the tidings as they roll,
And spread the truth from pole to pole.

What, though in solemn silence all
Move round this dark terrestrial ball!
What, though no real voice nor sound[2]
Amid their radiant orbs be found!
In Reason's ear they all rejoice,
And utter forth a glorious voice;
For ever singing as they shine,
"The hand that made us is divine."

Addison.

THE SLEEPING BABE.[3]

"She is not dead, but sleepeth." Luke viii. 52.

The baby wept;
The mother took it from the nurse's arms,
And soothed its grief, and stilled its vain alarms,
And baby slept.

---

(1) *Tale*—The idea of the Creation declaring, as if in speech, the goodness and greatness of God is preserved throughout the poem, by the use of the words "proclaim," "publish," "tell," "story," "tidings," &c.

(2) *What though, &c.*—Bishop Horsley translates the 3rd verse of the 19th Psalm thus:—

"There is no speech, no words,
No voice of them is heard;
Yet their sound goes throughout the earth;"

which is nearly the same rendering as Cranmer's in the Book of Common Prayer.

(3) The simple beauty of these lines well deserves attention; particularly the striking use made of the double meaning of the word *sleep*. The change in the tense from the past to present, heightens the climax, which is almost sublime.

Again it weeps,
And God doth take it from the mother's arms,
From present **pain, and** future unknown harms,
And baby sleeps.

Hinds.

TO THE **RAINBOW**.

TRIUMPHAL arch,[1] that fill'st the sky
   When storms prepare to part,[2]
I ask not proud Philosophy
   To teach me what thou art ;—

Still seem, as to my childhood's sight,
   A midway station given
For happy spirits to alight,
   Betwixt the earth and heaven.

Can all that optics teach unfold
   Thy form to please me so,
As when I dreamt of gems and gold
   Hid in thy radiant bow ?

When Science from Creation's face
   Enchantment's veil withdraws,
What lovely visions yield their place
   To cold material laws ![3]

And yet,[4] fair bow, no fabling dreams,
   But words of the Most High,
Have told why thy first robe of **beams**
   Was woven in the sky.

---

(1) *Triumphal arch*—There is something **very fine in** the conception of the **rainbow** being a triumphal arch, **raised to celebrate** the peace which follows the war of the elements. One copy **of this poem in** a popular collection reads " triumphant arch," to the utter confusion **of the sense.**

(2) *Part*—*i. e.* to depart. Gray, in his " Elegy " (see p. 60), writes :—

" The curfew tolls **the** knell of parting (*i. e.* departing or dying) day."

(3) Akenside has expressed a very different opinion on this point. See Appendix, Note C.

(4) ***And** yet, &c.*—*i.e.* though fiction may **be** sometimes more agreeable than fact, **yet here** the fact itself is especially interesting.

When o'er the green undeluged[1] earth,
  Heaven's covenant[2] thou didst shine,
How came the world's grey fathers[3] forth,
  To watch thy sacred sign!

And when its yellow lustre smiled
  O'er mountains yet untrod,
Each mother held aloft her child
  To bless the bow of God.

Methinks, thy jubilee to keep,
  The first-made anthem[4] rang
On earth, delivered from the deep,
  And the first poet sang.

Nor ever shall the Muse's eye,
  Unraptured greet thy beam:
Theme of primeval prophecy,
  Be still the poet's theme![5]

The earth to thee her incense yields,
  The lark thy welcome sings,
When glittering in the freshened fields,
  The snowy mushroom springs.

How glorious is thy girdle, cast
  O'er mountain, tower, and town!
Or mirrored in the ocean vast,
  A thousand fathoms down!

As fresh as yon horizon dark,
  As young thy beauties seem,
As when the eagle from the ark,
  First sported in thy beam.

---

(1) *Undeluged*—no longer overwhelmed by the deluge. The prefix *un* in this word does not fully convey the meaning of the writer; *un* is simply *not*, without that reference to a previous state which is implied by the prefix *dis*.

(2) *Heaven's covenant*—strictly speaking, the rainbow is not the covenant, but the sign or token of it. See Gen. ix. 13.

(3) *The world's grey fathers*—This beautiful expression is borrowed from Henry Vaughan, a poet of the 17th century. See Appendix, Note D.

(4) *Anthem*—literally *anti-hymn*—a piece of music arranged to be sung in parts, answering to each other—music for a cathedral choir.

(5) In the ordinary copies we have "*poet's* theme," as above; the reading, however, in the standard edition of Campbell's poems is "*prophet's* theme," a less appropriate expression, though not inconsistent with the first-named; inasmuch as the original idea of a poet included that of a prophet, or one who was, as it were, inspired to sing of things eternally true—of things past, present, and future.

> For, faithful to its sacred page,
>   Heaven still rebuilds thy span;
> Nor lets the type grow pale with age,
>   That first spoke peace to man.   *Campbell.*

THE THAMES.[1]

My eye descending from the Hill,[2] surveys
Where Thames among the wanton valleys strays:
Thames! the most loved of all the ocean's sons
By his old sire, to his embraces runs,
Hasting to pay his tribute to the sea,
Like mortal life to meet eternity;[3]
Though with those streams he no resemblance hold,
Whose foam is amber, and their gravel gold.[4]
His genuine and less guilty wealth to explore,
Search not his bottom, but survey his shore,
O'er which he kindly spreads his spacious wing,
And hatches plenty for the ensuing spring:
Nor then destroys it with too fond a stay,
Like mothers which their infants overlay,
Nor with a sudden and impetuous wave,
Like profuse kings, resumes the wealth he gave.[5]
No unexpected inundations spoil
The mower's hopes, nor mock the ploughman's toil;
But godlike his unwearied bounty flows,
First loves to do,[6] then loves the good he does.
Nor are his blessings to his banks confined,
But free and common as the sea or wind;

---

(1) The poem entitled "Cooper's Hill," from which this extract is made, was written in 1643. The date may account in part for the quaintness of the style.

(2) *The hill*—Cooper's Hill, near Windsor.

(3) This idea is beautifully amplified by Cowper (see p. 80), in the lines beginning,

"The lapse of time and rivers is the same."

(4) The rivers Pactolus and Hermus, in Asia Minor, were said by the ancient poets to roll down sand mingled with gold.

(5) *Resumes, &c.—i. e.* does not first by his overflow create abundance, and then by a second inundation destroy his own creation. The figures in the last few lines display more ingenuity than taste; they are incongruous and unnecessarily multiplied.

(6) *Loves to do—i. e.* loves to do good. The allusion here seems to be to Gen. i. 31.

When[1] he, to boast or to disperse his stores,
Full of the tributes of his grateful shores,
Visits the world, and in his flying towers
Brings home to us, and makes both Indies ours;
Finds wealth where 'tis, bestows it where it wants,
Cities in deserts, woods in cities plants;
So that to us no thing, no place is strange,
While his fair bosom is the world's exchange.
Oh, could I flow like thee! and make thy stream
My great example, as it is my theme:
Though deep, yet clear; though gentle, yet not dull;
Strong, without rage; without o'erflowing, full.[2]
Denham.

THE COMMON LOT.[3]

Once in the flight of ages past
  There lived a man—and who was he?
Mortal! howe er thy lot be cast,
  That man resembled thee!

Unknown the region of his birth,
  The land in which he lived unknown;
His name hath perished from the earth;
  This truth survives alone:—

That joy[4] and grief,[4] and hope and fear,
  Alternate triumphed in his breast;
His bliss and woe, a smile, a tear!
  Oblivion hides the rest.

---

(1) *When*—seems here to mean inasmuch, seeing that; and the sense of the passage to be, that the blessings of the Thames are unlimited, inasmuch as, through the agency of the ships—"his flying towers," that he sends forth laden with English produce and manufacture—he visits the world, and brings home both Indies to us, by making their produce and wealth ours.

(2) The last two lines have been much admired for the exquisite taste displayed in the choice of words. They embody, with happy brevity, the main characteristics of a finished literary style, which should be, "though deep, yet clear," &c. "*Strong, without rage,*" means strong without the ostentatious display of strength.

(3) The lot or condition which is common to all mankind—with its hopes and fears, its pleasures and pains.

(4) *Joy, delight,* and *bliss,* may be thus distinguished:—
    Joy—is vivid
    Delight—absorbing } and therefore transient, pleasure.
    Bliss—complete and abiding happiness.
A similar distinction holds between *grief* and *woe:*—

The bounding pulse, the languid limb,
    The changing spirits' rise and fall,
We know that these were felt by him,
    For these are felt by all.

He suffered—but his pangs are o'er;
    Enjoyed—but his delights are fled;
Had friends—his friends are now no more;
    And foes—his foes are dead.

He loved—but whom he loved the grave
    Hath lost in its unconscious womb;
Oh! she was fair, but nought could save
    Her beauty from the tomb.

The rolling seasons, day and night,
    Sun, moon, and stars, the earth and main,
Erewhile[1] his portion, life and light,
    To him[2] exist in vain.

He saw whatever thou hast seen;
    Encountered all that troubles thee;
He was—whatever thou hast been;
    He is—what thou shalt be.

The clouds and sunbeams o'er his eye
    That once their shade and glory threw,
Have left, in yonder silent sky,
    No vestige[3] where they flew!

The annals[4] of the human race,
    Their ruins since the world began,
Of him afford no other trace
    Than this—THERE LIVED A MAN.

Montgomery.

Grief—is intense and overwhelming, but brief, *sorrow.*
Woe—complete, absorbing, and abiding misery.

Hence we may speak of "transports of joy or grief," "ecstacies of delight," "perfect bliss," "speechless woe." In the above poem, "joy" and "grief" are correctly said to "triumph," &c., "delights" to be "fled," but "bliss" and "woe" are less correctly employed, inasmuch as bliss properly belongs only to heaven, and woe "lies too deep for tears."

(1) *Erewhile*—a while before—some time ago.
(2) *To him*—for him, as far as he is concerned.
(3) *Vestige*—from the Latin *vestigium*, a footmark—hence track, trace.
(4) *Annals, &c.*—neither the written history of mankind, nor the ruins they have left behind them, afford any other trace, &c.

THE LION HUNT.[1]

Mount—mount for the hunting—with musket and spear!
Call our friends to the field—for the lion is near!
Call Arend[2] and Ekhard and Groepe to the spoor;[3]
Call Muller and Coetzer and Lucas Van Vuur.

Ride up Eildon-Cleugh, and blow loudly the bugle:
Call Slinger and Allie and Dikkop and Dugal;
And George with the elephant-gun on his shoulder—
In a perilous pinch none is better or bolder.

In the gorge[4] of the glen lie the bones of my steed,
And the hoofs of a heifer of fatherland's[5] breed:
But mount, my brave boys! if our rifles prove true,
We'll soon make the spoiler his ravages rue.

Ho! the Hottentot lads have discovered the track—
To his den in the desert we'll follow him back;
But tighten your girths, and look well to your flints,
For heavy and fresh are the villain's foot-prints.

Through the rough rocky kloof[6] into Grey Huntley-Glen,
Past the wild olive clump where the wolf has his den,
By the black eagle's rock at the foot of the fell,[7]
We have tracked him at length to the buffalo's well.

Now mark yonder brake where the bloodhounds are howling;
And hark that hoarse sound—like the deep thunder growling;
'Tis his lair—'tis his voice!—from your saddles alight;
He's at bay in the brushwood, preparing for fight.

---

(1) The circumstances described in this very spirited poem, came under the personal observation of the writer, Mr. Pringle, and may be read in detail in the 8th chapter of his interesting "Narrative of a Residence in South Africa."

(2) The names in this piece are—with the exception of "the Rennies," who were Scottish friends of the author—those of Mulatto farmers, and Hottentot and Dutch servants, residing in the neighbourhood.

(3) *Spoor*—a Dutch word—track, the lion's track.

(4) *Gorge*—the throat or narrow passage at the opening of a defile.

(5) *Fatherland*—here means Scotland, which was the native country of the emigrants.

(6) *Kloof*—a Dutch word—a small valley opening into a larger one.

(7) *Fell*—a Scandinavian word—a rocky hill.

Leave the horses behind—and be still every man:
Let the Mullers and Rennies advance in the van:
Keep fast in your ranks;—by the yell of yon hound,
The savage, I guess, will be out with a bound.

He comes! the tall jungle before him loud crashing,
His mane bristled fiercely, his fiery eyes flashing;
With a roar of disdain, he leaps forth in his wrath,
To challenge the foe that dare 'leaguer[1] his path.

He couches—ay, now we'll see mischief, I dread:
Quick—level your rifles—and aim at his head:
Thrust forward the spears, and unsheath every knife—
St. George! he's upon us! Now fire, lads, for life!

He's wounded—but he'll draw blood ere he falls—
Ha! under his paw see Bezuidenhout sprawls—
Now Diederik! Christian! right in the brain
Plant each man his bullet—HURRA! he is slain!

Bezuidenhout—up, man!—'tis only a scratch—
(You were always a scamp, and have met with your match!)
What a glorious lion!—what sinews—what claws—
And seven-feet-ten from the rump to the jaws!

His hide, with the paws and the bones of his skull,
And the spoils of the leopard and buffalo bull,
We'll send to Sir Walter![2]—Now boys, let us dine,
And talk of our deeds o'er a flask of old wine.
Pringle.

SOLITUDE.

DEEP solitude I sought. There was a dell
Where woven shades shut out the eye of day,
While, towering near, the rugged mountains made
Dark background 'gainst the sky. Thither I went,
And bade my spirit taste that lonely[3] fount

---

(1) *Leaguer*—for beleaguer—to besiege, beset.
(2) Sir Walter Scott, a friend of the author.
(3) *Lonely*—synonymous with *alone*—feeling alone, habitually without company; *alone*—by one's self, actually without company. Hence we may speak of a "lonely fount," and of "being alone."

For which it long had thirsted 'mid the strife
And fever of the world.—I thought to be
There without witness. But the violet's eye[1]
Looked up to greet me. The fresh wild-rose smiled,
And the young pendant vine-flower kissed my cheek.
There were glad voices too.—The garrulous brook,
Untiring, to the patient pebbles told
Its history.—Up came the singing breeze,
And the broad leaves of the tall poplar spake
Responsive, every one. Even busy life
Woke in that dell. The dextrous spider threw,
From spray to spray, the silver-tissued snare;
The thrifty ant, whose curving pincers pierced
The rifled grain, toiled towards her citadel;[2]
To her sweet hive went forth the loaded bee;
While from her wind-rocked nest, the mother bird
Sang to her nurslings.
          Yet I strangely thought
To be alone and silent in thy realm,
Spirit of light and love!—it might not be!—
There is no solitude in thy domains,[3]
Save what man makes, when in his selfish breast
He locks his joy, and shuts out others' grief.
Thou hast not left thyself in this wide world
Without a witness. Even the desert place
Speaketh thy name. The simple flowers and stream
Are social and benevolent, and he
Who holdeth converse in their language pure,
Roaming among them at the cool of day,
Shall find, like him who Eden's garden dress'd,
His Maker there, to teach the listening[4] heart.
                              Mrs. Sigourney.

---

(1) The personification of the different inanimate objects is very delicately and gracefully managed.

(2) *Citadel*—an ingenious application of the term to the ant-hill, as being the insect's place of refuge, or stronghold.

(3) Compare Byron's lines on Solitude, p. 181.

(4) *Listening*—synonymous with *hearing*—endeavouring or being disposed to hear; *hearing*—simply catching a sound, whether voluntary or not. Hence we may listen without hearing, and hear without listening—but we never listen without giving attention. The "listening heart" is disposed to hear the voice of God speaking from the midst of his works.

SCHOOL-DAYS.

Be it a weakness, it deserves some praise,
We love the play-place of our early days;
The scene is touching, and the heart is stone
That feels not at that sight, and feels at none.[1]
The wall on which we tried our graving[2] skill,
The very name we carved[2] subsisting still;
The bench on which we sat while deep employed,
Though mangled, hacked,[2] hewed,[2] not yet destroyed;
The little ones, unbuttoned, glowing hot,
Playing our games, and on the very spot;
As happy as we once, to kneel and draw
The chalky ring, and knuckle down at taw;
To pitch the ball into the grounded hat,
Or drive it devious[3] with a dextrous pat.
The pleasing spectacle at once excites
Such recollection of our own delights,
That, viewing it, we seem almost to obtain,
Our innocent, sweet, simple years again.
This fond attachment to the well-known place,
Whence first we started into life's long race,
Maintains its hold with such unfailing sway,
We feel it even in age, and at our latest day.

Cowper.

---

(1) The inversion of the style occasions some obscurity in this passage. The meaning is—that the heart that feels not at that sight is stone, and feels, or can feel at no sight whatever.

(2) *Grave, carve, hack, hew,* all different modes of cutting, may be thus distinguished:—

To *grave* is to cut into, or hollow out, with a view to execute some design. To *carve* is to cut a thing so as to shape it into some new form. To *hack* is to cut for the purpose of injuring or destroying the existing form. To *hew* is to cut down, or off, for the purpose of removal. Hence, we may correctly say that the names were " graven " or " carved," and the bench " hacked," or notched and " hewed."

(3) *Devious,* from Latin *de* and *via,* from or out of the way; here, on one side, not straight forward. Dryden (see p. 359) wittily says:—

"The rest to some faint meaning make pretence,
But Shadwell never deviates into sense."

THE SPANISH CHAMPION.[1]

The warrior bowed his crested head, and tamed his heart of fire,
And sued the haughty king to free his long imprisoned sire,[2]
"I bring thee here my fortress keys,[3] I bring my captive train,
I pledge the faith, my liege, my lord!—oh break my father's chain!"

"Rise, rise! even now thy father comes, a ransomed man this day;
Mount thy good horse, and thou and I will meet him on his way."
Then lightly rose that loyal son, and bounded on his steed,[4]
And urged, as if with lance in rest, the charger's[4] foamy speed.

And lo! from far, as on they pressed, there came a glittering band,
With one that 'midst them stately rode, as a leader in the land:
"Now haste, Bernardo, haste! for there, in very truth, is he,—
The father whom thy faithful heart hath yearned so long to see."

His dark eye flashed, his proud breast heaved, his cheek's blood came and went;
He reached that grey-haired chieftain's side, and there dismounting, bent;
A lowly knee to earth he bent—his father's hand he took,—
What was there in his touch that all his fiery spirit shook?

That hand was cold—a frozen thing—it drooped from his like lead;
He looked up to the face above—the face was of the dead!
A plume waved o'er the noble brow—that brow was fixed and white;—
He met at last his father's eyes—but in them was no sight!

---

(1) The celebrated Spanish champion, Bernardo del Carpio, renowned for his exploits against the no less famous French hero Roland, as well as against the Moors in Spain, lived in the reign of Alonzo II., King of Leon.

(2) *Sire*—the count of Saldana, Bernardo's father, who had been imprisoned by the king for many years.

(3) *Fortress keys*—Bernardo, after many ineffectual efforts to procure his father's release, had taken up arms in despair, but at length assented to the king's proposal to give up the person of his father in exchange for the Castle of Carpio.

(4) *Steed, charger*—a steed is a horse for the stud, of fine shape and high mettle; a charger, a heavy war-horse, used for bearing down upon, or charging the enemy in battle.

Up from the ground he sprang, and gazed, but who could paint that gaze?
They hushed their very hearts that saw its horror and amaze;
They might have chained him, as before that stony form he stood,
For the power was stricken from his arm, and from his lip the blood.

"Father!" at length he murmured low—and wept like childhood then,—
Talk not of grief till thou hast seen the tears of warlike men!—
He thought on all his glorious hopes, and all his young renown;
He flung the falchion from his side, and in the dust sat down.

Then covering with his steel-gloved hands his darkly-mournful brow,
"No more, there is no more," he said, "to lift the sword for now:
My king is false, my hope betrayed, my father, oh! the worth,
The glory, and the loveliness, are passed away from earth!

"I thought to stand where banners waved, my sire! beside thee yet;
I would that there our kindred blood on Spain's free soil had met,—
Thou wouldst have known my spirit then,—for thee my fields were won,—
And thou hast perished in thy chains, as though thou hadst no son!"

Then, starting from the ground once more, he seized the monarch's rein,
Amidst the pale and wildered looks of all the courtier train;
And with a fierce o'ermastering grasp, the rearing war-horse led,
And sternly set them face to face,—the king before the dead!

"Came I not forth upon thy pledge, my father's hand to kiss?—
Be still! and gaze thou on, false king! and tell me what is this?
The voice, the glance, the heart I sought—give answer, where are they?—
If thou wouldst clear thy perjured soul, send life through this cold clay!

"Into these glassy eyes put light,—be still! keep down thine ire—
Bid these white lips a blessing speak—this earth is *not* my sire!
Give me back him for whom I strove, for whom my blood was shed,—
Thou canst not—and a king?—His dust be mountains on thy head!"

c

He loosed the steed; his slack hand fell,—upon the silent face
He cast one long, deep, troubled look,—then turned from that sad
    place;
His hope was crushed, his after-fate untold in martial strain,—
His banner led the spears no more amidst the hills of Spain.
Mrs. Hemans.

TO THE CUCKOO.[1]

O BLITHE new-comer! I have heard,
   I hear thee and rejoice:
O Cuckoo! shall I call thee bird,
   Or but a wandering voice?

While I am lying on the grass,
   Thy loud note smites my ear!
It seems to fill the whole air's space;
   At once far off and near!

I hear thee babbling[2] to the vale
   Of sunshine and of flowers;
But unto me thou bring'st a tale
   Of visionary hours.

Thrice welcome, darling of the spring!
   Even yet thou art to me
No bird, but an invisible thing,
   A voice, a mystery.

---

(1) Some elegant lines on the same subject, by the Scottish poet, Logan, may be found in "Select Poetry for Children," p. 7. The above poem is of a higher order than Logan's—though scarcely superior in point of interest and execution—because it is more suggestive, that is, awakens a less obvious train of thought, though when pointed out, not less natural and pleasing. Many hear the cuckoo and are pleased with that well-known note, which is so associated with the return of spring;—Wordsworth hears it, and is reminded, in addition, of "the golden time"—the spring-tide of his youth—when the bird was first an object of intense interest to the boy.

(2) *Babbling*—from Hebrew *Babel*, where confusion of tongues first arose; hence, to *bubble* is to talk confusedly and inarticulately. There is much beauty in the use of the word here. Thou babblest—confusedly talkest—to the vale, but to me thy language is distinct and definite, reminding me of my early years,—which appear as it were in a vision, and are here called "visionary hours."

The same whom in my school-boy days
  I listened to; that cry
Which made me look a thousand ways,
  In bush, and tree, and sky.

To seek thee did I often rove
  Through woods and on the green;
And thou wert still a hope, a love;
  Still longed for, never seen!

And I can listen to thee yet;
  Can lie upon the plain
And listen till I do beget[1]
  That golden time again.

O blessed bird! the earth we pace
  Again appears to be
An unsubstantial, fairy place;
  That is fit home for thee![2]

Wordsworth.

ADDRESS TO AN EGYPTIAN MUMMY.[3]

AND thou hast walked about—how strange a story!—
  In Thebes's streets three thousand years ago;
When the Memnonium[4] was in all its glory,
  And time had not begun to overthrow
Those temples, palaces, and piles stupendous,
Of which the very ruins are tremendous.

---

(1) *Beget, &c.*—recall, and as it were create anew, the scenes of boyhood. This faculty, which the mind possesses of reviving a train of scenes and circumstances, long past, on the recollection of some one of them, is usually called the *association of ideas*—the above poem is a pleasing illustration of the phenomenon. Akenside (in his "Pleasures of Imagination") thus refers to it:—

"A song, a flower, a name, at once restore
  Those long-connected scenes where first they moved
  The attention."

(2) *Fit home, &c.*—the vision of the "golden time" so fills the mind, that the earth seems to change into a fairy place, well suited to the mysterious and unreal character fancifully attributed to the cuckoo.

(3) "This poem has been deservedly admired for its picturesque vigour, combined with richness and felicity of historical allusion."—*Encyclopædia Britannica.*

(4) *Memnonium*—the name given to a temple now in ruins, supposed to have been dedicated to Memnon, an ancient king of Egypt.

Speak! for thou long enough hast acted dummy;
  Thou hast a tongue, come, let us hear its tune;
Thou'rt standing on thy legs, above ground, Mummy!
  Revisiting the glimpses of the moon;
Not like thin ghosts, or disembodied creatures,
But with thy bones, and flesh, and limbs, and features.

Tell us—for doubtless thou canst recollect—
  To whom should we assign the Sphinx's[1] fame?
Was Cheops,[2] or Cephrenes,[2] architect
  Of either pyramid that bears his name?
Is Pompey's pillar[3] really a misnomer?
Had Thebes[4] a hundred gates, as sung by Homer?

Perhaps thou wert a mason,[5] and forbidden
  By oath to tell the mysteries of thy trade;
Then say what secret melody[6] was hidden
  In Memnon's statue which at sunrise played?
Perhaps thou wert a priest—if so, my struggles
Are vain—Egyptian priests ne'er owned their juggles.[7]

Perchance that very hand, now pinioned flat,
  Has hob-a-nobbed[8] with Pharaoh, glass to glass;

---

(1) *Sphinx*—an Egyptian monster, with a virgin's face and a quadruped's body; said to have proposed riddles, and destroyed those who could not solve them.

(2) *Cheops, Cephrenes*—two ancient kings of Egypt, to whom Herodotus attributes the building of the two largest pyramids.

(3) *Pompey's pillar*—the column at Alexandria, which is thus named, is supposed to have been erected long after Pompey's time—in the reign of Diocletian. The name it bears is, therefore, a misnomer.

(4) *Thebes*—in the Bible called No, or No Ammon—was situated in Upper Egypt. Homer (Iliad ix. 381, &c.) calls it "the city with a hundred gates," each of which, he says, sent out two hundred men, with horses and chariots.

(5) *Mason*—i. e. a freemason; one of a company or society of men calling themselves by that name, and professing to maintain, as a condition of membership, some awful secrets, which they are sworn never to divulge.

(6) *Secret melody, &c.*—It seems clear that at sunrise certain sounds did issue from a particular statue, called Memnon's head, but in what manner the Egyptian priests contrived this "juggle?"—for such it doubtless was—is unknown.

(7) *Juggle*—probably from the Latin *jocus*, a joke or sport, whence *joculer, joculator*, and the old Anglo-Norman *jegelour* (used by Chaucer), one who plays tricks or makes sport.

(8) *Hob-a-nob*—supposed to be the same as *hab or nab*, i. e. have or not have; formerly used in asking a person whether he would have a glass of wine or not, or, as above, applied to the fact of drinking together. Halliwell considers it "the act of touching glasses in pledging a health."

Or dropt a halfpenny in Homer's hat,
   Or doffed[1] thine own to let Queen Dido pass,
Or held, by Solomon's own invitation,
A torch at the great Temple's dedication.

I need not ask thee if that hand, when armed,
   Has any Roman soldier mauled[2] or knuckled;
For thou wert dead, and buried, and embalmed,
   Ere Romulus and Remus had been suckled!
Antiquity appears to have begun
Long after thy primeval race was run.

Thou couldst develop, if that withered tongue
   Might tell us what those sightless orbs have seen,
How the world looked when it was fresh and young,
   And the great Deluge still had left it green;
Or was it then so old, that History's pages
Contained no record of its early ages?

Still silent, incommunicative elf?
   Art sworn to secrecy? then keep thy vows;
But, prythee, tell us something of thyself,
   Reveal the secrets of thy prison-house!
Since in the world of spirits thou hast slumbered,
What hast thou seen, what strange adventures numbered?

Since first thy form was in this box extended,
   We have, above-ground, seen some strange mutations;
The Roman empire has begun and ended,
   New worlds have risen—we have lost old nations;
And countless kings have into dust been humbled,
While not a fragment of thy flesh has crumbled.

Didst thou not hear the pother[3] o'er thy head,
   When the great Persian conqueror, Cambyses,

---

(1) *Doff*—to do off, or put off, as *don* is to do on, or put on, and *dout*, to do out, or put out.

(2) *Mauled*—to maul is to beat with a *mall* or large hammer, or in a secondary sense, to beat severely, so as to occasion bruises.

(3) *Pother*—same as *pudder* or *powder*, dust, as raised by a horse running swiftly. Shakspere (in "Lear") writes:—

      "Let the great gods,
   That keep this dreadful *pudder* o'er our heads,
   Find out their enemies now."

Marched armies o'er thy tomb with thundering tread,
    O'erthrew Osiris, Orus, Apis, Isis,[1]
And shook the Pyramids with fear and wonder,
    When the gigantic Memnon fell asunder?

If the tomb's secrets may not be confessed,
    The nature of thy private life unfold:—
A heart has throbbed beneath that leathern breast,
    And tears adown that dusty cheek have rolled;
Have children climbed those knees, and kissed that face?
What was thy name, and station, age, and race?

Statue of flesh[2]—Immortal of the dead!
    Imperishable type of evanescence!
Posthumous man, who quitt'st thy narrow bed,
    And standest undecayed within our presence!
Thou wilt hear nothing till the judgment morning,
When the great trump shall thrill thee with its warning!

Why should this worthless tenement endure,
    If its undying guest be lost for ever?
Oh! let us keep the soul embalmed and pure
    In living virtue; that, when both must sever,
Although corruption may our frame consume,
The immortal spirit in the skies may bloom!

Horace Smith.

THE ALPS AT DAY-BREAK.

The sun-beams streak the azure skies,
    And line with light the mountain's brow:
With hounds and horns the hunters rise,
    And chase the roebuck through the snow.

From rock to rock with giant-bound,
    High on their iron poles they pass;
Mute,[3] lest the air convulsed by sound,
    Rend from above the frozen mass.[4]

---

(1) *Osiris, &c.*—names of Egyptian divinities, worshipped under various forms.

(2) *Statue of flesh, &c.*—this is a very striking passage. The opposition in the terms excites and interests the mind. Statue of what? Marble? No—flesh. Immortal—undying—of the dead. Imperishable—undecaying—type of decay.

(3) *Mute*—i. e. at particular spots, where danger was to be apprehended.

(4) *Frozen mass*—an avalanche or huge mass of snow.

The goats wind slow their wonted way,[1]
  Up craggy **steeps** and ridges **rude;**
Marked by the **wild** wolf **for** his prey,
  From desert **cave** or hanging wood.

And while the torrent thunders **loud,**
  And as the echoing cliffs reply,
The huts peep o'er the mountain cloud,
  Perched, like an eagle's nest, on high.

Rogers.

THE CALENDAR OF FLORA.[2]

FAIR rising from her icy couch,
  Wan herald[3] of the floral year,
The snow-drop marks the Spring's approach,
  Ere yet the primrose groups appear,
Or peers the arum[4] from its spotted veil,
Or odorous violets scent the cold capricious **gale.**

Then thickly strewn in woodland bowers,
  Anemones[5] their stars unfold,
There spring the sorrel's veined flowers,
  And rich in vegetable gold,[6]

(1) *Way*—this line, **and** that in the **first** stanza, "With hounds and horns **the hunters rise,**" supply instances of what is called *alliteration*, or the frequent recurrence of the same initial letter. It is an artifice of composition which ought to be very judiciously **employed to satisfy** a cultivated taste—though its occasional introduction is pleasing. The poet **Churchill has at once** ingeniously ridiculed and exemplified it in the following line :—

"*And apt alliteration's artful aid.*"

(2) In the "Calendar of **Flora,**" the **flowers,** by their appearance at different parts of the year, serve as a sort of register, or calendar, of the seasons.

(3) *Herald*—synonymous with *harbinger* and *messenger.* All these words convey the idea of *going before*, but differ in the purpose.

A *herald* is one who goes before to declare something. A *harbinger* is one who goes before to procure a harbour or lodging for some important personage. A *messenger* is one who goes before to take a message.

(4) *Arum maculatum*—spotted arum, or cuckoo-pint.

(5) *Anemones*—called also wind-flowers. The *anemone nemorosa* is here referred to.

(6) *Vegetable gold*—an expression **borrowed** from Milton (Paradise Lost, iv. 218), and somewhat affectedly employed here to denote the golden colour of the cowslips.

From calyx pale the freckled cowslips born,
Receive in jasper cups the fragrant dews of morn.

Lo! the green thorn her silver buds
   Expands to May's enlivening beam;
Hottonia[1] blushes on the floods;
   And, where the slowly trickling stream
Mid grass and spiry rushes stealing glides,
Her lovely fringed flowers fair menyanthes[2] hides.

In the lone copse, or shadowy dale,
   Wild clustered knots of harebells grow,
And droops the lily of the vale
   O'er vinca's[3] matted leaves below.
The orchis race with varied beauty charm,
And mock the exploring bee or fly's aërial form.

Wound o'er the hedge-row's oaken boughs,
   The woodbine's tassels float in air,
And, blushing, the uncultured rose
   Hangs high her beauteous blossoms there;
Her fillets there the purple nightshade weaves,
And pale bryonia[4] winds her broad and scalloped leaves.

To later summer's fragrant breath
   Clematis' feathery garlands dance;
The hollow foxglove nods beneath;
   While the tall mullein's yellow lance—
Dear to the mealy moth of evening—towers;
And the weak galium[5] weaves its myriad fairy flowers.

Sheltering the coot's or wild duck's nest,
   And where the timid halcyon[6] hides,
The willow-herb, in crimson drest,
   Waves with arundo o'er the tides;
And there the bright nymphæa[7] loves to lave,
Or spreads her golden orbs upon the dimpling wave.

   (1) *Hottonia*—the water violet.
   (2) *Menyanthes*—the buck-bean or bog-bean.
   (3) *Vinca*—periwinkle.
   (4) *Bryonia*—bryony.
   (5) *Galium*—the yellow bed-straw.
   (6) *Halcyon*—the king-fisher.
   (7) *Nymphæa*—the white water-lily; the "golden orbs," in the next line, belong to the yellow species.

And thou, by pain and sorrow blest,
    Papaver![1] that an opiate dew
Conceal'st beneath thy scarlet vest,
    Contrasting with the corn-flower blue,
Autumnal months behold thy gauzy leaves
Bend in the rustling gale amid the tawny sheaves.

From the first bud, whose venturous head
    The Winter's lingering tempest braves,
To those which, 'midst the foliage dead,
    Sink latest to their annual graves,
Are all for health, for use, for pleasure given,
And speak, in various ways, the bounteous hand of Heaven.
                              Charlotte Smith.

THE HOROLOGE[2] OF FLORA.

In every copse and sheltered dell
Unveiled to the observant eye,
Are faithful monitors, who tell
How pass the hours and seasons by.

The green-robed children of the spring
Will mark the periods as they pass,
Mingle with leaves Time's feathered wing,
And wreathe with flowers his silent glass.

Mark where transparent waters glide,
Soft flowing o'er their tranquil bed,
There, cradled on the dimpling tide,
Nymphæa rests her lovely head.

But, conscious of the earliest beam,
She rises from her humid nest,
And sees reflected on the stream,
The virgin whiteness of her breast,

---

(1) *Papaver*—poppy. There seems to be an error here; it is the white poppy, *papaver somniferum*, which produces opium—the "opiate dew" of the text.

(2) *Horologe*—(from Lat. *horologium*, which is from ὥρα, an hour, and λέγειν, to tell), that which tells the hour, a clock, a watch, &c. In the "Horologe of Flora," or, as it is sometimes called, "the dial of flowers," certain flowers, which open or shut at regular intervals, fancifully serve the purpose of a time-piece.

Till the bright day-star to the west
Declines, in ocean's surge to lave,
Then, folded in her modest vest,
She slumbers on the rocking wave.

See hieracium's[1] various tribe
Of plumy[2] seed and radiate[3] flowers,
The course of time their bloom describe,
And wake or sleep appointed hours.

Broad o'er its imbricated[4] cup,
The goatsbeard spreads its golden rays,
But shuts its cautious petals up,
Retreating from the noontide blaze.

Pale as a pensive cloistered[5] nun,
The bethlem-star her face unveils,
When o'er the mountain peers the sun,
But shades it from the vesper gales.

Among the loose and arid sands,
The humble arenaria[6] creeps,
Slowly the purple star expands,
But soon within its calyx[7] sleeps.

And those small bells so lightly rayed,
With young Aurora's rosy hue,
Are to the noontide sun displayed,
But shut their plaits[8] against the dew.

---

(1) *Hieracium*—hawkweed.

(2) *Plumy*—feathery, from the Latin *pluma*, a feather.

(3) *Radiate*—from the Latin *radius*, the spoke of a wheel, or a line or ray of light emitted from a luminous body. As a botanical term, the adjective "radiate" signifies having florets set round a disk in the form of a star.

(4) *Imbricated*—from the Latin *imbrex*, a gutter-tile for carrying off rain—cut or indented like a gutter-tile.

(5) *Cloistered*—shut up in a cloister; from the Latin *claustrum*, an enclosed place.

(6) *Arenaria*—from the Latin *arena*, sand, which is from *arere*, to be dry—sandwort.

(7) *Calyx*—another form of the Latin *calix*, a cup—the outer covering of a flower.

(8) *Plaits*—folds; from the Latin *plicare*, to fold, through the French *plier*. In old English the word was *plite*. Chaucer writes:—"to sewe (*i.e.* to sew) and plite."

On upland slopes the shepherds mark
The hour, when, as the dial true,
Chicorium[1] to the towering lark
Lifts her soft eyes, serenely blue.

And thou! "Wee crimson-tipped flower,"[2]
Gatherest thy fringed mantle round
Thy bosom, at the closing hour,
When night-drops bathe the turfy ground;

Unlike silene,[3] who declines
The garish[4] noontide's blazing light.
But when the evening crescent shines,
Gives all her sweetness to the night.

Thus in each flower and simple bell
That in our path untrodden lie,
Are sweet remembrancers, who tell
How fast the winged moments fly.

A SPANISH BULL-FIGHT.

The lists[5] are oped, the spacious area cleared,
Thousands on thousands piled are seated round;
Long ere the first loud trumpet's note is heard,
No vacant seat for lated[6] wight is found.
Hushed is the din of tongues—on gallant steeds,
With milk-white crest, gold spur, and light-poised lance,
Four cavaliers prepare for venturous deeds,
And lowly bending to the lists advance;
The crowd's loud shout their prize, and ladies' lovely glance.

---

(1) *Chicorium*—chicory or succory.
(2) The daisy. In allusion to the poem by Burns, beginning with the above words. (See p. 76.)
(3) *Silene noctiflora*—the night-flowering catch-fly.
(4) *Garish*—from old English *gaure*, or *gare*, to stare, used thus by Chaucer—"Now gaureth all the people on her." Hence the adjective may mean, staringly, fine, gay, showy, oppressively bright.
(5) *Lists*, from Anglo-Saxon *lis-an*, to collect together. *List* is the Anglicised past participle, and means primarily that which is collected together, *i. e.* a collection, as in the expression "a list of names;" in a secondary sense, and in the plural number, it denotes the enclosure round which the company collected sit to behold a public spectacle, and also the barriers of rope, cloth, or board, which serve as the boundary.
(6) *Lated*—for *belated*—arriving too late.

In costly sheen and gaudy cloak arrayed,
But all afoot, the light-limbed Matadore[1]
Stands in the centre, eager to invade
The lord of lowing herds; but not before
The ground, with cautious tread, is traversed o'er,
Lest aught unseen should lurk to thwart his speed:
His arms a dart, he fights aloof,[2] nor more[3]
Can man achieve without his friendly steed—
　Alas! too oft condemned for him to bear and bleed.

Thrice sounds the clarion; lo! the signal falls,
The den expands, and expectation mute[4]
Gapes round the silent circle's[4] peopled walls.
Bounds with one lashing spring[5] the mighty brute,
And, wildly staring, spurns, with sounding foot,
The sand, nor blindly rushes on his foe:
Here, there, he points his threatening front, to suit
His first attack, wide waving to and fro
　His angry tail;—red rolls his eye's dilated glow.

Sudden he stops; his eye is fixed: away,
Away, thou heedless boy![6] prepare the spear:
Now is thy time, to perish, or display
The skill that yet may check his mad career.

　(1) *Matadore*—from the Spanish *matador*, a murderer, from the Latin *mactator*, which is from *mactare*, to kill. The office of the matadore is obvious from the context.

　(2) *Aloof*—*i. e. all off*—entirely separate.

　(3) *Nor more, &c.*—*i. e.* nor more can a man, thus lightly armed, do than fight aloof, without his friendly steed.

　(4) *Mute*—synonymous with *silent* and *dumb*. He is silent who *does* not speak; dumb, who *cannot* speak; and mute, who is compelled by circumstances to be silent. The epithet silent is often applied to *things* that admit no sound, as here, "the silent circle."

　(5) *Lashing spring*—a peculiar use of the term "lashing." The noun "lash" is derived from the French *lascher*, to let loose, and signifies that which is cast loose or thrown. A lashing spring, therefore, may be a leap all abroad, free, unchecked, enormous—or which, as it were, lashes the air.

　(6) *Away, thou heedless boy, &c.*—There is great beauty in the sudden change of the narrator into an actual sharer in the scene itself. He seems so intensely interested in the scene he is describing that he cannot refrain from calling out to warn the "heedless boy" of his danger, and the reader's sympathy is proportionately quickened.

With well-timed croupe[1] the nimble coursers veer;
On foams the bull, but not unscathed he goes;
Streams from his flank the crimson torrent clear:
He flies, he wheels, distracted with his throes;
Dart follows dart; lance, lance; loud bellowings speak his woes.

Again he comes;—nor lance nor darts avail,
Nor the wild plunging of the tortured horse;
Though man and man's avenging arms assail,
Vain are his weapons, vainer is his force.
One gallant steed is stretched a mangled corse;
Another, hideous sight! unseamed appears,
His gory chest unveils life's panting source;
Though death-struck, still his feeble frame he rears;
Staggering, but stemming all, his lord unarmed he bears.

Foiled,[2] bleeding, breathless, furious to the last,
Full in the centre stands the bull at bay,
Mid wounds, and clinging darts, and lances brast,[3]
And foes disabled in the brutal fray:
And now the Matadores around him play,
Shake the red cloak, and poise the ready brand:
Once more through all he bursts his thundering way—
Vain rage! the mantle quits the cunning hand,
Wraps his fierce eye—'tis past—he sinks upon the sand!

Where his vast neck just mingles with the spine,
Sheathed in his form the deadly weapon lies.
He stops—he starts—disdaining to decline:
Slowly he falls, amidst triumphant cries,
Without a groan, without a struggle dies.
The decorated car appears—on high
The corse is piled—sweet sight for vulgar eyes!
Four steeds that spurn the rein, as swift as shy,
Hurl the dark bulk along, scarce seen in dashing by.

Such the ungentle sport that oft invites
The Spanish maid, and cheers the Spanish swain.

(1) *Croupe* or *croupade*—a particular leap, taught in the *manège*, or riding-school—it is higher than that called the curvet.

(2) *Foiled*—to *foil*, is thus distinguished from to *baffle*; to foil, signifies to defeat one's adversary by disabling him; to baffle, to defeat him by perplexing or counteracting his plans.

(3) *Brast*—an old form of *burst*, from the Anglo-Saxon *berst-an*, to break out or forth, or generally, to break; hence, "brast" is broken.

Nurtured in blood betimes, his heart delights
In vengeance, gloating[1] on another's pain.
What private feuds the troubled village stain!
Though now one phalanxed host[2] should meet the foe,
Enough, alas! in humbler homes remain,
To meditate 'gainst friends the secret blow,
For some slight cause of wrath, whence life's warm stream must flow.

Byron.

SPRING.

Mindful of disaster past,
And shrinking at the northern blast,
The sleety storm returning still,
The morning hoar, the evening chill,
Reluctant comes the timid Spring:
Scarce a bee, with airy ring,
Murmurs the blossomed boughs around
That clothe the garden's southern bound:[3]
Scarce the hardy primrose peeps[4]
From the dark dell's entangled steeps:
O'er the field of waving broom
Slowly shoots[4] the golden bloom:
And but by fits the furze-clad dale
Tinctures the transitory gale.
Scant along the ridgy land
The beans their new-born ranks expand;
The fresh-turned soil, with tender blades,
Thinly the sprouting barley shades;
Fringing the forest's devious[5] edge
Half-robed appears the hawthorn hedge;

---

(1) *Gloating*—connected with *glowing*—looking at anything with ardent or eager eyes, that indicate pleasure in the sight.

(2) *Phalanxed host*—an army drawn up in a phalanx or dense square body.

(3) *Southern bound*—it has been objected to this line, that the wall which has the southern aspect will be the northern, not the southern boundary.

(4) *Peeps, shoots*—these words serve well to show the animation that is given to language by the use of metaphors. It might have been said that the primrose could scarcely be "seen" or "found" in the dark dell, but this would have been tame and inexpressive; whereas a sort of human interest is conferred upon the little flower by the word "peeps." Again, how vividly is the sudden effect of the blossoming broom on the eye painted by the word "shoots!"

(5) *Devious*—see note 3, p. 15.

Or to the distant eye displays,
Weakly green,[1] its budding sprays.
The swallow, for a moment seen,
Skims in haste the village green;
From the gray moor, on feeble wing,
The screaming plovers idly spring;
The butterfly, gay-painted, soon
Explores awhile the tepid noon;
And fondly[2] trusts its tender dyes
To fickle suns and flattering skies.

Fraught[3] with a transient frozen shower,
If a cloud should haply lower,[4]
Sailing o'er the landscape dark,
Mute on a sudden is the lark;
But, when gleams the sun again
O'er the pearl-besprinkled plain,
And from behind his watery veil
Looks through the thin descending hail,
She mounts, and lessening to the sight,
Salutes the blithe return of light,
And high her tuneful track pursues
Mid the dim rainbow's scattered hues.[5]
Beneath a willow long forsook[6]
The fisher seeks his 'ccustomed nook,
And, bursting through the crackling sedge
That crowns the current's caverned edge,
Startles from the bordering wood
The bashful wild-duck's early brood.
His free-born vigour yet unbroke,
By lordly man's usurping yoke,

(1) *Weakly green*—The poet Gray, in one of his letters, speaks of "that *tender emerald green*, which one usually sees only a fortnight in the opening of the spring."

(2) *Fondly*—foolishly—this is the ancient meaning of the word. Chaucer says—

"The rich man full fond is, I wis,
That weneth (fancies) that he loved is."

(3) *Fraught*—connected in derivation with *freight*—laden, completely filled.

(4) *Lower*, or *lour*—from *low*—to become low as if about to fall, hence to be heavy, dark, stormy, or threatening.

(5) *Hues*—A beautiful couplet; the lark, just before mute, now tunefully pursues her flight amongst the very fragments, as it were, of the rainbow, floating about in the air.

(6) *Long forsook*—that is, only throughout the winter, for it was the fisherman's accustomed nook.

The bounding colt forgets to play,
Basking beneath the noon-tide ray,
And stretched among the daisies pied[1]
Of a green dingle's sloping side:
While far beneath, where nature spreads
Her boundless length of level meads,
In loose luxuriance taught to stray,
A thousand tumbling rills inlay[2]
With silver veins the vale, or pass
Redundant through the sparkling grass.

Yet, in these presages rude,
Midst her pensive solitude,
Fancy,[3] with prophetic glance,
Sees the teeming[4] months advance;
The field, the forest, green and gay,
The dappled[5] slope, the tedded hay;
Sees the reddening orchard blow,
The harvest wave, the vintage flow;
Sees June unfold his glossy robe
Of thousand hues o'er all the globe;
Sees Ceres grasp her crown of corn,[6]
And Plenty load her ample horn.[7]

T. Warton.

---

(1) *Pied*—party-coloured or variegated like the *pie*, a bird so named.

(2) *Inlay*—a beautiful fancy; the rills, like veins of silver, inlay the vale. The passage, however, is much marred by the sudden abandonment of the metaphor—the expression "pass through," which follows, being purely literal.

(3) *Fancy, &c.*—i. e. fancy discovers the future in the present. She sees in the opening buds of spring the full-blown flowers of summer, and the ripe fruits of autumn.

(4) *Teeming*—from the Anglo-Saxon *tym-an*, to bring forth abundantly.

(5) *Dappled*—some derive this word from *apple*, as if streaked or spotted like an apple; but this etymology is doubtful. The word is more probably a diminutive of *dab* or *daub*, to spot or smear, as *nibble* of *nip*, and *waddle* of *wade;* hence, to dabble or dapple, is to spot or streak many times, or in many places.

(6) *Crown of corn*—Ceres, the goddess of agriculture, is usually represented with a chaplet of wheat around her temples.

(7) *Ample horn*—the horn of plenty, also called Cornucopiæ. The allusion is derived from ancient mythology, which informs us that Jupiter's nurse filled a goat's horn, which had been accidentally broken off, with fruits, and wreathing it with flowers, gave it to the babe, who, when he grew up and became powerful, made the horn the emblem of fertility. See Ovid, Fasti. lib. v. 115—128.

THE DYING MOTHER AND HER BABE.[1]

The room I well remember, and the bed
On which she lay; and all the faces, too,
That crowded dark and mournfully around.
Her father there, and mother, bending stood
And down their aged cheeks fell many drops
Of bitterness. Her husband too was there,
And brothers, and they wept; her sisters, too,
Did weep and sorrow comfortless; and all
Within the house was dolorous and sad.
This I remember well—but better still
I do remember, and will ne'er forget,
The dying eye!—That eye alone was bright,
And brighter grew, as nearer death approached;
As I have seen the gentle little flower
Look fairest in the silver beam, which fell
Reflected from the thunder-cloud, that soon
Came down, and o'er the desert scattered far
And wide its loveliness.[2] She made a sign
To bring her babe;—'twas brought, and by her placed.
She looked upon its face, that neither smiled
Nor wept, nor knew who gazed upon it; and laid
Her hand upon its little breast, and sought
For it—with looks that seemed to penetrate
The heavens—unutterable blessings, such
As God to dying parents only grants
For infants left behind them in the world.
"God keep my child!" we heard her say, and heard
No more. The angel of the covenant
Was come, and faithful to his promise, stood
Prepared to walk with her through death's dark vale.[3]
And now her eyes grew bright, and brighter still—
Too bright for ours to look upon, suffused

(1) This passage, though occasionally deformed by prosaic expressions and unmusical rhythm, depicts a deeply interesting scene in a very touching manner.

(2) The interruption of the narrative at such a point, by a long simile, is in very questionable taste. The effect of the supernatural brightness of the "dying eye," upon the reader's mind, ought not to have been thus neutralized.

(3) "Though I walk through the valley of the shadow of death, I will fear no evil: for thou art with me." Psalm xxiii 4.

With many tears—and closed without a cloud.
They set as sets the morning star, which goes
Not down behind the darkened west, nor hides
Obscured among the tempests of the sky,
But melts away into the light of heaven.[1]

Pollock

VENI CREATOR.[2]

CREATOR Spirit! by whose aid
The world's foundations first were laid,
Come visit every pious mind;
Come pour thy joys on human kind;
From sin and sorrow set us free,
And make thy temples[3] worthy thee.

O source of uncreated light,
The Father's promised Paraclete![4]
Thrice holy fount, thrice holy fire,
Our hearts with heavenly love inspire;
Come, and thy sacred unction bring,
To sanctify us while we sing.

Plenteous of grace descend from high,
Rich in thy sevenfold energy!
Thou strength of his almighty hand,
Whose power does heaven and earth command!
Proceeding Spirit,[5] our defence,
Who dost the gift of tongues dispense,
And crown'st thy gift with eloquence,

---

(1) The comparison of the eye, whose brightness melted, as it were, into the light of an eternal day, to the morning star, is very beautiful, and it is clothed in most felicitous language. A similar thought occurs in Montgomery's poem entitled "Friends;" speaking of friends as stars that pass away as the morning advances, he says (see p. 215):—

"Nor sink those stars in empty night,—
They hide themselves in heaven's own light."

Hide themselves in *light!*—a very striking and picturesque expression.

(2) *Veni Creator*—"Come, Creator," the first two words of a Latin hymn used in the Roman Catholic church.

(3) *Temples*—"Know ye not that ye are the *temples* of God, and that the Spirit of God dwelleth in you?" 1 Cor. iii. 16.

(4) *Paraclete*—the Greek word for "Comforter."

(5) "The spirit of truth, which *proceedeth* from the father." John xv. 26.

Refine and purge our earthly parts;
But, oh! inflame and fire our hearts;
Our frailties help, our vice control,
Submit the senses to the soul;
And when rebellious they are grown,
Then lay thy hand, and hold them down.

Chase from our minds the infernal foe,
And peace, the fruit of love, bestow;
And lest our feet should step astray,
Protect and guide us in the way.

Make us eternal[1] truths receive,
And practise all that we believe:
Give us thyself, that we may see
The Father, and the Son, by thee.

Immortal[1] honour, endless[1] fame,
Attend the Almighty Father's name:
The Saviour Son be glorified,
Who for lost man's redemption died:
And equal adoration be,
Eternal Paraclete, to thee! *Dryden.*

THE POPLARS.

The poplars are felled;—farewell to the shade,
And the whispering sound of the cool colonnade;[2]
The winds play no longer and sing in the leaves,
Nor Ouse[3] on its bosom their image receives.

---

(1) *Eternal, immortal, endless, everlasting,* all convey the idea of perpetual existence—they differ in the modification of that idea. That is *eternal* which always is, and cannot cease to be; *immortal*, which always lives, which can never die; *endless*, which has no termination; *everlasting* which has neither interruption nor termination. These words are very appropriately employed in the phrases "*eternal* truths," "*immortal* honour" (a figurative expression, since honour is not a living being), "*endless* fame," *i. e.* glory without end, "*everlasting* happiness."

(2) *Colonnade*—an architectural term designating a range of columns; here ingeniously applied to trees regularly disposed like pillars.

(3) *Ouse*—the Great Ouse in Buckinghamshire.

Twelve years have elapsed since I last took a view
Of my favourite field, and the bank where they grew:
And now in the grass behold they are laid,
And the tree is my seat that once lent me a shade.

The blackbird has fled to another retreat,
Where the hazels afford him a screen from the heat;
And the scene where his melody charmed me before,
Resounds with the sweet-flowing ditty no more.

My fugitive years are all hasting away,
And I must ere long lie as lowly as they,
With a turf on my breast, and a stone at my head,
Ere another such grove shall arise in its stead

The change both my heart and my fancy employs;
I reflect on the frailty of man and his joys;
Short-lived as we are, yet our pleasures, we see,
Have a still shorter date, and die sooner than we.
Cowper.

TO THE WEATHERCOCK.[1]

The dawn has broke, the morn is up,
   Another day begun,
And there thy poised and gilded spear
   Is flashing in the sun,
Upon that steep and lofty tower
   Where thou thy watch[2] hast kept,
A true and faithful sentinel,
   While all around thee slept.

For years upon thee there has poured
   The summer's noon-day heat,
And through the long, dark, starless night,
   The winter storms have beat;

---

(1) The good sense of these lines, and the originality with which a trite subject is treated, are more conspicuous than their strictly poetical merits. The style in some parts is almost prosaic, and the rhymes are occasionally incorrect, but the poem is nevertheless on the whole well worthy of preservation. It is the production of an American poet.

(2) *Watch*—originally identical with *wake*, as *ditch* with *dike* or *dyke*. In Wycliffe's Testament we have "Wake ye and preie," &c., for "Watch ye and pray," &c. Mark xiv. 38. To watch, therefore, is to keep awake—to observe; hence the meaning of the noun is obvious.

But yet thy **duty has** been done,
  By day and night **the** same;
Still thou hast watched and **met** the storm,
  Whichever way it came.

No chilling blast in wrath has swept
  Along the distant heaven,
But thou hast watch upon it kept,
  And instant warning given;
And when Midsummer's sultry beams
  Oppress all living things,
Thou dost announce each breeze that comes
  With health upon its wings.

How oft I've **seen** at **early dawn,**
  Or twilight's[1] quiet **hour,**
The swallows, in their joyous glee,
  Come darting round thy tower,
As if, with thee, to hail the sun,
  And catch his earliest light,
And offer ye the morn's salute,
  Or bid ye both—good **night.**

And when around thee, or above,
  No breath of air has stirred,
Thou seemst to watch the circling flight
  Of each free happy bird;
Till, after twittering round thy head,
  In many a mazy track,
The whole delighted company
  Have settled on thy back.

Then, if perchance amid their mirth
  A gentle breeze has sprung,
And, prompt to mark its first approach,
  Thy eager form has swung,
I've thought I **almost** heard thee **say,**
  As far aloft they flew,
" **Now all** away!—here ends **our play,**
  For **I** have work to do!"

Men slander thee, my honest **friend,**
  And call thee, in their pride,
An emblem of their fickleness,
  Thou ever faithful guide!

---

(1) *Twilight*—from the Anglo-Saxon *tweonliht*, doubtful light.

Each week, unstable human mind
    A "weathercock" they call:
And thus, unthinkingly, mankind
    Abuse thee, one and all.

They have no right to make thy name
    A by-word for their deeds:
They change their friends, their principles,
    Their fashions and their creeds;
While thou hast ne'er, like them, been known
    Thus causelessly to range,
But when thou *changest sides*, canst give
    Good reason for the change.

Thou, like some lofty soul, whose course
    The thoughtless oft condemn,
Art touched by many airs from heaven
    Which never breathe on them;
And moved by many impulses
    Which they can never know,
Who, round their earth-bound circles, plod
    The dusty paths below.

Through one more dark and cheerless night
    Thou well hast kept thy trust,
And now in glory o'er thy head
    The morning light has burst:
And unto earth's true watcher[1] thus,
    When his dark hours have passed,
Will come the "day-spring[2] from on high,"
    To cheer his path at last.

Bright symbol of *fidelity*,
    Still may I think of thee;
And may the lesson thou dost teach
    Be never lost on me:
But still in sunshine or in storm,
    Whatever task is mine,
May I be faithful to my trust,
    As thou hast been to thine.   *A. G. Greene.*

(1) *Earth's true watcher*—one who faithfully watches on earth; an allusion probably to the precept of our Saviour, "Watch ye, therefore: for ye know not when the master of the house cometh." Mark xiii. 35.

(2) *Day-spring*—the springing or rising of day—the dawn; figuratively employed here to denote the dawn of a heavenly day, which, after the dark hours of his life, will burst on the view of the faithful watcher, *i. e* the true Christian.

CHEVY CHACE.[1]

God prosper long our noble king,
    Our lives and safeties all:
A woeful hunting once there did
    In Chevy Chace[2] befal:

To drive the deer with hound and horn
    Earl Percy took his way:
The child may rue that is unborn,
    The hunting of that day.[3]

The stout earl of Northumberland
    A vow to God did make,
His pleasure in the Scottish woods
    Three summer days to take;

(1) This fine old ballad, which is in fact a modernised edition of a more ancient one, received its present form, it is thought, about the beginning of James the First's reign. The name of the author of the ancient song is Richard Sheale; that of the moderniser is unknown.

"The fine heroic song of **Chevy Chace**," writes Bishop Percy, "has ever been admired by competent judges. Those genuine strokes of natural and artless passion which have endeared it to the most simple readers, have recommended it to the most refined; and it has equally been the amusement of our childhood, and the favourite of our riper years."

Sir Philip Sidney, in his "Defense of Poesy," writes thus respecting this ancient ballad:—"I never heard the old song of Percy and Douglas that I found not my heart moved more than with a trumpet; and yet is sung (*i. e.* even when it is sung) but by some blind crowder (*fiddler*), with no rougher voice than rude style."

Addison, too, has eulogized the beauties of this poem—the modern version—in two numbers (70 and 74) of the "Spectator."

As it may interest some readers to see a specimen of the ancient ballad, the following lines, which form the first stanza, are subjoined:—

"The Perse owt off Northombarlande,
    And a bowe to God mayd he,
That he wolde hunte in the mountayns
    Off Chyviat within dayes iii.,
In the magger of doughte Dogles,
    And all that ever with him be."

(2) *Chevy Chace*—or Cheviot Chace, a preserve for game on the Cheviot Hills in Northumberland, then within the Scottish boundary.

(3) Addison invites us to admire this couplet, for the simple manner in which the remote consequences are suggested.

The chiefest harts in Chevy Chace
    To kill and bear away.—
These tidings to Earl Douglas came,
    In Scotland where he lay;

Who sent Earl Percy present word[1]
    He would prevent his sport:
The English earl not fearing that,
    Did to the woods resort,

With fifteen hundred bowmen bold,
    All chosen men of might,
Who knew full well in time of need,
    To aim their shafts aright.

The gallant greyhounds swiftly ran,
    To chase the fallow[2] deer;
On Monday they began to hunt
    When daylight did appear;

And long before high noon, they had
    A hundred fat bucks slain;
Then, having dined, the drovers went
    To rouse the deer again.

The bowmen mustered on the hills,
    Well able to endure;[3]
And all their rear with special care,
    That day was guarded sure.

The hounds ran swiftly through the woods,
    The nimble deer to take,
And with their cries the hills and dales
    An echo shrill did make.

Lord Percy to the quarry[4] went
    To view the slaughtered deer

---

(1) *Sent present word*—sent word at once, or immediately.

(2) *Fallow*—from Anglo-Saxon *fealo*, yellow.

(3) *Endure*—to go on with their sport, and yet be ready for the foe they expected.

(4) *Quarry*—The etymology of this word is doubtful. Some derive it from the Latin *quæro*, to seek or pursue, and thus *quarry* would mean the prey or game aimed at; others connect it with the verb *to carry*, and consider it as the booty carried off (the field); others again trace it to the French *quarrée* or *carrée*, the square or inclosure into which the game was driven, hence it might afterwards signify the prey thus caught, then game of every kind. The last derivation best suits the present passage, which evidently refers to an inclosure of some sort.

Quoth he, "Earl Douglas promised
   This day to meet me here:

"But if I thought he would not come,
   No longer would I stay."—
With that, a brave young gentleman
   Thus to the Earl did say:

"Lo! yonder doth Earl Douglas come,
   His men in armour bright:
Full twenty hundred Scottish spears
   All marching in our sight;

"All men of pleasant Tividale,[1]
   Fast by the river Tweed."—
"Then cease your sports," Earl Percy said,
   "And take your bows with speed:

"And now with me, my countrymen,
   Your courage forth advance;
For never was there champion yet,
   In Scotland or in France,

"That ever did on horseback come,
   But if my hap it were,
I durst encounter, man for man,
   With him to break a spear."

Earl Douglas on his milk-white steed,
   Most like a baron bold,
Rode foremost of the company,
   Whose armour shone like gold.[2]

"Show me," said he, "whose men you be,
   That hunt so boldly here;
That, without my consent, do chase
   And kill my fallow deer."

The first man that did answer make,
   Was noble Percy, he;
Who said, "We list not[3] to declare,
   Nor show whose men we be:

---

(1) *Tividale*—Teviotdale. The Teviot is a tributary of the Tweed.

(2) *Whose armour*—*i.e.* and his armour; *who is*, in old English, often used for *and he*, or *and they*. The Latin *qui* is constantly employed in the same way.

(3) *We list not*—we care not—we are not disposed.

"Yet will we spend our dearest blood,
  Thy chiefest harts to slay."
Then Douglas swore a solemn oath,
  And thus in rage did say:—

"Ere thus I will out-braved be,
  One of us two shall die:
I know thee well, an earl thou art,
  Lord Percy, so am I.

"But trust me, Percy, pity it were,
  And great offence, to kill
Any of these our guiltless men,
  For they have done no ill.

"Let thou and I the battle try,
  And set our men aside."—
"Accursed be he," Earl Percy said,
  "By whom this is denied."

Then stepped a gallant squire forth,
  Witherington was his name,
Who said, "I would not have it told
  To Henry our king, for shame,

"That e'er my captain fought on foot,
  And I stood looking on.—
You be two earls," quoth Witherington,
  "And I a squire alone:

"I'll do the best that do I may,
  While I have strength to stand;
While I have power to wield my sword,
  I'll fight with heart and hand."

Our English archers bent their bows,
  Their hearts were good and true;
At the first flight of arrows sent,
  Full fourscore Scots they slew.

Yet bides Earl Douglas on the bent,[1]
  As chieftain stout and good;
As valiant captain, all unmoved,
  The shock he firmly stood.

---

(1) *Bent*—hill-side, declivity, field of battle.

His host he parted had in three,
  As leader ware[1] and tried;
And soon his spearmen on their foes
  Bore down on every side.

Throughout the English archery
  They dealt full many a wound;
But still our valiant Englishmen
  All firmly kept their ground;

And throwing straight their bows away,
  They grasped their swords so bright:
And now sharp blows, a heavy shower,
  On shields and helmets light.[2]

They closed full fast on every side,
  No slackness there was found;
And many a gallant gentleman
  Lay gasping on the ground.

And oh! it was a grief to see,
  And likewise for to hear
The cries of men lying in their gore,
  And scattered here and there.

At last these two stout earls did meet,
  Like captains of great might:
Like lions wode,[3] they laid on load,[4]
  And made a cruel fight.

They fought until they both did sweat,
  With swords of tempered steel;
Until the blood, like drops of rain,
  They trickling down did feel.

---

(1) *Ware*—wary, **cautious**.

(2) The four preceding stanzas, somewhat altered from the ancient ballad, were introduced by Bishop **Percy**, in the place of "the unmeaning lines" of the modernised edition, which are given here as a puzzle for the ingenious:—

> "To drive the deer, with hound and horn,
>   Douglas bade on the bent;
> Two captains moved with **mickle** might,
>   Their spears to shivers went."

(3) *Wode*—mad, fierce, **wild**; connected with Woden, the Anglo-Saxon god of war, who is identical with the Scandinavian Odin.

(4) *They laid on load*—they struck violently and repeatedly.

"Yield thee, Lord Percy," Douglas said,
　"In faith I will thee bring
Where thou shalt high advanced be,
　By James, our Scottish king:[1]

"Thy ransom I will freely give,
　And this report of thee,
Thou art the most courageous knight
　That ever I did see."

"No, Douglas," quoth Earl Percy then,
　"Thy proffer I do scorn;
I will not yield to any Scot
　That ever yet was born."

With that there came an arrow keen
　Out of an English bow,
Which struck Earl Douglas to the heart,
　A deep and deadly blow;

Who never spoke more words than these,
　"Fight on my merry men[2] all;
For why, my life is at an end;
　Lord Percy sees my fall."[3]

Then leaving life, Earl Percy took
　The dead man by the hand,
And said, "Earl Douglas, for thy life
　Would I had lost my land!

---

(1) *James our Scottish king*—There is much difficulty in fixing the date of the hunting in Chevy Chace. Mention is here made of "James our Scottish king," and a little before, of "Henry our (the English) king." Now it appears that James I. of Scotland came to the throne in 1424, just two years after the accession of Henry VI. of England, so that, in accordance with these data, the hunting must have taken place *after* 1424, and yet reference is made in the poem to the *subsequent* battle of Homildon Hill, which we know was fought in 1402, in the reign of Henry IV., when Robert III., father of James I., was alive. The only possible way of reconciling these discrepancies is to suppose that the author of the ancient ballad mistook Robert for James.

(2) *My merry men*—a common expression in old ballads, nearly equivalent to "my brave fellows."

(3) *Lord Percy sees my fall*—The introduction of this aggravating circumstance is much commended by Addison, as also Earl Percy's taking the dead man by the hand.

"Ah me! my very heart doth bleed
   With sorrow for thy sake;
For sure a more redoubted[1] knight
   Mischance did never take."

A knight amongst the Scots there was,
   Which saw Earl Douglas die,
Who straight in wrath did vow revenge
   Upon the Lord Percy:

Sir Hugh Montgomery was he called;
   Who with a spear most bright,
Well mounted on a gallant steed,
   Ran fiercely through the fight;

And passed the English archers all,
   Without all dread or fear:
And through Earl Percy's body then
   He thrust his hateful spear:[2]

With such a vehement force and might
   He did his body gore,
The spear went through the other side
   A large cloth-yard, and more.

So thus did both these nobles die,
   Whose courage none could stain:
An English archer then perceived
   The noble earl was slain;

He had a bow bent in his hand,
   Made of a trusty tree;
An arrow of a cloth-yard long
   Up to the head drew he:

Against Sir Hugh Montgomery
   So right the shaft he set,
The grey-goose wing that was thereon
   In his heart's blood was wet.

---

(1) *Redoubted*—formidable; from the French, *redouter*, to fear, dread.
(2) Each earl died, it will be observed, by the national weapon of his enemy—the Scot by an English arrow, the Englishman by a Scottish spear.

This fight did last from break of day
  Till setting of the sun,[1]
For when they rung the evening bell,
  The battle scarce was done.

With stout Earl Percy there was slain
  Sir John of Egerton,
Sir Robert Ratcliffe, and Sir John,
  Sir James that bold baron:

And, with Sir George, and stout Sir James,
  Both knights of good account,
Good Sir Ralph Raby there was slain,
  Whose prowess did surmount.

For Witherington needs must I wail,
  As one in doleful dumps,[2]
For when his legs were smitten off,
  He fought upon his stumps.

And with Earl Douglas there was slain
  Sir Hugh Montgomery,
Sir Charles Murray, that from the field
  One foot would never flee.

---

(1) *From break of day, &c.*—This is not consistent with the opening of the ballad, where we are told of the huntsman having *dined* before the arrival of Douglas and his men. In the old song this inconsistency is absent:

    "This battle begun in Cheviot
      An hour before the none (*noon*),
    And when even-song bell was rung,
      The battle was not half done."

It would appear from this quotation that the evening bell, or curfew, was substituted by the moderniser, after the Reformation, for the vesper bell of the ancient writer.

(2) *Doleful dumps—i. e.* "I, as one in deep concern, must lament." This expression, which has now become ludicrous, was formerly only employed in the sense given above. Dump is by some derived from *dumb*, and thought to express the silent grief which arises from deep affliction. It sometimes signifies a melancholy strain of music. The moderniser has not in this instance improved upon the pathetic simplicity of the original, which runs thus:—

    "For Witherington my heart is woe,
      That ever he slain should be;
    For when both his legs were hewn in two,
      Yet he knelt and fought on his knee."

Sir Charles Murray of Ratcliffe, too,
   His sister's son was he;
Sir David Lamb, so well esteemed,
   But saved he could not be.

And the Lord Maxwell, in like case,
   Did with Earl Douglas die;
Of twenty hundred Scottish spears,
   Scarce fifty-five did fly.

Of fifteen hundred Englishmen,
   Went home but fifty-three;
The rest in Chevy Chace were slain,
   Under the greenwood tree.

Next day did many widows come,
   Their husbands to bewail;
They washed their wounds in brinish tears,
   But all would not prevail.

Their bodies, bathed in purple gore,
   They bore with them away;
They kissed them dead a thousand times,
   Ere they were clad in clay.

The news was brought to Edenborrow,
   Where Scotland's king did reign,
That brave Earl Douglas suddenly
   Was with an arrow slain:

"O heavy news!" King James did say,
   "Scotland can witness be,
I have not any captain more
   Of such account as he."

Like tidings to King Henry came,
   Within as short a space,
That Percy of Northumberland
   Was slain in Chevy Chace.

"Now God be with him," said our king,
   "Sith[1] 'twill no better be;
I trust I have within my realm,
   Five hundred as good as he.

---

(1) *Sith*—since. Another form is *sithence*, whence came since.

"Yet shall not Scots nor Scotland say,
　But I will vengeance take:
I'll be revenged on them all,
　For brave Earl Percy's sake."

This vow full well the king performed,
　After, at Humbledown;¹
In one day fifty knights were slain,
　With lords of high renown;

And of the rest of small account
　Did many hundreds die.—
Thus endeth² the hunting of Chevy Chace,
　Made by the Earl Percy.

God save the king! and bless this land,
　With plenty, joy, and peace;
And grant, henceforth, that foul debate³
　'Twixt noblemen may cease.

FEMALE NAMES.

In Christian world MARY the garland wears;
REBECCA sweetens on a Hebrew's ear;
Quakers for pure PRISCILLA are more clear;
And the light Gaul by amorous NINON swears.

---

(1) *Humbledown*—Humbleton, or Homildon Hill, in Northumberland, where a battle took place in 1402, in which the Earl of Northumberland and his son Hotspur gained a complete victory over the Scots.

(2) *Thus endeth*—This battle at Homildon Hill, which was occasioned by the hunting in Chevy Chace, is called the ending of the hunting.

(3) *Debate*—this word, formerly used to denote every kind of contest, has in course of time come to mean verbal strife only.

Having displayed in the beginning of this ballad the tributes of praise which its merits have elicited, it is but fair to add, at the close, a contrary opinion delivered by a great authority. Dr. Johnson, in his "Life of Addison," while ridiculing Addison for having praised the ballad in the "Spectator," speaks of the "chill and lifeless imbecility of the poem;" and adds—"the story cannot possibly be told in a manner that shall make less impression on the mind:" an opinion which, when compared with Dr. Percy's, given in a former note, proves how widely "doctors" may "differ."

Among the lesser lights how LUCY[1] shines!
What air of fragrance ROSAMOND throws round!
How like a hymn doth sweet CECILIA sound!
Of MARTHAS, and of ABIGAILS, few lines
Have bragged in verse. Of coarsest household stuff
Should homely JOAN be fashioned. But can
You BARBARA resist, or MARIAN?
And is not CLARE for love excuse enough?
Yet, by my faith in numbers, I profess,
These all, than Saxon EDITH, please me less.

Lamb.

SWIMMING.[2]

CHEERED by the milder beam, the sprightly youth
Speeds to the well-known pool, whose crystal depth
A sandy bottom shows. Awhile he stands
Gazing[3] the inverted landscape, half afraid
To meditate the blue profound below;
Then plunges headlong down the circling flood.
His ebon tresses and his rosy cheek
Instant emerge; and through the obedient wave,
At each short breathing by his lip repelled,
With arms and legs according well, he makes,
As humour leads, an easy winding path;
While, from his polished sides, a dewy light
Effuses on the pleased spectators round.
   This is the purest exercise of health,
The kind refresher of the summer heats;
Nor, when cold Winter keens the brightening flood,
Would I, weak-shivering, linger on the brink.

---

(1) *Lucy*—from the Latin *lux, lucis*, light. The graceful ingenuity displayed in this and the next two lines well deserves attention. "Among the lesser *lights* how *Lucy shines*," is exceedingly apt; and scarcely less so, "What air of *fragrance Rosamond* (from the Latin *rosa*, rose, and *munda*, pure or sweet) throws round."

(2) This passage is extracted from the "Summer" of Thomson's "Seasons."

(3) *Gazing—i. e.* gazing at. This license of leaving out words is very frequently employed by Thomson. See below, "headlong down the circling flood," *i. e.* into the flood; and "the limbs knit." *i. e.* became knit or compacted into strength.

Thus life redoubles; and is oft preserved
By the bold swimmer, in the swift illapse[1]
Of accident disastrous. Hence the limbs
Knit into force; and the Roman arm
That rose victorious o'er the conquered earth,
First learned, while tender, to subdue the wave.
Even[2] from the body's purity, the mind
Receives a secret sympathetic aid.

Thomson.

ON A TEAR.

Oh! that the chemist's magic art
   Could crystalize this sacred treasure!
Long should it glitter near my heart,
   A secret source of pensive pleasure.

The little brilliant, ere it fell,
   Its lustre caught from Chloe's eye;
Then, trembling, left its coral cell—
   The spring of sensibility.

Sweet drop of pure and pearly light!
   In thee the rays of virtue shine;[3]
More calmly clear, more mildly bright
   Than any gem that gilds the mine.

Benign restorer of the soul,
   Who ever fliest to bring relief,
When first we feel the rude control
   Of love or pity, joy or grief.[4]

---

(1) *Illapse*—sliding into occurrence. This "swift illapse of accident disastrous," is a very pedantic and unpleasing expression.

(2) *Even*—The word "even" belongs to the next clause, though for convenience' sake placed here. The construction in prose would be, From the body's purity, even the mind, &c.

(3) *Rays of virtue shine*—because tears are frequently the indication of repentance.

(4) *Love or pity, &c.*—all which passions, though so diverse in their character, find relief through the same natural channel.

The sage's and the poet's theme,[1]
  In every clime, in every age;
Thou charm'st in fancy's idle dream,
  In reason's philosophic page.

That very law[2] which moulds a tear,
  And bids it trickle from its source,
That law preserves the earth a sphere,
  And guides the planets in their course.

Rogers.

A PSALM OF LIFE.[3]

"Be up and doing."

TELL me not, in mournful numbers,
  Life is but an empty dream!
For the soul is dead that slumbers,
  And things are not what they seem.

Life is real! Life is earnest!
  And the grave is not its goal;
"Dust thou art, to dust returnest,"
  Was not spoken of the soul.

Not enjoyment, and not sorrow,
  Is our destined end or way;
But to act that each to-morrow
  Finds us farther than to-day.

Art is long, and Time is fleeting,
  And our hearts, though stout and brave,
Still, like muffled drums, are beating
  Funeral marches to the grave.

---

(1) *The sage's, &c.*—The tear which stimulates the poet's fancy, impels the philosopher to inquire scientifically into its origin, the cause of its shape, trickling down, &c.

(2) *Law*—the law of gravitation.

(3) "No poet has more beautifully expressed the depth of his conviction, that life is an earnest reality, something with eternal issues and dependencies; that this earth is no scene of revelry, a market of sale, but an arena of contest, and a hall of doom. This is the inspiration of his [Longfellow's] 'Psalm of Life.'"—*Gilfillan.*

In the world's broad field of battle,
   In the bivouac of Life,
Be not like dumb, driven cattle
   Be like heroes in the strife!

Trust no Future, howe'er pleasant!
   Let the dead Past bury its dead!
Act—act in the living Present!
   Heart within, and God o'erhead!

Lives of great men all remind us
   We can make our lives sublime,
And, departing, leave behind us
   Footprints on the sands of time;

Footprints, that perhaps another,
   Sailing o'er life's solemn main,
A forlorn and shipwrecked brother,
   Seeing, shall take heart again.

Let us, then, be up and doing,
   With a heart for any fate;
Still achieving, still pursuing,
   Learn to labour and to wait.

Longfellow.

EXCELSIOR.[1]

"Onward and upward."

THE shades of night were falling fast,
As through an Alpine village passed
A youth, who bore, 'mid snow and ice,
A banner, with the strange device,
   "Excelsior!"

His brow was sad; his eye beneath
Flashed like a falchion from its sheath,
And like a silver clarion rung
The accents of that unknown tongue,
   "Excelsior!"

[1] "'Excelsior' is Life and its Psalm personified. Longfellow has written in it his glowing hopes of the future, as well as his theory of the past. That figure climbing the evening Alps, in defiance of danger, of man's remonstrance, and the far deeper fascination of woman's love, is a type of man struggling, triumphing, purified by suffering, perfected in death."—*Gilfillan.*

In happy homes he saw the light
Of household fires gleam warm and bright;
Above the spectral glaciers shone,
And from his lips escaped a groan,
   "Excelsior!"

"Try not the pass!" the old man said,
"Dark lowers the tempest overhead,
The roaring torrent is deep and wide!"
And loud that clarion voice replied,
   "Excelsior!"

"O stay!" the maiden said, "and rest
Thy weary head upon this breast!"
A tear stood in his bright blue eye,
But still he answered, with a sigh,
   "Excelsior!"

"Beware the pine-tree's withered branch!
Beware the awful avalanche!"
This was the peasant's last good night!
A voice replied, far up the height,
   "Excelsior!"

At break of day, as heavenward,
The pious monks of St. Bernard
Uttered the oft-repeated prayer,
A voice cried through the startled air,
   "Excelsior!"

A traveller, by the faithful hound,
Half-buried in the snow was found,
Still grasping in his hand of ice
That banner with the strange device,
   "Excelsior!"

There, in the twilight, cold and gray,
Lifeless, but beautiful, he lay,
And from the sky, serene and far,
A voice fell, like a falling star,
   "Excelsior!"   *Longfellow.*

THE OCEAN.[1]

Roll on, thou deep and dark blue Ocean—roll!
Ten thousand fleets sweep over thee in vain;
Man marks the earth with ruin—his control
Stops with the shore;—upon the watery plain
The wrecks are all thy deed, nor doth remain
A shadow of man's ravage, save his own,
When, for a moment, like a drop of rain,
He sinks into thy depths, with bubbling groan,
Without a grave, unknell'd, uncoffin'd, and unknown.

His steps are not upon thy paths,—thy fields
Are not a spoil for him,—thou dost arise
And shake him from thee; the vile strength he wields
For earth's destruction thou dost all despise,
Spurning him from thy bosom to the skies,
And send'st him, shivering in thy playful spray
And howling, to his gods, where haply lies
His petty hope in some near port or bay,
And dashest him again to earth:—there let him lay.[2]

Thy shores are empires, changed in all save thee—
Assyria, Greece, Rome, Carthage, what are they?[3]
Thy waters wasted them while they were free,
And many a tyrant since; their shores obey
The stranger, slave, or savage; their decay

---

(1) This passage has been much criticised both in a friendly spirit and otherwise. Its general effect cannot but be considered as striking, even though the taste displayed in the details be questioned. The assailants of the poet's genius quote with some plausibility a passage from "Corinne," to prove that even the "original and fundamental theme," was borrowed from Madame de Staël, who speaks of—" Le spectacle de cette superbe mer, sur laquelle l'homme ne peut imprimer sa trace. La terre," she goes on to say, " est travaillée par lui, les montagnes sont coupées par ses routes, les rivières se reserrent en canaux pour porter ses marchandises; mais si les vaisseaux sillonnent un moment les ondes, la vague vient effacer aussitôt cette légère marque de servitude, et la mer reparaît telle qu'elle fût au premier jour de la création."

(2) The cynical tone and awkward phraseology of this stanza are brought to a climax in the solecism here perpetrated. "There let him lay," is quite unpardonable.

(3) "On those shores were the four great empires of the world: the Assyrian, the Persian, the Grecian, and the Roman. All our religion, almost all our law, almost all our arts, almost all that sets us above savages, has come to us from the shores of the Mediterranean."— *Dr. Johnson, in Boswell's Life.*

Has dried up realms to deserts :—not so thou,
Unchangeable save to thy wild waves' play—
Time writes no wrinkle on thine azure brow—
Such as creation's dawn beheld, thou rollest now.

Thou glorious mirror, where the Almighty's form
Glasses itself in tempests ; in all time,
Calm or convulsed—in breeze, or gale, or storm,
Icing the pole, or in the torrid clime
Dark-heaving ;—boundless, endless, and sublime—
The image of Eternity—the throne
Of the Invisible ; even from out thy slime
The monsters of the deep are made ; each zone
Obeys thee ; thou goest forth, dread, fathomless, alone.

And I have loved thee, Ocean ! and my joy
Of youthful sports was on thy breast to be
Borne, like thy bubbles, onward ; from a boy
I wanton'd with thy breakers—they to me
Were a delight ; and if the fresh'ning sea
Made them a terror—'twas a pleasing fear,
For I was as it were a child of thee,
And trusted to thy billows far and near,
And laid my hand upon thy mane, as I do here.

Byron.

WOMAN.[1]

Through many a land and clime a ranger,[2]
  With toilsome steps I've held my way,
A lonely unprotected stranger,[3]
  To all the stranger's ills a prey.

While steering thus my course precarious,
  My fortune still has been to find
Men's hearts and dispositions various,
  But gentle Woman ever kind ;

---

(1) The sentiments which are above so tastefully versified may be found in the journal of Ledyard the traveller. See his interesting "Life and Travels," p. 348.

(2) *Ranger*—Ledyard was the companion of Cook in his last voyage, and travelled much besides in the north of Europe and in Africa.

(3) *Stranger*—from the Latin *extraneus*, out'side, foreign ; the word is thus formed : **ex,** *extro*, *extraneus*, *estrange* (old French), *strange*, *stranger*.

Alive to every tender feeling,
    To deeds of mercy ever prone;
The wounds of pain and sorrow healing,
    With soft compassion's sweetest tone.

No proud delay, no dark suspicion
    Stints the free bounty of their heart;
They turn not from the sad petition,
    But cheerful aid at once impart.

Formed in benevolence of nature,
    Obliging, modest, gay, and mild,
Woman's the same endearing creature,
    In courtly town and savage wild.

When parched with thirst, with hunger wasted,
    Her friendly hand refreshment gave;
How sweet the coarsest food has tasted,
    What cordial in the simple wave![1]

Her courteous looks, her words caressing,
    Shed comfort on the fainting soul;
Woman's the stranger's general blessing
    From sultry India to the Pole!

                        Barbauld.

HUMAN FRAILTY.

Weak and irresolute is man;
    The purpose of to-day,
Woven with pains into his plan,
    To-morrow rends away.

The bow[2] well bent, and smart the spring;
    Vice seems already slain!
But passion rudely snaps the string,
    And it revives again.

---

(1) *Wave*—The precise words of the journal are:—"These actions have been performed in so free and kind a manner that, if I was dry, I drank the sweet draught, and, if hungry, ate the coarse morsel with a double relish."

(2) *Bow*—the "bow" is reason, whose decisions are too often thwarted by passion.

Some foe to his upright intent
    Finds out his weaker part,
Virtue engages his assent,
    But pleasure wins his heart.

'Tis here the folly of the wise,
    Through all his art[1] we view;
And while his tongue the charge denies,
    His conscience owns it true.

Bound[2] on a voyage of awful length,
    And dangers little known,
A stranger to superior strength,
    Man vainly trusts his own.

But oars alone can ne'er prevail
    To reach the distant coast;
The breath of heaven must swell the sail,
    Or all the toil is lost.

Cowper.

DEATH'S FINAL CONQUEST.[3]

The glories of our blood and state[4]
    Are shadows, not substantial things;
There is no armour against fate;
    Death lays his icy hand on kings.
        Sceptre and crown
        Must tumble down,
And in the dust be equal made
With the poor crooked scythe and spade.

Some men with swords may reap the field,
    And plant fresh laurels where they kill;[5]

---

(1) *His art*—the art with which he attempts to conceal his inconsistency and folly.

(2) *Bound, &c.*—These last two stanzas are beautifully simple; the figure is well carried out, and in the line "The breath of heaven," &c., becomes particularly striking.

(3) This poem was written about the beginning of the 17th century.

(4) *Blood and state*—high birth and actual rank.

(5) *Where they kill*—plant laurels for themselves on the blood they have spilt.

But their strong nerves at last must yield;
  They tame but one another still.[1]
    Early or late,
    They stoop to fate,
And must give up their murmuring breath,
When they, pale captives, creep to Death.

The garlands wither on your brow:
  Then boast no more your mighty deeds!
Upon Death's purple altar now
  See where the victor-victim bleeds!
    Your heads must come
    To the cold tomb;
Only the actions of the just
Smell sweet, and blossom in their dust.

Shirley.

HELVELLYN.[2]

I CLIMBED the dark brow of the mighty Helvellyn,
Lakes and mountains beneath me gleamed misty and wide;
All was still, save by fits, when the eagle was yelling,
And, starting, around me the echoes replied.
On the right, Striden-edge round the Red-tarn[3] was bending,
And Cathedicam its left verge was defending,
One huge nameless rock in the front was impending,
When I marked the sad spot where the wanderer[4] had died.

Dark green was that spot 'mid the brown mountain heather,
Where the pilgrim[5] of nature lay stretched in decay,
Like the corpse of an outcast abandoned to weather,
Till the mountain winds wasted the tenantless clay:

---

(1) *Tame, &c.*—but cannot tame the great conqueror, Death.

(2) *Helvellyn*—A lofty mountain in Cumberland. Striden-edge and Cathedicam are parts of it.

(3) *Red-tarn*—a "tarn" is a small lake high up in the bosom of a mountain.

(4) *Wanderer*—Mr. Charles Gough, of Manchester, perished in the spring of 1805, by losing his way over the mountain Helvellyn.

(5) *Pilgrim*—from the Italian *pellegrino*, which is from the Latin *peregrinus*, i. e. one who goes about *per agrum*—through the country. Hence, originally, a pilgrim was, generally, a wanderer, a traveller; then, one who travelled with a devotional purpose to some sacred spot. A "pilgrim of nature," therefore, is one who visits the shrines, i. e. the choice beauties and sublimities, of nature.

Nor yet quite deserted though lonely extended,
For, faithful in death, his mute favourite[1] attended,
The much-loved remains of her master defended,
And chased the hill-fox and the raven away.

How long didst thou think that his silence was slumber?
When the wind waved his garment, how oft didst thou start?
How many long days and long nights didst thou number,
Ere he faded before thee, the friend of thy heart?
And oh! was it meet that—no requiem[2] read o'er him,
No mother to weep, and no friend to deplore him,
And thou, little guardian, alone stretched before him—
Unhonoured the pilgrim from life should depart?

When a prince to the fate of a peasant has yielded,
The tapestry waves dark round the dim-lighted hall;
With scutcheons[3] of silver the coffin is shielded,
And pages stand mute by the canopied pall;
Through the courts, at deep midnight, the torches are gleaming,
In the proudly-arched chapel the banners are beaming,
Far adown the long aisle sacred music is streaming,
Lamenting a chief of the people should fall.

But meeter for thee, gentle lover of nature,
To lay down thy head, like the meek mountain lamb,
When 'wildered, he drops from some cliff high in stature,
And draws his last sob by the side of his dam;
And more stately thy couch by this desert[4] lake lying,
Thy obsequies[5] sung by the gay plover flying,
With one faithful friend but to witness thy dying,
In the arms of Helvellyn and Cathedicam.

Walter Scott.

(1) *Mute favourite*—a terrier, which for three months guarded the dead body of her master.

(2) *Requiem*—from the Latin *requies*, rest—strictly a mass for the dead, which begins with the words " *Requiem æternam.*" It is used here with some latitude for, funeral service.

(3) *Scutcheon*—from the Latin *scutum*, shield—originally the actual shield worn in battle, on which, for the sake of distinction, various devices were engraven; hence it signifies any field or ground on which are blazoned the armorial bearings of a family.

(4) *Desert*—for deserted, lonely.

(5) *Obsequies—funeral*—A common interment is a *funeral: obsequies* are pompous funeral ceremonies, with processions, &c. To "sing obsequies" is scarcely a correct expression, even allowing for poetic licence.

ELEGY

WRITTEN IN A COUNTRY CHURCHYARD.[1]

The curfew[2] tolls the knell of parting day,
   The lowing herd winds slowly o'er the lea,[3]
The ploughman homeward plods his weary way,
   And leaves the world to darkness[4] and to me.

Now fades the glimmering landscape on the sight,
   And all the air a solemn stillness holds,[5]
Save where the beetle wheels his droning flight,
   And drowsy tinklings lull the distant folds;

Save, that from yonder ivy-mantled tower,
   The moping owl does to the moon complain
Of such as, wandering near her secret bower,[6]
   Molest her ancient solitary reign.

Beneath those rugged elms,[7] that yew-tree's shade,
   Where heaves the turf in many a mouldering heap,
Each in his narrow cell for ever laid,
   The rude forefathers of the hamlet sleep.

---

(1) This well-known poem is perhaps unequalled for the skill with which the pathetic and the picturesque are combined, to excite our interest in the "simple annals of the poor." The language, too, is eminently tasteful and expressive, and furnishes a rich store of those apt quotations which—like snatches of some favourite air—touch the heart with a momentary, yet most exquisite pleasure. The "country churchyard" is said to be that of Stoke Pogeis, in Buckinghamshire, the scenery in and around which harmonizes well with that described in the poem. Gray spent much of his early life in the neighbourhood of this village, and here too he was buried.

(2) *Curfew*—the "curfew" here simply means any bell—time indefinite—sounding in the evening, and fancifully considered as announcing the death of the day.

(3) *Lea*—from the Anglo-Saxon *leag, laid* land—land that *lies* untilled—a meadow or pasture. Lea is connected with *ley, leigh,* and *legh,* which are found in proper names, as Elmsley, Stoneleigh, &c.

(4) *Darkness*—not absolute darkness, but the shade of evening in contrast with the brightness of day. If taken strictly, it would be inconsistent with "fades" and "glimmering" in the second stanza, and "moon" in the third.

(5) *Holds*—i. e. the stillness holds or fills all the air.

(6) *Bower*—from the Anglo-Saxon *bur,* a retired apartment—any place of retirement; hence a lady's bower is her own private room.

(7) *Beneath, &c.*—With this stanza, after the prelude of the three preceding, which are purely descriptive, that human interest is infused into the poem, which pervades it henceforth to its close.

The breezy call[1] of incense-breathing morn,
  The swallow twittering from the straw-built shed,[2]
The cock's shrill clarion, or the echoing horn,
  No more shall rouse them from their lowly bed.[3]

For them no more the blazing hearth shall burn,
  Or busy housewife ply her evening care;
No children run[4] to lisp their sire's return,
  Or climb his knees the envied kiss[5] to share.

Oft did[6] the harvest to their sickle yield,
  Their furrow oft the stubborn glebe has broke;
How jocund did they drive their team afield!
  How bowed the woods beneath their sturdy stroke!

Let not ambition mock their useful toil,
  Their homely joys and destiny obscure;
Nor grandeur hear with a disdainful smile
  The short and simple annals of the poor.

[The thoughtless[7] world to majesty may bow,
  Exalt the brave and idolize success;
But more to innocence their safety owe,
  Than power or genius e'er conspired to bless]

(1) *Breezy call, &c.*—A beautiful stanza, though perhaps slightly marred by the echoing sounds of "*breezy*" and "*breathing.*" A similar fault occurs in the last stanza, "*heaves*" and "*heap.*"

(2) *The straw-built shed*—i. e. the shed or *shade* formed by the projecting thatch.

(3) *Lowly bed*—of course the actual bed is meant, but the expression has been mistaken for the bed of death, the grave.

(4) *Run*—run home to tell the news.

(5) *Envied kiss, &c.*—It is impossible not to quote here the beautiful lines of Lucretius (iv. 907), which probably suggested the above passage:—

"At jam non domus accipiet te læta, neque uxor
  Optima, nec dulces occurrent oscula nati
  Præripere!"

How pretty is "oscula præripere," to snatch the first kiss!

(6) *Oft did, &c.*—Each line of this stanza aptly describes a class of agricultural labourers—the reapers, the ploughmen, &c.

(7) *The thoughtless, &c.*—This and the other stanzas enclosed in brackets are taken from the early editions, or from the MS. left by Gray. They are much too beautiful to be either lost or banished, and the present editor has therefore ventured to find a place for them.

The boast of heraldry, the pomp of power,
  And all that beauty, all that wealth e'er gave,
Await alike the inevitable hour :—
  The paths of glory lead but to the grave.

Nor you, ye proud! impute to these[1] the fault,
  If memory o'er their tomb no trophies raise,
Where through the long-drawn aisle and fretted vault,
  The pealing anthem swells the note of praise.

Can storied[2] urn, or animated bust,
  Back to its mansion call the fleeting breath?
Can honour's voice provoke[3] the silent dust,
  Or flattery soothe the dull, cold ear of death?

Perhaps in this neglected spot is laid
  Some heart once pregnant with celestial fire;
Hands that the rod of empire might have swayed,
  Or waked to ecstasy the living lyre:

But knowledge to their eyes her ample page,
  Rich with[4] the spoils of time, did ne'er unrol:
Chill penury repressed their noble rage,[5]
  And froze the genial current of the soul.

Full many a gem[6] of purest ray serene
  The dark unfathomed caves of ocean bear:

---

(1) *Impute to these, &c.*—*i. e.* do not suppose that these poor men do not *deserve* "trophies" as well as you.

(2) *Storied*—embossed with figures, or bearing an inscription relating to the story and history of the deceased. Milton, in "Il Penseroso" (see p. 310), has—

    "And storied windows, richly dight,
      Casting a dim religious light."

(3) *Provoke*—from the Latin *provoco*, I challenge or call forth; here, call back again to life.

(4) *Rich with, &c.*—containing the riches which time, like a conqueror, has gathered together. A noble expression!

(5) *Rage*—ardour, enthusiasm. This use of the word was once common. Thus Pope writes:—

    "So just thy skill, so regular my *rage*."

(6) Dr. Thomas Brown considers the reference to "gems" of the ocean inconsistent with the other illustrations of the poem, which are all drawn with great taste from rural scenes and circumstances.

Full many a flower[1] is born to blush unseen,
   And waste its sweetness on the desert air.

Some village Hampden, that, with dauntless breast,
   The little tyrant of his fields withstood,
Some mute, inglorious Milton, here may rest,
   Some Cromwell, guiltless of his country's blood.

The applause of listening senates to command,
   The threats of pain and ruin to despise,
To scatter plenty o'er a smiling land,
   And read their history[2] in a nation's eyes,

Their lot forbade: nor circumscribed alone
   Their growing virtues, but their crimes confined!—
Forbade to wade through slaughter to a throne,
   And shut the gates of mercy on mankind;

The struggling pangs[3] of conscious truth to hide,
   To quench the blushes of ingenuous shame,
Or heap the shrine of luxury and pride
   With incense kindled at the muse's flame.

Far from[4] the madding crowd's ignoble strife—
   Their sober wishes never learned to stray;
Along the cool sequestered vale of life
   They kept the noiseless tenor of their way.

[Hark! how the sacred calm that breathes around
   Bids every fierce tumultuous passion cease;
In still small accents whispering from the ground
   A grateful earnest of eternal peace.]

---

(1) *Many a flower, &c.*—Every word here seems the choicest possible, and the conception, so beautiful in itself, thus appears invested with a double charm.

(2) *Read their history, &c.*—Remarkable for the fulness of meaning condensed into a few words.

(3) *The struggling pangs, &c.*—It has been justly observed that this stanza rather weakens than increases the interest excited by the last, and comes in laggingly after that sonorous couplet, "Forbade to wade, &c.," which certainly ought to have closed the passage. The sense is—Their lot forbade their learning those mean arts by which men rise, as it is called, in the world, and which too frequently involve the abandonment of truth and honour.

(4) *Far from, &c.*—i. e. living far from the influence of the "ignoble strife," their wishes never strayed towards it. The "far from," has, of course, no grammatical connection with "stray."

Yet even[1] these bones from insult to protect,
  Some frail memorial still[2] erected nigh,
With uncouth rhymes and shapeless sculpture deckt,
  Implores the passing tribute of a sigh.

Their name, their years, spelt by the unlettered muse,
  The place of fame and elegy supply:
And many a holy text around she strews,
  To teach the rustic moralist to die.

For[3] who to dumb forgetfulness a prey,
  This pleasing, anxious being e'er resigned,
Left the warm precincts of the cheerful day,
  Nor cast one longing, lingering look behind?

On some fond breast the parting soul relies,
  Some pious drops[4] the closing eye requires;
Even from the tomb the voice of nature cries,
  Even in our ashes[5] live their wonted fires.

For thee, who,[6] mindful of the unhonoured dead,
  Dost in these lines their artless tale relate;
If, 'chance, by lonely contemplation led,
  Some kindred spirit shall inquire thy fate,

---

(1) *Yet even, &c.*—The direct train of thought, which has been long interrupted, is here resumed from the stanza beginning, " Nor you, ye proud," and may be thus connected:—Though these poor people have no monuments in cathedrals, yet even they love to have some memorial, however frail, raised near their bones, to bespeak the sympathy of passers-by.

(2) *Still*—always, continually; as if put for, " you will constantly find." A somewhat rare use of the word, if this be indeed its meaning here, which is not certain.

(3) *For, &c.*—This stanza is connected with the last but one; the last being in parenthesis.

(4) *Pious drops*—affectionate tears; taken in the sense of the Latin *pius*, dutiful to relations.

(5) *Even in our ashes, &c.*—even in the grave, that desire for affectionate sympathy which we evinced when alive, is expressed by the " frail memorial still erected nigh." Chaucer writes:—

    " Yet in our ashen cold is fire y-reken (*smoking*)."

(6) *For thee, &c.*—i. e. as to thee. The remainder of the poem refers to the character and circumstances of the author, who, by reflecting on the condition and fate of others, is naturally reminded of his own.

Haply some hoary-headed swain may say—
  "Oft have we seen him, at the peep of dawn,
Brushing with hasty steps the dews away,
  To meet the sun upon the upland lawn.

' There, at the foot of yonder nodding beech,
  That wreathes its old fantastic roots so high,
His listless length at noon-tide would he stretch,
  And pore upon the brook that babbles by.

["Him have we seen[1] the greenwood side along,
  While o'er the heath we hied, our labour done,
Oft as the woodlark piped her farewell song,
  With wistful eyes pursue the setting sun.]

" Hard by yon wood, now smiling as in scorn,
  Muttering his wayward fancies he would rove;
Now drooping woeful wan, like one forlorn,
  Or crazed with care, or crossed in hopeless love.

"One morn I missed him on the accustomed hill,
  Along the heath, and near his favourite tree;
Another came; nor yet beside the rill,
  Nor up the lawn, nor at the wood was he:

" The next, with dirges due, in sad array,
  Slow through the church-way path we saw him borne:—
Approach, and read (for thou canst read) the lay
  Graved on the stone beneath yon aged thorn.

["There scattered[2] oft, the earliest of the year,
  By hands unseen, are showers of violets found;
The redbreast loves to build and warble there,
  And little footsteps lightly print the ground."]

THE EPITAPH.

Here rests his head upon the lap of earth
  A youth, to fortune and to fame unknown:

---

(1) *Him have we seen, &c.*—This stanza, the "Doric delicacy" of which is praised by Mason, completes the poet's day, by supplying the evening. It is taken from Gray's first manuscript.

(2) *There scattered, &c.*—This exquisite stanza was printed in the earlier editions, but afterwards omitted by the author "because he thought it was too long a parenthesis in this place." The judgment is perhaps correct, but it is re-admitted here, notwithstanding, for the reason given in note 7, p. 61.

Fair Science[1] frowned not on his humble birth,
  And Melancholy[2] marked him for her own.

Large was his bounty,[3] and his soul sincere;[4]
  Heaven did a recompense as largely send:
He gave to misery all he had, a tear;
  He gained from Heaven ('twas all he wished) a friend.[5]

No further seek his merits to disclose,
  Or draw his frailties from their dread abode,
(There[6] they alike in trembling hope repose,)
  The bosom of his Father and his God.   *Gray.*

TO A WATER-FOWL.

Whither, midst falling dew,[7]
While glow the heavens with the last steps of day,
Far, through their rosy depths, dost thou pursue
  Thy solitary way?

Vainly the fowler's eye
Might mark thy distant flight to do thee wrong,
As darkly painted on the crimson sky,
  Thy figure floats along.

---

(1) *Fair Science, &c.*—i. e. the lowliness of his birth (not, however, that Gray's birth was actually humble) did not interfere with his successful pursuit of science and knowledge.

(2) Gray was of a grave temperament, and yet, like Cowper, wrote some particularly humorous poems.

(3) *Bounty*—The word usually refers to actual generosity, but here it seems to mean generosity of heart.

(4) *Sincere*—open and capable of friendship.

(5) *Friend*—probably the poet refers to his friend Mason.

(6) *There*—in their "dread abode," the bosom, i. e. the mercy of God, to which he refers both his merits and his frailties.

These notes may properly conclude with Dr. Johnson's judgment on the poem, that it "abounds with images which find a mirror in every mind, and with sentiments to which every bosom returns an echo." See "Life of Gray."

(7) *Falling dew*—This marks the time; for the bird being high in the air, was not, of course, in the midst of "falling dew."

Seek'st thou the plashy[1] brink
Of weedy lake, or marge of river wide,
Or where the rocky billows rise and sink
    On the chafed ocean side?

There is a power[2] whose care
Teaches thy way along that pathless coast[3]—
The desert and illimitable air—
    Lone wandering, but not lost.

All day thy wings have fanned,
At that far height, the cold thin atmosphere,
Yet stoop not, weary, to the welcome land,
    Though the dark night is near.

And soon that toil shall end;
Soon shalt thou find a summer-home, and rest,
And scream among thy fellows; reeds shall bend,
    Soon, o'er thy sheltered nest.

Thou'rt gone—the abyss of heaven
Hath swallowed up thy form; yet, on my heart,
Deeply hath sunk the lesson thou hast given,
    And shall not soon depart.

He, who from zone to zone
Guides through the boundless sky thy certain flight,
In the long way, that I must tread alone,
    Will lead my steps aright.

Bryant.

---

(1) *Plashy*—from the noun *plash*. The termination *ash*, according to Dr. Wallis, denotes a sharp, sudden motion, gradually subsiding, as in **crash**, *flash*, **plash**, *&c.* See his "Grammatica Linguæ Anglicanæ," p. 160.

(2) *There is a power, &c.*—*i. e.* the inquiries in the last stanza seem to impute vagueness and indecision to thy movements, but **such** is not their character;—There is a power that teaches thee thy way, &c.

(3) *Coast*—A peculiar but striking use of the word, as if the bird were skirting the very vault of the sky.

ALEXANDER SELKIRK'S SOLILOQUY.[1]

I AM monarch[2] of all I survey,
   My right there is none to dispute;
From the centre all round to the sea,
   I am lord of the fowl and the brute.
O solitude! where are the charms
   That sages have seen in thy face?
Better dwell in the midst of alarms,
   Than reign in this horrible place.

I am out of humanity's[3] reach,
   I must finish my journey alone,
Never hear the sweet music of speech—
   I start at the sound of my own.
The beasts that roam over the plain
   My form with indifference see;
They are so unacquainted with man,
   Their tameness is shocking to me.

Society, friendship, and love,
   Divinely[4] bestowed upon man,
Oh! had I the wings of a dove,
   How soon would I taste you again:
My sorrows I then might assuage
   In the ways of religion and truth;
Might learn from the wisdom of age,
   And be cheered by the sallies of youth.

Religion! what treasure untold
   Resides in that heavenly word!
More precious than silver and gold,
   Or all that this earth can afford.

---

(1) Alexander Selkirk was a sailor, who having quarrelled with his captain, was set on shore by him, in the year 1704, on the uninhabited island of Juan Fernandez, and remained there more than four years.

(2) *Monarch, sovereign*—The former word—from the Greek μόνος, alone, and ἀρχός, a governor—signifies one who has *sole* authority; *sovereign*—from the Latin *supremus* (through the old English, *sovran*), highest—one who has the highest authority. As there was no question of rank in Selkirk's case, the aptness of the word "monarch" is obvious.

(3) *Humanity*—human nature, mankind.

(4) *Divinely*—as the Latin *divinitus*, by divine providence, from heaven.

But the sound of the church-going bell[1]
   These valleys and rocks never heard;
Never sighed at the sound of a knell,
   Or smiled when a Sabbath appeared.

Ye winds! that have made me your sport,[2]
   Convey to this desolate shore
Some cordial endearing report
   Of a land I shall visit no more.
My friends, do they now and then send
   A wish or a thought after me?
Oh! tell me I yet have a friend,
   Though a friend I am never to see.

How fleet is a glance of the mind!
   Compared with the speed of its flight,
The tempest itself lags behind,
   And the swift-winged arrows of light
When I think of my own native land,
   In a moment I seem to be there;
But, alas! recollection at hand,
   Soon hurries me back to despair.

But the sea-fowl is gone to her nest,
   The beast is laid down in his lair;[3]
Even here is a season of rest,
   And I to my cabin repair.
There's mercy in every place,
   And mercy, encouraging thought!
Gives even affliction a grace,
   And reconciles man to his lot.   *Cowper.*

THE HAPPY MAN.[4]

How happy is he born and taught[5]
   That serveth not another's will;
Whose armour is his honest thought,[6]
   And simple truth his highest skill;

---

(1) *The church-going bell*—This expression ought by analogy to mean the bell that goes to church, and is therefore censured by Wordsworth in the Appendix to his "Lyrical Ballads."

(2) *Sport*—This implies that the author supposed that Selkirk had been shipwrecked, which, as just explained, was not the fact.

(3) *Lair*—See note 1, p. 4.

(4) Sir Henry Wotton, the author of this quaint and excellent poem, was a friend and contemporary of Milton.

(5) *Born and taught*—i. e. both by birth and education.

(6) *Honest thought*—honesty of purpose.

Whose soul is still[1] prepared for death;
  Whose passions not his masters are;
Untied[2] unto the world by care
  Of public fame or private breath;

Who envies none that chance doth raise,
  Or vice; who never understood
How deepest wounds are given with praise;[3]
  Nor[4] rules of state, but rules of good:

Who hath his life from rumours freed;[5]
  Whose conscience is his strong retreat;
Whose state can neither flatterers feed,
  Nor ruin make oppressors great;

Who God doth late and early pray
  More of his grace than gifts to lend;
And entertains the harmless day
  With a religious book or friend:—

This man is freed[6] from servile bands
  Of hope to rise, or fear to fall;
Lord of himself, though not of lands,
  And having nothing, yet hath all.

Sir H. Wotton.

ODE ON THE SPRING.[7]

Lo! where the rosy-bosomed Hours,[8]
  Fair Venus' train, appear,

(1) *Still*—always. (See note 2, p. 64.)

(2) *Untied, &c.*—not connected with the world by anxiety about either public or private applause.

(3) *Praise*—flattery.

(4) *Nor, &c.*—i. e. who never understood rules of policy, but rules of right.

(5) *Rumours freed*—free from cares and anxieties. The remaining lines of this stanza are at once simple and vigorous.

(6) *Freed, &c.*—from the slavish bonds both of hope and fear, for hope is no less enthralling than fear.

(7) "The 'Ode on the Spring' is an epitome of everything beautiful upon this subject."—*Gilbert Wakefield.*

(8) *Hours*—These fair damsels are represented in Homer and Hesiod, with the epithets "golden-armed" and "fair-haired," as forming the train of Venus. Their office here—opening the flowers and waking the year, as messengers of the Queen of Beauty—is most tastefully conceived. "Rosy-bosomed," says Wakefield, means, "with bosoms full of roses," perhaps rather, beautiful-bosomed.

Disclose the long-expecting[1] **flowers,**
   And **wake** the purple[2] year!
The Attic warbler[3] pours her throat
Responsive to the cuckoo's note,
   The **untaught** harmony[4] of spring;
While, whispering pleasures as they fly,
Cool zephyrs through the clear blue sky
   Their gathered fragrance fling.

Where'er the oak's thick branches stretch
   A broader, browner shade;
Where'er the rude and moss-grown beech
   O'er-canopies **the** glade,
Beside some **water's** rushy **brink**
With me the muse shall sit, **and** think
   (At ease reclined in rustic state)
How vain the ardour of the crowd,[5]
How low,[6] how little are the proud,
   How indigent[7] the great!

Still is the toiling hand of care;
   The panting[8] herds repose

---

(1) *Expecting*—In some editions "**expected**" is found; obviously **a very inferior** reading.

(2) *Purple*—Virgil uses the expression "*ver purpureum*," meaning nothing **more** than the "bright and beautiful spring," and this is probably the sense in **which** the word "purple" is often employed by poets of the 18th century.

(3) *Attic warbler*—the nightingale. We find in Milton ("Paradise Regained," **iv. 245):—**

    "The Attic bird
 Trills her thick-warbled notes the summer long."

It is called the "Attic bird" because Philomela, who was changed, as the fables say, into a nightingale, was an Athenian maiden.

(4) *Harmony, melody*—The difference between these **words is** that the latter denotes a succession, the former a combination, of musical **notes.**

(5) *Ardour of the crowd*—equivalent **to** the "madding crowd's ignoble strife." See the "Elegy," note 4, p. 63.

(6) *How low, &c.*—These lines appeared thus in the first edition:—

    "**How** low, how indigent the **proud,**
    How little are the great!"

but were subsequently altered "to avoid **the sort of** pun upon 'little' and 'great.'"

(7) *Indigent*—because **they** lack the **pure pleasures** of nature.

(8) *Panting*—It may perhaps be objected to this epithet, and to parts of the last **stanza,** "at ease reclined," &c., that they **are more** suitable to summer than to spring.

Yet hark, how through the peopled air
  The busy murmur glows![1]
The insect youth are on the wing,
Eager to taste the honeyed[2] spring,
  And float amid the liquid noon:
Some lightly o'er the current skim,
Some show their gaily-gilded trim,
  Quick-glancing to the sun.

To Contemplation's[3] sober eye,
  Such is the race of man;
And they that creep, and they that fly,
  Shall end where they began.
Alike the busy and the gay
But flutter through life's little day,
  In fortune's varying colours drest;
Brushed by the hand of rough mischance,
Or chilled by age, their airy dance
  They leave, in dust to rest.

Methinks I hear, in accents low,
  The sportive kind[4] reply;—
"Poor moralist! and what art thou?
  A solitary fly!
Thy joys no glittering female[5] meets,
No hive hast thou of hoarded sweets,
  No painted[6] plumage to display;
On hasty wings thy youth is flown;
Thy sun is set, thy spring[7] is gone—
  We frolic while 'tis May."

Gray.

(1) *Glows*—a daring, not to say audacious, word;—a murmur *glows!*

(2) *Honeyed*—Dr. Johnson has censured the use of adjectives of this class, which look like participles, but are really derived from nouns. Such forms are, however, congenial to the spirit of our language; thus we find "slippered pantaloon," "tapestried hall," "spiced cup," "daisied bank," &c.

(3) *To Contemplation's, &c.*—"This stanza furnishes the most curious specimen of a continued metaphor—the happiest intermixture of the simile and the subject—that the whole compass of poetry, ancient and modern, can produce."—*Gilbert Wakefield.*

(4) *Sportive kind*—i. e. the sportive insects; an awkward expression.

(5) *Glittering female*—In allusion, perhaps, to the glow-worm, the female of which is a wingless insect, and emits its light, it is thought, to attract the winged male.

(6) *Painted*—Phædrus has "*picta plumæ*"—painted feathers.

(7) *Thy sun is set, thy spring, &c.*—It is a very common metaphor to represent life as a day or a year. Thus we speak of the dawn, morning, noon, sunset

TO THE BUTTERFLY.[1]

Child of the sun! pursue thy rapturous flight,
Mingling with her thou lovest in fields of light,
And where the flowers of Paradise unfold,
Quaff fragrant nectar from their cups of gold:
There shall thy wings, rich as an evening sky,[2]
Expand and shut with silent ecstasy:
Yet wert thou once a worm—a thing that crept
On the bare earth, then wrought a tomb and slept.
And such is man—soon from his cell of clay
To burst a seraph in the blaze of day.

Rogers.

THE CRUSADE.[3]

Bound for holy Palestine,
Nimbly we brushed the level brine,
All in azure steel arrayed;
O'er the waves[4] our banners played,
And made the dancing billows glow;
High upon the trophied[5] prow,
Many a warrior-minstrel swung
His sounding harp, and boldly sung.

(as here), evening, and night of **life; as well as of its spring** (as here), summer, autumn, and winter. This ode must, notwithstanding its many beauties, be regarded as unfinished, inasmuch as it omits all consideration of those "glorious hopes" which raise man beyond the reach of any comparison with the brutes that perish. How different the close of the next piece!

(1) The thought and diction of these lines are equally rich and beautiful. They are alive with a light that warms while it illumines.

(2) *Rich as an evening sky*—Happily descriptive—an expression far transcending the "painted plumage" of Gray. See preceding page.

(3) "The 'Crusade,'" says Campbell, "has a genuine air of martial and minstrel enthusiasm."

(4) *Waves, billows*—A wave (from the Anglo-Saxon *wæg*, which is connected, perhaps, with *weg-an*, to weigh or balance), "may be defined," says Taylor, "a ridge of water in a state of oscillation." A billow (from the Anglo-Saxon *bilig*, a bulge or belly) is a wave that swells or *bulges* out more than others.

(5) *Trophied*—Adorned with trophies or memorials of victory.

"Syrian virgins, wail and weep,
English Richard ploughs the deep!
Tremble, watchmen, as ye spy,
From distant towers, with anxious eye,
The radiant range of shield and lance
Down Damascus' hills advance;
From Zion's turrets, as afar
Ye ken[1] the march of Europe's war![2]
Saladin, thou paynim[3] king,
From Albion's isle revenge we bring:
On Acco's[4] spiry citadel,
Though to the gale thy banners swell,
Pictured with the silver moon,[5]
England shall end thy glory soon
In vain to break our firm array,
Thy brazen drums[6] hoarse discord bray;
Those sounds our rising fury fan;
English Richard in the van,
On to victory we go,
A vaunting infidel the foe."

Blondel led the tuneful band,
And swept the wire with glowing hand.
Cyprus, from her rocky mound,
And Crete, with piny verdure crowned,
Far along the smiling[7] main
Echoed the prophetic strain.

(1) *Ken*—from the Anglo-Saxon *cenn-an*, to know by the senses, especially sight, to descry; to know generally. The word also means, to be able; thus implying the affirmation that "knowledge is power."

(2) *War*—put here for "forces," as in Milton's "Paradise Lost," xii. 213:—

"On their embattled ranks the waves return,
And overwhelm their *war*."

(3) *Paynim*—from the Latin *paganus*, through the French *payen*. The word originally meant merely a countryman, then one who, as living remote from the civilising influence of towns, clung to old superstitions and errors, hence an unbeliever. It was also applied as a term of contempt by the Crusaders to the Mahometans.

(4) *Acco*—the ancient Ptolemais and the modern Acra

(5) *Silver moon*—The Turkish crescent.

(6) *Brazen drums*—To increase the din, Saladin had brass kettle-drums beaten during one of the battles.

(7) *Smiling*—i. e. sparkling in the sun. Æschylus, in the "Prometheus Vinctus," beautifully refers to "the ocean-waves' unnumbered smiles."

Soon we kissed the sacred earth
That gave the suffering Saviour birth:
Then with ardour fresh endued
Thus the solemn song renewed:—

"Lo, the toilsome voyage past,
Heaven's favoured hills appear at last!
Object of our holy[1] vow,
We tread the Syrian valleys now.
From Carmel's almond-shielded steep
We feel the cheering fragrance creep:
O'er Engaddi's[2] shrubs of balm
Waves the date-empurpled[3] palm.
See Lebanon's aspiring head
Wide his immortal umbrage[4] spread!

"Hail, Calvary, thou mountain[5] hoar,
Where sin's dread load the Saviour bore!
Ye trampled tombs, ye fanes forlorn,
Ye stones, by tears of pilgrims worn;
Your ravished honours to restore,
Fearless we climb the hostile shore.
And thou, the sepulchre of God![6]
By mocking pagans rudely trod,
Bereft of every awful rite,
And quenched thy lamps that beamed so bright;
For thee, from Britain's distant coast,
Lo, Richard leads his faithful host!
Aloft in his heroic hand,
Blazing like the beacon's brand,

(1) *Holy*—a very much abused word when employed with reference to the Crusades generally.

(2) *Engaddi*—an ancient city which stood on the western coast of the Dead Sea. We learn from Josephus that it was once famous for palm-trees and balsams, or balm-shrubs, but "at present," says Dr. Robinson, who visited the spot in 1838, "not a palm-tree exists there."

(3) *Date-empurpled*—adorned with dates. A very artificial epithet. (See note 2, p. 71.)

(4) *Immortal umbrage*—in allusion to the remarkable longevity of the cedars of Lebanon. The natives, and some travellers, believe the most ancient of these trees to be the survivors of those cut down by Solomon for the building of the Temple.

(5) *Mountain*—It is difficult to understand how Calvary got the name of "mountain." The word means a "skull," and seems to have been given to a small hillock of that shape. Nothing that deserves the name of mountain can be found, and there is no scriptural authority for the term.

(6) *Sepulchre of God*—the Church of the Holy Sepulchre, originally built by Constantine. That referred to in the text was built by the first Crusaders.

O'er the far-affrighted fields,
Resistless Kaliburn[1] he wields.
Proud Saracen, pollute no more
The shrines by martyrs built of yore!
From each wild mountain's trackless crown
In view thy gloomy castles frown:
Thy battering-engines,[2] huge and high,
In vain our steel-clad steeds defy;
And, rolling in terrific state,
On giant-wheels[3] harsh thunders grate.

"Salem,[4] in ancient majesty
Arise, and lift thee to the sky!
Soon on thy battlements divine
Shall wave the badge of Constantine.[5]
Ye barons, to the sun unfold
Our cross with crimson wove and gold."

T. Warton.

TO A MOUNTAIN DAISY,

ON TURNING ONE DOWN WITH THE PLOUGH.[6]

Wee,[7] modest, crimson-tipped flower,
Thou's met me in an evil hour;
For I maun crush amang the stoure[8]
        Thy slender stem;
To spare thee now is past my power,
        Thou bonnie[9] gem.

---

(1) *Kaliburn*—the sword of King Arthur, which, according to the monkish historians, came into the possession of Richard. See an account of the wonderful performances of Kaliburn in Geoffrey of Monmouth's "British History," book ix.

(2) *Battering-engines*—battering-rams.

(3) *Giant-wheels*—The word "giant" is used in some compounds in the sense of "very large." (See "giant-bound," p. 22.) "Horse" seems to bear the same interpretation, in horse-chestnut, horse-leech, horse-laugh, &c.

(4) *Salem*—the ancient name of Jerusalem. It signifies "peace."

(5) *Badge of Constantine*—This refers to the "*labarum*," as the magnificent banner was called, which Constantine, after his conversion, adopted as the imperial standard. It bore a cross woven in gold upon *purple* cloth; not crimson, as implied in the text.

(6) "The verses to the 'Mouse' and 'Mountain Daisy' were composed," says the poet's brother, "on the occasions mentioned, and while the author was holding the plough."

(7) *Wee*—little.　　(8) *Stoure*—dust.　　(9) *Bonnie*—beautiful.

Alas! it's no thy neebor[1] sweet,
The bonnie lark,[2] companion meet,
Bending thee 'mang the dewy weet,[3]
    Wi' speckled breast,
When upward springing, blithe, to greet
    The purpling east.

Cauld blew the bitter-biting north
Upon thy early, humble birth;
Yet cheerfully thou glinted[4] forth
    Amid the storm,
Scarce reared above the parent earth
    Thy tender form.

The flaunting flowers our garden yields
High sheltering woods and wa's[5] maun shield;
But thou, beneath the random bield[6]
    O' clod or stane,
Adorns[7] the histie stibble-field,[8]
    Unseen, alane.

There, in thy scanty mantle clad,
Thy snawie bosom sunward spread,
Thou lifts thy unassuming head
    In humble guise:
But now the share uptears thy bed,
    And low thou lies!

Such fate to suffering worth is given,
Who long with wants and woes has striven,
By human pride or cunning driven
    To misery's brink,
Till, wrenched of every stay but Heaven,
    He, ruined, sink!

---

(1) *Neebor*—neighbour.

(2) *Lark*—"I have seldom," says Mackenzie, "met with an image more truly pastoral, than that of the lark in the second stanza."

(3) *Weet*—rain, wetness.   (4) *Glinted*—peeped.

(5) *Wa's*—walls. It is a characteristic of the lowland Scotch to elide the *l* in many words, thus, *wa'* for wall, *a'* for all, &c.

(6) *Random bield*—casual shelter.

(7) *Thou adorns*—In the northern dialect of the English language, to which the lowland Scotch is akin, all the persons, both singular and plural, of the present tense, are alike, and all end in *s*; thus I adorns, thou adorns, he adorns, we adorns, &c. So in the second line, "thou's met," for, thou hast met.

(8) *Histie stibble-field*—dry stubble-field.

Even thou who mourn'st the daisy's fate,
That fate is thine—no distant date;
Stern Ruin's ploughshare[1] drives elate[2]
                Full on thy bloom,
Till crushed beneath the furrow's weight,
                Shall be thy doom!

Burns.

TO A MOUSE,

ON TURNING HER UP IN HER NEST WITH THE PLOUGH.[3]

WEE, sleekit,[4] cowerin', timorous beastie,[5]
Oh, what a panic's in thy breastie!
Thou needna start awa sae hasty,
           Wi' bickering brattle![6]
I wad be laith[7] to rin an' chase thee,
           Wi' murdering pattle![8]

I'm truly sorry man's dominion
Has broken nature's social union,
An' justifies that ill opinion,
           Which maks thee startle
At me, thy poor earth-born companion,
           An' *fellow mortal!*

I doubt na whyles,[9] but thou may thieve;
What then? poor beastie, thou maun live!
A daimen-icker[10] in a thrave[11]
           'S a sma' request:
I'll get a blessin' wi' the lave,[12]
           And never miss't!

---

(1) *Ruin's ploughshare*—a bold figure and strikingly in keeping with the subject. It is borrowed from Young's "Night Thoughts" (see p. 408).

(2) *Elate*—triumphantly.

(3) "The charm," says Lord Jeffrey, "of these fine lines will be found to consist in the simple tenderness of the delineation;" and also, it may be added, in the hearty human sympathies which are interwoven with it. The words "fellow mortal," touch this chord with powerful effect.

(4) *Sleekit*—sleek, sly.

(5) *Beastie*—little beast. The termination *ie* marks the diminutive.

(6) *Bickering brattle*—hasty run.   (7) *Laith*—loth; as *baith*, both.

(8) *Pattle*—a small spade to clean the plough.   (9) *Whyles*—sometimes.

(10) *Daimen-icker*—an ear of corn met with occasionally.

(11) *Thrave*—shock of corn.   (12) *Lave*—leaving, the rest.

Thy wee bit housie,[1] too, in ruin!
Its silly wa's the win's[2] are strewin'!
An' naething now, to big[3] a new ane,
        O' foggage[4] green!
An' bleak December's wind ensuin',
        Baith snell[5] an' keen!

Thou saw the fields laid bare an' waste,
An' weary winter comin' fast,
An' cozie here, beneath the blast,
        Thou thought to dwell,
Till crash! the cruel coulter past
        Out-thro' thy cell.

That wee bit heap o' leaves an' stibble,
Has cost thee mony a weary nibble!
Now thou's turned out for a' thy trouble,
        But[6] house or hald,[7]
To thole[8] the winter's sleety dribble
        And cranreuch[9] cauld!

But, Mousie, thou art no thy lane,[10]
In proving foresight may be vain:
The best laid schemes o' *mice an' men*,
        Gang aft a-gley,[11]
An' lea'e us nought but grief and pain,
        For promised joy.

Still thou art blest, compared wi' me!
The present only touches thee:
But, och! I backward cast my e'e
        On prospects drear!
An' forward, tho' I canna see,
        I guess an' fear.   *Burns.*

---

(1) *Wee bit housie*—little bit of a house.
(2) *Win's*—winds. The final consonant is often omitted, as *an'* for and, *o'* for of, &c.
(3) *Big*—build.   (4) *Foggage*—long grass.
(5) *Snell*—bitter.   (6) *But*—without.
(7) *Hald*—abiding place, home.   (8) *Thole*—endure.
(9) *Cranreuch*—hoar-frost.   (10) *No thy lane*—not alone.
(11) *Gang aft a-gley*—often go wrong.

A COMPARISON.[1]

The lapse of time and rivers is the same,
Both speed their journey with a restless stream:
The silent pace with which they steal away,
No wealth can bribe, no prayers persuade to stay:
Alike irrevocable both when past,
And a wide ocean swallows both at last.
Though each resembles each in every part,
A difference strikes, at length, the musing heart:
Streams never flow in vain; where streams abound,
How laughs the land with various plenty crowned!
But time, that should enrich the nobler mind,[2]
Neglected, leaves a dreary waste behind. *Cowper.*

THE MESSIAH.[3]

A SACRED ECLOGUE.

Ye nymphs of Solyma![4] begin the song:
To heavenly themes sublimer[5] strains belong.
The mossy fountains and the sylvan shades,
The dreams of Pindus,[6] and the Aonian maids,
Delight no more—O Thou[7] my voice inspire,
Who touched Isaiah's hallowed lips with fire!

(1) A similar thought is found in the piece entitled "Thames" (see p. 9), but there it is merely suggested, here it is amply developed.

(2) *Nobler mind*—the soil of the mind, which is far nobler and more important than that of the land.

(3) "The idea of uniting the sacred prophecies and grand imagery of Isaiah with the mysterious visions and pomp of numbers in the Pollio of Virgil, thereby combining both sacred truth and heathen mythology in predicting the coming of the Messiah, is one of the happiest subjects for producing emotions of sublimity that ever occurred to the mind of a poet."—*Roscoe.*

(4) *Solyma*—same as Salem, supposed to be the ancient name of Jerusalem.

(5) *Sublimer*—i. e. than those required by common subjects. A comparative sometimes, in English as well as in Latin, has the force of an emphatic positive; "sublimer" therefore means, truly sublime.

(6) Mount Pindus, in Thessaly, and Aonia, a district of Bœotia, are celebrated as "haunts of the muses." This fanciful designation thus arises:—the lovely scenery of many parts of Greece suggested beautiful conceptions to the minds of the poets, who, in their turn, personified the influences which thus affected themselves, and gave them the name of muses. Hence, the muses are said to inspire the poet—that is, to sing his song to him—while he merely wrote it down.

(7) *O Thou, &c.*—i. e. the classic muses of Greece are unequal to such a subject, and, therefore, do Thou, &c.

Rapt into future times, the bard[1] begun:—
A Virgin shall conceive, a Virgin bear a son!
From Jesse's[2] root behold a branch arise,
Whose sacred flower with fragrance fills the skies;
The etherial Spirit o'er its leaves shall move,
And on its top descend the mystic Dove.
Ye heavens![3] from high the dewy nectar pour,
And in soft silence shed the kindly shower!
The sick and weak the healing plant shall aid,[4]
From storms a shelter, and from heat a shade.
All crimes shall cease, and ancient fraud shall fail;
Returning Justice[5] lift aloft her scale;
Peace o'er the world her olive wand extend,
And white-robed Innocence from heaven descend.
Swift fly the years, and rise the expected morn!
Oh, spring to light, auspicious Babe, be born!
See nature hastes her earliest wreaths to bring,
With all the incense of the breathing spring:
See lofty Lebanon his head advance,
See nodding forests on the mountains dance:
See spicy clouds from lowly Sharon rise,
And Carmel's flowery top[6] perfume the skies!

Hark! a glad voice the lonely desert cheers;
"Prepare the way![7] a God, a God appears!"
"A God, a God!" the vocal hills reply,
The rocks proclaim the approaching Deity.
Lo, earth receives him from the bending skies!
Sink down, ye mountains! and ye valleys, rise!
With heads declined, ye cedars, homage pay;
Be smooth, ye rocks! ye rapid floods, give way!
The Saviour comes! by ancient bards foretold:
Hear him, ye deaf! and all ye blind, behold![8]

(1) *The bard—i. e.* Isaiah, or the poet supposed to be endowed from above with the same inspiration.

(2) Isaiah xi. 1.   (3) Isaiah xlv. 8.   (4) Isaiah xxv. 4.

(5) *Returning Justice*—Astrea, the goddess of justice, according to the fable, left the earth in the iron age, being unable to endure the sinfulness of mankind; in this new golden age she will return. See also Isaiah ix. 7.

(6) *Carmel's flowery top*—" The good qualities of the soil of Carmel," says a modern traveller, "are apparent from the fact that many odoriferous plants and flowers, as hyacinths, jonquils, tazettos, anemones, &c., grow wild upon the mountain."   (7) Isaiah xl. 3, 4.

(8) *Hear him, &c.*—so striking an expression that it were to be wished that the next four lines had been omitted, as they only tamely repeat the same idea.

He from thick films shall purge the visual ray,
And on the sightless eyeball pour the day:
'Tis he the obstructed paths of sound shall clear,
And bid new music charm the unfolding ear:
The dumb[1] shall sing, the lame his crutch forego,
And leap exulting, like the bounding roe:
No sigh, no murmur, the wide world shall hear,
From every face he wipes off every tear:
In adamantine[2] chains shall death be bound,
And hell's grim tyrant feel the eternal wound.

As the good shepherd tends his fleecy care,
Seeks freshest pasture and the purest air,
Explores the lost, the wandering sheep directs,
By day o'ersees them, and by night protects;
The tender lambs he raises in his arms,
Feeds from his hand, and in his bosom warms:
Thus shall mankind his guardian care engage,
The promised father[3] of the future age.

No more shall nation[4] against nation rise,
Nor ardent warriors meet with hateful eyes:
Nor fields with gleaming steel be covered o'er,
The brazen trumpets kindle rage no more;
But useless lances into scythes shall bend,
And the broad falchion[5] in a ploughshare end.

Then palaces shall rise: the joyful son[6]
Shall finish what his short-lived sire begun;
Their vines a shadow to their race shall yield,
And the same hand that sowed, shall reap the field.
The swain in barren deserts with surprise
Sees lilies spring, and sudden verdure rise;
And starts amid the thirsty winds to hear
New falls of water murmuring in his ear.

---

(1) Isaiah xxxv. 5, 6.

(2) *Adamantine*—from the Greek ἀδάμας (in old Greek, *steel*), which is from α, not, and δαμάω, to tame or subdue—that which cannot be overpowered or broken, indissolubly strong.

(3) Isaiah ix. 6.   (4) Isaiah ii. 4.

(5) *Falchion*—from the Latin *falx*, a reaping-hook or sickle—a hooked or arched sword.

(6) Isaiah lxv. 21, 22.

On rifted rocks, the dragon's late abodes,
The green reed trembles,[1] and the bulrush[2] nods.
Waste sandy valleys,[3] once perplexed with thorn,
The spiry fir and stately box adorn;
To leafless shrubs the flowering palms succeed,
And odorous myrtle to the noisome weed.
The lambs with wolves shall grace the verdant mead,
And boys in flowery bands the tiger lead.[4]
The steer and lion at one crib shall meet,
And harmless serpents lick the pilgrim's feet.[5]
The smiling infant in his hand shall take
The crested basilisk[6] and speckled snake;
Pleased the green lustre of their scales survey,
And with their forky tongue shall innocently play.

Rise, crowned with light, Imperial Salem, rise![7]
Exalt thy towery[8] head, and lift thy eyes!
See a long race thy spacious courts adorn;[9]
See future sons, and daughters, yet unborn,
In crowding ranks on every side arise,
Demanding life, impatient for the skies!
See barbarous nations at thy gates attend,[10]
Walk in thy light, and in thy temple bend;
See thy bright altars thronged with prostrate kings,
And heaped with products of Sabæan[11] springs!
For thee Idume's spicy forests blow,
And seeds of gold in Ophir's mountains glow.

(1) Isaiah xxxv. 1, 7.

(2) *Bulrush*—The prefix *bul*, for *bull*, is augmentative—a bulrush is a *large* rush. "Horse" is used in the same manner, see note 3. p. 76. It may be remarked that the Greeks employed the corresponding words, $βοῦς$ and $ἵππος$, in a similar way: thus the epithet $βοῶπις$, ox-eyed, applied by Homer to Juno and others, means, having large and beautiful eyes

(3) Isaiah xli. 19; lv. 13.   (4) Isaiah xi. 6, 7, 8.   (5) Isaiah lxv. 25.

(6) *Basilisk*—from the Greek $βασιλίσκος$, a little king—a serpent with a crest which was fancifully thought like a crown. Some think the spectacle-snake of India is the species intended. A glance from the basilisk's eyes was vulgarly said to be fatal.   (7) Isaiah lx. 1.

(8) *Towery*—may either mean literally fortified with towers, or figuratively, rising like a tower; lofty.

(9) Isaiah lx. 4.

(10) Isaiah lx. 3.

(11) *Sabæan*—Sabæa was a district of Arabia Felix, noted for its frankincense, myrrh, balsam, &c. It is supposed to be the Sheba of Scripture.

See heaven its sparkling portals wide display,
And break upon thee in a flood of day.
No more the rising sun shall gild the morn,
Nor evening Cynthia fill her silver horn;
But lost, dissolved in thy superior rays,
One tide of glory, one unclouded blaze,
O'erflow thy courts: the LIGHT HIMSELF shall shine
Revealed, and God's eternal day be thine!

The seas shall waste, the skies in smoke decay,
Rocks fall to dust, and mountains melt away;
But fixed his word, his saving power remains;
Thy realm for ever lasts, thy own Messiah reigns!![1]

Pope.

SONNET.

ON FIRST LOOKING INTO CHAPMAN'S HOMER.[2]

MUCH have I travelled in the realms of gold,
  And many goodly states and kingdoms seen;
  Round many western islands have I been,
Which bards in fealty to Apollo hold.
Oft of one wide expanse have I been told
  That deep-browed Homer ruled as his demesne:
  Yet never did I breathe its pure serene
Till I heard Chapman speak out loud and bold:
Then felt I like some watcher of the skies,
  When a new planet swims into his ken;
Or, like stout Cortez, when with eagle eyes
  He stared at the Pacific—and all his men
Look'd at each other with a wild surmise—
  Silent, upon a peak in Darien.   *Keats.*

---

(1) Isaiah li. 6; liv. 10.

(2) The pleased surprise of one, who, after exploring many fields of literature, *discovered* Homer, is here described with much felicity both of conception and phraseology; but Chapman, after all, is only a dim reflection of the noble features of the original.

THE MEMORY OF THE BRAVE.[1]

How sleep[2] the brave, who sink to rest,
By all their country's wishes blest!
When Spring, with dewy fingers cold,
Returns to deck their hallowed mould,
She there shall dress a sweeter sod[3]
Than Fancy's feet have ever trod.

By fairy hands[4] their knell is rung;
By forms unseen[4] their dirge is sung:
There Honour comes, a pilgrim grey,[5]
To bless the turf that wraps their clay;
And Freedom[6] shall awhile repair,
And dwell, a weeping hermit, there. *Collins.*

HOHENLINDEN.[7]

On Linden, when the sun was low,
All bloodless lay the untrodden snow,
And dark as winter was the flow
 Of Iser,[8] rolling rapidly.

(1) Montgomery has said, perhaps with some degree of pardonable exaggeration, that these stanzas "are almost unrivalled in the association of poetry with picture, pathos with fancy, grandeur with simplicity, and romance with reality." See "Lectures on Poetry," p. 200.

(2) *How sleep, &c.*—"Not," says Montgomery, "how sweetly, soundly, happily, for all these are included in the simple apostrophe, '*How* sleep the brave!'"

(3) *Sweeter sod*—Why sweeter? Because of the *moral* interest associated with it, as the grave of those who died for their country.

(4) *Fairy hands, forms unseen*—These expressions, as well as the personifications of Honour and Freedom, refer to the influence which the memory of brave patriots diffuses over both the present and the future. The "fairy hands" and "forms unseen," are the feelings of gratitude, admiration, and pity, which affect the heart as mournful music does the ear.

(5) *A pilgrim grey*—A "pilgrim," because Honour comes from far—from other countries—to visit the shrine; "grey," because in distant years to come their memory shall still survive.

(6) *Freedom, &c.*—Freedom repairs thither—to weep alone ("a weeping *hermit*") because they are his children; "awhile" only, because he has other children still alive, and because time heals sorrow.

(7) *Hohenlinden*—A village of Germany, about twenty miles from Munich, where General Moreau completely defeated the combined army of Austrians and Bavarians, on the 3rd of December, 1800.

(8) *Iser*, or *Isar*—a tributary of the Danube.

But Linden saw another sight,
When the drum beat, at dead of night,
Commanding fires of death to light
   The darkness of her scenery.

By torch and trumpet fast array'd,
Each horseman drew his battle-blade,
And furious every charger neigh'd,
   To join the dreadful revelry.

Then shook the hills with thunder riven,
Then rush'd the steed to battle driven,
And louder than the bolts of heaven,
   Far flash'd the red artillery.

But redder yet that light shall glow
On Linden's hills of stained snow,
And bloodier yet the torrent flow
   Of Iser, rolling rapidly.

'Tis morn, but scarce yon level sun
Can pierce the war-clouds, rolling dun,
Where furious Frank, and fiery Hun,[1]
   Shout in their sulphurous canopy.

The combat deepens. On, ye brave,
Who rush to glory or the grave!
Wave, Munich! all thy banners wave!
   And charge with all thy chivalry!

Few, few, shall part where many meet!
The snow shall be their winding-sheet,
And every turf beneath their feet
   Shall be a soldier's sepulchre.   *Campbell.*

YE MARINERS OF ENGLAND;[2]

A NAVAL ODE.

Ye mariners of England!
   That guard our native seas;
Whose flag has braved, a thousand years,
   The battle and the breeze!

---

(1) *Hun*—the Austrian force.
(2) This spirited lyric well deserves to take rank with "Rule Britannia" (see p. 190). The main blemish in both is the want of a specific recognition of Almighty power as the only source of our own.

Your glorious standard launch again
   To match another foe!
And sweep through the deep,
   While the stormy winds do blow;
While the battle rages loud and long,
   And the stormy winds do blow.

The spirits of your fathers
   Shall start from every wave!—
For the deck it was their field of fame,
   And Ocean was their grave:
Where Blake and mighty Nelson fell,
   Your manly hearts shall glow,
As ye sweep through the deep,
   While the stormy winds do blow;
While the battle rages loud and long,
   And the stormy winds do blow.

Britannia needs no bulwarks,
   No towers along the steep;
Her march is o'er the mountain-waves,
   Her home is on the deep.
With thunders from her native oak,
   She quells the floods below,—
As they roar on the shore,
   When the stormy winds do blow;
When the battle rages loud and long,
   And the stormy winds do blow.

The meteor flag of England
   Shall yet terrific burn;
Till danger's troubled night depart,
   And the star of peace return.
Then, then, ye ocean warriors!
   Our song and feast shall flow
To the fame of your name,
   When the storm has ceased to blow;
When the fiery fight is heard no more,
   And the storm has ceased to blow.

Campbell.

THE MOTHER'S SACRIFICE.

"What shall I render Thee, Father Supreme,
For thy rich gifts, and this the best of all?"
Said a young mother, as she fondly watched
Her sleeping babe. There was an answering voice
That night in dreams:—

"Thou hast a little bud
Wrapt in thy breast, and fed with dews of love:
Give me that bud. 'Twill be a flower in heaven."[1]
But there was silence. Yea, a hush so deep,
Breathless, and terror-stricken, that the lip
Blanched in its trance.

"Thou hast a little harp—
How sweetly would it swell the angel's hymn:
Give me that harp." There burst a shuddering sob,
As if the bosom by some hidden sword
Were cleft in twain.

Morn came. A blight had struck
The crimson velvet of the unfolding bud;
The harp-strings rang a thrilling strain and broke—
And that young mother lay upon the earth,
In childless agony.

Again the voice
That stirred her vision:—"He who asked of thee
Loveth a cheerful giver." So she raised
Her gushing eyes, and, ere the tear-drop dried
Upon its fringes, smiled—and that meek smile,
Like Abraham's faith, was counted righteousness.

Mrs. Sigourney.

---

(1) This beautiful metaphor is also found in Coleridge's "Epitaph on an Infant:"—

"Ere sin could blight and sorrow fade,
Death came with friendly care,
The opening bud to heaven conveyed,
And bade it blossom there."

SONG FOR THE WANDERING JEW.[1]

Though the torrents from their fountains
Roar down many a craggy steep,
Yet they find among the mountains
Resting-places calm and deep.

Clouds that love through air to hasten
Ere the storm its fury stills,
Helmet-like themselves will fasten
On the heads of towering hills.

What, if through the frozen centre
Of the Alps the chamois bound,
Yet he has a home to enter
In some nook of chosen ground.

And the sea-horse, though the ocean
Yield him no domestic cave,
Slumbers, without sense of motion,
Couched upon the rocking wave.

If on windy days the raven
Gambol like a dancing skiff,
Not the less she loves her haven
In the bosom of the cliff.

The fleet ostrich till day close
Vagrant over desert sands,
Brooding on her eggs reposes
When chill night that care demands.

Day and night *my* toils redouble,
Never nearer to the goal;
Night and day I feel the trouble
Of the Wanderer in my soul. *Wordsworth.*

---

(1) The legend of the Wandering Jew is of great, but unknown, antiquity. He was, the fable informs us, Pilate's porter, and when the soldiers were dragging the Saviour out of the judgment-hall, struck him on the back, saying, "Go faster, Jesus, go faster; why dost thou linger?" upon which Christ said to him, "I indeed am going, but thou shalt tarry till I come." He was soon after converted, but the doom rested upon him, and even so lately as 1228, an Armenian bishop visiting England, professed with all sincerity to have dined recently with the man. See Percy's "Reliques of Ancient English Poetry," vol iii. p. 133.

OLD AGE.

The seas are quiet[1] when the winds give o'er;
So calm[1] are we when passions are no more.
For then we know how vain it was to boast
Of fleeting things so certain to be lost.

Clouds of affection[2] from our younger eyes
Conceal that emptiness which age descries,
The soul's dark cottage,[3] battered and decayed,
Lets in new light through chinks that time has made.

Stronger by weakness,[4] wiser, men become,
As they draw near to their eternal home:
Leaving the old, both worlds at once they view,
That stand upon the threshold of the new.

Waller.

THE BURIAL OF SIR JOHN MOORE.[5]

Not a drum was heard, not a funeral note,
As his corse to the rampart we hurried;
Not a soldier discharged his farewell shot
O'er the grave where our hero we buried.

(1) *Quiet, calm*—That is *quiet* which is made so by circumstances, and is, therefore, superficially at rest; that is *calm* which is quiet by constitution—or which is altogether at rest. An angry man may be quiet externally, but certainly not calm.

(2) *Affection*—i. e. love for the "fleeting things" of the world.

(3) *Soul's dark cottage*—i. e. the body, called in Job iv. 19, "a house of clay," and in 2 Cor. v. 1, "our earthly house of this tabernacle;" or, more correctly, "this earthly house, this tabernacle."

(4) *Stronger by weakness*—because the soul's strength increases as the body's decays. Milton, in his "Prose Works," employs a very fine expression, something like this of Waller's, when he speaks of "the martyrs, with the *unresistable might of weakness*, shaking the powers of darkness."

(5) This poem is doubtless one of the most affecting of its kind ever written. The conceptions, the language, the rhythm, all unite in forcibly impressing the reader with the *reality* of the scene, and making him not a spectator merely, but a sharer in the mournful ceremony. Sir John Moore died January 16th, 1809, at Corunna, of a wound which he received in the battle which took place there between the English under his command, and the French headed by Marshal Soult.

We buried him darkly, at dead of night,
The sod with our bayonets turning,
By the struggling moonbeam's misty light,
And the lantern dimly burning.

No useless coffin enclosed his breast,
Nor in sheet nor in shroud we wound him;
But he laid like a warrior taking his rest,
With his martial cloak around him.[1]

Few and short were the prayers we said,
And we spoke not a word of sorrow;
But we steadfastly gazed on the face of the dead,[2]
And we bitterly thought of the morrow.[3]

We thought, as we hollowed his narrow bed,[4]
And smoothed down his lonely pillow,
That the foe and the stranger would tread o'er his head,
And we far away on the billow!

Lightly they'll talk of the spirit that's gone,
And o'er his cold ashes upbraid him;—
But little he'll reck, if they let him sleep on
In the grave where a Briton has laid him.

But half of our heavy task was done,
When the clock struck the hour for retiring;
And we heard the distant and random gun
Of the enemy sullenly firing.[5]

(1) Lord Byron, who considered this poem one of the finest in our language, pronounced this stanza perfect, particularly the last two lines. The art with which the writer, under the semblance of a figure, displays the actual circumstances, is very striking. It reminds one of the Grecian artist's picture of a curtain, which was taken for the curtain itself.

(2) *Face of the dead*—some copies read "face that was dead," which is discarded from the text, first, because we can scarcely with propriety speak of "a dead face," and secondly, if we could, the meaning is unnecessarily restricted by confining the triumph of death to a part only of the once active frame.

(3) *The morrow*—because the British troops were to embark the next morning.

(4) *Narrow bed*—the conception of the bed and pillow gracefully harmonizes with that of the warrior "taking his rest."

(5) *Sullenly firing*—As if in spite, because they had been defeated. One of the readings of these two lines is:—

" And we heard by the distant and random gun
That the foe were suddenly firing."

That is, we heard by the firing that the enemy was *suddenly firing*, which is either a redundant expression, or else implies that the report of the guns notified a sudden, that is, a new attack, which, however, is inconsistent with the facts.

Slowly and sadly we laid him down,
From the field of his fame fresh and gory;
We carved not a line, and we raised not a stone—
But we left him alone with his glory!

Wolfe.

THE HAUNTED HOUSE.[1]

A ROMANCE.

Some dreams we have are nothing else but dreams,
Unnatural, and full of contradictions;
Yet others of our most romantic schemes
   Are something more than fictions.

It might be only on enchanted ground;
It might be merely by a thought's expansion;
But, in the spirit or the flesh, I found
   An old deserted mansion;

A residence for woman, child, and man,
A dwelling-place—and yet no habitation;
A house—but under some prodigious ban
   Of excommunication.

Unhinged, the iron gates half open hung,
Jarred by the gusty gales of many winters,
That from its crumbled pedestals had flung
   One marble globe in splinters.

No dog was at the threshold, great or small;
No pigeon on the roof—no household creature—
No cat demurely dozing on the wall—
   Not one domestic feature.

No human figure stirr'd, to go or come,
No face looked forth from shut or open casement;
No chimney smoked—there was no sign of home
   From parapet to basement.

---

(1) The extract here given is a portion only of a poem of Hood's with the above title, but it gives us a good idea of the author's skill in the choice of details which, by accumulation, make up a striking picture. The aptness, too, of the epithets, which give tone and colour to the picture, and the musical flow of the verse, evince a high degree of artistical ingenuity.

With shatter'd panes the grassy court was starr'd;
The time-worn coping stone had tumbled after;
And through the ragged roof the sky shone, barr'd
   With naked beam and rafter.

O'er all there hung a shadow and a fear;
A sense of mystery the spirit daunted,
And said, as plain as whisper in the ear,
   The place is haunted!

The flower grew wild and rankly as the weed,
Roses with thistles struggled for espial,[1]
And vagrant plants of a parasitic breed
   Had overgrown the dial.

But gay or gloomy, steadfast or infirm,
No heart was there to heed the hour's duration;
All times and tides were lost in one long term
   Of stagnant desolation.

The wren had built within the porch—she found
Its quiet loneliness so sure and thorough;
And on the lawn, within its turfy mound,
   The rabbit made his burrow:

The rabbit wild and grey, that flitted through
The shrubby clumps, and frisked, and sat, and vanished;
But leisurely and bold, as if he knew
   His enemy was banished.

The weary crow, the pheasant from the woods,
Lulled by the still and everlasting sameness,
Close to the mansion, like domestic broods,
   Fed with a "shocking tameness."

The coot was swimming in the reedy pond,
Beside the water-hen, so soon affrighted;
And in the weedy moat the heron, fond
   Of solitude, alighted;

The moping heron, motionless and stiff,
That on a stone, as silently and stilly,
Stood, an apparent sentinel, as if
   To guard the water-lily.

---

(1) *i. e.* to try which could look over the other.

No sound was heard, except, from far away,
The ringing of the whitwall's shrilly laughter,
Or now and then the chatter of the jay,
    That echo murmur'd after.

But echo never mock'd the human tongue;
Some mighty crime, that heaven could not pardon,
A secret curse on that old building hung,
    And its deserted garden.

The beds were all untouch'd by hand or tool;
No footstep marked the damp and mossy gravel;
Each walk was green as is the mantled pool,
    For want of human travel.

The vine unpruned, and the neglected peach,
Droop'd from the wall with which they used to grapple;
And on the canker'd tree, in easy reach,
    Rotted the golden apple.

But awfully the truant shunn'd the ground,
The vagrant kept aloof, and daring poacher;
In spite of gaps, that through the fences round
    Invited the encroacher.

For over all there hung a cloud of fear,
A sense of mystery the spirit daunted,
And said as plain as whisper in the ear,
    The place is haunted!

The pear and quince lay squandered on the grass;
The mound was purpled with unheeded showers
Of bloomy plums—a wilderness it was
    Of fruits, and weeds, and flowers.

The marigold amidst the nettles blew,
The gourd embraced the rose-bush in its ramble,
The thistle and the stock together grew,
    The hollyhock and bramble.

The bear-bine with the lilac interlaced,
The sturdy bur-dock choked its slender neighbour,
The spicy pink. All tokens were effaced
    Of human care and labour.

The very yew formality had train'd
To such a rigid **pyramidal stature,**
For want of trimming had almost regained
   The **raggedness** of nature.

The fountain was a-dry—**neglect and time**
Had marr'd the work of artizan and mason,
And efts and croaking frogs, **begot of slime,**
   Sprawl'd in the ruin'd bason.

The statue, fallen from its marble base,
Amidst the refuse leaves, and herbage rotten,
Lay like the idol of some bygone race,
   Its name and rites forgotten.

On every side **the aspect was the same,**
All ruin'd, **desolate, forlorn, and savage;**
No hand or foot within the precinct came
   To rectify or ravage.

For over all **there** hung a cloud **of fear,**
A sense of mystery the spirit **daunted,**
And said as plain **as** whisper in the ear,
   The place is haunted!
     *   *   *   *   *   *Hood.*

MAY MORNING.[1]

Now the bright morning star, day's harbinger,
Comes dancing from the East, and leads with her
The flowery May, **who from her** green lap[2] **throws**
The yellow cowslip, and the pale primrose.
   Hail, bounteous May, that dost inspire
   Mirth, and youth, and warm desire;
   Woods and groves[3] **are** of thy dressing,
   Hill and dale doth boast thy blessing.
Thus we salute thee with our early **song,**
And welcome thee, and wish thee long.   *Milton.*

(1) **Not the** least charm **of this** graceful salutation to May morning is **the** sudden change of the metre in the fifth line, which seems as it were to introduce us at once into the presence of **the** fair vision, whose approach is indicated by the previous passage.

(2) *Green lap*—Spenser describes " faire May " as " throwing flowers out of her lap around."

(3) *Woods and groves, &c.*—i. e. thou deckest them with verdure.

LAVINIA.

The lovely young Lavinia once had friends;
And fortune smiled deceitful on her birth:
For, in her helpless years deprived of all,
Of every stay, save innocence and Heaven,
She, with her widowed mother, feeble, old,
And poor, lived in a cottage, far retired
Among the windings of a woody vale;
By solitude and deep surrounding shades,
But more by bashful modesty, concealed.
Together thus they shunned the cruel scorn
Which virtue, sunk to poverty, would meet
From giddy passion, and low-minded pride;
Almost on Nature's bounty fed,
Like the gay birds that sung them to repose,
Content, and careless of to-morrow's fare.
Her form was fresher than the morning rose,
When the dew wets its leaves; unstained and pure,
As is the lily or the mountain snow.
The modest virtues mingled in her eyes,
Still on the ground dejected,[1] darting all
Their humid beams into the blooming flowers;
Or when the mournful tale her mother told,
Of what her faithless fortune promised once,
Thrilled in her thought, they, like the dewy star
Of evening, shone in tears. A native grace
Sat fair-proportioned on her polished[2] limbs,
Veiled in a simple robe, their best attire,
Beyond the pomp of dress; for loveliness
Needs not the foreign aid of ornament,
But is, when unadorned, adorned the most.
Thoughtless of beauty, she was beauty's self,
Recluse amidst the close-embowering woods:

---

(1) *Dejected*—cast down, referring to the eyes, not to the feelings—a very peculiar application of the term.

(2) *Polished*—Dr. Johnson has proposed a critical canon, which though not universally true, may perhaps be considered as applicable here: it is, that "an epithet or metaphor drawn from nature ennobles art; an epithet or metaphor drawn from art degrades nature."

As in¹ the hollow breast of Apennine,
Beneath the shelter of encircling hills,
A myrtle rises, far from human eye,
And breathes its balmy fragrance o'er the wild;
So flourished, blooming, and unseen by all,
The sweet Lavinia.

Thomson.

STONEHENGE.²

Thou noblest monument of Albion's isle!
  Whether by Merlin's³ aid from Scythia's shore,
  To Amber's fatal plain⁴ Pendragon⁵ bore,
Huge frame of giant-hands, the mighty pile,
  To entomb his Britons slain by Hengist's guile;.
  Or Druid priests, sprinkled with human gore,
  Taught mid thy massy maze their mystic lore;
Or Danish chiefs, enriched with savage spoil,
  To victory's idol vast, an unhewn shrine,
Reared the rude heap; or, in thy hallowed round,
  Repose the kings of Brutus'⁶ genuine line;
Or here those kings in solemn state were crowned:
  Studious to trace thy wondrous origin,
We muse on many an ancient tale renowned.⁷

Thomas Warton.

(1) *As in, &c.*—Compare this beautiful passage with Gray's lines, beginning " Full many a gem," p. 62.

(2) This word, though the name of an ancient British memorial, seems to be Anglo-Saxon, and signifies *hanging* or *hung up* stones See Philological Society's Journal, No. 130.

(3) *Merlin*—a renowned enchanter, as he was called, who lived in the times of King Arthur, and who is fabulously said to have transported these stones from Africa, first to Ireland, and thence to Salisbury Plain.

(4) *Amber's fatal plain*—so called from Ambrose, the uncle of King Arthur; styled "fatal" from the massacre of the Britons, which is said to have taken place here.

(5) *Pendragon*—Dragon's head—a name of office; here probably meant for Uther Pendragon, the father of Arthur.

(6) *Brutus*—The great-grandson of Æneas, who is fabulously said to have landed at Totnes, in Devonshire, and made himself king of the island, giving it the name of Britain from his own. See Milton's " History of Britain."

(7) " Nothing can be more admirable than the learning here displayed, or the inference from it, that it is of no use but as it leads to interesting thought and reflection."—*Hazlitt.*

THE FIRMAMENT.[1]

When I survey the bright
    Celestial sphere,
So rich with jewels hung, that night
Doth like an Ethiop bride appear,

My soul her wings doth spread,
    And heavenward flies,
The Almighty's mysteries to read
In the large volumes of the skies.

For the bright firmament
    Shoots forth no flame
So silent, but is eloquent
In speaking the Creator's name.

No unregarded star
    Contracts its light
Into so small a character,
Removed far from our human sight,

But if we steadfast look,
    We shall discern
In it, as in some holy book,
How man may heavenly knowledge learn.

Habington.

BEES.[2]

Ye musical hounds of the fairy king,
    Who hunt for the golden dew,
Who track for your game the green coverts of spring,
Till the echoes, that lurk in the flower-bells, ring
    With the peal of your elfin[3] crew!

---

(1) These fine lines—and the first four especially deserve the epitaph—were written in the early part of the seventeenth century.

(2) This little poem presents a new and graceful handling of a trite subject. The first and last stanzas are original and striking.

(3) *Elfin*—from the Anglo-Saxon *ælf*, an elf, fairy. The Anglo-Saxons had their dun, or mountain elves, wood elves, water elves, &c.

How joyous your life, if its pleasures ye knew,
   Singing ever from bloom to bloom!
Ye wander the summer year's paradise through,
The souls of the flowers are the viands for you,
   And the air that you breathe, perfume.

But unenvied your joys, while the richest you miss,
   And before you no brighter life lies:
Who would part with his cares for enjoyment like this,
When the tears[1] that embitter the pure spirit's bliss
   May be pearls in the crown of the skies!

MUSIC ON THE WATERS.[2]

The foot of music is on the waters,
Hark! how fairly, sweetly it treads,
As in the dance of Orestes' daughters,[3]
Now it advances and now recedes;

Now it lingers among the billows,
Where some one fonder than the rest,
Clasps the rover in passing, and pillows
Her softly upon its heaving breast.

Oft she flies, and her steps, though light,
Make the green waves all tremble beneath her;
Now the quick ear cannot follow her flight,
And the flood is unstirred as the calm blue ether.

(1) *The tears, &c.*—i. e. the sorrows of earth may be appointed by God as the very means of fixing the affections on heaven.

(2) The measure of these lines very aptly illustrates their subject; this is effected by an artful and ingenious intermingling of various metrical feet. The following scheme of the first stanza will exemplify the remark. The — points out the accented syllables.

$$\smile | - | - \smile | - \smile | - |$$
$$\smile | - \smile | - \smile | -$$
$$- \smile | - \smile | \smile | \smile$$
$$- \smile | - \smile | - | -$$

The advancing and receding in the last line are most skilfully represented.

(3) *Orestes' daughters*—It is difficult to say who Orestes' daughters were; probably the Oreades or mountain nymphs are meant.

GREECE.[1]

He who hath bent him o'er the dead,
Ere the first day of death is fled,
Before decay's effacing fingers
Have swept the lines where beauty lingers;
And marked the mild angelic air,
The rapture of repose that's there,
The fixed yet tender traits that streak
The languor of the placid cheek;
And but for that sad shrouded eye,
That fires not—wins not—weeps not—now;
And but for that chill, changeless brow,
Where cold obstruction's[2] apathy
Appals the gazing mourner's heart,
As if to him it could impart
The doom he dreads, yet dwells upon;—
Yes, but for these, and these alone,
Some moments, aye, one treacherous hour,
He still might doubt the tyrant's power:
So fair, so calm, so softly sealed,
The first—last look—by death revealed!
Such is the aspect of this shore—
'Tis Greece—but living Greece no more![3]
So coldly sweet, so deadly fair,
We start—for soul is wanting there.
Hers is the loveliness in death,
That parts not quite with parting breath,
But beauty with that fearful bloom,
That hue which haunts it to the tomb—

---

(1) There is, perhaps, no instance in our poetical literature in which a continued simile is so beautifully sustained, as that which runs through these lines. The affecting picture of the lovely form, no longer animated by the living spirit, deeply touching in itself, derives a new interest from its exquisite adaptation to the subject which suggested it. The music of the rhythm too—so soft, so delicately modulated—floats like a requiem over the whole, and leaves nothing to be desired in consummating the effect.

(2) *Cold obstruction*—This expression is taken from Shakspere, who speaks of the dead as "lying in cold obstruction," in allusion to the *stoppage* of the animal functions.

(3) The following passage, from Gillies' "History of Greece," is thought to have suggested the above comparison:—"The present state of Greece, compared to the ancient, is the silent obscurity of the grave contrasted with the vivid lustre of active life."

Expression's last receding ray,
A gilded halo hovering round decay,
The farewell beam of feeling past away!
Spark of that flame—that flame of heavenly birth—
Which gleams—but warms no more its cherished earth!

    Clime of the unforgotten brave![1]
Whose land from plain to mountain-cave
Was freedom's home or glory's grave!
Shrine of the mighty! can it be,
That this is all remains of thee?
Approach, thou craven crouching slave,
    Say, is not this Thermopylæ?[2]
These waters blue that round you lave,
    Oh, servile offspring of the free,
Pronounce what sea, what shore is this?
The gulf, the rock of Salamis![2]
These scenes, their story not unknown,
Arise, and make again your own;
Snatch from the ashes of your sires
The embers of their former fires;
And he who in the strife expires
Will add to theirs a name of fear
That tyranny shall quake to hear,
And leave his sons a hope, a fame,
They too will rather die than shame:
For freedom's battle once begun,
Bequeathed by bleeding sire to son,
Though baffled oft is ever won.
Bear witness, Greece, thy living page,
Attest it many a deathless age!
While kings, in dusty darkness hid,
Have left a nameless pyramid,
Thy heroes, though the general doom
Hath swept the column from their tomb,
A mightier monument command,
The mountains of their native land!

(1) The transition here to another variation of the same theme, by a change of key, as it were, is very striking. The energy of these lines is as remarkable as the pathos of the preceding.

2) *Thermopylæ, Salamis*—An instance of the suggestive power of a name. No description is given of the deeds for which these places were remarkable—the simple mention of them is enough.

There points thy Muse to stranger's eye,
The graves of those that cannot die!—
'Twere long to tell, and sad to trace
Each step from splendour to disgrace;
Enough—no foreign foe could quell
Thy soul, till from itself it fell;
Yes! self-abasement paved the way
To villain-bonds and despot sway.

Byron.

THERMOPYLÆ.

They fell devoted, but undying;
The very gale their name seemed sighing;
The waters murmured of their name,
The woods were peopled with their fame;
The silent pillar, lone and grey,
Claimed kindred with their sacred clay;
Their spirits wrapped the dusky mountain,
Their memory sparkled o'er the fountain;
The meanest rill, the mightiest river,
Rolls mingling with their fame for ever.

Byron.

TO A SKYLARK.[1]

Ethereal minstrel! pilgrim of the sky!
Dost thou despise the earth, where cares abound?
Or, while the wings aspire, are heart and eye
Both with thy nest upon the dewy ground?
The nest which thou canst drop into at will,
Those quivering wings composed, that music still!

To the last point of vision, and beyond,
Mount, daring warbler!—that love-prompted strain
('Twixt thee and thine a never-failing bond)
Thrills not the less the bosom of the plain:
Yet might'st thou seem,[2] proud privilege! to sing
All independent of the leafy spring.

---

(1) It is difficult to conceive anything more exquisitely graceful than these lines; the last two especially, and that beginning, "A privacy of," &c., may be characterized as perfect.

(2) *Yet might'st thou seem, &c.—i. e.* yet you mount so high, that you might seem to have lost all connection with earth, and not to be inspired by the genial influences of spring, which prompt the songs of other birds.

Leave to the nightingale her shady wood;
A privacy of glorious light is thine;
Whence thou dost pour upon the world a flood
Of harmony, with instinct more divine;
Type of the wise who soar, but never roam;
True to the kindred points of heaven and home!
Wordsworth.

THE CATARACT AND THE STREAMLET,[1]

OR POWER AND GENTLENESS.

NOBLE the mountain stream,
Bursting in grandeur from its 'vantage ground;[2]
  Glory is in its gleam
Of brightness—thunder in its deafening sound:

  Mark, how its foamy spray,
Tinged by the sunbeams with reflected dyes,
  Mimics the bow of day,
Arching in majesty the vaulted skies;

  Thence, in a summer shower,
Steeping the rocks around;—Oh! tell me where
  Could majesty and power
Be clothed in forms more beautifully fair?

  Yet lovelier, in my view,
The Streamlet, flowing silently serene;
  Traced by the brighter hue,
And livelier growth[3] it gives; itself unseen!

  It flows through flowery meads,
Gladdening the herds which on its margin browse;
  Its quiet beauty feeds
The alders that o'ershade it with their boughs.

(1) The excellent moral of this piece is recommended by its tasteful style and versification. The closing stanza is finely expressed:

(2) *'Vantage ground*—'vantage is a contraction of *advantage*, and the expression is equivalent to, position of advantage, *i. e.* an elevated and commanding position.

(3) *Livelier growth.*—Cowper speaks of the rills that—

> "Lose themselves at length
> In matted grass, that with a livelier green
> Betrays the secret of their silent course."

    Gently it murmurs, by
The village churchyard, in low plaintive tone,
    A dirge-like melody
For worth and beauty modest as its own.

    More gaily now it sweeps
By the small school-house, in the sunshine bright;
    And o'er the pebbles leaps,
Like happy hearts by holiday made light.

    May not its course express,
In characters which they who run may read,
    The charms of gentleness,
Were but its still small voice allowed to plead?

    What are the trophies gained
By power, alone, with all its noise and strife,
    To that meek wreath, unstained,
Won by the charities[1] that gladden life?

    Niagara's streams might fail,
And human happiness be undisturbed:
    But Egypt would turn pale,
Were her still Nile's o'erflowing bounty curbed!
Bernard Barton.

GOD'S WATCHFUL CARE.

The insect, that with puny wing
    Just shoots along one summer ray,
The floweret which the breath of spring
    Wakes into life for half a day,
The smallest mote, the tenderest hair,
All feel a heavenly Father's care.

E'en from the glories of his throne
    He bends to view this earthly ball;
Sees all as if that all were one,
    Loves one as if that one were all;
Rolls the swift planets in their spheres,
And counts the sinner's lonely tears.
Cunningham.

---

(1) *Charities*—from the Greek χάρις, favour, love—the domestic affections.

THE VANITY OF HUMAN WISHES [1]
ABRIDGED.

Let observation, with extensive view,
Survey mankind from China to Peru ;[2]
Remark each anxious toil, each eager strife,
And watch the busy scenes of crowded life ;
Then say how hope and fear, desire and hate,
O'erspread with snares the clouded maze of fate,
Where wavering man, betrayed by venturous pride
To tread the dreary paths without a guide,
As treacherous phantoms in the midst delude,
Shuns fancied ills, or chases airy good.
How rarely reason guides the stubborn choice,
Rules the bold hand, or prompts the suppliant voice !
How nations sink, by darling schemes opprest,
When vengeance listens to the fool's request !
Fate wings with every wish the afflictive dart,
Each gift of nature, and each grace of art ;
With fatal heat impetuous courage glows,
With fatal sweetness elocution flows,
Impeachment[3] stops the speaker's powerful breath,
And restless fire precipitates on death.

The needy traveller, serene and gay,
Walks the wild heath, and sings his toil away.
Does envy seize thee ? crush the upbraiding joy—
Increase his riches, and his peace destroy :
Now fears in dire vicissitude invade,
The rustling brake alarms, and quivering shade,
Nor light nor darkness brings his pain relief,
One shows the plunder and one hides the thief.

In full-blown dignity, see Wolsey stand,
Law in his voice, and fortune in his hand :

---

(1) "The Vanity of Human Wishes" is an imitation—not a translation—of the 10th Satire of Juvenal, and notwithstanding occasional tautology and needless pomposity of style, is a nervous and energetic poem. Sir Walter Scott praises its "deep and pathetic morality ;" and Lord Byron calls it "a grand poem," though he does not "much admire the opening."

(2) On this couplet Coleridge justly remarks, that it is as much as to say, "let observation with extensive observation observe mankind."

(3) *Impeachment*—from the French *empécher*, to hinder, arrest—a charge of grave importance brought against a public character.

To him the church, the realm, their powers consign,
Through him the rays of regal bounty shine,
Turned by his nod the stream of honour flows,
His smile alone security bestows.
Still to new heights his restless wishes tower;
Claim leads to claim, and power advances power;
Till conquest, unresisted, ceased to please,
And rights submitted left him none to seize:
At length his Sovereign frowns—the train of state
Mark the keen glance, and watch the sign to hate:
Where'er he turns he meets a stranger's eye,
His suppliants scorn him, and his followers fly;
Now drops at once the pride of awful state—
The golden canopy, the glittering plate,
The regal palace, the luxurious board,
The liveried army, and the menial lord.[1]
With age, with cares, with maladies opprest,
He seeks the refuge of monastic rest.
Grief aids disease, remembered folly stings,
And his last sighs reproach the faith of kings.

Speak, thou whose thoughts at humble peace repine,
Shall Wolsey's wealth with Wolsey's end be thine?
Or livest thou now, with safer pride content,
The wisest justice on the banks of Trent?
For why did Wolsey, near the steeps of fate,
On weak foundations raise the enormous weight?
Why but to sink beneath misfortune's blow,
With louder ruin to the gulfs below.

On what foundation stands the warrior's pride,
How just his hopes, let Swedish Charles decide.
A frame of adamant, a soul of fire,
No dangers fright him, and no labours tire;
O'er love, o'er fear, extends his wide domain,
Unconquered lord of pleasure and of pain;
No joys to him pacific sceptres yield,
War sounds the trump, he rushes to the field;
Behold surrounding kings their power combine,
And one capitulate,[2] and one resign;

---

(1) *Menial lord*—the lord of the menials, the steward of the household.

(2) *And one capitulate, &c.*—Charles XII. compelled the King of Denmark to sue for peace, and the King of Poland to resign his crown.

Peace courts his hand, but spreads her charms in vain;
"Think nothing gained," he cries, "till nought remain:
On Moscow's walls till Gothic standards fly,
And all be mine beneath the polar sky."
The march begins in military state,
And nations on his eye suspended wait;
Stern famine guards the solitary coast,
And winter barricades the realms of frost;
He comes—nor want, nor cold, his course delay;
Hide, blushing glory, hide Pultowa's[1] day:
The vanquished hero leaves his broken bands,
And shows his miseries in distant lands:[2]
Condemned a needy supplicant to wait,
While ladies interpose, and slaves debate.
But did not chance at length her error mend?
Did no subverted empire mark his end?
Did rival monarchs give the fatal wound?
Or hostile millions press him to the ground?
His fall was destined to a barren strand,
A petty fortress,[3] and a dubious hand;
He left the name at which the world grew pale,
To point a moral, or adorn a tale.

In gay hostility and barbarous pride,
With half mankind embattled at his side,
Great Xerxes came to seize the certain prey,
And starves exhausted regions[4] in his way;
Attendant flattery counts his myriads o'er,
Till counted myriads soothe his pride no more;
Fresh praise is tried till madness fires his mind,
The waves he lashes, and enchains the wind;
New powers are claimed, new powers are still bestowed,
Till rude resistance lops the spreading god;
The daring Greeks deride the martial show,
And heap their valleys with the gaudy foe;

(1) *Pultowa*—At the battle of Pultowa, a town in Russia, Charles was completely defeated by his rival, Peter the Great.

(2) *Distant lands*—He retired into the Turkish territory, to Bender, on the Dniester, where he was liberally entertained, notwithstanding the absurdity of his behaviour there. See Voltaire's "Histoire de Charles XII."

(3) *Petty fortress*—Charles was struck dead by a shot from an unknown hand, while besieging Friedrichshall, in Norway.

(4) *Starves exhausted regions*—This is a Latinism, like "captum interfecit," he took and killed him; so here, he exhausts and starves the regions.

The insulted sea with humbler thoughts he gains,
A single skiff to speed his flight remains;
The encumbered oar[1] scarce leaves the dreaded coast
Through purple billows and a floating host.

But grant,[2] the virtues of a temperate prime
Bless with an age exempt from scorn or crime;
An age that melts with unperceived decay,
And glides with modest innocence away;
Whose peaceful day benevolence endears,
Whose night congratulating conscience cheers;
The general favourite as the general friend;
Such age there is, and who shall wish its end?

Yet even on this her load misfortune flings,
To press the weary minutes' flagging wings;
New sorrow rises as the day returns,
A sister sickens, or a daughter mourns;
Now kindred merit fills the sable bier,
Now lacerated friendship claims a tear;
Year chases year, decay pursues decay,
Still drops some joy from withering life away;
New forms arise, and different views engage,
Superfluous[3] lags the veteran on the stage,
Till pitying nature signs the last release,
And bids afflicted worth retire to peace.

But few there are whom hours like these await,
Who set unclouded in the gulfs of fate.
From Lydia's monarch[4] should the search descend,
By Solon cautioned to regard his end,
In life's last scene what prodigies surprise,
Fears of the brave and follies of the wise!
From Marlborough's[5] eyes the streams of dotage flow,
And Swift[6] expires a driveller and a show.

(1) *The encumbered oar, &c.*—Though extravagant, the language of this couplet presents a very striking picture of the scene.

(2) *But grant*—i. e. but suppose that, &c.

(3) *Superfluous, &c.*—A striking metaphor, ingenious, clear, and admirably expressed.

(4) *Lydia's monarch*—Crœsus.

(5) *Marlborough's, &c.*—He was afflicted with paralysis: "but," says a writer in the 'Penny Cyclopædia,' "without at all seriously impairing his faculties;" so that the above line is, at least, a poetical exaggeration.

(6) *Swift*—For some time before his death Swift's mind gave way, and he at length died in a state of quiet idiotcy.

Where then shall hope and fear their objects find?
Must dull suspense corrupt the stagnant mind?
Must helpless man in ignorance sedate,
Roll darkling down the torrent of his fate?
Must no dislike alarm, nor wishes rise,
No cries invoke the mercies of the skies?
Inquirer, cease! petitions yet remain,
Which heaven may hear, nor deem religion vain.
Still raise for good the supplicating voice,
But leave to heaven the measure and the choice.
Safe in His power, whose eyes discern afar
The secret ambush of a specious[1] prayer.
Implore His aid, in His decisions rest,
Secure whate'er He gives, He gives the best.
Yet when the sense of sacred presence fires,
And strong devotion to the skies aspires,
Pour forth thy fervours for a healthful mind,
Obedient passions, and a will resigned;
For love, which scarce collective man[2] can fill;
For patience, sovereign o'er transmuted ill;[3]
For faith, that, panting for a happier seat,
Counts death kind nature's signal of retreat:
These goods for man the laws of heaven ordain,
These goods He grants, who grants the power to gain;
With these celestial wisdom calms the mind,
And makes the happiness she does not find. *Johnson.*

LUCY.[4]

Three years she grew in sun and shower,
Then Nature said, "A lovelier flower
  On earth was never sown;
This child I to myself will take;
She shall be mine, and I will make
  A lady of my own.

(1) *Secret ambush, &c.*—*i. e.* the lurking danger connected with the attainment of what may seem to you very desirable. See note 4, p. 1.

(2) *Collective man*—the whole human race.

(3) *Transmuted ill*—*i. e.* evil changed by the power of patience into good.

(4) These lines describe, in a very graceful manner, the supposed operation of natural influences in developing the faculties both of mind and body. The conception is, of course, intended to be fanciful, but it embodies, nevertheless, much truth, for there is an influence in natural scenery which insensibly both "kindles and restrains" the taste and the affections.

"Myself will to my darling be
Both law and impulse;[1] and with me[2]
    The girl, in rock and plain,
In earth and heaven, in glade and bower,
Shall feel an overseeing power
    To kindle or restrain.

"She shall be sportive[3] as the fawn,
That wild with glee across the lawn
    Or up the mountain springs;
And hers shall be the breathing balm,
And hers the silence[4] and the calm[4]
    Of mute insensate things.

"The floating clouds their state shall lend
To her; for her the willow bend;
    Nor shall she fail to see
Even in the motions of the storm,
Grace that shall mould the maiden's form
    By silent sympathy.

"The stars of midnight shall be dear
To her; and she shall lean her ear
    In many a secret place
Where rivulets[5] dance their wayward round,
And beauty, born of murmuring sound,
    Shall pass into her face.

"And vital feelings of delight
Shall rear her form to stately height,[6]
    Her virgin bosom swell;
Such thoughts to Lucy I will give,
While she and I together live
    Here in this happy dell."

(1) *Law and impulse*—These words and the synonymous phrase, a "power to kindle or restrain," are admirably chosen to denote the apparently opposite, yet really harmonious results produced in the mind by external nature.

(2) *With me, &c.*—*i. e.* while she is in company with me among the "rocks," &c., she shall be conscious of my superintending power to animate and tranquillize the mind.

(3) *She shall be sportive, &c.*—This stanza beautifully exemplifies the last.

(4) *Silence, calm*—See note 1, p. 90.

(5) *Where rivulets, &c.*—A very picturesque line, and most delicately versified. Try the effect of substituting some word of two syllables for "rivulets."

(6) *Stately height, &c.*—Joy, it is well known, expands and elevates the form, while sorrow depresses it.

Thus Nature spake. The work was done—
How soon my Lucy's race was run!
 She died, and left to me
This heath, this calm, and quiet scene;
The memory of what has been,
 And never more will be.

Wordsworth.

PRIDE AND HUMILITY.[1]

The self-applauding bird, the peacock, see—
Mark what a sumptuous Pharisee is he!
Meridian sunbeams tempt him to unfold
His radiant glories, azure, green, and gold:
He treads as if, some solemn music near,
His measured step were governed by his ear;
And seems to say—Ye meaner fowl, give place,
I am all splendour, dignity, and grace!
 Not so the pheasant on his charms presumes,
Though he too has a glory in his plumes.
He, Christian-like, retreats with modest mien
To the close copse, or far-sequestered green,
And shines without desiring to be seen.

Cowper.

THE COTTAGER.

Yon cottager, who weaves[2] at her own door—
Pillow and bobbins all her little store—
Content, though mean, and cheerful if not gay,[3]
Shuffling her threads about the live-long day,
Just earns a scanty pittance, and at night
Lies down secure, her heart and pocket light:
She, for her humble sphere by nature fit,
Has little understanding, and no wit;

---

(1) "The comparison of the proud and humble believer to the peacock and the pheasant, and the parallel between Voltaire and the poor cottager, are exquisite pieces of eloquence and poetry."—*Hazlitt.*

(2) *Weaves—i. e.* weaves lace with bobbins upon a pillow.

(3) *Cheerful, gay*—He is *cheerful* who is habitually lively; *gay*, who is occasionally or accidentally so. Cheerfulness is an evergreen; gaiety a passing flower, more brilliant for a time, but not permanent.

Receives no praise; but though her lot be such,
(Toilsome and indigent,) she renders much;[1]
Just knows, and knows no more, her Bible true—
A truth the brilliant Frenchman[2] never knew;
And in that charter reads, with sparkling eyes,
Her title to a treasure in the skies.
O happy peasant! O unhappy bard!
His the mere tinsel, hers the rich reward;
He, praised perhaps for ages yet to come,
She, never heard of half a mile from home;
He, lost in errors his vain heart prefers,
She, safe in the simplicity of hers.

Cowper.

THE HERMIT.

At the close of the day, when the hamlet is still,
   And mortals the sweets of forgetfulness prove;
When nought but the torrent is heard on the hill,
   And nought but the nightingale's song in the grove;
'Twas thus, by the cave of the mountain afar,
   While his harp rang symphonious,[3] a hermit began;
No more with himself or with nature at war,
   He thought as a sage, though he felt as a man:—

"Ah! why, all abandoned to darkness and woe;
   Why, lone Philomela,[4] that languishing fall?
For spring shall return, and a lover bestow,
   And sorrow no longer thy bosom enthral.
But, if pity inspire thee, renew the sad lay,
   Mourn, sweetest complainer, man calls thee to mourn;
Oh soothe him, whose pleasures, like thine, pass away:
   Full quickly they pass—but they never return.

"Now, gliding remote on the verge of the sky,
   The moon, half-extinguished, her crescent displays;
But lately I marked, when majestic on high
   She shone, and the planets were lost in her blaze.

---

(1) *Much*—much praise to God.
(2) *Frenchman*—Voltaire, who was a scoffer at religion.
(3) *Symphonious*—from the Greek σύν, together, and φωνή, a sound—making one sound, accordant; the harp sounded at the same time with the voice.
(4) *Philomela*—See note 3, p. 71.

Roll on, thou fair orb, and with gladness pursue
    The path that conducts thee to splendour again;
But man's faded glory what change shall renew?
    Ah, fool! to exult in a glory so vain!

" 'Tis night, and the landscape is lovely no more:
    I mourn; but, ye woodlands, I mourn not for you;
For morn is approaching, your charms to restore,
    Perfumed with fresh fragrance, and glittering with dew:
Nor yet for the ravage of winter I mourn;
    Kind nature the embryo blossom shall save:
But when shall spring visit the mouldering urn?
    Oh when shall it dawn on the night of the grave?—

" 'Twas thus, by the light of false science betrayed,
    That leads to bewilder, and dazzles to blind,
My thoughts wont[1] to roam from shade onward to shade,
    Destruction before me, and sorrow behind;
Oh pity, great Father of light, then I cried,
    Thy creature, that fain would not wander from thee;
Lo, humbled in dust, I relinquish my pride:
    From doubt and from darkness thou only canst free.

" And darkness and doubt are now flying away;
    No longer I roam in conjecture forlorn;
So breaks on the traveller, faint and astray,
    The bright and the balmy effulgence of morn.
See Truth, Love, and Mercy, in triumph descending,
    And nature all glowing in Eden's first bloom!
On the cold cheek of death smiles and roses are blending,
    And beauty immortal awakes from the tomb."

Beattie.

THE DESTRUCTION OF SENNACHERIB'S ARMY.

The Assyrian came down like a wolf on the fold,
And his cohorts[2] were gleaming in purple and gold;
And the sheen of their spears was like stars on the sea,
When the blue wave rolls nightly on deep Galilee.

---

(1) *Wont*—i. e. were once wont.
(2) *Cohorts.*—A cohort is strictly a troop of Roman soldiers only; it is here employed in a general sense, like the Greek word phalanx.

Like the leaves of the forest when summer is green,[1]
That host with their banners at sunset were seen;
Like the leaves of the forest when autumn hath blown,
That host on the morrow lay withered and strown.

For the angel of death spread his wings on the blast,
And breathed in the face of the foe as he past;
And the eyes of the sleepers waxed deadly and chill,
And their hearts but once heaved—and for ever grew still.

And there lay the steed with his nostril all wide,
But through it there rolled not the breath of his pride,
And the foam of his gasping lay white on the turf,
And cold as the spray of the rock-beating surf.

And there lay the rider, distorted and pale,
With the dew on his brow, and the rust on his mail;
And the tents were all silent—the banners alone—
The lances unlifted—the trumpets unblown.

And the widows of Asshur are loud in their wail,
And the idols are broke in the temple of Baal;
And the might of the Gentile,[2] unsmote by the sword,
Hath melted like snow in the glance of the Lord!

Byron.

THE POET'S PLEA,

WHEN LONDON WAS THREATENED WITH ASSAULT.[3]

CAPTAIN, or Colonel, or Knight in arms,
   Whose chance on these defenceless doors[4] may seize,
   If deed of honour did thee ever please,
Guard them, and him within protect from harms.
He can requite thee, for he knows the charms[5]

---

(1) The comparison of the living and dead host respectively to the spring and autumn leaves is very apt and impressive.

(2) *And the might, &c.*—This couplet forms a splendid close to the poem.

(3) This exquisite sonnet was written in 1642, when the King's army, by its near approach, alarmed the citizens of London.

(4) Milton was then living in Aldersgate Street, London.

(5) *Charms that call, &c.*—The poet's power is like that attributed to the charms and spells of the magician—he can make thee famous—spread thy name, &c.

That call fame on such gentle acts as these,
And he can spread thy name o'er lands and seas,
Whatever clime the sun's bright circle warms.
Lift not thy spear against the Muses' bower:
The great Emathian conqueror[1] bid spare
The house of Pindarus,[2] when temple and tower
Went to the ground: and the repeated[3] air
Of sad Electra's poet had the power
To save the Athenian walls[4] from ruin bare.

Milton.

TO A LADY, WITH A ROSE.[5]

Go, lovely rose!
Tell her that wastes her time, and me,
That now she knows,
When I resemble her to thee,
How sweet and fair she seems to be.

Tell her that's young,
And shuns to have her graces spied,
That hadst thou sprung
In deserts where no men abide,
Thou must have uncommended died.

Small is the worth
Of beauty from the light retired;
Bid her come forth,
Suffer herself to be desired,
And not blush so to be admired.

---

(1) *Emathian conqueror*—Alexander the Great, so called from Emathia, the original name of Macedonia.

(2) *Pindarus*—When Alexander took Thebes—Pindar's native city—he ordered the poet's family to be respected, and his house to be left untouched.

(3) *Repeated*—recited. Plutarch relates that when Lysander had taken Athens, and was meditating its total destruction, the recitation, at a banquet, of some fine verses from the "Electra" of Euripides, induced him and his officers to forego their resolution.

(4) *Walls*—i. e. the houses and buildings of the city; for the external walls and fortifications were destroyed by Lysander's order.

(5) These lines furnish a favourable specimen of the flattering sentimental poetry of Waller, in much of which the result gained is singularly disproportionate to the pains taken.

>   Then die! that she
>   The common fate of all things rare
>   May read in thee:
>   How small a part of time they share,
>   That are so wondrous sweet and fair!
>
>   [Yet though¹ thou fade,
>   From thy dead leaves let fragrance rise;
>   And teach the maid
>   That goodness time's rude hand defies,
>   That virtue lives when beauty dies.]
>
>   *Waller.*

THE BATTLE OF IVRY.²

Now glory to the Lord of Hosts, from whom all glories are!
And glory to our sovereign liege, King Henry of Navarre!
Now let there be the merry sound of music and of dance,
Through thy corn-fields green, and sunny vines, oh pleasant land
      of France!
And thou, Rochelle!—our own Rochelle! proud city of the waters,
Again let rapture light the eyes of all thy mourning daughters;
As thou wert constant in our ills, be joyous in our joy,
For cold, and stiff, and still, are they, who wrought thy walls annoy.³
Hurrah! hurrah! a single field hath turned the chance of war,
Hurrah! hurrah! for Ivry, and Henry of Navarre!

Oh! how our hearts were beating, when, at the dawn of day,
We saw the army of the League drawn out in long array;
With all its priest-led citizens and all its rebel peers,
And Appenzel's stout infantry, and Egmont's Flemish spears!
There rode the brood of false Lorraine, the curses of our land;
And dark Mayenne was in the midst, a truncheon in his hand:
And as we looked on them, we thought of Seine's empurpled flood,
And good Coligni's hoary hair, all dabbled with his blood;
And we cried unto the living God, who rules the fate of war,
To fight for his own holy name, and Henry of Navarre.

(1) This last stanza was added by Kirke White, in a copy of Waller's poems.

(2) *Ivry*—A town of Normandy, near which Henry IV., at the head of the Huguenot army, defeated the forces of the League or Catholic party. Henry was "Henry of Navarre" by virtue of his mother's right.

(3) *Annoy*—In allusion to the severe siege sustained by the Huguenots in that city, in which, after the awful massacre of St. Bartholomew's day, 1572, the survivors had taken refuge.

The King is come to marshal us, in all his armour drest,
And he has bound a snow-white plume upon his gallant crest.
He looked upon his people, and a tear was in his eye;
He looked upon the traitors, and his glance was stern and high.
Right graciously he smiled on us, as rolled from wing to wing,
All down our line a deafening shout, "God save our lord, the King!"
"And if my standard-bearer fall, as fall full well he may,
For never saw I promise yet of such a bloody fray,
Press where ye see my white plume shine, amidst the ranks of war,
And be your oriflamme[1] to-day, the helmet of Navarre."

Hurrah! the foes are moving. Hark to the mingled din
Of fife, and steed, the trump, and drum, and roaring culverin.[2]
The fiery duke is pricking fast across Saint André's plain,
With all the hireling chivalry of Guelders and Almayne.[3]
Now by the lips of those ye love, fair gentlemen of France,
Charge for the golden lilies—upon them with the lance!
A thousand spurs are striking deep, a thousand spears in rest,
A thousand knights are pressing close behind the snow-white crest;
And in they burst, and on they rushed, while, like a guiding star,
Amidst the thickest carnage blazed the helmet of Navarre.

Now God be praised, the day is ours! Mayenne hath turned his rein;
D'Aumale hath cried for quarter; the Flemish count is slain;
Their ranks are breaking like thin clouds before a Biscay gale;
The field is heaped with bleeding steeds, and flags, and cloven mail;
And then we thought on vengeance, and all along our van,
"Remember Saint Bartholomew!" was passed from man to man.
But out spake gentle Henry, "No Frenchman is my foe;
Down, down with every foreigner, but let your brethren go."
Oh! was there ever such a knight, in friendship or in war,
As our sovereign lord, King Henry, the soldier of Navarre?

Ho! maidens of Vienna; ho! matrons of Lucerne;
Weep, weep, and rend your hair for those who never shall return.
Ho! Philip, send for charity thy Mexican pistoles,
That Antwerp monks may sing a mass for thy poor spearmen's
    souls.

(1) *Oriflamme*—from the Latin *aurea flamma*, golden flame; the name given to the great standard of France, reputed to have been brought from heaven by an angel, and given to the monks of St. Denis. It was a blazing flag of blue cloth, besprinkled over with golden fleurs-de-lis, and quartered with a cross of scarlet cloth.

(2) *Culverin*—from the Latin *coluber*, a serpent, through the French *coulevrine*,—a piece of ordnance long and thin, like the body of a serpent.

(3) *Almayne*—Allemagne, Germany; Austria is particularly indicated.

Ho! gallant nobles of the League, look that your arms be bright;
Ho! burghers of Saint Genevieve, keep watch and ward to-night:
For our God hath crushed the tyrant, our God hath raised the slave,
And mocked the counsel of the wise, and the valour of the brave.
Then glory to His holy name, from whom all glories are;
And glory to our sovereign lord, King Henry of Navarre!
Macaulay.

THE DAFFODILS.[1]

I WANDERED lonely as a cloud
That floats on high o'er vales and hills,
When all at once I saw a crowd,
A host of golden daffodils;
Beside a lake, beneath the trees,
Fluttering and dancing in the breeze.

Continuous as the stars that shine
And twinkle on the milky-way,
They stretched in never-ending line
Along the margin of a bay;
Ten thousand saw I at a glance,
Tossing their heads in sprightly dance.

The waves beside them danced, but they
Outdid the sparkling waves in glee:
A poet could not but be gay
In such a jocund company.
I gazed, and gazed, but little thought
What wealth the show to me had brought.

For oft when on my couch I lie
In vacant or in pensive mood,
They flash upon that inward eye,
Which is[2] the bliss of solitude;
And then my heart with pleasure fills,
And dances with the daffodils. *Wordsworth.*

---

(1) The leading idea suggested by these simple, yet philosophical lines, is also conveyed in the "Lines on revisiting the Wye," by the same author, in which the following passage occurs:

> "Here I stand, not only with the sense
> Of present pleasure, but with pleasing thoughts
> That in this moment there is life and food
> For future years."

(2) *Which is, &c.*—which makes or furnishes, &c.

A CALM WINTER'S NIGHT.

How beautiful this night! the balmiest sigh,
Which vernal zephyrs breathe in evening's ear,
Were discord to the speaking quietude[1]
That wraps this moveless scene. Heaven's ebon vault,
Studded with stars unutterably bright,
Through which the moon's unclouded grandeur rolls,
Seems like a canopy which love has spread
To curtain her sleeping world. Yon gentle hills,
Robed in a garment of untrodden snow—
Yon darksome rocks, whence icicles depend,
So stainless that their white and glittering spires
Tinge not the moon's pure beam—yon castled steep,
Whose banner[2] hangeth o'er the time-worn tower
So idly, that rapt fancy deemeth it
A metaphor of peace,—all form a scene
Where musing solitude might love to lift
Her soul above this sphere of earthliness;
Where silence undisturbed might watch alone,
So cold, so bright, so still.

Shelley.

MARCH.

Like as that lion through the green woods came,
With roar which startled the hushed solitude,
Yet soon as he saw Una,[3] that fair dame
To virtue wedded, quieted his rude
And savage heart, and at her feet sank tame
As a pet lamb—so March, though his first mood
Was boisterous and wild, feeling that shame
Would follow his fell steps, if Spring's young brood

---

(1) *Speaking quietude*—This metaphor is by no means new, but its fitness to illustrate the subject renders it particularly striking here.

(2) *Whose banner, &c.*—An exquisite fancy. The poet's touch converts the emblem of war into a symbol of peace, and thus blends it into harmony with the other features of this calm, still, beautiful scene.

(3) *Una*—See the extracts from Spenser's "Faerie Queene," in the second part of this work.

Of buds and blossoms withered where he trod—
Calmed his fierce ire. And now blue violets
Wake to new life; the yellow primrose sits
Smiling demurely from the wayside clod;
And early bees are all day on the wing,
And work like labour, yet like pleasure sing.
Cornelius Webbe.

"ON THE RECEIPT OF MY MOTHER'S PICTURE."[1]

Oh that those lips had language! Life has past
With me but roughly since I heard thee last.[2]
Those lips are thine—thine own sweet smile I see,
The same that oft in childhood solaced me;
Voice only fails, else how distinct they say,
"Grieve not, my child, chase all thy fears away!"
The meek intelligence of those dear eyes—
Blessed be the art that can immortalize,
The art that baffles time's tyrannic claim
To quench it[3]—here shines on me still the same.

Faithful remembrancer of one so dear,
O welcome guest, though unexpected here!
Who bidd'st me honour with an artless song,
Affectionate, a mother lost so long.
I will obey, not willingly alone,
But gladly, as the precept were her own:
And, while that face renews my filial grief,
Fancy shall weave a charm for my relief,
Shall steep me in Elysian reverie,
A momentary dream, that thou art she.

---

(1) The tenderness and pathos of these lines have never been surpassed. The "charm," which the poet's fancy "weaves for his relief," cannot but entangle and hold every reader of refined feeling and taste.

The picture was sent him by his cousin, Mrs. Bodham. In his letter acknowledging the receipt of it he says:—"The world could not have furnished you with a present so acceptable as the picture which you have so kindly sent me. ....I kissed it, and hung it where it is the last object that I see at night, and, of course, the first on which I open my eyes in the morning."

(2) *Heard thee last*—These lines were written by Cowper more than fifty years after his mother's death, which occurred when he was about six years old.

(3) *It*—*i. e.* the meek intelligence, &c.

My mother! when I learned that thou wast dead,
Say, wast thou conscious[1] of the tears I shed?
Hovered thy spirit o'er thy sorrowing son,
Wretch even then, life's journey just begun?
Perhaps thou gavest me, though unfelt, a kiss;
Perhaps a tear, if souls can weep in bliss.
Ah, that maternal smile! it answers—Yes.
I heard the bell tolled on thy burial day,
I saw the hearse that bore thee slow away;
And turning from my nursery window, drew
A long, long sigh, and wept a last adieu!
But was it such?—It was.—Where thou art gone,
Adieus and farewells are a sound unknown.
May I but meet thee on that peaceful shore,
The parting word shall pass my lips no more!
Thy maidens, grieved themselves at my concern,
Oft gave me promise of thy quick return.
What ardently I wished, I long believed,
And, disappointed still, was still deceived:
By expectation every day beguiled,
Dupe of to-morrow even from a child!
Thus many a sad to-morrow came and went,
Till all my stock of infant sorrow spent
I learned at last submission to my lot,
But, though I less deplore thee, ne'er forgot.

   Where once we dwelt, our name is heard no more.
Children not thine have trod my nursery floor;
And where the gardener, Robin, day by day,
Drew me to school along the public way,
Delighted with my bauble coach, and wrapt
In scarlet mantle warm, and velvet-capt,
'Tis now become a history little known,
That once we called the pastoral house[2] our own.
Short-lived possession! but the record fair,
That memory keeps of all thy kindness there,
Still outlives many a storm that has effaced
A thousand other themes less deeply traced.

(1) *Conscious*—from the Latin *con*, together, and *scio*, I know—knowing within oneself. The word is incorrectly used in this passage. We may be *aware of* the thoughts and actions of others, but we can be *conscious* only of our own.

(2) *Pastoral house*—The parsonage house of Great Berkhampstead, in Hertfordshire, of which place Cowper's father was rector, and where he himself was born in the year 1731.

Thy nightly visits to my chamber made
That thou mightst know me safe and warmly laid;
Thy morning bounties ere I left my home,
The buiscuit, or confectionary plum;
The fragrant waters on my cheeks bestowed
By thy own hand, till fresh they shone and glowed;—
All this, and more endearing still than all,
Thy constant flow of love, that knew no fall,
Ne'er roughened by those cataracts and breaks,
That humour interposed too often makes;—
All this still legible in memory's page,
And still to be so to my latest age,
Adds joy to duty, makes me glad to pay
Such honours to thee as my numbers may;
Perhaps a frail memorial, but sincere,
Not scorned in heaven, though little noticed here

 Could time, his flight reversed, restore the hours,
When, playing with thy vesture's tissued flowers,
The violet, the pink, and jessamine,
I pricked them into paper with a pin,
(And thou wast happier than myself the while,
Wouldst softly speak, and stroke my head, and smile,)
Could those few pleasant days again appear,
Might one wish bring them, would I wish them here?
I would not trust my heart—the dear delight
Seems so to be desired, perhaps I might—
But no—what here we call our life is such,
So little to be loved, and thou so much,
That I should ill requite thee to constrain
Thy unbound spirit into bonds again.

 Thou, as a gallant bark from Albion's coast
(The storms all weathered and the ocean crossed)
Shoots into port at some well-havened isle,
Where spices breathe, and brighter seasons smile,
There sits quiescent on the floods, that show
Her beauteous form reflected clear below,
While airs impregnated with incense play
Around her, fanning light her streamers gay;—
So thou, with sails how swift! hast reached the shore
"Where tempests never beat, nor billows roar,"[1]

---

(1) *Where tempests, &c.*—This line is taken (Cowper himself tells us in a note) from a poem by Dr. Garth.

And thy loved consort on the dangerous tide
Of life, long since, has anchored by thy side.
But me, scarce hoping to attain that rest,
Always from port withheld, always distrest—
Me howling blasts drive devious, tempest-tost,
Sails ripped, seams opening wide, and compass lost,
And day by day some current's thwarting force
Sets me more distant from a prosperous course.
But oh! the thought, that thou art safe, and he!
That thought is joy, arrive[1] what may to me.
My boast is not that I deduce my birth
From loins enthroned and rulers of the earth;
But higher far my proud pretensions rise—
The son of parents past into the skies!
And now, farewell!—time unrevoked has run
His wonted course, yet what I wished is done.
By contemplation's help, not sought in vain,
I seem to have lived my childhood o'er again;
To have renewed the joys that once were mine,
Without the sin of violating thine;
And while the wings of fancy still are free,
And I can view the mimic show of thee,
Time has but half succeeded in his theft—
Thyself removed, thy power to soothe me left.

Cowper.

ODE

ON A DISTANT PROSPECT OF ETON COLLEGE.

Ye[2] distant spires! ye antique towers!
   That crown the watery glade,
Where grateful Science still adores
   Her Henry's[3] holy shade;
And ye[4] that from the stately brow
Of Windsor's heights the expanse below

---

(1) *Arrive*—a Gallicism, from the French *arriver*, to happen.

(2) *Ye*, &c.—The first fourteen lines form a sort of complicated vocative case, the grammatical construction remaining incomplete until we reach the line, "I feel the gales," &c.

(3) *Henry's holy shade*—Henry VI. founded Eton College, in 1441. "*Holy* shade," on account of the saintliness of character attributed to him.

(4) *Ye*—*i. e.* ye towers of Windsor Castle.

Of grove, of lawn, of mead survey,
Whose turf,[1] whose shade, whose flowers among
Wanders the hoary Thames along
   His silver-winding[2] way;—

Ah, happy hills! ah, pleasing shade!
   Ah, fields beloved in vain![3]
Where once my careless childhood strayed,
   A stranger yet to pain!
I feel the gales that from you blow
A momentary bliss bestow,
As waving fresh their gladsome wing,
My weary soul they seem to soothe,
And, redolent[4] of joy and youth,
   To breathe a second spring.

Say, father Thames![5] for thou hast seen
   Full many a sprightly race,
Disporting on thy margent green,
   The paths of pleasure trace,
Who foremost now delight to cleave
With pliant arm thy glassy wave?
   The captive linnet[6] which enthral?
What idle progeny succeed
To chase the rolling circle's speed,
   Or urge the flying ball?

---

(1) *Whose turf, &c.*—These nouns pair with those in the previous line, thus:—the turf of whose lawn, the shade of whose grove, the flowers of whose mead. In a similar style Shakspere writes:—

"The courtier's, soldier's, scholar's eye, tongue, sword."

(2) *Silver-winding*—literally, winding like silver, which would be absurd. The word means shining like silver as it winds along.

(3) *In vain*—to no purpose, since he was obliged to leave them

(4) *Redolent*—from the Latin *redolens*, emitting a smell—smelling sweetly. The word is here used metaphorically, and means, in connection with "of joy and youth," fraught with the influences of, &c. A beautiful expression.

(5) *Father Thames*—Dr. Johnson pettishly says that "this supplication is useless and puerile. Father Thames has no better means of knowing than himself." The great critic, however, in his own "Rasselas," makes one of the characters thus address the Nile:—"Great father of waters! tell me," &c.

(6) *The captive, &c.*—Some think this expression tautologous, but it may perhaps be thus explained:—Who imprison the captive (or captured) linnet? *i. e.* who catch and cage the linnet? A somewhat similar idiom is pointed out in note 4, p. 107.

While some, on earnest business bent,
   Their murmuring labours ply,
'Gainst graver hours that bring constraint
   To sweeten liberty,
Some bold adventurers disdain
The limits of their little reign,
   And unknown regions dare descry;
Still as they run they look behind,
They hear a voice in every wind,
   And snatch a fearful joy.[1]

Gay hope is theirs, by fancy fed,
   Less pleasing when possest;
The tear forgot as soon as shed,
   The sunshine of the breast;
Theirs buxom[2] health of rosy hue,
Wild wit, invention ever new,
   And lively cheer, of vigour born;
The thoughtless day, the easy night,
The spirits pure, the slumbers light,
   That fly the approach of morn.

Alas! regardless of their doom,
   The little victims play!
No sense have they of ills to come,
   No care beyond to-day;
Yet see how all around them wait
The ministers[3] of human fate,
   And black Misfortune's baleful train!
Ah, show them where in ambush stand,
To seize their prey, the murderous band!
   Ah! tell them[4] they are men.

---

(1) *Snatch a fearful joy*—A happy combination of words. A fearful joy!

(2) *Buxom*—in Old English, *boughsome; i. e.* easily bent or *bowed* to one's will: hence, obedient, pliant, easily moved, elastic, merry.

(3) *Minister*—from the Latin *minister*, an attendant—an official servant. "The ministers of human fate" are the dangers of human life, appointed by the Supreme Power, who is here, somewhat heathenishly, called fate.

(4) *Ah! tell them, &c.*—The conception of the grim ministers of **fate**—the murderous band—awaiting in ambush the approach of their heedless victim, is very striking, whatever opinion may be formed of the view of life which it suggests.

These[1] shall the fury passions[2] tear,
  The vultures of the mind,
Disdainful Anger, pallid Fear,
  And Shame that skulks behind:
Or pining Love shall waste their youth;
Or Jealousy, with rankling tooth,
  That inly gnaws the secret heart;
And Envy wan, and faded Care,
Grim-visaged, comfortless Despair,
  And Sorrow's piercing dart.[3]

Ambition this shall tempt to rise,
  Then whirl the wretch from high,
To bitter Scorn a sacrifice
  And grinning Infamy:
The stings of Falsehood those shall try,
And hard Unkindness' altered eye,
  That mocks the tear it forced to flow;
And keen Remorse, with blood defiled,
And moody Madness,[4] laughing wild,
  Amid severest woe.

Lo! in the vale of years beneath
  A grisly troop are seen,—
The painful family of Death,[5]
  More hideous than their queen:[6]
This racks the joints, this fires the veins,
That every labouring sinew strains,

(1) *These*—some of these—in contrast with "this" and "those" in the next stanza.

(2) *Fury passions*—This stanza presents, in a short compass, a graphic sketch of the passions—those "vultures of the mind." They are mostly characterized by their effects, as "pallid Fear," *i. e.* fear that makes pale; "faded Care," *i. e.* care that makes the cheek fade, &c.

(3) *Sorrow's piercing dart*—An instance of anti-climax, or bathos. A climax to an ascending series of thoughts or illustrations, rising in interest from one step to another. An anti-climax, on the contrary, is a descending series. In the present case, "sorrow" is tame after the bold personification of

"Grim-visaged, comfortless Despair."

(4) *Moody Madness, &c.*—In contrast with the close of the last stanza, this may be characterized as a very striking climax.

(5) *Family of Death*—diseases.

(6) *Queen*—There is a fault here in making Death feminine; and it is believe

Those in the deeper vitals rage:
Lo! Poverty, to fill the band,
That numbs the soul with icy hand,
   And slow-consuming Age.

To each his sufferings: all are men,
   Condemned alike to groan,
The tender for another's pain,
   The unfeeling for his own.
Yet, ah! why should they know their fate,
Since sorrow never comes too late,
   And happiness too swiftly flies?
Thought would destroy their paradise:
No more:—where ignorance is bliss
   'Tis folly to be wise.

Gray.

INSCRIPTIONS.

I. FOR THE ENTRANCE TO A WOOD.[1]

STRANGER, if thou hast learned a truth which needs
No school of long experience, that the world
Is full of guilt and misery; and hast known
Enough of all its sorrows, crimes, and cares,
To tire thee of it—enter this wild wood,
And view the haunts of Nature. The calm shade
Shall bring a kindred calm, and the sweet breeze,
That makes the green leaves dance, shall waft a balm
To thy sick heart. Thou wilt find nothing here
Of all that pained thee in the haunts of men,

---

that no other such instance occurs in our literature. One cannot but be reminded of Milton's grand conception of Death in the "Paradise Lost," book ii.:—

> " The other shape,
> If shape it might be call'd that shape had none
> Distinguishable in member, joint, or limb;
> Or substance might be call'd that shadow seemed.
> For each seem'd either: black it stood as Night,
> Fierce as ten Furies, terrible as hell,
> And shook a dreadful dart; what seem'd his head,
> The likeness of a kingly crown had on."

(1) An inscription should be simple, short, and eminently suggestive. That given above is simple and suggestive, but its length is somewhat inconsistent with the imaginary purpose for which such a composition is written, and yet we could hardly wish to lose any part of what is so graceful and beautiful.

And made thee loathe their life. The primal curse
Fell, it is true, upon the unsinning earth,
But not in vengeance. God hath yoked to guilt[1]
Her pale tormentor, misery. Hence,[2] these shades
Are still the abodes of gladness; the thick roof
Of green and stirring branches is alive
And musical with birds, that sing and sport
In wantonness of spirit; while below,
The squirrel, with raised paws and form erect,
Chirps merrily. Throngs of insects in the shade[3]
Try their thin wings, and dance in the warm beam
That waked them into life. Even the green trees
Partake the deep contentment; as they bend
To the soft winds, the sun from the blue sky
Looks in, and sheds a blessing on the scene.
Scarce less the cleft-born[4] wild-flower seems to enjoy
Existence, than the winged plunderer
That sucks its sweets. The massy rocks themselves,
And the old and ponderous trunks of prostrate trees,
That lead from knoll[5] to knoll a causey[6] rude,
Or bridge the sunken brook, and their dark roots
With all their earth upon them twisting high,
Breathe fixed tranquillity. The rivulet
Sends forth glad sounds, and tripping o'er its bed
Of pebbly sands, or leaping down the rocks,
Seems, with continuous laughter, to rejoice
In its own being. Softly tread the marge,
Lest from her midway perch thou scare the wren,
That dips her bill in water. The cool wind,
That stirs the stream in play, shall come to thee,
Like one that loves thee, nor will let thee pass
Ungreeted, and shall give its light embrace.

Bryant.

(1) *To guilt*—*i. e.* to guilt only. The inseparable connection between guilt and misery is vividly denoted by the imagery of the text.

(2) *Hence*—*i. e.* because guilt haunts not these shades, they are still, &c.

(3) *Shade*—*i. e.* not among the branches, but below; a somewhat unfortunate word, since, if taken strictly, it contradicts the next line.

(4) *Cleft-born*—springing from a cleft, or fissure in the rock.

(5) *Knoll*—from the Anglo-Saxon *cnoll*, a head or top—a little round hill.

(6) *Causey or causeway*—from the French *chaussée*, which is either from the Latin *calcata*, trodden down, or *calceata*, shod or protected by a hard covering of wood or stone. See Philological Society's Journal, vol. v. p. 39.

II. FOR A COLUMN AT TRUXILLO.[1]

Pizarro here was born: a greater name
The list of glory boasts not. Toil and pain,
Famine and hostile elements, and hosts
Embattled, failed to check him in his course;—
Not to be wearied, not to be deterred,
Not to be overcome. A mighty realm
He overran, and with relentless arm
Slew or enslaved its unoffending sons,
And wealth, and power, and fame, were his rewards.
There is another world beyond the grave,
According to their deeds where men are judged.
O reader! if thy daily bread be earned
By daily labour—yea, however low,
However wretched be thy lot assigned,
Thank thou, with deepest gratitude, the God
Who made thee, that thou art not such as he.
Southey.

III. FOR A COLUMN AT RUNNIMEDE.[2]

Thou who the verdant plain dost traverse here,
While Thames among his willows from thy view
Retires, O stranger, stay thou, and the scene
Around contemplate well. This is the place
Where England's ancient barons, clad in arms,
And stern with conquest, from their tyrant king—
Then rendered tame—did challenge and secure
The charter of thy freedom. Pass not on
Till thou hast blest their memory, and paid
Those thanks which God appointed the reward
Of public virtue. And if 'chance thy home
Salute thee with a father's honoured name,
Go call thy sons, instruct them what a debt
They owe their ancestors, and make them swear
To pay it, by transmitting down entire
Those sacred rights to which themselves were born.
Akenside.

---

(1) A town of Estramadura, in Spain.
(2) The pure, classical, and severely simple tone of these lines is admirable.

IV. FOR A FOUNTAIN ON A HEATH.[1]

This sycamore, oft musical with bees—
Such tents the patriarchs loved!—oh long unharmed
May all its aged boughs o'er-canopy
The small round basin, which this jutting stone
Keeps pure from falling leaves! Long may this spring,
Quietly as a sleeping infant's breath,
Send up cold waters to the traveller
With soft and even pulse! Nor ever cease
Yon tiny cone of sand[2] its soundless dance,
Which at the bottom, like a fairy's page—
As merry and no taller—dances still,
Nor wrinkles the smooth surface of the fount.
Here twilight is and coolness; here is moss,
A soft seat, and a deep and ample shade;
Thou may'st toil far and find no second tree.
Drink, pilgrim, here; here rest; and if thy heart
Be innocent, here too shalt thou refresh
Thy spirit, listening to some gentle sound,
Or passing gale, or hum of murmuring bees. *Coleridge.*

V. FOR A STATUE OF CHAUCER AT WOODSTOCK.

Such was old Chaucer, such the placid mien
Of him who first with harmony informed[3]
The language of our fathers. Here he dwelt
For many a cheerful day. These ancient walls
Have often heard him while his legends blithe
He sang of love and knighthood, or the wiles
Of homely life, through each estate and age,
The fashions and the follies of the world
With cunning hand portraying. Though, perchance,
From Blenheim's towers, O stranger! thou art come,
Glowing with Churchill's[4] trophies; yet in vain
Dost thou applaud them, if thy breast be cold
To him this other hero, who, in times
Dark and untaught, began with charming verse
To tame the rudeness of his native land. *Akenside.*

(1) This inscription, compared with the last, is as a painting to a statue—it has colour as well as form; but both are very beautiful.

(2) The reference to this minute and characteristic circumstance shows that the picture was drawn from close observation of nature.

(3) *Informed*—from the Latin *informare*, to give form to any thing—to mould, shape, animate; it is much used in this sense by our older writers.

(4) *Churchill*—the family name of the Duke of Marlborough.

VI. FOR A NATURAL GROTTO NEAR A DEEP STREAM.

HEALTH, rose-lipped cherub, haunts this spot:—
She slumbers oft in yonder nook;
If in the shade you trace her not,
Plunge—and you'll find her in the brook!

Anonymous.

VII. FOR A NATURAL SPRING.

HERE quench your thirst, and mark in me
   An emblem of true charity;
Who, while my bounty I bestow,
   Am neither heard nor seen to flow.

T. Warton.

LORD BACON.[1]

PHILOSOPHY, the great and only heir
   Of all that human knowledge which has been
   Unforfeited by man's rebellious sin,
Though full of years he do appear,
   Has still been kept in nonage till of late,
   Nor managed or enjoyed his vast estate:
Instead of carrying him to see
The riches which do hoarded for him lie
In Nature's endless treasury,
   They chose his eye to entertain
   With painted scenes, and pageants of the brain.[2]

BACON at last, a mighty man! arose,
Whom a wise King[3] and Nature chose
Lord Chancellor of both their laws,
And boldly undertook the injured pupil's[4] cause.

---

(1) *Lord Bacon* flourished just before Cowley's time. These lines are extracted from a poem of Cowley's, addressed "To the Royal Society."

(2) One of the main principles of Lord Bacon's philosophy was, that science ought to be based on the firm ground of experiment, and not, as had been too much the case previously, on fanciful surmises and conjectures.

(3) *Wise King*—James I.

(4) *Injured pupil, &c.*—*i e.* Philosophy, who was before spoken of as wrongfully kept in nonage. A pupil—from the Latin *pupilus,* a child—is one under guardianship, a ward.

Authority, which did a body boast,
Though 'twas but air condensed, and stalked about
Like some old giant's more gigantic ghost,
To terrify the learned rout,[1]
With the plain magic of true Reason's light,[2]
He chased out of our sight,
Nor suffered men to be misled
By the vain shadows of the dead;—
To graves, from whence it rose, the conquered phantom fled.
From words, which are but pictures of the thought—
Though we our thoughts from them perversely drew—
To things, the mind's right object, he it brought;
Like foolish birds to painted grapes we flew—
He sought and gathered for our use the true.
From these, and all long errors of the way
In which our wandering predecessors went,
And, like the old Hebrews, many years did stray
In deserts but of small extent,
Bacon, like Moses, led us forth at last;
The barren wilderness he passed,
Did on the very border stand
Of the blest promised land,
And from the mountain top of his exalted wit,
Saw it himself, and showed us it.

Cowley.

THE EVE OF THE BATTLE.[3]

There was a sound of revelry by night,[4]
And Belgium's capital had gathered then
Her beauty and her chivalry, and bright
The lamps shone o'er fair women and brave men;
A thousand hearts beat happily; and when

---

(1) *Rout*—from the Latin *rota*, wheel or circle—a circle or body of men; used here, and in the early writers, in a grave sense.

(2) *Reason's light, &c.*—i. e. the simple magic of true Reason's light dissipated the misty phantom of Authority;—the thought is here very boldly and vividly developed.

(3) The battle of Quatre Bras is here referred to, not that of Waterloo, which took place two days after.

(4) On the night previous to the action, a ball was given at Brussels, by the Duchess of Richmond. Most of the English officers were present, but retired—pursuant to directions previously received from the Duke of Wellington—at ten o'clock, to take the posts assigned them.

Music arose with its voluptuous swell,
Soft eyes looked love to eyes which spake again,
And all went merry as a marriage bell;
But hush! hark! a deep sound strikes like a rising knell!

Did ye not hear it?—No; 'twas but the wind,
Or the car rattling o'er the stony street;
On with the dance! let joy be unconfined;
No sleep till morn, when youth and pleasure meet
To chase the glowing hours with flying feet.
But hark!—that heavy sound breaks in once more,
As if the clouds its echo would repeat;
And nearer, clearer, deadlier than before!
Arm! arm! it is—it is—the cannon's opening roar!

Within a windowed niche of that high hall
Sate Brunswick's fated chieftain; he did hear
That sound the first amidst the festival,
And caught its tone with death's prophetic ear;
And when they smiled because he deemed it near,
His heart more truly knew that peal too well
Which stretched his father on a bloody bier,[1]
And roused the vengeance blood alone could quell:
He rushed into the field, and, foremost fighting, fell.

Ah! then and there was hurrying to and fro,
And gathering tears, and tremblings of distress,
And cheeks all pale, which but an hour ago
Blushed at the praise of their own loveliness;
And there were sudden partings, such as press
The life from out young hearts; and choking sighs,
Which ne'er might be repeated: who could guess
If ever more should meet those mutual eyes,
Since upon night so sweet such awful morn could rise!

And there was mounting in hot haste; the steed,
The mustering squadron and the clattering car,
Went pouring forward with impetuous speed,
And swiftly forming in the ranks of war;
And the deep thunder, peal on peal, afar;
And, near, the beat of the alarming drum
Roused up the soldier ere the morning star;

---

(1) The Duke of Brunswick's father received his death-wound at the battle of Jena.

While thronged the citizens with terror dumb,
Or whispering with white lips—"The foe! They come! they come!"

And wild and high the "Camerons' gathering" rose;
The war-note of Lochiel, which Albyn's[1] hills
Have heard—and heard, too, have her Saxon foes:—
How in the noon of night that pibroch[2] thrills,
Savage and shrill! But, with the breath which fills
Their mountain-pipe, so fill the mountaineers
With the fierce native daring which instils
The stirring memory of a thousand years;
And Evan's, Donald's[3] fame, rings in each clansman's ears.

And Ardennes[4] waves above them her green leaves,
Dewy with nature's tear-drops, as they pass,
Grieving, if aught inanimate e'er grieves,
Over the unreturning brave—alas!
Ere evening to be trodden like the grass,
Which now beneath them, but above shall grow
In its next verdure, when this fiery mass
Of living valour, rolling on the foe
And burning with high hope, shall moulder cold and low.

Last noon beheld them full of lusty life,
Last eve in beauty's circle proudly gay,
The midnight brought the signal sound of strife,
The morn, the marshalling in arms—the day,
Battle's magnificently stern array!
The thunder-clouds close o'er it, which, when rent,
The earth is covered thick with other clay,
Which her own clay shall cover, heaped and pent,
Rider, and horse, friend, foe, in one red burial blent.[5]

Byron.

(1) *Albyn*—an ancient name of the Scottish Highlands.
(2) *Pibroch*—the bagpipe—sometimes the music played upon it.
(3) Sir Evan Cameron and his descendant Donald, who were conspicuous in the rebellion of the year 1745.
(4) *Ardennes*—put here for the wood of Soignies, which was thought to have anciently formed part of the Sylva Arduenna, afterwards called the Forest of Ardennes.
(5) "Childe Harold, though he shuns to celebrate the victory of Waterloo, gives us here a most beautiful description of the evening which preceded the battle of Quatre Bras, the alarm which called out the troops, and the hurry and confusion which preceded their march. I am not sure that any verses in our language surpass, in vigour and in feeling, this most beautiful description."—*Sir Walter Scott.*

CHRISTMAS.

Heap on more wood!—the wind is chill;
But let it whistle as it will,
We'll keep our Christmas merry still.
Each age has deemed the new-born year
The fittest time for festal cheer;
Even, heathen yet, the savage Dane
At Iol[1] more deep the mead did drain;
High on the beach his galleys drew,
And feasted all his pirate crew;
Then in his low and pine-built hall,
Where shields and axes decked the wall,
They gorged upon the half-dressed steer,
Caroused in seas of sable beer;
While round, in brutal jest, were thrown
The half-gnawed rib, and marrow-bone;
Or listened all, in grim delight,
While Scalds[2] yelled out the joys of fight.
Then forth in frenzy would they hie,
While wildly loose their red locks fly,
And, dancing round the blazing pile,
They make such barbarous mirth the while,
As best might to the mind recall
The boisterous joys of Odin's[3] hall.

And well our Christian sires of old
Loved when the year its course had rolled,
And brought blithe Christmas back again,
With all its hospitable train.
Domestic and religious rite
Gave honour to the holy night:
On Christmas-eve the bells were rung;
On Christmas-eve the mass was sung:

---

(1) *Iol*, or Jul—hence our *Yule*, the old word for Christmas. It is a Scandinavian word, and means *time of festivity*, and specially of the festivities in honour of the god Frey, or the sun.

(2) *Scalds*—bards, poets.

(3) *Odin*—the Jupiter of the North, called Woden by the Anglo-Saxons. We have traces of the name in Wednesday, Wednesbury, Wanborough, &c. See Dr. Leo's treatise "On Anglo-Saxon Names," p. 4.

That only night in all the year,
Saw the stoled priest the chalice rear.
The damsel donned her kirtle sheen;[1]
The hall was dressed with holly green;
Forth to the wood did merry men go,
To gather in the mistletoe.
Then open wide the Baron's hall
To vassal, tenant, serf,[2] and all;
Power laid his rod of rule aside,
And Ceremony doffed his pride.
The heir, with roses in his shoes,[3]
That night might village partner choose;
The lord, underogating,[4] share
The vulgar game of "post and pair."[5]
All hailed with uncontrolled delight,
And general voice, the happy night,
That to the cottage, as the crown,
Brought tidings of salvation down.

The fire, with well-dried logs supplied,
Went roaring up the chimney wide;
The huge hall-table's oaken face—
Scrubbed till it shone, the day to grace—
Bore then upon its massive board
No mark to part the squire and lord.
Then was brought in the lusty brawn,
By old blue-coated serving man;
Then the grim boar's head frowned on high,
Crested with bays and rosemary.
Well can the green-garbed ranger tell,
How, when, and where, the monster fell;
What dogs before his death he tore,
And all the baiting of the boar.

(1) *Donned her kirtle sheen*—put on her gay holiday gown. Kirtle, from the Anglo-Saxon *cyrtel*, is connected with *gird*, and denotes a flowing garment for man or woman, requiring to be restrained by a belt or girdle.

(2) *Vassal—tenant—serf*—A vassal is a dependent upon a superior lord, and owes service; a *tenant* holds land or houses of another, and owes rent; a *serf* is a slave, and owes himself and all he has.

(3) *Roses in his shoes*—The roses were decorations made of ribbon, like what are now called *rosettes*.

(4) *Underogating*—without derogating from, or lessening, his dignity

(5) *Post and pair*—a game at cards, common in early times.

The wassail[1] round, in good brown bowls,
Garnished with ribbons, blithely trowls;[2]
There the huge sirloin reeked; hard by
Plum-porridge stood, and Christmas pie:
Nor failed old Scotland to produce,
At such high tide, her savoury goose.
Then came the merry masquers in,
And carols roared with blithesome din;
If unmelodious was the song,
It was a hearty note, and strong.
Who lists may in their mumming[3] see
Traces of ancient mystery;[4]
White shirts supplied the masquerade,
And smutted cheeks the visors[5] made;
But oh! what masquers, richly dight,[6]
Can boast of bosoms half so light!
England was merry England, when
Old Christmas brought his sports again.
'Twas Christmas broached the mightiest ale;
'Twas Christmas told the merriest tale;
A Christmas gambol oft could cheer
The poor man's heart through half the year.
Walter Scott.

THE OMNIPRESENCE OF GOD.

Thou art, O God! the life and light
  Of all this wondrous world we see;
Its glow by day, its smile by night,
  Are but reflections caught from thee:
Where'er we turn thy glories shine,
And all things fair and bright are thine.

(1) *Wassail*—according to Webster, from the Anglo-Saxon *wæs hæl*, health-liquor—a beverage formerly much used at feasts.
(2) *Trowls*—or trolls—moves about, goes round.
(3) *Mumming*—from the German *mumme*, a mask—masking, or performing in masks.
(4) *Ancient mystery*—A mystery was a sort of dramatic performance, on some religious subject, common in the middle ages.
(5) *Visor*—from the Latin *visus*, through the French *visière*—a mask to protect the face, forming part of the helmet: also the upper part of the same, which was perforated to *see through*—hence the name.
(6) *Dight*—from the Anglo-Saxon *gediht*, set in order—dressed, decked.

When day, with farewell beam, delays
  Among the opening shades of even,
And we can almost think we gaze
  Through golden vistas[1] into heaven;
Those hues, that mark the sun's decline,
So soft, so radiant, Lord! are thine.

When night, with wings of starry gloom,
  O'ershadows all the earth and skies,
Like some dark, beauteous bird, whose plume
  Is sparkling with unnumbered eyes;
That sacred gloom, those fires divine,
So grand, so countless, Lord! are thine.

When youthful spring around us breathes,
  Thy spirit warms her fragrant sigh;
And every flower the summer wreathes,
  Is born beneath that kindling eye:
Where'er we turn thy glories shine,
And all things fair and bright are thine.

Moore.

GRONGAR HILL.[2]

Silent Nymph![3] with curious eye,
Who, the purple evening, lie[4]
On the mountain's lonely van,
Beyond the noise of busy man,
Painting fair the form of things,
While the yellow linnet sings;
Or the tuneful nightingale
Charms the forest with her tale;

---

(1) *Vista*—from the Italian *vistá*, a sight—a view or prospect seen through an opening.

(2) Grongar Hill claims a high place among descriptive poems. It is vivid, clear, and picturesque: which qualities may in part be due to the writer's profession, which was, in early youth, that of a painter. Dr. Johnson says of this popular poem:—"The scenes which it displays are so pleasing, the images which they raise so welcome to the mind, and the reflections of the writer so consonant to the general sense and experience of mankind, that when it is once read, it will be read again."

(3) *Silent nymph!*—The poet here calls in painting to aid poetry—her "sister muse"—in depicting the landscape. It may be, however, remarked that there is no classical muse of Painting.

(4) The grammar halts here; it should be "liest" to be consistent with the phrase "*thy* various hues" which follows.

Come, with all thy various hues,
Come, and aid thy sister muse;
Now, while Phœbus, riding high,
Gives lustre to the land and sky!
Grongar Hill[1] invites my song,
Draw the landscape bright and strong;
Grongar! in whose mossy cells,
Sweetly musing, Quiet dwells;
Grongar! in whose silent shade,
For the modest muses made,
So oft I have, the evening still,
At the fountain of a rill,
Sat upon a flowery bed,
With my hand beneath my head,
While strayed my eyes o'er Towy's flood,
Over mead and over wood,
From house to house, from hill to hill,
Till Contemplation had her fill.

About his chequered sides I wind,
And leave his brooks and meads behind,
And groves and grottoes, where I lay,
And vistas shooting beams of day.
Wide and wider spreads the vale,
As circles on[2] a smooth canal:
The mountains round—unhappy fate,
Sooner or later, of all height—
Withdraw their summits from the skies,
And lessen as the others[3] rise.
Still the prospect wider spreads,
Still it widens, widens still,
And sinks the newly risen hill.

Now I gain the mountain's brow:
What a landscape lies below!
No clouds, no vapours intervene;
But the gay, the open scene,
Does the face of nature show
In all the hues of heaven's bow;

---

(1) *Grongar Hill*—an eminence in Caermarthenshire, near the banks of the Towy.

(2) *Wide and wider, &c.*—*i. e.* as the traveller mounts the hill the limits of his prospect extend as circles, &c.

(3) *The others*—the others which lie beyond, and which come into view as you ascend the hill.

And, swelling to embrace the light,
Spreads around beneath the sight.
  Old castles on the cliffs arise,
Proudly towering in the skies;
Rushing from the woods, the spires
Seem from hence ascending fires;
Half his beams Apollo sheds
On the yellow mountain-heads,
Gilds the fleeces of the flocks,
And glitters on the broken rocks.
  Below me trees unnumbered rise,
Beautiful in various dyes:
The gloomy pine, the poplar blue,
The yellow beech, the sable yew:
The slender fir that taper grows,
The sturdy oak with broad-spread boughs;
And, beyond the purple grove,
Haunt of Phillis, queen of love!
Gaudy as the opening dawn,
Lies a long and level lawn,
On which a dark hill, steep and high,
Holds and charms the wandering eye.
Deep are his feet[1] in Towy's flood;
His sides are clothed in waving wood,
And ancient towers crown his brow,
That cast an awful look below!
Whose ragged walls the ivy creeps,
And with her arms from falling keeps:
So both a safety from the wind
In mutual dependence find.
  'Tis now the raven's bleak abode,
'Tis now the apartment of the toad;
And there the fox securely feeds,
And there the poisonous adder breeds,
Concealed in ruins, moss, and weeds;
While, ever and anon, there falls
Huge heaps[2] of hoary, mouldered walls.
Yet time has seen, that lifts the low,
And level lays the lofty brow,

---

(1) *Deep are his feet*—Though this is a common-place metaphor in itself, yet its use here in pointing out the precise situation of the hill is very effective.

(2) *There falls huge heaps*—This is a very anomalous, but perhaps not an entirely ungrammatical, form; at least, Shakspere writes, "there is tears for his love," which has met with defenders.

Has seen this broken pile complete,
Big with the vanity of state:
But transient is the smile of fate!
A little rule, a little sway,
A sunbeam in a winter's day,
Is all the proud and mighty have
Between the cradle and the grave.

And see the rivers, how they run
Through woods and meads, in shade and sun,
Sometimes swift, sometimes slow,
Wave succeeding wave, they go
A various journey to the deep,
Like human life, to endless sleep!
Thus is nature's vesture wrought,
To instruct our wandering thought;
Thus she dresses green and gay,
To disperse our cares away.

Ever charming, ever new,
When will the landscape tire the view?
The fountain's fall, the river's flow,
The woody valleys, warm and low,
The windy summit, wild and high,
Roughly rushing on the sky!
The pleasant seat, the ruined tower,
The naked rock, the shady bower;
The town and village, dome and farm,
Each gives each a double charm,
As pearls[1] upon an Ethiop's arm.

See on the mountain's southern side,
Where the prospect opens wide,
Where the evening gilds the tide,
How close and small the hedges lie!
What streaks of meadows cross the eye!
A step, methinks, may pass the stream,
So little distant dangers seem:
So we mistake the future's face,[2]
Eyed through Hope's deluding glass;

---

(1) *As pearls, &c.*—One of the happiest similes to be met with in poetry—terse, brief, and particularly ingenious.

(2) It has been both asserted and denied that this passage suggested the well-known lines near the beginning of Campbell's "Pleasures of Hope:"—

"'Tis distance lends enchantment to the view,
    And robes the mountain in its azure hue."

As yon summits, soft and fair,
Clad in colours of the air,
Which, to those who journey near,
Barren, brown, and rough appear;
Still we tread the same coarse way;
The present's still a cloudy day.

Oh may I with myself agree,
And never covet what I see!
Content me with an humble shade,
My passions tamed, my wishes laid:
For while our wishes wildly roll,
We banish quiet from the soul:
'Tis thus the busy beat the air,
And misers gather wealth and care.

Now, e'en now, my joys run high,
As on the mountain turf I lie;
While the wanton zephyr sings,
And in the vale perfumes his wings;
While the waters murmur deep;
While the shepherd charms[1] his sheep;
While the birds unbounded fly,
And with music fill the sky;
Now, e'en now, my joys run high.

Be full, ye courts! be great who will;
Search for peace with all your skill;
Open wide the lofty door,
Seek her on the marble floor:
In vain ye search, she is not there:
In vain ye search the domes of Care!
Grass and flowers Quiet treads,
On the meads and mountain-heads,
Along with Pleasure close allied,
Ever by each other's side;
And often, by the murmuring rill,
Hears the thrush, while all is still,
Within the groves of Grongar Hill.

Dyer.

---

(1) *Charms*—sings to. The word *charm*, from the Latin *carmen*, a song, was once used specifically for a song or singing;—thus Milton writes, "with *charm* of earliest birds."

THE CLOUD.[1]

I BRING fresh showers for the thirsting flowers,
    From the seas and the streams;
I bear light shade for the leaves when laid
    In their noon-day dreams.
From my wings are shaken the dews that waken
    The sweet birds every one,
When rocked to rest on their mother's[2] breast,
    As she dances about the sun.
I wield the flail of the lashing hail,
    And whiten the green plains under;
And then, again, I dissolve it in rain,
    And laugh as I pass in thunder.

I sift the snow on the mountains below,
    And their great pines groan aghast;
And all the night, 'tis my pillow white
    While I sleep in the arms of the blast.
Sublime on the towers of my skyey bowers
    Lightning, my pilot,[3] sits;
In a cavern under is fettered the thunder,
    It struggles and howls by fits;
Over earth and ocean, with gentle motion,
    This pilot is guiding me,
Lured by the love of the genii that move
    In the depths of the purple sea;
Over the rills, and the crags, and the hills,
    Over the lakes and the plains,
Wherever he dream, under mountain or stream,
    The spirit he loves, remains;
And I all the while bask in heaven's blue smile,
    Whilst he is dissolving in rains.

(1) The fanciful conceptions of which this poem consists are embodied in richly coloured and most musical language. The obscurity, however, of some passages is a material drawback on the reader's pleasure.

(2) *Their mother, &c.*—*i. e.* the earth's breast, as she rapidly revolves—"dances" —around the sun.

(3) *Lightning, my pilot, &c.*—There seems to be here an allusion, which is carried on to the end of the stanza, to the formation of clouds by the absorption of moisture from the earth, and, perhaps, also to the influence of electricity in occasioning the movement of the clouds and producing rain.

The[1] sanguine[2] sunrise, with his meteor eyes,
  And his burning plumes outspread,
Leaps on the back of my sailing rack[3]
  When the morning star shines dead;[4]
As on the jag of a mountain crag,
  Which an earthquake rocks and swings,
An eagle alit one moment may sit
  In the light of its golden wings.
And when sunset may breathe, from the lit sea beneath,
  Its ardours[5] of rest and love,
And the crimson pall of eve may fall
  From the depth of heaven above,
With wings folded I rest on mine airy nest,
  As still as a brooding dove.

That orbed maiden, with white fire laden,
  Whom mortals call the moon,
Glides glimmering o'er my fleece-like floor,
  By the midnight breezes strewn;
And wherever the beat of her unseen feet,
  Which only the angels bear,
May have broken the woof of my tent's thin roof,
  The stars peep behind her and peer:
And I laugh to see them whirl and flee,
  Like a swarm of golden bees,
When I widen the rent in my wind-built tent,
  Till the calm river, lakes, and seas,
Like strips of the sky fallen through me on high,
  Are each paved with the moon and these.

I bind[6] the sun's throne with a burning zone,
  And the moon's with a girdle of pearl:

---

(1) *The, &c.*—The first eight lines of the stanza represent the cloud in motion in the morning; the last six represent it when motionless in the evening.

(2) *Sanguine*—from the Latin *sanguis*, blood—of a blood-red colour.

(3) *Rack*—from the Anglo-Saxon, *rec-an*, to smoke, to cast forth vapours—a vapour, mist, exhalation; sometimes, as here, a body of vapours forming a large cloud. Shakspere's expression, "Leave not a *rack* behind," is well known. (See p. 284.)

(4) *Shines dead*—i. e. waxes dim or faint: a singular expression.

(5) *Its ardours of, &c.*—its warm sympathies with, &c.

(6) *I bind, &c.*—The whirlwinds unfurling the banner of the clouds—the clouds forming a bridge from mountain to mountain—the triumphal procession beneath the rainbow's arch—are all conceptions of remarkable beauty.

The volcanoes are dim, and the stars reel and swim,
    When the whirlwinds my banner unfurl.
From cape to cape, with a bridge-like shape,
    Over a torrent sea,
Sunbeam-proof, I hang like a roof,
    The mountains its columns be.
The triumphal arch through which I march,
    With hurricane, fire, and snow,
When the powers of the air are chained to my chair,
    Is the million-coloured bow;
The sphere-fire[1] above its soft colours wove,
    While the moist earth was laughing below.

I am the daughter of the earth and water,
    And the nursling of the sky;
I pass through the pores of the ocean and shores;
    I change, but I cannot die.
For after the rain, when, with never a stain,
    The pavilion of heaven is bare,
And the winds and sunbeams, with their convex gleams,
    Build up the blue dome of air—
I silently laugh at my own cenotaph,[2]
    And out of the caverns of rain,
Like a child from the womb, like a ghost from the tomb,
    I rise and unbuild it again.

                            Shelley.

THE MITHERLESS BAIRN.[3]

When a' ither bairnies[4] are hushed to their hame
By aunty, or cousin, or frecky[5] grand-dame,
Wha stands last an' lanely, an' sairly forfairn?[6]
'Tis the puir dowie[7] laddie—the mitherless bairn!

---

(1) *Sphere-fire*—i. e. a light from the spheres, not earthly light.

(2) *Cenotaph*—from the Greek κενός, empty, τάφος, tomb—a tomb erected in honour of some one buried elsewhere. In this passage the sky—the proper region of the clouds—being, after the rain, empty of them, seems to be called on this account their cenotaph.

(3) This pathetic ballad was written by a poor weaver named Thom, still living at Inverury, in Aberdeenshire. The words not explained here will be found in pp. 76—79.   (4) *Bairnie*—diminutive of *bairn*, a child.

(5) *Frecky*—eager, ready.   (6) *Sairly forfairn*—sorely distressed, destitute.

        (7) *Dowie*—worn out with grief.

The mitherless bairnie creeps to his lane bed,
Nane covers his cauld back, or haps[1] his bare head;
His wee hackit heelies[2] are hard as the airn,[3]
An' litheless[4] the lair o' the mitherless bairn!

Aneath his cauld brow, siccan[5] dreams hover there,
O' hands that wont kindly to kaim his dark hair!
But morning brings clutches[6] a' reckless an' stern,
That lo'e[7] na the locks o' the mitherless bairn!

The sister wha sang o'er his saftly rocked bed,
Now rests in the mools[8] where their mammie is laid;
While the father toils sair his wee bannock[9] to earn,
An' kens na the wrangs o' his mitherless bairn!

Her spirit that passed in yon hour of his birth
Still watches his lone lorn wanderings on earth,
Recording in heaven the blessings they earn,
Wha couthilie[10] deal wi' the mitherless bairn!

Oh! speak him na harshly—he trembles the while,
He bends to your bidding, and blesses your smile:
In their dark hour o' anguish the heartless shall learn,
That God deals the blow for the mitherless bairn!

Thom.

ENGLISH RIVERS.[11]

Rivers, arise! whether thou be the son
Of utmost Tweed, or Ouse, or gulfy Dun,
Or Trent, who, like some earth-born giant, spreads
His thirty arms[12] along the indented meads;

---

(1) *Haps*—wraps, covers up. (2) *Hackit heelies*—heels chapped with the cold.
(3) *Airn*—iron (4) *Litheless*—comfortless. (5) *Siccan*—such.
(6) *Cutches*—i.e. pulls at his hair. (7) *Lo'e*—love. (8) *Mools*—dust.
(9) *Bannock*—barley-cake. (10) *Couthilie*—kindly.
(11) On comparing Milton's lines with Pope's, which follow, it will be observed that all the epithets employed by the former *individualise* the rivers, while Pope's, where they are his own, are frequently vague and general.

(12) *Thirty arms*—The word Trent is here, according to an old tradition, considered as derived from the Latin *triginta*, thirty, and on this fancy several conceits respecting it were based.

Or sullen Mole[1] that runneth underneath;
Or Severn swift, guilty of maiden's death;[2]
Or rocky Avon, or of sedgy Lea,
Or coaly Tyne, or ancient hallowed Dee;[3]
Or Humber loud, that keeps the Scythian's name;[4]
Or Medway smooth, or royal-towered Thame.[5]

Milton.

THE THAMES AND ITS TRIBUTARIES.

From his oozy bed,
Old Father Thames advanced his reverend head:
Around his throne the sea-borne brothers stood,
Who swell with tributary urns his flood.
First the famed authors of his ancient name,
The winding Isis and the fruitful Thame;
The Kennet swift, for silver eels renowned;
The Loddon slow, with verdant alders crowned;
Colne, whose dark streams his flowery islands lave;
And chalky Wey, that rolls a milky wave:
The blue, transparent Vandalis[6] appears;
The gulfy Lea his sedgy tresses rears;
And sullen Mole, that hides his diving flood;
And silent Darent, stained with Danish blood.

Pope.

HOME.

There is a land, of every land the pride,
Beloved by heaven o'er all the world beside;
Where brighter suns disperse serener light,
And milder moons emparadise the night;

---

(1) *Mole*—This river sinks in the summer time into a "subterraneous and invisible channel," between Dorking and Letherhead, in Surrey. For a discussion of the causes of this phenomenon see Brayley's "History of Surrey," vol. i. pp. 175—185.

(2) *Maiden's death*—In allusion to the legend of Sabrina, referred to in "Comus," and detailed in Milton's "History of Britain," book i.

(3) *Hallowed Dee*—so called from its being fabulously considered the haunt of magicians, &c. (See extract from Milton's "Lycidas," p. 299.)

(4) *Scythian's name*—Humber is said to have been the name of a Scythian king, who was drowned in the river.

(5) *Royal-towered Thame*—in allusion to the royal towers of Windsor.

(6) *Vandalis*—the Wandle, a river in Surrey.

A land of beauty, virtue, valour, truth,
Time-tutored age, and love-exalted youth.
The wandering mariner, whose eye explores
The wealthiest isles, the most enchanting shores,
Views not a realm so bountiful and fair,
Nor breathes the spirit of a purer air;
In every clime the magnet of his soul,
Touched by remembrance, trembles to that pole;
For in this land of Heaven's peculiar grace,
The heritage of nature's noblest race,
There is a spot of earth supremely blest—
A dearer, sweeter spot than all the rest,
Where man, creation's tyrant, casts aside
His sword and sceptre, pageantry and pride,
While in his softened looks benignly blend
The sire,[1] the son, the husband, brother, friend.
Here woman reigns; the mother, daughter, wife,
Strews with fresh flowers the narrow way of life!
In the clear heaven of her delightful eye,
An angel-guard[2] of loves and graces lie;
Around her knees domestic duties meet,
And fireside pleasures gambol at her feet.
Where shall that land, that spot of earth be found?
Art thou a man?—a patriot?—look around!
Oh thou shalt find, howe'er thy footsteps roam,
That land THY COUNTRY, and that spot THY HOME!

O'er China's garden-fields and peopled floods;
In California's pathless world of woods;
Round Andes' heights, where Winter, from his throne,
Looks down in scorn upon the summer zone;
By the gay borders of Bermuda's isles,
Where Spring, with everlasting verdure, smiles;
On pure Madeira's vine-robed hills of health;
In Java's swamps of pestilence and wealth;
Where Babel stood, where wolves and jackals drink,
Midst weeping willows on Euphrates' brink;

---

(1) *Sire, husband*—The *sire*—from the Latin *senior*, elder, through the French *sieur*—is the head of the family, the master of the house; *husband*—from the Anglo-Saxon *hus*, house, and *band*, bond—though its meaning is now restricted, had originally the same signification, the bond or support of the house. A man, therefore, as in the above line, may be called a *sire* in relation to his house and family, and a *husband* in relation to his wife.

(2) *An angel-guard, &c.*—The reference here to woman in her domestic circle is particularly elegant.

On Carmel's crest; by Jordan's reverend stream,
Where Canaan's glories vanished like a dream;
Where Greece, a spectre, haunts her heroes' graves,
And Rome's vast ruins darken Tiber's waves;
Where broken-hearted Switzerland bewails
Her subject mountains and dishonoured vales;
Where Albion's rocks exult amidst the sea,
Around the beauteous isle of Liberty;—
Man, through all ages of revolving time,
Unchanging man, in every varying clime,
Deems his own land of every land the pride,
Beloved by heaven o'er all the world beside;
His home the spot of earth supremely blest,
A dearer, sweeter spot than all the rest. *Montgomery.*

PROVIDENCE.[1]
FROM THE ITALIAN OF FILICAJA.

EVEN as a mother o'er her children bending
Yearns with maternal love—her fond embraces,
And gentle kiss to each in turn extending,
One at her feet, one on her knees she places,
And from their eyes, and voice, and speaking faces,
Their varying wants and wishes comprehending,
To one a look, to one a word addresses,
Even with her frowns a mother's fondness blending;
So o'er us watches Providence on high,
And hope to some, and help to others lends,
And yields alike to all an open ear,
And when she seems her favours to deny,
She for our prayers[2] alone the boon suspends,
Or, seeming to deny, she grants the prayer.

HYMN BEFORE SUNRISE IN THE VALE OF CHAMOUNI.[3]

HAST thou a charm to stay the morning-star
In his steep course? so long he seems to pause

---

(1) This sonnet is extracted from the "Edinburgh Review," January, 1835.

(2) *For our prayers*—on account of the wrong spirit of our prayers.

(3) This noble composition, which is said to be, for the most part, a translation from the German, is a suitable companion for Milton's "Morning Hymn" (see p. 358) and Thomson's "Hymn of the Seasons" (see p. 387).

On thy bald awful head, O sovran Blanc!
The Arvé and Arveiron at thy base
Rave ceaselessly; but thou, most awful form!
Risest from forth thy silent sea of pines
How silently! Around thee and above
Deep is the air, and dark, substantial, black,
An ebon mass: methinks thou piercest it,
As with a wedge! but when I look again,
It is thine own calm home, thy crystal shrine,
Thy habitation from eternity!
O dread and silent mount! I gazed upon thee,
Till thou, still present to the bodily sense,
Didst vanish from my thought: entranced in prayer
I worshipped the invisible alone.

Yet, like some sweet beguiling melody,
So sweet, we know not we are listening to it,
Thou, the meanwhile, wast blending with my thoughts,
Yea, with my life, and life's own secret joy:
Till the dilating soul,[1] enrapt, transfused,
Into the mighty vision passing—there,
As in her natural form, swelled vast to heaven!

Awake, my soul! not only passive praise
Thou owest! not alone these swelling tears,
Mute thanks and secret ecstasy! Awake,
Voice of sweet song! Awake, my heart, awake!
Green vales and icy cliffs, all join my hymn.

Thou first and chief, sole sovran of the vale!
O struggling with the darkness all the night,
And visited all night by troops of stars,
Or when they climb the sky, or when they sink;
Companion of the morning-star at dawn,
Thyself earth's rosy star,[2] and of the dawn

---

(1) *The dilating soul, &c.*—*i. e.* the soul expanding, as it were, with the conceptions suggested by the sublime scene, to its natural dimensions, swelled even to heaven. A similar thought occurs in "Childe Harold" (canto iv. 155), in reference to the effect produced on the mind by the view of St. Peter's at Rome:

> "Thy mind,
> Expanded by the genius of the spot,
> Has grown colossal."

(2) *Thyself earth's rosy star*—Mont Blanc is here spoken of as a *star*, because of the height of its summit above the vale—a *rosy star* because its peak is flushed at dawn with the rosy tints reflected from the clouds, so that it becomes in this way co-herald of the dawn, with the morning-star.

Co-herald! wake, O wake, and utter praise!
Who sank thy sunless pillars deep in earth?
Who filled thy countenance with rosy light?
Who made thee parent of perpetual streams?
   And you, ye five wild torrents,[1] fiercely glad!
Who called you forth from night and utter death,
From dark and icy caverns called you forth,
Down those precipitous, black, jagged rocks,
For ever shattered and the same for ever?
Who gave you your invulnerable life,[2]
Your strength, your speed, your fury and your joy,
Unceasing thunder and eternal foam?
And who commanded—and the silence came—
"Here let the billows stiffen, and have rest?"
   Ye ice-falls! ye that from the mountain's brow
Adown enormous ravines slope amain—
Torrents, methinks, that heard a mighty voice,
And stopped at once amid their maddest plunge!
Motionless torrents! silent cataracts!
Who made you glorious as the gates of heaven,
Beneath the keen full moon? Who bade the sun
Clothe you with rainbows? Who, with living flowers[3]
Of loveliest blue, spread garments at your feet?—
God! let the torrents, like a shout of nations,
Answer; and let the ice-plains echo, God!
God! sing, ye meadow-streams, with gladsome voice!
Ye pine-groves, with your soft and soul-like sounds![4]
And they too have a voice, yon piles of snow,
And in their perilous fall shall thunder—GOD!
   Ye living flowers that skirt the eternal frost!
Ye wild goats sporting round the eagle's nest!
Ye eagles, playmates of the mountain storm!
Ye lightnings, the dread arrows of the clouds!

---

(1) "Besides the rivers Arvé and Arveiron, which have their sources in the foot of Mont Blanc, five conspicuous torrents rush down its sides."—*Coleridge.*

(2) *Invulnerable life*—The conception of some of the torrents as endued with "invulnerable life," and exhibiting all the attributes of human power, passion, and joy, is finely contrasted with that below of others "stopped at once," and converted into   "Motionless torrents! silent cataracts!"

(3) *Living flowers, &c.*—The *Gentiana major*, with its lovely blue corolla, is one of the flowers found in countless myriads "skirting the eternal frost" like a garland.

(4) *Soul-like sounds*—i. e. such aërial sounds as might be fancifully attributed to invisible spirits.

Ye signs and wonders of the elements!
Utter forth God, and fill the hills with praise!
  Thou too, hoar mount! with thy sky-pointing peaks,
Oft from whose feet, the avalanche, unheard,[1]
Shoots downward, glittering through the pure serene
Into the depth of clouds that veil thy breast—
Thou too again, stupendous mountain! thou
That as I raise my head, awhile bowed low
In adoration, upward from thy base
Slow-travelling, with dim eyes suffused with tears,
Solemnly seemest, like a vapoury cloud,
To rise before me—rise, O ever rise,
Rise, like a cloud of incense, from the earth!
Thou kingly spirit, throned among the hills,
Thou dread ambassador from earth to heaven,
Great hierarch! tell thou the silent sky,
And tell the stars, and tell yon rising sun,
Earth, with her thousand voices, praises God!

                                   Coleridge.

ODE TO EVENING.[2]

If aught of oaten stop,[3] or pastoral song,
  May hope, O pensive Eve, to soothe thine ear,
      Like thy own brawling springs,
      Thy springs, and dying gales,

O nymph reserved! while now the bright-haired sun
  Sits in yon western tent, whose cloudy skirts,
      With brede[4] ethereal wove,
      O'erhang his wavy bed;

---

(1) *Unheard*—from its great height.

(2) Sir Egerton Brydges says of this ode:—"Such a scene of enchanting repose was never exhibited by Claude, or any other among the happiest of painters. It is vain to attempt to analyse the charm of this ode; it is so subtle, that it escapes analysis. Its harmony is so perfect, that it requires no rhyme. The objects are so happily chosen, and the simple epithets convey ideas and feelings so congenial to each other, as to throw the reader into the very mood over which the personified being so beautifully designed presides. No other poem on the same subject has the same magic."

(3) *Oaten stop*—The ancient shepherd's pipe was sometimes made of oat-straw.

(4) *Brede* (or *braid*) *ethereal wove*—The clouds, woven into a sort of airy fringe, hang like a curtain over the sea—the sun's "wavy bed;" an exquisite conception.

Now air is hushed,[1] save where the weak-eyed bat,
With short shrill shriek, flits by on leathern wing,
  Or where the beetle winds
  His small but sullen horn,

As oft he rises, 'midst the twilight path,
Against the pilgrim borne in heedless hum:
  Now teach me, maid composed,
  To breathe some softened strain,

Whose numbers, stealing through thy darkening vale,
May not unseemly with its stillness suit,
  As, musing slow, I hail
  Thy genial, loved return!

For[2] when thy folding-star arising shows
His paly circlet, at his warning lamp
  The fragrant Hours, and Elves
  Who slept in buds the day,

And many a Nymph who wreathes her brows with sedge,
And sheds the freshening dew, and, lovelier still,
  The pensive Pleasures sweet,
  Prepare thy shadowy car.

Then let me rove some wild and healthy scene,
Or find some ruin 'midst its dreary dells,
  Whose walls more awful nod
  By thy religious gleams.

Or, if chill blustering winds, or driving rain,
Prevent my willing feet, be mine the hut,
  That, from[3] the mountain's side,
  Views wilds and swelling floods,

And hamlets brown, and dim-discovered spires;
And hears their simple bell, and marks o'er all
  Thy dewy fingers draw
  The gradual dusky veil.

---

(1) *Now air, &c.*—i. e. and now while, &c., teach me, maid composed, &c.

(2) *For, &c.*—i. e. let me aid by some "softened strain" to celebrate thy loved return, *for*—inasmuch as—other votaries of thine—the hours, elves, &c.—are now preparing to greet thee too.

(3) *That, from, &c.*—"In what short and simple terms does he (Collins) open a wide and majestic landscape to the mind, such as we might view from Benlomond or Snowdon, when he speaks of 'the hut that, from,' &c."—*Campbell.*

While Spring[1] shall pour his showers, as oft he wont,
And bathe thy breathing[2] tresses, meekest Eve!
  While Summer loves to sport
  Beneath thy lingering light;

While sallow Autumn fills thy lap with leaves;
Or Winter, yelling through the troublous air,
  Affrights thy shrinking train,
  And rudely rends thy robes;

So long, regardful of thy quiet rule,
Shall Fancy, Friendship, Science, smiling Peace,
  Thy gentlest influence own,
  And love thy favourite name.   *Collins.*

TO THE MEMORY OF THOMSON.[3]

While virgin Spring, by Eden's flood,
 Unfolds her tender mantle green,
Or pranks the sod in frolic mood,
 Or tunes Æolian strains[4] between;

While Summer, with a matron grace,
 Retreats to Dryburgh's cooling shade,
Yet oft, delighted, stops to trace
 The progress of the spiky blade;

While Autumn, benefactor kind,
 By Tweed erects his aged head,
And sees, with self-approving mind,
 Each creature on his bounty fed;

While maniac Winter rages o'er
 The hills whence classic[5] Yarrow flows,
Rousing the turbid torrent's roar,
 Or sweeping, wild, a waste of snows;

---

(1) *While Spring, &c.*—It has been remarked that to these three last verses Burns was indebted for the leading idea contained in the next poem. He had been reading Collins at the time he wrote it.

(2) *Breathing*—i. e. breathing perfume; in allusion perhaps to the fragrance exhaled in the evening from trees, shrubs, and flowers (the "tresses"), after a shower.

(3) These lines were written on occasion of the crowning of the bust of Thomson, at Ednam, Roxburghshire, the place of his birth. The rivers named in the poem are in the same district.

(4) *Æolian strains*—strains like those of the Æolian harp.

(5) *Classic*—because the Yarrow has been much celebrated in poetry.

So long, sweet Poet of the year,
    Shall bloom that wreath thou well hast won:
While Scotia, with exulting tear,
    Proclaims that THOMSON was her son.

Burns.

ISAAC ASHFORD, THE ENGLISH PEASANT.[1]

To pomp and pageantry in nought allied,
A noble peasant, Isaac Asford died.
Noble he was, contemning all things mean;
His truth unquestioned, and his soul serene:
Of no man's presence Isaac felt afraid,
At no man's question Isaac looked dismayed:
Shame knew him not, he dreaded no disgrace;
Truth, simple truth, was written in his face:
Yet while the serious thought his soul approved,
Cheerful he seemed, and gentleness he loved:
To bliss domestic he his heart resigned,
And, with the firmest, had the fondest, mind.
Were others joyful, he looked smiling on,
And gave allowance, where he needed none;
Good he refused with future ill to buy,
Nor knew a joy that caused reflection's sigh:
A friend to virtue, his unclouded breast
No envy stung, no jealousy distrest;
Yet was he far from stoic pride removed:
He felt humanely, and he warmly loved:
I marked his action when his infant died,
And his old neighbour for offence was tried:
The still tears, stealing down that furrowed cheek,
Spoke pity plainer than the tongue can speak.
If pride were his, 'twas not their vulgar pride,
Who, in their base contempt, the great deride;
Nor pride in learning, though my clerk agreed,
If fate should call him, Ashford might succeed;
Nor pride in rustic skill, although he knew
None his superior, and his equals few;

---

(1) The power of Crabbe's delineations of character depends much on accumulation. The respective traits are often tame and uninteresting, while their combined effect is bold and striking. The passage here given will illustrate this remark.

But if that spirit in his soul had place,
It was the jealous pride that shuns disgrace:
A pride in honest fame, by virtue gained,
In sturdy boys to virtuous labours trained;
Pride in the power that guards his country's coast,
And all that Englishmen enjoy and boast;
Pride in a life that slander's tongue defied,
In fact, a noble passion, misnamed pride.

In times severe, when many a sturdy swain
Felt it his pride, his comfort, to complain;
Isaac their wants would soothe, his own would hide,
And feel in *that* his comfort and his pride.

I feel his absence in the hours of prayer,
And view his seat and sigh for Isaac there;
I see no more those white locks, thinly spread
Round the bald polish of that honoured head:
No more that awful glance on playful wight,
Compelled to kneel and tremble at the sight,
To fold his fingers, all in dread the while,
Till "Mister Ashford" softened to a smile;
No more that meek and suppliant look in prayer,
Nor the pure faith, to give it force, are there;
But he is blest, and I lament no more,
A wise, good man contented to be poor.

Crabbe.

THE RIVAL STATESMEN.[1]

To mute and to material things
New life revolving summer brings;
The vernal sun new life bestows
E'en on the meanest flower that blows;
But vainly, vainly may he shine
Where glory weeps o'er Fox's shrine;
And vainly pierce the solemn gloom
That shrouds, O Pitt, thy hallowed tomb!
For ne'er held marble in its trust
Of two such wondrous men the dust.

With more than mortal powers endowed,
How high they soared above the crowd!

---

(1) This extract is taken from the introduction to the first canto of "Marmion."

Theirs was no common party race,
Jostling by dark intrigue for place;
Like fabled gods, their mighty war
Shook realms and nations in its jar;
Beneath each banner proud to stand,
Looked up the noblest of the land,
Till through the British world were known
The names of Pitt and Fox alone.
Now—taming thought to human pride!—
The mighty chiefs sleep side by side.[1]
Drop upon Fox's grave the tear,
'Twill trickle to his rival's bier:
O'er Pitt's the mornful requiem sound,
And Fox's shall the notes rebound.
The solemn echo seems to cry,
" Here let their discord with them die:
Speak not for those a separate doom,
Whom Fate made brothers in the tomb;
But search the land of living men,
Where wilt thou find their like again?"
Walter Scott.

CLOUDLAND;

OR, FANCY IN NUBIBUS.

Oh! it is pleasant with a heart at ease,
  Just after sunset, or by moonlight skies,
To make the shifting clouds be what you please,
  Or let the easily persuaded eyes
Own each quaint likeness, issuing from the mould
  Of a friend's fancy; or, with head bent low,
And cheek aslant, see rivers flow of gold
  'Twixt crimson banks; and then, a traveller, go
From mount to mount through Cloudland, gorgeous land!
  Or listening to the tide, with closed sight,
Be that blind bard, who, on the Chian strand,[2]
  By those deep sounds possessed with inward light,
Beheld[3] the Iliad and Odysse
  Rise to the swelling of the voiceful sea. <i>Coleridge.</i>

---

(1) *Side by side*—in Westminster Abbey.
(2) *Chian strand*—It was an ancient tradition that Homer was born at Chios.
(3) *Beheld*—i. e. with his mental eye conceived the plan of the famous poems above mentioned.

AT A SOLEMN MUSIC.[1]

BLEST pair of Sirens, pledges[2] of heaven's joy,
Sphere-born harmonious sisters, Voice and Verse,
Wed your[3] divine sounds, and mixed power[4] employ,
Dead things with imbreathed sense able to pierce;
And to our high-raised phantasy[5] present
That undisturbed song of pure concent,[6]
Aye[7] sung before the sapphire-coloured throne
To him that sits thereon,
With saintly shout and solemn jubilee:
Where the bright seraphim, in burning row,
Their loud uplifted angel-trumpets blow;
And the cherubic host, in thousand quires,
Touch their immortal harps of golden wires,
With those just Spirits that wear victorious palms,
Hymns devout and holy psalms
Singing everlastingly;
That we on earth, with undiscording voice,
May rightly answer that melodious noise;[8]
As once we did, till disproportioned[9] sin
Jarred against nature's chime, and with harsh din
Broke the fair music that all creatures made
To their great Lord, whose love their motion swayed
In perfect diapason,[10] whilst they stood
In first obedience, and their state of good.

---

(1) *At a solemn music*—i. e. lines written at, or on, a sacred concert or oratorio.

(2) *Pledges*—i. e. earnests or foretastes of the joys of heaven.

(3) *Wed your, &c.*—Milton speaks in his "L'Allegro," of airs "married to immortal verse." (See p. 309.)

(4) *Mixed power, &c.*—i. e. employ your united power, which is able to penetrate and breathe life even into dead things, and to our, &c.

(5) *Phantasy*—the old spelling for *fancy*.

(6) *Concent*—from the Latin *con*, together, and *centus* (for *cantus*), singing, harmony—in allusion to Plato's conceit of the music of the spheres.

(7) *Aye*—always, ever.

(8) *Noise*—music. So the word used to be sometimes employed in prose. See Psalm xlvii. 5: "God is gone up with a merry noise, and the Lord with the sound of the trumpet."—*Cranmer's version*.

(9) *Disproportioned*—mismatched, disorderly.

(10) *Diapason*—from the Greek διά, through, and πασῶν, of all—"the interval of the octave, so called because it includes all admitted musical sounds"—here, metaphorically, full harmony.

Oh! may we soon again renew that song,
  And keep in tune with heaven, till God ere long
 To his celestial concert us unite,
  To live with him, and sing in endless morn of light!
                                                Milton.

ON THE LATE MASSACRE IN PIEDMONT.[1]

Avenge, O Lord! thy slaughtered saints, whose bones
  Lie scattered on the Alpine mountains cold;
  Even them who kept thy truth so pure of old,[2]
  When all our fathers worshipped stocks and stones,
Forget not: in thy book record their groans
  Who were thy sheep, and in their ancient fold
  Slain by the bloody Piedmontese, that rolled
  Mother with infant down the rocks. Their moans[3]
The vales redoubled to the hills, and they
  To Heaven. Their martyred blood and ashes sow
  O'er all the Italian fields, where still doth sway
The triple tyrant;[4] that from these may grow
  A hundred-fold, who, having learned thy way,
  Early may fly the Babylonian woe.[5]
                                                Milton.

TO A FRIEND.

When we were idlers with the loitering rills
The need of human love we little noted:
Our love was nature, and the peace that floated
On the white mist, and dwelt upon the hills,

---

(1) *This* sublime prayer, *as it may truly be called,* was written on occasion of the barbarous massacre in 1655, inflicted by the Duke of Savoy on his Protestant subjects, the Vaudois.

(2) *So pure of old*—The Vaudois appear to have kept themselves separate from the church of Rome from time immemorial.

(3) *Their moans, &c.*—The simplicity of the expression, the fulness of meaning, and the fine movement of the verse, make this sentence truly sublime.

(4) *The triple tyrant*—the Pope. So designated, probably, from his wearing the triple crown.

(5) *Babylonian woe*—the woe denounced on the spiritual Babylon, which is by many considered to be the Roman Catholic church.

To sweet accord subdued our wayward wills:
One soul was ours, one mind, one heart devoted,
That, wisely doting,[1] asked not why it doted,
And ours the unknown joy, which knowing kills.[2]
But now I find how dear thou wert to me;
That man is more than half of nature's treasure,
Of that fair beauty, which no eye can see,
Of that sweet music which no eye can measure;
And now the streams may sing for others' pleasure,
The hills sleep on in their eternity!
Hartley Coleridge.

THE DEATH-BED.

WE watched her breathing through the night,
   Her breathing soft and low,
As in her breast the wave of life
   Kept heaving to and fro.

So silently we seemed to speak,
   So slowly moved about,
As we had lent her half our powers
   To eke her living out.

Our very hopes belied our fears,
   Our fears our hopes belied—
We thought her dying when she slept,
   And sleeping when she died.

For when the morn came, dim and sad,
   And chill with early showers,
Her quiet eyelids closed—she had
   Another morn than ours.
Hood.

---

(1) *Wisely doting*—to *dote*, connected with the Dutch *dutten*, and the French *doter*, *radoter*, probably meant originally to sleep, or dream, then to rave, to talk or act foolishly: hence the pointed antithesis, in the above phrase.

(2) This beautiful line reminds us of Gray's expression (see p. 127)—

> "Where ignorance is bliss
> 'Tis folly to be wise;"

and also of the exquisite story of Cupid and Psyche, as told by Apuleius (book iv. 28). Psyche was perfectly happy in the love of Cupid, or Eros, until her curiosity prompted her to try to ascertain who he was—and then he vanished for ever!

NIGHT.

Night is the time for rest;—
How sweet! when labours close,
To gather round an aching breast
The curtain of repose;
Stretch the tired limbs and lay the head
Upon our own delightful bed!

Night is the time for dreams;—
The gay romance of life;
When truth that is, and truth that seems,
Blend in fantastic strife;
Ah! visions less beguiling far
Than waking dreams by daylight are!

Night is the time for toil;—
To plough the classic field,
Intent to find the buried spoil
Its wealthy furrows yield;
Till all is ours that sages taught,
That poets sang, or heroes wrought.

Night is the time to weep;—
To wet with unseen tears
Those graves of memory where sleep
The joys of other years;
Hopes that were angels in their birth,
But perished young, like things of earth.

Night is the time for care;—
Brooding on hours misspent,
To see the spectre of despair
Come to our lonely tent;
Like Brutus,[1] 'midst his slumbering host,
Startled by Cæsar's stalworth[2] ghost.

---

(1) *Like Brutus*—In allusion to the phantom of Cæsar, which is said to have appeared to Brutus before the battle of Philippi.

(2) *Stalworth*—from the Anglo-Saxon *stæl-weorth*, worth stealing or taking, and therefore (says Richardson), by inference—brave, strong, daring. Jamieson derives its equivalent *stalwart* from the Anglo-Saxon *stalferhth*, steel mind or spirit—a much more probable derivation.

Night is the time to pray;—
Our Saviour oft withdrew
To desert mountains far away;
So will his followers do;
Steal from the throng to haunts untrod,
And hold communion there with God.

Night is the time for death;—
When all around is peace,
Calmly to yield the weary breath,
From sin and suffering cease;
Think of heaven's bliss and give the sign
To parting friends—such death be mine!
Montgomery.

DEATH OF AN INFANT.[1]

DEATH found strange beauty on that infant brow,
And dashed it out. There was a tint of rose
On cheek and lip. He touched the veins with ice,
And the rose faded. Forth from those blue eyes
There spake a wishful tenderness, a doubt
Whether to grieve or sleep, which innocence
Alone may wear. With ruthless haste he bound
The silken fringes of those curtaining lids
For ever. There had been a murmuring sound
With which the babe would claim its mother's ear,
Charming her even to tears. The spoiler set
His seal of silence. But there beamed a smile
So fixed, so holy, from that cherub brow,
Death gazed and left it there;—he dared not steal
The signet ring of heaven.
Mrs. Sigourney.

EARLY RISING AND PRAYER.[2]

WHEN first thine eyes unveil, give thy soul leave
  To do the like; our bodies but forerun
The spirit's duty; true hearts spread and heave
  Unto their God, as flowers do to the sun;

---

(1) This subject has not often been more gracefully and tenderly handled than in the above lines. The picture here presented matches with that by the same elegant hand in p. 88.

(2) The author of these striking lines was a Welsh private gentleman who lived in the 17th century. It is rare to find so much meaning in so few words.

Give Him thy first thoughts then, so shalt thou keep
Him company all day, and in him sleep.

Yet never sleep the sun up;[1] prayer should
    Dawn with the day; there are set awful hours
'Twixt heaven and us; the manna was not good
    After sun-rising; fair day sullies flowers.
Rise to prevent[2] the sun: sleep doth sins glut,
And heaven's gate[3] opens when this world's is shut.

Walk with thy fellow-creatures:[4] note the hush
    And whisperings amongst them. Not a spring
Or leaf but hath this morning hymn; each bush
    And oak doth know I Am.[5] Canst thou not sing?
Oh leave thy cares and follies! go this way,[6]
And thou art sure to prosper all the day.

Serve God before the world; let him not go
    Until thou hast a blessing; then resign
The whole unto him, and remember who
    Prevailed[7] by wrestling ere the sun did shine;
Pour oil upon the stones, weep for thy sin,
Then journey on, and have an eye to heaven.[8]

Mornings are mysteries; the first world's youth,
    Man's resurrection, and the future's bud,
Shroud in[9] their births; the crown of life, light, truth,
    Is styled their star; the store and hidden food:
Three blessings wait upon them; one of which
    Should move: they make us holy, happy, rich.

(1) *The sun up*—i. e. when the sun is up.

(2) *Prevent*—from the Latin *præ*, before, and *venire*, to come or go—to go before. This is the primitive signification of the word, and was common in the 17th century and earlier, as is evident from the Liturgy:—" Prevent us, O Lord, by thy continual grace."

(3) *Heaven's gate, &c.*—It is difficult to conceive of a more beautiful mode of suggesting the charms and benefits of early rising. Many a long poem on the subject is less eloquent than this one line.

(4) *Fellow-creatures*—i. e. the trees, flowers, birds, &c., created by the same hand.

(5) *I Am*—See Exodus iii. 14.

(6) *Go this way*—i. e do as they do—praise God early in the morning.

(7) *Who prevailed, &c.*—See Genesis xxxii. 26.

(8) *Heaven*—rhymes here, by a most extraordinary licence, with *sin*.

(9) *Shroud in, &c.*—are wrapt in, or symbolized by; as when we speak of the morning of the world, of the resurrection, &c.

When the world's up, and every swain abroad,
　　Keep well thy temper, mix not with each clay;
Despatch necessities; life hath a load
　　Which must be carried on and safely may;
Yet keep those cares without thee; let the heart
Be God's alone, and choose the better part.
Vaughan.

CHANGES.[1]

The lopped tree in time may grow again,
　　The naked plants renew both leaf and flower;
The sorriest wight may find release of pain,
　　The driest soil suck in some moistening shower.
Times go by turns, and changes come by course,
From foul to fair, from better hap to worse.

Not always fall of leaf, nor always spring,
　　Not endless night, yet not eternal day:
The saddest birds a season find to sing,
　　The roughest storm a calm may soon allay.
Thus, with succeeding turns, God tempereth all,
That man may hope to rise, yet fear to fall.

A chance may win that[2] by mischance was lost,
　　The net that holds no great, takes little fish;
In some things all, in all things none are crost;
　　Few all they need, but none have all they wish!
Unmingled joys here to no man befal:
Who least, hath some, who most, hath never all
Southwell.

THE IDEA OF A STATE.

IN IMITATION OF ALCÆUS.

What constitutes a State?
　　Not high-raised battlement or laboured mound,
Thick wall, or moated gate;
　　Not cities proud, with spires and turrets crowned;
Not bays and broad-armed ports,
　　Where, laughing at the storm, rich navies ride;

---

(1) The pithiness of these lines countenances Pope's assertion that poetry is emphatically the language of brevity. They are of the same date as the last.
(2) *That*—that which.

Not starred and spangled courts,
  Where low-bred baseness wafts perfume to pride:
No—men, high-minded men,
  With powers as far above dull brutes endued,
In forest, brake, or den,
  As beasts excel cold rocks and brambles rude:
Men, who their duties know,
  But know their rights; and, knowing, dare maintain;
Prevent the long-aimed blow,
  And crush the tyrant, while they rend the chain.
These constitute a State;
  And sovereign Law,[1] that state's collected will,
O'er thrones and globes elate,
  Sits empress, crowning good, repressing ill.
Smit by her sacred frown,
  The fiend Dissension like a vapour sinks;
And e'en the all-dazzling Crown
  Hides his faint rays, and at her bidding shrinks.
                                        Sir Wm. Jones.

THE NEW MOON.[2]

When, as the garish day is done,
Heaven burns with the descended sun,
  'Tis passing sweet to mark
Amid that flush of crimson light,
The new moon's modest bow grow bright,
  As earth and sky grow dark.

Few are the hearts too cold to feel
A thrill of gladness o'er them steal,
  When first the wandering eye
Sees faintly, in the evening blaze,
That glimmering curve of tender rays
  Just planted in the sky.

---

(1) It may not be inappropriate to quote here Hooker's eulogy on Law ("Ecclesiastical Polity," book i.)—"Of law there can be no less acknowledged than that her seat is the bosom of God, her voice the harmony of the world; all things in heaven and earth do her homage, the very least as feeling her care, and the greatest as not exempted from her power."

(2) The quiet beauty of these lines well befits their subject, and reminds us of the similar tone of Campbell's "Rainbow" (see p. 7), and Montgomery's "Daisy" (see "Select Poetry for Children," p. 220).

The sight of that young crescent brings
Thoughts of all fair and youthful things—
  The hopes of early years;
And childhood's purity and grace,
And joys that like a rainbow chase
  The passing shower of tears.

The captive yields him to the dream
Of freedom, when that virgin beam
  Comes out upon the air;
And painfully the sick man tries
To fix his dim and burning eyes
  On the soft promise there.

And there do thoughtful men behold
A type[1] of errors, loved of old,
  Forsaken and forgiven;
And thoughts and wishes not of earth,
Just opening in their early birth,
  Like that new light in heaven.

Bryant.

EPISTLE TO JOSEPH HILL, ESQ.[2]

Dear Joseph, five and twenty years ago—
Alas, how time escapes!—'tis even so—
With frequent intercourse, and always sweet,
And always friendly, we were wont to cheat
A tedious hour—and now we never meet!
As some grave gentleman in Terence says
('Twas therefore much the same in ancient days),
Good lack, we know not what to-morrow brings—
Strange fluctuation of all human things!
True. Changes will befall, and friends may part,
But distance only cannot change the heart;
And, were I called to prove the assertion true,
One proof should serve—a reference to you.
  Whence comes it then, that, in the wane of life,
Though nothing have occurred to kindle strife,
We find the friends we fancied we had won,
Though numerous once, reduced to few or none?

---

(1) *A type, &c.*—The new moon is a type of purification and restoration.

(2) "The epistle to Hill is quite Horatian."—*Quarterly Review.* Horace's epistles are characterized by freedom and ease of style, liveliness of tone, and apt delineation of character.

Can gold grow worthless that has stood the touch?
No; gold they seemed, but they were never such.
　Horatio's servant once, with bow and cringe,
Swinging the parlour-door upon its hinge,
Dreading a negative, and overawed
Lest he should trespass, begged to go abroad.
"Go, fellow!—whither?"—turning short about—
"Nay—stay at home—you're always going out."—
"'Tis but a step, Sir, just at the street's end."—
"For what?"—"An't[1] please you, Sir, to see a friend."—
"A friend!" Horatio cried, and seemed to start—
"Yea, marry[2] shalt thou, and with all my heart:
And fetch my cloak; for, though the night be raw,
I'll see him too—the first I ever saw!"
　I knew the man, and knew his nature mild,
And was his plaything often when a child;
But somewhat at that moment pinched him close,
Else he was seldom bitter or morose.
Perhaps his confidence just then betrayed,
His grief might prompt him with the speech he made;
Perhaps 'twas mere good humour gave it birth,
The harmless play of pleasantry and mirth:
Howe'er it was, his language, in my mind,
Bespoke at least a man that knew mankind.
　But not to moralize too much, and strain
To prove an evil of which all complain,
(I hate long arguments verbosely spun);
One story more, dear Hill, and I have done.
Once on a time an emperor, a wise man,
No matter where, in China or Japan,
Decreed, that whosoever should offend
Against the well-known duties of a friend,
Convicted once should ever after wear
But half a coat, and show his bosom bare;
The punishment importing this, no doubt,
That all was naught within, and all found out.
　O happy Britain! we have not to fear
Such hard and arbitrary measures here;
Else could a law like that which I relate
Once have the sanction of our triple state,

---

(1) *An't* for *an it*, which is an obsolete expression for *if it*.
(2) *Marry*—a corruption of the word Mary, formerly employed as a kind of oath, "By Mary." It is used above in the sense of *indeed, to be sure.*

Some few that I have known in days of old
Would stand most dreadful risk of catching cold;
While you, my friend, whatever wind should blow,
Might traverse England safely to and fro,
An honest man, close-buttoned to the chin,
Broad-cloth without, and a warm heart within.

Cowper.

EPITAPHS.

I. ON A YOUNG LADY.

UNDERNEATH this stone doth lie
As much virtue as could die;
Which when alive did vigour give
To as much beauty as could live.

Ben Jonson.

II. ON THE COUNTESS OF PEMBROKE.[1]

UNDERNEATH this marble hearse
Lies the subject of all verse,
Sidney's sister, Pembroke's mother;—
Death! ere thou hast slain another,
Learned and fair and good as she,
Time shall throw his dart at thee!

Ben Jonson.

III. INTENDED FOR SIR ISAAC NEWTON.

NATURE and Nature's laws lay hid in night:
God said, "Let Newton be!" and all was light.

Pope.

IV. FOR THE TOMB OF MR. HAMILTON.

PAUSE here, and think: a monitory rhyme
Demands one moment of thy fleeting time.
Consult life's silent clock, thy bounding vein;
Seems it to say—"Health here has long to reign?"
Hast thou the vigour of thy youth? an eye
That beams delight? a heart untaught to sigh?
Yet fear. Youth, ofttimes healthful and at ease,
Anticipates a day it never sees;
And many a tomb, like Hamilton's, aloud
Exclaims, "Prepare thee for an early shroud!"

Cowper.

---

(1) This accomplished lady was the sister of Sir Philip Sidney, who has been styled by Coleridge " the star of serenest brilliancy in the glorious constellation of Elizabeth's court."

THE EMIGRANTS.

Where the remote Bermudas ride
In ocean's bosom unespied,
From a small boat that rowed along,
The listening winds received this song:—

"What should we do but sing His praise,
That led us through the watery maze,
Unto an isle so long unknown,
And yet far kinder than our own!

"Where He the huge sea monsters racks,
That lift the deep upon their backs,
He lands us on a grassy stage,
Safe from the storm and prelates'[1] rage.

"He gives us this eternal spring,
Which here enamels everything;
And sends the fowls to us, in care,
On daily visits through the air.

"He hangs in shades the orange bright,
Like golden[2] lamps in a green night,
And does in the pomegranate close[3]
Jewels more rich than Ormus shows.

"He makes the figs our mouths to meet,
And throws the melons at our feet;
With cedars chosen by His hand,
From Lebanon, He stores the land.

"He cast—of which we rather boast—
The Gospel's pearl[4] upon our coast,
And, in these rocks, for us did frame
A temple where to sound His name.

"Oh! let our voice His praise exalt,
Till it arrive at heaven's vault,
Which thence perhaps resounding, may
Echo beyond the Mexique bay."

(1) *Prelates' rage*—See note 4 below.
(2) *Like golden, &c.*—No one can have seen an orangery, even in our own country, who will not acknowledge the truth and beauty of this line.
(3) *Close*—enclose.
(4) *Gospel's pearl, &c.*—The emigrants had left their country to avoid persecution for their religious opinions;—hence their thankfulness that here they would be unmolested.

Thus sang they in the English boat
A holy and a cheerful note,
And all the way, to guide their chime,
With falling oars they kept the time.

Andrew Marvell.

LYRICS FROM THE OLDER WRITERS.

I. THE SONGS OF BIRDS.

What bird so sings, yet so does wail?
Oh 'tis the ravished nightingale!
"Jug, jug, jug, tereu!" she cries,
And still her woes at midnight rise.
Brave prick song![1] Who is't now we hear?
None but the lark so shrill and clear;
Now at heaven's gates[2] she claps her wings,
The morn not waking till she sings.
Hark! hark! with what a pretty throat
Poor robin-redbreast tunes his note!
Hark! how the jolly cuckoos sing!
Cuckoo! to welcome in the spring.
Cuckoo! to welcome in the spring.

Lyly (born 1553).

II. THE FAIRY'S SONG.

Over hill, over dale,
  Thorough bush, thorough brier;
Over park, over pale,
  Thorough flood, thorough fire,
I do wander everywhere,
Swifter than the moon's sphere;
And I serve the Fairy Queen,
To dew her orbs[3] upon the green;

---

(1) *Prick song*—elaborate and ornamented music pricked out in harmony—as distinguished from plain song, which consisted of simple melody.

(2) *Heaven's gates*—See the "Réveillé," p. 172, where we find Shakspere using the same expression—probably borrowed from Lyly. Milton also adopts it (see p. 340):—

"Ye birds
That singing up to heaven's gate ascend."

(3) *To dew her orbs, &c.*—The orbs are the *fairy rings*, as they are popularly called, and the fairy's office was to dew or water them after they had been worn dry by the merry little dancers.

The cowslip tall her pensioners[1] be;
In their gold coat spots you see—
These be rubies, fairy favours,
In those freckles live their savours:
I must go seek some dewdrops here,
And hang a pearl in every cowslip's ear.
Shakspere (*born* 1564).

III. WINTER.

When icicles hang by the wall,
  And Dick the shepherd blows his nail,
And Tom bears logs into the hall,
  And milk comes frozen home in pail,
When blood is nipt, and ways be foul,[2]
Then nightly sings the staring owl,
    Tu-whoo!
Tu-whit! tu-whoo! a merry note,
While greasy Joan doth keel[3] the pot.

When all aloud the wind doth blow,
  And coughing drowns the parson's saw,[4]
And birds sit brooding in the snow,
  And Marian's nose looks red and raw,
When roasted crabs[5] hiss in the bowl,
Then nightly sings the staring owl,
    Tu-whoo!
Tu-whit! tu-whoo! a merry note,
While greasy Joan doth keel the pot.
Shakspere.

IV. INGRATITUDE.

Blow, blow, thou winter wind,
Thou art not so unkind
  As man's ingratitude;
Thy tooth is not so keen
Because thou art not seen,
  Although thy breath be rude.

---

(1) *Pensioners*—Body-guard. "They were" (says Charles Knight) "Queen Elizabeth's favourite attendants. They were the handsomest men of the first families—tall as the cowslip was to the fairy, and shining in their spotted gold coats like that flower under an April sun."

(2) *Ways be foul*—the roads are dirty.

(3) *Keel*—skim, according to some; others say it means to cool.

(4) *Saw*—from *say*, a saying. Shakspere, in "The Seven Ages" (see p. 283), speaks of "wise *saws*, and modern instances."

(5) *Crabs*—*i. e.* apples, which it was usual to put into the wassail-bowl.

Freeze, freeze, thou bitter sky,
  Thou dost not bite so nigh
    As benefits forgot;
  Though thou the waters warp,
  Thy sting is not so sharp
    As friend remembered not.

Shakspere.

V. THE REVEILLE.

Hark! hark! the lark at heaven's gate sings,
  And Phœbus 'gins arise,
His steeds[1] to water at those springs
  On chaliced flowers that lies;[2]
And winking marybuds begin
  To ope their golden eyes;
With everything that pretty bin;[3]
  My lady sweet, arise;
    Arise, arise!

Shakspere.

VI. ARIEL'S SONG.

Where the bee sucks there suck I;
  In a cowslip's bell I lie;
There I couch when owls do cry;
  On the bat's wing I do fly
    After summer, merrily;
Merrily, merrily, shall I live now,
  Under the blossom that hangs on the bough.

Shakspere.

VII. AMIENS' SONG.

Under the greenwood tree,
Who loves to lie with me,
And tune his merry note
Unto the sweet bird's throat,
Come hither, come hither, come hither;
  Here shall we see
  No enemy
But winter and rough weather.

---

(1) *His steeds, &c.*—i. e. the sun begins to drink up the dew from the cups of the flowers; a more exquisite application of the mythological fable can scarcely be conceived.

(2) *That lies*—i. e. the springs that lies. See a remark on a similar expression in note 2, p. 110.

(3) *Bin*—an old form of the 3rd person, for which we now have *is* and *are*.

> Who doth ambition shun
> And loves to live in the sun,
> Seeking the food he eats,
> And pleased with what he gets,
> Come hither, come hither, come hither;
> There shall he see
> No enemy
> But winter and rough weather.   *Shakspere.*

VIII. HYMN TO DIANA.[1]

> Queen and huntress, chaste and fair,
> Now the sun is laid to sleep,
> Seated in thy silver car,
> State in wonted manner keep;
>   Hesperus[2] entreats thy light,
>   Goddess excellently bright!
>
> Earth, let not thy envious shade
> Dare itself to interpose;
> Cynthia's shining orb was made
> Heaven to clear when day did close:
>   Bless us then with wishèd sight,
>   Goddess excellently bright!
>
> Lay thy bow of pearl apart,
> And thy crystal shining quiver;
> Give unto the flying hart
> Space to breathe, how short soever;
>   Thou that makest a day of night,
>   Goddess excellently bright!
>   *Ben Jonson (born 1574).*

IX. TO FANCY, AT NIGHT.

> Break, Fancy, from thy cave of cloud,
>   And spread thy purple wings;
> Now all thy figures are allowed,
>   And various shapes of things;
> Create of airy forms a stream,
>   It must have blood[3] and nought of phlegm;
> And though it be a waking dream,

---

(1) *Diana* is here addressed as the moon, though reference is incidentally made to her functions as goddess of hunting.

(2) *Hesperus*—God of evening.

(3) *It must have, &c.*—The "stream" or procession of airy forms must have warmth and animation, and not consist merely of cold and unimpressive figures. See note on Milton's "Il Penseroso," p. 315.

Yet let it like an odour rise[1]
  To all the senses here,
And fall like sleep upon their eyes,
  Or music on their ear.

Ben Jonson.

X. TO BLOSSOMS.

Fair pledges of a fruitful tree,
  Why do you fall so fast?
  Your date is not so past,
But you may stay yet here awhile,
  To blush and gently smile,
    And go at last.

What! were ye born to be
  An hour or half's delight,
  And so to bid good night?
'Twas pity nature brought ye forth
  Merely to show your worth,
    And lose you quite.

But you are lovely leaves, where we
  May read how soon things have
  Their end, though ne'er so brave:[2]
And after they have shown their pride,
  Like you, awhile they glide
    Into the grave.

Herrick (born 1591).

XI. TO DAFFODILS.

Fair daffodils, we weep to see
You haste away so soon;
As yet the early rising sun
Has not attained his noon;
  Stay, stay
    Until the hastening day
  Has run
    But to the even song;
And having prayed together, we
  Will go with you along.

---

(1) *Like an odour, &c.*—The closing lines remind us of the rising of Pandemonium, "like an exhalation," in Milton's magnificent description. (See p. 324.)

(2) *Brave*—in the old sense—fine, gay, glorious.

We have short time to stay, as you;
We have as short a spring,
As quick a growth to meet decay,
　As you, or anything;
　　We die
　As your hours do; and dry
　　Away
Like to the summer's rain,
Or as the pearls of morning dew,
　Ne'er to be found again.

Herrick.

THE DYING BOY.

I KNEW a boy, whose infant feet had trod
Upon the blossoms of some seven springs,
And when the eighth came round, and called him out
To gambol in the sun, he turned away,
And sought his chamber, to lie down and die!
'Twas night—he summoned his accustomed friends,
And, on this wise, bestowed his last bequest—

　"Mother! I'm dying now—
There is deep suffocation in my breast,
As if some heavy hand my bosom prest;
　And on my brow

　"I feel the cold sweat stand;
My lips grow dry and tremulous, and my breath
Comes feebly up. Oh! tell me, is this death?
　Mother! your hand—

　"Here—lay it on my wrist,
And place the other thus, beneath my head;
And say, sweet mother—say, when I am dead,
　Shall I be missed?

　"Never beside your knee
Shall I kneel down again at night to pray,
Nor with the morning wake, and sing the lay
　You taught to me!

"Oh, at the time of prayer,
When you look round and see a vacant seat,
You will not wait then for my coming feet—
    You'll miss me there!"

"Father! I'm going home!
To the good home you speak of, that blest land
Where it is one bright summer always, and
    Storms do not come.

"I must be happy then,
From pain and death you say I shall be free—
That sickness never enters there, and we
    Shall meet again!"

"Brother!—the little spot
I used to call *my* garden, where long hours
We've stayed to watch the budding things and flowers,
    Forget it not!

"Plant there some box or pine—
Something that lives in winter, and will be
A verdant offering to my memory,
    And call it mine!"

"Sister! my young rose-tree—
That all the spring has been my pleasant care,
Just putting forth its leaves so green and fair,
    I give to thee.

"And when its roses bloom,
I shall be gone away—my short life done!
But will you not bestow a single one
    Upon my tomb?"

"Now, mother! sing the tune
You sang last night—I'm weary and must sleep!
Who was it called my name?—Nay, do not weep,
    You'll all come soon!"

Morning spread over earth her rosy wings—
And that meek sufferer, cold and ivory pale,
Lay on his couch asleep! The gentle air
Came through the open window, freighted with
The savoury odours of the early spring—
He breathed it not!—The laugh of passers-by
Jarred like a discord in some mournful tune,
But marrèd not his slumbers—he was dead!

Mrs. Sigourney.

THE STAR OF BETHLEHEM.

When marshalled on the nightly plain,
    The glittering host bestud the sky,
One star alone of all the train
    Can fix the sinner's wandering eye:
Hark! hark! to God the chorus breaks,
    From every host, from every gem,
But one alone the Saviour speaks—
    It is the star of Bethlehem!

Once on the raging seas I rode;
    The storm was loud, the night was dark;
The ocean yawned, and rudely blowed
    The wind that tossed my foundering bark;
Deep horror then my vitals froze,
    Death-struck, I ceased the tide to stem;
When suddenly a star arose—
    It was the star of Bethlehem!

It was my guide, my light, my all,
    It bade my dark forebodings cease;
And, through the storm and danger's thrall,
    It led me to the port of peace:
Now, safely moored, my perils o'er,
    I'll sing, first in night's diadem,
For ever and for evermore—
    The star—the star of Bethlehem!

Kirke White.

METRICAL FEET.

Trōchĕē trīps frŏm lōng tŏ shŏrt;
From long to long, in solemn sort,
Slōw Spŏndeē stālks; strōng foōt! yet ill able
Ĕvĕr tŏ cōme ŭp wĭth Dāctȳl trĭsȳll'blĕ.
Ĭāmbĭcs mārch frŏm shŏrt tŏ lōng;
Wĭth ă leāp ănd ă boūnd thē swĭft Ānăpæsts thrŏng;
One syllable long, with one short at each side,
Ămphĭbrāchȳs hāstes wĭth ă stātelȳ strīde;
Fīrst ănd lāst bēĭng lōng, mĭddlĕ shŏrt, Āmphĭmācer
Strīkes hĭs thŭndĕrĭng hoōfs līke ă proūd hĭgh-brĕd rācer

Coleridge.

THE HOMERIC HEXAMETER DESCRIBED AND EXEMPLIFIED.[1]

FROM THE GERMAN OF SCHILLER.

Strongly it bears us along in swelling and limitless billows,
Nothing before and nothing behind but the sky and the ocean.

Coleridge.

THE OVIDIAN ELEGIAC METRE DESCRIBED AND EXEMPLIFIED.[2]

FROM THE GERMAN OF SCHILLER.

In the Hexameter rises the fountain's silvery column;
In the Pentameter aye falling in melody back.

Coleridge.

ON A CATARACT.[3]

FROM THE GERMAN OF STOLBERG.

Unperishing Youth![4]
Thou leapest from forth
The cell of thy hidden nativity;
Never mortal saw
The cradle of the strong one;

---

(1) Though brief, these specimens of versification are of rare beauty, and finely exemplify the flexibility of our native tongue.

The scheme is:—

　　⏑⏑ | ⏑⏑ | — — | ⏑⏑ | ⏑⏑ | — —
　　⏑⏑ | — — | ⏑⏑ | ⏑⏑ | ⏑⏑ | — —

The original German is subjoined:—

"Schwindelnd trägt er dich fort auf rastlos strömenden Wogen;
Hinter dir siehst du, du siehst vor dir nur Himmel und Meer."

(2) The scheme here is:—

　　⏑⏑ | ⏑⏑ | ⏑⏑ | — — | ⏑⏑ | — —
　　⏑⏑ | ⏑⏑ | — | ⏑⏑ | ⏑⏑ | —

The German is:—

"Im Hexameter steigt des Springquells flüssige Säule;
Im Pentameter drauf fällt sie melodisch herab."

(3) These lines—a transfusion rather than a translation of Stolberg's conception—as a specimen of pure rhythm without rhyme, are perhaps unparalleled in the English language. They are musical, vigorous, and in every sense adapted to the subject; even, perhaps, in their occasional obscurity.

(4) *Unperishing youth*—*i. e.* the torrent is boldly personified as a sort of infant Hercules.

Never mortal heard
The gathering of his voices;
The deep murmured[1] charm of the son of the rock,
That is lisped evermore at his slumberless fountain.
There's a cloud at the portal, a spray-woven veil
At the shrine of his ceaseless renewing;
It embosoms[2] the roses of dawn,
It entangles the shafts of the noon,
And into the bed of its stillness
The moonshine sinks down as in slumber,
That the son of the rock, that the nursling of heaven,
May be born in a holy twilight!
Coleridge.

AGAINST CRUELTY TO ANIMALS.

The heart is hard in nature, and unfit
For human fellowship, as being void
Of sympathy, and therefore dead alike
To love and friendship both, that is not pleased
With sight of animals enjoying life,
Nor feels their happiness augment his own.
I would not enter on my list of friends
(Though graced with polished manners and fine sense,
Yet wanting sensibility), the man
Who needlessly sets foot upon a worm.
An inadvertent step may crush the snail
That crawls at evening in the public path;
But he that has humanity, forewarned,
Will tread aside, and let the reptile live.
Ye, therefore, who love mercy, teach your sons
To love it too. The spring time of our years
Is soon dishonoured and defiled in most
By budding ills, that ask a prudent hand
To check them. But, alas! none sooner shoots,
If unrestrained, into luxuriant growth,
Than cruelty, most devilish of them all.
Mercy to him that shows it,[3] is the rule
And righteous limitation of its act,

---

(1) *Deep murmured, &c.*—the gurgling of the water on issuing from the spring.
(2) *Embosoms, &c.*—*i. e.* the veil of mist catches the rosy tints of the morning, as well as the more direct beams of noon.
(3) "Blessed are the merciful: for they shall obtain mercy." Matt. v. 7.

By which heaven moves in pardoning guilty man;
And he that shows none, being ripe in years,
And conscious of the outrage he commits,
Shall seek it, and not find it in his turn.

Cowper

THE SOUTH AFRICAN DESERT.[1]

Afar in the desert I love to ride,
With the silent bush-boy alone by my side:
Away—away from the dwellings of men,
By the wild deer's haunt, by the buffalo's glen;
By valleys remote, where the oribi[2] plays,
Where the gnu, the gazelle, and the hartebeest graze,
And the kudu and eland unhunted recline
By the skirts of grey forests o'erhung with wild vine;
Where the elephant browses at peace in his wood,
And the river-horse gambols unscared in the flood,
And the mighty rhinoceros wallows at will
In the fen where the wild ass is drinking his fill.
There is rapture to vault on the champing steed,
And to bound away with the eagle's speed,
With the death-fraught firelock in my hand—
The only law of the desert land.

Afar in the desert I love to ride,
With the silent bush-boy alone by my side:
O'er the brown Karroo, where the bleating cry
Of the springbok's fawn sounds plaintively;
Where the zebra wantonly tosses his mane
As he scours with his troop o'er the desolate plain;
And the timorous quagga's shrill whistling neigh
Is heard by the fountain at twilight grey;
And the fleet-footed ostrich over the waste
Speeds like a horseman who travels in haste,
Hieing away to the home of her rest,
Where she and her mate have scooped their nest,
Far hid from the pitiless plunderer's view,
In the pathless depths of the parched Karroo.

(1) The desert in South Africa referred to in these spirited lines is the great Karroo.
(2) *Oribi, &c.*—The animals named in this and in the next two lines are all species of antelopes.

And here while the night-winds around me sigh,
And the stars burn bright in the midnight sky,
As I sit apart by the desert stone,
Like Elijah at Horeb's cave alone,
"A still small voice" comes through the wild—
Like a father consoling his fretful child—
Which banishes bitterness, wrath and fear,
Saying—"MAN IS DISTANT, BUT GOD IS NEAR!"
Pringle.

A MOONLIGHT NIGHT.

How calmly gliding through the dark blue sky
The midnight moon ascends! her placid beams
Through thinly scattered leaves and boughs grotesque,
Mottle with mazy shades the orchard slope;
Here, o'er the chestnut's fretted foliage grey
And massy, motionless they spread; here, shine
Upon the crags, deepening with blacker night
Their chasms; and there the glittering argentry[1]
Ripples and glances on the confluent streams.
A lovelier, purer light than that of day
Rests on the hills; and oh, how awfully
Into that deep and tranquil firmament
The summits of Auseva rise serene!
The watchman on the battlements partakes
The stillness of the solemn hour; he feels
The silence of the earth, the endless sound
Of flowing water soothes him; and the stars,
Which, in that brightest moonlight well-nigh quenched,
Scarce visible, as in the utmost depth
Of yonder sapphire infinite, are seen,
Draw on with everlasting influence
Towards eternity the attempered mind. *Southey.*

SOLITUDE.

To sit on rocks, to muse o'er flood and fell,
To slowly trace the forest's shady scene,
Where things that own not man's dominion dwell,
And mortal foot hath ne'er or rarely been;

---

(1) *Argentry*—from the Latin *argentum*, silver—the silvery radiance.

To climb the trackless mountain all unseen,
With the wild flock that never needs a fold;
Alone o'er steeps and foaming falls to lean;—
'This is not solitude—'tis but to hold
Converse with Nature's charms, and view her stores unrolled.

But 'midst the crowd, the hum, the shock of men,[1]
To hear, to see, to feel, and to possess,
And roam along, the world's tired denizen,[2]
With none who bless us, none whom we can bless;
Minions of splendour, shrinking from distress!
None that, with kindred consciousness endued,
If we were not, would seem to smile the less,
Of all that flattered, followed, sought, and sued;—
This is to be alone; this, this is solitude! *Byron.*

THE FLOWERS OF THE FIELD.

Sweet nurslings of the vernal skies,
    Bathed in soft airs, and fed with dew,
What more than magic in you lies,
    To fill the heart's fond view!
In childhood's sports, companions gay,
In sorrow, on life's downward way,
How soothing! in our last decay
    Memorials prompt and true.

Relics ye are of Eden's bowers,
    As pure, as fragrant, and as fair,
As when ye crowned the sunshine hours
    Of happy wanderers there.
Fallen all beside—the world of life
How is it stained with fear and strife!
In reason's world what storms are rife,
    What passions rage and glare!

---

(1) "For," says Lord Bacon, "a crowd is not company, and faces are but a gallery of pictures:" and he quotes in confirmation the Latin adage, "Magna civitas, magna solitudo." See "Essay on Friendship."

(2) *Denizen*—supposed to be connected with the French *donaison*, a gift or present—one who has obtained enfranchisement, a stranger made free. The "world's denizen" is one admitted to the rights and privileges of the world, but still feeling that he is an alien, and not a native.

Ye fearless in your nests abide—
  Nor may we scorn, too proudly wise,
Your silent lessons, undescried
  By all but lowly eyes:
For ye could draw the admiring gaze[1]
Of Him who worlds and hearts surveys;
Your order wild, your fragrant maze,
  He taught us how to prize.

Alas! of thousand bosoms kind
  That daily court you and caress,
How few the happy secret find
  Of your calm loveliness!
"Live for to-day; to-morrow's light
To-morrow's cares shall bring to sight;
Go sleep like closing flowers at night,
  And heaven thy morn will bless."   *Keble.*

THE SPANISH ARMADA.[2]

A FRAGMENT.

ATTEND, all ye who list to hear our noble England's praise;
I tell of the thrice-famous deeds she wrought in ancient days,
When that great Fleet Invincible against her bore in vain
The richest spoils of Mexico, the stoutest hearts of Spain.
  It was about the lovely close of a warm summer day,
There came a gallant merchant-ship full sail to Plymouth bay;
Her crew hath seen Castile's black fleet, beyond Aurigny's isle,[3]
At earliest twilight, on the waves lie heaving many a mile;
At sunrise she escaped their van, by God's especial grace,
And the tall Pinta,[4] till the noon, had held her close in chace.
Forthwith a guard at every gun was placed along the wall,
The beacon blazed upon the roof of Edgecumbe's lofty hall;
Many a light fishing-bark put out to pry along the coast;
And with loose rein and bloody spur rode inland many a post.

  (1) *Admiring gaze, &c.*—See Matt. vi. 28—30.
  (2) It is needless to point out the life and spirit which pervade these lines, and soon draw the reader under their spell. The poet's imagination—like the alarm-fire he depicts—lights up tower after tower, and hill after hill, until night becomes "as bright and busy as the day."
  (3) *Aurigny's isle*—the isle of Alderney.
  (4) *Pinta*—a Spanish vessel of war built for fast sailing.

With his white hair unbonneted the stout old sheriff comes;
Behind him march the halberdiers,[1] before him sound the drums;
His yeomen round the market-cross make clear an ample space,
For there behoves him to set up the standard of Her Grace.
And haughtily the trumpets peal, and gaily dance the bells,
As slow upon the labouring wind the royal blazon swells.
Look how the Lion of the sea lifts up his ancient crown,
And underneath his deadly paw treads the gay lilies down!
So stalked he when he turned to flight, on that famed Picard field,[2]
Bohemia's plume, and Genoa's bow, and Cæsar's eagle shield;
So glared he when at Agincourt in wrath he turned to bay,
And crushed and torn beneath his claws the princely hunters lay.
Ho! strike the flagstaff deep, sir knight: ho! scatter flowers, fair maids:
Ho! gunners, fire a loud salute: ho! gallants, draw your blades:
Thou sun, shine on her joyously—ye breezes, waft her wide;
Our glorious SEMPER EADEM[3]—the banner of our pride.

The freshening breeze of eve unfurled that banner's massy fold;
The parting gleam of sunshine kissed that haughty scroll of gold;
Night sunk upon the dusky beach, and on the purple sea—
Such night in England ne'er had been, nor e'er again shall be.
From Eddystone to Berwick bounds, from Lynn to Milford Bay,
That time of slumber was as bright and busy as the day;
For swift to east and swift to west the warning radiance spread;
High on St. Michael's Mount it shone, it shone on Beachy Head.
Far on the deep the Spaniard saw, along each southern shire,
Cape beyond cape, in endless range, those twinkling points of fire.
The fisher left his skiff to rock on Tamar's glittering waves;
The rugged miners poured to war from Mendip's sunless caves:
O'er Longleat's towers, o'er Cranbourne's oaks, the fiery herald flew:
He roused the shepherds of Stonehenge, the rangers of Beaulieu.
Right sharp and quick the bells all night rang out from Bristol town,
And ere the day three hundred horse had met on Clifton down;
The sentinel on Whitehall Gate looked forth into the night,
And saw o'erhanging Richmond Hill the streak of blood-red light.
Then bugle's note and cannon's roar the death-like silence broke,
And with one start, and with one cry, the royal city woke.

(1) *Halberdier*—one who carried a halberd, which in early times was a long pole, terminating in a battle-axe. This word is thought by some to be a corruption of *helm-barte* or *helm-axe*, so called from its original use.

(2) *Picard field*—Crecy is in the province of Picardy.

(3) *Semper Eadem*—" Always the same "—Queen Elizabeth's motto.

At once on all her stately gates arose the answering fires;
At once the wild alarum clashed from all her reeling¹ spires;
From all the batteries of the Tower pealed loud the voice of fear,
And all the thousand masts of Thames sent back a louder cheer;
And from the farthest wards² was heard the hush of hurrying feet,
And the broad streams of flags and pikes dashed down each roaring street:
And broader still became the blaze, and louder still the din,
As fast from every village round the horse came spurring in;
And eastward straight from wild Blackheath the warlike errand went,
And roused in many an ancient hall the gallant squires of Kent.
Southward from Surrey's pleasant hills flew those bright couriers forth;
High on bleak Hampstead's swarthy moor they started for the north;
And on, and on, without a pause, untired they bounded still:
All night from tower to tower they sprang—they sprang from hill to hill,
Till the proud Peak unfurled the flag o'er Darwin's rocky dales—
Till like volcanoes flared to heaven the stormy hills of Wales—
Till twelve fair counties saw the blaze on Malvern's lonely height—
Till streamed in crimson on the wind the Wrekin's crest of light—
Till broad and fierce the star came forth on Ely's stately fane,
And tower and hamlet rose in arms o'er all the boundless plain;
Till Belvoir's lordly terraces the sign to Lincoln sent,
And Lincoln sped the message on o'er the wide vale of Trent;
Till Skiddaw saw the fire that burned on Gaunt's embattled pile;³
And the red glare on Skiddaw roused the burghers of Carlisle.

*   *   *   *   *

Macaulay.

KING'S COLLEGE CHAPEL, CAMBRIDGE.⁴

Tax not the royal saint⁵ with vain expense—
With ill-matched aims the architect who planned—

---

(1) *Reeling*—a bold use of the word, to denote the shaking of the steeples by the bells.

(2) *Wards*—districts or divisions of the city.

(3) *Gaunt's embattled pile*—Lancaster Castle.

(4) **These are** noble lines on a noble subject, and may, without much question, be admitted amongst those—

      "Whose very sweetness yieldeth proof
        That they were born for immortality."

(5) *Royal saint*—Henry VI. (See note 3, p. 123.)

Albeit labouring for a scanty band
Of white-robed scholars only—this immense
And glorious work of fine intelligence!
Give all thou canst; high heaven rejects the lore
Of nicely calculated less or more;
So deemed the man who fashioned for the sense
These lofty pillars, spread that branching roof
Self-poised, and scooped into ten thousand cells,
Where light and shade repose, where music dwells
Lingering—and wandering on as loth to die;
Like thoughts whose very sweetness yieldeth proof
That they were born for immortality.

They dreamt not of a perishable home
Who thus could build! Be mine, in hours of fear
Or grovelling thought, to seek a refuge here;
Or through the aisles of Westminster to roam;
Where bubbles burst, and folly's dancing foam
Melts if it cross the threshold; where the wreath[1]
Of awe-struck wisdom droops:—or let my path
Lead to that younger pile,[2] whose sky-like dome
Hath typified by reach of daring art
Infinity's embrace; whose guardian crest,
The silent cross, among the stars shall spread
As now, when she hath also seen her breast
Filled with mementoes, satiate[3] with its part
Of grateful England's overflowing dead.

Wordsworth.

TO SLEEP.[4]

How many of my poorest subjects
Are at this hour asleep! Sleep, gentle sleep,

---

(1) *Where the wreath, &c.—i. e.* where man's boasted wisdom sinks into insignificance—a very impressive metaphor.

(2) *Younger pile*—St. Paul's.

(3) *Satiate, &c.—i. e.* when her breast shall have received its full share, &c.

(4) These lines are put into the mouth of the usurper, Henry IV. Independently of the striking character of the thoughts themselves, the versification is deliciously melodious. The cadence of the line beginning, "And steep," &c., is most aptly modulated; while that beginning, "And lulled," &c., exhibits the most harmonious correspondence between sound and sense—ending in a beautiful "dying fall."

Nature's soft nurse, how have I frighted thee,
That thou no more wilt weigh my eyelids down,
And steep my senses in forgetfulness?
Why rather, sleep, liest thou in smoky cribs,
Upon uneasy pallets stretching thee,
And hushed with buzzing night-flies to thy slumber;
Than in the perfumed chambers of the great,
Under the canopies of costly state,
And lulled with sounds of sweetest melody?
O thou dull god! why liest thou with tne vile,
In loathsome beds; and **leavest**[1] the kingly couch,
A watch-case, or a common 'larum bell?
Wilt thou upon the high and giddy mast
Seal up the ship-boy's eyes, and rock his brains
In cradle of the rude imperious surge,
And in the visitation[2] of the winds,
Who take the ruffian billows by the top,
Curling their monstrous heads and hanging them
With deafening clamours in the slippery[3] clouds,
That, with the hurly,[4] death itself awakes?
Canst thou, O partial sleep! give thy repose
To the wet sea-boy, in an hour so rude,
And in the calmest and most stillest[5] night,
With all appliances and means to boot,
Deny it to a king? Then, happy low-lie-down![6]
Uneasy lies the head that wears a crown.

Shakspere.

(1) *And leavest, &c.*—This difficult passage may perhaps be thus interpreted:—Thou, O sleep, forsakest the kingly couch—a luxurious and inviting place of repose—as if it were a place designed for wakefulness, like a watch-case, or sentry-box, or an alarm-bell, the very name of which suggests disturbance and inquietude.

(2) *And in the visitation, &c.*—i. e. and wilt thou keep his eyes sealed up at a time when the boisterous winds are roaring round him ("in the visitation"), and taking "the ruffian billows by the top and curling," &c.

(3) *Slippery*—because the clouds do not hold them, but let them, as it were, slip down again.

(4) *Hurly*—a word of uncertain derivation—disturbance, confusion, din.

(5) *Most stillest*—this double superlative is common in our early writers.

(6) *Happy low-lie-down*—the common reading is "happy low, lie down," the meaning of which is obscure. Dr. Warburton altered the text on his own authority, to "happy, lowly clown;" that given above is from Knight's text, and was suggested by Coleridge, taking "low-lie-down" as a sort of compound appellative. The meaning then would be, "Then happy is he whose head lies low," &c.

THE FLIGHT OF XERXES.

I saw him on the battle-eve,
  When, like a king he bore him—
Proud hosts were there in helm and greave,
  And prouder chiefs before him:
The warrior, and the warrior's deeds—
The morrow, and the morrow's meeds—
  No daunting thought came o'er him;
He looked around him, and his eye
Defiance flashed to earth and sky!

He looked on ocean—its broad breast
  Was covered with his fleet:
On earth—and saw from east to west,
  His bannered millions meet;
While rock, and glen, and cave, and coast,
Shook with the war-cry of that host,
  The thunder of their feet!
He heard the imperial echoes ring—
He heard—and felt himself a king!

I saw him next alone—nor camp,
  Nor chief his steps attended;
Nor banner blazed, nor courser's tramp
  With war-cries proudly blended.
He stood alone, whom fortune high
So lately seemed to deify;
  He, who with Heaven contended,
Fled, like a fugitive and slave!
Behind—the foe; before—the wave!

He stood—fleet, army, treasure gone—
  Alone, and in despair!
While wave and wind swept ruthless on,
  For *they* were monarchs there;
And Xerxes in a single bark,
Where late his thousand ships were dark,[1]
  Must all their fury dare;—
What a revenge—a trophy this—
For thee, immortal Salamis!

Miss Jewsbury.

(1) *Were dark*—darkened the waters.

THE HOUR OF DEATH.[1]

Leaves have their time to fall,
And flowers to wither[2] at the north wind's breath,
   And stars to set; but all—
Thou hast *all* seasons for thine own, O Death!

Day is for mortal care;
Eve for glad meetings round the joyous hearth;
   Night for the dreams of sleep, the voice of prayer—
But all for thee, thou mightiest of the earth!

The banquet has its hour,
Its feverish hour of mirth, and song, and wine;
   There comes a day for grief's o'erwhelming power,
A time for softer tears—but all are thine!

Youth and the opening rose
May look like things too glorious for decay,[2]
   And smile at thee—but thou art not of those
Who wait the ripened bloom to seize their prey.

We know when moons shall wane,
When summer birds from far shall cross the sea,
   When autumn's hue shall touch the golden grain—
But who shall teach us when to look for thee?

Is it when spring's first gale
Comes forth to whisper where the violets lie?
   Is it when roses in our path grow pale?
They have *one* season—*all* are ours to die!

Thou art where billows foam;
Thou art where music melts upon the air;
   Thou art around us in our peaceful home;
And the world calls us forth—and thou art there!

(1) The measure in which these fine verses are written, though peculiar, considerably enhances the effect of the impressive thoughts they embody.

(2) *Wither, decay, fade*—These words may perhaps be thus distinguished:—a plant *withers* when it loses its proper form and shrivels up; *fades* when it loses its proper colour; *decays* when it loses its vital strength. We may say correctly—the leaf withers, the flower fades, and the entire plant decays.

Thou art where friend meets friend,
Beneath the shadow of the elm to rest—
  Thou art where foe meets foe, and trumpets rend
The skies, and swords beat down the princely crest.

Leaves have their time to fall,
And flowers to wither at the north wind's breath,
  And stars to set; but all—
Thou hast *all* seasons for thine own, O Death!

Mrs. Hemans.

RULE BRITANNIA [1]

When Britain first at Heaven's command,
  Arose from out the azure main,
This was the charter of the land,
  And guardian angels sang this strain:
    "Rule, Britannia, rule the waves,
    Britons never will be slaves!"

The nations not so blest as thee,
  Must in their turns to tyrants fall;
While thou shalt flourish, great and free,
  The dread and envy of them all.

Still more majestic shalt thou rise,
  More dreadful from each foreign stroke;
As the loud blast that tears the skies,
  Serves but to root thy native oak.

Thee haughty tyrants ne'er shall tame:
  All their attempts to bend thee down
Will but arouse thy generous flame—
  But work their woe and thy renown.

To thee belongs the rural reign;
  Thy cities shall with commerce shine;
All thine shall be the subject main:
  And every shore it circles thine.

---

(1) Allowing for some exaggeration—and what British heart will not make the allowance?—this truly national song well deserves its fame. The third stanza is particularly noble. Its greatest fault is the want of a more direct and explicit reference to God, as the source of all power and prosperity.

The Muses still[1] with freedom found,
  Shall to thy happy coast repair;
Blest isle! with matchless beauty crowned,
  And manly hearts to guard the fair:
    "Rule, Britannia, rule the waves,
    Britons never will be slaves!"   *Thomson.*

THE PALACE OF ICE.

         No forest fell,
Imperial mistress of the fur-clad Russ,[2]
When thou wouldst build; no quarry sent its stores
To enrich thy walls; but thou didst hew the floods,
And make thy marble of the glassy wave.
In such a palace poetry might place
The armoury of Winter; where his troops,
The gloomy clouds, find weapons—arrowy sleet,
Skin-piercing volley, blossom-bruising hail,
And snow, that often blinds the traveller's course,
And wraps him in an unexpected tomb.

Silently[3] as a dream the fabric rose;
No sound of hammer or of saw was there;
Ice upon ice, the well adjusted parts
Were soon conjoined, no other cement asked
Than water interfused to make them one.
Lamps gracefully disposed, and of all hues,
Illumined every side: a watery light
Gleamed through the clear transparency, that seemed
Another moon new risen, or meteor fallen
From heaven to earth, of lambent[4] flame serene.
So stood the brittle prodigy; though smooth
And slippery the materials, yet frost-bound[5]

(1) *Still*—ever (see note 2, p. 64).
(2) *Imperial mistress, &c.*—The celebrated Catherine, Empress of Russia.
(3) *Silently, &c.*—This fine line reminds us both of Milton's Pandemonium rising "like an exhalation" (see p. 324), and of the beautiful passage in Heber's "Palestine," referring to the building of the Temple:—

    "No workman steel, no ponderous axes rung:
    Like some tall palm the noiseless fabric sprung;—
    Majestic silence."

(4) *Lambent*—from the Latin *lambens*, licking; touching lightly, as if with the tongue.
(5) *Yet frost-bound*—i. e. yet when bound together by the frost.

Firm as a rock. Nor wanted aught within,
That royal residence might well befit,
For grandeur or for use. Long wavy wreaths
Of flowers, that feared no enemy but warmth,
Blushed on the panels. Mirror needed none
Where all was vitreous; but in order due
Convivial table and commodious seat
(What seemed at least commodious seat) were there;
Sofa and couch, and high-built throne august.
The same lubricity was found in all,
And all was moist to the warm touch: a scene
Of evanescent glory, once a stream,
And soon to slide into a stream again.
Alas![1] 'twas but a mortifying stroke
Of undesigned severity, that glanced
(Made by a monarch) on her own estate,
On human grandeur, and the courts of kings.
'Twas transient in its nature, as in show
'Twas durable; as worthless, as it seemed
Intrinsically precious; to the foot
Treacherous and false; it smiled, and it was cold.
Cowper.

THE BELLS.[2]

I.

HEAR the sledges with the bells—
　　Silver bells!
What a world of merriment their melody foretells!
　How they tinkle, tinkle, tinkle,
　　In the icy air of night!
　While the stars that oversprinkle
　All the heavens, seem to twinkle
　　With a crystalline delight;

---

(1) *Alas, &c.*—This abrupt and striking transition to the moral bearings of the subject is in Cowper's most characteristic manner.

(2) This remarkable composition is presented as a rare specimen of the music of poetry—a sort of literary curiosity; marked, it is true, by many defects and imperfections, but abounding, nevertheless, in very choice beauties and graces. Let it be read aloud, carefully and spiritedly, and it will plead its own cause. It was written by a young American of highly promising talents, whose wretched career of dissipation was closed by an early death, in the year 1849.

Keeping time, time, **time**,
   In a sort of Runic rhyme,[1]
To the tintinnabulation that **so** musically wells
  From **the bells**, bells, **bells, bells,**
    Bells, bells, bells—
From the jingling and the tinkling of the bells.

II.

Hear the mellow wedding-bells,
   Golden bells!
What a world of happiness their harmony foretells!
  Through the balmy air of night
  How they ring out **their** delight!
  From the molten **golden note**,
    And **all in tune**,
What a liquid ditty floats
To the turtle-dove that listens, while **she gloats**
    On the moon!
  Oh, from out the sounding cells
What a gush of euphony voluminously wells!
    How it swells—
    How it dwells
On the Future! how it tells
Of the rapture that impels
To the swinging and the ringing
   Of the bells, bells, bells—
   Of the bells, bells, bells, bells,
    Bells, bells, bells—
To the rhyming and the chiming of the bells!

III.

Hear the **loud** alarum bells—
   Brazen bells!
What a tale of terror, now, their **turbulency tells!**[2]
  In the startled **ear** of night
  How they scream out their affright!
    Too much horrified to speak
    They can only **shriek**, shriek,
    Out of tune,

---

(1) *Runic rhyme*—The Runes were the most ancient Scandinavian alphabetical characters, and so much admired in an age of ignorance that even magical qualities were attributed to them—hence Runic often means magical or mysterious.

(2) Notice here, and in other parts of the poem, the use made by the writer of "apt alliteration's artful aid."

In a clamorous appealing to the mercy of the fire,
In a mad expostulation with the deaf and frantic fire—
    Leaping higher, higher, higher,
    With a desperate desire
And a resolute endeavour
Now—now to sit or never,
By the side of the pale-faced moon.
  Oh, the bells, bells, bells!
What a tale their terror tells
    Of Despair!
How they clang, and clash, and roar,
What a horror they outpour
On the bosom of the palpitating air!
  Yet the ear it fully knows,
    By the twanging,
    And the clanging,
How the danger ebbs and flows;
Yet the ear distinctly tells,
    In the jangling,
    And the wrangling,
How the danger sinks and swells,
By the sinking or the swelling in the anger of the bells—
    Of the bells—
  Of the bells, bells, bells, bells,
    Bells, bells, bells—
In the clamour and the clangour of the bells!

IV.

Hear the tolling of the bells—
    Iron bells!
What a world of solemn thought their monody compels!
  In the silence of the night
  How we shiver with affright
At the melancholy menace of their tone!
  For every sound that floats
  From the rust within their throat
    Is a groan.
And the people—ah, the people—
They that dwell up in the steeple,
    All alone,
And who, tolling, tolling, tolling,
  In that muffled monotone,
Feel a glory in so rolling
  On the human heart a stone—

They are neither man nor woman—
They are neither brute nor human—
  They are Ghouls;
 And their king it is who tolls;
 And he rolls, rolls, rolls,
  Rolls
 A pæan from the bells!
And his merry bosom swells
 With the pæan of the bells!
And he dances, and he yells!
Keeping time, time, time,
In a sort of Runic rhyme,
 To the pæan of the bells—
  Of the bells:
Keeping time, time, time,
In a sort of Runic rhyme,
 To the throbbing of the bells—
Of the bells, bells, bells,
 To the sobbing of the bells;
Keeping time, time, time,
 As he knells, knells, knells,
In a happy Runic rhyme,
 To the rolling of the bells—
Of the bells, bells, bells,
 To the tolling of the bells,
Of the bells, bells, bells, bells—
  Bells, bells, bells—
To the moaning and the groaning of the bells.

Edgar Poe.

TO THE PAST.[1]

Thou unrelenting Past!
Strong are the barriers round thy dark domain,
 And fetters sure and fast,
Hold all that enter thy unbreathing reign.

 Far in thy realm withdrawn,
Old empires sit in sullenness and gloom,
 And glorious ages gone,
Lie deep within the shadow of thy womb.

---

(1) The striking conception embodied in this poem is sustained with great force and beauty—if it may not sometimes be called sublimity—throughout. The pathos, too, in parts is most touching.

Childhood with all its mirth,
Youth, manhood, age, that draws us to the ground,
And last, man's life on earth,
Glide to thy dim domains, and are bound.

Thou hast my better years,
Thou hast my early friends—the good—the kind,
Yielded to thee with tears—
The venerable form—the exalted mind.

My spirit yearns to bring
The lost ones back—yearns with desire intense,
And struggles hard to wring
Thy bolts apart and pluck thy captives thence.

In vain[1]—thy gates deny
All passage save to those who hence depart;
Nor to the streaming eye
Thou givest them back—nor to the broken heart.

In thy abysses hide
Beauty and excellence unknown—to thee
Earth's wonder and her pride
Are gathered, as the waters to the sea;

Labours of good to man,
Unpublished charity—unbroken faith—
Love, that 'midst grief began,
And grew with years, and faltered not in death.

Full many a mighty name
Lurks in thy depths, unuttered, unrevered;
With thee are silent fame,
Forgotten arts, and wisdom disappeared.

Thine for a space are they—
Yet shalt thou yield thy treasures[2] up at last;
Thy gates shall yet give way,
Thy bolts shall fall, inexorable Past!

All that of good and fair
Has gone into thy womb from earliest time,
Shall then come forth, to wear
The glory and the beauty of its prime.

(1) *In vain, &c.*—this verse in particular exemplifies the remarks just made.
(2) *Yet shalt, &c.*—The anticipations of the sea's "giving up her dead," solemn as it is, seems faint and limited when compared with the image here brought before us—the awful portals of the shadowy Past opening and revealing all its dread secrets.

They have not perished—No!
Kind words, remembered **voices once so sweet,**
  Smiles, radiant long ago,
And **features, the** great soul's **apparent**[1] seat;

  All shall come back, each tie
Of pure affection shall be knit again;
  Alone shall evil die,
And sorrow dwell[2] a prisoner in thy **reign.**   *Bryant.*

WOMAN.[3]

SHE was a phantom of delight
When first she gleamed upon **my sight;**
A lovely apparition, sent
To be a moment's ornament;
Her eyes as stars of twilight fair;
Like twilight's, too, her dusky **hair;**
But all things else about her drawn
From May-time and the cheerful **dawn;**
A dancing shape, an image gay,
To haunt, to startle, and waylay.

I saw her upon nearer view,
A spirit, yet a woman too!
Her household motions light and free,
And steps of virgin-liberty:
A countenance[4] in which did meet
Sweet **records,** promises as sweet!
A creature not too bright or good
For human nature's daily food;

---

(1) *Apparent*—there is much significance in this word:—the features of the countenance are the seat or spot in which the soul reveals or displays itself.

(2) *Sorrow dwell, &c.*—A fine personification of sorrow left behind as the only prisoner in the silent dungeon of the past.

(3) Rarely, if ever, has a more lovely picture been drawn of woman in her threefold relation to the beautiful, the social, and the spiritual.

(4) *A countenance, &c.*—The *countenance,* as distinguished from the *face,* is the "soul's apparent seat" (see note 1, above), and belongs only to intellectual **man;** —a brute may have a face, but not a countenance. "Record" too is a very expressive word here. It is from the Latin, *re,* again, and *cor,* the heart—something that the heart or mind dwells upon; an authentic memorial of the past.

For transient sorrows, simple wiles,
Praise, blame, love, kisses, tears, and smiles.

And now I see with eye serene
The very pulse of the machine;
A being breathing thoughtful breath,
A traveller betwixt life and death;
The reason firm, the temperate will,
Endurance, foresight, strength, and skill—
A perfect woman, nobly planned
To warn, to comfort, and command;
And yet a spirit still, and bright,
With something of an angel-light.   *Wordsworth.*

VICTORIA'S TEARS.[1]

"O MAIDEN! heir of kings!
　A king has left his place!
The majesty of Death has swept
　All other from his face!
And thou upon thy mother's breast
　No longer lean adown,
But take the glory for the rest,[2]
And rule the land that loves thee best!"
　　She heard and wept—
　　She wept to wear a crown!

They decked her courtly halls;
　They reined her hundred steeds;
They shouted at her palace gate,
　"A noble Queen succeeds!"
Her name has stirred the mountain's sleep,
　Her praise has filled the town,
And mourners God had stricken deep,
Looked hearkening up, and did not weep.
　　Alone she wept,
　　Who wept to wear a crown!

---

(1) When her present Majesty was first informed of her accession to the throne, she was so affected with the consciousness of the responsibilities which had in a moment fallen upon her that she wept;—it is to this circumstance that the above simple and beautiful stanzas owe their origin.

(2) *For the rest*—*i. e.* in the place of the rest and retirement hitherto enjoyed.

  She saw no purples shine,
   For tears had dimmed her eyes;
  She only knew her childhood's flowers
   Were happier pageantries!
  And while her heralds played their part
   Those million shouts to drown—
  "God save the Queen!" from hill to mart—
  She heard through all her beating heart,
   And turned and wept,—
   She wept to wear a crown!

   God save thee, weeping Queen!
    Thou shalt be well beloved!
  The tyrant's sceptre cannot move,
   As those pure tears have moved!
  The nature in thine eyes we see
   That tyrants cannot own—
  The love that guardeth liberties!
  Strange blessing on the nation lies
    Whose sovereign wept—
   Yea! wept to wear its crown!

   God bless thee, weeping Queen,
    With blessing more divine!
  And fill with happier love than earth's
   That tender heart of thine!
  That when the thrones of earth shall be
   As low as graves brought down,
  A pierced hand may give to thee
  The crown which angels shout to see!
    Thou wilt not *weep*
   To wear that heavenly crown!

Elizabeth Browning.

WAR.

   'Twas Man himself
Brought Death into the world; and Man himself
Gave keenness to his darts, quickened his pace,
And multiplied destruction on mankind.
 First Envy,[1] eldest born of hell, imbrued
Her hands in blood, and taught the sons of men

  (1) *First Envy, &c.*—In allusion to the murder of Abel.

To make a death which Nature never made,
And God abhorred: with violence rude to break
The thread of life ere half its length was run,
And rob a wretched brother of his being.
With joy Ambition saw, and soon improved
The execrable deed. 'Twas not enough
By subtle fraud to snatch a single life:
Puny impiety! whole kingdoms fell
To sate the lust of power; more horrid still,
The foulest stain and scandal of our nature
Became its boast. One murder[1] made a villain,
Millions a hero. Princes were privileged
To kill, and numbers sanctified the crime.
Ah! why will kings forget that they are men?
And men, that they are brethren? Why delight
In human sacrifice? Why burst the ties
Of Nature, that should knit their souls together
In one soft bond of amity and love?
Yet still they breathe destruction, still go on
Inhumanly ingenious to find out
New pains for life, new terrors for the grave.
Artificers of Death! Still monarchs dream
Of universal empire growing up
From universal ruin. Blast the design,
Great God of Hosts, nor let thy creatures fall
Unpitied victims at Ambition's shrine!

   Yet say, should tyrants learn at last to feel,
And the loud din of battle cease to bray;
Should dove-eyed Peace o'er all the earth extend
Her olive branch, and give the world repose,
Would Death be foiled? Would health, and strength, and youth,
Defy his power? Has he no arts in store,
No other shafts, save those of War? Alas!
Even in the smile of Peace—that smile which sheds
A heavenly sunshine o'er the soul—there basks
The serpent Luxury. War its thousands slays;
Peace its ten thousands. In the embattled plain
Though Death exults, and claps his raven wings,
Yet reigns he not ev'n there so absolute,

---

(1) *One murder, &c.*—This line and the two following are remarkable for compactness and force of expression. The antithesis between "one murder" and "millions," "villain" and "hero," is very striking. The words "privileged" and "sanctified" are happily sarcastic, and remind us of Cowper.

So merciless, as in yon frantic scenes
Of midnight revel and tumultuous mirth,
Where, in the intoxicating draught concealed,
He snares the simple youth, who nought suspecting,
Means to be blest—but finds himself undone!
Porteus.

GINEVRA.[1]

If thou shouldst ever come to Modena
Stop at a palace near the Reggio-gate,
Dwelt in of old by one of the Orsini.[2]
Its noble gardens, terrace above terrace,
And numerous fountains, statues, cypresses,
Will long detain thee; but before thou go,
Enter the house—prythee, forget it not—
And look awhile upon a picture there.

'Tis of a lady in her earliest youth;—
She sits inclining forward as to speak,
Her lips half-open, and her finger up,
As though she said, "Beware!"—her vest of gold
Broidered with flowers, and clasped from head to foot—
An emerald stone in every golden clasp;
And on her brow, fairer than alabaster,
A coronet of pearls. But then her face,
So lovely, yet so arch, so full of mirth,
The overflowings of an innocent heart—
It haunts me still, though many a year has fled,
Like some wild melody!—Alone it hangs
Over a mouldering heirloom,[3] its companion,
An oaken chest, half-eaten by the worm.

She was an only child; from infancy
The joy, the pride, of an indulgent sire.
Her mother dying of the gift she gave,
That precious gift, what else remained to him?
The young Ginevra was his all in life,
Still as she grew, for ever in his sight.

---

(1) The affecting incident narrated in these lines is understood to have been a real occurrence.

(2) *Orsini*—A noble Italian family.

(3) *Heirloom*—a *loom* or piece of furniture (still the meaning of the word in Cheshire) for the *heir*—any movable article that by law descends to the heir along with the freehold.

She was all gentleness, all gaiety,
Her pranks the favourite theme of every tongue.
But now the day was come, the day, the hour;
And in the lustre of her youth, she gave
Her hand, with her heart in it, to Francesco.

Great was the joy; but at the bridal feast,
When all sat down, the bride was wanting there—
Nor was she to be found! Her father cried,
"'Tis but to make a trial of our love!"
And filled his glass to all; but his hand shook,
And soon from guest to guest the panic spread.
'Twas but that instant she had left Francesco,
Laughing and looking back, and flying still,
Her ivory tooth imprinted on his finger.
But now, alas! she was not to be found;
Nor from that hour could anything be guessed,
But that she was not! Weary of his life,
Francesco flew to Venice, and forthwith
Flung it away in battle with the Turk.
Orsini lived; and long mightst thou have seen
An old man wandering as in quest of something,
Something he could not find—he knew not what.
When he was gone, the house remained awhile
Silent and tenantless—then went to strangers.

Full fifty years were past, and all forgot,
When on an idle day, a day of search
'Mid the old lumber in the gallery,
That mouldering chest was noticed; and 'twas said,
By one as young, as thoughtless, as Ginevra,
"Why not remove it from its lurking-place?"
'Twas done as soon as said; but on the way
It burst—it fell; and lo! a skeleton;
And here and there a pearl, an emerald-stone,
A golden clasp, clasping a shred of gold.
All else had perished—save a nuptial ring,
And a small seal, her mother's legacy,
Engraven with a name, the name of both—
"GINEVRA."—There then had she found a grave!
Within that chest had she concealed herself,
Fluttering with joy, the happiest of the happy;
When a spring-lock that lay in ambush there,
Fastened her down for ever!

Rogers.

THE MARTYRS.

PATRIOTS have toiled, and in their country's cause
Bled nobly; and their deeds, as they deserve,
Receive proud recompence. We give in charge
Their names to the sweet lyre. The historic muse,
Proud of the treasure, marches with it down
To latest times; and sculpture, in her turn,
Gives bond in stone, and ever-during brass
To guard them, and to immortalize her trust:
But fairer wreaths are due, though never paid,
To those who, posted at the shrine of Truth,
Have fallen in her defence. A patriot's blood,
Well spent in such a strife, may earn indeed,
And for a time ensure, to his loved land
The sweets of liberty and equal laws;
But martyrs struggle for a brighter prize,
And win it with more pain. Their blood is shed
In confirmation of the noblest claim—
Our claim to feed upon immortal truth,
To walk with God, to be divinely free,
To soar, and to anticipate[1] the skies.
Yet few remember them. They lived unknown
Till persecution dragged[2] them into fame,
And chased them up to heaven. Their ashes flew—
No marble tells us whither. With their names
No bard embalms and sanctifies his song:
And history,[3] so warm on meaner themes,
Is cold on this. She execrates indeed
The tyranny that doomed them to the fire,
But gives the glorious sufferers little praise.

Cowper.

(1) *Anticipate, hope, expect*—We *anticipate* (or receive beforehand) either evil or good; we *hope* only for good; we *expect* (or look out for) the coming event, whatever may be its complexion. To "anticipate the skies," therefore, is to enjoy the happiness of heaven while upon earth.

(2) *Dragged*—a well chosen word. They were undesirous of public notice, but persecution *dragged* them into fame.

(3) *History, &c.*—In allusion to the cool tone in which Hume in his History of England speaks of the noble men whose fate was sealed with their blood.

THE POET ON HIS BLINDNESS.[1]

When I consider[2] how my light is spent
  Ere half my days, in this dark world and wide,
  And that one talent which is death to hide,
  Lodged with me useless, though my soul more bent
To serve therewith my Maker, and present
  My true account, lest He, returning, chide;—
  "Doth God exact day-labour, light denied?"
I fondly[3] ask: but Patience, to prevent
That murmur, soon replies:—"God doth not need
  Either man's work, or his own gifts; who best
  Bear his mild yoke, they serve him best: his state
Is kingly; thousands at his bidding speed,
  And post o'er land and ocean without rest;
  They also serve who only stand and wait."

Milton.

THE PLEASURE ARISING FROM VICISSITUDE.[4]

Now the golden morn aloft
Waves her dew-bespangled wing;
With vermeil cheek, and whisper soft,
She woos the tardy spring;
Till April starts, and calls around
The sleeping fragrance from the ground;
And lightly o'er the living scene
Scatters his freshest, tenderest green.[5]

(1) Some consider this the finest of Milton's sonnets. Its merits are of a very refined order, and appear more striking on every re-perusal. The touching subject, the manly and noble tone in which it is treated, and the selectness of the diction, form altogether a rare combination of moral and intellectual beauty.

(2) *When I consider, &c.*—*i. e.* when I consider myself as a labourer in God's field having a given task to perform, and yet deprived of the light necessary for its performance, I repiningly ask, "Doth God," &c.

(3) *Fondly*—foolishly or repiningly. (See note 2, p. 31).

(4) These elegant lines were left unfinished by their author, and perhaps on that account have obtained less notice than they deserve. The stanza, however, beginning, "See the wretch," &c., is very often quoted, and always with admiration.

(5) *Tenderest green*—See note 1, p. 31.

New-born flocks, in rustic dance,
Frisking ply their feeble feet;
Forgetful of their wintry trance
The birds his presence greet:
But chief, the skylark warbles high
His trembling, thrilling, ecstasy;
And, lessening from the dazzled sight,
Melts into air and liquid light.

Yesterday the sullen year[1]
Saw the snowy whirlwind fly;
Mute was the music of the air,
The herd stood drooping by:
Their raptures now that wildly flow,
No yesterday nor morrow know;
'Tis man alone that joy descries
With forward and reverted eyes.

Smiles on[2] past misfortune's brow
Soft reflection's hand can trace,
And o'er the cheek of sorrow throw
A melancholy grace;
While hope prolongs our happier hour,
Or deepest shades,[3] that dimly lower
And blacken round our weary way,
Gilds with a gleam of distant day.

Still where[4] rosy pleasure leads,
See a kindred grief pursue;
Behind the steps that misery treads,
Approaching comfort view;
The hues of bliss more brightly glow,
Chastised by sabler tints of woe;
And blended form, with artful strife,
The strength and harmony of life.

---

(1) *The sullen year*—i. e. the sullen season—the gloomy weather.

(2) *Smiles on, &c.*—This stanza is intended to illustrate the last. Reflection enables man to "descry" with "reverted," and hope with "forward" eyes.

(3) *Deepest shades*—governed, in construction, by "gilds."

(4) *Still where, &c.*—This stanza, in which the general principle is laid down, that our joys are enhanced by contrast with our sorrows, is scarcely inferior to the well-known lines, forming the illustration, which follow.

See the wretch that long has tost
On the thorny bed of pain,
At length repair his vigour lost,
And breathe and walk again :
The meanest floweret of the vale,
The simplest note that swells the gale,
The common sun, the air, the skies,
To him are opening paradise.

Humble Quiet builds her cell
Near the source whence pleasure flows;
She eyes the clear crystalline well,
And tastes it as it goes.
While far below the madding crowd
Rush headlong to the dangerous flood,
Where broad and turbulent it sweeps,
And perish in the boundless deeps.[1]   *Gray.*

THE DYING GLADIATOR.[2]

I see before me the Gladiator lie:
He leans upon his hand—his manly brow
Consents to death, but conquers agony,
And his drooped head sinks gradually low;
And through his side the last drops ebbing slow
From the red gash, fall heavy, one by one,
Like the first of a thunder shower; and now
The arena swims around him—he is gone,
Ere ceased the inhuman shout which hailed the wretch who won.

He heard it, but he heeded not—his eyes
Were with his heart, and that was far away;
He recked not of the life he lost, nor prize,
But where his rude hut by the Danube lay—

---

(1) The last four lines were added by Mason, Gray's most intimate friend.

(2) These beautiful lines have often been quoted as an instance of the superior range of poetry as compared with sculpture. The sculptor or the painter might embody all that is suggested by the first stanza, but here, as Mr. Montgomery remarks, "They have reached their climax;" but "poetry goes further than both," and "reveals that secret of the sufferer's breaking heart, which neither of them could intimate by any visible sign." "The poet has turned the marble into man, and endowed it with human affections."

There were his young barbarians all at play,
There was their Dacian[1] mother—he, their sire,
Butchered to make a Roman holiday!—
All this rushed with his blood.   *Byron.*

TIME'S SONG.

O'er the level plain, where mountains greet me as I go;
O'er the desert waste, where fountains at my bidding flow;
On the boundless beam by day, and on the cloud by night,
I am rushing hence away;—who will chain my flight?

War his weary watch was keeping;—I have crushed his spear:
Grief within her bower was weeping;—I have dried her tear.
Pleasure caught a minute's hold;—then I hurried by,
Leaving all her banquet cold, and her goblet dry.

Power had won a throne of glory;—where is now her fame?
Genius said—"I live in story;"—who hath heard his name?
Love beneath a myrtle bough whispered—"Why so fast?"
And the roses on his brow withered as I past.

I have heard[2] the heifer lowing o'er the wild waves' bed,
I have seen the billow flowing where the cattle fed;—
Where began my wanderings?—Memory will not say!
Where will rest my weary wings?—Science turns away!
                                                Anonymous.

THE POWER OF STEAM.[3]

The giant-power, from earth's remotest caves,
Lifts with strong arm her dark reluctant waves;
Each caverned rock, and hidden den explores,
Drags her dark coals, and digs her shining ores.
Next, in close cells of ribbed oak confined,
Gale after gale, he crowds the struggling wind;
The imprisoned storms[4] through brazen nostrils roar,
Fan the white flame, and fuse the sparkling ore.

---

(1) *Dacian.*—The ancient Dacia included the modern Transylvania, Moldavia, Wallachia, and part of Hungary.

(2) *I have heard, &c.*—In allusion to the geological changes in the earth's surface.

(3) These lines very ingeniously master the difficulty of subjecting scientific details to poetic numbers.

(4) *Storms*—a strong hyperbole for the blasts of the forge-bellows.

Here high in air the rising stream he pours
To clay-built cisterns, or to lead-lined towers;
Fresh through a thousand pipes the wave distils,
And thirsty cities drink the exuberant rills.
There the vast mill-stone, with inebriate whirl,
On trembling floors his forceful fingers twirl,
Whose flinty teeth the golden harvests grind,
Feast without blood, and nourish human kind.
   Now his hard hands on Mona's[1] rifted crest,
Bosomed in rock, her azure ores[2] arrest;
With iron lips his rapid rollers seize
The lengthening bars, in thin expansion squeeze;
Descending screws, with ponderous fly-wheels wound
The tawny plates, the new medallions round;
Hard dies of steel the cupreous circles cramp,
And with quick fall his massy hammers stamp.
The Harp,[3] the Lily, and the Lion join,
And George and Britain guard the sterling coin.
   Soon shall thy arm,[4] unconquered Steam! afar
Drag the slow barge, or drive the rapid car;
Or on wide waving wings expanded bear
The flying chariot through the fields of air.

Darwin.

ANCIENT BRITAIN.

Now borne upon the wings of truth sublime,
Review thy dim original and prime.
This island, spot of unreclaimed rude earth,
The cradle that received thee at thy birth,
Was rocked by many a rough Norwegian blast,
And Danish howlings scared thee as they passed;
For thou wast born amid the din of arms,
And sucked a breast that panted with alarms.

---

(1) *Mona*—the Isle of Anglesea. It is noted for its mineral riches, both in copper and lead.

(2) *Azure ores*—the ores of copper are of a bluish tint.

(3) *The harp, &c.*—The characteristic emblems of Ireland, France, and England. The *fleur-de-lis* was erased from the standard of England in 1802.

(4) *Soon shall thy arm, &c.*—These lines are curious and interesting, viewed as a kind of prophecy, for they were written several years before steam-boats and steam-carriages had come into use.

While yet thou wast a grovelling puling chit,
Thy bones not fashioned, and thy joints not knit,
The Roman taught thy stubborn knee to bow,
Though twice a Cæsar could not bend thee now.
His victory was that of orient light,
When the sun's shafts disperse the gloom of night.
Thy language at this distant moment shows
How much the country to the conqueror owes;
Expressive, energetic, and refined,
It sparkles with the gems he left behind:
He brought thy land a blessing when he came,
He found thee savage, and he left thee tame;
Taught thee to clothe thy pinked[1] and painted hide,
And grace thy figure with a soldier's pride;
He sowed the seeds of order where he went,
Improved thee far beyond his own intent;
And, while he ruled thee by the sword alone,
Made thee at last a warrior like his own.
Religion, if in heavenly truths attired,
Needs only to be seen to be admired;
But thine, as dark as witcheries of the night,
Was formed to harden hearts and shock the sight;
Thy Druids struck the well-hung harps they bore
With fingers deeply dyed in human gore;
And while the victim slowly bled to death,
Upon the rolling chords rang out his dying breath.

Cowper.

THE PROCESSION OF RIVERS.[2]

And afterwards the famous rivers came,
Which do the earth enrich and beautify:
The fertile Nile, which creatures new[3] doth frame;
Long Rhodanus,[4] whose source springs from the sky;
Fair Ister, flowing from the mountains high;
Divine Scamander, purpled yet with blood

---

(1) *Pinked*—pierced with small holes—punctured: in allusion to the custom of tattooing, practised by our British ancestors. See "Pictorial History of England," vol. i. p. 129.

(2) An extract from "The Faerie Queene," book iv. canto xi.

(3) *Creatures new, &c.*—The mud of the Nile used to have a fabulous reputation for producing, in consequence of its singular richness, new and monstrous animals.

(4) *Rhodanos*—the Rhone.

P

Of Grecks and Trojans, which therein did die ;
Pactolus,[1] glistring with his golden flood ;
And Tigris fierce, whose streams of none may be withstood ;

Great Ganges, and immortal Euphrates ;
Deep Indus, and Mæander intricate ;
Slow Peneus, and tempestuous Phasides ;[2]
Swift Rhine, and Alpheus, still immaculate ![3]
Araxes, fearéd for great Cyrus' fate ;
Tibris, renownéd for the Romans' fame ;
Rich Orinoko, though but knowen late ;
And that huge river which doth bear his name
Of warlike Amazons which do possess the same.

The noble Thames, with all his noble train ;
The Ouse, whom men do rightly Isis name ;
The bounteous Trent, that in himself enseams[4]
Both thirty[5] sorts of fish, and thirty streams ;
The chalky Kennet, and the Thetis[6] grey ;
The moorish Colne, and the soft-sliding Breane ;[7]
The wanton Lea, that oft doth lose his way ;
And the still Darent, in whose waters clean
Ten thousand fishes play, and deck his pleasant stream.

There was the speedy Tamar, which divides
The Cornish and the Devonish confines,
Through both whose borders swiftly down it glides,
And meeting Plym, to Plymouth thence declines ;
And Dart, nigh choked with sands of tinny mines ;
But Avon marchéd in more stately path,
Proud of his adamants[8] with which he shines
And glistens wide, as als[9] of wondrous Bath,
And Bristol fair, which on his waves he buildeth hath.

(1) *Pactolus*—see note 4, p. 9.
(2) *Phasides*—The Phasis of ancient Colchis.
(3) *Immaculate*—in allusion to the fable of this river passing under the sea to Sicily without mingling its waters. This epithet properly signifies *unspotted*.
(4) *Enseams*—Critics are not agreed whether this word means here, encloses, or fattens, nourishes.
(5) *Thirty, &c.*—See note 12, p. 146.
(6) *Thetis*—it is difficult to say what river is meant here.
(7) *Breane*—perhaps the Brent is intended.
(8) *Adamants*—the quartz crystals found at Clifton, and usually called Bristol diamonds. (See also p. 82, note 2.)
(9) *Als*—also.

Next these the plenteous **Ouse** came far from land,
By many a city and by many a town,
And many rivers taking underhand
Into his waters, as he passeth down—
The Cle, the Were, the Guant, the **Stour**, the Rowne;
Thence doth by **Huntingdon** and Cambridge flit[1]—
My mother Cambridge,[2] whom as with a crown
He doth adorn, and is adorned of it
With many a gentle muse, and many a learned wit.

Next these came Tyne, along whose stony bank
That Roman monarch[3] built a brazen wall,
Which might the feeble Britons strongly flank
Against the Picts, that swarméd over all,
Which **yet thereof** Gualsever[4] **they do** call;
And Tweed, the limit betwixt Logris'[5] land
And Albany; and Eden, though but small,
Yet **often stained with blood of many a** band
Of Scots and **English both, that tyned**[6] **on** his strand.

Spenser.

THE CATARACT OF LODORE.[7]

How does the water come down at Lodore?[8]

Here it comes sparkling,[9]
And there it lies darkling;
Here smoking and frothing,
Its tumult and wrath **in,**

(1) *Cambridge flit*—The Cam is a tributary of the Ouse, but poetically the Ouse may be said to flow past Cambridge.

(2) Spenser was educated at Cambridge, and hence regarded it **as his** *Alma Mater*. (See p. 253.)

(3) *Monarch*—Severus.

(4) *Gualsever*—Wall of Severus. Gwal, or gual, is British for *wall*.

(5) *Logris*—or Lœgria—an old poetical name of England, as Albany was of Scotland.

(6) *Tyned*—fought, or perished.

(7) This poem is **a** literary curiosity—showing the fertility and energy of our native tongue. We have here at least one hundred and fifty adjectives applied to **water** dashing **down a** cascade, and nearly every one of them apt and expressive—**many very** happily descriptive.

(8) *Lodore*—a waterfall, one hundred feet in height, near Keswick, in Cumberland.

(9) **Dr. Wallis, in his** valuable English grammar—written in Latin—shows **that in the formation of** many English words there is a remarkable correspond-

It hastens along, conflicting, strong,
  Now striking and raging,
  As if a war waging,
Its caverns and rocks among.

  Rising and leaping,
  Sinking and creeping,
  Swelling and flinging,
  Showering and springing,
  Eddying and whisking,
  Spouting and frisking,
  Twining and twisting,
    Around and around,
  Collecting, disjecting,
    With endless rebound;
  Smiting and fighting,
  A sight to delight in;
  Confounding, astounding,
Dizzing and deafening the ear with its sound.

  Reeding and speeding,
  And shocking and rocking,
  And darting and parting,
  And threading and spreading,
  And whizzing and hissing,
  And dripping and skipping,
  And whitening and brightening,
  And quivering and shivering,
  And hitting and splitting,
  And shining and twining,
  And rattling and battling,
  And shaking and quaking,
  And pouring and roaring,
  And waving and raving,
  And tossing and crossing,
  And flowing and growing,
  And running and stunning,
  And hurrying and skurrying,
  And glittering and flittering,
  And gathering and feathering,

ence between the sound and the sense. Thus words beginning with *sp*, as "sparkling," denote, says he, "dispersion or expansion;" with *sm* and *sw*, as "smoking," and "swelling," "a sort of noiseless agitation or gentle lateral motion;" with *str*, as "strong," "energy, strength, effort," &c. The above lines will furnish many illustrations of the general principle.

  And dinning and spinning,
  And foaming and roaming,
  And dropping and hopping,
  And working and jerking,
  And heaving and cleaving,
  And thundering and floundering;

And falling and crawling and sprawling,
And driving and riving and striving,
And sprinkling and twinkling and wrinkling,
And sounding and bounding and rounding,
And bubbling and troubling and doubling,
Dividing and gliding and sliding,
And grumbling and rumbling and tumbling,
And clattering and battering and shattering;

And gleaming and steaming and streaming and beaming,
And rushing and flushing and brushing and gushing,
And flapping and rapping and clapping and slapping,
And curling and whirling and purling and twirling,
Retreating and beating and meeting and sheeting,
Delaying and straying and playing and spraying,
Advancing and prancing and glancing and dancing,
Recoiling, turmoiling and toiling and boiling,
And thumping and flumping and bumping and jumping,
And dashing and flashing and splashing and clashing;
And so never ending, but always descending,
Sounds and motions for ever and ever are blending
All at once and all o'er, with a mighty uproar—
And this way the water comes down at Lodore.

Southey.

PATRIOTISM.

BREATHES there the man with soul so dead,
Who never to himself hath said,
 "This is my own—my native land!"
Whose heart hath ne'er within him burned,
As home his footsteps he hath turned,
 From wandering on a foreign strand?
If such there breathe, go, mark him well!
For him no minstrel's raptures swell;
High though his titles, proud his name,
Boundless his wealth as wish can claim;

Despite those titles, power, and pelf,
The wretch concentred all in self,
Living, shall forfeit fair renown,
And, doubly dying, shall go down
To the vile dust from whence he sprung,
Unwept, unhonoured, and unsung!
Walter Scott.

GOD, THE ONLY COMFORTER!

Oh, thou! that driest the mourner's tear,
  How dark this world would be,
If, when deceived and wounded here,
  We could not fly to thee!

The friends who in our sunshine live,
  When winter comes are flown;
And he who has but tears to give,
  Must weep those tears alone.

But thou wilt heal the broken heart,
  Which, like the plants that throw
Their fragrance from the wounded part,
  Breathes sweetness out of woe.

When joy no longer soothes or cheers,
  And even the hope that threw
A moment's sparkle o'er our tears,
  Is dimmed and vanished too;

Then sorrow, touched by thee, grows bright
  With more than rapture's ray;
As darkness shows[1] us worlds of light
  We could not see by day.
Moore.

FRIENDS.

Friend after friend departs;
  Who hath not lost a friend?
There is no union here of hearts
  That finds not here an end:
Were this frail world our final rest,
Living or dying none were blest.

---

(1) *As darkness shows,* &c.—A most ingenious and striking adaptation of a scientific truth to a moral purpose.

Beyond the flight of time—
   Beyond the reign of death—
There surely is some blessed clime
   Where life is not a breath;
Nor life's affections transient fire,
Whose sparks fly upward and expire!

There is a world above
   Where parting is unknown—
A long eternity of love,
   Formed for the good alone;
And faith beholds the dying here
Translated to that glorious sphere.

Thus star[1] by star declines,
   Till *all* are passed away;
As morning high and higher shines
   To pure and perfect day:
Nor sink those stars in empty night,
But hide themselves in Heaven's own light.
                      Montgomery.

TO ENGLAND.

O NE'ER enchained, nor wholly vile,
O Albion! O my Mother Isle!
Thy valleys, fair as Eden's bowers,
Glitter green with sunny showers!
Thy grassy upland's gentle swells
Echo to the bleat of flocks;
Those grassy hills, those glittering dells,
Proudly ramparted with rocks:
And OCEAN, mid his uproar wild,
Speaks safety to his ISLAND-CHILD!
Hence, through many a fearless age,
Has social Freedom loved the Land,
Nor alien Despot's jealous rage,
Or warped thy growth, or stamped the servile brand.
                      Coleridge.

---

(1) *Thus star, &c.*—The close of this beautiful stanza has been already characterized. (See note 1, p. 34.)

THE MAN OF ROSS.[1]

Rise, honest muse! and sing the Man of Ross:
Pleased Vaga[2] echoes through her winding bounds,
And rapid Severn hoarse applause resounds.
Who hung with woods yon mountain's sultry brow?
From the dry rock who bade the waters flow?
Not to the skies in useless columns tost,
Or in proud falls magnificently lost,
But clear and artless,[3] pouring through the plain
Health to the sick, and solace to the swain.
Whose causeway parts the vale with shady rows?
Whose seats the weary traveller repose?
Who taught that heaven-directed spire to rise?
"The Man of Ross!" each lisping babe replies.
Behold the market-place with poor o'erspread!
The Man of Ross divides the weekly bread:
He feeds yon almshouse, neat, but void of state,
Where age and want sit smiling at the gate;
Him portioned maids, apprenticed orphans blest,
The young who labour, and the old who rest.
Is any sick? the Man of Ross relieves,
Prescribes, attends, the medicine makes, and gives.
Is there a variance? enter but his door,
Baulked are the courts, and contest is no more.
Despairing quacks with curses fled the place,
And vile attorneys, now a useless race.

Thrice happy man! enabled to pursue
What all so wish, but want the power to do!
Oh say, what sums that generous hand supply?
What mines, to swell that boundless charity?

Of debts,[4] and taxes, wife and children clear,
This man possessed—five hundred pounds a year!

---

(1) Ross is a town on the banks of the Wye, in Herefordshire; and the Man of Ross was a philanthropic individual, of the name of John Kyrle, who, after a life of benevolence, died in the year 1724, at the age of 90.

(2) *Vaga*—the Latin name of the Wye.

(3) *Artless*—i. e. not forced by art into fountains or cascades. This word is generally applied to persons, not to things, as here.

(4) *Of debts, &c.*—This line is ambiguous; it may mean either that he had no wife and children, or that after their expenses were paid, he had £500 a year. The former is the more probable interpretation.

Blush, grandeur, blush! proud courts, **withdraw your blaze**;
Ye little stars! hide your diminished **rays**.

And what! no monument, inscription, **stone**?
His race, his form, his name almost **unknown**?

Who builds a church to God, and not to Fame,
Will never mark the marble with his name:
Go, **search it** there, where[1] to be born and die,
Of rich and poor makes all the history;
Enough, that virtue filled the space between;
Proved, by the ends of being, to have been. *Pope.*

THE TRAVELLER'S HYMN OF GRATITUDE.[2]

How are thy servants blest, O Lord!
    How sure is their defence!
Eternal wisdom is their guide,
    Their **help**, Omnipotence.

In foreign realms, and lands remote,
    Supported by thy care,
Through burning climes I passed unhurt,
    And breathed in tainted air.

Thy mercy sweetened every soil,
    Made every region please;
The hoary Alpine hills it warmed,
    And smoothed the Tyrrhene seas.[3]

Think, O my soul, devoutly think,
    How, with affrighted eyes,
Thou saw'st the wide-extended deep
    In all its horrors rise:

---

(1) *There, where, &c.*—*i. e.* in the parish registry.

(2) "The earliest composition," says Burns, speaking of his eleventh or twelfth year, "that I recollect taking pleasure in, was the 'Vision of Mirza,' and a hymn of Addison's beginning:—

'How are thy servants blest, O Lord!'

I particularly remember one half-stanza, which was music to my ear:—

'For though in dreadful whirls we hung
High on the broken wave.'"

(3) *Tyrrhene sea*—this sea, called also the Tuscan Sea, was accounted very dangerous by the Romans. It means here, of course, any dangerous sea.

    Confusion dwelt in every face,
        And fear in every heart;
    When waves on waves, and gulfs on gulfs,
        O'ercame the pilot's art.

    Yet then from all my griefs, O Lord,
        Thy mercy set me free;
    Whilst in the confidence of prayer
        My soul took hold on thee.

    For though in dreadful whirls we hung
        High on the broken wave,
    I knew thou wert not slow to hear,
        Nor impotent to save.

    The storm was laid, the winds retired,
        Obedient to thy will;
    The sea that roared at thy command,
        At thy command was still.

    In midst of dangers, fears, and death,
        Thy goodness I'll adore;
    And praise thee for thy mercies past,
        And humbly hope for more.

    My life, if thou preserv'st my life,
        Thy sacrifice shall be;
    And death, when death shall be my doom,
        Shall join my soul to thee.   *Addison.*

SAMSON'S LAMENT OVER HIS BLINDNESS.[1]

O loss of sight, of thee I most complain!
Blind among enemies, O worse than chains,
Dungeon, or beggary, or decrepit age!
Light, the prime[2] work of God, to me is extinct,
And all her various objects of delight
Annulled, which might in part my grief have eased;

---

(1) Some of Milton's most pathetic passages are due to his loss of sight. He was blind for the last twenty-two years of his life, during which period "Paradise Lost," "Paradise Regained," and "Samson Agonistes" (from which the above passage is extracted), were published.

(2) *Prime*—first; in allusion to the creation of light, which was the work of the first day, and there is perhaps a reference to its importance also.

Inferior to the vilest now become
Of man or worm; the vilest here excel me—
They creep, yet see; I, dark in light, exposed
To daily fraud, contempt, abuse, and wrong,
Within doors, or without, still as a fool,
In power of others, never in my own;
Scarce half I seem to live, dead more than half.
O dark, dark, dark,[1] amid the blaze of noon,
Irrecoverably dark, total eclipse
Without all hope of day!
O first created beam, and thou great Word,
"Let there be light, and light was over all,"
Why am I thus bereaved thy prime decree?
The sun to me is dark
And silent as the moon,[2]
When she deserts the night,
Hid in her[3] vacant interlunar cave.
Since light so necessary is to life,
And almost life itself, if it be true
That light is in the soul,
She all in every part, why was the sight
To such a tender ball as the eye confined,
So obvious and so easy to be quenched?
And not, as feeling, through all parts diffused,
That she might look at will through every pore?
Then had I not been thus exiled from light,
As in the land of darkness, yet in light,
To live a life half dead, a living death,
And buried: but O yet more miserable!
Myself my sepulchre, a moving grave,
Buried, yet not exempt
By privilege of death and burial
From worst of other evils, pains, and wrongs,
But made hereby obnoxious more
To all the miseries of life,
Life in captivity
Among inhuman foes. *Milton.*

(1) *O dark, dark, &c.*—"Few passages in poetry," says Sir E. Brydges, "are so affecting as this; and the tone of expression is peculiarly Miltonic."

(2) *Silent as the moon*—a singular expression taken from the Latin "*silens luna*," the silent moon, *i. e.* the moon when she does not shine.

(3) *Hid in her, &c.*—Hidden idly (" vacant") in the cave to which she (poetically) retires between one lunation and another.

THE MEDAL.

See the wild waste of all devouring years!
How Rome her own sad sepulchre appears!
With nodding arches, broken temples spread;
The very tombs now vanished like their dead!
Imperial wonders[1] raised on nations spoiled,
Where, mixed with slaves, the groaning martyr toiled;
Huge theatres, that now unpeopled woods,
Now drained[2] a distant country of her floods;
Fanes, which admiring gods with pride survey;
Statues of men, scarce less alive than they!
Some felt the silent stroke of mouldering age,
Some hostile fury, some religious rage:
Barbarian blindness, Christian zeal conspire,
And Papal piety, and Gothic fire.
Perhaps, by its own ruins saved from flame,
Some buried marble half preserves a name;
That name, the learn'd with fierce disputes pursue,
And give to Titus[3] old Vespasian's due.

   Ambition sighed; she found it vain to trust
The faithless column, and the crumbling bust;
Huge moles, whose shadow stretched from shore to shore—
Their ruins perished, and their place no more!
Convinced, she now contracts her vast design,
And all her triumphs shrink into a coin.
A narrow orb each crowded conquest keeps—
Beneath her palm[4] here sad Judea weeps.
Now scantier limits the proud arch confine,
And scarce are seen the prostrate Nile or Rhine;
A small Euphrates through the piece is rolled,
And little eagles wave their wings in gold.

(1) *Imperial wonders*—The poet here refers to the circuses, amphitheatres, &c., of Rome.

(2) *Drained, &c.*—In allusion to the naumachiæ, or mock sea-fights, which used to be represented in the Circus Maximus, the water for which, although derived immediately from the Tiber, might poetically be said to drain a distant country.

(3) *Give to Titus, &c.*—i. e. mistake a statue of Vespasian for one of Titus.

(4) *Beneath her palm*—the medals struck to commemorate the conquest of Judea represent a female figure sitting, bowed in sorrow, beneath a palm-tree.

The Medal, faithful to its charge of fame,
Through climes and ages bears each form and name;
In one short view subjected to our eye,
Gods, emperors, heroes, sages, beauties lie.
With sharpened sight pale antiquaries pore,
The inscription value, but the rust adore;
This the blue[1] varnish, that the green endears,
The sacred rust of twice ten hundred years!
To gain Pescennius[2] one employs his schemes;
One grasps a Cecrops in ecstatic dreams:
Poor Vadius, long with learned spleen devoured,
Can taste no pleasure since his shield was scoured;
And Curio, restless by the fair one's side,
Sighs for an Otho, and neglects his bride.   *Pope.*

JERUSALEM BEFORE THE SIEGE.[3]

Titus speaks.

It must be—
And yet it moves me, Romans! it confounds
The counsel of my firm philosophy,
That ruin's merciless ploughshare[4] must pass o'er,
And barren salt be sown on, yon proud city.
As on this olive-crownéd hill[5] we stand,
Where Kedron at our feet its scanty waters
Distils from stone to stone with gentle motion,
As through a valley sacred to sweet peace,
How boldly doth it front us! how majestically!
Like a luxurious vineyard, the hill-side
Is hung with marble fabrics, line o'er line,
Terrace o'er terrace, nearer still, and nearer

---

(1) *This the blue, &c.*—The blue tinge marks the silver, and the green, the copper medals.

(2) *To gain Pescennius, &c.*—In this and the following lines, the deep anxieties of the virtuoso antiquary are glanced at with happy raillery. The medals named are of course such as are very scarce and difficult to procure. Pescennius was a Roman Consul. The other names need no explanation.

(3) This fine view of Jerusalem is almost altogether taken from that given by Josephus. The description of the Temple, especially, is nearly verbatim.

(4) *Ruin's merciless, &c.*—This bold metaphor is also employed by Burns (see p. 78), and both writers probably derived it from Young. (See p. 407.)

(5) *Olive-crowned hill*—Mount Olivet, east of Jerusalem.

To the blue heavens. There bright and sumptuous palaces,
With cool and verdant gardens interspersed;
There towers of war that frown in massy strength;
While over all hangs the rich purple eve,
As conscious of its being her last farewell
Of light and glory to that faded city.
And as our clouds of battle, dust, and smoke,
Are melted into air, behold the Temple
In undisturbed and lone serenity,
Finding itself a solemn sanctuary
In the profound of heaven! It stands before us
A mount of snow, fretted with golden pinnacles.
The very sun, as though he worshipped there,
Lingers upon the gilded cedar roofs,
And down the long and branching porticoes;
On every flowery-sculptured capital
Glitters the homage of his parting beams. *Milman.*

THE TRANQUILLITY OF NATURE.

Eve's lingering clouds extend in solid bars
Through the grey west; and lo! these waters, steeled
By breezeless air to smoothest polish, yield
   A vivid repetition of the stars;
   Jove—Venus—and the ruddy crest of Mars,
Amid his fellows, beauteously revealed
At happy distance from earth's groaning field,
   Where ruthless mortals wage incessant wars.
Is it a mirror?—or the nether sphere
   Opening its vast abyss, while fancy feeds
On the rich show!—But list! a voice is near;
   Great Pan[1] himself low-whispering through the reeds,
    "Be thankful thou; for, if unholy deeds
Ravage the world, tranquillity is here!" *Wordsworth.*

(1) *Pan*—Pan, among the Greeks, was the God of universal Nature, and the name was used frequently, as we use the word Nature, for the invisible cause of the beauties of creation.

TWILIGHT.

Hail, Twilight! sovereign of one peaceful hour!
  Not dull art thou as undiscerning Night!
  But studious only to remove from sight
Day's mutable distinctions.—Ancient Power!
'Thus did the waters gleam, the mountains lower
  To the rude Briton, when, in wolf-skin vest,
  Here roving wild, he laid him down to rest
On the bare rock, or through a leafy bower
  Looked ere his eyes were closed. By him was seen
The self-same vision which we now behold,
  At thy meek bidding, shadowy Power, brought forth:—
  These mighty barriers and the gulf between;
The floods,—the stars;—a spectacle as old
  As the beginning of the heavens and earth!
                                Wordsworth.

TO THE NIGHTINGALE.[1]

Sweet bird! thou sing'st away the early hours!
  Of winters past or coming void of care,
  Well pleaséd with delights which present are,—
Fair seasons, budding sprays, sweet smelling flowers!
To rocks, to springs, to rills from leafy bowers,
  Thou thy Creator's goodness dost declare,
  And what dear gifts[2] on thee he did not spare.
Oh stain[3] to human sense, in sin that lowers!
  What soul can be so sick, which by thy songs,
  (Attired in sweetness,) sweetly is not driven
  Quite to forget earth's turmoils, spites, and wrongs,
And lift a reverend eye and thought to heaven!
  Sweet artless songster! thou my mind dost raise
  To airs of spheres,[4] yea, and to angels' lays!
                                Drummond.

(1) **The** writer of this and the following beautiful sonnet was a friend and contemporary of Ben Jonson.

(2) *And what dear gifts, &c.*—i. e. and the precious gifts that he lavished on thee.

(3) *Oh stain, &c.*—Oh what a reproach to men is the sin which debases ("lowers") them, and prevents their praising God as you do

(4) *Airs of spheres-* the fancied music of the spheres.

THE PLEASURES OF RETIREMENT.

Thrice happy he who by some shady grove,
  Far from the clamorous world, doth live his own:[1]
Though solitary, who is not alone,
But doth converse with that eternal love!
  Oh, how more sweet is bird's harmonious moan,
Or the hoarse sobbings of the widowed dove,
  Than those smooth whisperings near a prince's throne,
Which good make doubtful, do the evil prove!
  Oh, how more sweet is zephyr's wholesome breath,
And sighs embalmed which new-born flowers unfold,
  Than that applause vain honour doth bequeath!
How sweet are streams to poison[2] drunk in gold!
  The world is full of honours, troubles, slights;—
Woods' harmless shades have only true delights.
                                      Drummond.

DIRGE OVER FIDELE'S TOMB.[3]

To fair Fidele's grassy tomb,
  Soft maids and village hinds shall bring
Each opening sweet of earliest bloom,
  And rifle all the breathing Spring.

No wailing ghost shall dare appear
  To vex with shrieks this quiet grove;
But shepherd lads assemble here,
  And melting virgins own their love.

No withered witch shall here be seen,
  No goblins lead their nightly crew;
The female fays shall haunt the green,
  And dress thy grave with pearly dew!

---

(1) *His own*—by himself.
(2) *To poison, &c.*—Compared to poison.
(3) This exquisite poem seems to have been suggested by the funeral chant over the body of Imogen, under the assumed name of Fidele, in Shakspere's "Cymbeline." Sir E. Brydges commends its "simplicity and pathos," its "highly poetical thought and tone," its "exquisite polish, without one superfluous, one prosaic word." He continues thus:—"The extreme transparency of the words and thoughts would induce a vulgar reader to consider them [such poems] trite, while they are the expression of a genius so refined as to be all essence of spirit."

The redbreast oft,[1] at evening hours,
    Shall kindly lend his little aid,
With hoary moss, and gathered flowers,
    To deck the ground where thou art laid.

When howling winds and beating rain
    In tempests shake the sylvan cell;
Or 'midst the chace, on every plain,
    The tender thought on thee shall dwell;

Each lonely scene shall thee restore;
    For thee the tear be duly shed;
Beloved, till life can charm no more,
    And mourned, till Pity's self be dead.

Collins.

TO MAY.[2]

Though many suns have risen and set
    Since thou, blithe May, wert born,
And bards, who hailed thee, may forget
    Thy gifts, thy beauty scorn,
There are who to a birthday strain
    Confine not harp and voice,
But evermore throughout thy reign
    Are grateful and rejoice.

Earth, sea, thy presence feel—nor less,
    If yon ethereal blue
With its soft smile the truth express,
    The heavens have felt it too.
The inmost heart of man, if glad,
    Partakes a livelier cheer;
And eyes that cannot but be sad
    Let fall a brightened tear.

---

(1) *The redbreast, &c.*—It is thought that Gray was indebted to this stanza for the lines in the "Elegy" (see p. 65) beginning—

    "There scattered oft," &c.

(2) Among the many beautiful poems of the same author, there is not perhaps a more finished composition than this—not one more noticeable for the "*curiosa felicitas*,"—that "grace beyond the reach of art,"—which evinces the perfect mastery of the artist.

Since thy return, through days and weeks
  Of hope that grew by stealth,
How many wan and faded cheeks
  Have kindled into health!
The old, by thee revived, have said,
  "Another year is ours!"
And wayworn wanderers, poorly fed,
  Have smiled upon thy flowers.

Who tripping lisps a merry song
  Amid his playful peers?
The tender infant, who was long
  A prisoner of fond fears;
But now, when every sharp-edged blast
  Is quiet in its sheath,
His mother leaves him free to taste
  Earth's sweetness in thy breath.

Lo! streams that April could not check
  Are patient of thy rule;
Gurgling[1] in foamy water-break,
  Loitering in glassy pool:
By thee, thee only, could be sent
  Such gentle mists as glide,
Curling[2] with unconfirmed intent,
  On that green mountain's side.

How delicate the leafy veil
  Through which yon House of God
Gleams 'mid the peace of this deep dale,
  By few but shepherds trod!
And lowly huts, near beaten ways,
  No sooner stand attired
In thy fresh wreaths, than they for praise
  Peep forth, and are admired.

Season of fancy and of hope,
  Permit not for one hour
A blossom from thy crown to drop,
  Nor add to it a flower!

---

(1) *Gurgling, &c.*—In one line of this couplet we may almost *hear* the "gurgling," and in the other almost *feel* the stillness, of the water.

(2) *Curling, &c.*—One of those "felicities" of phrase alluded to in the first note.

Keep lovely May [1] as if by touch
   Of self-restraining art,
This modest charm of not too much,
   Part seen, imagined part!   *Wordsworth.*

THE POET.

Ages elapsed ere Homer's lamp appeared,
And ages ere the Mantuan swan[2] was heard.
To carry nature lengths unknown before,
To give a Milton birth, asked ages more.
Thus genius rose and set at ordered times,
And shot a day-spring into distant climes,
Ennobling every region that he chose;
He sank in Greece, in Italy he rose;
And, tedious years of Gothic darkness past,
Emerged all splendour in our isle at last:
Thus lovely halcyons dive into the main,
Then show far off their shining plumes again.
  Nature, exerting an unwearied power,
Forms, opens, and gives scent to every flower;
Spreads the fresh verdure of the field, and leads
The dancing Naiads through the dewy meads:
She fills profuse ten thousand little throats
With music, modulating all their notes;
And charms the woodland scenes, and wilds unknown,
With artless airs and concerts of her own;
But seldom (as if fearful of expense)
Vouchsafes to man a poet's just pretence—
Fervency, freedom, fluency of thought,
Harmony, strength, words exquisitely sought;
Fancy, that from the bow that spans the sky,
Brings colours dipt in heaven[3] that never die;

---

(1) *Keep, lovely May, &c.*—The most satisfactory test of superlative excellence, in point of composition, of such lines as this and the following, would be afforded by the attempt to improve them by the alteration or addition of even a single word. The success of Horace himself in such an endeavour would have been extremely doubtful.

(2) *Mantuan swan*—Virgil, so called because he was born at Mantua, in Italy. A particular species of swans had the reputation among the ancients of singing very beautifully—hence poets were figuratively styled *swans*.

(3) "*Colours dipt in heaven*"—an expression borrowed from "Paradise Lost."

A soul exalted above earth; a mind
Skilled in the characters that form mankind;
And as the sun, in rising beauty drest,
Looks to the westward from the dappled east,
And marks, whatever clouds may interpose,
Ere yet his race begins, its glorious close;
An eye like his to catch the distant goal;
Or, ere the wheels of verse begin to roll,
Like his to shed illuminating rays
On every scene and subject it surveys:
Thus graced, the man asserts a poet's name,
And the world cheerfully admits the claim.

Cowper.

MORAL MAXIMS, EPIGRAMS, &c.

I. LIVE WHILE YOU LIVE.[1]

"Live while you live," the epicure would say,
"And seize the pleasures of the present day."
"Live while you live," the sacred preacher cries,
"And give to God each moment as it flies."
Lord! in my views let both united be;
I live in pleasure when I live to Thee.   *Doddridge.*

II. LINES UNDER MILTON'S PORTRAIT.

Three poets in three distant ages born,
Greece, Italy, and England, did adorn.
The first in loftiness of thought surpassed;
The next in majesty; in both the last.
The force of nature could no further go,
To make a third she joined the former two.

Dryden.

III. HOPE.

The wretch, condemned with life to part,
　Still, still on hope relies;
And every pang that rends the heart
　Bids expectation[2] rise.

---

(1) Dr. Johnson has pronounced this epigram the finest in the language.

(2) *Expectation*—is here employed in precisely the same sense as *hope*: for the distinction between them, see note 1, p. 203.

  Hope, like the¹ glimmering taper's light,
   Adorns and cheers the way;
  And still, as darker grows the night,
   Emits a brighter ray.   *Goldsmith.*

IV. LINES WRITTEN BY LORD BYRON IN HIS BIBLE.²

  WITHIN this awful volume lies
  The mystery of mysteries:
  Happiest they of human race,
  To whom their God has given grace
  To read, to fear, to hope, to pray,
  To lift the latch—to force the way;
  But better had they ne'er been born
  Who read to doubt, or read to scorn.
         Walter Scott.

V. VIGOUR OF MIND.

 THE wise and active conquer difficulties
 By daring to attempt them: sloth and folly
 Shiver and shrink at sight of toil and hazard,
 And make the impossibility they fear.
         Rowe.

VI. SKATING.

 O'ER crackling ice, o'er gulfs profound,
  With nimble glide the skaters play:
 O'er treacherous pleasure's flowery ground,
  Thus lightly skim and haste away.
         Dr. Johnson.

VII. GUARD THE TONGUE.

 IF thou wishest to be wise,
 Keep these words before thine eyes:—
 What thou speak'st, and *how*, beware!
 Of whom—*to* whom—when—and where.

---

(1) *Like the, &c.*—It is scarcely necessary to point out the singular beauty of this stanza, "which," as Mr. Montgomery has remarked, "like the taper itself, grows clearer and brighter the more it is contemplated."

(2) These lines may be found in one of Sir Walter Scott's tales; their application to a worthier subject is said to be originally due to Lord Byron, as above stated.

VIII. THE SAME SUBJECT.
From the Persian of Hafiz.

Two ears and but a single tongue
By nature's law to man belong!
The lesson she would teach is clear—
" Repeat but half of what you hear."

IX. CONQUER BY KINDNESS.

Safer to reconcile a foe, than make
A conquest of him, for the conquest's sake;
This tames the *power* of doing present ill,
But that disarms him of the very *will*.

Byrom.

X. INNOCENCE.

What stronger breast-plate than a heart untainted?
Thrice is he armed that hath his quarrel just:
And he but naked, though locked up in steel,
Whose conscience with injustice is corrupted.

Shakspere.

XI. LOVE YOUR NEIGHBOUR.
From the German of Wernicke.

Friend, do not crouch to those above,
  And do not tread on those below;
Love *those*, they're worthy of thy love;
  Love *these*, and thou wilt make them so.

XII. SUNSET AND SUNRISE.
From the Latin of Milton.

Contemplate when the sun declines
  Thy death, with deep reflection;
And when again he rising shines,
  The day of resurrection!

Cowper.

XIII. THE WORLD'S WEALTH.

The swelling of an outward fortune can
Create a prosperous, not a happy man;
A peaceful Conscience is the true Content,
And Wealth is but her golden ornament.

Quarles.

XIV. CARPE DIEM.

From the Latin of Martial.

"To-morrow I will live," the fool doth say—
To-day itself's too late: the wise lived yesterday.
Cowley.

XV. LET TRUE WORTH BE SEEN.

To hide true worth from public view,
Is burying diamonds in their mine;
All is not gold that shines, 'tis true;
But all that *is* gold—*ought to shine!*
Bishop.

XVI. OPPORTUNITY.

There is a tide in the affairs of men,
Which, taken at the flood, leads on to fortune;
Omitted, all the voyage of their life
Is bound in shallows and in miseries.
Shakspere.

XVII. GRATITUDE.

What is grandeur, what is power?
Heavier toil, superior pain.
What the bright reward we gain?
The grateful memory of the good.

Sweet is the breath of vernal shower,
The bee's collected treasures sweet,
Sweet Music's melting fall; but sweeter yet
The still small voice of Gratitude.
Gray.

XVIII. "CHARMS AND KNOTS."

Who read a chapter when they rise,
Shall ne'er be troubled with ill eyes.

Who shuts his hand hath lost his gold;
Who opens it hath it twice told.

Who goes to bed and doth not pray,
Maketh two nights to every day.

Who by aspersions throw a stone
At the head of others, hit their own.
Herbert.

XIX. WISDOM AND KNOWLEDGE.

KNOWLEDGE descries alone; Wisdom applies;
That makes some fools, this maketh none but wise.
In my afflictions, Knowledge apprehends
Who is the author, what the cause, and ends:
It finds that Patience is my sad relief,
And that the hand that caused can cure my grief.
To rest contented here is but to bring
Clouds without rain, and heat without a spring;
But sacred Wisdom doth apply that good
Which simple Knowledge barely understood.
Wisdom concludes, and in conclusion proves,
That wheresoever God corrects, he loves.

Quarles.

XX. SIC VITA.

LIKE to the falling of a star,
Or as the flights of eagles are;
Or like the fresh spring's gaudy hue,
Or silver drops of morning dew;
Or like a wind that chafes the flood,
Or bubbles which on water stood:
Even such is man, whose borrowed light
Is straight called in, and paid to-night.
The wind blows out, the bubble dies;
The spring entombed in autumn lies;
The dew dries up, the star is shot;
The flight is past—and man forgot!

H. King.

END OF PART I.

STUDIES IN ENGLISH POETRY.

PART II.

Poems and Extracts Chronologically Arranged,

WITH
BIOGRAPHICAL AND CRITICAL NOTICES.

CHAUCER.

PRINCIPAL EVENTS OF HIS LIFE.—Geoffrey Chaucer—the Father of English Poetry—was born in the year 1328, and died in 1400; so that his era comprehends the reigns of Edward III. and Richard II. It was the age of Gower and Wycliffe in England, of Dante (who died in 1321), Boccacio, and Petrarch in Italy, and of Froissart in France; but amongst these eminent names, that of Chaucer shines with no feeble lustre. He was

> " Our morning-star of song, that led the way
> To welcome the long-after coming beam
> Of Spenser's light, and Shakspere's perfect day."

Chaucer was born in London, and learnedly educated at either Oxford or Cambridge, it is uncertain which, for both claim him; he may perhaps have passed from the one to the other. When rather more than thirty years of age, he appears in public life as a soldier, and moreover as a prisoner, during the invasion of France by Edward III. When he was liberated is not known; but we soon after find him honoured with the patronage and friendship of John of Gaunt, with whom he became subsequently more closely connected by the marriage of his wife's sister with that prince. In 1372 he visited Italy, as an envoy of the government; and during this journey he is thought to have formed an acquaintance with Petrarch at Padua. He resided many years at Woodstock, in a house granted him by the king ;[1] and here, when more than sixty years of age, he wrote his principal work—"The Canterbury Tales." His attachment—in common with John of Gaunt—to the religious tenets of Wycliffe (which however he in after life abjured), involved him in the political factions of the age, and on one occasion he was for some time obliged to conceal himself on the continent from the pursuit of the court party. It is doubtful whether he viewed this religious question in any other than a political light, though old John Foxe, the martyrologist, says, that he "no doubt, saw in religion as much almost as even we doe now, and uttereth in his workes no lesse, and seemeth to be a right Wiclevian, or els was never any." Chaucer died on the 25th of October, 1400, and was buried in that part of Westminster Abbey which is now known as "Poets' Corner."

PRINCIPAL WORKS.—The chief works of Chaucer are the "Romaunt of the Rose," "Troilus and Creseide," "The House of Fame," "The Flower and the Leaf," and the "Canterbury Tales." This last work consists of tales told in turn by a number of pilgrims to the shrine of Thomas-à-Becket, according to an agreement entered into at the suggestion of the host of the Tabard Inn (now the Talbot), in Southwark, at whose "hostelrie" they had all assembled previous to setting out. The introductory part of the poem is called the Prologue. It furnishes us with graphic and discriminative sketches of the twenty-nine individuals who formed the party. The tales then follow.

CHARACTERISTIC SPIRIT AND STYLE.—"In elevation and elegance, in harmony and perspicuity of versification, he surpasses his predecessors in an infinite proportion : his genius was universal, and adapted to themes of unbounded variety : his merit was not less in painting familiar manners with humour and propriety, than in moving the passions, and in representing the beautiful or the grand objects of nature with grace and sublimity. In a word, he appeared with all the lustre and dignity of a true poet, in an age which compelled him to struggle with a barbarous language, and a natural want of taste, and when to write verses at all was regarded as a singular qualification."[2]

"What an intimate scene of English life in the fourteenth century do we enjoy in those tales, beyond what history displays, by glimpses, through the stormy atmosphere of her scenes, or the antiquary can discover by the cold light of his researches! Our ancestors are restored to us, not as phantoms from the field of

---

(1) See Akenside's "Inscription for a Statue to Chaucer," p. 130 of this volume.
(2) Warton. "History of English Poetry," § xviii. last Ed.

battle, or the scaffold, but in the full enjoyment of their social existence. After four hundred years have closed over the mirthful features which formed the living originals of the poet's descriptions, his pages impress the fancy with the momentary credence that they are still alive; as if Time had rebuilt his ruins, and were reacting the lost scenes of existence."[1]

"He speaks of what he wishes to describe with the accuracy, the discrimination, of one who relates what has happened to himself, or has had the best information from those who have been eye-witnesses of it. The strokes of his pencil always tell. He dwells only on the essential, on that which would be interesting to the persons really concerned; yet as he never omits any material circumstance, he is prolix from the number of points on which he touches, without being diffuse on any one; and is sometimes tedious from the fidelity with which he adheres to his subject, as other writers are from the frequency of their digressions from it. He is contented to find grace and beauty in truth. He exhibits, for the most part, the naked object, with little drapery thrown over it. His metaphors, which are few, are not for ornament, but use, and as like as possible to the things themselves. He does not affect to show his power over the reader's mind, but the power which his subject has over his own. There were none of the commonplaces of poetic diction in our author's time, no reflected lights of fancy, no borrowed roseate tints; he was obliged to inspect things for himself, to look narrowly, and almost to handle the object, as in the obscurity of morning we partly see and partly grope our way. The picturesque and the dramatic are in him closely blended together, and hardly distinguishable; for he principally describes external appearances as indicating character—as symbols of internal sentiment."[2]

"I take unceasing delight in Chaucer. His manly cheerfulness is especially delicious to me in my old age. How exquisitely tender he is, and yet how perfectly free from the least touch of sickly melancholy or morbid drooping!"[3]

VERSIFICATION.—The versification of Chaucer has been considered, on the great authority of Dryden, rude and inharmonious; but modern researches into the rhythmical capabilities of our language have led to a different conclusion.[4] There are some

---

(1) Campbell. "Specimens of the British Poets," p. 5, last Ed.
(2) Hazlitt. "Lectures on the English Poets," p. 46, 8vo. Ed.
(3) Coleridge. "Table Talk," p. 290, 12mo. Ed.
(4) See Tyrwhitt's Essay on Chaucer's versification prefixed to his edition of the "Canterbury Tales," and also Mr. R. H. Horne's ingenious introduction to "Chaucer Modernized."

peculiarities for which it is certainly difficult to account, but in general his rhythm is highly musical. Three main characteristics, however, should be borne in mind:—

I. He frequently introduces a foot of three syllables, where modern usage generally requires a dissyllable, thus:—

"And of her smiling was ful simple and coy."

Here "simple and" must be read by delicately blending the "ple" as a sort of *appoggiatura*, or grace-note, with the next syllable. This licence is of the same kind as that employed by Milton in—

"To whom thus Eve, with perfect beauty adorned."

II. He makes the final *e*, which, as in the word "serve," is now mute, and the *es* of the plural, significant in the pronunciation whenever the verse requires it, thus:—

"And smalé foulés maken melodie."

III. He varies the accentuation of syllables at pleasure,[1] thus:—

"Of which vertùe engendred is the flour."

EXTRACTS FROM THE CANTERBURY TALES.[2]

THE GATHERING.

Whanné[3] that April with his shourés[4] soté[5]
The droughte of March hath percéd to the rote,[6]
And bathéd every veine in swiche[7] licòur,[8]
Of which vertùe engendred is the flour;
Whan Zephirus eké[9] with his soté brethe
Enspiréd hath in every holt[10] and hethe

---

(1) Both the latter usages may be traced to the strong tincture of French which the old Saxon language had received from the Norman invasion.
(2) The extracts from Chaucer and Spenser are accented for the convenience of the reader. The acute accent (´) is employed to denote that the syllable over which it is placed is to be pronounced; the grave (`) to denote an unusual accentuation.
(3) *Whanne*—When.   (4) *Shoures*—Showers.   (5) *Sote* or *swote*—Sweet.
(6) *Rote*—Root; so *dore* and *mone* have become door and moon.   (7) *Swiche*, for *swilke*—Such.   (8) *In swiche licour, &c.*—With such moisture, as by its virtue or efficacy gives life to the flower.   (9) *Eke*—Also.   (10) *Holt*—Grove.

The tendre croppés,[1] and the yongé sonne[2]
Hath in the Ram his halfé cours yronne,[3]
And smalé foulés maken[4] melodie,
That slepen allé night with open eye,
So priketh hem[5] natùre in hir coràges;[6]
Than longen folk to gon[7] on pilgrimàges,
And palmeres for to seken strangé strondes,[8]
To servé[9] halwes couthe[10] in sondry londes;
And specially, from every shirés[11] ende
Of Englelond,[12] to Canterbury they wende,[13]
The holy blisful martyr[14] for to seke,
That hem hath holpen, whan that they were seke.[15]
 Befelle,[16] that, in that seson, on a day,
In Southwerk at the Tabard[17] as I lay,
Redy to wenden on my pilgrimàge
To Canterbury with devoute coràge,
At night was come into that hostelrie[18]
Wel nine and twenty in a compagnie
Of sondry folk, by àventure[19] yfalle
In felawship, and pilgrimes were they alle,
That toward Canterbury wolden ride.
The chambres and the stables weren wide,
And wel we weren eséd[20] atté beste.
 And shortly, whan the sonne was gon to reste,

(1) *Croppes*—Shoots. (2) *Sonne*—Sun. (3) *Yronne*—Run. The past participle in old English frequently has the prefix *y* (which is a softened form of the Anglo-Saxon *ge*), as *ycleped*, called; *yclad*, clothed. (4) *Maken*—Make. The old English plural of the verb ends in *en* for all persons, as *we maken, ye maken, they maken*. The *n* is, however, frequently dropt. (5) *So priketh hem, &c.*—i. e. they sleep all night with open eyes, because nature prompts or stirs them so much in their spirits, or makes them so cheerful and lively; *hem* is them, and *hir* their. (6) *Corage*—from the French *cœur*, heart—mind, spirit. (7) *Gon*—To go. The old English infinitive usually ended in *en* or *n*, which, however, was frequently dropt. Sometimes the infinitive sign *to* and the termination were both used. (8) *Strange strondes*—Foreign shores. (9) *To serve halwes, &c.*—i. e. to pay homage to saints known or famous in different countries. (10) *Couthe*—Known, is from the old English *connen*, to know, the past participle of which is conned—connde=conde=coude=couthe. (11) *Shires*—shire's. This is the old possessive case, which was formed by adding *se* or *s*. (12) *Englelond*—Angles-land, England. (13) *Wende*—Go. (14) *Martyr*—Thomas-à-Becket. (15) *Seke*—Sick. (16) *Befelle*—It befel, happened. (17) *Tabard*—Now the Talbot Inn in the Borough. A tabard was a jacket, or sleeveless coat, worn by heralds. (18) *Hostelrie*—An inn or lodging-house. (19) *By aventure, &c.*—By accident (*par aventure*) fallen into company. Observe the French phraseology here and elsewhere employed by Chaucer. (20) *Wel we weren, &c.*—i. e. we were well accommodated with the best.

So hadde I spoken with hem everich[1] on
That I was of hir felawship anon,[2]
And madé forword[3] erly for to rise,
To take oure way ther as I you devise.[4]

THE KNIGHT.

A KNIGHT ther was, and that a worthy man,
That fro the timé that he firste began
To riden out, he lovéd chevalrie,[5]
Trouthe and honòur, fredom and curtesie.
Ful worthy was he in his Lordés werre,[6]
And thereto had he ridden, no man ferre,[7]
As wel in Cristendom as in Hethenesse,[8]
And ever honoured for his worthinesse.
  At mortal battailles hadde he ben fiftene,
And foughten for our faith at Tramissene[9]
In listés[10] thriés,[11] and ay slain his fo.
This ilké[12] worthy knight hadde ben also
Somtimé with the Lord of Palatie,[13]
Agen[14] another hethen in Turkie:
And evermore he hadde a sovereine pris.[15]
And though that he was worthy he was wise,
And of his port as meke as is a mayde.
He never yet no vilanie[16] ne[17] sayde
In alle his lif, unto no manere wight:[18]
He was a veray parfit gentil[19] knight.
  But for to tellen you of his araie,[20]
His hors was good, but he ne was not gaie.

---

(1) *Everich*—Every. (2) *Anon*—Soon. (3) *Forword*—*i. e.* foreword; promise or engagement. (4) *Devise*—Relate. (5) *Chevairne*—Chivalry—"the manners, exercises, and valiant exploits of a knight." (6) *His Lordes werre*—his Lord's war—the Holy war. (7) *Ferre*—further, comparative of *fer*, far. (8) *Hethenesse*—country of heathens. (9) *Tramissene*—a city in Barbary. (10) *Listes*—See note 5, p. 27. (11) *Thries*—thrice. (12) *Ilke*—same. (13) *Palatie*—Palathia, a city in Asia Minor. (14) *Agen*—against. (15) *Sovereine pris*—the highest praise. The words *prize, price,* and *praise,* are nearly identical in original signification. (16) *Vilanie*—"anything unbecoming a gentleman." (17) *Never, ne*—Double negatives were used by Chaucer as they now are in French. (18) *No manere wight*—no sort of person. (19) *Gentil*—nobly born, gentlemanlike. (20) *Araie*—equipment.

Of fustiàn he weréd[1] a gipon,[2]
Allé besmotred[3] with his habergeou,[4]
For he was late ycome fro his viàge,[5]
And wenté for to don[6] his pilgrimage.

THE SQUIER.

WITH him ther was his sone a yonge SQUIER,
A lover, and a lusty[7] bacheler,
With lockés crull[8] as they were laide in presse.
Of twenty yere of age he was I gesse.
Of his stature he was of even[9] lengthe,
And wonderly deliver,[10] and grete of strengthe.
And he hadde be somtime in chevachie,[11]
In Flaundres, in Artois, and in Picardie,
And borne him wel, as of so litel space,[12]
In hope to stonden in his ladies grace.
Embrouded[13] was he, as it were a mede[14]
Alle ful of fresshé flourés, white and rede.
Singing he was, or floyting[15] alle the day,
He was as fresshe as is the moneth of May.
Shorte was his goune, with slevés long and wide.
Wel coude he sitte on hors, and fayré[16] ride.
He coudé songés make, and well endite,[17]
Juste[18] and eke dance, and wel pourtraie[19] and write.
So hote he lovéd, that by nightertale[20]
He slep no more than doth the nightingale.
Curteis he was, lowly, and servisable,[21]
And carf[22] before his fader at the table.

(1) *Wered*—wore. (2) *Gipon*—a short cassock or frock; it is the French *jupon*, and Scotch *jupe*. (3) *Besmotred*—smutted, soiled. (4) *Habergeon*—a coat of mail; a diminutive of *hauberk*. (5) *Viage*—voyage, journey. (6) *Don*, to do, perform.
(7) *Lusty*—strong, stout. (8) *Lockes crull, &c.*—Locks curled as if they had been laid in a press. (9) *Even*—middle, common. (10) *Wonderly deliver*—remarkably nimble; *deliver*, from the French *libre*, free. (11) *Chevachie*—from the French *cheval*, a horse—military expedition. (12) *As of so litel space*—considering the short time that he had been a soldier. (13) *Embrouded*—embroidered. (14) *Mede*—Meadow. (15) *Floyting*—Fluting, playing on the flute. (16) *Fayre*—skilfully. (17) *Endite*—compose or dictate. (18) *Juste*—joust or tilt at tournaments. (19) *Pourtraie*—portray, draw. (20) *Nightertale*—night time. (21) *Servisable*—disposed to do services, obliging. (22) *Carf*—carved.

THE PRIORESSE.

Ther was also a Nonne,[1] a Prioresse,
That of hire[2] smiling was ful simple and coy;
Hire gretest othe[3] n'as but[4] by Seint Eloy,[5]
And she was clepéd[6] Madame Eglentine.
Ful wel she sangé the servìce devìne,
Entunéd in hire nose ful swetély;
And French she spake ful fayre and fetisly,[7]
After the scole of Stratford[8] atté Bow,
For Frenche of Paris was to hire unknowe.[9]
At meté[10] was she wel ytaughte withalle;
She lette no morsel from her lippés falle,
Ne wette hire fingres in hire saucé depe.
Wel coude she carie a morsel, and wel kepe,
Thatté no drop ne fell upon hire brest.
In curtesie[11] was sette ful moche hire lest.[12]
Hire over-lippé wipéd she so clene,
That in hire cuppé was no ferthing sene
Of gresé,[13] whan she dronken hadde hire draught.
Ful semély[14] after hire mete she raught.[15]
And sikerly[16] she was of grete disport,[17]
And ful plesànt, and amiable of port,
And peinéd hire[18] to contrefeten chere[19]
Of court, and ben estatelich of manère,
And to ben olden digne[20] of reverence.
But for to speken of hire consciènce,
She was so charitable and so pitoùs[21]
She woldé wepe if that she saw a mous

---

(1) *Nonne*—Nun.   (2) *Hire*—her.   (3) *Othe*—oath.   (4) *N'as but*—was not but, was only; like the French *n'était que*.   (5) *Seint Eloy*—Warton and Tyrwhitt both say this is Saint Louis, but others say Saint Eligius is meant. (6) *Clepéd*—called.   (7) *Fetisly*—neatly, properly.   (8) *Stratford*—At Stratford, near Bow, Essex, there seems to have been anciently a Benedictine nunnery; the French taught at this fashionable seminary is above satirically distinguished from the French of Paris.   (9) *Unknowe*—unknown.   (10) *Mete*—dinner.   (11) *In curtesie, &c.*—i. e. she prided herself on her gentility. (12) *Lest*—pleasure.   (13) *No ferthing of grese*—not the smallest spot of grease: *ferthing*—a farthing, any very small thing.   (14) *Semely*—seemly, in a polite manner.   (15) *Raught*—reached, bent forward to.   (16) *Sikely*—certainly. (17) *Disport*—cheerfulness.   (18) *Peined hire*—it peined (in the French sense) her—she took pains; not "it pained her," as interpreted in "Chaucer Modernized." (19) *To contrefeten, &c.*—To imitate or assume court manners, and to be stately in her carriage.   (20) *Digne*—worthy.   (21) *Pitous*—piteous.

Caught in a trappe, if it were ded or bledde.
Of smalé houndés[1] hadde she, that she fedde
With rosted flesh, and milk, and wastel brede.[2]
But sore wept she if on[3] of hem were dede,
Or if men smote it with a yerdé[4] smert:[5]
And all was consciènce and tendre herte.

Ful semély hire wimple[6] ypinchéd[7] was;
Hire nose tretìs,[8] hire eyen[9] grey as glas;
Hire mouth ful smale, and therto[10] soft and red,
But sikerly she hadde a fayre forehèd.
It was almost a spanné brode I trowe;
For hardily[11] she was not undergrowe.

Ful fetise[12] was hire cloke, as I was ware.
Of smale coràll aboute hire arm she bare
A pair of bedés, gauded[13] all with grene;
And thereon heng[14] a broche of gold ful shene,[15]
On which was first ywriten a crounéd A,[16]
And after, *Amor vincit omnia.*[17]

THE PERSONE.[18]

A GOOD man ther was of religiòun,
That was a pouré PERSONE[19] of a toun:
But riche he was of holy thought and werk.
He was also a lerned man, a Clerk,
That Cristés gospel trewely woldé preche.
His parishens[20] devoutly wolde he teche.

---

(1) *Of smale houndes*—some little dogs; *of* is here used in the partitive sense, like the French *de*. (2) *Wastel brede*—cake-bread, fine bread. The word "wastel" is connected in origin with the French *gasteau=gâteau*—a cake. (3) *On*—one. (4) *Yerde*—rod, stick. (5) *Smert*—smartly. (6) *Wimple*—a hood or veil, or, as others say, a covering for the neck. (7) *Ypinched*—crimped up. (8) *Tretis*—straight and long. (9) *Eyen*—eyes; the old plural. (10) *Therto*—in addition to that, moreover. (11) *Hardily, &c.*—Certainly she was not of low stature. (12) *Ful fetise, &c.*—Very handsome was her cloak, I observed. (13) *Gauded*—ornamented. (14) *Heng*—hung. (15) *Shene*—sheen, bright. (16) *A crouned A*—for *Amor*, love, with a crown above it to symbolise the motto in the next line. (17) *Amor vincit, &c.*—"Love subdues all things;" to denote the religious service to which she was then dedicated.

(18) The above striking lines are the original of Dryden's "Good Priest" (see p. 360), and seem to have suggested the Village Clergyman of Goldsmith's "Deserted Village" (see p. 446). (19) *Persone*—Parson: "He is called," says Blackstone, "*parson, persona,* because by his *person* the Church, which is an invisible body, is represented." (20) *Parishens*—parishioners.

Benigne he was, and wonder[1] diligent,
And in adversitee ful patient:
And swiche he was ypreved often[2] sithes.
Ful loth were him to cursen for his tithes,
But rather wolde he yeven,[3] out of doute,
Unto his pouré parishens aboute,
Of his offring, and eke of his substànce.
He coude in litel thing have suffisance.[4]
Wide was his parish, and houses fer asonder,
But he ne left nought for no rain ne thonder,
In sikenesse and in mischief[5] to visìte
The ferrest in his parish, moche and lite,[6]
Upon his fete, and in his hand a staf.
This noble ensample to his shepe he yaf,[7]
That first he wrought, and afterward he taught.
Out of the Gospel he the wordés caught,
And this figùre he added yet therto,
That if gold rusté, what shuld iren do?
For if a preest be foule,[8] on whom we trust,
No wonder is a lewed[9] man to rust.
Wel ought a preest ensample for to yeve,
By his cleennessé, how his shepe shulde live.

He setté not his benefice to hire,
And lette[10] his shepe acombred[11] in the mire,
And ran unto Londòn, unto Seint Poules,
To seken him a chanterie[12] for soules,
Or with[13] a brotherhede to be withold;
But dwelt at home, and kepte wel his fold,
So that the wolf ne made it not miscarie.
He was a shepherd, and no mercenàrie.
And though he holy were, and vertuous,
He was to sinful men not dispitòus,[14]
Ne of his speché dangerous[15] ne digne,[16]
But in his teching discrete and benigne.
To drawen folk to heven with faireness,
By good ensample, was his besinesse:

(1) *Wonder*—wonderfully. (2) *Ypreved often, &c.*—Proved often since. (3) *Yeven*—give. (4) *Suffisance*—sufficiency. (5) *Mischief*—trouble. (6) *Moche and lite*—great and small. (7) *Yaf*—gave. (8) *Foule*—soiled, defiled. (9) *Lewed*—ignorant; connected with *low*. *Lewed-man*=layman. (10) *Lette* —left. (11) *Acombred*—encumbered. (12) *Chanterie*—a singing for souls, an endowment for that purpose. (13) *Or with, &c.*—Or be kept from the world with a brotherhood of monks, or friars. (14) *Dispitous*—inexorable, angry to excess. (15) *Dangerous*—sparing. (16) *Digne*—proud, disdainful.

But it were[1] any persone obstinat,
What so he were of highe, or **low estat,**
Him wolde he snibben[2] sharply for the nonés.[3]
A better preest I trowe that nowher non[4] is.
He waited after no pompe ne reverence,
Ne makéd him no spicéd conscience,[5]
But Cristés lore, and his apostles **twelve,**
He taught, but first he folwed it **himselve.**

THE TALE OF THE ENCHANTED STEED.[6]

At Sarra, in the lond of Tartarie,
Ther dwelt a king that werreiéd[7] Russie,
Thurgh[8] which ther diéd many a doughty man:
This noble king **was** clepéd Cambuscan,
Which in his time was **of so gret renoun,**
That ther n' as no wher in no regioùn
So excellent a lord in allé thing:
Him lacked nought that longeth[9] to a king,
As of the secte[10] of which that he was borne.
He kept his lay[11] to which he was ysworne;
And, therto, he was hardy, wise, and **riche,**
And pitöus, and just; and alway yliche;[12]

(1) *But it were*—But if there were. (2) *Snibben*—snub, reprove. (3) *For the nones*—for the occasion, implying that he did not generally reprove sharply. (4) *Non*—no one. (5) *Spiced conscience*—a conscience embalmed in sophistries.

(6) **This** romantic story—usually called "The Squire's Tale"—seems to have been a favourite with Milton, who in the "Il Penseroso" characterizes Chaucer as—

"Him that left half-told
The story of Cambuscan bold,
Of Camball, and of Algarsife,
And who had Canace to wife,
That **owned** the virtuous ring and glass,
And of the wondrous horse of **brass,**
On which the Tartar king did **ride."**

"The imagination," says **Warton** ("**History of English Poetry,**" § xv.), "**of this** story, consists in Arabian fiction, engrafted on Gothic chivalry."

The **story, as above intimated, is in the original only** "**half** told," but to fit it for this selection, the fragment **has been** somewhat abridged—the part left out, however, being a wearisome specimen of that "tediousness" which even Chaucer sometimes "bestows" upon **his readers.**

(7) *Werreied*—made war **against.** (8) *Thurgh*—through. (9) *Longeth*—belongeth. (10) *As of the secte, &c.*—As suitable to the rank in life to which he was born. (11) *Lay*—law, that which is *laid* down, as *saw* is that which is *said*.
(12) *Yliche*—alike, the same.

Trewe of his word, benigne and honouràble;
Of his coràge as any centre, stable;
Yong, fresh, and strong; in armés desiroùs,
As any bacheler of all his hous.
A faire persòn he was, and fortunate,
And kept alway so well reàl[1] estat,
That ther n' as no wher swiche another man.

This noble king, this Tartre Cambuscàn,
Haddé two sones by Elfeta his wif,
Of which the eldest highté[2] Algarsif,
That other was yclepéd Camballo.

A daughter had this worthy king also,
That yongest was, and highté Canace:
But for to tellen you all hire beautee,
It lith[3] not in my tonge, ne in my conning;
I dare not undertake so high a thing:
Min English, eke, is unsufficient;
It musté ben a rethor[4] excellent,
That coude[5] his colours longing for[6] that art,
If he shuld hire descriven ony part:
I am not swiche; I mote[7] speke as I can.

And so befell, that when this Cambuscàn
Hath twenty winter borne his diademe,
As he was wont fro yere to yere, I deme,
He let the feste[8] of his nativitee,
Don crién, thurghout Sarra his citee,
The last Idus of March,[9] aftér the yere.

Phebus the sonne ful jolif was and clere,
For he was nigh his exaltatïòn
In Martés face, and in his mansiòn
In Aries, the colerike hote signe:
Ful lusty[10] was the wether, and benigne;
For which the foules again[11] the sonné shene,
(What for the seson and the yonge grene),
Ful loudé songen hir affectiòns;[12]
Hem semed[13] han gatten hem protectiòns

---

(1) *Real*—royal, from the Latin *regalis*. (2) *Highte*—was called. (3) *Lith*—lieth. (4) *Rethor*—rhetorician, one highly skilled in composition. (5) *Coude*—knew. (6) *Longing for, &c.*—belonging to that art. (7) *Mote*—must. (8) *Let the feste, &c.*—ordered the feast of his nativity to be proclaimed. (9) *Idus of March*—the 15th day, by the Roman computation. (10) *Lusty*—vigorous, inspiriting. (11) *Again*—against, in front of. (12) *Affections*—gratitude. (13) *Hem semed, &c.*—i. e. they seemed to have got, &c.

Again the swerd[1] of winter kene and cold.
   This Cambuscàn, of which I have you told,
In real vestiments, sits on his deis[2]
With diademe, ful high in his paleis;
And holt[3] his feste so solempne and so riche,
That in this world ne was ther non it liche,
Of which if I shal tellen all the array,
Than wold it occupie a somers day;
And, eke, it nedeth not for to devise
At every cours the order of hir service:
I wol not tellen of hir strangé sewes,[4]
Ne of hir swannés, ne hir heronsewes.[5]
Eke, in that lond, as tellen knightés old,
Ther is som mete that is ful daintee hold,
That in this lond men reeche[6] of it ful smal:
Ther n' is no man that may reporten al.
I wol not tarien you, for it is prime,[7]
And for it is no fruit, but losse of time,
Unto my purpose I wol have recours.
   And so befell, that after the thridde[8] cours,
While that this king sit thus in his noblèy,[9]
Herking his minstrallés hir thingés pley
Beforne him at his bord deliciously,
In at the hallé dore, al sodenly,
Ther came a knight upon a stede of bras,
And in his hond a brod[10] mirroùr of glas;
Upon his thombe he had of gold a ring;
And by his side a naked swerd hangìng,
And up he rideth to the highé bord.
In all the halle ne was ther spoke a word,
For mervaille of this knight; him to behold
Ful besily they waiten, yong and old.
   This strangé knight that come thus sodenly
Al armed, save his hed, ful richély,
Salueth[11] king and quene, and lordés alle,
By order as they saten in the halle,

---

(1) *Swerd*—sword. (2) *Deis*—dais, the elevated part of an ancient dining hall, where the principal persons sat under a canopy (3) *Holt*—held. (4) *Hir strange sewes*—their strange or dainty dishes. (5) *Heronsewes*—young herons. (6) *Reeche of it, &c.*—Reck or care for it very little. (7) *It is prime*, either means, it is now the first quarter of the day (or early in the morning), and therefore I must be quicker with my story; or it is used metaphorically for the season of action and business. (8) *Thridde*—third. (9) *In his nobley*—in his splendour, or, among his nobility. (10) *Brod*—broad. (11) *Salueth*—saluteth.

With so high reverence and óbservance,
As wel in speche as in contenance,
That Gawain[1] with his oldé curtesie,
Though he were come agen out of faerie,
Ne coude him not amenden with a word.
And, after this, beforn the highé bord,
He with a manly vois sayd his messàge,
After the forme uséd in his langàge,
Withouten vice of sillable or of letter.
And for[2] his talé shuldé seme the better,
Accordant to his wordés was his chere,[3]
As techeth art of speche hem that it lere:[4]
Al be it that I cannot soune his stile,[5]
Ne cannot climben over so high a stile,[5]
Yet say I this, as to comùn entent,[6]
Thus much amounteth al that ever he ment,
If it so be[7] that I have it in mind.

He sayd: "The King of Arabie and of Inde,
My liegé Lord! on this solempné day,
Salueth you as he best can and may;
And sendeth you, in honour of your feste,
By me, that am al redy at your heste,[8]
This stede of bras, that esily and wel
Can in the space of a day naturel,
(This is to sayn, in four and twenty houres),
Wher so you list, in drought or ellés shoures,
Beren your body into every place,
To which your herté willeth for to pace,[9]
Withouten wemme of you,[10] thurgh foule or faire.
Or if you list to fleen[11] as high in the aire
As doth an egle, whan him list[12] to sore,
This samé stede shal bere you evermore,

---

(1) *Gawain*—a nephew to King Arthur, and described as a model of knightly courtesy. (2) *And for, &c.*—And in order that this tale, &c. (3) *Chere*— appearance, the expression of his countenance. (4) *Lere*—learn; hence the noun, *lore*. (5) *Stile*—the two words thus written above, and given as rhymes, are of different origin—the former is from the Latin *stylus*, the writing implement of the Romans; the latter from the Anglo-Saxon *stigh-el*, something *raised*. (6) *Comun entent*—the general meaning or scope. (7) *If it so be, &c.*—If at least I understand it well myself. (8) *Heste*—command. (9) *Pace*—pass, go. (10) *Withouten wemme of you*—without spot or any injury to you. (11) *Fleen*—to fly. (12) *Him list*—this verb is generally used in old authors, as in the above examples, impersonally. It is the same as *lest*, used two lines below; its past tense was *luste*.

Withouten harme, till ye be ther you lest,
(Though that ye slepen on his back or rest,)
And turne again with writhing[1] of a pin.
He that it wrought, he conde[2] many a gin;
He waited[3] many a constellatiön
Or he had don this operatiön,
And knew ful many a sele and many a bond.
This mirrour, eke, that I have in min hond,
Hath swiche a might, that men may in it see
When ther shal falle ony adversitee
Unto your regne, or to yourself also,
And openly, who is your frend or fo.
And, over all this, if any lady bright
Hath set her herte on any maner wight,
If he be false, she shal his treson see,
His newé love, and all his subtiltee,
So openly, that ther shal nothing hide.
Wherfore, again this[4] lusty somer tide,
This mirrour and this ring that ye may see,
He hath sent to my lady Canace,
Your excellenté doughter that is here.
"The vertue of this ring, if ye wol here,
Is this, that if hire list it for to were
Upon hire thombe, or in hire purse it bere,
Ther is no foule that fleeth under heven,
That she ne shal wel understond his steven,[5]
And know his mening openly and plaine,
And answere him in his langàge again:
And every gras that groweth upon rote
She shal eke know, and whom it wol do bote,[6]
Al be his woundes never so depe and wide.
This naked swerd, that hangeth by my side,
Swiche vertue hath, that what man that it smite,
Thurghout his armure it wol kerve[7] and bite,
Were it as thicke as a braunchéd oke;
And what man that is wounded with the stroke

---

(1) *Writhing*—turning. (2) *He coude, &c.*—He knew many a contrivance.
(3) *He waited, &c.*—*i. e.* he waited until the stars were favourable to him.
(4) *Again this, &c.*—Against this pleasant summer-time. (5) *Steven*—from the
Anglo-Saxon *stefn-ian*, to set up, institute; hence *steven* is *instituted* language,
speech. (6) *Bote*—from the Anglo-Saxon *bot-an*, to superadd, satisfy—satisfaction, help, remedy; *do bote*, cure. The words *boot*, in "*to boot*" and *bootless*, are
derived from this word. (7) *Kerve*—carve, cut.

Shal never be hole, til that you list of grace[1]
To stroken him with the platte[2] in thilke[3] place
Ther[4] he is hurt; this is as much to sain,
Ye moten[5] with the platté swerde again
Stroken him in the wound, and it wol close.
This is the veray soth,[6] withouten glose;[7]
It faileth not, while it is in your hold."

And whan this knight hath thus his talé told,
He rideth out of halle, and down he light:
His stedé, which that shone as sonné bright,
Stant in the court as stille as any ston.
This knight is to his chambre ladde[8] anon,
And is unarmed,[9] and to the mete ysette.
Thise presents ben ful richélich[10] yfette,[11]
This is to sain, the swerd and the mirroùr,
And borne anon into the highé tour
With certain officers ordained therfore;
And unto Canace the ring is bore
Solempnély, ther she sat at the table;
But, sikerly, withouten any fable,
The hors of bras, that may not be remued;[12]
It stant, as it were to the ground yglued:
Ther may no man out of the place it drive
For non engine, of windlas, or polive;[13]
And causé why, for they con[14] not the craft,
And therfore in the place they han it laft,
Til that the knight hath taught hem the manère
To voiden[15] him, as ye shul after here.

Gret was the prees[16] that swarméd to and fro,
To gauren[17] on this hors that stondeth so;
For it so high was, and so brod and long,
So wel proportionéd for to be strong,
Right as it were a stede of Lumbardie;
Therwith[18] so horsly,[19] and so quik of eye,

---

(1) *That you list of grace*—that you please, as an act of favour. (2) *Platte*—the flat part. (3) *Thilke*—the same. (4) *Ther*—where. (5) *Ye moten*—you must. (6) *Soth*—sooth, truth. (7) *Glose*—deceit. (8) *Ladde*—led. (9) *Unarmed*—we should now write "disarmed." (10) *Richélich*—richly, with much ceremony. (11) *Yfette*—fetched. (12) *Remued*—from the French *remuer*, to stir—removed. (13) *Polive*—pulley. (14) *Con*—know. (15) *Voiden*—remove. (16) *Prees*—press. (17) *Gauren*—gaze. (18) *Therwith*—with that, at the same time. (19) *Horsly*—here applied to a horse, as *manly* is to a man.

As it a gentle Poileis courser[1] were;
For certes,[2] fro his tayle unto his ere,
Nature ne art ne coud him not amend
In no degree, as all the peple wend.[3]
    But evermore hir mosté wonder was,
How that it coudé gon, and was of bras;
It was of faerie, as the peple semed.
Diversé folk diversély han demed;
As many heds, as many wittés ben.
They murmuréd, as doth a swarme of been,[4]
And maden skillés[5] after hir fantasies,
Rehersing of the oldé poetries,
And sayd it was ylike the Pegasee,
The hors that haddé wingés for to flee;
Or, elles, it was the Grekés[6] hors Sinon,
That broughté Troyé to destruction,
As men moun[7] in thise oldé gestés[8] rede.
    "Min herte," quod[9] on, "is evermore in drede;
I trowe[10] some men of armés ben therin,
That shapen hem[11] this citee for to win:
It were right good that al swiche thing were know."
Another rowned[12] to his felaw low,
And sayd, "He lieth, for it is rather like
An apparence ymade by some magike,
As jogelours[13] plaien at thise festés grete."
    Now after mete there goth this noble king
To seen this hors of bras, with all a route[14]
Of lordés and of ladies him aboute.
Swiche wondring was ther on this hors of bras,
That sin the gret assege of Troyé was,
Ther as[15] men wondred on an hors also,
Ne was ther swiche a wondring as was tho.[16]
But, finally, the king askèth the knight

---

(1) *Poileis courser*—a horse of Apulia, in Italy, which in old French was called Poille. The horses of that country were much esteemed. (2) *Certes*—certainly, surely. (3) *Wend*—weened, thought. (4) *Been*—bees. (5) *Maden skilles*—made or gave reasons. (6) *The Grekes, &c.*—Sinon the Greek's horse. (7) *Moun*—for *mowen*, may. (8) *Gestes*—from the Latin *gestum*, an achievement—adventures. (9) *Quod*—quoth. (10) *Trowe*—believe. (11) *Shapen hem*—prepare themselves, make ready. (12) *Rowned*—whispered. (13) *Jogelours*—jugglers (see noet 7, p. 20.) (14) *Route*—company (see note 1, p. 132). (15) *Ther as*—whereas on which occasion. (16) *Tho*—then.

The vertue of this courser, and the might,
And praiéd him to tell his governaunce.¹
   This hors, anon, gan for to trip and daunce,
Whan that the knight laid hond upon his rein;
And saidé, "Sire! ther n' is no more to sain,
But whan you list to riden any where,
Ye moten trill² a pin, stant³ in his ere,
Which I shal tellen you betwixt us two;
Ye moten nempne⁴ him to what place also,
Or to what contree, that you list to ride.
And when ye come ther as you list⁵ abide,
Bid him descend, and trill another pin,
(For therin lieth the effect of all the gin,⁶)
And he wol doun descend and don your will,
And in that place he wol abiden still:
Though al the world had the contràry swore,
He shall not thennes be drawe ne be bore.⁷
Or if you list to bid him thennés gon,
Trillé this pin, and he wol vanish anon
Out of the sight of every maner wight,
And come agen, be it by day or night,
Whan that you list to clepen⁸ him again,
In swiche a guise as I shal to you sain
Betwixen you and me, and that ful sone.
Ride whan you list, ther n' is no more to done."
   Enfourméd whan the king was of the knight,
And hath conceivéd in his wit aright
The maner and the forme of all this thing,
Ful glad and blith, this noble doughty king
Repaireth to his revel, as beforne.
The bridel is in to the tour yborne,
And kept among his jewels lefe⁹ and dere;
The hors vanisht, I n'ot¹⁰ in what manere,
Out of hir sight; ye get no more of me:
But this I lete,¹¹ in lust¹² and jolitee,

---

(1) *His governaunce*—the mode of governing him.   (2) *Trill*—twirl, turn round. This word is akin to *drill, thrill, twirl, tirl* (see an article on the meaning and origin of the verb *to tirl*, by Sir G. C. Lewis, in the "Classical Museum," vol. i. pp. 113—124).   (3) *Stant*—i. e. which stands.   (4) *Moten nempne*—must name.   (5) *Ther as you list, &c.*—Where you wish to stop.   (6) *Gin*—engine.   (7) *Bore*—borne.   (8) *Clepen*—call.   (9) *Lefe*—pleasing, beloved.   (10) *N'ot*—know not.   (11) *Lete*—let, leave.   (12) *Lust*—connected with *list* and *lest*—pleasure.

This Cambuscán his lordés festeying,
Til that wel nigh the day began to spring.

GOOD COUNSAIL OF CHAUCER.[2]

Fly fro the prease,[3] and dwell with sothfastnesse,[4]
Suffise unto[5] thy good though it be small,
For horde hath hate, and climbing tikelnesse,[6]
Prease hath envy, and wele[7] is blent over all,
Savour[8] no more than thee behové shall,
Rede[9] well thy selfe that other folk canst rede,
And trouth thee shall deliver, it is no drede.[10]

Peiné thee not ech crooked to redresse,
In trust of her that tourneth[11] as a ball;
Great rest standèth in little businesse,
Beware[12] also to spurne againe a nall,[13]
Strive not as doth a crocké[14] with a wall,

(1) Thus concludes what is called the first part of the story. The second describes the rising of Canace at daybreak, to try the effect of her ring. The sunrise is thus simply and freshly painted;—

"The vapour, which that fro the earthé glode (*glided*),
Maketh the sonne to semé rody and brode;
But nathéles it was so faire a sight,
That it made all hir hertes for to light (*lighten*)
What for the seson, and the morwening (*morning*)
And for the foulés that she herdé sing:
For right anon she wisté what they ment,
Right by hir song, and knew al hir entent."

Her attention is soon attracted to a falcon, whose pitiful lamentation extends over nearly two hundred lines, and is for the most part very prolix and wearisome. Shortly after the piece abruptly closes, being evidently left—if we judge by the plan which the author lays down—even less than "half told." Spenser, in the "Faerie Queene" (book iv. cantos 2 and 3), afterwards attempted to supply the deficiency.

(2) This is said to have been Chaucer's last composition, and written upon his death-bed, "when he was in great anguish." (3) *Prease*—press, crowd. (4) *Sothfastnesse*—truth. (5) *Suffise unto, &c.*—Be satisfied with thy wealth. (6) *Tikelnesse*—uncertainty. (7) *Wele is, &c.*—Wealth or riches are blind (*blent*) or deceitful above all things. (8) *Savour*—taste, affect. (9) *Rede*—counsel. (10) *It is no drede*—there is no fear or doubt. (11) *Her that tourneth, &c.*—Fortune. (12) *Beware*—take care not, like the French *gardez-vous de*. (13) *Nall*—nail. (14) *Crocke*—earthen pitcher.

Demé¹ thy selfe that demest others dede,²
And trouth thee shall deliver, it is no drede.

That thee is sent receive in buxomnesse,³
The wrastling of this world asketh a fall,
Here is no home, here is but wildernesse,
Forth, pilgrime! forth, beast, out of thy stall!
Looke up on high, and thanké God of all!
Weivé⁴ thy lusts, and let thy ghost⁵ thee lede,
And trouth thee shall deliver, it is no drede.

SPENSER.

PRINCIPAL EVENTS OF HIS LIFE.—Edmund Spenser—"The Prince of Poets in his time,"⁶—was, like Chaucer, a native of London. He was born in East Smithfield, in 1553. He was educated at Cambridge, and early in life became the friend of the accomplished Sir Philip Sidney, and a dependent on the powerful Earl of Leicester, Sidney's uncle. By this nobleman he was, in 1580, sent to Ireland, as secretary to Lord Grey of Wilton, who had been appointed the Lord Deputy of that country. For his services in this capacity, he subsequently obtained of the crown the grant of an estate in Cork, named Kilcolman, with a castle of the same name. During his residence here, his great poem, "The Faerie Queene," was probably begun; and here he was visited by Sir Walter Raleigh, who, after Sir Philip Sidney's death, had become Spenser's principal friend and patron, and who is said to have introduced him to Queen Elizabeth. His success as a courtier was doubtful, if we may believe his own experience, thus recorded:—

> "Full little knowest thou, that hast not tride,
>   What hell it is, in suing long to bide:
>   To loose good dayes that might be better spent,
>   To wast long nights in pensive discontent;
>   To speed to-day, to be put back to-morrow;
>   To feed on hope, to pine with feare and sorrow;
>   To have thy princes grace, yet want her peeres;
>   To have thy asking, yet waite manie yeeres;

---

(1) *Deme*—judge.   (2) *Others dede*—others' deed, that which is done by others.   (3) *Buxomnesse*—obedience (see note 2, p. 125).   (4) *Weive*—waive, forsake.   (5) *Ghost*—spirit.
(6) So styled in the inscription on his tomb.

> To fret thy soule with crosses and with cares;
> To eate thy heart through comfortlesse dispaires;
> To fawne, to crowche, to ride, to waite, to ronne;
> To spend, to give, to want, to be undonne."

Spenser's earthly career ended very mournfully. In the rebellion of Tyrone, his castle was attacked, and to conclude in Ben Jonson's words, "The Irish having robbed Spenser's goods, and burnt his house, and a little child new-born, he and his wife escaped; and after, he died for lake (*lack*) of bread, in King Street, and refused twenty pieces sent to him by my lord of Essex, adding, 'He was sorrie he had no time to spend them.'" He died in 1598, and was buried, at his own request, near Chaucer, in Westminster Abbey, and the most celebrated poets of the time followed the hearse, and threw "mournful elegies" into his grave.

PRINCIPAL WORKS.—Spenser's most important poems are "The Shepheards Calender," "An Hymne of Heavenly Love," "An Hymne of Heavenly Beautie," "Prothalamion" and "Epithalamion" (both nuptial poems), two elegies entitled "Daphnaïda" and "Astrophel," "The Ruines of Rome," "The Ruines of Time," "Muiopotmos, or the Fate of the Butterfly;" and far transcending all the rest, both in extent and merit, "The Faerie Queene" The subject of this poem is thus described by Dr. Aikin:[1]—"His 'Faery Queen' is by much the most considerable allegorical poem in our language; and in many respects it deserves the reputation which through two centuries it has enjoyed. Its plan, indeed, is most singularly perplexed and incoherent; and as the work is unfinished, it would be entirely unintelligible had not the author himself given a prefatory explanation of it. The term *faery* is used by him to denote something existing only in the regions of fancy, and the *Faery Queen* is the abstract idea of Glory personified. The knights of faery-land are the twelve virtues, who are the champions or servants of the Queen. The British Prince Arthur, who is the subject of so many fabulous legends, becomes enamoured of the Faery Queen in a vision, and comes to seek her in faery-land. He is the image of perfect excellence, and is regarded as the general hero of the piece. Each book, however, has its particular hero, who is one of the virtues above mentioned, and who goes through a course of adventures modelled upon the tales of chivalry, and having for their object the relief of some distressed damsel, or other sufferer under wrong and oppression. He encounters giants, monsters, enchanters, and the like, who are the allegorised foes of the particular virtue of which he is the representative; and prince

---

[1] "Letters on English Poetry," p. 212.

Arthur, the general hero, occasionally appears as his auxiliary when he is hard pressed.

"Thus far there is some consistency in the plan; but the poet had the further view of paying his court to Queen Elizabeth, the great topic of all the learned adulation of the age. She is therefore typified by the person of the Faery Queen, and several incidents of her history are related under the veil of allegory: the principal personages of her court are likewise occasionally alluded to in the characters of the faery knights. Moreover, the supposed real history of Arthur and other British princes is interwoven with the tissue of fictitious adventure. It is impossible to conceive a more tangled skein of narrative, and the author could scarcely expect that any reader would take the pains to unravel it. In fact, no one at present regards this poem in any other light than as a gallery of allegorical pictures, no otherwise connected than by the relation several of them bear to one common hero. It would be no easy matter to form one consistent allegory of any single book, and to explain the emblematical meaning of every adventure ascribed to its particular knight."

CHARACTERISTIC SPIRIT AND STYLE.—"His command of imagery is wide, easy, and luxuriant. He threw the soul of harmony into our verse, and made it more warmly, tenderly, and magnificently descriptive than it ever was before, or, with a few exceptions, than it has ever been since. It must certainly be owned, that in description he exhibits nothing of the brief strokes and robust power which characterise the very greatest poets; but we shall nowhere find more airy and expansive images of visionary things, a sweeter tone of sentiment, or a finer flush in the colours of language, than in this Rubens of English poetry. His fancy teems exuberantly in minuteness of circumstance, like a fertile soil sending bloom and verdure through the utmost extremities of the foliage which it nourishes. On a comprehensive view of the whole work, we certainly miss the charm of strength, symmetry, and rapid or interesting progress; for though the plan which the poet designed is not completed, it is easy to see that no additional cantos could have rendered it less perplexed. But still there is a richness in his materials, even where their coherence is loose, and their disposition confused. The clouds of his allegory may seem to spread into shapeless forms, but they are still the clouds of a glowing atmosphere. Though his story grows desultory, the sweetness and grace of his manner still abide by him. He is like a speaker whose tones continue to be pleasing, though he may speak too long; or like a painter who makes us forget the defect of his design by the magic of his colouring. We always rise from perusing him with melody in the mind's ear, and with pictures of romantic beauty impressed on the imagination.

"Succeeding generations have acknowledged the pathos and richness of his strains, and the new contour and enlarged dimensions of grace which he gave to English poetry. He is the poetical father of a Milton and a Thomson. Gray habitually read him when he wished to frame his thoughts for composition, and there are few eminent poets in the language who have not been essentially indebted to him.

> "'Hither, as to their fountain, other stars
> Repair, and in their urns draw golden light.'"[1]

The following testimony from Pope will confirm the remarks just cited:—"After my reading," said he, "a canto of Spenser, two or three days ago, to an old lady, between seventy and eighty, she said that I had been showing her a collection of pictures. She said very right; and I know not how it is, but there is something in Spenser that pleases one as strongly in one's old age as it did in one's youth. I read the 'Faery Queen' when I was about twelve with a vast deal of delight, and I think it gave me as much when I read it over about a year or two ago."[2]

Spenser accounted himself the poetical son of Chaucer; and, to do honour to his parentage, adopted a style and diction belonging to a previous stage of the language.[3] He was, therefore, in his own times, taunted with "affecting the ancients," with his "Chaucerisms," and with his "new grafts of old withered words and exploded expressions." "One might imagine," says Mr. Campbell, "the difference of Spenser's style from that of Shakspere's, whom he so shortly preceded, to indicate that his gothic subject and story made him lean towards words of the elder time. At all events, much of his expression is now become antiquated; though it is beautiful in its antiquity, and like the moss and ivy on some majestic building, covers the fabric of his language with romantic and venerable associations."[4]

VERSIFICATION.—The stanza employed by Spenser in the "Faerie Queene" was borrowed from the Italian; the poet, however, made it his own by the addition of an Alexandrine, or long

---

(1) Campbell. "Specimens," &c., Introduction, p. liv.
(2) "Literary History," &c., vol. ii. p. 334.
(3) In the "Faerie Queene" (book iv. canto 2), Spenser speaks of Chaucer, as

"Don Chaucer, well of English undefyled,
On fame's eternall beadroll worthie to be fyled."

(4) Campbell. "Specimens," &c., Introduction, p. lv.

line, which closes the whole with a majestic cadence. This style of versification—subsequently called the Spenserian—has been, notwithstanding its difficulty, adopted with much success by Thomson, in "The Castle of Indolence"—Beattie, in "The Minstrel"—and Byron, in "Childe Harold."

EXTRACTS FROM THE FAERIE QUEENE.

UNA AND THE RED-CROSS KNIGHT.[1]

A gentle knight[2] was pricking[3] on the plaine,
  Ycladd in mightie armes[4] and silver shielde,
Wherein old dints[5] of deepe woundes did remaine,
  The cruel markes of many a bloody fielde;
  Yet armes till that time did he never wield:
His angry steede did chide his foming bitt,
  As much disdayning to the curbe to yield:
Full iolly[6] knight he seemd, and faire did sitt,
As one for knightly giusts[7] and fierce encounters fitt.

And on his brest a bloodie crosse he bore,
  The deare remembrance of his dying Lord,
For whose sweete sake that glorious badge he wore,
  And dead, as living ever,[8] him adored:
Upon his shield the like was also scored,
  For soveraine hope,[9] which in his helpe he had.
Right faithfull, true he was in deede and word;
  But of his cheere[10] did seeme too solemne sad;[11]
Yet nothing did he dread, but ever was ydrad.[12]

---

(1) "Faerie Queene," book I. canto 1. This extract is the commencement of the poem. (2) *Gentle knight*—the Red-Cross knight, St. George, the tutelary Saint of England, who represents True Holiness. (3) *Pricking*—riding fast, or rather here, spurring his horse, but at the same time checking him to keep the pace of the lady upon her "palfrey slow." (4) *Mightie armes, &c.*—The armour of the Christian, described in Ephes. vi. 13—17, is here intended. (5) *Dints*—marks. (6) *Iolly*—from the French *joli*—handsome. (7) *Giusts*—jousts, or tilting matches. (8) *Dead, as living ever*—i. e. though dead, yet alive for evermore (see Rev. i. 18). (9) *For soveraine, &c.*—On account of the supreme hope, &c. (10) *Cheere*—countenance, appearance. (11) *Sad*—grave—not mournful. Old writers talk of a *sad* dress, *sad* colour, &c. (12) *Ydrad*—dreaded.

Upon a great adventure he was bond,[1]
 That greatest Gloriana[2] to him gave
 (That greatest glorious Queene of Faery lond),
 To winne him worshippe, and her grace to have,
 Which of all earthly things he most did crave:
 And ever, as he rode, his hart did earne[3]
 To prove his püissance[4] in battell brave
 Upon his foe, and his new force to learne[5]
Upon his foe, a dragon[6] horrible and stearne.

A lovely ladie[7] rode him faire beside,
 Upon a lowly asse more white then snow;
 Yet she much whiter; but the same did hide
 Under a vele, that wimpled[8] was full low;
 And over all a blacke stole[9] shee did throw,
 As one that inly mournd; so was she sad,
 And heavie sate upon her palfrey slow;
 Seeméd in heart some hidden care she had;
And by her in a line a milke-white lambe she lad.

So pure and innocent, as that same lambe,
 She was in life and every vertuous lore;
 And by descent from royall lynage[10] came
 Of ancient kinges and queenes, that had of yore
 Their scepters stretcht from east to westerne shore,
 And all the world in their subjection held;
 Till that infernal feend, with foule uprore,
 Forwasted[11] all their land, and them expeld;
Whom to avenge, she had this knight from far compeld.[12]

Behind her farre away a dwarfe did lag,
 That lasie seemd, in being ever last,
 Or wearied with bearing of her bag
 Of needments[13] at his backe. Thus as they past,
 The day with cloudes was suddeine overcast,

---

(1) *Bond*—bound. (2) *Gloriana*—Glory—the "Faery Queene." (3) *Earne*—yearn. (4) *Püissance* (three syllables here)—power. (5) *Learne*—in its old sense—teach, show, manifest. (6) *Dragon*—this is intended to represent Error. (7) *Lovely ladie*—this is Una, or Truth, the representative of the *one* true church. (8) *Wimpled*—plaited or folded over. (9) *Stole*—a long robe or garment. (10) *Lynage*—lineage. (11) *Forwasted*—i. e. forth wasted, thoroughly laid waste. (12) *Compeld*—from the Latin *compellare*, to address—called on. (13) *Needments*—necessaries.

And angry Iove[1] an hideous storme of raine
Did poure into his lemans[2] lap so fast,
That everie wight to shroud[3] it did constrain;
And this faire couple eke to shroud themselves were fain.[4]

Enforst to seeke some covert nigh at hand,
A shadie grove not farr away they spide,
That promist ayde the tempest to withstand;
Whose loftie trees, yclad with sommers pride,
Did spred so broad, that heavens light did hide,
Not perceable[5] with power of any starr;
And all within were pathes and alleies wide,
With footing worne, and leading inward farr:
Faire harbour that them seems; so in they entred ar.

And foorth they passe, with pleasure forward led,
Joying to heare the birdes sweete harmony,
Which therein shrouded from the tempest dred,
Seemed in their song to scorne the cruell sky.
Much can they praise[6] the trees so straight and hy,
The sayling Pine, the Cedar proud and tall,
The vine-propp Elme,[7] the Poplar never dry,
The builder Oake, sole king of forrests all,
The Aspine good for staves, the Cypresse funerall;

The Laurell, meed of mightie conquerours,
And poets sage; the Firre that weepeth still;
The Willow, worne of forlorne paramours,[8]
The Eugh,[9] obedient to the benders will,
The Birch for shafts, the Sallow for the mill,
The Mirrhe sweete-bleeding[10] in the bitter wound,
The warlike[11] Beech, the Ash for nothing ill,
The fruitful Olive, and the Platane[12] round,
The carver Holme,[13] the Maple seldom inward sound.

(1) *Jove*—the air or atmosphere is frequently so named in the Classics. (2) *Leman*—from the Anglo-Saxon *leof*, loved, and *man*, one—a loved one, sweetheart. (3) *Shroud*—shelter. (4) *Fain*—glad. (5) *Not perceable, &c.*—"It was an ancient superstition," says Warton, "that stars had a malign influence on trees. Hence Milton, in 'Arcades:'—

'Under the shady roof
Of branching elm *star-proof.*'"

(6) *Much can they praise*—i. e. much they praise. (7) *Vine-propp elme*—i. e. the elm that props up and supports the vine. (8) *Forlorne paramours*—forsaken lovers. (9) *Eugh*—yew. (10) *Sweete-bleeding, &c.*—In allusion to the healing virtues of myrrh. (11) *Warlike beech*—war-chariots used to be made of beech. (12) *Platane*—the plane-tree. (13) *Holme*—the holm oak.

Led with delight, they thus beguile the way,
  Untill the blustring storme is overblowne;
  When, weening[1] to returne, whence they did stray,
  They cannot find that path, which first was showne,
  But wander too and fro in waies unknowne,
  Furthest from end then, when they neerest weene,
  That makes them doubt their wits be not their own;
  So many pathes, so many turnings seene,
That which of them to take in diverse doubt they been.

THE HOUSE OF SLEEP.[2]

He,[3] making speedy way through spersed[4] ayre,
  And through the world of waters wide and deepe,
  To Morpheus house[5] doth hastily repaire;
  Amid the bowels of the earthe full steepe
  And low, where dawning day doth never peepe,
  His dwelling is; there Tethys[6] his wet bed
  Doth ever wash, and Cynthia still doth steepe
  In silver deaw his ever-drouping hed,
Whiles sad Night over him her mantle black doth spred;

Whose double gates he findeth locked fast;
  The one faire[7] framed of burnisht yvory,
  The other all with silver overcast;
  And watchful dogges before them farre doe lye,
  Watching to banish Care, their enimy,
  Who oft is wont to trouble gentle Sleepe.
  By them the sprite doth passe in quietly,
  And unto Morpheus comes, whom drownéd deepe
In drowsie fit he findes; of nothing he takes keepe.

---

(1) *Weening*—imagining, thinking.
(2) "Faerie Queene," book i. canto 1. "What can be more solitary, more shut up in itself, than his description of the House of Sleep? It is as if 'the honey-dew of slumber' had settled on his pen in writing these lines."—*Hazlitt*.
(3) *He*—a sprite sent on a mission by Archimago, or Fraud, the enchanter.
(4) *Spersed*—dispersed. (5) *Morpheus house*—in the classical writers Somnus, and not Morpheus, is the god of Sleep, the latter being one of the children of Somnus. (6) *Tethys*—the mythological wife of the ocean; here put for the ocean itself. (7) *The one faire, &c.*—Homer and Virgil represent the gates of Sleep's palace as made of ivory and horn respectively; the former for false, and the latter for true, dreams.

And more to lull him in his slumber soft,
　A trickling streame from high rock tumbling downe,
　And ever drizling raine upon the loft,
　Mixt with a murmuring winde, much like the sowne[1]
　Of swarming bees, did cast him in a swowne.[2]
　No other noyse, nor peoples troublous cryes,
　As still are wont to annoy the walled towne,
　Might there be heard: but careless Quiet lyes
Wrapt in eternall silence, farre from enimyes.

UNA AND THE LION.[3]

One day, nigh wearie of the yrkesome way,
　From her unhastie beast she did alight;
　And on the grasse her dainty limbs did lay
　In secrete shadow, far from all men's sight;
　From her fayre head her fillet she undight,[4]
　And layd her stole aside: her angels face,
　As the great eye of heaven, shyned bright,
　And made a sunshine[5] in the shady place:
Did never mortal eye behold such heavenly grace.

It fortunéd, out of the thickest wood
　A ramping lyon rushéd suddeinly,
　Hunting full greedy after salvage[6] blood;
　Soone as the royall virgin he did spy,
　With gaping mouth at her ran[7] greedily,
　To have attonce[8] devourd her tender corse:
　But to the pray when as he drew more ny,
　His bloody rage aswagéd, with remorse,
And, with the sight amazed, forgat his furious forse.

---

(1) *Sowne*—sound.　　　　　(2) *Swowne*—swoon.

(3) "Faerie Queene," book i., canto 3. "What a picture!" says Professor Wilson, in reference to this passage. "We have seen it painted, and beautifully too, by colours on canvas; but never nearly so beautiful as here in the light of words."—*Blackwood's Magazine*, Nov. 1834.

(4) *Undight*—loosened, untied.

(5) *And made a sunshine, &c.*—"A line," says the writer just quoted, "of itself sufficient to make the whole world in love with Truth."

(6) *Salvage*—savage.

(7) *Ran*—i. e. he ran; the ellipsis of the personal pronoun is very common in the old writers. See another instance in the last line of this stanza.

(8) *Attonce*—at once.

Instead thereof he kist her weary feet,
   And lickt her lilly hands with fawning tong;
   As he her wronged innocence did weet.[1]
O how can beautie maister the most strong,
And simple truth subdue avenging wrong!
Whose yielded pride and proud submissiòn,
   Still dreading death, when she had markéd loug,
   Her heart gan melt in great compassiòn;
And drizling teares did shed for pure affectiòn.

"The lyon, lord of everie beast in field,"
   Quoth she, "his princely puissance doth abate,
   And mightie proud to humble weake does yield,
Forgetfull of the hungry rage, which late
Him prickt, in pittie of my sad estate:—
But he, my lyon, and my noble lord,[2]
   How does he find in cruell hart to hate
   Her, that him loved, and ever most adord
As the god of my life? why hath he me abhord?"

Redounding[3] tears did choke th' end of her plaint,
   Which softly ecchoed from the neighbour wood;
   And, sad to see her sorrowful constraint,
The kingly beast upon her gazing stood;
With pittie calmd, downe fell his angry mood.
At last, in close hart shutting up her payne,
   Arose the virgin borne of heavenly brood,
   And to her snowy palfrey[4] got agayne,
To seeke her strayéd champion if she might attayne.

The lyon would not leave her desolate,
   But with her went along, as a strong gard
   Of her chast person, and a faythfull mate
Of her sad troubles and misfortunes hard:
Still, when she slept, he kept both watch and ward;
And when she wakt, he wayted diligent,
   With humble service to her will prepard;
   From her fayre eyes he took commandément,
And ever by her lookes conceivéd her intent.

(1) *Weet*—from the Anglo-Saxon *wit-an*, to know—recognise. (2) *My noble lord*—the Red-Cross Knight, from whom Una had been separated by Archimago's devices. (3) *Redounding*—from the Latin *redundare*, to flow over—abounding. (4) *Palfrey*—from the French *par le frein*, by the bridle—a lady's horse, led by the squire. The word here refers to the ass before named.

MAN THE CARE OF ANGELS.[1]

And is there care in heaven? And is there love
 In heavenly spirits to these creatures base,
 That may compassion of their evils move?
 There is:—else much more wretched were the case
 Of men then[2] beasts: but O the exceeding grace
 Of Highest God! that loves his creatures so,
 And all his workes with mercy doth embrace,
 That blessed angels he sends to and fro,
To serve to[3] wicked man, to serve his wicked foe!

How oft do they their silver bowers leave,
 To come to succour us that succour want!
 How oft do they with golden pinions cleave
 The flitting skyes,[4] like flying pursuivant,[5]
 Against fowle feendes to ayd us militant![6]
 They for us fight, they watch, and dewly ward,
 And their bright squadrons round about us plant;
 And all for love, and nothing for reward;
O why should hevenly God to men have such regard!

THE BOWER OF BLISS.[7]

There the most daintie paradise on ground[8]
 Itselfe doth offer to his[9] sober eye,
 In which all pleasures plenteously abownd,
 And none does others happinesse envye;
 The painted flowers; the trees upshooting hye;
 The dales for shade; the hilles for breathing space;
 The trembling groves; the christall running by;
 And, that which all faire works doth most aggrace,[10]
The art,[11] which all that wrought, appeared in no place.

(1) "Faerie Queene," book ii. canto 8. "These," says Dr. Jortin, "are fine lines, and would not suffer by being compared with anything that Milton has said upon this subject."

(2) *Then*—than. (3) *Serve to*—this is the old syntax. (4) *Flitting skyes*—the floating clouds (see note 4, p. 5). (5) *Pursuivant*—from the French *poursuivre*, to follow up—a state messenger. (6) *Militant*—from the Latin *militare*, to serve as a soldier—fighting, engaged in warfare.

(7) "Faerie Queene," book ii. canto 12. (8) *On ground*—on earth. (9) *His*—i. e. Sir Guyon, or Temperance. (10) *Aggrace*—favour, enhance. (11) *The art, &c.*—The old maxim—*artis est celare artem*, the perfection of art consists in concealing it, seems to be here hinted at.

One would have thought (so cunningly the rude
  And scornéd parts were mingled with the fine,)
That Nature had for wantonesse ensude[1]
Art, and that Art at Nature did repine;
So striving each the other to undermine,
Each did the others worke more beautify;
So differing both in wills, agreed in fine:[2]
So all agreed, through sweete diversity,
This gardin to adorne with all variety.

And in the midst of all a fountaine stood,
  Of richest substance that on earth might bee,
So pure and shiny, that the silver flood
Through every channell running one might see;
Most goodly it with curious ymageree
Was overwrought, and shapes of naked boys,
Of which some seemed with lively iollitee
To fly about, playing their wanton toyes,
Whylest others did themselves embay[3] in liquid ioyes.

And over all, of purest gold, was spred
  A trayle of yvie in his native hew;
For the rich metall was so colouréd,
That wight, who did not well avised it vew,
Would surely deeme it to bee yvie trew:
Low his lascivious[4] armes adown did creepe,
That themselves dipping in the silver dew,
Their fleecy flowres they fearefully did steepe,
Which drops of christall seemed for wantones to weep.

Infinit streames continually did well
  Out of this fountain, sweete and faire to see,
The which into an ample laver fell,
And shortly grew to so great quantitie
That like a little lake it seemd to bee;
Whose depth exceeded not three cubits hight,
That through the waves one might the bottom see,
All pavd beneath with jaspar shining bright,
That seemd the fountaine in that sea did sayle upright.

---

(1) *Ensude*—followed.   (2) *Fine*—end.   (3) *Embay*—bathe.   (4) *Lascivious*—loose, hanging loose.

Eftsoones[1] they heard a most melodious sound
  Of all that mote delight a daintie ear,
  Such as attonce might not on living ground,
  Save in this paradise, be heard elsewhere:
  Right hard it was for wight which did it heare
  To read[2] what manner musicke that mote bee:
  For all that pleasing is to living eare,
  Was there consorted in one harmonee;
Birdes, voices, instruments, windes, waters, all agree:

The ioyous birdes, shrouded in chearefull shade,
  Their notes unto the voice attempred sweet;
  The angelical soft trembling voyces made
  To the instruments divine respondence meet;
  The silver-sounding instruments did meet
  With the base[3] murmure of the waters fall:
  The waters fall, with difference discreet,
  Now soft, now loud, unto the wind did call:
The gentle warbling wind low answeréd to all.

MASQUE OF THE SEASONS.[4]

So forth issèwed the Seasons of the yeare:
  First, lusty[5] Spring, all dight in leaves of flowres
  That freshly budded and new bloosmes did beare,
  In which a thousand birds had built their bowers
  That sweetly sung to call forth paramours;
  And in his hand a iavelin he did beare,
  And on his head (as fit for warlike stoures[6])
  A guilt engraven morion[7] he did weare;
That as some did him love, so others did him feare.

Then came the iolly Sommer, being dight
  In a thin silken cassock coloured greene,
  That was unlyned all, to be more light;
  And on his head a girlond well beseene[8]
  He wore, from which as he had chauffèd[9] been
  The sweat did drop; and in his hand he bore
  A bowe and shaftes, as he in forrest greene

---

(1) *Eftsoones*—soon efter or after, presently. (2) *Read*—guess. (3) *Base*—low. (4) " Faerie Queene," canto 7 (of " Mutabilitie "). (5) *Lusty*—" Beautiful, lovely."—*Todd*. (6) *Stoures*—assaults, battles. (7) *Morion*—an ancient steel cap or helmet. (8) *Well beseene*—beautiful to be seen. (9) *Chauffed*—heated.

Had hunted late the libbard[1] or the bore,
And nowe would bathe his limbes, with labor heated sore.

Then came the Autumne, all in yellow clad,
  As though he ioyéd in his plenteous store,
  Laden with fruits that made him laugh, full glad
  That he had banisht hunger, which to-fore[2]
  Had by the belly oft him pinchéd sore;
  Upon his head a wreath, that was enrold[3]
  With ears of corne of every sort, he bore;
  And in his hand a sickle he did holde,
To reape the ripened fruits the which the earth had yold.[4]

Lastly came Winter, cloathed all in frize,
  Chattering his teeth for cold that did him chill;
  Whilst on his hoary beard his breath did freese,
  And the dull drops, that from his purpled bill
  As from a limbeck[5] did adown distill:
  In his right hand a tippéd staffe he held,
  With which his feeble steps he stayéd still;
  For he was faint with cold and week with eld;[6]
That scarse his looséd limbes he hable was to weld.[7]

THE BUTTERFLY.[8]

Thus the fresh Clarion,[9] being readie dight,
  Unto his iourney did himselfe addresse,
And with good speed began to take his flight;
  Over the fields, in his frank lustinesse,
  And all the champaine[10] o're he soared light;
  And all the country wide he did possesse,
Feeding upon their pleasures bounteouslie,
That none gainsaid, nor none did him envie.

The woods, the rivers, and the meadowes greene,
  With his aire-cutting wings he measured wide;
Ne did he leave the mountaines bare unseene,
  Nor the rank grassie fennes delights untride:

---

(1) *Libbard*—the leopard. (2) *To-fore*—before this. (3) *Enrold*—surrounded.
(4) *Yold*—yielded. (5) *Limbeck*—an alembic or still. (6) *Eld*—old age.
(7) *Weld*—wield, govern.
(8) "Muiopotmos; or, the Fate of the Butterflie," vv. 145—232. (9) *Clarion*—the name of the butterfly. (10) *Champaine*—from the French *champagne*, Italian *campagna*, Latin *campanus*, and all from *campus*, a plain—open country.

But none of these, however sweet they beene,
  Mote please his fancie, nor him cause to abide:
His choicefull sense with every change doth flit;
No common things may please a wavering wit.

To the gay gardins his unstaid desire
  Him wholly caried, to refresh his sprights:
There, lavish Nature, in her best attire,
  Powres forth sweete odors and alluring sights;
And Arte, with her contending, doth aspire
  To excell the naturall with made delights:
And all that faire or pleasant may be found,
In riotous excesse doth there abound.

There he arriving, round about doth flie
  From bed to bed, from one to other border;
And takes survey, with curious busie eye,
  Of every flowre and herbe there set in order;
Now this, now that, he tasteth tenderly,
  Yet none of them he rudely doth disorder,
Nor with his feete their silken leaves deface,
But pastures on the pleasures of each place.

And evermore, with most varietie
  And change of sweetness (for all change is sweete),
He casts[1] his glutton sense to satisfy;
  Now sucking of the sap of herbe most meet,
Or of the deaw which yet on them does lie,
  Now in the same bathing his tender feete:
And then he pearcheth on some braunch thereby,[2]
To weather him,[3] and his moyst wings to dry.

And then again he turneth to his play,
  To spoyle[4] the pleasures of that Paradise;
The wholesome Saulge,[5] and Lavender still gray,
  Ranke-smelling Rue, and Cummin good for eyes,
The Roses raigning in the pride of May,
  Sharp Isope[6] good for green[7] wounds remedies,
Faire Marigoldes, and bees-alluring Thime,
Sweet Marjoram and Daysies decking prime;

---

(1) *He casts*—he casts in *his mind*, contrives how.   (2) *Thereby*—Close by.
(3) *To weather him*—to expose himself to the air.   (4) *Spoyle*—make a spoil of.
(5) *Saulge*—from the Latin *salvere*, to be in good health—the herb sage, so called from its salutary properties.   (6) *Isope*—hyssop.   (7) *Green*—fresh.

Coole Violets, and Orpine growing still,
    Embathéd Balme, and chearfull Galingale,
Fresh Costmarie, and breathfull Camomill,
    Dull Poppy, and drink-quickning Setuale,
Veyne-healing Verven, and hed-purging Dill,
    Sound Savorie, and Bazil hartie-hale,
Fat Colworts, and comforting Perseline,[1]
Cold Lettuce, and refreshing Rosmarine.

And what so else of vertue good or ill
    Grewe in this gardin, fetcht from farre away,
Of every one he takes and tastes at will,
    And on their pleasures greedily doth pray,
Then when he had both plaid, and fed his fill,
    In the warme sunne he did himselfe embay,[2]
And there him rests in riotous suffisaunce,
Of all his gladfulnes, and kingly ioyaunce.[3]

What more felicitie can fall to creature
    Than to enjoy delight with libertie,
And to be lord of all the works of nature,
    To raigne in the air from the earth to highest skie,
To feed on flowres and weeds of glorious feature,
    To take whatever thing doth please the eie?
Who rests not pleaséd with such happines,
Wel worthy he to taste of wretchednes.

But what on earth can long abide in state?
    Or who can him assure of happy day?
Sith morning faire may bring fowle evening late,
    And least mishap the most blisse alter may!
For thousand perills lie in close awaite
    About us daylie, to worke our decay;
That none except a God, or God him guide,
May them avoyde, or remedie provide.

And whatso heavens in their secret doome
    Ordained have, how can fraile fleshly wight
Forecast,[4] but it must needs to issue come?
    The sea, the aire, the fire, the day, the night,

---

(1) *Perseline*—parsley.   (2) *Embay*—bathe, delight.   (3) *Ioyaunce*—the word must be pronounced here *io-y-aunce* for the sake of the metre.   (4) *Forecast*—foresee, provide against.

And the armies of their creatures all and some
    Do serve to them, and with impórtune might
Warre against us the vassals of their will.
Who then can save what they dispose to spill?

THE RUINS OF ROME.[1]

Thou stranger! which for Rome in Rome here seekest,
And nought of Rome in Rome perceivst at all,
These same olde walls, olde arches which thou seest,
Olde palaces, is that which Rome men call.
Beholde what wreake, what ruine, and what wast,
And how that She, which with her mightie powre
Tamed all the world, hath tamed herselfe at last;—
The pray of Time, which all things doth devowre!
Rome now of Rome is the onely funeral,
And onely Rome of Rome hath victorie;
Ne ought save Tyber, hastening to his fall,
Remains of all: O worlds inconstancie!
That which is firme doth flit[2] and fall away,
And that is flitting doth abide and stay.

Thou that at Rome astonisht doth behold
The antique pride which menacéd the skie,
These haughtie heaps, these palaces of olde,
These wals, these arcks, these baths, these temples hie!
Judge, by these ample ruines vew,[3] the rest,
The which injurious Time hath quite outworne,
Since of all workmen held in reckning best;
Yet these olde fragments are for paternes borne:
Then also mark how Rome, from day to day,
Repayring her decayéd fashiòn,
Renewes herselfe with buildings rich and gay,
That one would judge[4] that the Romaìne dæmòn
Doth yet himselfe with fatal hand enforce,
Againe on foot to reare her pouldred[5] corse.

---

(1) From the poem of this name, stanzas 4, 27—29.   (2) *Flit*—to fly away rapidly.   (3) *These ample ruines vew*—the sight of these ample ruins.   (4) *One would judge, &c.*—i. e. one would imagine that the genius or spirit of Rome were striving to reanimate the mouldering body.   (5) *Pouldred*—powdered, mouldering.

He that hath seene a great oke drie and dead,
Yet clad with reliques of some trophees olde,
Lifting to heaven her aged hoarie head,
Whose foot on ground hath left but feeble holde,
But halfe disboweld lies above the ground,
Shewing her wreathéd rootes and naked armes,
And on her trunk, all rotten and unsound,
Onely supports herself for meate of wormes;
And, though she owe her fall[1] to the first winde,
Yet of the dèvout people is adored,
And manie yong plants spring out of her rinde:—
Who such an oke hath seene, let him record
That such this cities honour was of yore,
And mongst all cities florishéd much more.[2]

All that which Ægypt whilome[3] did devise,
All that which Greece, their temples to embrave,[4]
After the Ionick, Atticke, Doricke guise,
Or Corinth, skild in curious works to grave;
All that Lysippus practique[5] art could forme,
Apelles wit,[6] or Phidias his skill;
Was wont this auncient citie to adorne,
And the heaven itselfe with her wide wonders fill:
All that which Athens ever brought forth wise,
All that which Afrike ever brought forth strange,
All that which Asia ever had of prise,[7]
Was here to see. O mervelous great change!
Rome, living, was the worlds sole ornament,
And dead, is now the worlds sole moniment.

(1) *Owe her fall*—*i. e.* her fall is, as it were, due—she is doomed to fall by the first wind. (2) *Much more*—*i. e.* than the oak does amongst trees. (3) *Whilome* —formerly. "In the antiquated word *whilom*, at times we have a remnant of the old dative in *m*. The sense of the word is adverbial; its form, however, is that of a dative case."—*Latham*. (4) *Embrave*—make brave or fine, adorn. (5) *Practique*—skilful, cunning. (6) *Wit*—ingenuity or genius. (7) *Prise*—praise, value.

SHAKSPERE.

PRINCIPAL EVENTS OF HIS LIFE.—William Shakspere—called by Coleridge the "myriad-minded man"—was born in 1564, at Stratford-upon-Avon, in Warwickshire. So scanty is our information respecting the events of his life, that we may without much exaggeration say in the language of one of his critics:[1] "All that is known with any degree of certainty concerning Shakspere is, that he was born at Stratford-upon-Avon; married and had children there; went to London, where he commenced actor, and wrote poems and plays; returned to Stratford, made his will, died, and was buried." The few additional items which modern research has furnished, give little further aid in illustrating Shakspere's character, either as a man or a poet.[2] The important events of his life were, in truth, the publications from time to time of those famous works with which his name has become inseparably connected. These, however, rather exhibit to us the universal range and capabilities, than the characteristic features of his mind, so that our attention is confined rather to what he did, than what he was; as we enjoy the genial light of the sun by feeling its reflection from objects around us, rather than by gazing at the luminary itself. He died in 1616, eight years after the birth of Milton. Shakspere's was an era of distinguished men—the age of Spenser, Sidney, Raleigh, Ben Jonson, and Beaumont and Fletcher in England; of Tasso in Italy, of Cervantes in Spain, and of Camoens in Portugal.

PRINCIPAL WORKS.—Shakspere wrote a few miscellaneous poems and many dramatical works, of which the "Midsummer Night's Dream," "Romeo and Juliet," the "Merchant of Venice," "Lear," "Timon of Athens," "Othello," the "Tempest," "Macbeth," and "Hamlet," are the most admired.

CHARACTERISTIC SPIRIT AND STYLE.—"He [Shakspere] was the man, who of all modern and perhaps ancient poets, had the largest and most comprehensive soul. All the images of nature were still present to him, and he drew them not laboriously but

---

[1] Steevens.

[2] "How much," says Mr. Hallam ("Edinburgh Review," 1808), "has been written upon *Shakspeare* and *Shakespere*—what long pedigrees of the Halls, Harts, and Hathaways—while the reader, amidst the profusion of learning, searches in vain for a vestige of the manners and opinions of him, in whom alone he is interested! *Pars minima est ipse poeta sui.*"

luckily; when he describes anything, you more than see it, you feel it too. Those who accuse him to have wanted learning, give him the greater commendation; he was naturally learned; he needed not the spectacles of books to read nature; he looked inwards, and found her there. I cannot say he is everywhere alike: were he so, I should do him injury to compare him with the greatest of mankind; he is many times flat and insipid; his comic wit degenerating into clenches, his serious swelling into bombast. But he is always great when great occasion is presented to him. No man can say he ever had a fit subject for his wit, and did not then raise himself as high above the rest of poets—

'Quantum lenta solent inter viburna cupressi.'"[1]

"Criticism goes back for names worthy of being put into competition with his, to the first great masters of dramatic invention; and even in the points of dissimilarity between them and him, discovers some of the highest indications of his genius. Compared with the classical composers of antiquity, he is to our conceptions nearer the character of a universal poet; more acquainted with man in the real world, and more terrific and bewitching in the præternatural. He expanded the magic circle of the drama beyond the limits that belonged to it in antiquity; made it embrace more time and locality; filled it with larger business and action, with vicissitudes of gay and serious emotion which classical taste had kept divided; with characters which developed humanity in stronger lights and subtler movements; and with a language more widely, more playfully diversified by fancy and passion, than was ever spoken on any stage. Like nature herself, he presents alternations of the gay and the tragic: and his mutability, like the suspense and precariousness of real existence, often deepens the force of our impression."[2]

"When Aristotle defined it to be the province of Tragedy to move pity and terror, he did not intend that the excitement of these emotions was its ultimate use. These are the instruments it employs to impress its moral. It woos and urges thus our attention and sympathy. Where, then, can such a Tragic Bard be found as this? Where can we trace the same power to soften and to alarm the heart? Where are the same strokes of pathos and images of horror? Never was simplicity more sweet, never was pomp more magnificent. Beauty unfolds before us, modest as

---

(1) Dryden. "Essay on Dramatic Poesy."
(2) Campbell. "Specimens," &c., Introduction, p. lxi.

the violet, fair as the lily, lovely as the rose; greatness rises up, fearful as the incantation, daring as the battle, terrible as the storm. He is everything that he describes; wand could not wave more awfully from magician's hand, crook could not recline more easily on shepherd's arm, diadem could not rest more gracefully around monarch's brow, wing could not flap more buoyantly in spirit's flight. The mask is no portion of his tragic paraphernalia; and he but strikes, for his most touching and most stirring chords, the strings of the human heart."[1]

"He has a magic power over words: they come winged at his bidding; and seem to know their places. They are struck out at a heat, on the spur of the occasion, and have all the truth and vividness which arise from an actual impression of the objects. His epithets and single phrases are like sparkles thrown off from an imagination fired by the whirling rapidity of its own motion. His language is hieroglyphical. It translates thoughts into visible images. It abounds in sudden transitions and illiptical expressions. This is the source of his mixed metaphors, which are only abbreviated forms of speech. These, however, give no pain from long custom, they have, in fact, become idioms in the language. They are the building, and not the scaffolding to thought. We take the meaning and effect of a well-known passage entire, and no more stop to scan and spell out the particular words and phrases than the syllables of which they are composed."[2]

VERSIFICATION.—"His versification is no less powerful, sweet, and varied. It has every occasional excellence of sullen intricacy, crabbed and perplexed, or of the smoothest and loftiest expansion—from the ease and familiarity of measured conversation to the lyrical sounds

> . . . . . . 'Of ditties highly penned,
> Sung by a fair queen in a bower of beauty,
> With ravishing division to her lute.'"[3]

"It is the only blank verse in the language, except Milton's, that for itself is readable. It is not stately and uniformly swelling like his, but varied and broken by the inequalities of the ground it has to pass over in its uncertain course."[4]

(1) Dr. Hamilton. "Nugæ Literariæ," p. 233.
(2) Hazlitt. "Lectures," &c., p. 107.
(3) Id.
(4) Id., p. 108.

EXTRACTS FROM VARIOUS PLAYS.

WOLSEY'S FALL.[1]

FAREWELL, a long farewell, to all my greatness!
This is the state of man: To-day he puts forth
The tender leaves of hope, to-morrow blossoms,
And bears his blushing honours thick upon him;
The third day comes a frost, a killing frost,
And—when he thinks, good easy man, full surely
His greatness is a-ripening—nips his root,
And then he falls—as I do. I have ventured,
Like little wanton boys that swim on bladders,
This many summers in a sea of glory;
But far beyond my depth: my high-blown[2] pride
At length broke under me; and now has left me,
Weary, and old with service, to the mercy
Of a rude stream,[3] that must for ever hide me.
Vain pomp and glory of this world, I hate ye!
I feel my heart new opened.[4] Oh, how wretched
Is that poor man that hangs on princes' favours!
There is, betwixt that smile we would aspire to,
That sweet aspèct of princes, and their ruin,
More pangs and fears than wars or women have;
And, when he falls, he falls like Lucifer,
Never to hope again.

Cromwell, I did not think to shed a tear
In all my miseries; but thou hast forced me,
Out of thy honest truth, to play the woman.
Let's dry our eyes; and thus far hear me, Cromwell:
And—when I am forgotten, as I shall be,
And sleep in dull cold marble, where no mention
Of me more must be heard of—say, I taught thee;
Say, Wolsey—that once trod the ways of glory,
And sounded all the depths and shoals of honour—

---

(1) "Henry VIII.," Act iii., scene 2. Wolsey is here addressing Cromwell, Earl of Essex.
(2) *High-blown*—puffed up and swollen like a bladder.
(3) *Rude stream*—i. e. that which was a sea of glory has suddenly become a boisterous and hostile ocean of billows—that which before held me up buoyantly floating on its surface, now overwhelms and hides me.
(4) *New opened*—i. e. now I see things as they are.

Found thee a way, out of his wreck, to rise in;
A sure and safe one, though thy master missed it.
Mark but my fall, and that that ruined me.
Cromwell, I charge thee, fling away ambition;
By that sin fell the angels; how can man, then,
The image of his Maker, hope to win by't?
Love thyself last; cherish those hearts that hate thee;
Corruption wins not more than honesty.[1]
Still in thy right hand carry gentle peace,
To silence envious tongues. Be just, and fear not;
Let all the ends thou aim'st at be thy country's,
Thy God's, and truth's; then, if thou fall'st, O Cromwell,
Thou fall'st a blessed martyr! Serve the king,
And—pr'ythee, lead me in:——
There, take an inventory of all I have,
To the last penny; 'tis the king's: my robe,
And my integrity to Heaven, is all
I dare now call my own. O Cromwell, Cromwell,
Had I but served my God with half the zeal
I served my king, He would not in mine age
Have left me naked to mine enemies!

WOLSEY'S DEATH.[2]

At last, with easy roads,[3] he came to Leicester,
Lodged in the abbey; where the reverend abbot,
With all his convent, honourably received him;
To whom he gave these words: "O FATHER ABBOT,
AN OLD MAN, BROKEN WITH THE STORMS OF STATE,
IS COME TO LAY HIS WEARY BONES AMONG YE;
GIVE HIM A LITTLE EARTH FOR CHARITY!"
So went to bed: where eagerly his sickness
Pursued him still; and, three nights after this,
About the hour of eight (which he himself
Foretold should be his last) full of repentance,
Continual meditations, tears, and sorrows,
He gave his honours to the world again,
His blessed part to Heaven, and slept in peace.

---

(1) *Honesty*—from the Latin *honestas*, honour, virtue—uprightness, integrity.
(2) "Henry VIII.," Act iv., scene 2.
(3) *Roads*—as we now say, journeys.

WOLSEY'S CHARACTER.[1]

The dark side.

He was a man
Of an unbounded stomach,[2] ever ranking
Himself with princes; one that by suggestion[3]
Tied all the kingdom: simony[4] was fair play;
His own opinion was his law; i' th' presence[5]
He would say untruths; and be ever double,
Both in his words and meaning. He was never,
But where he meant to ruin, pitiful:
His promises were, as he then was, mighty;
But his performance, as he is now, nothing.
Of his own body he was ill, and gave
The clergy ill example.

The bright side.

This Cardinal,
Though from an humble stock, undoubtedly
Was fashioned to much honour from his cradle.
He was a scholar, and a ripe and good one;
Exceeding wise, fair spoken, and persuading;
Lofty and sour to them that loved him not,
But, to those men that sought him, sweet as summer.
And though he were unsatisfied in getting,
(Which was a sin,) yet in bestowing, madam,
He was most princely: ever witness for him
Those twins of learning that he raised in you,
Ipswich and Oxford![6] one which fell with him,
Unwilling to out-live the good that did[7] it;
The other, though unfinished, yet so famous,

---

(1) "Henry VIII.," Act iv., scene 2. Queen Katharine describes the evil, and Griffith, her gentleman-usher, the good, of Wolsey's character.

(2) *Stomach*—in the old sense—arrogance, haughtiness.

(3) *By suggestion, &c.*—By secret influence ruled all the kingdom. Some take *tied* to mean *tithed*.

(4) *Simony*—the buying or selling of church preferment; so called from Simon Magus. See Acts viii. 20.

(5) *I' th' presence*—from the Latin *in præsentia*, at the present time—to suit his immediate purpose; or perhaps it means, in the king's presence.

(6) *Ipswich and Oxford*—Wolsey founded a college, which had a very brief existence, in his native town of Ipswich, as well as the noble college of Cardinal's, now called Christ Church, Oxford.

(7) *That did it*—that made or founded it.

So excellent in art, and still so rising,
That Christendom shall ever speak his virtue.
His overthrow heaped happiness upon him;
For then, and not till then, he felt himself,[1]
And found the blessedness of being, little;
And, to add greater honours to his age
Than man could give him, he died fearing God.

BEES.[2]

So work the honey bees;
Creatures that, by a rule in nature, teach
The act of order to a peopled kingdom.
They have a king,[3] and officers of sorts;
Where some, like magistrates, correct at home;
Others, like merchants, venture trade abroad;
Others, like soldiers, arméd in their stings,
Make boot upon[4] the summer's velvet buds;
Which pillage they with merry march bring home,
To the tent-royal of their emperor;
Who, busied in his majesty, surveys
The singing masons building roofs of gold;
The civil citizens kneading up the honey;
The poor mechanic porters crowding in
Their heavy burdens at his narrow gate;
The sad-eyed justice, with his surly hum,
Delivering o'er to executors pale
The lazy yawning drone.

LIFE AND DEATH.[5]

To be, or not to be, that is the question:—
Whether 'tis nobler in the mind, to suffer
The slings and arrows of outrageous fortune,
Or to take arms against a sea of troubles,[6]

---

(1) *He felt himself*—i. e. he felt himself little, and found the blessedness of being so.   (2) "Henry V.," Act i., scene 2.

(3) *King*—king seems here used in the general sense of sovereign—the reference is of course to the queen bee.

(4) *Make boot upon*—despoil, feed on.   (5) "Hamlet," Act iii., scene 1.

(6) *Sea of troubles*—Pope proposed to alter this into "a *siege* of troubles," upon which Mr. Knight, in his pictorial edition, remarks, "Surely the metaphor of the *sea*, to denote an overwhelming flood of troubles, is highly beautiful." This is unquestionable. The difficulty, however, lies in the expression, "to *take arms* against a sea," which, strictly speaking, presents an incongruous image. If we consider the words "a sea" as unemphatic, and merely used for "a host" or great number, the whole will be harmonized.

And, by opposing, end them? To die—to sleep—
No more;[1]—and, by a sleep, to say we end
The heart-ache, and the thousand natural shocks
That flesh is heir to!—'tis a consummation
Devoutly to be wished. To die—to sleep—
To sleep!—perchance to dream!—ay, there's the rub;
For in that sleep of death what dreams may come,
When we have shuffled off this mortal coil,[2]
Must give us pause:—there's the respect
That makes calamity of so long life:
For who would bear the whips and scorns of time,
The oppressor's wrong, the proud man's contumely,
The pangs of despised love, the law's delay,
The insolence of office, and the spurns
That patient merit of the unworthy takes,
When he himself might his quietus[3] make
With a bare bodkin?[4] Who would fardels[5] bear,
To grunt[6] and sweat under a weary life,
But that the dread of something after death—
The undiscovered country from whose bourn
No traveller returns—puzzles the will,
And makes us rather bear those ills we have,
Than fly to others that we know not of?
Thus conscience does make cowards of us all;
And thus the native hue of resolution
Is sicklied o'er with the pale cast of thought;
And enterprises of great pith and moment,
With this regard,[7] their currents turn awry,
And lose the name of action.

(1) *No more—i. e.* to die is no **more than to sleep**; this was Hamlet's first notion, which he afterwards corrects.

(2) *Coil*—rope wound into **a ring**, hence, perhaps, from the noise made in coiling a rope—stir, murmur, **tumult.** "To shuffle off this mortal coil" is to get free from the entanglements and perplexities of life, or, in a secondary **sense, from** its busy stir.

(3) *Quietus*—**a law** term—final discharge, complete acquittance.

(4) *Bodkin*—a small sword.

(5) *Fardels*—from the French *fardeau*, a parcel—burdens.

(6) *Grunt*—lament loudly. This, and not *groan*, is the true reading.

(7) *With this regard—i. e.* **from** this view of the object—in consequence of the check which conscience gives.

DOVER CLIFFS.[1]

How fearful
And dizzy 'tis to cast one eyes so low!
The crows, and choughs, that wing the midway air,
Show scarce so gross as beetles: half-way down
Hangs one that gathers samphire[2]—dreadful trade!
Methinks he seems no bigger than his head:
The fishermen, that walk upon the beach,
Appear like mice; and yon tall anchoring bark,
Diminished to her cock;[3] her cock, a buoy,
Almost too small for sight: the murmuring surge,
That on the unnumbered idle pebbles chafes,
Cannot be heard so high:—I'll look no more,
Lest my brain turn, and the deficient[4] sight
Topple down headlong.

ANTONY'S FUNERAL ORATION OVER CÆSAR'S BODY.[5]

Friends, Romans, Countrymen, lend me your ears!
I come to bury Cæsar, not to praise him.
The evil that men do lives after them;
The good is oft interred with their bones;
So let it be with Cæsar! Noble Brutus
Hath told you Cæsar was ambitious;
If it were so, it was a grievous fault,
And grievously hath Cæsar answered it.

(1) "King Lear," Act iv., scene 6.
These lines are generally considered as an actual description, but a reference to the connection in which they occur will show that, though suggested by the scenery of the Dover Cliffs, they only represent an imaginary picture. This consideration may serve to account for the discrepancy which is usually felt between the actual scene and this description.
(2) *Samphire*—a plant used for pickling.
(3) *Cock*—a small man-of-war's boat.
(4) *And the deficient, &c.*—i. e. and I, my sight failing me, topple down headlong.
(5) "Julius Cæsar," Act iii., scene 3.
This speech is a masterpiece of oratory, exhibiting in one view nearly all the resources of the art. The ingenuity with which Antony "wields at will" the fickle populace of Rome in the midst of their greatest excitement, dextrously concealing his purpose until they were prepared themselves voluntarily to aid it, can hardly be too much admired, while his success by such means confirms the truth of the dogma, that "Reason and Rhetoric have nothing in common."

Here, under leave of Brutus and the rest—
For Brutus is an honourable man,
So are they all, all honourable men—
Come I to speak in Cæsar's funeral.
He was my friend, faithful and just to me;
But Brutus says he was ambitious;
And Brutus is an honourable man.
He hath brought many captives home to Rome,
Whose ransoms did the general coffers fill;
Did this in Cæsar seem **ambitious**?
When that the poor have cried, Cæsar hath wept;
Ambition should be made of sterner stuff.
Yet Brutus says, he was ambitious;
And Brutus is an honourable man.
You all did see, that, on the **Lupercal**,[1]
I thrice presented him a kingly crown;
Which he did thrice refuse. Was this ambition?
Yet Brutus says, he was ambitious;
And, sure, he is an honourable man.
I speak not to disprove what Brutus spoke,
But here I am to speak what I do know.
You all did love him once—not without cause—
What cause withholds you then to mourn for him?
O judgment! thou art fled to brutish beasts,
And men have lost their reason!—Bear with me;—
My heart is in the coffin there with Cæsar,
And I must pause till it come back to me.

But yesterday, the word of Cæsar might
Have stood against the world: now lies he there,
And none so poor[2] to do him reverence.
O masters! if I were disposed to stir
Your hearts and minds to mutiny and rage,
I should do Brutus wrong, and Cassius wrong,
Who, you all know, are honourable men:
I will not do them wrong; I rather choose
To wrong the dead, to wrong myself, and you,
Than I will wrong such honourable men.

(1) *Lupercal*—a spot at the foot of Mount Aventine, at Rome, where the Lupercalia (games commemorative of the founder of Rome) were annually celebrated. Perhaps "on the Lupercal" refers only to the day, and not to the place.

(2) *None so poor*—*i. e.* "the meanest man is now too high to do reverence to Cæsar."—*Dr. Johnson.*

But here's a parchment with the seal of Cæsar;
I found it in his closet, 'tis his will;
Let but the commons[1] hear this testament
(Which, pardon me, I do not mean to read),
And they would go and kiss dead Cæsar's wounds,
And dip their napkins in his sacred blood;
Yea, beg a hair of him, for memory,
And, dying, mention it within their wills,
Bequeathing it, as a rich legacy,
Unto their issue.

If you have tears, prepare to shed them now.
You all do know this mantle; I remember
The first time ever Cæsar put it on—
'Twas on a summer's evening in his tent,
That day he overcame the Nervii—
Look! in this place ran Cassius' dagger through;
See what a rent the envious Casca made!—
Through this the well-beloved Brutus stabbed;
And as he plucked his cursed steel away
Mark how the blood of Cæsar followed it!
As rushing out of doors, to be resolved[2]
If Brutus so unkindly knocked, or no:
For Brutus, as you know, was Cæsar's angel:
Judge, O you gods! how dearly Cæsar loved him:
This was the most unkindest cut of all:
For when the noble Cæsar saw him stab,
Ingratitude, more strong than traitors' arms,
Quite vanquished him; then burst his mighty heart;
And, in his mantle muffling up his face,
Even at the base of Pompey's statua,[3]
Which all the while ran blood,[4] great Cæsar fell.
Oh, what a fall was there, my countrymen!
Then I, and you, and all of us fell down,
Whilst bloody treason flourished[5] over us.
Oh! now you weep; and I perceive you feel
The dint[6] of pity: these are gracious drops.

(1) *The commons*—the common people, or *plebs Romana*.
(2) *To be resolved*—to have the doubt resolved, to ascertain the point.
(3) *Statua*—This word was once much used for *statue*.
(4) *All the while*—i. e. "the blood of Cæsar flew upon the statue, and trickled down it."—*Dr. Johnson.*
(5) *Flourished*—i. e. flourished or brandished *the sword*—triumphed.
(6) *Dint*—mark, impression.

Kind souls! What! weep you when you but behold
Our Cæsar's vesture wounded? Look you here!
Here is himself, marred, as you see, with traitors.

Good friends, sweet friends, let me not stir you up
To any sudden flood of mutiny.
They that have done this deed are honourable:
What private griefs they have, alas! I know not,
That made them do it; they are wise and honourable,
And will, no doubt, with reasons answer you.
I come not, friends, to steal away your hearts;
I am no orator, as Brutus is;
But, as you know me all, a plain blunt man,
That loved my friend; and that they know full well
That gave me public leave to speak of him.
For I have neither wit, nor words, nor worth,
Action, nor utterance, nor the power of speech,
To stir men's blood; I only speak right on:
I tell you that which you yourselves do know;
Show you sweet Cæsar's wounds, poor, poor dumb mouths!
And bid them speak for me: but were I Brutus,
And Brutus Antony, there were[1] an Antony
Would ruffle up your spirits, and put a tongue
In every wound of Cæsar, that should move
The stones of Rome to rise and mutiny.

OTHELLO'S COURTSHIP.[2]

Related before the Senate of Venice.

Most potent, grave, and reverend signiors,
My very noble and approved good masters,
That I have ta'en away this old man's daughter,
It is most true; true, I have married her;
The very head and front of my offending
Hath this extent—no more. Rude am I in speech,
And little blest with the soft phrase of peace;

---

(1) *There were, &c.*—*i. e.* I would prove such an Antony as would ruffle, &c.
(2) "Othello," Act i., scene 3.
  This simple and beautiful narrative affords many instances of the influence which Shakspere's phraseology has had upon our language. His words and expressions, from their aptness and pithiness, have truly become "household terms" amongst us, still keeping their sharp and fresh appearance, like ancient coins in high preservation.

For since these arms of mine had seven years' pith,
Till now some nine moons wasted they have used
Their dearest action in the tented field;
And little of this great world can I speak,
More than pertains to fears of broil and battle;
And little therefore shall I grace my cause
In speaking for myself. Yet, by your gracious patience,
I will a round unvarnished tale deliver
Of my whole course of love: what drugs, what charms,
What conjuration, and what mighty magic
(For such proceeding I am charged withal),
I won his daughter with.
   Her father loved me; oft invited me;
Still questioned me the story of my life,
From year to year; the battles, sieges, fortunes,
That I have past.
I ran it through, even from my boyish days,
To the very moment that he bade me tell it:
Wherein I spoke of most disastrous chances,
Of moving accidents by flood and field;
Of hairbreadth 'scapes in the imminent deadly breach;
Of being taken by the insolent foe,
And sold to slavery; of my redemption thence
And portance[1] in my travel's history:
Wherein of antres[2] vast, and deserts idle,
Rough quarries, rocks, and hills, whose heads touch heaven,
It was my hint to speak;—such was the process:
And of the cannibals that each other eat,
The anthropophagi,[3] and men whose heads
Do grow beneath their shoulders. These things to hear
Would Desdemona seriously incline;
But still the house affairs would draw her thence;
Which ever as she could with haste dispatch,
She'd come again, and with a greedy ear
Devour up my discourse: which I observing,
Took once a pliant hour, and found good means
To draw from her a prayer of earnest heart,
That I would all my pilgrimage dilate,
Whereof by parcels she had something heard,

---

(1) *Portance*—port, bearing, conduct.
(2) *Antres*—from the Latin *antrum*, a cavern—caves.
(3) *Anthropophagi*—from the Greek ἄνθρωπος, a man, and φαγεῖν, to eat—man-eaters.

But not intentively.¹   I did consent,
And often did beguile her of her tears,
When I did speak of some distressful stroke
That my youth suffered. My story being done,
She gave me for my pains a world of sighs;
She swore, in faith, 'twas strange, 'twas passing strange,
'Twas pitiful, 'twas wondrous pitiful—
She wished she had not heard it;—yet she wished
That heaven had made her such a man :—she thanked me,
And bade me, if I had a friend that loved her,
I should but teach him how to tell my story,
And that would woo her. Upon this hint I spake;
She loved me for the dangers I had past,
And I loved her that she did pity them.
This only is the witchcraft I have used.

THE SEVEN AGES OF MAN.²

ALL the world's a stage,
And all the men and women merely players;
They have their exits and their entrances;
And one man in his time plays many parts—
His acts being seven ages. At first, the infant,
Mewling and puking in the nurse's arms.
And then the whining schoolboy, with his satchel,
And shining morning face, creeping like a snail
Unwillingly to school. And then the lover,
Sighing like furnace, with a woful ballad³
Made to his mistress' eyebrow. Then the soldier,
Full of strange oaths, and bearded like the pard,⁴
Jealous in honour, sudden and quick in quarrel,
Seeking the bubble reputation
Even in the cannon's mouth. And then the justice,
In fair round belly, with good capon lined,
With eyes severe, and beard of formal cut,
Full of wise saws⁵ and modern instances;⁶

(1) *Intentively*—with diligent, undivided attention.
(2) "As You Like It," Act ii., scene 7.
(3) *Ballad*—a song or sonnet.
(4) *Pard*—leopard.
(5) *Saws*—see note 4, p. 171.
(6) *Modern instances*—instances of the folly of the age in which he lives, in comparison with the "good old times."

And so he plays his part. The sixth age shifts
Into the lean and slippered pantaloon,
With spectacles on nose, and pouch on side :
His youthful hose, well saved, a world too wide
For his shrunk shanks ; and his big manly voice,
Turning again towards childish treble, pipes
And whistles in his sound. Last scene of all,
That ends this strange eventful history,
Is second childishness, and mere oblivion ;
Sans[1] teeth, sans eyes, sans taste, sans everything.

END OF ALL EARTHLY GLORIES.[2]

Our revels now are ended : these our actors,
As I foretold you, were all spirits, and
Are melted into air, into thin air ;
And, like the baseless fabric of this vision,
The cloud-capt towers, the gorgeous palaces,
The solemn temples, the great globe itself,
Yea, all which it inherit, shall dissolve ;
And, like this unsubstantial pageant faded,
Leave not a rack[3] behind !

SOLITUDE AND ADVERSITY.[4]

Now my co-mates and brothers in exile,
Hath not old custom made this life more sweet
Than that of painted pomp ? Are not these woods
More free from peril than the envious court ?
Here feel we but the penalty of Adam,
The season's difference ; as the icy fang
And churlish chiding of the winter's wind ;
Which, when it bites and blows upon my body,
Even till I shrink with cold, I smile and say,
"This is no flattery ; these are counsellors
That feelingly persuade me what I am."

---

(1) *Sans*—a French word—*without*.
(2) "The Tempest," Act iv., scene 1.
This is said by Prospero, who by magical arts had raised a vision of a masque or scenic entertainment.
(3) *Rack*—see note 3, p. 141.
(4) "As You Like It," Act ii., scene 2.
Spoken by an old nobleman who had retired from the world.

Sweet are the uses of adversity,
Which, like the toad, ugly and venomous,
Wears yet a precious jewel in his head:
And this our life, exempt from public haunt,
Finds tongues in trees, books in the running brooks,
Sermons in stones, and good in every thing.

QUEEN MAB.[1]

O then, I see Queen Mab hath been with you!
She is the fairies' midwife; and she comes
In shape no bigger than an agate-stone
On the fore-finger of an alderman;
Drawn with[2] a team of little atomies
Athwart men's noses as they lie asleep:
Her wagon-spokes made of long spinner's legs;
The cover, of the wings of grasshoppers;
The traces, of the smallest spider's web;
The collars, of the moonshine's watery beams;
Her whip, of cricket's bone; the lash of film;
Her wagoner, a small grey-coated gnat,
Not half so big as a round little worm,
Pricked from the lazy finger of a maid:
Her chariot is an empty hazel-nut,
Made by the joiner squirrel, or old grub—
Time out of mind the fairies' coachmakers—
And in this state she gallops, night by night,
Through lovers' brains, and then they dream of love;
On courtiers' knees, that dream on courtesies straight;
O'er lawyers' fingers, who straight dream on fees;
O'er ladies' lips, who straight on kisses dream,
Which oft the angry Mab with blisters plagues,
Because their breaths with sweetmeats tainted are.
Sometimes she gallops o'er a courtier's nose,
And then dreams he of smelling out a suit:[3]
And sometimes comes she with a tithe-pig's tail,
Tickling a parson's nose as 'a[4] lies asleep;
Then dreams he of another benefice.

(1) "Romeo and Juliet," Act i., scene 4.
(2) *Drawn with, &c.*—Drawn by a team of little atoms.
(3) *Suit*—a solicitation for some place or office at court.
(4) *As 'a*—as he.

Sometimes she driveth o'er a soldier's neck,
And then he dreams of cutting foreign throats,
Of breaches, ambuscadoes, Spanish blades,[1]
Of healths five-fathom deep; and then anon
Drums in his ear, at which he starts, and wakes;
And, being thus frighted, swears a prayer or two
And sleeps again. This is that very Mab
That plats the manes of horses in the night;
And bakes the elf-locks[2] in foul sluttish hairs,
Which, once untangled, much misfortune bodes.

MERCY.[3]

THE quality of mercy is not strained:
It droppeth as the gentle rain from heaven
Upon the place beneath. It is twice blest;
It blesseth him that gives, and him that takes.
'Tis mightiest in the mightiest; it becomes
The thronéd monarch better than his crown:
His sceptre shows the force of temporal power,
The attribute to awe and majesty,
Wherein doth sit[4] the dread and fear of kings;
But mercy is above this sceptred sway,
It is enthronéd in the hearts of kings,
It is an attribute to God himself;
And earthly power doth then show likest God's,
When mercy seasons justice. Therefore, Jew,[5]
Though justice be thy plea, consider this—
That, in the course of justice, none of us
Should see salvation; we do pray[6] for mercy;
And that same prayer doth teach us all to render
The deeds of mercy.

ONE FRIEND UPBRAIDING ANOTHER.[7]

INJURIOUS Hermia, most ungrateful maid!
Have you conspired, have you with these contrived

---

(1) *Spanish blades*—The Toledo blades were once very famous for their temper.
(2) *Elf-locks*—locks of hair entangled and clotted ("baked") by wicked elves or fairies. Such was the superstition.
(3) "Merchant of Venice," Act iv., scene 1.
(4) *Wherein doth sit*—which inspire.
(5) *Jew*—this is addressed to Shylock, the Jew.
(6) *We do pray, &c.*—i. e. in the Lord's Prayer; "Forgive us our trespasses," &c.
(7) "Midsummer Night's Dream," Act iii., scene 2.

To bait me with this foul derision?
Is all the counsel that we two have shared,
The sisters' vows, the hours that we have spent,
When we have chid the hasty-footed time
For parting us—oh! and is all forgot?
All school-day's friendship, childhood innocence?
We, Hermia, like two artificial gods,
Have with our needls[1] created both one flower,
Both on one sampler, sitting on one cushion;
Both warbling of one song, both in one key;
As if our hands, our sides, voices, and winds,[2]
Had been incorporate. So we grew together,
Like to a double cherry, seeming parted,
But yet an union in partition;
Two lovely berries moulded on one stem:
So with two seeming bodies, but one heart;
And will you rend our ancient love asunder,
To join with men in scorning your poor friend?
It is not friendly, 'tis not maidenly:
Our sex, as well as I, may chide you for it,
Though I alone do feel the injury.

MUSIC.[3]

Lorenzo and Jessica speak.

How sweet the moonlight sleeps[4] upon this bank!
Here will we sit, and let the sounds of music
Creep in our ears; soft stillness and the night
Become the touches of sweet harmony.
Sit, Jessica; look how the floor of heaven
Is thick inlaid with patines[5] of bright gold;
There's not[6] the smallest orb which thou behold'st,
But in his motion like an angel sings,
Still quiring[7] to the young-eyed cherubims;
Such harmony is in immortal souls;

(1) *Neelds*—needles.
(2) *Winds*—breath.
(3) "Merchant of Venice," Act v., scene 1.
(4) *Sleeps*—There is an exquisite propriety and beauty in the metaphorical use of the word "sleeps" in this passage.
(5) *Patines*—from the Latin *patina*, a plate or dish—a bright round object.
(6) *There's not, &c.*—This and the two following lines refer to the fanciful notion of the music of the spheres.
(7) *Still quiring*—continually singing as in a choir.

But whilst this muddy vesture[1] of decay
Doth grossly close it in, we cannot hear it.—
Come, ho,[2] and wake Diana with a hymn:
With sweetest touches pierce your mistress' ear,
And draw her home with music.
    Jes. I'm never merry when I hear sweet music.
    Lor. The reason is, your spirits are attentive;[3]
For do but note a wild and wanton herd,
Or race of youthful and unhandled colts,
Fetching mad bounds, bellowing and neighing loud—
Which is the hot condition of their blood—
If they perchance but hear a trumpet sound,
Or any air of music touch their ears,
You shall perceive them make a mutual stand;
Their savage eyes turned to a modest gaze,
By the sweet power of music. Therefore the poet
Did feign that Orpheus drew trees, stones, and floods;
Since nought so stockish, hard, and full of rage,
But music for the time doth change his nature.
The man that hath no music in himself,
Nor is not moved with concord of sweet sounds,
Is fit for treasons, stratagems, and spoils;
The motions of his spirit are dull as night,
And his affections dark as Erebus:
Let no such man be trusted.

IMAGINATION.[4]

Lovers and madmen have such seething[5] brains,
Such shaping fantasies, that apprehend
More than cool reason ever comprehends.
The lunatic, the lover, and the poet,
Are of imagination[6] all compact:
One sees more devils than vast hell can hold;
That is, the madman; the lover, all as frantic,

---

(1) *This muddy vesture, &c.*—In allusion to the Platonic doctrine that the body is the earthly prison of the soul.

(2) *Come, ho, &c.*—This is addressed to some musicians.

(3) *Attentive—i. e.* to the music, entirely absorbed by its influence.

(4) "Midsummer Night's Dream," Act v., scene 1.

(5) *Seething*—boiling, heated.

(6) *Are of imagination, &c.*—Are altogether made up, or filled with imagination. This sense appears to be justified by another passage, in which Shakspere writes, " Love is a spirit *all compact* of fire."

Sees Helen's beauty in a brow of Egypt;
The poet's eye, in a fine frenzy rolling,
Doth glance from heaven to earth, from earth to heaven;
And as imagination bodies forth
The forms of things unknown, the poet's pen
Turns them to shape, and gives to airy nothing
A local habitation and a name.

MILTON.

PRINCIPAL EVENTS OF HIS LIFE.—John Milton—emphatically the Sublime Poet—was born in Bread Street, London, on the 9th of December, 1608. He was early distinguished for his love of learning, so that in the beginning of his sixteenth year he left St. Paul's School, where his education had been carried on, for several years, and entered Christ's College, Cambridge. On leaving college, he returned to his father's house, at Horton, in Buckinghamshire, and here for five years he pursued a course of unremitting study, which comprehended, it is said, all the Greek and Roman classics. Here too he wrote "Comus," "Lycidas," "L'Allegro," and "Il Penseroso." In the year 1638, he visited the continent, and was introduced at Paris to the famous Hugo Grotius, at that time ambassador from Christina, Queen of Sweden, to the French court; at Naples to Manso, Marquis of Villa, the friend and patron of Tasso; and at Florence, to the renowned Galileo, "a prisoner to the Inquisition," to use Milton's own words, "for thinking in astronomy otherwise than the Franciscan and Dominican licensers thought." On his return to England, after an absence of fifteen months, he settled in London, and devoted himself to the instruction of youth. He soon, however, became involved in the political agitation of the times, and was ultimately appointed Latin Secretary to the Council of State, which office he held for several years. It was during this period that he entirely lost his sight. On the restoration of Charles II., in 1660, he was included in the act of indemnity, and devoted the retirement now afforded him to composing—it cannot be called writing, since it was all dictated by the blind bard—the noblest epic poem of that or any other age—the "Paradise Lost," which was published in 1667, when he was in his sixtieth year. He died with great calmness, on the 8th of November, 1674, and was buried in the chancel of St. Giles's, Cripplegate.

In reference to the tone of his mind during his later years, an eminent modern writer thus speaks :[1]—"The strength of his mind overcame every calamity. Neither blindness, nor gout, nor age, nor penury, nor domestic afflictions, nor political disappointments, nor abuse, nor proscription, nor neglect, had power to disturb his sedate and majestic patience. His spirits do not seem to have been high, but they were singularly equable. His temper was serious, perhaps stern; but it was a temper which no sufferings could render sullen or fretful. Such as it was, when, on the eve of great events, he returned from his travels, in the prime of health and manly beauty, loaded with literary distinctions, and glowing with patriotic hopes; such it continued to be, when, after having experienced every calamity which is incident to our nature, old, poor, sightless, and disgraced, he retired to his hovel to die!"

PRINCIPAL WORKS.—Besides "Comus," "Lycidas," "L'Allegro," "Il Penseroso," and "Paradise Lost," already mentioned, Milton wrote "Paradise Regained," "Samson Agonistes," and many miscellaneous poems and sonnets. He also wrote in Latin prose the two famous "Defences of the People of England;" and in English "A Tractate on Education;" "Areopagitica, A Speech for the Liberty of Unlicensed Printing;" "History of England to the Conquest;" and many other works both political and literary.

CHARACTERISTIC SPIRIT AND STYLE.—"In speaking of the intellectual qualities of Milton, we may observe, that the very splendour of his poetic fame has tended to obscure or conceal the extent of his mind, and the variety of its energies and attainments. To many, he seems only a poet, when in truth he was a profound scholar, a man of vast compass of thought, imbued thoroughly with all ancient and modern learning, and able to master, to mould, to impregnate with his own intellectual power, his great and various acquisitions. He had not learned the superficial doctrines of a later day—that poetry flourishes most in an uncultivated soil, and that imagination shapes its brightest visions from the mists of a superstitious age; and he had no dread of accumulating knowledge, lest it should oppress and smother his genius. He was conscious of that within him which could quicken all knowledge, and wield it with ease and might; which could give freshness to old truths, and harmony to discordant thoughts; which could bind together by living ties and mysterious affinities the most remote discoveries, and rear fabrics of glory and beauty from the rude

---

(1) Macaulay. "Edinburgh Review," vol. xlii., p. 323.

materials which other minds had collected. Milton had that universality which marks the highest order of intellect. Though accustomed almost from infancy to drink at the fountains of classical literature, he had nothing of the pedantry and fastidiousness which disdains all other draughts. His healthy mind delighted in genius, on whatever soil or in whatever age it burst forth and poured out its fulness. He understood too well the rights, the dignity, and pride of creative imagination, to lay on it the laws of the Greek or Roman school. Parnassus was not to him the only holy ground of genius. He felt that poetry was as a universal presence. Great minds were everywhere his kindred. He felt the enchantment of oriental fiction, surrendered himself to the strange creations of 'Araby the Blest,' and delighted still more in the romantic spirit of chivalry, and in the tales of wonder in which it was embodied. Accordingly, his poetry reminds us of the ocean, which adds to its own boundlessness contributions from all regions under heaven. Nor was it only in the department of imagination that his acquisitions were vast. He travelled over the whole field of knowledge as far as it had then been explored. His various philological attainments were used to put him in possession of the wisdom stored in all countries where the intellect had been cultivated."[1]

"In Milton there may be traced obligations to several minor English poets; but his genius had too great a supremacy to belong to any school. Though he acknowledged a filial reverence for Spenser as a poet, he left no Gothic irregular tracery in the design of his own great work, but gave a classical harmony of parts to its stupendous pile. It thus resembles a dome, the vastness of which is at first sight concealed by its symmetry, but which expands more and more to the eye while it is contemplated. His early poetry seems to have neither disturbed nor corrected the bad taste of the age. 'Comus' came into the world unacknowledged by its author, and 'Lycidas' appeared at first only with his initials. Almost a century elapsed before his minor works obtained their proper fame. Even when 'Paradise Lost' appeared, though it was not neglected, it attracted no crowd of imitators, and made no visible change in the poetical practice of the age. He stood alone and aloof above his times, the bard of immortal subjects; and, as far as there is perpetuity in language, of immortal fame. There is something that overawes the mind in conceiving his long deliberated selection of that theme—his attempting it when his eyes were shut upon the face of nature—his dependence, we might almost say,

---

(1) Dr. Channing. "Remarks on the Character and Writings of John Milton."

on supernatural inspiration; and in the calm air of strength with which he opens 'Paradise Lost,' beginning a mighty performance without the appearance of an effort. Taking the subject all in all, his powers could nowhere else have enjoyed the same scope. It was only from the 'height of this great argument' that he could look back upon eternity past, and forward upon eternity to come. Still the subject had precipitous difficulties. It obliged him to relinquish the warm, multifarious interests of human life. For these, indeed, he could substitute holier things; but a more insuperable objection to the theme was, that it involved a representation of a war between the Almighty and his created beings. To the vicissitudes of such a warfare it was impossible to make us attach the same fluctuations of hope and fear, the same curiosity, suspense, and sympathy which we feel amidst the battles of the 'Iliad,' and which make every brave young spirit long to be in the midst of them.

"Milton has certainly triumphed over one difficulty of his subject—the paucity and the loneliness of its human agents; for no one, in contemplating the garden of Eden, would wish to exchange it for a more populous world. His earthly pair could only be represented, during their innocence, as beings of simple enjoyment and negative virtue, with no other passions than the fear of heaven and the love of each other. Yet from these materials what a picture has he drawn of their homage to the Deity, their mutual affection, and the horrors of their alienation! By concentrating all exquisite ideas of external nature in the representation of their abode—by conveying an inspired impression of their spirits and forms, whilst they first shone under the fresh light of creative heaven—by these powers of description he links our first parents, in harmonious subordination, to the angelic natures—he supports them in the balance of poetical importance with their divine coadjutors and enemies, and makes them appear at once worthy of the friendship and envy of gods."[1]

"He had considered creation in its whole extent, and his descriptions are therefore learned. He had accustomed his imagination to unrestrained indulgence, and his conceptions therefore were extensive. The characteristic quality of his poem is sublimity. He sometimes descends to the elegant, but his element is the great. He can occasionally invest himself with grace; but his natural port is gigantic loftiness. He can please when pleasure is required; but it is his peculiar power to astonish.

"He seems to have been well acquainted with his own genius, and to know what it was that nature had bestowed upon him more

---

(1) Campbell. "Specimens," &c., Introduction, p. lxxx.

bountifully than upon others—the power of displaying the vast, illuminating the splendid, enforcing the awful, darkening the gloomy, and aggravating the dreadful: he therefore chose a subject on which too much could not be said; on which he might tire his fancy without the censure of extravagance.

"The appearances of nature, and the occurrences of life, did not satiate his appetite of greatness. To paint things as they are, requires a minute attention, and employs the memory rather than the fancy. Milton's delight was to sport in the wide regions of possibility; reality was a scene too narrow for his mind. He sent his faculties out upon discovery, into worlds where only imagination can travel; and delighted to form new modes of existence, and furnish sentiment and action to superior beings, to trace the counsels of hell, or accompany the choirs of heaven."[1]

"We often hear of the magical influence of poetry. The expression in general means nothing, but, applied to the writings of Milton, it is most appropriate. His poetry acts like an incantation. Its merit lies less in its obvious meaning than in its occult power. There would seem, at first sight, to be no more in his words than in other words. But they are words of enchantment. No sooner are they pronounced than the past is present and the distant near. New forms of beauty start at once into existence, and all the burial-places of the memory give up their dead. Change the structure of the sentence, substitute one synonyme for another, and the whole effect is destroyed."[2]

VERSIFICATION.—"Milton's blank verse is the only blank verse in the language, except Shakspere's, that deserves the name of verse. Dr. Johnson, who had modelled his ideas of versification on the regular sing-song of Pope, condemns the 'Paradise Lost' as harsh and unequal. I shall not pretend to say that this is not sometimes the case; for where a degree of excellence beyond the mechanical rules of art is attempted, the poet must sometimes fail. But I imagine that there are more perfect examples in Milton of musical expression, or of an adaptation of the sound and movement of the verse to the meaning of the passage, than in all our other writers, whether of rhyme or blank verse, put together (with the exception already mentioned). Spenser is the most harmonious of our poets, as Dryden is the most sounding and varied of our rhymists; but in neither is there anything like the same ear for music, the same power of approximating the varieties of poetical to those of musical rhythm, as there is in our great epic poet. The

---

(1) Dr. Johnson. "Life of Milton."
(2) Macaulay. "Edinburgh Review," vol. xlii., p. 311.

sound of his lines is moulded into the expression of the sentiment, almost of the very image. They rise or fall, pause or hurry rapidly on, with exquisite art, but without the least trick of affectation, as the occasion seems to require."[1]

"Was there ever anything so delightful as the music of the 'Paradise Lost?' It is like that of a fine organ; has the fullest and the deepest tones of majesty, with all the softness and elegance of the Dorian flute; variety without end, and never equalled, unless perhaps by Virgil."[2]

HYMN ON THE NATIVITY.[3]

(ABRIDGED.)

It was the winter wild,
While the heaven-born child
   All meanly wrapt in the rude manger lies;
Nature, in awe to him,
Hath dofft her gaudy trim,
   With her great Master so to sympathize:
It was no season then for her
To wanton with the sun, her lusty paramour.

Only with speeches fair
She woos the gentle air,
   To hide her guilty front with innocent snow,
And on her naked shame,
Pollute with sinful blame,
   The saintly veil of maiden white to throw;
Confounded, that her Maker's eyes
Should look so near upon her foul deformities.

---

(1) Hazlitt. "Lectures," &c., p. 120.
(2) Cowper. "Letters."
(3) Written in 1629, when Milton was only twenty-one years old. This poem, though occasionally disfigured by conceits more befitting the muse of Cowley than that of Milton, is melodious and beautiful, and in every sense a worthy harbinger of "L'Allegro" and "Il Penseroso," which soon followed it. Sir E. Brydges even "ventures" (an appropriate word!) "to pronounce this poem far superior to the 'L'Allegro' and 'Il Penseroso,'" though, as he sagaciously forbodes, "the popular taste may not concur with him."

But He, her fears to cease¹
Sent down the meek-eyed Peace:
  She, crowned with olive-green, **came softly sliding**
Down through the turning sphere,
His **ready harbinger,**
  With turtle wing the amorous clouds dividing;
And **waving wide her** myrtle wand,
She strikes a universal peace² through sea and land.

No war,³ or battle's sound
Was heard the world around:
  The idle spear and shield were high up hung;
The hooked chariot stood
Unstained with **hostile** blood;
  The trumpet spake not to the arméd throng:
And **kings sat** still **with awful eye,**
As if they surely knew their sovran Lord was by.

But peaceful was the night,
Wherein the Prince of Light
  His reign of peace upon the earth began:
The winds with wonder whist,⁴
Smoothly the waters kissed,
  Whispering new joys to the mild ocëan
Who now hath quite forgot to rave,
While birds of calm sit brooding **on** the charméd wave.

The shepherds on the lawn,
Or e'er⁵ the point of dawn,
  Sat simply chatting in a **rustic row;**
Full little thought they than⁶
That the mighty Pan⁷
  Was kindly come **to live with them below;**

---

(1) *Cease*—i. e. to make to cease, to allay.

(2) *Universal peace*—in allusion to the peace which **ensued** after the battle of Actium, and the establishment of Augustus upon the throne of Rome.

(3) *No war, &c.*—"There is **a** dignity and simplicity in these lines [i. e. in this stanza] worthy of the maturest years **and best** times."—*Warton.*

(4) *Whist*—past participle of the old **verb** *to whist*, to still **or** hush—hushed.

(5) *Or e'er*—before. (6) *Than*—the old form of "then."

(7) **Pan**—Though the introduction of the name of a heathen deity in such a connection offends the ear and the taste, yet it should be remembered that as Pan **was** mythologically the god of universal nature, and also of shepherds, so our **Saviour** was in a far higher sense at once the Creator of all things, and the great **Shepherd of** his people.

Perhaps their loves, or else their sheep,
Were all that did their silly[1] thoughts so busy keep;

When such music sweet
Their hearts and ears did greet,
  As never was by mortal fingers strook;
Divinely warbled voice
Answering the stringéd noise,[2]
  As all their souls in blissful rapture took;
The air, such pleasures loth to lose,
With thousand echoes still prolongs each heavenly close.

At last surrounds their sight
A globe of circular light,
  That with long beams the shame-faced night arrayed;
The helmed Cherubim,
And sworded Seraphim,
  Are seen in glittering ranks with wings displayed,
Harping in loud and solemn quire,
With unexpressive[3] notes, to Heaven's new-born heir.

Such music, as 'tis said,
Before was never made,
  But when of old the sons of morning sung,
While the Creator great
His constellations set,
  And the well-balanced world on hinges hung,
And cast the dark foundations deep,
And bid the weltering waves their oozy channel keep.

The oracles[4] are dumb;
No voice or hideous hum
  Runs through the arched roof in words deceiving:
Apollo from his shrine
Can no more divine,
  With hollow shriek the steep of Delphos leaving:
No nightly trance, or breathéd spell,
Inspires the pale-eyed priest from the prophetic cell.

---

(1) *Silly*—simple, innocent; the original meaning of the word.
(2) *Noise*—music. (See note 8, p. 153.)
(3) *Unexpressive*—inexpressible, such as cannot be described.
(4) *The oracles, &c.*—All the heathen oracles are said to have ceased at the coming of Christ. "Attention," says Dr. Warton, "is irresistibly awakened and engaged by the air of solemnity and enthusiasm that reigns in this stanza, and some that follow."

The lonely mountains o'er,
And the resounding shore,
  A voice of weeping[1] heard, and loud lament:
From haunted spring and dale,
Edgéd with poplar pale,
  The parting Genius is with sighing sent;
With flower-inwoven tresses torn,
The nymphs in twilight shade of tangled thickets mourn.

In consecrated earth,
And on the holy hearth,
  The Lars and Lemures[2] moan with midnight plaint;
In urns and altars round,
A drear and dying sound
  Affright the Flamens[3] at their service quaint;
And the chill marble seems to sweat,
While each peculiar Power foregoes his wonted seat.

Peor and Baälim
Forsake their temples dim,
  With that twice-battered god[4] of Palestine;
And mooned Ashtaroth,
Heaven's queen and mother both,
  Now sits not girt with tapers' holy shine;
The Lybic Hammon[5] shrinks his horn;
In vain the Tyrian maids their wounded Thammuz mourn.

And sullen Moloch, fled,
Hath left in shadows dread
  His burning idol[6] all of blackest hue;
In vain with cymbals' ring,
They call the grisly king,
  In dismal dance about the furnace blue:

---

(1) *Weeping, &c.*—The lamentations of the fabulous tenants of the woods and glades—the dryads, fauns, nymphs, &c.—at leaving their favorite haunts.

(2) *Lars and Lemures*—domestic gods of the Romans, representing the departed spirits of their ancestors.

(3) *Flamen*—the officiating priest of a particular deity and temple.

(4) *Twice-battered god*—Dagon. See 1 Sam. v. 3, 4.

(5) *Lybic Hammon*—Jupiter was worshipped at the Hammonium, in Lybia (the oasis now called Siwah), under the form of a ram.

(6) *Burning idol, &c.*—The brazen idol of Moloch used to be filled with fire, and into its hands, extended for the purpose, infants were put as victims, which soon sank down through the hollow arms into the fire, and perished there. The cymbals were to drown the children's cries.

The brutish gods of Nile as fast,
Isis and Orus, and the dog Anubis, haste.

Nor is Osiris seen
In Memphian grove or green,
   Trampling the unshowered grass with lowings loud:
Nor can he be at rest
Within his sacred chest;
   Nought but profoundest hell can be his shroud;
In vain with timbreled anthems dark
The sabled-stoléd sorcerers bear his worshipped ark.

He feels from Judah's land
The dreaded Infant's hand;
   The rays of Bethlehem blind his dusky eyne;
Nor all the gods beside
Longer dare abide,
   Nor Typhon huge ending in snaky twine:
Our Babe, to show his Godhead true,
Can in his swaddling bands[1] control the damnéd crew.

So, when the sun in bed,[2]
Curtained with clouded red,
   Pillows his chin[3] upon an orient wave,
The flocking shadows pale
Troop to the infernal jail;
   Each fettered ghost slips to his several grave;
And the yellow-skirted fayes
Fly after the night-steeds,[4] leaving their moon-loved maze.

But see, the Virgin blest
Hath laid her Babe to rest;

---

(1) *Swaddling bands, &c.*—In allusion to the story of the infant Hercules, who strangled two serpents in his cradle.

(2) *So when the sun, &c.*—"Our author has here beautifully applied the vulgar superstition of spirits disappearing at the break of day as the groundwork of a comparison. All the false gods of every species of heathen religion depart at the birth of Christ, as spectres and demons vanish when the morning dawns."—*Warton.*

(3) *Pillows his chin, &c.*—"The words 'pillows' and 'chin' throw an air of burlesque and familiarity over a comparison most exquisitely conceived and adapted."—*Warton.*

(4) *Fly after the night-steeds*—i. e. the fairies depart at the approach of morning.

Time is our tedious song should here have ending:
Heaven's youngest-teemed[1] star
Hath fixed her polished car,
Her sleeping Lord with handmaid lamp attending:
And all about the courtly stable
Bright-harnessed[2] angels sit in order serviceable.

LYCIDAS.[3]

(ABRIDGED.)

YET once more,[4] O ye laurels, and once more
Ye myrtles brown, with ivy never sere,
I come to pluck your berries harsh and crude,
And, with forced fingers rude,

(1) *Youngest-teemed*—last created. (See note 4, p. 32.)

(2) *Bright-harnessed*—equipped in bright armour.

(3) This monody was written on occasion of the death of Milton's friend, Mr. Edward King, who was drowned in the Irish Sea in 1637. It was published in 1638.

It is aptly remarked by Dr. Warton, with regard to this beautiful poem, that "He who wishes to know whether he has a true taste for poetry or not, should consider whether he is highly delighted or not with the perusal of Milton's Lycidas." "Nothing," says an able critic ("Quarterly Review," vol. xxxvi., p. 45), "was ever so *unearthly* as Milton's poetry. The most unpromising subject, after passing through his heated mind, comes out purged, and purified, and refined: the terrestrial body dissolves in the process, and we behold in its stead a glorified body. That which was by nature a frail and perishable flower, when transplanted to his fancy becomes 'immortal amaranth.'" The same writer, after referring to "Comus" as an illustration of this remark, thus also adduces "Lycidas:"—"His friend perishes by sea as he passes from Chester to Ireland. Again, Milton clothes this naked fact in imagery of his own; and Mr. King is no longer his college companion, but the shepherd with whom he had been accustomed 'to drive a-field under the opening eyelids of the morn'—and the crazy vessel is no more a material hulk, but capable of perfidy, and rigged with curses, and built in an eclipse:—and his fellow-students are not besought to honour his memory with their funeral songs, but the muses who loved him are called upon to purple the ground where, in imagination at least, he lies, with fresh flowers, and to lavish upon it the embroidery of spring. The mind of Milton was perfect fairyland; and every thought which entered it, whether grave or gay, magnificent or mean, quickly partook of a fairy form. We do not believe that he loved his friend less because he chose to call him Lycidas instead of Mr. King. He thought in Romance: the daily occurrences of life were translated into romance, almost before his mind could act upon them."

(4) *Yet once more, &c.*—The poet begins as if he were called on by this sad and unexpected occasion, to break a resolution he had previously made, to refrain

Shatter your leaves before the mellowing year.
Bitter constraint, and sad occasion dear,
Compels me to disturb your season due:
For Lycidas is dead, dead ere his prime,
Young Lycidas, and hath not left his peer.
Who would not sing for Lycidas? he knew
Himself to sing, and build the lofty rhyme.[1]
He must not float upon his watery bier
Unwept, and welter to the parching wind,
Without the meed of some melodious tear.
Begin then, Sisters[2] of the sacred well,
That from beneath the seat of Jove doth spring,
Begin, and somewhat loudly sweep the string.
Hence with denial vain, and coy excuse:
So may some gentle Muse
With lucky words[3] favour my destined urn,
And, as he passes, turn,
And bid fair peace be to my sable shroud.
For we were nurst upon[4] the selfsame hill,
Fed the same flock,[5] by fountain, shade, and rill.
Together both, ere the high lawns appeared
Under the opening eyelids of the morn,
We drove a-field,[6] and both together heard
What time the gray-fly winds her sultry horn,
Battening[7] our flocks with the fresh dews of night,
Oft till the star that rose at evening, bright,
Toward heaven's descent had sloped his westering wheel.
Meanwhile the rural ditties were not mute,

from poetry until his genius should be more matured. Hence he speaks of "berries harsh and crude," or unripe. The laurels, myrtles, and ivy, perhaps mark the poetical, affectionate, and mournful character of the composition. Some, however, refer the crudeness and immaturity to Mr. King's youth.

(1) *Rhyme*—i. e. verse, as opposed to prose.

(2) *Sisters, &c.*—The muses, who haunt the fountain Hippocrene, which flows from Mount Helicon, on which there was an altar to Jupiter.

(3) *Lucky words*—words of benediction or blessing.

(4) *We were nurst upon, &c.*—i. e. we both studied at the same place.

(5) *Fed the same flock, &c.*—All the imagery throughout this poem which represents Mr. King, or the author, as shepherds, refers to their character as students of literature, perhaps especially of classical poetry.

(6) *We drove a-field*—i. e. we drove *our flocks* a-field, or began our studies together. Having thus alluded to their studies in the morning, in the next few lines he indicates that they were carried on together throughout the day until late in the night.

(7) *Battening*—making fat.

Tempered to the oaten flute;
Rough satyrs danced, and fauns with cloven heel
From the glad sound would not be absent long;
And old Damœtas loved to hear our song.

But oh, the heavy change, now thou art gone!
Now thou art gone, and never must return!
Thee, shepherd, thee, the woods, and desert caves,
With wild thyme and the gadding[1] vine o'ergrown,
And all their echoes, mourn.
The willows, and the hazel copses green,
Shall now no more be seen
Fanning their joyous leaves to thy soft lays.
As killing as the canker to the rose,
Or taint-worm to the weanling herds that graze,
Or frost to flowers, that their gay wardrobe wear
When first the whitethorn blows;—
Such, Lycidas, thy loss to shepherd's ear.

Where were ye, Nymphs, when the remorseless deep
Closed o'er the head of your loved Lycidas?
For neither were ye playing on the steep,
Where your old bards,[2] the famous Druids, lie,
Nor on the shaggy top of Mona[3] high,
Nor yet where Deva[4] spreads her wizard stream;
Ay me! I fondly dream!
Had ye been there[5]—for what could that have done?
What could the Muse herself that Orpheus bore,
The Muse herself, for her enchanting son,
Whom universal nature did lament,
When, by the rout that made the hideous roar,
His gory visage down the stream was sent,
Down the swift Hebrus to the Lesbian shore?

Alas! what boots it with incessant care
To tend the homely, slighted, shepherd's trade,
And strictly meditate[6] the thankless Muse?
Were it not better done as others use,

---

(1) *Gadding*—connected with the verb *to go*—going about, wandering, straying.

(2) *Where your old bards, &c.*—The Druid sepulchres in the mountains of Denbighshire are referred to here.

(3) *Mona*—the Isle of Anglesey.

(4) *Deva*—the Dee. (See note 3, p. 147.)

(5) *Had ye been there, &c.*—i. e. as Warton interprets—"I will suppose you had been there—but why should I suppose it—for what would that have availed?"

(6) *Meditate*—in the Latin sense, practise. Milton here imitates Virgil (see "Ecl." i. 2):—"Silvestrem tenui Musam meditaris."

To sport with Amaryllis in the shade,
Or with the tangles of Neæra's hair?
Fame is the spur that the clear spirit doth raise—
That last infirmity of noble mind—
To scorn delights, and live laborious days;
But the fair guerdon when we hope to find,
And think to burst out into sudden blaze,
Comes the blind Fury[1] with the abhorréd shears,
And slits the thin-spun life. "But not the praise,"
Phœbus replied, and touched my trembling ears;
"Fame is no plant that grows on mortal soil,
Nor in the glistering foil
Set off to the world, nor in broad rumour lies:
But lives and spreads aloft by those pure eyes,
And perfect witness of all-judging Jove;
As he pronounces lastly on each deed,
Of so much fame in Heaven expect thy meed."

O fountain Arethusé, and thou honoured flood,
Smooth-sliding Mincius,[2] crowned with vocal reeds!
That strain I heard was of a higher mood:
But now my oat proceeds,
And listens to the herald of the sea
That came in Neptune's plea;
He asked the waves, and asked the felon winds,
What hard mishap hath doomed this gentle swain?
And questioned every gust of rugged wings,
That blows from off each beaked promontory;
They knew not of his story,
And sage Hippotades[3] their answer brings,
That not a blast was from his dungeon strayed;
The air was calm, and on the level brine
Sleek Panope[4] with all her sisters played.
It was that fatal and perfidious bark,
Built in the eclipse, and rigged with curses dark,
That sunk so low that sacred head of thine.

Return, Alpheus; the dread voice is past,
That shrunk[5] thy streams; return, Sicilian Muse,

---

(1) *Fury*—i. e. destiny.
(2) *Mincius*—a river near Mantua, where Virgil was born.
(3) *Hippotades*—Æolus, the son of Hippotas, the fabulous king of the winds.
(4) *Panope*—a sea-nymph.
(5) *That shrunk, &c.*—i. e. "that silenced my pastoral poetry," as Mr. Warton interprets.

And call the vales, and bid them hither cast,
Their bells and flowerets of a thousand hues.
Ye valleys low, where the mild whispers use[1]
Of shades, and wanton winds, and gushing brooks,
On whose fresh lap the swart-star[2] sparely looks,
Throw hither all your quaint enamelled eyes,
That on the green turf suck the honied showers,
And purple all the ground with vernal flowers,
Bring the rathe[3] primrose that forsaken dies,
The tufted crow-toe, and pale jessamine,
The white pink, and the pansy freaked with jet,
The glowing violet,
The musk-rose, and the well-attired woodbine,
With cowslips wan that hang the pensive head,
And every flower that sad embroidery wears:
Bid amarantus all his beauty shed,
And daffodillies fill their cups with tears,
To strow the laureat hearse where Lycid lies.
For, so to interpose, a little ease,
Let our frail thoughts dally with false surmise.
Ay me! Whilst thee the shores and sounding seas
Wash far away, where'er thy bones are hurled,
Whether beyond the stormy Hebrides,
Where thou, perhaps, under the whelming tide,
Visit'st the bottom of the monstrous world;[4]
Or whether thou, to our moist vows denied,
Sleep'st by the fable of Bellerus old,[5]
Where the great vision of the guarded mount[6]
Looks toward Namancos[7] and Bayona's hold;
Look homeward, Angel, now, and melt with ruth:
And, O ye Dolphins, waft the hapless youth.

(1) *Use*—i. e. frequent, inhabit.
(2) *Swart-star*—"The dog-star is called the swart-star, by turning the effect into the cause. *Swart* is swarthy, brown, &c."—*Warton.*
(3) *Rathe*—early, too soon; hence the adverb *rather*, sooner, before.
(4) *Monstrous world*—the world of monsters, the sea.
(5) *Bellerus old*—a fabulous giant of that name, renowned in Cornish mythology, or a rugged cliff so named: some say the Land's End is intended.
(6) *Where the great vision of the guarded mount*—i. e. the apparition of St. Michael, who gives name to St. Michael's Mount, which looks towards Spain, as intimated in the next line.
(7) *Namancos*—this place appears, Mr. Todd informs us, in old maps, as a castle on the coast of Galicia in Spain. Some think Numantia is intended.

    Weep no more, woful shepherds, weep no more,
For Lycidas, your sorrow, is not dead,
Sunk though he be beneath the watery floor;
So sinks the day-star in the ocean bed,
And yet anon repairs his drooping head,
And tricks his beams, and with new spangled ore
Flames in the forehead of the morning sky;
So Lycidas sunk low but mounted high,
Through the dear might of Him that walked the waves,
Where other groves and other streams along,
With nectar pure his oozy locks he laves,
And hears the unexpressive nuptial song,
In the blest kingdoms meek of joy and love.
There entertain him all the saints above,
In solemn troops, and sweet societies,
That sing, and singing in their glory move,
And wipe the tears for ever from his eyes.
Now, Lycidas, the shepherds weep no more;
Henceforth thou art the genius of the shore,
In thy large recompence, and shalt be good
To all that wander in that perilous flood.
    Thus sang the uncouth swain to the oaks and rills,
While the still morn went out with sandals grey,
He touched the tender stops of various quills,
With eager thought[1] warbling his Doric lay:
And now the sun had stretched out all the hills,
And now was dropt into the western bay;
At last he rose, and twitched his mantle blue;
To-morrow to fresh woods, and pastures new.

L'ALLEGRO.[2]

Hence, loathed Melancholy!
Of Cerberus and blackest Midnight born,
In Stygian cave forlorn,
'Mongst horrid shapes, and shrieks, and sights unholy:

---

(1) *Thought*—anxiety, serious solicitude, a nearly obsolete use of the word. Old writers speak of persons " dying of thought."

(2) L'Allegro—" The cheerful man."

The design of this and the following poem is to represent in a connected series of pictures, the most obvious images respectively associated with the cheerful and the melancholy temperament. The tone, spirit, and scenery all exquisitely

Find out some **uncouth cell,**
Where brooding **Darkness** spreads his jealous wings;
And the night **raven sings;**
There under ebon shades, and low-browed rocks,
As ragged as thy locks,
In dark **Cimmerian** desert ever dwell.
   But come, thou goddess fair and free,
In heaven ycleped Euphrosyne,[1]
And by men, heart easing Mirth,
Whom lovely Venus at a birth,
With two sister Graces more,
To ivy-crowned Bacchus bore;
Or whether (as some sager[2] sing)
The frolic wind that breathes the **spring,**
Zephyr, with Aurora **playing,**
As he **met** her once a-maying,
There on beds of violets blue,
And **fresh-blown roses** washed in dew,
Filled her with thee, a daughter fair,
So buxom, blithe, and debonair.
   Haste thee, Nymph, and bring with thee
Jest, and youthful Jollity,
Quips, and Cranks, and wanton Wiles,
Nods, and Becks, and wreathed[3] Smiles
Such as hang on Hebe's cheek,
And love to live in dimple sleek;

---

combine in accomplishing the poet's purpose. "They are indeed," as Mr. Macaulay remarks, "not so much poems, as collections of hints, from each of which the reader is to make out a poem for himself. **Every epithet is a text for** a canto."

  The first ten lines, in contrast with the ten that follow, afford one of the finest specimens that can be found of the expressive music of verse. In reading them aloud, the voice is at first encumbered and detained amongst artful pauses, long syllables, **and clusters of harsh** consonants, until, at the tenth line, it is almost lost in the sombre gloom; in the next, it bursts as **it were at once** into life and light, and the very tone and beat of the verse are in the highest degree animating and picturesque.

  (1) *Euphrosyne*—It must be remarked that the cheerfulness illustrated in this **poem** is not obstreperous and vulgar merriment, but such **as it befits one of the Graces to inspire.**

  (2) **As** *some sager, &c.*—The allegory should be observed; on the one supposition, Mirth **is the** offspring of sensuality—on the other, the wiser conjecture, of exercise, **and** the breezes of the early morning, betokened by Zephyr and Aurora.

  (3) *Wreathed*—in allusion to the curling or curving of the features in the act of smiling, giving what is called an *arch* look.

x

Sport that wrinkled Care derides,
And Laughter holding both his sides.
Come and trip it as you go
On the light fantastic toe;
And in thy right-hand lead with thee
The mountain-nymph,[1] sweet Liberty;
And if I give thee honour due,
Mirth, admit me of thy crew,
To live with her, and live with thee,
In unreproved[2] pleasures free:
To hear the lark begin its flight,
And singing startle the dull night,
From his watch-tower in the skies,
Till the dappled[3] dawn doth rise;
Then to come,[4] in spite of sorrow,
And at my window bid good-morrow,
Through the sweetbrier or the vine,
Or the twisted eglantine:[5]
While the cock, with lively din,
Scatters the rear of darkness thin,
And to the stack, or the barn-door,
Stoutly struts his dames before;
Oft listening[6] how the hounds and horn
Cheerly rouse the slumbering morn,
From the side of some hoar hill,
Through the high wood echoing shrill:

(1) *Mountain-nymph*—Either because, as Dr. Newton conjectures, "mountainous countries are favourable to political liberty;" or because, as T. Warton thinks, Liberty, like an oread, loves the inaccessible and uncultivated scenes of nature, as "adapted to her free and uninterrupted range."

(2) *Unreproved*—i. e. unreprovable—not subject to reproof, blameless, innocent. Spenser has, "unreproved truth."

(3) *Dappled*—See note 5, p. 32.

(4) *Then to come, &c.*—It would be inconsistent with the lark's habits to come to a window; the meaning, therefore, seems to be:—After he has from his watch-tower awakened the night, his glad notes in descending, heard from my window, will seem to bid me good-morrow, and make me cheerful, in spite of any sadness which may at the time oppress me.

(5) *Eglantine*—properly the sweetbrier; here, as the critics in their difficulty say, it must mean the honeysuckle.

(6) *Oft listening, &c.*—The construction is:—Mirth, admit me oft listening, &c., as a follower of thee—i. e. let me derive cheerful pleasure from listening, &c., and also from walking, not unseen, to behold the sun rise.

Sometime walking, not unseen,[1]
By hedge-row elms, on hillocks **green,**
Right against the eastern **gate,**
Where the great sun begins his state,[2]
Robed in flames and amber light,
The clouds in thousand liveries dight;
While the ploughman, near **at** hand,
Whistles o'er the furrowed land;
And the milk-maid singeth blithe,
And the mower whets his scythe,
And every shepherd tells his tale,[3]
Under the hawthorn in the dale.

Straight mine eye[4] hath caught new pleasures,
Whilst the lanscape round it measures;
Russet lawns, and fallows **grey,**
Where **the** nibbling **flocks do stray;**
Mountains, on **whose barren breast**
The labouring clouds do often rest:
Meadows trim with daisies pied;[5]
Shallow brooks and rivers wide;
Towers and battlements it sees
Bosomed high in tufted trees,
Where perhaps some beauty lies,
The Cynosure[6] of neighbouring eyes.

Hard by a cottage chimney smokes,
From betwixt two aged oaks,
Where Corydon[7] and Thyrsis met,
Are at their savoury dinner set

(1) *Not unseen*—*i. e.* in the open air, in full view of others; not as the melancholy man (see "Il Penseroso," p. 312), walking

"*Unseen*
On the dry smooth-shaven green."

(2) *State*—this word is now nearly obsolete in the above sense; *to begin his state* means to hold his court. Jonson in like manner (see p. 173) bids Diana—

"State in wonted manner keep."

(3) *Tells his tale*—this may mean—1st. Tells his tale *of love;* 2nd. Tells tales, *or stories;* 3rd. Tells his tale *of sheep—i. e.* counts them. The last is perhaps the true interpretation, as helping to indicate the time of day.

(4) *Straight mine eye, &c.*—The early morn is now over, forenoon has arrived, and the landscape is quite clear.

(5) *Pied*—many-coloured, variegated. (See note 1, p. 32.)

(6) *Cynosure*—the pole-star; the point at which many gaze.

(7) *Corydon, Thyrsis, Phyllis, Thestylis*—the names of farmers and rustics, borrowed from Theocritus, Virgil, and other writers of pastorals.

Of herbs, and other country messes,
Which the neat-handed Phyllis dresses;
And then in haste her bower[1] she leaves
With Thestylis to bind the sheaves;
Or, if the earlier season lead,
To the tanned haycock in the mead.
Sometimes, with secure delight,
The upland hamlets will invite,
When the merry bells ring round,
And the jocund rebecks[2] sound
To many a youth and many a maid,
Dancing[3] in the chequered shade:
And young and old come forth to play
On a sunshine holiday,
Till the livelong daylight fail;
Then to the spicy nut-brown ale,
With stories told of many a feat,
How faery Mab[4] the junkets eat;
She[5] was pinched, and pulled, she said,
And he,[6] by friar's lantern led,
Tells how the drudging Goblin sweat,
To earn his cream-bowl duly set,
When in one night, ere glimpse of morn,
His shadowy flail had threshed the corn,
That ten day-labourers could not end;
Then lies him down the lubber[7] fiend,
And, stretched out all the chimney's length,
Basks at the fire his hairy strength;
And cropful out of doors he flings
Ere the first cock his matin rings.
Thus done the tales, to bed they creep,
By whispering winds soon lulled asleep.

(1) *Bower*—The words *bower* here, and *din* (" the cock, with lively *din*") in a previous line, seem by their unexpectedness, and, strictly speaking, inappropriateness, to be intended to vary and enliven the style. A bower is strictly a lady's apartment or chamber.

(2) *Rebeck*—an ancient kind of fiddle.

(3) *Dancing*—This suggests the after part of the day, perhaps afternoon and evening.

(4) *Faery Mab*—See p. 285.

(5) *She, &c*—persons who tell the stories to the company.

(6) *And he, &c.*—i. e. and he, one of the men, tells how at one time he was led astray by Will-o'-the-Wisp; and how, another time, Puck, or Robin Goodfellow, sweated to earn, &c.

(7) *Lubber*—lazy; here, perhaps, tired.

Towered cities please us then,[1]
And the busy hum of men,
Where throngs of knights and barons bold,
In weeds of peace[2] high triumphs[3] hold,
With stores of ladies, whose bright eyes
Rain influence, and judge the prize
Of wit or arms, while both contend
To win her grace whom all commend.[4]
There let Hymen oft appear
In saffron robe, with taper clear,
And pomp, and feast, and revelry,
With mask and antique pageantry;
Such sights as youthful poets dream
On summer-eves by haunted stream.
Then to the well-trod stage anon,
If Jonson's learned sock[5] be on,
Or sweetest Shakspere, Fancy's child,
Warble his native wood-notes wild.

And ever, against eating cares,
Lap me in soft Lydian airs,
Married to immortal verse;
Such as the melting soul may pierce,
In notes, with many a winding bout[6]
Of linkéd sweetness long drawn out,
With wanton heed, and giddy cunning,
The melting voice[7] through mazes running,

(1) *Then*—i. e. says Mr. Warton, "at night," and adds "*then* is in this line a repetition of the first *then*—'then to the spicy,' &c." In referring *then*, however, to night at all, we are met by the difficulty that the passage that follows seems to describe a tournament, which of course would not be held in a nocturnal assembly. If we consider *then* in this line as a correlative of *then* fourteen lines below, like the Latin *tunc—tunc*, we may interpret them both *sometimes*, and refer them to entirely different views of the subject. After all, the solution is difficult to find.

(2) *Weeds of peace*—splendid dresses. "Weeds" in this sense still remains in the expression, "widow's weeds."

(3) *Triumphs*—i. e. "Shows, such as masks, revels," &c.— *Warton.* The word is used in the classical sense—*triumphus* meant, originally, a grand procession or pageant.

(4) *Whom all commend*—i. e. the Queen of Beauty, the lady who presided at the tournament.

(5) *Sock*—the shoe worn by the Roman comedians; here put for comedy itself.

(6) *Bout*—a fold or twist.

(7) *The melting voice, &c.*—i.e. "As the voice of the singer runs through the manifold mazes or intricacies of sound, all the chains are untwisted which imprison and entangle the hidden soul, the essence, or perfection, of harmony."— *Warton.*

Untwisting all the chains that tie
The hidden soul of harmony;
That Orpheus' self may heave his head,
From golden slumber on a bed
Of heaped Elysian flowers, and hear
Such strains as would have won the ear
Of Pluto, to have quite set free
His half-regained Eurydice.

These delights, if thou canst give,
Mirth, with thee I mean to live.

IL PENSEROSO.[1]

HENCE, vain deluding joys,
The brood of Folly, without father bred!
How little you bestead,[2]
Or fill the fixéd mind with all your toys!
Dwell in some idle brain,
And fancies fond with gaudy shapes possess,
As thick and numberless
As the gay motes that people the sunbeams,
Or likest hovering dreams,
The fickle pensioners[3] of Morpheus' train.

(1) *Il Penseroso*—"The thoughtful, melancholy man." Both this poem and the preceding were written before Milton was thirty years of age. It is not difficult to perceive that "Il Penseroso" more especially embodies the poet's own experience and sympathies. Beautiful though "L'Allegro" is, "Il Penseroso" is still more exquisitely refined and graceful. But both may be considered as masterpieces of the poetic art, and every attempt that has been made to imitate them has only served by the contrast to enhance the superlative excellence and beauty of the originals. The riches of the present poem are glanced at in the following synopsis:—"The portrait of contemplation," says Dr. Symmons; "the address to Philomel; the image of the moon, wandering through heaven's pathless way; the slow swinging of the curfew over some wide-watered shore; the flaming of the night-lamp in some lonely tower; the unsphering of the spirit of Plato to disclose the residence of the unbodied soul; the arched walks of twilight groves; the mysterious dream by the murmuring waters; the sweet music of the friendly spirit of the wood; the pale and studious cloister; the religious light thrown through the storied windows; the pealing organ, and finally, the peaceful hermitage, form together such a mass of poetic imagery as was never before crowded into an equal space; the impression made by it on the imagination is to be felt, and not explained."

(2) *Bestead*—avail.

(3) *Pensioners*—attendants, retinue.

But hail, thou goddess, sage and holy,
Hail, divinest Melancholy!
Whose saintly visage is too bright
To hit the sense of human sight;
And therefore to our weaker view
O'erlaid with black, staid Wisdom's hue;
Black, but such as in esteem
Prince Memnon's sister[1] might beseem;
Or that starred Ethiop queen[2] that strove
To set her beauty's praise above
The sea-nymphs, and their powers offended:
Yet thou art higher far descended:
Thee, bright-haired[3] Vesta, long of yore,
To solitary Saturn bore;
His daughter she—in Saturn's reign
Such mixture was not held a stain—
Oft in glimmering bowers and glades
He met her, and in secret shades
Of woody Ida's inmost grove,
Whilst yet[4] there was no fear of Jove.

Come, pensive nun, devout and pure,
Sober, stedfast, and demure,
All in a robe of darkest grain,
Flowing with majestic train,
And sable stole of Cyprus lawn,[5]
Over thy decent shoulders drawn.
Come, but keep thy wonted state,
With even step, and musing gait,
And looks commercing with the skies,
Thy rapt soul sitting in thine eyes:
There, held in holy passion still,
Forget thyself to marble, till

---

(1) *Memnon's sister*—i. e. "**An Ethiopian princess, or sable beauty.** This lady is a creation of the poet."—*Dunster.*

(2) *Starred Ethiop queen*—Cassiope or **Cassiopea,** who pretended to vie with the **Nereids in** beauty;—*starred* because she was transformed into the constellation which bears her name.

(3) *Thee, bright-haired, &c.*—i. e. says Warton, "Melancholy is the daughter of **Genius,** which is typified by the bright-haired goddess of the eternal fire. Saturn, **the father,** is the god of saturnine disposition, of pensive and gloomy minds."

(4) *Whilst yet, &c.*—i. e. before Jupiter rebelled against his father.

(5) **Cyprus** *lawn*—a fine fabric made at Cyprus; generally, but not always, of a **black colour.** Some read "cypress" in reference to the shrub so called, which is **of a dark hue.**

With a sad leaden downward cast
Thou fix them on the earth as fast;
And join with thee calm Peace and Quiet,
Spare Fast, that oft[1] with gods doth diet,
And hears the Muses in a ring,
Aye round about Jove's altar sing,
And add to these retired Leisure,
That in trim gardens takes his pleasure:
But first, and chiefest with thee bring,
Him that yon soars on golden wing,
Guiding the fiery-wheeled throne,[2]
The cherub Contemplation:
And the mute Silence hist[3] along,
'Less Philomel will deign a song;
In her sweetest, saddest plight,
Smoothing the rugged brow of Night,
While Cynthia checks[4] her dragon yoke,
Gently o'er the accustomed oak.
Sweet bird that shunn'st the noise of folly,
Most musical, most melancholy![5]
Thee, chantress, oft the woods among
I woo, to hear thy even song;
And, missing thee, I walk unseen
On the dry smooth-shaven green,
To behold the wandering moon
Riding near her highest noon,
Like one that had been led astray,
Through the heaven's wide pathless way;
And oft, as if her head she bowed,
Stooping through a fleecy cloud.
 Oft, on a plat of rising ground,
I hear the far-off curfew sound,

---

(1) *Spare Fast, that oft, &c.*—To imply that temperance is favourable to poetical enthusiasm.

(2) *The fiery-wheeled throne*—the throne of God or Providence, guided by calm and comprehensive forethought.

(3) *Hist*—hu-hed; the same as "whist." (See note 4, p. 295.) Sir E. Brydges thus speaks of this and the seventeen following lines: "There is a spell in it (this passage) which goes far beyond mere description, it is the very perfection of ideal, and picturesque, and contemplative poetry."

(4) *Cynthia checks, &c.*—*i. e.* the Moon stops to hear the nightingale.

(5) Coleridge blames Milton for speaking of the nightingale as "melancholy;" he calls it the "merry nightingale."

Over some wide-watered shore,
Swinging slow with sullen roar :¹
Or, if the air will not permit,
Some still removed² place will fit,
Where glowing embers through the room
Teach light to counterfeit a gloom;
Far from all resort of mirth,
Save the cricket on the earth;
Or the bellman's drowsy charm,
To bless the doors from nightly harm.
Or let my lamp, at midnight hour,
Be seen in some high lonely tower,
Where I may oft out-watch the Bear,³
With thrice-great Hermes; or unsphere
The spirit⁴ of Plato, to unfold
What worlds or what vast regions hold
The immortal mind, that hath forsook
Her mansion in this fleshy nook;
And of those⁵ demons that are found
In fire, air, flood, or under ground,
Whose power hath a true⁶ consent
With planet, or with element.
    Sometimes let gorgeous Tragedy⁷
In sceptered pall come sweeping by,
Presenting Thebes, or Pelops' line,
Or the tale of Troy divine;
Or what (though rare⁸) of later age
Ennobled hath the buskined stage.⁹

---

(1) Observe the peculiar aptness of every word in this line, and the music of its rhythm when read aloud.

(2) *Removed*—remote, unfrequented.

(3) *Out-watch the Bear, &c.*—i. e. study till past midnight the works of Hermes Trismegistus (the Mercury of the Egyptians), or of Plato.

(4) *Unsphere the spirit, &c.*—Awake it from its sphere or mansion, and bid it tell me where the soul goes when it leaves the body.

(5) *And of, &c.*—i. e. "unfold," or give me information of, or concerning those demons, &c. The construction here is very peculiar.

(6) *Hath a true, &c.*—i. e. works or co-operates, with planetary or elemental influences.

(7) *Gorgeous tragedy, &c.*—i. e. the famous tragedies of the Greeks, founded, generally, on the distresses of kings; *pall* here means, a flowing robe.

(8) *Though rare*—"Just glancing at Shakspere."—*Hurd.*

(9) *Buskined stage*—the *buskin* symbolises tragedy, as the *sock* does comedy. (See note 5, p. 309.)

But, O sad virgin, that thy power
Might raise Musæus[1] from his bower!
Or bid the soul of Orpheus sing
Such notes, as, warbled to the string,
Drew iron tears down Pluto's cheek,
And made hell grant what love did seek.
Or call up him that left[2] half-told
The story of Cambuscan bold,
Of Camball, and of Algarsife,
And who had Canace to wife,
That owned the virtuous ring and glass;
And of the wondrous horse of brass,
On which the Tartar king did ride;
And if aught else[3] great bards beside
In sage and solemn tunes have sung,
Of tourneys, and of trophies hung,
Of forests and enchantments drear,
Where more is meant[4] than meets the ear.

Thus, Night,[5] oft see me in thy pale career,
Till civil-suited[6] morn appear;
Not tricked and frounced[7] as she was wont
With the Attic boy[8] to hunt,
But kercheft in a comely cloud,
While rocking winds are piping loud,
Or ushered with a shower still,
When the gust hath blown his fill,
Ending on the rustling leaves,
With minute-drops[9] from off the eaves.

(1) *Musæus*—a celebrated Greek poet whose works are lost.

(2) *Him that left*, &c.—Chaucer. The story may be found in the extracts from that poet, pp. 243—251. Spenser endeavoured to complete it in the "Faerie Queene," book iv. It is difficult to see the propriety of this reference to a story which is rather romantic and fanciful than sad.

(3) *And if aught else*, &c.—i. e. O mournful virgin, relate to me anything else that great bards, &c. He here refers to Spenser and the "Faerie Queene."

(4) *Where more is meant*, &c.—In reference to the allegorical meaning of the "Faerie Queene."

(5) *Thus, Night*, &c.—"Hitherto we have seen the night of the melancholy man; here his day commences."—*Warton*.

(6) *Civil-suited*—soberly attired, not splendidly adorned, as in "L'Allegro."

(7) *Tricked and frounced*—dressed and frizzled, or curled.

(8) *Attic boy*—Cephalus, with whom Aurora fell in love as he was hunting.

(9) *Minute-drops*—drops falling at intervals, as we say *minute-guns*, and *minute-bells*.

And, when the sun begins to fling
His flaring beams, me, goddess, bring
To arched walks of twilight groves,
And shadows brown, that Sylvan loves,
Of pine, or monumental[1] oak,
Where the rude axe, with heavéd stroke,
Was never heard the nymphs to daunt,
Or fright them from their hallowed haunt.
There, in close covert, by some brook,
Where no profaner eye may look,
Hide me from day's garish eye,
While the bee with honeyed thigh,[2]
That at her flowery work doth sing,
And the waters murmuring,
With such concert as they keep,
Entice the dewy feathered Sleep:
And let some strange,[3] mysterious dream
Wave at his wings in airy stream
Of lively portraiture displayed,
Softly on my eyelids laid:
And, as I wake, sweet music breathe
Above, about, or underneath,
Sent by some spirit to mortals good,
Or the unseen Genius of the wood.
   But let my due feet never fail
To walk the studious cloisters' pale,[4]
And love the high-embowéd roof,
With antique pillars massy proof,[5]

(1) *Monumental*—perhaps so called from the great age to which the oak lives; surviving, as it were, like a monument of bygone times.

(2) *Honeyed thigh*—this is slightly incorrect: the bee collects honey in a bag, and wax on its thigh.

(3) *Let some strange, &c.*—i. e. let some strange, mysterious dream wave at or rustle the wings of Sleep with an airy stream of visionary figures, vividly portrayed to my fancy. The meaning of this passage may perhaps be illustrated by comparing Jonson's song "To Fancy, at Night." (See p. 173.) Statius, in his beautiful soliloquy to Sleep ("Ad Somnum"), speaks of the feathers of sleep—

    "Nec ne totas infundere pennas
    Luminibus compello meis."

(4) *Pale*—this may mean either as an adjective dim, or shaded; or as a substantive, the pale, or enclosure, of the cloister.

(5) *Massy proof*—i. e. massy *and* proof, or immovable. This explanation seems justified, as Dr. Mant remarks, by the parallel expression used by Milton in "Samson Agonistes," where he speaks of a "frock of mail" being "adamantean proof," that is adamantean *and* proof, or impenetrable.

And storied windows richly dight,
Casting a dim religious light.
There let the pealing organ blow
To the full-voiced quire below,
In service high, and anthems clear,
As may with sweetness, through mine ear,
Dissolve me into ecstasies,
And bring all heaven before mine eyes.

And may at last my weary age
Find out the peaceful hermitage,
The hairy gown and mossy cell,
Where I may sit and rightly spell
Of every star that heaven doth shew,
And every herb that sips the dew;
Till old experience do attain
To something like prophetic strain.[1]

These pleasures, Melancholy, give,
And I with thee will choose to live.

EXTRACTS FROM PARADISE LOST.[2]

THE EXORDIUM.

Of Man's first disobedience, and the fruit
Of that forbidden tree, whose mortal taste
Brought death into the world, and all our woe,
With loss of Eden, till one greater Man
Restore us, and regain the blissful seat,

---

(1) *Till old experience, &c.*—A pregnant couplet. The man of large experience of the past is able to predict the future, because he has risen from the observation of particular and individual facts to the contemplation of general truths, which belong equally to all time, past, present, and future. On the same principle the Latin word *vates* signified *prophet*, as well as *poet* and *priest*.

(2) *Paradise Lost*—the most sublime work of imagination ever presented to the world, was published in 1667, when Milton was in his sixtieth year. He had been blind several years when he began to compose it, but neither this calamity, nor the troublous times in which he lived and suffered, daunted him in prosecuting to its close a work which he hoped "the world would not willingly let die."

The calm dignity and majesty of this exordium give us an exalted idea of the poet's mental power; he rises to the "height of his great argument" with scarcely an effort, and thus at once assures the reader, and stamps the character of the poem.

Sing, heavenly Muse![1] that on the secret[2] top
Of Oreb, or of Sinai, didst inspire
That shepherd, who first taught the chosen seed,
In the beginning, how the heavens and earth
Rose out of chaos: or, if Sion hill[3]
Delight thee more, and Siloa's brook that flowed
Fast by the oracle of God,[4] I thence
Invoke thy aid to my adventurous song,
That with no middle flight intends to soar
Above the Aonian mount,[5] while it pursues
Things unattempted yet in prose or rhyme.[6]

And chiefly thou, O SPIRIT! that dost prefer
Before all temples the upright heart and pure,
Instruct me, for thou knowst; thou from the first
Wast present, and with mighty wings outspread,
Dove-like, sat'st brooding[7] on the vast abyss,
And mad'st it pregnant: what in me is dark,
Illumine; what is low, raise and support;
That to the height of this great argument
I may assert eternal Providence,
And justify the ways of God to men.

SATAN MUSTERING THE REBEL ANGELS.[8]

THUS Satan, talking to his nearest mate,
With head uplift above the wave, and eyes

(1) *Heavenly Muse*—The Holy Spirit is addressed both here and below under different aspects: here, as the source of the divine poetry of Moses and David; below, as the source of spiritual energy and strength.

(2) *Secret*—in allusion to the secresy of the interview between God and Moses. Bentley proposed to alter *secret* to "sacred."

(3) *Sion hill*—Here stood David's palace, and thus the reference to David's poetry is indicated.

(4) *Oracle of God*—the Temple.

(5) *Above the Aonian mount*—i. e. beyond the range of the classical poets. Aonia was that part of Bœotia in which were Mount Helicon and the fountains Aganippe and Hippocrene, all celebrated haunts of the Muses.

(6) *Rhyme*—from the Greek $\dot{\rho}v\theta\mu\acute{o}\varsigma$, measured motion, rhythm—verse. (See note 1, p. 300.)

(7) *Brooding*—the true meaning of the word translated "moved" in Genesis i. 2.

(8) The conception of Satan is, perhaps, the most magnificent in all poetry. He rises in vague and indefinite grandeur before the mind, standing "like a tower," and seeming "alone the antagonist of Heaven." As the personification of the Spirit of Evil, he is justly represented as possessing high mental energy, a daring will, and an unconquerable aversion to the supremely good, fair, and great.

That sparkling blazed; his other parts besides
Prone on the flood,[1] extended long and large,
Lay floating many a rood; in bulk as huge
As whom the fables name of monstrous size,
Titanian,[2] or Earth-bòrn, that warred on Jove,
Briareos, or Typhon, whom the den
By ancient Tarsus[3] held; or that sea-beast
Leviathan,[4] which God of all his works
Created hugest,[5] that swim the ocean stream.

    Forthwith upright he rears from off the pool
His mighty stature; on each hand the flames,
Driven backward, slope their pointing spires, and, rolled
In billows, leave in the midst a horrid vale.
Then with expanded wings he steers his flight
Aloft, incumbent on the dusky air,
That felt unusual weight, till on dry land
He lights, if it were land that ever burned
With solid, as the lake with liquid fire.
                    His ponderous shield,
Ethereal temper, massy, large, and round,
Behind him cast; the broad circumference
Hung on his shoulders, like the moon, whose orb
Through optic glass the Tuscan artist[6] views
At evening, from the top of Fesolé,
Or in Valdarno,[7] to descry new lands,
Rivers, or mountains, in her spotty globe.
His spear—to equal which the tallest pine
Hewn on Norwegian hills, to be the mast
Of some great ammiral,[8] were but a wand—

(1) *Prone on the flood, &c.*—The numerous monosyllables in this and the next line, detain the voice in reading, and give an idea of the sense through the sound.

(2) *Titanian*—According to the mythology it was the giants, and not the Titans, "that warred on Jove."

(3) *Ancient Tarsus*—Tarsus, in Cilicia, Asia Minor.

(4) *Leviathan*—In Job this word means the crocodile, but here the whale.

(5) *Created hugest, &c.*—"What a force of imagination," says Hazlitt, "is there in this expression! What an idea it conveys of that hugest of created beings, as if it shrunk up the ocean to a stream. Force of style is one of Milton's greatest excellences."

(6) *Tuscan artist*—Galileo, the inventor or improver of the "optic glass," or telescope.

(7) *Valdarno*—Val d' Arno—Vale of Arno. Florence is seated in the bosom of the Val d' Arno.

(8) *Ammiral*—the admiral's ship; any large ship. Some derive this word from the eastern title, *Emir*.

He walked with, to support uneasy steps
Over the burning marle; not like those steps
On heaven's azure: and the torrid clime
Smote on him sore besides, vaulted with fire:
Nathless[1] he so endured, till on the beach
Of that inflaméd sea he stood, and called
His legions,[2] angel forms, who lay entranced,
Thick as autumnal leaves that strow the brooks
In Vallombrosa,[3] where the Etrurian shades
High overarched embower; or scattered sedge
Afloat, when with fierce winds Orion armed[4]
Hath vexed the Red Sea coast, whose waves o'erthrew
Busiris[5] and his Memphian chivalry,
While with perfidious hatred they pursued
The sojourners of Goshen, who beheld
From the safe shore their floating carcases
And broken chariot wheels: so thick bestrown,
Abject and lost lay these, covering the flood,
Under amazement of their hideous change.
He called so loud, that all the hollow deep
Of Hell resounded:—

     "Princes, potentates,
Warriors, the flower of heaven, once yours, now lost,
If such astonishment as this can seize
Eternal spirits!—or have ye chosen this place
After the toil of battle to repose

(1) *Nathless*—nevertheless.

(2) *Called his legions, &c.*—"If there is one circumstance more than another which sets him [Milton] above Virgil and Homer, it is this, that he takes more violent possession of the mind of his reader, by crowding upon him a phalanx of thick-coming thoughts. Satan's legions lie entranced upon the sea of fire, 'thick as the leaves in the brooks of Vallombrosa.' Here another poet might have ended. Not so Milton:—they are, moreover, like the scattered sedge on the coast of the Red Sea, when Orion hath vexed it with fierce winds. Still something is wanted, not to complete the simile, but to overwhelm the reader;—and in throng Busiris and the Memphian chivalry, and floating carcases, and broken chariot wheels."—*Quarterly Review*, vol. xxxvi. p. 56.

(3) *Vallombrosa*—from the Latin *Vallis umbrosa*, shady vale, a valley in Tuscany.

(4) *Orion armed, &c.*—"Orion is a constellation represented in the figure of an armed man, and supposed to be attended with stormy weather."—*Newton*.

(5) *Busiris, &c.*—Milton thus styles, not without authority, Pharaoh and his horsemen, who pursued the Israelites *perfidiously*, since he had previously agreed to allow them to depart unmolested.

Your wearied virtue,[1] for the ease you find
To slumber here, as in the vales of heaven?
Or in this abject posture have you sworn
To adore the Conqueror? who now beholds
Cherub and seraph rolling in the flood
With scattered arms and ensigns, till anon
His swift pursuers from Heaven gates discern
The advantage, and, descending, tread us down
Thus drooping, or with linkéd thunderbolts
Transfix us to the bottom of this gulf.
Awake!—arise!—or be for ever fallen!"
  They heard, and were abashed, and up they sprung
Upon the wing: as when men wont to watch
On duty, sleeping found by whom they dread,
Rouse and bestir themselves ere well awake.
Nor did they not perceive[2] the evil plight
In which they were, or the fierce pains not feel;
Yet to[3] their general's voice they soon obeyed
Innumerable. As when the potent rod
Of Amram's son, in Egypt's evil day,
Waved round the coast, up called a pitchy cloud
Of locusts, warping[4] on the eastern wind,
That o'er the realm of impious Pharaoh hung
Like night, and darkened all the land of Nile:
So numberless were those bad angels seen,
Hovering on wing under the cope of hell,
'Twixt upper, nether, and surrounding fires;
Till, as a signal[5] given, the uplifted spear
Of their great sultan, waving to direct
Their course, in even balance down they light
On the firm brimstone, and fill all the plain;
A multitude, like which the populous north
Poured never from her frozen loins, to pass
Rhene or the Danaw, when her barbarous sons
Came like a deluge on the south, and spread
Beneath Gibraltar to the Libyan sands.
  Forthwith from every squadron and each band,

---

(1) *Virtue*—as the Latin *virtus*—courage, strength.

(2) *Nor did they not perceive*—a Latinism for, they did perceive.

(3) *Yet to, &c.*—"To obey to" is frequently found in our old authors.

(4) *Warping*—a sea term—working laboriously forward, with a sort of sidelong motion.

(5) *As a signal*—Another reading is, "at a signal given." If that given in the text is correct, the spear of Satan itself gave the signal, which is more poetical.

The heads and leaders thither haste, where stood
Their great commander; godlike shapes, and forms
Excelling human, princely dignities,
And powers that erst[1] in heaven sat on thrones;
Though of their names in heavenly records now
Be no memorial, blotted out and rased,
By their rebellion, from the Book of Life.

All these and more came flocking, but with looks
Downcast and damp;[2] yet such wherein appeared
Obscure some glimpse of joy, to have found their chief
Not in despair, to have found themselves not lost
In loss itself; which[3] on his countenance cast
Like doubtful hue; but he, his wonted pride
Soon recollecting, with high words that bore
Semblance of worth, not substance, gently raised
Their fainting courage, and dispelled their fears:
Then straight commands, that, at the warlike sound
Of trumpets loud and clarions,[4] be upreared
His mighty standard: that proud honour claimed
Azazel as his right, a cherub tall;
Who forthwith from the glittering staff unfurled[5]
The imperial ensign; which, full high advanced,
Shone like a meteor streaming to the wind,
With gems and golden lustre rich emblazed,
Seraphic arms and trophies; all the while
Sonorous metal blowing martial sounds:
At which the universal host up-sent
A shout that tore hell's concave, and beyond
Frighted the reign of Chaos and old Night.
All in a moment through the gloom were seen
Ten thousand banners rise into the air,
With orient colours waving: with them rose
A forest huge of spears; and thronging elms
Appeared, and serried[6] shields in thick array

(1) *Erst*—or *erest*, superlative of Anglo-Saxon *ær*, before.

(2) *Damp*—depressed, dispirited.

(3) *Which*—which *circumstance*—*i. e.* the twofold expression of their countenances, cast on his *like* doubtful hue.

(4) *Clarion*—from the Latin *clarus*, clear—a clear-sounding, shrill kind of trumpet.

(5) *Unfurled, &c.*—Addison particularly mentions Azazel's unfurling the standard, and the shout of the rebel angels, as "wonderfully poetical, and instances of that sublime genius so peculiar to the author."

(6) *Serried*—from the French *serrer*, to lock—locked, or clasped together.

Y

Of depth[1] immeasurable: anon they move
In perfect phalanx to the Dorian mood[2]
Of flutes and soft recorders;[3] such as raised
To height of noblest temper heroes old
Arming to battle; and, instead of rage,
Deliberate valour breathed, firm and unmoved
With dread of death to flight or foul retreat:
Nor wanting power to mitigate and swage
With solemn touches troubled thoughts, and chase
Anguish, and doubt, and fear, and sorrow, and pain,
From mortal or immortal minds. Thus they,
Breathing united force, with fixéd thought
Moved on in silence to soft pipes, that charmed
Their painful steps o'er the burnt soil; and now,
Advanced in view they stand, a horrid[4] front
Of dreadful length and dazzling arms, in guise
Of warriors old with ordered[5] spear and shield,
Awaiting what command their mighty chief
Had to impose. He through the arméd files
Darts his experienced eye, and soon travèrse[6]
The whole battalion views, their order due,
Their visages and stature as of gods;
Their number last he sums. And now his heart
Distends with pride, and hardening in his strength,
Glories: for never, since created man,[7]
Met such embodied force.
      He, above[8] the rest,
In shape and gesture proudly eminent,

(1) *Of depth, &c.*—The rhythmical beat of this verse is remarkable. The word "immeasurable" closes the sentence most fitly, and gives occasion for a pause, which however is soon broken by the commencement of the march. The words "anon they move," &c., not only describe, but *represent* the movement.

(2) *Dorian mood.*—"There seems to have been three principal modes or measures among the ancients: the Lydian, the Phrygian, and the Dorian. The Lydian was the most doleful, the Phrygian was the most sprightly, and the Dorian the most grave and majestic."—*Newton.*

(3) *Recorders*—pipes, flageolets.

(4) *Horrid*—in the Latin sense—bristling.

(5) *Ordered*—in regular order, or equipment.

(6) *Traverse*—transversely, obliquely.

(7) *Since created man*—a Latinism—since man was created, or, since the creation of man.

(8) *He above, &c.*—"There is no single passage," says Addison, "in the whole poem worked up to a greater sublimity than that wherein his [Satan's] person is described in those celebrated lines, He above, &c."

Stood like a tower;[1] his form had yet not lost
All her original brightness, nor appeared
Less than archangel ruined, and the excess
Of glory obscured: as when the sun,[2] new risen,
Looks through the horizontal misty air
Shorn of his beams; or from behind the moon,
In dim eclipse, disastrous twilight sheds
On half the nations, and with fear of change
Perplexes monarchs; darkened so, yet shone
Above them all the archangel: but his face
Deep scars of thunder had intrenched; and care
Sat on his faded cheek, but under brows
Of dauntless courage, and considerate pride
Waiting revenge; cruel his eye, but cast
Signs of remorse and passion,[3] to behold
The fellows of his crime—the followers rather—
(Far other once beheld in bliss!) condemned
For ever now to have their lot in pain:
Millions of spirits for his fault amerced[4]
Of heaven, and from eternal splendours flung
For his revolt; yet faithful[5] how they stood,
Their glory withered: as when heaven's fire
Hath scathed the forest oaks, or mountain pines,
With singéd top their stately growth, though bare,
Stands on the blasted heath. He now prepared
To speak; whereat their doubled ranks they bend
From wing to wing, and half enclose him round
With all his peers: attention held them mute.
Thrice he assayed, and thrice, in spite of scorn,
Tears, such as angels weep, burst forth: at last
Words, interwove with sighs, found out their way.

(1) *Like a tower*—It may be observed, that no possible limitation of Satan's dimensions could have equalled the effect produced by the indefiniteness of this image.

(2) *As when the sun, &c.*—" The fallen archangel is compared to the sun when he shines through the horizontal, misty air, shorn of his beams; this is a splendid picture in itself; but Milton does not think it enough; he presses on with another magnificent feature, the eclipse. Nor is this all: the concomitant horrors of the disasters it is believed to portend—perplexity to monarchs, and revolution to nations—are superadded, and then 'the charm's wound up.'"—*Quarterly Review*, *ubi supra*.

(3) *Passion*—feeling, sympathy.

(4) *Amerced*—deprived, as a punishment.

(5) *Yet faithful*—i. e. *to behold* how faithful they stood, though they were punished for his fault.

PANDEMONIUM, AND THE ASSEMBLING OF THE COUNCIL.

Anon, out of the earth a fabric huge
Rose like an exhalation, with the sound
Of dulcet symphonies and voices sweet;
Built like a temple, where, pilasters[1] round
Were set, and Doric pillars, overlaid
With golden architrave;[1] nor did there want
Cornice or frieze,[1] with bossy sculptures graven;
The roof was fretted gold. Not Babylon,
Nor great Alcairo, such magnificence
Equalled in all their glories, to enshrine
Belus or Serapis,[2] their gods, or seat
Their kings, when Egypt with Assyria strove
In wealth and luxury. The ascending pile
Stood fixed[3] her stately height: and straight the doors,
Opening their brazen folds, discover wide
Within her ample spaces o'er the smooth
And level pavement. From the archéd roof,
Pendent by subtle magic, many a row
Of starry lamps and blazing cressets,[4] fed
With naphtha and asphaltus, yielded light
As from a sky. The hasty multitude
Admiring entered; and the work some praise,
And some the architect: his hand was known
In heaven by many a towered structure high,
Where sceptred angels held their residence,
And sat as princes; whom the supreme King
Exalted to such power, and gave to rule,
Each to his hierarchy, the orders bright.
Nor was his name unheard or unadored
In ancient Greece; and in Ausonian land[5]
Men called him Mulciber; and how he fell
From heaven they fabled, thrown by angry Jove

(1) *Pilasters, architrave, &c.*—These architectural terms may be thus briefly explained:—*pilasters,* pillars jutting out from the wall; *architrave,* the chief beam resting immediately on the column; *frieze,* the part between the architrave and cornice of a column.

(2) *Serapis*—the usual quantity of this word is Serāpis.

(3) *Stood fixed, &c.*—Stood (with) her stately height (now) fixed.

(4) *Cresset*—from the French *croisette,* a little cross, because beacons had anciently crosses on their tops—any great light set on high.

(5) *Ausonian land*—Italy.

Sheer o'er the crystal battlements: from morn
To noon he fell, from noon to dewy eve,
A summer's day; and with the setting sun
Dropt from the zenith, like a falling star,
On Lemnos, the Ægean isle: thus they relate,
Erring; for he with this rebellious rout
Fell long before: nor aught availed him now
To have built in heaven high towers; nor did he 'scape
By all his engines, but was headlong sent
With his industrious crew to build in hell.
   Meanwhile, the wingéd heralds, by command
Of sovereign power, with awful ceremony
And trumpet's sound, throughout the host proclaim
A solemn council, forthwith to be held
At Pandemonium,[1] the high capital
Of Satan and his peers; their summons called
From every band and squared regiment,
By place or choice the worthiest; they anon
With hundreds and with thousands, trooping came,
Attended: all access was thronged; the gates
And porches wide, but chief the spacious hall
(Though like a covered field,[2] where champions bold
Wont ride in armed, and at the soldan's chair
Defied the best of Panim[3] chivalry
To mortal combat, or career with lance),
Thick swarmed, both on the ground and in the air,
Brushed[4] with the hiss of rustling wings. As bees
In spring-time, when the sun with Taurus rides,
Pour forth their populous youth about the hive
In clusters; they among fresh dews and flowers
Fly to and fro, or on the smoothéd plank,
The suburb of their straw-built citadel,
New rubbed with balm, expatiate,[5] and confer
Their state affairs: so thick the aëry crowd
Swarmed, and were straitened; till, the signal given,
Behold a wonder! They but now who seemed

---

  (1) *Pandemonium*—from the Greek πᾶν, every, and δαιμόνιον, a demon—the rendezvous of all the demons.

  (2) *Covered field*—i. e. enclosed or listed field—the lists.

  (3) *Panim*—Pagan. (See p. 74, note 3.)

  (4) *Brushed*—This line, by the abundance of sibilants, aptly illustrates the subject.

  (5) *Expatiate*—range at large, traverse to and fro.

In bigness to surpass earth's giant sons,
Now less than smallest dwarfs, in narrow room
Throng numberless, like that pigmëan race
Beyond the Indian mount; or fairy elves,
Whose midnight revels by a forest side
Or fountain, some belated peasant sees,
Or dreams he sees, while overhead the moon
Sits arbitress,[1] and nearer to the earth[2]
Wheels her pale course; they, on their mirth and dance
Intent, with jocund musick charm his ear;
At once with joy and fear his heart rebounds.
Thus incorporeal spirits to smallest forms
Reduced their shapes immense, and were at large,[3]
Though without number still, amidst the hall
Of that infernal court. But far within,
And in their own dimensions[4] like themselves,
The great seraphic lords and cherubim
In close recess and secret conclave sat;
A thousand demi-gods on golden seats,
Frequent[5] and full. After short silence then,
And summons read, the great consult began.

ADDRESS TO LIGHT.[6]

Hail, holy Light! offspring of heaven's first-born,
Or of the Eternal[7] co-eternal beam,
May I express thee unblamed? since God is light,
And never but in unapproached light

(1) *Arbitress*—witness, spectatress.

(2) *Nearer to the earth*—in allusion to the superstitious notion of witches and fairies having the power of drawing down the moon towards the earth.

(3) *At large*—at liberty, without restraint.

(4) *In their own dimensions, &c.*—Addison particularly admires the ingenuity of the poet in preserving the natural dimensions of the chiefs, while those of the common crowd are contracted.

(5) *Frequent*—in the Latin sense—crowded.

(6) "Paradise Lost," book iii. "Our author's address to Light, and lamentation of his own blindness, may perhaps be censured as an excrescence or digression not agreeable to the rules of epic poetry; but yet this is so charming a part of the poem that the most critical reader, I imagine, cannot wish it were omitted. One is even pleased with a fault, if it be a fault, that is the occasion of so many beauties, and acquaints us so much with the circumstances and character of the author."—*Newton*.

(7) *Or of the Eternal, &c.*—i. e. "or may I without blame call ("express") thee the co-eternal beam of the eternal God?"—*Newton*.

Dwelt from eternity, dwelt then in thee,
Bright effluence[1] of bright essence increate.
Or hear'st thou rather[2] pure ethereal stream,
Whose fountain who shall tell? Before the sun,
Before the heavens thou wert; and at the voice
Of God, as with a mantle, didst invest
The rising world of waters dark and deep,
Won from the void and formless infinite.
Thee I revisit now with bolder wing,
Escaped the Stygian pool;[3] though long detained
In that obscure sojourn, while in my flight
Through utter[4] and through middle darkness borne,
With other notes than to the Orphéan lyre,
I sung of Chaos and eternal Night;
Taught by the heavenly Muse to venture down
The dark descent, and up to reascend,
Though hard and rare:[5] thee I revisit safe,
And feel thy sovran vital lamp; but thou
Revisit'st not these eyes, that roll in vain
To find thy piercing ray, and find no dawn;
So thick a drop serene[6] hath quenched their orbs,
Or dim suffusion veiled. Yet not the more
Cease I to wander where the Muses haunt
Clear spring, or shady grove, or sunny hill,
Smit with the love of sacred song; but chief
Thee, Sion, and the flowery brooks[7] beneath,
That wash thy hallowed feet, and warbling flow,
Nightly I visit: nor sometimes forget[8]
Those other two[9] equalled with me in fate,

(1) *Bright effluence, &c.*—"Thou bright overflowing of that bright, uncreated, self-existent being."—*Richardson.*

(2) *Or hear'st thou rather*—a pure Latinism—dost thou delight rather to be called?

(3) *Escaped the Stygian pool, &c.*—i. e. having escaped from describing the burning lake in the first book, and Chaos and Night in the second book.

(4) *Through utter, &c.*—i. e. through hell, and the great gulf between heaven and hell.

(5) *Hard and rare*—difficult and seldom achieved.

(6) *Drop serene, &c.*—In reference to the *gutta serena,* "drop serene," or *amaurosis,* as it is now called, with which he was afflicted.

(7) *Brooks*—Kedron and Siloam.

(8) *Nor sometimes forget*—i. e. sometimes remember; *nor* being here, in imitation of the Latin idiom, equivalent to, *and not.*

(9) *Those other two*—Milton speaks of *two,* and then names *four.*—Newton's explanation is, "Though he mentions four, yet there are two whom he particularly

So were I equalled with them in renown,
Blind Thamyris, and blind Mæonides,[1]
And Tiresias,[2] and Phineus, prophets old:
Then feed on thoughts that voluntary move
Harmonious numbers;[3] as the wakeful bird
Sings darkling, and in shadiest covert hid
Tunes her nocturnal note. Thus, with the year
Seasons return, but not to me returns
Day, or the sweet approach of even or morn,
Or sight of vernal bloom or summer's rose,
Or flocks, or herds, or human face divine;
But clouds instead, and ever-during dark
Surrounds me, from the cheerful ways of men
Cut off, and for the book of knowledge fair
Presented with a universal blank
Of Nature's works, to me expunged and rased,
And wisdom[4] at one entrance quite shut out.
So much the rather thou, celestial Light,
Shine inward, and the mind through all her powers
Irradiate; there plant eyes, all mist from thence
Purge and disperse, that I may see and tell
Of things invisible to mortal sight.

SATAN'S MEETING WITH URIEL IN THE SUN.[5]

He soon
Saw within ken a glorious angel stand,
The same which John saw[6] also in the sun:
His back was turned, but not his brightness hid:

---

desires to resemble; and those he distinguishes both with the epithet 'blind' to make the likeness more striking." He adds, "It seems, therefore, as if Milton had intended at first to mention only these two, and then *currente calamo* had added the two others."

(1) *Mæonides*—Homer, so called from Mæonia, the supposed place of his birth.

(2) *And Tiresias, &c.*—Dr. Pearce proposes to correct the false accent in this line, by making "Tiresias" and "Phineus" change places.

(3) *Thoughts that voluntary, &c.*—This, it has been well observed, is perhaps one of the best definitions of poetry that could be framed.

(4) *And wisdom, &c.*—i.e and *presented with* wisdom, enfeebled and disparaged; or rather, perhaps, this is an instance of the nominative absolute, *wisdom being*, &c.

(5) "Paradise Lost," book iii. "The figures introduced here," remarks Hazlitt, "have all the elegance and precision of a Greek statue; glossy and impurpled, tinged with golden light."

(6) *John saw*—" And I saw an angel standing in the sun." Rev. xix. 17.

Of beaming sunny rays a golden tiar[1]
Circled his head; nor less his locks behind
Illustrious[2] on his shoulders, fledge with wings,
Lay waving round: on some great charge employed
He seemed, or fixed in cogitation deep.
Glad was the Spirit impure, as now in hope
To find who might direct his wandering flight
To Paradise, the happy seat of man,
His journey's end, and our beginning woe.[3]
But first he casts[4] to change his proper shape,
Which else might work him danger or delay:
And now a stripling cherub[5] he appears,
Not of the prime,[6] yet such as in his face
Youth smiled celestial, and to every limb
Suitable grace diffused, so well he feigned:
Under a coronet his flowing hair
In curls on either cheek played; wings he wore
Of many a coloured plume, sprinkled with gold;
His habit[7] fit for speed succinct, and held
Before his decent steps[8] a silver wand.
He drew not nigh unheard; the angel bright,
Ere he drew nigh, his radiant visage turned,
Admonished by his ear, and straight was known
The archangel Uriel, one of the seven
Who in God's presence, nearest to his throne,
Stand ready at command, and are his eyes[9]
That run through all the heavens, or down to th' earth
Bear his swift errands over moist and dry,
O'er sea and land.

(1) *Tiar*—tiara, or diadem—the ornamental head-dress of Eastern princes.
(2) *Illustrious*—bright, glossy.
(3) *Our beginning woe*—the first cause of woe to us—a Latinism.
(4) *Casts*—casts in *his mind*, contrives a plan.
(5) *Stripling cherub, &c.*—"A finer picture of a young angel," says Newton, "could not be drawn by the pencil of Raphael than is here by the pen of Milton."
(6) *Prime*—first or highest dignity.
(7) *His habit succinct*—i. e. his robe was tucked or looped up for freedom of action; he was prepared for motion.
(8) *Decent*—as the Latin *decens*, graceful, comely.
(9) *His eyes, &c.*—"Those seven, they are the eyes of the Lord, which run to and fro through the whole earth." Zech. iv. 10.

SATAN'S ADDRESS TO THE SUN.[1]

(Abridged.)

O thou! that, with surpassing glory crowned,
Look'st from thy sole dominion like the God
Of this new world;[2] at whose sight all the stars
Hide their diminished heads; to thee I call,
But with no friendly voice, and add thy name,
O Sun! to tell thee how I hate thy beams,
That bring to my remembrance from what state
I fell—how glorious once above thy sphere!—
Till pride and worse ambition[3] threw me down
Warring in Heaven against Heaven's matchless King.
Ah, wherefore! He deserved no such return
From me, whom he created what I was
In that bright eminence, and with his good
Upbraided none; nor was his service hard.
What could be less[4] than to afford him praise,
The easiest recompence, and pay him thanks,
How due! yet all his good proved ill in me,
And wrought but malice; lifted up so high
I 'sdained[5] subjection, and thought one step higher
Would set me highest, and in a moment quit
The debt immense of endless gratitude,
So burdensome,[6] still paying, still to owe:
Forgetful what from him I still received;
And understood not that a grateful mind
By owing owes not, but still pays, at once
Indebted and discharged; what burden then?
Oh! had his powerful destiny ordained
Me some inferior angel, I had stood

---

(1) "Paradise Lost," book iv. "The opening of this speech to the sun," says Addison, "is very bold and noble. It is, I think, the finest ascribed to Satan in the whole poem." The consummate skill, too, with which the poet describes the conflict of passions in the mind of Satan is commended by the same judicious critic.

(2) *This new world*—Satan has now alighted on earth, and from the top of Mount Niphates thus addresses the sun, which "sat high in his meridian tower." The ruined archangel, the mighty orb of day, the lone mountain-summit, each the greatest of its kind, present in their combination a magnificent picture.

(3) *Worse ambition*—worse, because it led to daring impiety and its retribution.

(4) *What could be, &c.*—i. e. what service could be less hard, &c.

(5) *I 'sdained*—I disdained.

(6) *So burdensome, &c.*—i. e. it being so burdensome, &c.

Then happy; no unbounded hope had raised
Ambition. Yet why not? some other power
As great might have aspired, and me, though mean,
Drawn to his part; but other powers as great
Fell not, but stand unshaken, from within
Or from without, to all temptations armed.
Hadst thou the same free will and power to stand?
Thou hadst. Whom hast thou then, or what, to accuse,
But Heaven's free love, dealt equally to all?
Be then his love accursed, since love or hate,
To me alike, it deals eternal woe.
Nay, cursed be thou; since against his thy will
Chose freely what it now so justly rues.
Me miserable! which way shall I fly
Infinite wrath, and infinite despair?
Which way I fly is hell; myself am hell!
And, in the lowest deep, a lower deep
Still threatening to devour me opens wide,
To which the hell I suffer seems a heaven.

PARADISE.[1]

So on he fares,[2] and to the border comes
Of Eden, where delicious Paradise,
Now nearer, crowns with her enclosure green,
As with a rural mound, the champaign head[3]
Of a steep wilderness, whose hairy sides
With thicket overgrown, grotesque and wild,

---

(1) "Paradise Lost," book iv. This beautiful description has been compared with the finest specimens of the same kind, as Homer's description of the gardens of Alcinous, and of Calypso's shady grotto, Ariosto's of the garden of Paradise, Tasso's of the garden of Armida, and Marino's of the garden of Venus, and though doubtless a general imitation of some of them, is thought greatly to exceed them all. In reference to Milton's power of delineating external scenery, Macaulay remarks ("Edinburgh Review," vol. xlii.):—"Neither Theocritus nor Ariosto had a finer or a more healthful sense of the pleasantness of external objects, or loved better to luxuriate amidst sunbeams and flowers, the song of nightingales, the juice of summer fruits, and the coolness of shady fountains. His poetry reminds us of the miracles of Alpine scenery. Nooks and dells, beautiful as fairyland, are embosomed in its most rugged and gigantic elevations. The roses and myrtles bloom unchilled on the verge of the avalanche."

(2) *Fares*—from the Anglo-Saxon *far-an*, to go—goes. We have the same element in "thoroughfare"—*i. e.* through-go.

(3) *Champaign head, &c.*—Open top or table-land of a steep hill, whose rough and prickly sides were covered with a wild growth of thickets and bushes.

Access denied; and overhead[1] up grew
Insuperable height of loftiest shade,
Cedar, and pine, and fir, and branching palm,
A sylvan scene; and, as the ranks ascend
Shade above shade, a woody theatre
Of stateliest view. Yet higher than their tops
The verdurous wall[2] of Paradise up sprung;
Which to our general sire gave prospect large
Into his nether empire neighbouring round:
And higher than that wall a circling row
Of goodliest trees, loaden with fairest fruit,[3]
Blossoms and fruits at once of golden hue,
Appeared with gay enamelled colours mixed;
On which the sun more glad impressed his beams,
Than in fair evening cloud, or humid bow,
When God hath showered the earth; so lovely seemed
That landscape: and of pure[4] now purer air
Meets his approach, and to the heart inspires
Vernal delight and joy, able to drive
All sadness but despair: now gentle gales,
Fanning their odoriferous wings, dispense
Native perfumes, and whisper whence they stole
Those balmy spoils. As when to them who sail
Beyond the Cape of Hope, and now are past
Mozambic, off at sea north-east winds blow
Sabæan odours from the spicy shore
Of Araby the blest; with such delay
Well pleased they slack their course, and many a league
Cheered with the grateful smell old Ocean smiles:
So entertained those odorous sweets the fiend
Who came their bane.

Beneath him with new wonder now he views,
To all delight of human sense exposed,
In narrow room, Nature's whole wealth, yea, more,

---

(1) *Overhead, &c.*—*i. e.* overhead above these thickets, on the side of the hill likewise, grew the loftiest trees, rising one above another like the seats of an amphitheatre.

(2) *Verdurous wall*—*i. e.* a sort of bank set with a green hedge, over which Adam could look downwards on Eden. All the scenery hitherto described is outside of the garden itself.

(3) *Fruit*—here used in the sense of produce, including both blossoms and fruit.

(4) *Of pure, &c.*—*Of* frequently implies change of circumstances, as in "Paradise Lost," book x., v. 720—"O miserable of happy."

A heaven on earth: for blissful Paradise
Of God the garden was, by him in the east
Of Eden planted; Eden stretched her line
From Auran[1] eastward to the royal towers
Of great Seleucia, built by Grecian kings;
Or where the sons of Eden long before
Dwelt in Telassar.[2] In this pleasant soil
His far more pleasant garden God ordained:
Out of the fertile ground he caused to grow
All trees of noblest kind, for sight, smell, taste;
And all amid them stood the Tree of Life,
High eminent, blooming ambrosial fruit
Of vegetable gold; and next to life,
Our death, the Tree of Knowledge, grew fast by;—
Knowledge of good bought dear by knowing ill!
Southward through Eden went a river large,
Nor changed his course, but through the shaggy hill
Passed underneath ingulfed: for God had thrown
That mountain as his garden-mould, high raised
Upon the rapid current, which, through[3] veins
Of porous earth with kindly thirst up-drawn,
Rose a fresh fountain, and, with many a rill
Watered the garden; thence united fell
Down the steep glade, and met the nether flood,
Which from his darksome passage now appears,
And now, divided into four main streams,
Runs diverse, wandering many a famous realm
And country, whereof here needs no account;
But rather to tell how, if art could tell,
How from that sapphire fount the crisped brooks
Rolling on orient pearl and sands of gold,
With mazy error under pendent shades
Ran nectar, visiting each plant, and fed
Flowers worthy of Paradise: which not nice art
In beds and curious knots, but nature boon
Poured forth profuse on hill, and dale, and plain;
Both where the morning sun first warmly smote
The open field, and where the unpiercéd shade

(1) *Auran*—i. e. Haran or Charræ, in Mesopotamia.
(2) *Telassar*—See Isaiah xxxvii. 12.
(3) *Which, through, &c.*—i. e. the water of the river being absorbed, it rose up through the mound placed upon it, and gushed out in the garden as a fountain—a feat of enchantment scarcely harmonizing with the general character of the scene, in which nature is elevated and adorned, but not violated.

Imbrowned the noon-tide bowers. Thus was this place
A happy rural seat of various view;
Groves,[1] whose rich trees wept odorous gums and balm;
Others whose fruit, burnished with golden rind,
Hung amiable (Hesperian fables[2] true,
If true, here only), and of delicious taste.
Betwixt them lawns, or level downs, and flocks
Grazing the tender herb, were interposed,
Or palmy hillock; or the flowery lap
Of some irriguous[3] valley spread her store;—
Flowers of all hue, and without thorn the rose.
Another side, umbrageous grots, and caves
Of cool recess, o'er which the mantling[4] vine
Lays forth her purple grape, and gently creeps
Luxuriant: meanwhile, murmuring waters fall
Down the slope hills, dispersed, or in a lake,
That to the fringéd bank with myrtle crowned
Her crystal mirror holds, unite their streams.
The birds their quire apply: airs, vernal airs,
Breathing the smell of field and grove, attune
The trembling leaves; while universal Pan,[5]
Knit with the Graces and the Hours in dance,
Led on the eternal Spring. Not that fair field
Of Enna, where Prosèrpine gathering flowers,
Herself a fairer flower, by gloomy Dis[6]
Was gathered, which cost Ceres all that pain
To seek her through the world; nor that sweet grove
Of Daphne[7] by Orontes, and the inspired
Castalian spring, might with this Paradise
Of Eden strive.

(1) *Groves, &c.*— "In the description of Paradise, the poet has observed Aristotle's rule of lavishing all the ornaments of diction on the weak, inactive parts of the fable, which are not supported by the beauty of sentiment and character."—*Addison.*

(2) *Hesperian fables, &c.*—i. e. "What is said of the Hesperian gardens is true here only; if all is not pure invention, this garden was meant."—*Richardson.*

(3) *Irriguous*—well-watered, full of springs and rills.

(4) *Mantling*—covering as with a mantle, spreading luxuriantly.

(5) *While universal Pan, &c.*—"The ancients personified everything. Pan is Nature, the Graces are the beautiful Seasons, and the Hours are the time for the production and perfection of things."—*Richardson.*

(6) *Dis*—Pluto.

(7) *Daphne*—"A grove near Antioch, in Syria, on the banks of the river Orontes; there also was the Castalian spring, of the same name with that in Greece, and extolled for its prophetic qualities."—*Newton.*

ADAM AND EVE IN PARADISE.[1]

Two of far nobler shape, erect and tall,
Godlike erect, with native honour clad,
In naked majesty seemed lords of all,
And worthy seemed; for in their looks divine
The image of their glorious Maker shone,
Truth, wisdom, sanctitude severe and pure
(Severe,[2] but in true filial freedom placed),
Whence[3] true authority in men; though both
Not equal, as their sex not equal seemed;
For contemplation he and valour formed;
For softness she, and sweet attractive grace;
He for God only, she for God in him:
His fair large front and eye sublime declared
Absolute rule; and hyacinthine[4] locks
Round from his parted forelock manly hung
Clustering, but not beneath his shoulders broad:
She, as a veil, down to the slender waist
Her unadorned golden tresses wore
Dishevelled, but in wanton ringlets waved
As the vine curls her tendrils; which implied
Subjection,[5] but required with gentle sway,
And by her yielded, by him best received,
Yielded[6] with coy submission, modest pride,
And sweet, reluctant, amorous delay.

So hand in hand they passed, the loveliest pair
That ever since in love's embraces met;

---

(1) "Paradise Lost," book iv. "The description of Adam and Eve, as they first appeared to Satan, is exquisitely drawn, and sufficient to make the fallen angel gaze upon them with all that astonishment and those emotions of envy, in which he is represented."—*Addison.*

(2) *Severe, &c.*—*i. e.* strict, but yet consistent with the freedom of children; "denoting," says Dr. Pearce, "a reverence rather than fear of the Deity."

(3) *Whence, &c.*—*i. e.* from the truth, wisdom, and holiness just mentioned, which, Dr. Pearce remarks, "are qualities that give to magistrates 'true authority,' that proper authority which they may want who yet have legal authority."

(4) *Hyacinthine*—a classical epithet, denoting black or dark brown chestnut.

(5) *Which implied subjection*—in reference to 1 Cor. xi. 10: "the woman ought to have *power* on her head," where the word ἐξουσίαν is interpreted in the margin, "a covering," a sign that she is under the power of her husband.

(6) *Yielded, &c.*—*i. e. when* yielded by her, &c.

Adam the goodliest[1] of men since born
His sons; the fairest of her daughters Eve.
Under a tuft of shade that on a green
Stood whispering soft, by a fresh fountain-side
They sat them down; and after no more toil
Of their sweet gardening labour than sufficed
To recommend cool zephyr, and made ease
More easy, wholesome thirst and appetite
More grateful, to their supper fruits they fell—
Nectarine[2] fruits, which the compliant boughs
Yielded them, side-long as they sat recline[3]
On the soft downy bank damasked with flowers.
The savoury pulp they chew, and in the rind,
Still as they thirsted, scoop the brimming stream.
About them frisking played
All beasts of the earth, since wild, and of all chace
In wood or wilderness, forest or den:
Sporting the lion ramped,[4] and in his paw
Dandled the kid; bears, tigers, ounces, pards,
Gamboled before them; the unwieldy elephant,
To make them mirth used all his might, and wreathed
His lithe proboscis; close the serpent sly
Insinuating wove with Gordian[5] twine
His braided train, and of his fatal guile
Gave proof unheeded; others on the grass
Couched, and now filled with pasture gazing sat,
Or bedward ruminating;[6] for the sun,
Declined, was hasting now with prone career
To the ocean isles,[7] and in the ascending scale[8]
Of heaven the stars that usher evening rose.

---

(1) *Adam the goodliest, &c.*—The superlative is here used for the comparative, as sometimes in Greek. The meaning of course is that Adam was a handsomer man than any of his sons, and Eve fairer than any of her daughters.

(2) *Nectarine*—as sweet as nectar.

(3) *Recline*—reclining.

(4) *Ramped*—"Stood on his two hinder legs in the posture of climbing; from the French *ramper*, to climb. In heraldry, a lion in this attitude is said to be *rampant.*"—*Richardson.*

(5) *Wove with Gordian, &c.*—Wove his twisted tail into a complicated braid, like the famous Gordian knot.

(6) *Bedward ruminating*—"Chewing the cud before they go to rest."—*Hume.*

(7) *Ocean isles*—the islands in the western ocean.

(8) *The ascending scale, &c.*—A metaphor for the changes of day and night, as if like a balance, the one ascended as the other sank.

EVENING IN PARADISE.

Now came[1] still evening on, and twilight grey
Had in her sober livery all things clad;
Silence accompanied; for beast and bird,
They to their grassy couch, these to their nests
Were slunk; all but the wakeful nightingale;
She all night long her amorous descant[2] sung.
Silence was pleased: now glowed the firmament
With living sapphires; Hesperus, that led
The starry host, rode brightest; till the moon,
Rising in clouded majesty, at length
Apparent queen, unveiled her peerless light,
And o'er the dark her silver mantle threw:
When Adam thus to Eve: "Fair consort! the hour
Of night, and all things now retired to rest
Mind us of like repose; since God hath set
Labour and rest, as day and night, to men
Successive; and the timely dew of sleep,[3]
Now falling with soft slumbrous weight, inclines
Our eyelids. Other creatures all day long
Rove idle, unemployed, and less need rest;
Man hath his daily work of body or mind
Appointed, which declares his dignity,
And the regard of heaven on all his ways;
While other animals unactive range,
And of their doings God takes no account.
To-morrow, ere fresh morning streak the east
With first approach of light, we must be risen,
And at our pleasant labour, to reform
Yon flowery arbours, yonder alleys green,
Our walk at noon, with branches overgrown,
That mock our scant manuring,[4] and require
More hands than ours to lop their wanton growth:

(1) *Now came, &c.*—"Words cannot furnish out a more lovely description. The greatest poets in all ages have, as it were, vied with one another in their descriptions of evening and night; but for the variety of numbers and pleasing images, I know of nothing parallel or comparable to this to be found among all the treasures of ancient or modern poetry."—*Newton.*

(2) *Descant*—a song with various modulations.

(3) *The timely dew of sleep*—"Did not the beauty of the poetry keep the mind awake, the words would lull the reader insensibly."—*Richardson.*

(4) *Manuring*—from the French *manœuvrer*, to work with the hands—manual labour;—a very unusual sense of the word.

These blossoms also, and those dropping gums,
That lie bestrown, unsightly and unsmooth,
Ask riddance, if we mean to tread with ease;
Meanwhile, as nature wills, night bids us rest."

To whom thus Eve, with perfect beauty adorned:
"My author[1] and disposer, what thou bidd'st,
Unargued I obey; so God ordains.
God is thy law, thou mine: to know no more
Is woman's happiest knowledge and her praise.
With thee conversing, I forget all time;
All seasons[2] and their change—all please alike.
Sweet is the breath[3] of morn, her rising sweet,
With charm[4] of earliest birds; pleasant the sun,
When first on this delightful land he spreads
His orient beams, on herb, tree, fruit, and flower.
Glistering with dew; fragrant the fertile earth
After soft showers; and sweet the coming on
Of grateful evening mild; then silent night,
With this her solemn bird,[5] and this fair moon,
And these the gems of heaven, her starry train:
But neither breath or morn, when she ascends
With charm of earliest birds; nor rising sun
On this delightful land; nor herb, fruit, flower,
Glistering with dew; nor fragrance after showers;
Nor grateful evening mild; nor silent night,
With this her solemn bird; nor walk by moon,
Or glittering star-light, without thee is sweet."

THE MORNING HYMN IN PARADISE.[6]

"THESE are[7] Thy glorious works, Parent of good,
Almighty! Thine this universal frame,

(1) *Author*—because Eve was made out of Adam.

(2) *Seasons*—the different periods and changes of the day, not of the year; this sense is determined by the lines that follow.

(3) *Sweet is the breath, &c.*—Addison remarks that " the variety of images in this passage is infinitely pleasing," and that "the recapitulation of each image, with a little varying of the expression, makes one of the finest turns of words" he had ever seen. See "Tatler," No. 114.

(4) *Charm*—i. e. song, from *carmen*, a song.

(5) *Solemn bird*—Milton calls the nightingale "most melancholy" in "Il Penseroso;" in both passages, referring rather to the circumstances under which the bird sings than to the tone of its music.

(6) "Paradise Lost," book v.

(7) *These are, &c.*—"The morning hymn is written in imitation of one of those psalms [the 148th for instance] where, in the overflowings of gratitude and praise,

Thus wondrous fair; Thyself how wondrous then!
Unspeakable, who sitt'st above these heavens,
To us invisible, or dimly seen
In these thy lowest works; yet these declare
Thy goodness beyond thought, and power divine.
Speak ye who[1] best can tell, ye, sons of light,
Angels! for ye behold Him, and with songs
And choral symphonies, day without night,
Circle his throne rejoicing; ye, in heaven—
On earth, join all ye creatures, to extol
Him first, him last, him midst, and without end.
Fairest of stars, last in the train of night,
If better thou belong not to the dawn,
Sure pledge of day, that crown'st the smiling morn
With thy bright circlet, praise him in thy sphere,
While day arises, that sweet hour of prime.
Thou sun, of this great world both eye and soul,
Acknowledge him thy greater; sound his praise
In thy eternal course, both when thou climb'st,
And when high noon hast gained, and when thou fall'st
Moon![2] that now meet'st the orient sun, now fliest,
With the fixed stars—fixed in their orb that flies;
And ye five other[3] wandering fires! that move
In mystic dance[4] not without song, resound
His praise, who out of darkness called up light.
Air, and ye elements! the eldest birth
Of nature's womb, that in quaternion[5] run
Perpetual circle, multiform, and mix
And nourish all things; let your ceaseless change
Vary to our great Maker still new praise.

the Psalmist calls not only upon the angels, but upon the most conspicuous parts of the inanimate creation, to join with him in extolling their common Maker. Invocations of this nature fill the mind with glorious ideas of God's works, and awaken that divine enthusiasm which is so natural to devotion."—*Addison.*

(1) *Speak ye who, &c.*—"He is unspeakable—no creature can speak worthily of him as he is, but speak *ye* who are best able, ye angels, &c."—*Newton.*

(2) *Moon, &c.*—The construction is:—Thou moon that now meetest and now fliest the orient sun, together with the fixed stars—fixed in their orb which flies—and ye five other wandering fires, or planets, &c.

(3) *Five other, &c.*—*i. e.* Mercury, Mars, Jupiter, Saturn, and Venus—considering the reference to the morning star as not marking any particular planet.

(4) *Mystic dance, &c.*—In allusion to the music of the spheres. (See extracts from Shakspere, p. 287.)

(5) *In quaternion run*—*i. e.* "that in a fourfold mixture and combination run a perpetual circle, one element continually changing into another."—*Newton.*

Ye mists and exhalations! that now rise
From hill or steaming lake, dusky or grey,
Till the sun paint your fleecy skirts with gold,
In honour to the world's great Author, rise;
Whether to deck with clouds the uncoloured sky,
Or wet the thirsty earth with falling showers,
Rising or falling, still advance his praise.
His praise, ye winds, that from four quarters blow,
Breathe soft or loud; and wave your tops, ye pines!
With every plant, in sign of worship, wave.
Fountains, and ye that warble[1] as ye flow,
Melodious murmurs, warbling tune his praise.
Join voices, all ye living souls![2] ye birds,
That singing, up to heaven-gate[3] ascend,
Bear on your wings, and in your notes his praise.
Ye that in waters glide, and ye that walk
The earth, or stately tread, or lowly creep,
Witness if I be silent, morn or even,
To hill or valley, fountain or fresh shade,
Made vocal by my song, and taught his praise.
Hail, universal Lord! be bounteous still
To give us only good; and if the night
Have gathered aught of evil, or concealed,
Disperse it, as now light dispels the dark!

THE SENTENCE OF EXPULSION FROM PARADISE.[4]

The archangel[5] soon drew nigh,
Not in his shape celestial, but as man
Clad to meet man: over his lucid arms
A military vest of purple flowed,
Livelier than[6] Melibœan, or the grain

---

(1) *Ye that warble, &c.*—i. e. ye streams that issue from the fountains, and warble forth melodious murmurs as ye flow, &c.

(2) *Souls*—creatures in general.

(3) *Up to heaven-gate, &c.*—Most probably taken from Shakspere's line (see p. 172), "Hark! hark! the lark at heaven's gate sings."

(4) "Paradise Lost," book xi.

(5) *The archangel*—Michael, whom the rabbinical writers name the minister of severity, is suitably chosen by Milton for the execution of God's sentence upon Adam and Eve. As a warrior he is represented in military costume, and as Addison remarks, "his person, his port, and behaviour, are suitable to a spirit of the highest rank, and exquisitely described in these lines."

(6) *Livelier than, &c.*—i. e. of a livelier colour and richer dye than the purple of Melibœa, in Thessaly, or Tyre (Sarra).

Of Sarra, worn by kings and heroes old
In time of truce:[1] Iris had dipped[2] the woof:
His starry helm unbuckled showed him prime
In manhood were youth ended; by his side,
As in a glistering zodiac,[3] hung the sword,
Satan's dire dread;[4] and in his hand[5] the spear.
Adam bowed low; he, kingly, from his state
Inclined not, but his coming thus declared:
"Adam, Heaven's high behest no preface needs:
Sufficient[6] that thy prayers are heard; and death,
Then due by sentence when thou didst transgress,
Defeated of his seizure; many days
Given thee of grace, wherein thou mayst repent,
And one bad act with many deeds well done
Mayst cover: well may then thy Lord, appeased,
Redeem thee quite from death's rapacious claim;
But longer in this Paradise to dwell
Permits not: to remove thee I am come,
And send thee from the garden forth, to till
The ground whence thou wast taken—fitter soil."

He added not; for Adam at the news
Heart-struck, with chilling gripe of sorrow stood,
That all his senses bound: Eve, who unseen
Yet all had heard, with audible lament
Discovered soon the place of her retire.[7]

"Oh unexpected stroke,[8] worse than of death!
Must I thus leave thee, Paradise? thus leave
Thee, native soil! these happy walks and shades,
Fit haunt of gods? where I had hope to spend,

(1) *In time of truce—i. e.* of peace. Milton speaks of "weeds of peace" in "L'Allegro"—meaning, as here, gorgeous and costly robes.

(2) *Iris had dipped, &c.*—The rainbow had dyed it in grain, and therefore more durably.

(3) *Zodiac*—zone or belt.

(4) *Satan's dire dread*—in allusion to its use in the great conflict between Satan and Michael, described in the sixth book of "Paradise Lost."

(5) *In his hand—i. e.* in his hand (*was*) the spear.

(6) *Sufficient, &c.*—The construction appears to be, It is sufficient that thy prayers are heard, that death is defeated of his seizure, and that many days are graciously given thee, &c.

(7) *Retire*—retirement.

(8) *Oh unexpected stroke, &c.*—"Eve's complaint," remarks Addison, "is wonderfully beautiful; the sentiments are not only proper to the subject, but have something in them particularly soft and womanish."

Quiet, though sad, the respite of that day
That must be mortal to us both. O flowers,
That never will in other climate grow—
My early visitation, and my last
At even—which I bred up with tender hand
From the first opening bud, and gave ye names!
Who now shall rear ye to the sun, or rank
Your tribes, and water from the ambrosial fount?
Thee, lastly, nuptial bower! by me adorned
With what to sight or smell was sweet! from thee
How shall I part, and whither wander down
Into a lower world, to this[1] obscure
And wild? How shall we breathe[2] in other air
Less pure, accustomed to immortal fruits?"

Whom thus the angel interrupted mild:—
"Lament not, Eve, but patiently resign
What justly thou hast lost; nor set thy heart,
Thus over-fond, on that which is not thine;
Thy going is not lonely; with thee goes
Thy husband; him to follow thou art bound;
Where he abides, think there thy native soil."

Adam by this from the cold sudden damp
Recovering, and his scattered spirits returned,
To Michael thus his humble words addressed:

"Celestial![3] whether among the thrones, or named
Of them the highest;—for such of shape may seem[4]
Prince above princes! gently hast thou told
Thy message, which might else in telling wound,
And in performing end us; what besides[5]
Of sorrow, and dejection, and despair,
Our frailty can sustain, thy tidings bring;

(1) *To this*—i. e. compared to this.

(2) *How shall we breathe, &c.*—The antithesis between "air" and "fruits" does not appear very apt, but there is an evident ellipsis, the sense of which may perhaps be thus given:—How shall we breathe the gross air [which nourishes only mortal fruits] after being accustomed, &c.

(3) *Celestial, &c.*—"Adam's speech," says Addison, "abounds with thoughts which are equally moving [with those in Eve's complaint], but of a more masculine and elevated turn. Nothing can be conceived more sublime and poetical than the following passage in it:—'This most afflicts me, &c.'"

(4) *Such of shape, &c.*—Such in appearance may he be who is a prince over princes.

(5) *What besides, &c.*—i. e. thou hast executed thy mission gently, and in so doing, thou hast forborne to wound or kill us; but setting this aside ("besides") thy tidings involve the extreme of sorrow, dejection, &c.

Departure from this happy place, our sweet
Recess, and only consolation left
Familiar to our eyes; all places else
Inhospitable appear, and desolate;
Nor knowing us, nor known: and, if by prayer
Incessant I could hope to change the will
Of Him who all things can, I would not cease
To weary him with my assiduous cries:
But prayer against his absolute decree
No more avails than breath against the wind,
Blown stifling back on him that breathes it forth:
Therefore to his great bidding I submit,
This most afflicts me, that, departing hence,
As from his face I shall be hid, deprived
His blessed countenance; here I could frequent
With worship place by place where he vouchsafed
Presence divine, and to my sons relate;—
On this mount he appeared—under this tree
Stood, visible—among these pines his voice
I heard—here with him at this fountain talked;—
So many grateful altars I would rear
Of grassy turf, and pile up every stone
Of lustre from the brook, in memory[1]
Or monument to ages, and thereon
Offer sweet-smelling gums, and fruits, and flowers.
In yonder nether world where shall I seek
His bright appearances, or footstep trace?
For though I fled him angry, yet, recalled
To life prolonged and promised race, I now
Gladly behold though but his utmost skirts
Of glory; and far off his steps adore."

CONCLUSION OF THE POEM.[2]

To their fixed station,[3] all in bright array,
The cherubim descended; on the ground
Gliding meteorous,[4] as evening-mist
Risen from a river o'er the marish[5] glides,

(1) *In memory, &c.*—As a memorial to himself, or as a monument to others, for ages.
(2) "Paradise Lost," book xii. "The lines which conclude the poem rise in a most glorious blaze of poetical expressions."—*Addison*.
(3) *Their fixed station*—*i. e.* to the position Michael had ordered them to occupy.
(4) *Meteorous*—like meteors, seeming as it were noiselessly to sweep the ground.
(5) *Marish*—an old word for *marsh*.

And gathers round fast at the labourer's heel
Homeward returning. High in front advanced
The brandished sword of God before them blazed,
Fierce as a comet; which with torrid heat,
And vapour as the Lybian air adust,[1]
Begin to parch that temperate clime; whereat
In either hand the hastening angel caught
Our lingering parents, and to the eastern gate
Led them direct, and down the cliff as fast
To the subjected plain;[2] then disappeared.
They, looking back, all the eastern side beheld
Of Paradise, so late their happy seat,
Waved over by that flaming brand; the gate
With dreadful[3] faces thronged, and fiery arms.
Some natural tears they dropped, but wiped them soon:
The world was all before them, where to choose
There place of rest, and Providence their guide.
They, hand in hand,[4] with wandering steps and slow,
Through Eden took their solitary way.

(1) *Adust*—from the Latin *adustus*, burnt up—parched, scorching.
(2) *Subjected plain*—a Latinism—the plain below.
(3) *With dreadful, &c.*—A very magnificent line.
(4) *They, hand in hand, &c.*—The poem closes with a simplicity worthy of its greatness; the conception, expression, and versification, all eminently conducing to the effect.

The following remarks upon the *moral* of "Paradise Lost" may not unsuitably close the notes upon that poem. "The moral which reigns in Milton is the most universal and most useful that can be imagined. It is in short this, that obedience to the will of God makes men happy, and that disobedience makes them miserable. This is visibly the moral of the principal fable, which turns upon Adam and Eve, who continued in Paradise while they kept the command that was given them, and were driven out of it as soon as they had transgressed. This is likewise the moral of the principal episode, which shows us how an innumerable multitude of angels fell from their state of bliss, and were cast into hell upon their disobedience. Besides this great moral, which may be looked upon as the soul of the fable, there are an infinity of under morals, which are to be drawn from the several parts of the poem, and which make this work more useful and instructive than any other poem in any language."—*Addison.*

EXTRACTS FROM PARADISE REGAINED.[1]

THE BANQUET.[2]

He spake no dream; for, as his words had end,
Our Saviour, lifting up his eyes, beheld
In ample space, under the broadest shade,
A table richly spread, in regal mode,
With dishes piled, and meats of noblest sort
And savour, beasts of chace, or fowl of game,
In pastry built, or from the spit, or boiled,
Gris-amber-steamed;[3] all fish from sea or shore,
Freshet,[4] or purling brook, of shell or fin,
And exquisitest name, for which was drained
Pontus and Lucrine bay,[5] and Afric coast.
(Alas! how simple to these cates compared,
Was that crude apple that diverted[6] Eve!)
And at a stately sideboard, by the wine
That fragrant smell diffused, in order stood

---

(1) "Paradise Regained" was published in 1671, and was, singularly enough, preferred by its author to "Paradise Lost,"—"a prejudice which," says Dr. Johnson, "Milton had to himself." The great critic afterwards remarks:—"Had this poem been written not by Milton, but by some imitator, it would have claimed and received universal praise." One of the main hindrances, it may be suggested, to its popularity, is its obvious theological deficiency According to Milton, Paradise is regained by the Saviour's triumph over the temptation of Satan, as recited in the first eleven verses of the fourth chapter of St. Matthew's gospel, while no reference whatever is made throughout the poem to the death of Christ, as an atonement for sin.

(2) "Our Lord is 'an hungered,' and through that appetite tempted of the devil. Narrow as this ground is, for Milton it is enough; and he forthwith raises a table in the wilderness, furnished from 'Pontus and Lucrine bay, and Afric coast;' and the charming pipes are heard to play, and Arabian odours and early flowers breathe around, and nymphs and naiads of Diana's train are summoned forth to dance beneath the shade; and the whole is combined into one of those splendid banquets with which nothing but a most perfect knowledge of antiquity could have supplied him."—*Quarterly Review*, vol. xxxvi., p. 55.

(3) *Gris-amber-steamed*—seasoned or flavoured with ambergris, which is said to have been formerly much employed in culinary operations.

(4) *Freshet*—a stream of fresh water.

(5) *Lucrine bay*—this Italian bay was famous for its oysters.

(6) *Diverted*—"is here used," says Dr. Newton, "in the Latin signification of *divertor*, 'to turn aside.'"

Tall stripling youths rich clad, of fairer hue
Than Ganymed or Hylas; distant more
Under the trees now tripped, now solemn stood,
Nymphs of Diana's train, and Naiades,
With fruits and flowers from Amalthea's horn,[1]
And ladies of the Hesperides,[2] that seemed,
Fairer than feigned of old, or fabled since
Of faery damsels met in forest wide
By knights of Logres,[3] or of Lyones,[3]
Lancelot,[4] or Pelleas, or Pellenore:
And all the while harmonious airs were heard
Of chiming strings, or charming pipes; and winds
Of gentlest gale Arabian odours fanned
From their soft wings, and Flora's earliest smells.

GLORY.[5]

For what is glory but the blaze of fame,
The people's praise, if always praise unmixed?
And what the people but a herd confused,
A miscellaneous rabble, who extol
Things vulgar, and, well weighed, scarce worth the praise.
They praise and they admire they know not what,
And know not whom, but as one leads the other;
And what delight to be by such extolled,
To live upon their tongues and be their talk,
Of whom to be dispraised were no small praise?—
His lot who dares be singularly good.
The intelligent among them and the wise
Are few, and glory scarce of few is raised.

(1) *Amalthea's horn*—See note 7, p. 32.

(2) *Ladies of the Hesperides*—the Hesperides were fabulous islands, where fruit-trees bore golden apples, and where the nymphs called Hesperides lived. (See also note 2, p. 334.)

(3) *Logres, Lyones*—the former an ancient name of England generally; the latter of Cornwall.

(4) *Lancelot, &c.*—The names of persons famous in the old romance of "Morte d'Arthur."

(5) This fine discourse is put into the mouth of our Saviour in answer to Satan's temptation to the pursuit of glory. "How admirably," remarks Thyer, "does Milton in this speech expose the emptiness and uncertainty of a popular character, and found true glory upon its only basis, the approbation of the God of Truth!"

This is true glory and **renown**, when God
Looking on the earth, with approbation marks
The just man, and **divulges** him through heaven
To all his angels, who, with **true applause**
Recount his praises: thus he did to Job,
When to extend his fame through heaven and earth,
As thou to thy reproach mayst **well remember,**
He asked thee, "Hast thou **seen my servant Job?**"
Famous he was in heaven, **on** earth less **known,**
Where glory is false glory, attributed
To things not glorious, men not worthy **of fame.**
They err who count it glorious to subdue
By conquest far and wide, to overrun
Large countries, and in field great battles **win,**
Great cities by assault: what do **these worthies**
But **rob and** spoil, burn, slaughter, **and enslave**
Peaceable nations, neighbouring or remote,
Made captive, yet deserving **freedom more**
Than those their conquerors, who leave behind
Nothing but ruin wheresoe'er they rove,
And all the flourishing works of peace destroy;
Then swell with pride, and must be titled gods,
Great benefactors of mankind, deliverers,
Worshipped with temple, priest, and sacrifice?
One is the[1] son of Jove, of Mars the other;
Till conqueror Death discover them scarce men,
Rolling in brutish vices, **and deformed,**
Violent or shameful death their due reward.
But if there be in glory aught of good,
It may by means far different be attained,
Without ambition, **war,** or violence;
By deeds of peace, **by** wisdom eminent,
By patience, temperance.   I mention still
Him whom thy wrongs, with saintly patience borne,
Made famous in a land and times obscure;
Who names not now with honour patient Job?
Poor Socrates (who next more memorable?)
By what he taught, and suffered for so doing,
For truth's sake suffering death unjust, lives now
Equal in fame to proudest conquerors.
Yet, if for fame and glory aught be done,
Aught suffered; if young African for fame

(1) *One is the, &c.*—Alexander and Romulus are intended.

His wasted country freed from Punic rage,
The deed becomes unpraised, the man at least,
And loses, though but verbal, his reward.
Shall I seek glory then, as vain men seek,
Oft not deserved? I seek not mine, but His
Who sent me, and thereby witness whence I am.

ROME.[1]

He brought our Saviour to the western side
Of that high mountain, whence he might behold
Another plain,[2] long, but in breadth not wide,
Washed by the southern sea; and on the north
To equal length backed with a ridge of hills,
That screened the fruits of the earth, and seats of men
From cold Septentrion blasts; thence in the midst
Divided by a river, of whose banks
On each side an imperial city stood,
With towers and temples proudly elevate
On seven small hills, with palaces adorned,
Porches[3] and theatres, baths, aqueducts,
Statues and trophies,[4] and triumphal arcs,
Gardens and groves, presented to his eyes,
Above the height of mountains interposed:
(By what strange parallax[5] or optic skill
Of vision, multiplied through air, or glass

---

(1) " And now, in her turn, Rome under Tiberius is depicted, with the spirit indeed of a poet, but with the accuracy of a contemporary annalist: and her imperial palaces, the houses of her gods, the conflux of divers nations and languages at her gates; the embassies from far crowding the Emilian and Appian roads; the prætors and proconsuls hasting to their provinces, or on their triumphant return, all fill the mind's eye."—*Quarterly Review, ubi supra.*

(2) *Another plain, &c.*—The " plain " is that part of Italy contained between the "southern sea," the Mediterranean, and the "ridge of hills," the " Apennines."

(3) *Porches*—from the Latin *porticus,* a portico—a walk covered with a roof and supported by columns, a colonnade. These erections were beautifully constructed both at Athens and Rome, and were the favourite resorts of the fashionable and literary circles. See note 3, p. 351; and also Dr. Smith's " Dictionary of Greek and Roman Antiquities," article " Porticus."

(4) *Trophies*—memorials or monuments of victory, consisting generally of the arms, shields, &c., of the enemy, fixed on some elevation.

(5) *Parallax*—from the Greek παράλλαξις, a difference — aberration, the distance between the true and the apparent place of a star; hence here, the elevation of the object to the eye, by which the city was seen "above the height of mountains interposed."

Of telescope, were curious to enquire)
And now the tempter thus his silence broke:—

"The city which thou seest no other deem
Than great and glorious Rome, queen of the earth,
So far renowned, and with the spoils enriched
Of nations; there the Capitol thou seest,
Above the rest lifting his stately head
On the Tarpeian rock, her citadel
Impregnable; and there mount Palatine,
The imperial palace, compass huge, and high
The structure, skill of noblest architects,
With gilded battlements, conspicuous far
Turrets and terraces, conspicuous far
Many a fair edifice besides, more like
Houses of gods (so well I have disposed
My aery microscope), thou mayst behold,
Outside and inside both, pillars and roofs,
Carved work, the hand of famed artificers
In cedar, marble, ivory, or gold.
Thence to the gates cast round thine eye, and see
What conflux issuing forth, or entering in;
Prætors, proconsuls to their provinces
Hasting,[1] or on return, in robes of state;
Lictors and rods, the ensigns of their power,
Legions and cohorts, turms[2] of horse and wings:
Or embassies from regions far remote
In various habits on the Appian road,[3]
Or on the Emilian; some from farthest south,
Syene, and where the shadow both way falls,
Meroe, Nilotic isle, and more to west,
The realm of Bocchus to the Blackmoor sea:
From the Asian kings, and Parthian among these;
From India and the golden Chersonese,[4]

---

(1) *Hasting*—"The rapacity of the Roman provincial governors, and their eagerness to take possession of their prey, is here strongly marked by the word 'hasting.'"—*Dunster.*

(2) *Turms*—from the Latin *turma*, a cavalry troop—troops of horse.

(3) *The Appian road, &c.*—The Appian road led south; the Emilian, north of Rome. The nations on the Appian road are enumerated in the seven lines beginning "Syene," &c.; those in the Emilian, in the three beginning "From Gallia," &c.

(4) *Golden Chersonese*—the Aurea Chersonesus, or Golden Peninsula, Malacca.

And utmost Indian isle, Taprobane,[1]
Dusk faces[2] with white silken turbans wreathed;
From Gallia, Gades,[3] and the British west;
Germans, and Scythians, and Sarmatians, north
Beyond Danubius to the Tauric pool.[4]
All nations now to Rome obedience pay,
To Rome's great emperor, whose wide domain
In ample territory, wealth, and power,
Civility of manners, arts, and arms,
And long renown, thou justly mayst prefer
Before the Parthian. These two thrones except,
The rest are barbarous, and scarce worth the sight,
Shared among petty kings too far removed;
These having shown thee, I have shown thee all
The kingdoms of the world, and all their glory."

ATHENS.[5]

"LOOK once more, ere we leave[6] this specular mount,
Westward, much nearer by south-west; behold
Where on the Ægean shore a city stands
Built nobly; pure the air, and light the soil;
Athens, the eye of Greece, mother of arts
And eloquence, native to[7] famous wits

(1) *Taprobane*—the island of Ceylon.
(2) *Dusk faces*—a line noted for its picturesqueness.
(3) *Gades*—Cadiz.
(4) *Tauric pool*—The Palus Mœotis, or Sea of Azoff.
(5) "It [the mind's eye] is again carried away to the westward, and the flowery hill of Hymettus offers itself to our notice; and Athens, with its picturesque suburbs, is unfolded with a perspicuity and precision that might challenge the most scrupulous critic to quarrel even with an epithet (so true is Milton to his Grecian masters); while her schools of philosophy, the sects into which they are divided, the dogmas they severally espoused, all pass in rapid review, leaving us confounded at the mental plentitude of this extraordinary man."—*Quarterly Review, ubi supra.*
(6) *Ere we leave, &c.*—It is Satan who speaks, after displaying from this "specular mount"—this hill of observation—the kingdoms of the world and the glory of them. "It would be impossible," remarks the Rev. A. P. Stanley, "for any one to describe the view from the summit of Hymettus more truly than in the words in which Milton has set forth his conception of Athens, not from ocular inspection, but such as, from the union of deep classical learning with his poetical faculty, he imagined it to have appeared in the vision from the specular mount in the 'Paradise Regained.'"—*Classical Museum*, vol. i., p. 57.
(7) *Native to, &c.*—i. e. a place noted for the famous men who were born there and ever ready to welcome eminent strangers.

Or hospitable, in her sweet recess,
City or suburban, studious walks and shades;
See there the olive grove of Academe,
Plato's retirement, where the Attic bird[1]
Trills her[2] thick-warbled notes the summer long;
There flowery hill Hymettus, with the sound
Of bees' industrious murmur, oft invites
To studious musing; there Ilissus rolls
His whispering stream: within the walls then view
The schools of ancient sages: his who bred
Great Alexander to subdue the world,
Lyceum[3] there, and painted Stoa next:
There shalt thou hear and learn the secret power
Of harmony in tones and numbers hit
By voice or hand, and various-measured verse,
Æolian charms[4] and Dorian lyric odes;
And his[5] who gave them breath, but higher sung,
Blind Melesigenes,[6] thence Homer[7] called,
Whose poem Phœbus challenged for his own.
Thence what the lofty grave tragedians taught[1]
In chorus or iambic,[8] teachers best
Of moral prudence, with delight received
In brief sententious precepts, while they treat
Of fate, and chance, and change in human life;
High actions, and high passions best describing.
Thence to the famous orators repair,
Those ancient,[9] whose resistless eloquence

(1) *Attic bird*—See note 3, p. 71.

(2) *Trills her, &c.*—" There never was," says Dr. Newton, "a verse more expressive of the harmony of the nightingale than this."

(3) *Lyceum, &c.*—The Lyceum was the school of Aristotle; the Stoa that of Zeno. The word Stoa answers to the latin *porticus*, or porch. (See note 3, p. 348.)

(4) *Æolian charms, &c.*—" Æolia carmina," verses such as those of Alcæus and Sappho, who were both of Mitylene, in Lesbos, an island belonging to the Æolians: "'Dorian lyric odes,'—such as those of Pindar."—*Newton.*

(5) *And his, &c.*—*i. e.* and his who not only cultivated those species of poetry, but the loftier field of epic.

(6) *Melesigenes*—*i. e.* born at or near Meles, a river of Asia Minor.

(7) *Thence Homer, &c.*—*i. e.* from his blindness, called ἀμυρός, blind; this is one of the many conjectures respecting the etymology of the name.

(8) *Iambic*—*i. e.* "the dialogue part of the tragedy, which was chiefly written in iambic measure, as distinguished from the chorus, which consisted of various measures."—*Newton.*

(9) *Ancient*—*i. e.* Pericles, Æschines, Demosthenes, &c.

Wielded at will that fierce democratie,
Shook the arsenal, and fulmined over Greece,
To Macedon and Artaxerxes' throne.
To sage Philosophy next lend thine ear,
From heaven descended to the low-roofed house
Of Socrates; see there his tenement,
Whom, well inspired, the oracle pronounced
Wisest of men; from whose mouth[1] issued forth
Mellifluous streams that watered all the schools
Of Academics[2] old and new, with those
Surnamed Peripatetics,[3] and the sect
Epicurean, and the Stoic severe;
These here resolve, or as thou likest, at home,
Till time mature thee to a kingdom's weight;
These rules[4] will render thee a king complete,
Within thyself; much more with empire joined."

THE THUNDER-STORM IN THE WILDERNESS.[5]

Darkness now rose
As day-light sunk, and brought in lowering Night,
Her shadowy offspring, unsubstantial both,
Privation mere of light and absent day.
Our Saviour, meek, and with untroubled mind
After his aery jaunt,[6] though hurried sore,
Hungry and cold betook him to his rest,
Wherever, under some concourse of shades,
Whose branching arms thick intertwined might shield
From dews and damps of night his sheltered head;
But sheltered, slept in vain, for at his head
The tempter watched, and soon with ugly dreams
Disturbed his sleep; and either tropic[7] now

(1) *From whose mouth, &c.*—i. e. who was the father and founder of moral philosophy among the Greeks.

(2) *Academics, &c.*—Plato was at the head of the old Academy, Carneades of the new.

(3) *Peripatetics*—from the Greek περί, about, and πατέω, I walk—the followers of Aristotle, who was accustomed to teach as he walked about with his disciples.

(4) *These rules*—as no rules have been mentioned, one critic proposes to read "their rules;" while another supposes Milton to refer to the "brief, sententious precepts" mentioned before.

(5) "One of the grandest descriptions in all poetry."—*Sir E. Brydges.*

(6) *After his aery jaunt*—after being borne through the air by Satan.

(7) *And either tropic, &c.*—i. e. from both tropics at once—from North and South.

'Gan thunder, and both ends¹ of heaven ; the clouds²
From many a horrid rift abortive poured
Fierce rain with lightning mixed, water with fire
In ruin³ reconciled ; nor slept the winds
Within their stony caves,⁴ but rushed abroad
From the four hinges of the world, and fell
On the vexed wilderness, whose tallest pines,
Though rooted deep as high, and sturdiest oaks,
Bowed their stiff necks, loaden with stormy blasts,
Or torn up sheer. Ill wast thou shrouded⁵ then,
O patient Son of God, yet only stood'st
Unshaken : nor yet stayed the terror there ;
Infernal ghosts, and hellish furies round
Environed thee ; some howled, some yelled, some shrieked :
Some bent at thee their fiery darts, while thou
Satst unappalled in calm and sinless peace.
Thus passed the night so foul, till morning fair
Came forth with pilgrim steps in amice⁶ grey,
Who with a radiant finger stilled the roar
Of thunder, chased the clouds, and laid the winds,
And grisly spectres, which the fiend had raised
To tempt the Son of God with terrors dire.
And now the sun, with more effectual beams,
Had cheered the face of earth, and dried the wet
From drooping plant, or dropping tree ; the birds
Who all things now behold more fresh and green,
After a night of storms so ruinous,
Cleared up their choicest notes in bush and spray,
To gratulate the sweet return⁷ of morn.

(1) *Both ends, &c.*—*i. e.* East and West. This and the last expression taken together imply, of course, that the thunder rolled all around.

(2) *The clouds, &c.*—*i. e.* the clouds from many a dreadful fissure ("rift") or opening in the sky, precipitately and with supernatural vehemence ("abortive") poured down their torrents.

(3) *Ruin*—used here in the original sense of the Latin *ruina*, downfall ; the sense, therefore, is—water and fire, two incongruous elements, were united in the one object of rushing down upon the earth.

(4) *Stony caves*—in allusion to the story of Æolus (see "Æneid").

(5) *Shrouded*—sheltered ; an ancient use of the word (see p. 258, note 3).

(6) *Amice*—literally, a sacerdotal habiliment used in the Romish Church—here employed in the general sense of a garment or robe.

(7) *Sweet return, &c.*—"The preceding description," remarks Dr. Warton, "exhibits some of the finest lines which Milton has written in all his poems."

A A

DRYDEN.

PRINCIPAL EVENTS OF HIS LIFE.—John Dryden, the founder of what is by some called the artificial style of English Poetry, was born in 1631, at Aldwinkle, in Northamptonshire. His father, who was a gentleman of some property, gave his son the benefit of a learned education, by placing him under the famous Dr. Busby, at Westminster School. He thence removed, in 1650, to Trinity College, Cambridge, where he resided three years after taking his degree of Master of Arts. In early life he was a friend and visitor of Milton, and seems to have been generally attached to the party of Cromwell, on whose death he wrote some highly eulogistic stanzas. The versatility, however, of his principles, was clearly evinced by the publication shortly afterwards of courtly strains of fulsome adulation in honour of Charles II. In 1666, he married Lady Elizabeth Howard, an alliance—like that subsequently formed by Addison with a lady of rank and title—which very little promoted the happiness of the poet. For some years before, and long after this epoch, he wrote for the stage. In 1668, he was appointed Poet Laureate, but appears at this time in the ranks of the political adversaries of the king's or high court party. Subsequently, with more ease than honour, he passed directly over to those whom he had previously assailed, and discovered for their benefit his powerful but hitherto unappreciated vein of satire, by writing the famous poem of "Absalom and Achitophel," which was soon succeeded by others of the same character. On the accession of James II., we find Dryden with suspicious, though in his case not remarkable, flexibility, attaching himself to the Roman Catholic Church. At the Revolution all his prospects were overclouded, and for the remainder of his life he was compelled to depend upon his literary labours for the means of subsistence. He died on the 1st of May, 1700, at his house in Gerard Street, London, and was buried at Westminster Abbey, between Chaucer and Cowley.

PRINCIPAL WORKS.—Dryden's most important miscellaneous poems are "Annus Mirabilis," "Ode to the Memory of Mrs. Anne Killigrew," and "Alexander's Feast;" of his dramatical works, the only two now considered above mediocrity are "Don Sebastian," and "All for Love;" as satires, "Absalom and Achitophel," the "Medal," and "Mac-Flecnoe," are best known, and perhaps "Religio Laici," and the "Hind and the Panther," may be referred to the same head. He translated the whole of Virgil, and paraphrased and modernised several of Chaucer's and Boccacio's tales.

CHARACTERISTIC SPIRIT AND STYLE.—"Dryden and Pope are the great masters of the artificial style of poetry in our language, as Chaucer, Spenser, Shakspere, and Milton, were of the natural; and though this artificial style is generally and very justly acknowledged to be inferior to the other, yet those who stand at the head of that class ought, perhaps, to rank higher than those who occupy an inferior place in a superior class."[1]

"He [Dryden] is a writer of manly and elastic character. His strong judgment gave force as well as direction to a flexible fancy; and his harmony is generally the echo of solid thoughts. But he was not gifted with intense or lofty sensibility, on the contrary, the grosser any idea is, the happier he seems to expatiate upon it. The transports of the heart, and the deep and varied delineations of the passions, are strangers to his poetry. He could describe character in the abstract, but could not embody it in the drama, for he entered into character more from clear perception than fervid sympathy. This great high priest of all the Nine was not a confessor to the finer secrets of the human breast."[2]

VERSIFICATION.—"What can be said of his versification will be little more than a dilatation of the praise given it by Pope:—

> 'Waller was smooth; but Dryden taught to join
> The varying verse, the full-resounding line,
> The long majestic march, and energy divine.'

"Some improvements had been already made in English numbers; but the full force of our language was not yet felt; the verse that was smooth was commonly feeble. If Cowley had sometimes a finished line, he had it by chance. Dryden knew how to choose the flowing and the sonorous words; to vary the pauses, and adjust the accents; to diversify the cadence, and yet preserve the smoothness of his metre."[3]

(1) Hazlitt. "Lectures," &c., p. 135.
(2) Campbell. "Specimens," &c., Introduction, p. lxxxv.
(3) Johnson. "Lives of the Poets."

CHARACTER OF SHAFTESBURY,

UNDER THE NAME OF ACHITOPHEL.[1]

Of these[2] the false Achitopel[3] was first;
A name to all succeeding ages curst;
For close designs and crooked counsels fit;
Sagacious, bold, and turbulent of wit;
Restless, unfixed in principles and place;
In power unpleased, impatient of disgrace;
A fiery soul, which, working out its way,
Fretted the pigmy body to decay,
And o'er-informed[4] the tenement of clay.
A daring pilot in extremity;
Pleased with the danger when the waves went high,
He sought the storms; but, for a calm unfit,
Would steer too nigh the sands to boast his wit.
Great wits[5] are sure to madness near allied,
And thin partitions do their bounds divide;
Else why should he, with wealth and honour blest,
Refuse his age the needful hours of rest?
Punish a body which he could not please;
Bankrupt of life, yet prodigal of ease?
And all to leave what with his toil he won,
To that unfeathered two legged thing, a son,
In friendship false, implacable in hate;
Resolved to ruin or to rule the State:

---

(1) *From the Satire of* "*Absalom and Achitophel*"—considered by many competent judges the finest poem of the kind in our language. It was written in 1681, to defend the king, Charles II., against the political factions raised by his own son, the Duke of Monmouth, and his crafty counsellor, the Earl of Shaftesbury.

(2) *Of these, &c.*—*i. e.* of those who had factiously risen against the monarch.

(3) *Achitophel*—The character of the original Achitophel, and his connection with Absalom, may be seen in 2 Sam. xvi. 23.

(4) *O'er-informed*—over-animated (see note 3, p. 130).

(5) *Great wits, &c.*—Charles Lamb thus controverts the above position:—"The greatest wits," says he, "will ever be found to be the sanest writers. It is impossible for the mind to conceive of a mad Shakspere. The greatness of wit, by which the poetic talent is here chiefly to be understood, manifests itself in the admirable balance of all the faculties. Madness is the disproportionate straining or excess of any one of them."

To compass this, the triple bond[1] he broke,
The pillars of the public safety shook,
And fitted Israel[2] for a foreign yoke:
Then seized with fear, yet still affecting[3] fame,
Usurped a patriot's all-atoning name.
So easy still it proves, in factious times,
With public zeal to cancel private crimes;
How safe is treason, and how sacred ill,
Where none can sin against the people's will!
Where crowds can wink, and no offence be known,
Since in another's guilt they find their own!
Yet fame deserved no enemy can grudge;
The statesman we abhor, but praise the judge.[4]
In Israel's courts ne'er sat an Abethdin[5]
With more discerning eyes, or hands more clean;
Unbribed, unsought, the wretched to redress,
Swift of despatch, and easy of access.
Oh! had he been content to serve the crown
With virtues only proper for the gown;
Or had the rankness of the soil been freed
From cockle,[6] that oppressed the noble seed;
David[7] for him his tuneful harp had strung,
And Heaven had wanted one immortal song.
But wild ambition loves to slide, not stand;
And fortune's ice prefers to virtue's land.
Achitopel, grown weary to possess
A lawful fame, and lazy happiness,
Disdained the golden fruit to gather free,
And lent the crowd his arm to shake the tree.

THE HOLY SCRIPTURES.[8]

WHENCE but from Heaven could men unskilled in arts,
In several ages born, in several parts,

(1) *The triple bond*—the alliance between England, Sweden, and Holland.
(2) *Israel*—England.
(3) *Affecting*—aiming at, seeking after.
(4) *Praise the judge*—Shaftesbury, as Lord Chancellor, is said to have given wise and impartial judgments, though unfurnished with legal knowledge.
(5) *Abethdin*—the title of one of the judges of the court of the Sanhedrim; here it means Lord Chancellor.
(6) *Cockle*—a weed that infests growing corn.
(7) *David*—Charles II.   (8) From "Religio Laici."

Weave such agreeing truths? or how or why
Should all conspire to cheat us with a lie?
Unasked their pains, ungrateful their advice,
Starving their gain, and martyrdom their price.

If on the book itself we cast our view,
Concurrent heathens prove the story true;
The doctrine, miracles, which must convince,
For Heaven in them appeals to human sense;
And though they prove not, they confirm the cause,
When what is taught agrees with nature's laws.

Then for the style; majestic and divine,
It speaks no less than God in every line;
Commanding words, whose force is still the same,
As the first fiat that produced our frame.

All faiths beside, or did by arms ascend,
Or sense indulged has made mankind their friend;
This only doctrine does our lusts oppose;
Unfed by nature's soil, on which it grows;
Cross to our interests, curbing sense and sin,
Oppressed without, and undermined within,
It thrives through pain, its own tormentors tires,
And with a stubborn patience still aspires.
To what can reason such effects assign,
Transcending nature, but to laws divine,
Which in that sacred volume are contained,
Sufficient, clear, and for that use ordained?

THE MONARCH OF DULNESS.[1]

ALL human things are subject to decay;
And, when Fate summons, monarchs must obey.
This Flecnoe found, who, like Augustus, young
Was called to empire: and had governed long;
In prose and verse was owned, without dispute,
Through all the realms of Nonsense, absolute.

---

(1) From "Mac-Flecnoe"—*i. e.* the son of Flecnoe; an expression employed to designate a poet of the day named Shadwell, who is in this poem satirised, not undeservedly it is thought, by Dryden. As a specimen of pungency and force it would be difficult to bring anything of the kind, ancient or modern, into comparison with the lines given above. Flecnoe was the true name of a dull, hackneyed poetaster of the day.

This aged prince, **now flourishing in peace,**
And blest with **issue of a large increase,**
Worn out **with business, did at length debate**
To settle **the succession of the State;**
And pondering which of all his sons was fit
To reign, and wage immortal war with wit,
Cried, "'Tis resolved; for Nature pleads, that he
Should only **rule who most** resembles **me.**
Shadwell, alone, my **perfect** image bears,
Mature in dulness from his tender years:
Shadwell, alone, of all **my** sons, is he,
Who stands confirmed in full stupidity.
The rest to some faint meaning make pretence,
But Shadwell never deviates[1] into sense.
Some **beams of wit on** other **souls may fall,**
Strike through, and make a lucid interval;
But Shadwell's genuine night admits no ray;
His rising fogs prevail upon[2] the day.
Besides, his goodly fabric[3] fills the eye,
And seems designed for thoughtless majesty:
Thoughtless as monarch oaks, that shade the plain,
And spread in solemn state, supinely reign. * * *"
Then thus continued he:[4] "My son, advance
Still in **new** impudence, new ignorance.
Success let others teach; learn thou, from me,
Pangs without birth, and fruitless industry.
Let Virtuosos[5] in five years be writ;
Yet not one thought **accuse** thy toil **of wit;**
And when false flowers of rhetoric **thou wouldst cull,**
Trust nature, do not labour **to be dull.**
Like mine, thy gentle numbers feebly **creep,**
Thy tragic muse gives smiles; thy **comic, sleep.**
With whate'er gall thou sett'st thyself **to write,**
Thy inoffensive **satires never bite.**
In thy felonious heart though venom lies,
It does but touch thy Irish pen, and dies.

(1) *Deviates*—Notice the peculiarly happy use of this word.
(2) *Prevail upon*, &c.—*i. e.* get the victory over and extinguish—an exceedingly witty expression.
(3) *Goodly fabric*—in allusion to the clumsy and obese person of Shadwell, who was a man of grossly intemperate habits.
(4) *Thus continued he*—this was after the inauguration, which is humorously but coarsely described by Dryden.
(5) *Virtuosos*—in allusion to a play of **Shadwell's.**

Thy genius calls thee not to purchase fame
In keen Iambics,[1] but mild Anagram.[2]
Leave writing plays, and choose for thy command
Some peaceful province in Acrostic land;
There thou mayst wings display, and altars raise,
And torture one poor word ten thousand ways.
Or, if thou wouldst thy different talents suit,
Set thy own songs, and sing them to thy lute."

THE CHARACTER OF A GOOD PARSON.[3]

(ABRIDGED.)

A PARISH priest was of the pilgrim train;
An awful, reverend, and religious man.
His eyes diffused a venerable grace,
And charity itself was in his face.
Rich was his soul, though his attire was poor
(As God had[4] clothed his own ambassador);
For such on earth his blest Redeemer bore.
Of sixty years he seemed; and well might last
To sixty more, but that he lived too fast;
Refined himself to soul, to curb the sense;
And made almost a sin of abstinence.
Yet had his aspect nothing of severe,
But such a face as promised him sincere:
Nothing reserved or sullen was to see,
But sweet regards and pleasing sanctity;
Mild was his accent, and his action free,
With eloquence innate his tongue was armed,
Though harsh the precept, yet the preacher charmed.

---

(1) *Iambics*—Satirical writings were generally composed in iambic verse.

(2) *Anagram, &c.*—This and the next five lines allude to the fantastic modes of verse-writing in which the small wits of the day indulged.

(3) This is a sort of translation, as Dryden himself calls it, of Chaucer's "Character of a Good Parson" (or which see p. 241), but it is so different in many respects from the original, that it is more correctly a new building upon the old foundation. It will be useful and interesting to the reader to compare them together.

(4) *As God had*—as if God had himself.

For, letting down the golden chain[1] from high,
He drew his audience upward to the sky.
He bore his great commission in his look;
But sweetly tempered awe, and softened all he spoke.
He preached the joys of Heaven and pains of hell,
And warned the sinner with becoming zeal;
But on eternal mercy loved to dwell.
He taught the gospel rather than the law,
And forced himself to drive, but loved to draw:
For fear but freezes minds; but love, like heat,
Exhales the soul sublime to seek her native seat.
To threats the stubborn sinner oft is hard;
Wrapped in his crimes, against the storm prepared;
But when the milder beams of mercy play,
He melts,[2] and throws his cumbrous cloak away;
Lightning and thunder (Heaven's artillery)
As harbingers before the Almighty fly;
Those but proclaim his style and disappear;
The stiller sound succeeds, and God is there!

    The tithes his parish freely paid, he took,
But never sued, or cursed[3] with bell and book:
With patience bearing wrong, but offering none,
Since every man is free to lose his own.
The country churls, according to their kind
(Who grudge their dues, and love to be behind),
The less he sought his offerings, pinched the more;[4]
And praised a priest contented to be poor.

    Yet of his little he had some to spare,
To feed the famished and to clothe the bare:
For mortified he was to that degree,
A poorer than himself he would not see.
"True priests," he said, "and preachers of the word,
Were only stewards of their Sovereign Lord;
Nothing was theirs, but all the public store;
Entrusted riches, to relieve the poor;

---

    (1) *The golden chain, &c.*—There is nothing of the kind in Chaucer. The idea is derived from the golden chain which is represented by Homer as attached to the foot of Jupiter's throne, and reaching to earth—a beautiful emblem of providential care.

    (2) *Melts, &c.*—This idea seems to be derived from Æsop's fable of "The Sun and the Wind."

    (3) *Cursed, &c.*—In allusion to an awful ceremony of the Romish Church, in which curses were chanted from a book, and a bell tolled at intervals.

    (4) *Pinched the more*—i. e. denied themselves to pay his dues.

Who, should they steal for want of his relief,
He judged himself accomplice with the thief."
  Wide was his parish, not contracted close
In streets, but here and there a straggling house;
Yet still he was at hand, without request,
To serve the sick, to succour the distressed:
Tempting, on foot alone, without affright,
The dangers of a dark, tempestuous night.
  The proud he tamed, the penitent he cheered,
Nor to rebuke the rich offender feared.
His preaching much, but more his practice wrought,
(A living sermon of the truths he taught):
For this by rules severe his life he squared,
That all might see the doctrine which they heard:
"For priests," he said, "are patterns for the rest;
(The gold of Heaven, who bear the God imprest);
But when the precious coin is kept unclean,
The Sovereign's image is no longer seen.
If they be foul, on whom the people trust,
Well may the baser brass contract a rust."
  The prelate for his holy life he prized;
The worldly pomp of prelacy despised.
His Saviour came not with a gaudy show,
Nor was his kingdom of the world below.
Patience in want, and poverty of mind,
These marks of church and churchmen he designed,
And living taught, and dying left behind.
The crown he wore was of the pointed thorn;
In purple he was crucified, not born.
They who contend for place and high degree,
Are not his sons, but those of Zebedee.
  Such was the saint, who shone with every grace,
Reflecting, Moses-like, his Maker's face.
God saw his image lively was expressed,
And his own work, as in creation, blessed.

POPE.

Principal Events of his Life.—Alexander Pope, the most distinguished of Dryden's followers and **disciples**, was born in London, in 1688. His attachment to **poetry was** very early developed. He says of himself—

> "As yet a child, and all unknown to fame,
> I lisped in numbers, for the numbers came."

As his father **was a** Roman Catholic, he did not **receive a** university education, but was carefully instructed both **at home** and at school by various **Romish** priests, until he reached the age of twelve, at which **time, with** singular decision **and perseverance,** "he formed," says Dr. Johnson, "a plan of study, which he completed with little **other incitement than the desire of excellence."** An important event in this early stage **of his life was his being taken, at his own** request, **to a** coffee-house frequented by Dryden, **to see the eminent** poet whose greatness was soon to be succeeded **by his own.** Dryden **died** about **three** weeks before Pope was **twelve** years old. His father, formerly **a** linen-draper in the **Strand,** had, some little time before this, retired from business **with a** considerable fortune, and **was** now residing at Binfield, in Windsor Forest; and here the youthful poet cultivated the genius of which he felt conscious, and ranged at will over **the** fair fields of ancient and modern literature. He soon became known as an author, **by** the publication of the "Pastorals," and subsequently, by the "Essay on Criticism," which at **once** formed for him the reputation **that he** maintained, by his **numerous** other writings, until his death, in 1744, **at** Twickenham.

Principal Works.—His first work was, as above intimated, the "Pastorals," or "Spring," "Summer," "Autumn," and "Winter," **which he** wrote at the age **of sixteen. His** most important subsequent poems were the "Essay **on Criticism,**" "Rape of the Lock," "Temple **of** Fame," "Windsor **Forest,**" translations of the "Iliad" **and** "Odyssey," "Epistle from Eloisa to Abelard," "Essay on Man," "The Messiah," "Imitations of Horace," "Moral Epistles," and "The Dunciad."

Characteristic Spirit and Style.—"In attempting to describe those characteristics which are peculiar to Pope, and by which he is more particularly distinguishable, both from those who preceded him and those who have followed him, we may, in the first place, observe in all his writings a striking, expressive, and energetic manner, so peculiar as to carry with it a conviction that no other person could have compressed the same sentiments into such narrow limits with such full effect. At the same time, he is always equal and consistent with himself; in whatever he attempts, he always succeeds; whether he rises or falls, he does it with equal grace; the one displays no effort, the other no weakness.

"2. He always goes directly to his point, and occupies no useless time. To his writings nothing can be added but what would be superfluous; from them nothing can be taken away but what would occasion a deficiency. He does not say all that can be said, but all that ought to be said.

"3. He is always alive and attentive to his subject, and he keeps his readers so. On whatever subject he writes, there is a continual and rapid variety, that plays upon the imagination, and surprises, elevates, softens, or in some other manner affects or delights the mind; yet this is never dwelt upon, so as to become tiresome or disgusting. A quick sense of propriety distinguishes all he says. His tact is sure. He feels for the reader, and never offers him anything but what is acceptable. This is a perpetual compliment to the good sense, or perhaps the self-love of the reader, who perceives that he is never treated with disrespect or neglect, and that the author has not only done all that was in his power, but all that was possible to be done, to gratify him.

"4. Though highly ornamented, he exhibits no ambitious love of ornament; nothing but what his subject demands. No unnecessary similes are introduced to illustrate a proposition which is sufficiently clear already. Pope well knew that the finest figures of speech, brought forward for their own sake, are an impertinence, not an ornament.

"5. But perhaps the superlative merit of Pope consists in the point and correctness of his language, which is truly English, and exhibits no instances of being debased or intermixed with the French or any other foreign idioms. It would not be too much to say that if every English writer were to be corrected, so as to bring him to a true standard, there would be less to alter in Pope than in any other.

"6. To these particular endowments of Pope, as a poet, we may add, the variety which he has displayed, not only in the choice of his subjects, but in the manner in which he has treated them. There is scarcely a subject, from the simplest description to the sublimest strains of devotion, or the deepest recesses of intellectual and moral truth, which has not engaged his attention, and on which his efforts have not been attended with the most acknowledged success.

"That the inventive powers of Pope were confined only to a few particular instances, is an assertion not founded on fact. Whether we apply that term to the construction of a fable, or continued narration of imagery and fictitious events, as in the 'Rape of the Lock,' or 'The Dunciad,' or to the illustration of any subject, whatever its nature may be, by the introduction of appropriate decoration and beautiful figures of speech, as in his moral and didactic writings, it cannot be denied that Pope has displayed the powers of imagination in a degree which entitles him to rank with the most celebrated poets in any age or country."[1]

"That Pope was neither so insensible to the beauties of nature, nor so indistinct in describing them, as to forget the character of a genuine poet, is what I mean to urge, without exaggerating his picturesqueness. But before speaking of that quality in his writings, I would beg leave to observe, in the first place, that the faculty by which a poet luminously describes objects of art, is essentially the same faculty which enables him to be a faithful describer of simple nature; in the second place, that nature and art are, to a greater degree, relative terms in poetical description than is generally recollected; and thirdly, that artificial objects and manners are of so much importance in fiction, as to make the exquisite description of them no less characteristic of genius than the description of simple physical appearances. The poet is 'creation's heir.' He deepens our social interest in existence. It is surely by the liveliness of the interest which he excites in existence, and not by the class of subjects which he chooses, that we most fairly appreciate the genius or the life of life which is in him. It is no irreverence to the external charms of nature to say, that they are not more important to a poet's study, than the manners and affections of his species. Nature is the poet's goddess; but by nature no one rightly understands her mere inanimate face, however charming it may be, or the simple landscape-painting of trees, clouds, precipices, and flowers. Why, then, try Pope, or any other poet, exclusively by his powers of describing inanimate phenomena? Nature, in the wide and proper sense of the word, means life in all its circumstances—nature, moral as well as external. As the subject of inspired fiction, nature includes artificial

---

(1) Roscoe's Edition of Pope's Works, vol. ii.

forms and manners. Richardson is no less a painter of nature than Homer. Homer himself is a minute describer of works of art; and Milton is full of imagery derived from it. Satan's spear is compared to the pine, that makes the 'mast of some great ammiral;' and his shield is like the moon, but like the moon artificially seen through the glass of the Tuscan artist. The 'spirit-stirring drum, the ear-piercing fife, the royal banner, and all the quality, pride, pomp, and circumstance of glorious war,' are all artificial images. When Shakspere groups into one view the most sublime objects of the universe, he fixes on the 'cloud-capt towers, the gorgeous palaces, the solemn temples.' Those who have ever witnessed the spectacle of the launching of a ship of the line, will perhaps forgive me for adding this to the examples of the sublime objects of artificial life. Of that spectacle I can never forget the impression, and of having witnessed it, reflected from the faces of ten thousand spectators. They seem yet before me. I sympathize with their deep and silent expectation, and with their final burst of enthusiasm. It was not a vulgar joy, but an affecting national solemnity. When the vast bulwark sprang from her cradle, the calm water on which she swung majestically round, gave the imagination a contrast of the stormy element in which she was soon to ride. All the days of battle and the nights of danger which she had to encounter, all the ends of the earth which she had to visit, and all that she had to do and to suffer for her country, rose in awful presentiment before the mind: and when the heart gave her a benediction, it was like one pronounced on a living being."[1]

VERSIFICATION.—"Pope gave our heroic couplet its strictest melody and tersest expression. He has a gracefully peculiar manner, though it is not calculated to be a universal one; and where, indeed, shall we find the style of poetry that could be pronounced an exclusive model for every composer? His pauses have little variety, and his phrases are too much weighed in the balance of antithesis. But let us look to the spirit that points his antithesis, and to the rapid precision of his thoughts, and we shall forgive him for being too antithetic and sententious."[2]

(1) Campbell. "Specimens." Introduction, p. lxxxvii.
(2) Ibid., p. lxxxvi.

EXTRACTS FROM THE ESSAY ON CRITICISM.[1]

NATURE FROM THE BASIS OF ART.[2]

First follow Nature, and your judgment frame
By her just standard, which is still the same:
Unerring Nature, still divinely bright,
One clear, unchanged, and universal light,
Life, force, and beauty, must to all impart,
At once[3] the source, and end, and test of art.
Art from that fund each just supply provides;
Works without show, and without pomp presides;
In some fair body thus the informing soul
With spirits feeds, with vigour fills the whole,
Each motion guides, and every nerve sustains;
Itself unseen, but in the effects remains.
Some, to whom Heaven in wit[4] has been profuse,
Want as much more to turn it to its use;
For wit and judgment often are at strife,
Though meant each other's aid, like man and wife.
'Tis more to guide, than spur the Muses' steed;
Restrain his fury, than provoke his speed;
The winged courser, like a generous horse,
Shows most true mettle when you check his course.
    Those rules, of old discovered, not devised,
Are nature still, but nature methodized;
Nature, like liberty,[5] is but restrained
By the same laws which first herself ordained.

(1) "One of his [Pope's] greatest, though of his earliest works, is the 'Essay on Criticism;' which, if he had written nothing else, would have placed him among the first critics and the first poets, as it exhibits every mode of excellence that can embellish or dignify didactic composition."—*Dr. Johnson.*

(2) The object of the writer in this passage is to show—1st. That nature is the foundation of art. 2nd. That rules of art are but nature methodised. 3rd. That the practice of the ancient classical writers confirms these positions.

(3) *At once, &c.*—*i. e.* the *source,* because art is founded on nature; the *end,* because it is the aim of art to resemble nature; the *test,* because art must be tried by its conformity to nature.

(4) *Wit*—this word bears a variety of meanings in Pope's writings, some of which have already become obsolete: it here signifies genius.

(5) *Nature, like liberty, &c.*—Most happily expressed;—the rules laid down by the great critics are derived from nature, and therefore obedience to them is, in fact, obedience to nature.

Hear how learn'd Greece[1] her useful rules indites,
When to repress, and when indulge our flights:
High on Parnassus' top her sons she showed,
And pointed out those arduous paths they trod;
Held from afar, aloft, the immortal prize,
And urged the rest by equal steps to rise;
Just precepts thus from great examples given,
She drew from them what they derived from Heaven.
The generous critic fanned the poet's fire,
And taught the world with reason to admire.
Then criticism the Muse's handmaid proved,
To dress her charms, and make her more beloved:
But following wits[2] from that intention strayed,
Who could not win the mistress, wooed the maid:
Against the poets their own arms they turned,
Sure to hate most the men from whom they learned.
Some on the leaves of ancient authors prey;
Nor time nor moths e'er spoiled so much as they:
Some drily plain, without invention's aid,
Write dull receipts how poems may be made:
These leave the sense, their learning to display,
And those explain the meaning quite away.
    You then, whose judgment the right course would steer,
Know well each Ancient's proper character;
His fable,[3] subject, scope, in every page;
Religion, country, genius of his age:
Without all these at once before your eyes,
Cavil you may, but never criticise.
Be Homer's works your study and delight:
Read them by day and meditate by night;
Thence form your judgment, thence your notions **bring**,
And trace the Muses upward to their spring.
Still with itself compared, his text peruse;
And let your comment be the Mantuan Muse.[4]

(1) *Learn'd Greece*—In reference especially to Aristotle's "Canons of Criticism."

(2) *Wits*—men of genius (see note 4, p. 367).

(3) *Fable*—in a strict sense this word means, the tissue of events that constitute the story, it is therefore quite distinct from the "subject," and from the species of composition so styled.

(4) *The Mantuan Muse*—Virgil's "Æneid:" it will serve as a comment, because it is, in fact, as Foster, in one of his "Essays," beautifully designates it, "a lunar reflection" of the "Iliad."

When first young Maro[1] in his boundless mind
A work to outlast immortal Rome[2] designed,
Perhaps he seemed above the critic's law,
And but from Nature's fountains scorned to draw:
But when to examine every part he came,
Nature and Homer were, he found, the same:
Convinced, amazed, he checks the bold design;
And rules as strict his laboured work confine,
As if the Stagirite[3] o'erlooked each line.
Learn hence for ancient rules a just esteem;
To copy nature is to copy them.

  Some beauties yet no precepts can declare,
For there's a happiness[4] as well as care.
Music resembles poetry; in each
Are nameless graces which no methods teach,
And which a master-hand alone can reach.
If, where the rules not far enough extend,
(Since rules were made but to promote their end),
Some lucky licence answers to the full
The intent proposed, that licence is a rule.
Thus Pegasus, a nearer way to take,
May boldly deviate from the common track.
Great wits sometimes may gloriously offend,
And rise to faults true critics dare not mend;
From vulgar bounds with brave disorder part,
And snatch a grace beyond the reach of art;
Which, without passing through the judgment, gains
The heart, and all its end at once attains.
In prospects, thus, some objects please our eyes,
Which out of nature's common order rise;
The shapeless rock, or hanging precipice.
But though the ancients thus their rules invade,
(As kings dispense with laws themselves have made),
Moderns, beware! or if you must offend
Against the precept, ne'er transgress its end;[5]

---

(1) *Maro*—Virgil.

(2) *To outlast immortal Rome*—*i. e.* Rome, self-styled "Eternal Rome;" without this limitation the expression in th text would be obviously absurd.

(3) *Stagirite*—Aristotle, who was born at Stagira, in Macedonia. He was the first, both in order of time and in rank, of the critics of antiquity.

(4) *Happiness*—a "curiosa felicitas," or "grace beyond the reach of art."

(5) *Ne'er transgress its end*—*i. e.* the end of critical canons must be obedience and conformity to nature; therefore never forget, that though you forsake certain rules, you must still keep close to nature.

Let it be seldom, and compelled by need;
And have at least their precedent to plead
The critic else proceeds without remorse,
Seizes your fame, and puts his laws in force.
  I know there are, to whose presumptuous thoughts
Those freer beauties, even in them, seem faults.
Some figures monstrous and misshaped appear,
Considered singly, or beheld too near,
Which, but proportioned to their light or place,
Due distance reconciles to form and grace.
A prudent chief[1] not always must display
His powers in equal ranks, and fair array,
But with the occasion and the place comply,
Conceal his force, nay, seem sometimes to fly.
Those oft are stratagems which errors seem,
Nor is it Homer nods,[2] but we that dream.
  Still green[3] with bays each ancient altar stands,
Above the reach of sacrilegious hands;
Secure from flames, from envy's fiercer rage,
Destructive war, and all-involving age.
See, from each clime the learned their incense bring;
Hear, in all tongues, consenting pæans[4] ring!
In praise so just let every voice be joined,
And fill the general chorus of mankind!
Hail, bards triumphant! born in happier days;
Immortal heirs of universal praise!
Whose honours with increase of ages grow,
As streams roll down, enlarging as they flow:

---

(1) *A prudent chief, &c.*—An ingenious writer, quoted by Dr. Warton ("Essay on Pope," p. 139), says, "If we consider that variety which, in all arts, is necessary to keep up attention, we may perhaps affirm with truth that *inequality* makes a part of the character of excellence; that something ought to be thrown into shade, in order to make the lights more striking."

(2) *Homer nods*—To account for certain discrepancies, the critics have good-humouredly given out that occasionally Homer nods; Pope here affirms that it is they that nod.

(3) *Still green, &c.*—This is a noble passage, displaying, with Pope's exquisite finish, more fervour of feeling and expression than he ordinarily discovers. "Still green with bays" conveys the same idea as the remarkable phraseology of Hobbes, that the ancient classical writers had "put off flesh and blood, and put on immortality;" and of Byron, who calls them,

> "The dead but sceptred monarchs,
> Who still rule our spirits from their urns."

(4) *Pæans*—songs of triumph and praise.

Nations unborn your mighty names shall sound,
And worlds applaud that must not yet be found!
Oh! may some spark of your celestial fire
The last, the meanest of your sons inspire,
That on weak wings, from far, pursues your flights;
Glows while he reads, but trembles as he writes;
To teach vain wits a science little known,
To admire superior sense, and doubt their own!

IMPEDIMENTS TO THE ATTAINMENT OF JUST TASTE.

Of all the causes[1] which conspire to blind
Man's erring judgment, and misguide the mind,
What the weak head with strongest bias rules,
Is Pride,[2] the never-failing vice of fools.
Whatever nature has in worth denied,
She gives in large recruits of needful pride;
For as in bodies, thus in souls we find
What wants in blood and spirits, filled with wind:
Pride, where wit fails, steps in to our defence,
And fills up all the mighty void of sense.
If once right reason drives that cloud away,
Truth breaks upon us with resistless day.
Trust not yourself; but your defects to know,
Make use of every friend, and every foe.

A little learning[3] is a dangerous thing;
Drink deep, or taste not the Piërian spring:
There shallow draughts intoxicate the brain,
And drinking largely sobers us again.
Fired at first sight with what the Muse imparts,
In fearless youth we tempt the heights of arts,
While from the bounded level of our mind,
Short views we take, nor see the lengths behind,

---

(1) *Of all the causes, &c.*—The causes enumerated in this passage as interfering with a correct and enlarged taste are—1st. Pride, or rather vanity. 2nd. Imperfect learning. 3rd. Judging not by the whole, but by some particular feature, such as the fancies, or "conceits" struck out, the language, or the versification.

(2) *Pride—i. e.* self-esteem, vanity, conceit. The word "pride" is incorrectly employed here.

(3) *A little learning, &c.—i. e.* a little learning, if it usurp the place and credit of much, may prove dangerous to its possessor. Pope has been much censured for the sentiment conveyed here, as if he had asserted that a little learning was worse than none at all, but it is clear from the context that that is not his meaning.

But, more advanced, behold, with strange surprise
New distant scenes of endless science rise!
So pleased at first,[1] the towering Alps we try,
Mount o'er the vales, and seem to tread the sky,
The eternal snows appear already past,
And the first clouds and mountains seem the last:
But, those attained, we tremble to survey
The growing labours of the lengthened way,
The increasing prospect tires our wandering eyes,
Hills peep o'er hills, and Alps on Alps arise!
   A perfect judge will read each work of wit
With the same spirit that its author writ:
Survey the *whole*,[2] nor seek some faults to find,
Where nature moves, and rapture warms the mind;
Nor lose, for that malignant dull delight,
The generous pleasure to be charmed with wit.
But in such lays as neither ebb nor flow,
Correctly cold, and regularly low,
That shunning faults, one quiet tenour keep,
We cannot blame indeed—but we may sleep.
In wit, as nature, what affects our hearts
Is not the exactness of peculiar parts;
'Tis not a lip, or eye, we beauty call,
But the joint force, and full result of all.
Thus when we view some well-proportioned dome,
(The world's just wonder, and even thine, O Rome!)
No single parts unequally surprise;
All comes united to the admiring eyes;
No monstrous height, or breadth, or length appear;
The whole at once is bold and regular.
   Some to *Conceit*[3] alone their taste confine,
And glittering thoughts struck out at every line.

(1) *So pleased at first, &c.*—Dr. Johnson says of this simile, that it "is perhaps the best that English poetry can show: it assists the apprehension and elevates the fancy."

(2) *Survey the whole, &c.*—A work of art is to be judged of by the general impression stamped on the mind by the unity and completeness of the whole. Hence it is, as Coleridge has remarked, that the real merit of a poem may be tested by reading it *repeatedly* over. All the great master-pieces of music, painting, and poetry, have this in common, that the more they are scrutinized the more their *beauties* appear; whereas, in inferior works, close scrutiny only discovers their *defects*.

(3) *Conceit*—The fault here reproved is the want of that simplicity, both of air and manner, which is ever associated with true greatness—"the contortions of the Sibyl without her inspiration."

Pleased with a work where nothing's just or fit,
One glaring chaos and wild heap of wit.
Poets like painters, thus, unskilled to trace
The naked nature and the living grace,
With gold and jewels cover every part,
And hide with ornaments their want of art.
True wit is nature to advantage dressed;
What oft was thought, but ne'er so well expressed;
Something, whose truth convinced at sight we find,
That gives us back the image of our mind.
As shades more sweetly recommend the light,
So modest plainness sets off sprightly wit.
For works may have[1] more wit than does them good,
As bodies perish through excess of blood.

 Others for *Language* all their care express,
And value books, as women men, for dress;
Their praise is still—'the style is excellent:'
The sense, they humbly take upon content.
Words are like leaves; and where they most abound,
Much fruit of sense beneath is rarely found.
False eloquence,[2] like the prismatic glass,
Its gaudy colours spreads on every place;
The face of nature we no more survey,
All glares alike, without distinction gay;
But true expression, like the unchanging sun,
Clears, and improves whate'er it shines upon;
It gilds all objects, but it alters none.
Expression is the dress of thought, and still
Appears more decent, as more suitable.
A vile conceit, in pompous words expressed,
Is like a clown in regal purple dressed;
For different styles with different subjects sort,
As several garbs with country, town, and court.

---

(1) *Works may have, &c.*—An extraordinary assertion if understood literally, and "wit" be interpreted, as before, "genius;" inasmuch as true genius would mould and subordinate all the parts to their proper end, and therefore avoid the error here censured. "Wit," then, in this passage, appears to mean brilliancy and intensity of thought working incessantly, but uncontrolled by unity of purpose.

(2) *False eloquence*—"A principal device in the fabrication of this style [of mock eloquence] is to multiply epithets, dry epithets, laid on the surface, and into which no vitality of the sentiment is found to circulate." See Foster's "Essays," p. 252, where may be found a masterly description of mock eloquence.

But most by *Numbers*[1] judge a poet's song,
And smooth or rough, with them, is right or wrong;
In the bright Muse though thousand charms conspire,
Her voice is all these tuneful fools admire;
Who haunt Parnassus but to please their ear,
Not mend their minds; as some to church repair,
Not for the doctrine, but the music there.
These equal syllables alone require,
Though oft the ear the open vowels tire;
While expletives their feeble aid do join;
And ten low words oft creep in one dull line;
While they ring round the same unvaried chimes,
With sure returns of still-expected rhymes.
Where'er you find 'the cooling western breeze,'
In the next line, it 'whispers through the trees;'
If crystal streams 'with pleasing murmurs creep,'
The reader's threatened (not in vain) with 'sleep:'
Then, at the last and only couplet fraught
With some unmeaning thing they call a thought,
A needless Alexandrine ends the song,
That, like a wounded snake, drags its slow length along.
Leave such to tune their own dull rhymes, and know
What's roundly smooth, or languishingly slow;
And praise the easy vigour of a line,
Where Denham's strength, and Waller's sweetness join.
True ease in writing comes from art, not chance,
As those move easiest who have learned to dance:
'Tis not enough no harshness gives offence,
The sound must seem an echo to the sense.
Soft is the strain[2] when Zephyr gently blows,
And the smooth stream in smoother numbers flows;

(1) *Most by numbers, &c.*—The celebrated passage which follows, ingeniously exemplifies the faults which it seems to censure. In general it may be remarked that if these artifices of poetry constitute the aim of the writer, they are unquestionably vicious, but if subordinate to some higher end, they contribute legitimately to the pleasure of the reader. It may be further remarked, that whether versification is essential to poetry in the vague and general acceptation of that term, there can be little doubt that it is absolutely essential to poetry considered in its proper light as an *Art*. It is indeed to poetry what melody and time are to music, colour to painting, and form to sculpture.

(2) *Soft is the strain, &c.*—Pope's success in this and the subsequent illustrations has been both maintained and denied with much zeal. Dr. Johnson is against Pope, and declares that "the smooth strain runs with a perpetual clash of jarring consonants;" that in the lines which describe the efforts of Ajax, there is no

But when loud surges lash the sounding shore,
The hoarse, rough verse should like the torrent roar;
When Ajax strives some rock's vast weight to throw,
The line too labours, and the words move slow;
Not so, when swift Camilla scours the plain,
Flies o'er the unbending corn, and skims along the main.
Hear how Timotheus' varied lays[1] surprise,
And bid alternate passions fall and rise!
While, at each change, the son of Libyan Jove,
Now burns with glory, and then melts with love:
Now his fierce eyes with sparkling fury glow:
Now sighs steal out, and tears begin to flow:
Persians and Greeks like turns of nature found,
And the world's victor stood subdued by sound!

THE TOILET.[2]

And now, unveiled, the toilet stands displayed,
Each silver vase in mystic order laid.
First, robed in white, the nymph intent adores,
With head uncovered, the cosmetic[3] powers.
A heavenly image in the glass appears,
To that she bends, to that her eyes she rears:
The inferior priestess at her altar's side,
Trembling, begins the sacred rites of pride.
Unnumbered treasures ope at once, and here
The various offerings of the world appear;
From each she nicely culls with curious toil,
And decks the goddess with the glittering spoil.

particular heaviness and delay, "and that the swiftness of Camilla is rather contrasted than exemplified," adding, "why the verse should be lengthened to express speed will not easily be discovered." If, however, the verses be carefully read *aloud*, it may perhaps be admitted that the sibilants in the former line entirely overpower the "jarring consonants," which was the effect intended—that the monosyllables in the line "when Ajax strives," &c., sensibly detain the voice—and that Camilla does in the last cited instance majestically sweep over the plain with effectual, though not mechanical, velocity.

(1) *Timotheus' varied lays*—in allusion to Dryden's "Ode on St. Cecilia's Day."
(2) This extract, from "The Rape of the Lock," displays the power of Pope over the artificial and fanciful regions of poetry. Never before or since were the mysteries of the toilet so gracefully described.
(3) *Cosmetic*—from the Greek κόσμος, orderly arrangement, embellishment—belonging to the adornment of the person.

This casket India's glowing gems unlocks,
And all Arabia breathes from yonder box:
The tortoise here and elephant unite,
Transformed to combs, the speckled and the white.
Here files of pins extend their shining rows,
Puffs, powders, patches,[1] bibles, billet-doux.
Now awful beauty puts on all its arms;
The fair each moment rises in her charms,
Repairs her smiles, awakens every grace,
And calls forth all the wonders of her face;
Sees by degrees a purer blush arise,
And keener lightnings quicken in her eyes.
The busy sylphs surround their darling care,
These set the head, and those divide the hair,
Some fold the sleeve, whilst others plait the gown:
And Betty's praised for labours not her own.

EXTRACTS FROM THE ESSAY ON MAN.

MAN'S IGNORANCE.

HEAVEN from all creatures hides the book of fate,
All but the page prescribed, their present state;
From brutes what men, from men what spirits know;
Or who could suffer being here below?
The lamb[2] thy riot dooms to bleed to-day,
Had he thy reason, would he skip and play?
Pleased to the last, he crops the flowery food,
And licks the hand just raised to shed his blood.
Oh blindness to the future! kindly given,
That each may fill the circle marked by Heaven,
Who sees with equal eye, as God of all,
A hero perish or a sparrow fall;
Atoms, or systems, into ruin hurled,
And now a bubble burst, and now a world!

---

(1) *Patches*—small pieces of black silk, which fashionable ladies used once to stick upon their faces for the sake of ornament.

(2) *The lamb, &c.*—The tenderness and beauty of this illustration are admirable—its direct bearing on the argument is less obvious The "reason" of man does not prevent his "skipping and playing" often on the very brink of destruction. "In the midst of life we are in death."

Hope humbly then; with trembling pinions soar;
Wait the great teacher, Death, and God adore!
What future bliss, he gives not thee to know,
But gives that Hope to be thy blessing now.
Hope springs eternal in the human breast;
Man never is, but always to be blest;
The soul, uneasy and confined from home,
Rests and expatiates in a life to come.

What would this man? Now upward will he soar,
And little less than angel, would be more;
Now looking downwards, just as grieved appears,
To want the strength of bulls, the fur of bears.
Made for his use all creatures if he call,
Say, what their use, had he the powers of all?
Nature to these, without profusion, kind,
The proper organs, proper powers assigned;
Each seeming want compensated of course,
Here, with degrees of swiftness, there, of force;
All in exact proportion to the state;
Nothing to add, and nothing to abate.
Each beast, each insect, happy in its own,
Is heaven unkind to man, and man alone?
Shall he alone, whom rational we call,
Be pleased with nothing, if not blessed with all?

The bliss of man (could pride that blessing find)
Is not to act, or think, beyond mankind;
No powers of body or of soul to share,
But what his nature and his state can bear.
Why has not man a microscopic eye?
For this plain reason—man is not a fly.
Say, what the use, were finer optics given,
To inspect a mite, not comprehend the heaven?
Or touch, if tremblingly alive all o'er,
To smart and agonize at every pore?
Or quick effluvia darting through the brain,
Die of a rose in aromatic pain?
If nature thundered in his opening ears,
And stunned him[1] with the music of the spheres,
How would he wish that Heaven had left him still
The whispering zephyr, and the purling rill!

---

(1) *And stunned him, &c.*—"It is justly objected," remarks Dr. Warton, "that the argument required an instance drawn from real sound, and not from the imaginary music of the spheres."

Who finds not Providence all good and wise,
Alike in what it gives and what denies?

GRADATION OF THE SENSUAL AND MENTAL FACULTIES.

Far as creation's ample range extends,
The scale of sensual, mental powers ascends;
Mark how it mounts to man's imperial race
From the green myriads[1] in the peopled grass:
What modes of sight betwixt each wide extreme,
The mole's dim curtain, and the lynx's beam;
Of smell, the headlong lioness between,
And hound sagacious on the tainted green;
Of hearing, from the life that fills the flood,
To that which warbles through the vernal wood.
The spider's touch, how exquisitely fine!
Feels at each thread, and lives along the line:
In the nice bee, what sense, so subtly true,
From poisonous herbs extracts the healing dew!
How instinct varies in the grovelling swine,
Compared, half-reasoning elephant,[2] with thine!
'Twixt that and reason what a nice barrièr!
For ever separate, yet for ever near!
Remembrance and reflection[3] how allied!
What thin partitions sense from thought divide!
And middle natures, how they long to join,
Yet never pass the insuperable line!
Without this just gradation could they be
Subjected, these to those, or all to thee?
The powers of all subdued by thee alone,
Is not thy reason all these powers in one?

See, through this air, this ocean, and this earth,
All matter quick, and bursting into birth.

---

(1) *From the green myriads, &c.*—This and the eight following lines have elicited the warm eulogiums of Warton and Campbell, the latter of whom remarks, that "every epithet is a decisive touch."

(2) *Half-reasoning elephant*—There can be little doubt that animals possess to some extent the reasoning faculty. What they distinctively lack is the imaginative power—the ability to live out of and beyond the immediate sphere of the present moment.

(3) *Remembrance and reflection*—Remembrance is an involuntary, and reflection a voluntary, act of the mind: the former furnishes the materials on which the latter operates.

Above, how high progressive life may go!
Around how wide; how deep extend below!
Vast chain of being! which from God began,
Natures ethereal, human, angel, man,
Beast, bird, fish, insect, what no eye can see,
No glass can reach: from infinite to thee,
From thee to nothing.—On superior **powers**
Were we to press, inferior might on ours;
Or in the full creation leave a void,
Where, one step broken, the great scale's **destroyed**:
From nature's chain whatever link you strike,
Tenth, or ten thousandth, breaks the chain alike.

What if the foot, ordained the dust to tread,
Or hand to toil, aspired to be the head?
What if the head, the **eye, or ear** repined
To **serve** mere engines **to the ruling** mind?
Just as absurd, for any **part to claim**
To be another in this general frame:
Just as absurd, to mourn the tasks or pains
The great directing Mind of All ordains.

All are but parts[1] of one stupendous **whole**,
Whose body nature is, and God the **soul**;
That, changed through all, and yet in **all** the same,
Great **in** the earth as in the ethereal frame,
Warms in the sun, refreshes **in** the breeze,
Glows in the stars, and blossoms in the trees,
Lives through all life, extends through all extent,
Spreads undivided, operates **unspent**;
Breathes in our soul, informs **our** mortal part,
As full, as perfect, in a hair **as heart**;
As full, as perfect, **in** vile **man** that mourns,
As the rapt seraph that adores and burns;
To Him, no high, no low, no great, **no small**;
He fills, He bounds, connects, **and** equals all.

Cease then, nor Order Imperfection name:
Our proper bliss depends on what we blame.
Know thy own point: this kind, this due degree
Of blindness, weakness, Heaven bestows on thee.

---

(1) *All are but parts*, &c.—Our language scarcely **contains** a more striking representation of the Omnipresence of the Deity than that contained in these lines, " which have," as Dr. Warton remarks, " all the energy and harmony that **can be given** to rhyme."

Submit—in this, or any other sphere,
Secure to be as blest as thou canst bear:
Safe in the hand of one disposing Power,
Or in the natal, or the mortal hour.
All nature is but art, unknown to thee;
All chance, direction, which thou canst not see;
All discord, harmony not understood;
All partial evil, universal good.

HAPPINESS.

Know then this truth (enough for man to know),
"Virtue alone is happiness below;"
The only point where human bliss stands still,
And tastes the good without the fall to ill;
Where only[1] merit constant pay receives,
Is blest in what it takes, and what it gives:
The joy unequalled, if its end it gain,
And if it lose, attended with no pain:
Without satiety, though e'er so blest,
And but more relished as the more distressed.
The broadest mirth unfeeling folly wears,
Less pleasing far than virtue's very tears:
Good, from each object, from each place acquired,
For ever exercised, yet never tired;
Never elated, while one man's oppressed;
Never dejected, while another's blest;
And where no wants, no wishes can remain,
Since but to wish[2] more virtue is to gain.
See the sole bliss Heaven could on all bestow!
Which who but feels can taste, but thinks can know:
Yet poor with fortune, and with learning blind,
The bad must miss, the good untaught will find:
Slave to no sect, who takes no private road,
But looks through nature up to nature's God;
Pursues that chain which links the immense design,
Joins heaven and earth, and mortal and divine;
Sees that no being any bliss can know,
But touches some above, and some below;

---

(1) *Where only, &c.*—A sentiment equivalent to the well-known maxim, "Virtue is its own reward."

(2) *Since but to wish, &c.*—*i. e.* the very wish for more is more.

Learns from this union of the rising whole,
The first, last purpose of the human soul;
And knows where faith, law, morals, all began,
All end, in love of God, and love of man.
  For him alone hope leads from goal to goal,
And opens still, and opens on his soul;
Till lengthened on to faith,[1] and unconfined,
It pours the bliss that fills up all the mind.
He sees why nature plants in man alone
Hope of known bliss, and faith in bliss unknown:
(Nature, whose dictates to no other kind
Are given in vain, but what they seek, they find:)
Wise is her present; she connects in this
His greatest virtue with his greatest bliss;
At once his own bright prospect to be blest,
And strongest motive to assist the rest.
  Self-love thus pushed to social, to divine,
Gives thee to make thy neighbour's blessing thine:
Is this too little for the boundless heart?
Extend it, let thy enemies have part:
Grasp the whole worlds of reason, life, and sense,
In one close system of benevolence:
Happier as kinder, in whate'er degree;
And height of bliss but height of charity.
  God loves from whole to parts; but human soul
Must rise from individual to the whole.
Self-love[2] but serves the virtuous mind to wake,
As the small pebble stirs the peaceful lake;
The centre moved, a circle straight succeeds;
Another still, and still another spreads;
Friend, parent, neighbour, first it will embrace;
His country next, and next all human race;
Wide and more wide, the o'erflowings of the mind
Take every creature in of every kind;
Earth smiles around, with boundless bounty blest,
And Heaven beholds its image in his breast.

---

(1) *Lengthened on to faith—i. e.* Hope is extended or intensified until it becomes Faith.

(2) *Self-love, &c.*—The aptness and beauty of this simile cannot but be admired.

THOMSON.

PRINCIPAL EVENTS OF HIS LIFE.—James Thomson, the painter of the Seasons, was born in 1700, at Ednam, Roxburghshire, of which place his father was the minister. He received his early education at Jedburgh, previously to his entering the University of Edinburgh as a divinity student. Circumstances diverted his attention to other objects; and in 1725 he went up to London as a literary adventurer. At this time the manuscript of "Winter" was his only property. He gradually became known and appreciated, was patronized by the Lord Chancellor Talbot, and Frederick Prince of Wales, enjoyed from the government two or three small sinecure offices and pensions, wrote poems and plays, and died in 1748. He was buried in the churchyard of Richmond, Surrey.

PRINCIPAL WORKS.—Besides his great works, "The Seasons" and the "Castle of Indolence," he wrote the poems entitled, "Britannia" and "Liberty," several tragedies, and, in conjunction with Mallet, the masque of "Alfred," in which occurs the national song of "Rule Britannia," &c., which is generally ascribed to Thomson, while others claim it for his coadjutor.

CHARACTERISTIC SPIRIT AND STYLE.—"Habits of early admiration teach us all to look back upon this poet as the favourite companion of our solitary walks, and as the author who has first or chiefly reflected back to our minds a heightened and refined sensation of the delight which rural scenery affords us. The judgment of cooler years may somewhat abate our estimation of him, though it will still leave us the essential features of his poetical character to abide the test of reflection. The unvaried pomp of his diction suggests a most unfavourable comparison with the manly idiomatic simplicity of Cowper; at the same time the pervading spirit and feeling of his poetry is in general more bland and delightful than that of his great rival·in rural description. Cowper's image of nature is more curiously distinct and familiar; Thomson carries our associations through a wider circuit of speculation and sympathy. His touches cannot be more faithful than Cowper's, but they are more soft and select, and less disturbed by the intrusion of homely objects. Cowper was certainly much indebted to him; and though he elevates his style with more reserve and judgment than his predecessor, yet, in his highest moments, he seems to retain an imitative remembrance of him. It is almost stale to remark the beauties of a poem so universally felt; the truth and general interest with which he carries us through the life of the year; the harmony of succession which he gives to the casual phenomena of nature; his pleasing transition from native to foreign scenery; and the soul of exalted and unfeigned benevolence which accompanies his prospects of the creation. It is but equal justice to say, that amidst the feeling and fancy of 'The Seasons,' we meet with interruptions of declamation, heavy narrative, and unhappy digression. As long as he dwells in the pure contemplations of nature, and appeals to the universal poetry of the human breast, his redundant style comes to us as something venial and adventitious—it is the flowing vesture of the Druid; and, perhaps, to the general experience is rather imposing; but, when he returns to the familiar narrations or courtesies of life, the same diction ceases to seem the mantle of inspiration, and only strikes us by its unwieldy difference from the common costume of expression.

"To the 'Castle of Indolence' he brought not only the full nature but the perfect art of a poet. There he redeemed the jejune ambition of his style, and retained all its wealth and luxury without the accompaniment of ostentation. Every stanza of that charming allegory, at least of the whole first part of it, gives out a group of images from which the mind is reluctant to part, and a flow of harmony which the ear wishes to hear repeated."[1]

VERSIFICATION.—"As a writer, he is entitled to one praise of the highest kind; his mode of thinking, and of expressing his thoughts, is original. His blank verse is no more the blank verse of Milton, or of any other poet, than the rhymes of Prior are the rhymes of Cowley. His numbers, his pauses, his diction, are of his own growth, without transcription, without imitation."[2]

EXTRACTS FROM "THE SEASONS."

THE SUMMER MORNING.

WHEN now no more the alternate Twins are fired,
And Cancer reddens with the solar blaze,
Short is the doubtful empire of the night;
And soon, observant of approaching day,

(1) Campbell. "Specimens," &c., p. 403.
(2) Dr. Johnson. "Lives of the Poets."

The meek-eyed Morn appears, mother of dews;[1]
At first faint-gleaming in the dappled east,
Till far o'er ether spreads the widening glow,
And, from before the lustre of her face,
White break the clouds away. With quickened step
Brown night retires; young day pours in apace,
And opens all the lawny prospect wide.
The dripping rock, the mountain's misty top,
Swell on the sight, and brighten with the dawn.
Blue, through the dusk, the smoking currents shine;
And from the bladed field the fearful hare
Limps awkward; while along the forest-glade
The wild deer trip, and often turning gaze
At early passenger. Music awakes,[2]
The native voice of undissembled joy;
And thick around the woodland hymns arise.
Roused by the cock, the soon-clad shepherd leaves
His mossy cottage, where with peace he dwells;
And from the crowded fold, in order, drives
His flock, to taste the verdure of the morn.

    Falsely luxurious, will not man awake;
And, springing from the bed of sloth, enjoy
The cool, the fragrant, and the silent hour,
To meditation due and sacred song?
For is there aught in sleep can charm the wise?
To lie in dead oblivion, losing half
The fleeting moments of too short a life;
Total extinction of the enlightened soul!
Or else to feverish vanity alive,
Wildered and tossing through distempered dreams!
Who would in such a gloomy state remain
Longer than nature craves, when every muse
And every blooming pleasure wait without,
To bless the wildly-devious morning walk?
    But yonder comes the powerful king of day,

---

(1) *Mother of dews*—It is not easy to see the force of this characteristic. The dews are not produced by morning, whose influence only tends to dissipate them; they are, however, revealed by the morning rays, and this perhaps is the meaning of the passage. Thomson's descriptions must be judged of *in the whole*—the parts are often very tame and feeble.

(2) *Music awakes, &c.*—*i. e.* music, which is the native voice, &c. This is the pointing in Mr. Bolton Corney's beautiful edition of Thomson;—the common reading omits the comma after "awakes."

Rejoicing in the east.[1] The lessening cloud,
The kindling azure, and the mountain's brow
Illumed with fluid gold, his near approach
Betoken glad. Lo! now, apparent all,
Aslant the dew-bright earth and coloured air,
He looks in boundless majesty abroad,
And sheds the shining day, that burnished plays
On rocks, and hills, and towers, and wandering streams,
High-gleaming from afar. Prime cheerer, light![2]
Of all material beings first and best!
Efflux divine! Nature's resplendent robe!
Without whose vesting beauty all were wrapt
In unessential[3] gloom.

THE TRAVELLER LOST IN THE SNOW.

As thus the snows arise, and foul and fierce
All Winter drives along the darkened air,
In his own loose-revolving fields the swain
Disastered stands; sees other hills ascend,
Of unknown joyless brow; and other scenes,
Of horrid prospect, shag the trackless plain:
Nor finds the river, nor the forest, hid
Beneath the formless wild; but wanders on
From hill to dale, still more and more astray;
Impatient flouncing through the drifted heaps,
Stung with the thoughts of home; the thoughts of home
Rush on his nerves, and call their vigour forth,
In many a vain attempt. How sinks his soul!
What black despair, what horror fills his heart!
When for the dusky spot, which fancy feigned
His tufted cottage rising through the snow,
He meets the roughness of the middle waste,
Far from the track and blest abode of man!
While round him night resistless closes fast,
And every tempest, howling o'er his head,
Renders the savage wilderness more wild.
Then throng the busy shapes into his mind
Of covered pits, unfathomably deep,

---

(1) *Rejoicing in the east*—In reference probably to Psalm xix. 4, 5.

(2) *Prime cheerer, light, &c.*—Compare these lines with the commencement of Milton's " Address to Light," p. 326.

(3) *Unessential*—void of real being, unsubstantial, impalpable.

A dire descent! beyond the power of frost;
Of faithless bogs; of precipices huge,
Smoothed up with snow; and, what is land unknown,
What water, of the still unfrozen spring,
In the loose marsh or solitary lake,
Where the fresh fountain from the bottom boils.
These check his fearful steps; and down he sinks
Beneath the shelter of the shapeless drift,
Thinking o'er all the bitterness of death,
Mixed with the tender anguish nature shoots
Through the wrung bosom of the dying man—
His wife, his children, and his friends unseen.
In vain for him[1] the officious wife prepares
The fire fair blazing, and the vestment warm;
In vain his little children, peeping out
Into the mingling storm, demand their sire,
With tears of artless innocence. Alas!
Nor wife, nor children, shall he more behold,
Nor friends, nor sacred home. On every nerve
The deadly winter seizes; shuts up sense;
And, o'er his inmost vitals creeping cold,
Lays him along the snows a stiffened corse,
Stretched out, and bleaching in the northern blast.

  Ah! little think the gay licentious proud,
Whom pleasure, power, and affluence surround;
They, who their thoughtless hours in giddy mirth,
And wanton, often cruel, riot waste;
Ah! little think they, while they dance along,
How many feel, this very moment, death,
And all the sad variety of pain;
How many sink in the devouring flood,
Or more devouring flame; how many bleed
By shameful variance 'twixt man and man;
How many pine in want, and dungeon glooms,
Shut from the common air, and common use
Of their own limbs; how many drink the cup
Of baleful grief, or eat the bitter bread
Of misery; sore pierced by wintry winds,
How many shrink into the sordid hut
Of cheerless poverty; how many shake

---

(1) *In vain for him, &c.*—The tenderness of this passage is most touching; the conception is perhaps derived from Lucretius (see the passage quoted, note 5, p. 61), but the application of it is due to Thomson.

With all the fiercer tortures of the mind,
Unbounded passion, madness, guilt, remorse;
Whence, tumbled headlong from the height of life,
They furnish matter for the tragic muse;
Even in the vale, where wisdom loves to dwell,
With friendship, peace, and contemplation joined,
How many, racked with honest[1] passions, droop
In deep retired distress; how many stand
Around the death-bed of their dearest friends,
And point the parting anguish. Thought fond man[2]
Of these, and all the thousand nameless ills,
That one incessant struggle render life,
One scene of toil, of suffering, and of fate,
Vice in his high career would stand appalled,
And heedless rambling Impulse learn to think;
The conscious heart of Charity would warm,
And her wide wish Benevolence dilate;
The social tear would rise, the social sigh,
And into clear perfection, gradual bliss,
Refining still, the social passions work.

THE HYMN OF THE SEASONS.[3]

These, as they change, Almighty Father, these
Are but the varied God. The rolling year

---

(1) *Honest*—honourable, not debasing; this is the classical sense of the original word *honestus*.

(2) *Thought fond man, &c.*—*i. e.* if foolish man thought of these, &c. Some copies erroneously point the passage thus:—"Thought, fond man," &c., to the manifest violation of the sense.

(3) "This piece," **remarks Dr. Aikin,** "the sublimest production of its kind since the days of Milton, should be considered as the winding up of all the variety of matter and design contained in the preceding parts [*i. e.* the four seasons]: and thus is not only admirable as a separate composition, but is contrived with masterly skill to strengthen the unity and connection of the great whole."

Montgomery, too, designates this hymn as "unquestionably one of the most **magnificent specimens of verse in** any language, and only inferior to the inspired prototypes in the Book of Psalms, of which it is for the most part a paraphrase."—*Lectures on Poetry,* **p.** 182.

This fine poem should be compared with Coleridge's "Hymn before Sunrise in the Vale of Chamouni," p. 149, and Milton's "Morning Hymn," p. 338.

Is full of thee. Forth in the pleasing SPRING
Thy beauty walks, thy tenderness and love.
Wide flush the fields; the softening air is balm;
Echo the mountains round, the forest smiles;
And every sense, and every heart is joy.
Then comes thy glory in the SUMMER months,
With light and heat refulgent. Then thy sun
Shoots full perfection through the swelling year;
And oft thy voice in dreadful thunder speaks:
And oft at dawn, deep noon, or falling eve,
By brooks and groves, in hollow-whispering gales.
Thy bounty shines in AUTUMN unconfined,
And spreads a common feast for all that lives.
In WINTER awful thou! with clouds and storms
Around thee thrown, tempest o'er tempest rolled,
Majestic darkness! on the whirlwind's wing
Riding sublime, thou bidst the world adore,
And humblest nature with thy northern blast.

Mysterious round! what skill, what force divine,
Deep felt, in these appear! a simple train,
Yet so delightful mixed, with such kind art,
Such beauty and beneficence combined,
Shade, unperceived, so softening into shade,
And all so forming an harmonious whole,
That, as they still succeed, they ravish still.
But wandering oft, with brute unconscious gaze,
Man marks not thee, marks not the mighty hand,
That, ever busy, wheels the silent spheres;
Works in the secret deep; shoots, steaming, thence
The fair profusion that o'erspreads the Spring;
Flings from the sun direct the flaming day;
Feeds every creature; hurls the tempest forth;
And, as on earth this grateful change revolves,
With transport touches all the springs of life.

Nature attend! join every living soul,
Beneath the spacious temple of the sky,
In adoration join; and, ardent, raise
One general song! To Him, ye vocal gales,
Breathe soft, whose spirit in your freshness breathes;
Oh, talk of Him in solitary glooms,
Where, o'er the rock, the scarcely waving pine
Fills the brown shade with a religious awe.
And ye, whose bolder note is heard afar,
Who shake the astonished world, lift high to heaven

The impetuous song, and say from whom you rage.
His praise, ye brooks,[1] attune, ye trembling rills,[1]
And let me catch it as I muse along.
Ye headlong torrents,[1] rapid and profound;
Ye softer floods, that lead the humid maze
Along the vale; and thou, majestic main,
A secret world of wonders in thyself,
Sound His stupendous praise, whose greater voice
Or bids you roar, or bids your roarings fall.
Soft roll your incense, herbs, and fruits, and flowers,
In mingled clouds, to Him, whose sun exalts,
Whose breath perfumes you, and whose pencil paints.
Ye forests, bend, ye harvests, wave to Him;
Breathe your still song into the reaper's heart,
As home he goes beneath the joyous moon.
Ye that keep watch in heaven, as earth asleep
Unconscious lies, effuse your mildest beams,
Ye constellations, while your angels strike,
Amid the spangled sky, the silver lyre.
Great source of day, best image here below
Of thy Creator, ever pouring wide,
From world to world, the vital ocean round,
On nature write, with every beam, His praise.
The thunder rolls; be hushed the prostrate world,
While cloud to cloud returns the solemn hymn.
Bleat out afresh, ye hills; ye mossy rocks,
Retain the sound; the broad responsive low,
Ye valleys, raise; for the Great Shepherd reigns,
And His unsuffering kingdom yet will come.
Ye woodlands all, awake! a boundless song
Burst from the groves! and when the restless day,
Expiring, lays the warbling world asleep,
Sweetest of birds, sweet Philomela, charm
The listening shades, and teach the night His praise.
Ye chief, for whom the whole creation smiles,
At once the head, the heart, and tongue of all,
Crown the great hymn! in swarming cities vast,
Assembled men to the deep organ join

---

(1) *Brook, rill, torrent—A brook—*from the Anglo-Saxon *brcae-an*, to break—is water that breaks or bursts through from the ground; *a rill*—from the Latin *rivulus*, diminutive of *rivus*, a stream—is a little stream; *a torrent*—from the Latin *torrens*, foaming, boiling—is water that dashes impetuously along or down, foaming as it flows.

The long-resounding voice, oft breaking clear,
At solemn pauses, through the swelling bass;
And, as each mingling flame increases each,
In one united ardour rise to heaven.
Or if you rather choose the rural shade,
And find a fane in every sacred grove;
There let the shepherd's flute, the virgin's lay,
The prompting seraph, and the poet's lyre,
Still sing the God of Seasons, as they roll.
For me, when I forget the darling theme,
Whether the blossom blows, the Summer ray
Russets the plain, inspiring Autumn gleams,
Or Winter rises in the blackening east,
Be my tongue mute, my Fancy[1] paint no more,
And, dead to joy, forget my heart to beat!

   Should fate command me to the farthest verge
Of the green earth, to distant barbarous climes,
Rivers unknown to song, where first the sun
Gilds Indian mountains, or his setting beam
Flames on the Atlantic isles, 'tis nought to me;
Since God is ever present, ever felt,
In the void waste, as in the city full;
And where He vital breathes there must be joy.
When even, at last, the solemn hour shall come,
And wing my mystic flight to future worlds,
I cheerful will obey; there, with new powers,
Will rising wonders sing. I cannot go
Where Universal Love not smiles around,
Sustaining all yon orbs, and all their suns;
From seeming evil still educing good,
And better thence again, and better still,
In infinite progression. But I lose
Myself in Him, in Light ineffable;
Come then, expressive silence, muse His praise!

      (1) *My fancy*—*i. e.* may my fancy, &c.

DESCRIPTION OF THE CASTLE OF INDOLENCE.[1]

In lowly dale, fast by a river's side,
With woody hill o'er hill encompassed round,
A most enchanting wizard did abide,
Than whom a fiend more fell is nowhere found.
It was, I ween, a lovely spot of ground;
And there a season atween[2] June and May,
Half prankt[3] with spring, with summer half imbrowned,
A listless climate made, where, sooth to say,
No living wight could work, ne caréd e'en for play.

Was nought around but images of rest;
Sleep-soothing groves, and quiet lawns between;
And flowery beds, that slumbrous influence kest,[4]
From poppies breathed;[5] and beds of pleasant green,
Where never yet was creeping creature seen.
Meantime unnumbered glittering streamlets played,
And hurléd everywhere their waters sheen;
That, as they bickered[6] through the sunny glade,
Though restless still themselves, a lulling murmur made.

Joined to the prattle of the purling rills,
Were heard the lowing herds along the vale,
And flocks loud bleating from the distant hills,
And vacant shepherds piping in the dale:
And now and then sweet Philomel would wail,
Or stock-doves plain amid the forest deep,
That drowsy rustled to the sighing gale;

---

(1) The "Castle of Indolence," from which the above extract is made, is considered one of the most successful of the many imitations of the style and manner of Spenser. The conception, diction, and measure, harmonize together with singular aptness.

(2) *Atween, &c.—i. e.* combining the characteristic features of May with those of June.

(3) *Prankt*—from the German *prang-en,* to act proudly, display ostentatiously—gaudily arrayed or decked out.

(4) *Kest*—old English for *cast*.

(5) *From poppies, &c.—i. e.* which influence was from poppies breathed.

(6) *Bicker*—a word of uncertain origin—to skirmish; to quiver, or exhibit a tremulous motion.

And still a coil[1] the grasshopper did keep;
Yet all these sounds yblent inclinéd all to sleep.

Full in the passage of the vale, above,
A sable, silent, solemn forest stood;
Where nought but shadowy forms were seen to move,
As Idlesse fancied in her dreaming mood:
And up the hills, on either side, a wood
Of blackening pines, aye waving to and fro,
Sent forth a sleepy horror through the blood;
And where this valley winded out, below,
The murmuring main was heard, and scarcely heard, to flow.

A pleasing land of drowsy-head[2] it was,
Of dreams that wave before the half-shut eye;
And of gay castles in the clouds that pass,
For ever flushing round a summer sky:
There eke the soft delights, that witchingly
Instil a wanton sweetness through the breast,
And the calm pleasures, always hovered nigh;
But whate'er smacked of noyance or unrest,
Was far, far off expelled from this delicious nest.

The landscape such, inspiring perfect ease,
Where Indolence (for so the wizard hight)
Close hid his castle mid embowering trees,
That half shut out the beams of Phœbus bright,
And made a kind of checkered day and night.
Meanwhile, unceasing at the massy gate,
Beneath a spacious palm, the wicked wight
Was placed; and to his lute, of cruel fate,
And labour harsh, complained, lamenting man's estate.

The doors, that knew no shrill alarming bell,
Ne cursed knocker, plied by villain's[3] hand,
Self-opened into halls, where, who can tell
What elegance and grandeur wide expand,
The pride of Turkey and of Persia land?
Soft quilts on quilts, on carpets carpets spread,
And couches stretched around in seemly band;

---

(1) *Coil*—See note 2, p. 277.
(2) *Drowsy-head*—or drowsy-hed, as Spenser spells it—drowsiness.
(3) *Villain*—perhaps from the Latin *vilis*, mean, contemptible, though some derive it from *villanus*, a countryman—in the original sense, a farm-servant, or as here, a servant in general.

And endless pillows rise **to prop the** head ;
So that each spacious **room was one** full-swelling bed.

And everywhere **huge covered tables stood,**
With wines high-flavoured **and** rich viands crowned ;
Whatever sprightly juice **or** tasteful food
On the green bosom of this earth are found,
And all old ocean genders in his round :
Some **hand** unseen these **silently** displayed,
Even undemanded by a sign **or** sound ;
You need but wish, and, instantly obeyed,
Fair ranged the dishes rose, and thick the glasses played.

The rooms with costly tapestry were hung,
Where was inwoven many a gentle tale ;
Such **as** of old **the rural** poets **sung,**
Or **of Arcadian or Sicilian vale :**
Reclining lovers, in the lonely dale,
Poured forth at large the sweetly-tortured heart ;
Or, sighing tender passion, **swelled the** gale,
And **taught** charmed Echo to resound their smart,
While **flocks,** woods, streams, around, repose and peace impart.

Those pleased **the** most, where, by **a cunning** hand,
Depainted was the patriarchal age :
What time Dan[1] Abraham left the Chaldee land,
And pastured on from verdant stage to stage,
Where fields and fountains fresh could best engage.
Toil was not then. Of nothing took they heed,
But with wild beasts the sylvan war to wage,
And o'er vast plains their herds and flocks to feed ;
Blest sons of nature they ! true golden age **indeed !**

Sometimes the pencil, **in** cool airy halls,
Bade the gay bloom of vernal landscapes rise,
Or Autumn's **varied** shades imbrown the walls :
Now the black tempest strikes the astonished eyes,
Now down the steep the flashing torrent flies ;
The trembling sun now plays o'er ocean blue,
And now rude mountains frown amid the skies ;

---

(1) *Dan*—or Don, a corruption of the Latin *dominus*, a lord—a title of respect and honour, equivalent to Sir.

Whate'er Lorraine[1] light-touched with softening hue,
Or savage Rosa[2] dashed, or learned Poussin[3] drew.

Each sound, too, here to languishment inclined,
Lulled the weak bosom, and induced ease.
Aërial music in the warbling wind,
At distance rising, oft by small degrees,
Nearer and nearer came, till o'er the trees
It hung, and breathed such soul-dissolving airs,
As did, alas! with soft perdition please:
Entangled deep in its enchanting snares,
The listening heart forgot all duties and all cares.

A certain music,[4] never known before,
Here lulled the pensive melancholy mind;
Full easily obtained; behoves no more,
But sidelong, to the gently-waving wind,
To lay the well-tuned instrument reclined;
From which, with airy-flying fingers light,
Beyond each mortal touch the most refined,
The god of winds drew sounds of deep delight;
Whence, with just cause, the harp of Æolus it hight.

Ah, me! what hand can touch the string so fine?
Who up the lofty diapason[5] roll
Such sweet, such sad, such solemn airs divine,
Then let them down again into the soul?
Now rising love they fanned; now pleasing dole[6]
They breathed, in tender musings, through the heart;
And now a graver, sacred strain they stole,
As when seraphic hands a hymn impart:
Wild-warbling nature all, above the reach of art!

---

(1) *Lorraine*—Claude Lorraine, generally called Claude, an eminent French landscape painter, whose main characteristic was, perhaps, the "softening hue" cast over his pictures, which fuses down all inequality and roughness, and leaves only the graceful and beautiful behind.

(2) *Savage Rosa*—Salvator Rosa, an Italian painter, famed for depicting the wild and the terrible in nature.

(3) *Learned Poussin*—Nicholas Poussin, a very distinguished French painter, whose profound acquaintance with the principles of his art justly claims for him the epithet "learned."

(4) *A certain music, &c.*—Here follows a description of the Æolian harp.

(5) *Diapason*—See note 10, p. 155.

(6) *Dole*—melancholy.

Such the gay splendour, the luxurious state
Of caliphs old, who on the Tigris' shore,
In mighty Bagdad, populous and great,
Held their bright court, where was of ladies store;[1]
And verse, love, music, still the garland wore;
When sleep was coy, the bard in waiting there
Cheered the lone midnight with the muse's lore;
Composing music bade his dreams be fair,
And music lent new gladness to the morning air.

Near the pavilions where we slept, still ran
Soft-tinkling streams, and dashing waters fell,
And sobbing breezes sighed, and oft began
(So worked the wizard) wintry storms to swell,
As heaven and earth they would together mell;[2]
At doors and windows threatening seemed to call
The demons of the tempest, growling fell,
Yet the least entrance found they none at all;
Whence sweeter grew our sleep, secure in massy hall.

COLLINS.

PRINCIPAL EVENTS OF HIS LIFE.—William Collins was born in 1721, at Chichester. His early education at Winchester school, under Dr. Burton, prepared him for the collegiate course which he commenced in 1740, at Oxford. In 1743 or 1744 he came to London, a "literary adventurer," says Dr. Johnson, "with many projects in his head, and very little money in his pocket." Indolence and irresolution paralyzed his eminent powers, and often reduced him to a pitiable state of helplessness and want. He was, moreover, disappointed in the reception given by the public to the works which he did finish and send forth, and morbidly judged that he had "fallen on evil tongues and evil times." The result of these combined causes was his relapse into a state of imbecility, occasionally interrupted by paroxysms of frenzy, which lasted until his death, in 1756, at his native town.

(1) *Of ladies store*—An expression borrowed from Milton. See p. 309.
(2) *Mell* or *mall*—from the Latin *malleus*, a hammer—to bruise, crush.

PRINCIPAL WORKS.—Collins's poems are all of moderate compass and of the lyrical form. The most admired are the odes entitled "To Fear," "On the Poetical Character," "To Liberty," "To Evening," "The Passions," "On the Death of Thomson," and "On the Popular Superstitions of the Highlands of Scotland."

CHARACTERISTIC SPIRIT AND STYLE.—"Collins had employed his mind chiefly upon works of fiction, and subjects of fancy; and, by indulging some peculiar habits of thought, was eminently delighted with those flights of imagination which pass the bounds of nature, and to which the mind is reconciled only by a passive acquiescence in popular traditions. He loved fairies, genii, giants, and monsters; he delighted to rove through the meanders of enchantment, to gaze on the magnificence of golden palaces, to repose by the waterfalls of Elysian gardens."[1]

"A cloud of obscurity sometimes rests on his highest conceptions, arising from the fineness of his associations, and the daring sweep of his allusions; but the shadow is transitory, and interferes very little with the light of his imagery, or the warmth of his feeling. The absence of even this speck of mysticism from his 'Ode on the Passions' is perhaps the happy circumstance that secured its unbounded popularity.

"His genius loved to breathe rather in the preternatural and ideal element of poetry, than in the atmosphere of imitation, which lies closest to real life; and his notions of poetical excellence, whatever vows he might address to the manners, were still tending to the vast, the undefinable, and the abstract. Certainly, however, he carried sensibility and tenderness into the highest regions of abstracted thought: his enthusiasm spreads a glow even amongst 'the shadowy tribes of mind,' and his allegory is as sensible to the heart as it is visible to the fancy."[2]

(1) Dr. Johnson. "Lives of the Poets."
(2) Campbell. "Specimens," &c., p. 429.

ODE TO FEAR.[1]

Thou, to whom the world unknown,[2]
  With all its shadowy shapes is shown;
Who seest, appalled, the unreal scene,
While Fancy lifts the veil between;
  Ah Fear![3] ah, frantic Fear!
  I see, I see thee near.
I know thy hurried step, thy haggard eye!
Like thee I start; like thee disordered fly.
  For, lo! what monsters in thy train appear!
Danger,[4] whose limbs of giant mould
What mortal eye can fixed behold?
Who stalks his round, a hideous form,
Howling amidst the midnight storm;
Or throws him on the rigid steep
Of some loose-hanging rock to sleep:
And with him thousand phantoms joined,
Who prompt to deeds accursed the mind:
And those, the fiends, who, near allied,
O'er Nature's wounds and wrecks preside;
Whilst Vengeance, in the lurid air,
Lifts her red arm, exposed and bare;
On whom that ravening brood of Fate,
Who lap the blood of sorrow, wait:
Who, Fear, this ghastly train can see,
And look not madly wild, like thee?

---

(1) **Pity and Fear are represented by Aristotle as the** two great engines by whose "purging or **purifying** operation on the mind, the moral effects of the drama are to be produced." The various phenomena of Fear, especially as a dramatic agent, are allegorically represented in this fine ode.

(2) *Thou to whom, &c.*—In allusion to the influence of supernatural horrors on the mind, as displayed by Imagination (here incorrectly called Fancy), who lifts the veil between the actual and the ideal world.

(3) *Ah Fear, &c.*—The abruptness of these lines represents to us the painter of the passion so absorbed by its influence, that he becomes its victim.

(4) *Danger, &c.*—This bold personification is considered one of the most striking of its class in our literature. Every word is significant—the "limbs of giant mould," and the "hideous form," indicate that fear magnifies and exaggerates the reality; and what can be more happily conceived than his sleeping "on the ridgy steep of some loose-hanging rock?"

EPODE.

In earliest Greece, to thee, with partial choice,
    The grief-full Muse addrest her infant tongue;
The maids and matrons, on her awful voice,
    Silent and pale, in wild amazement hung.

Yet he, the bard[2] who first invoked thy name,
    Disdained in Marathon its power to feel:
For not alone he nursed the poet's flame,
    But reached from Virtue's hand the patriot's steel.

But who is he, whom later garlands grace,
    Who left awhile o'er Hybla's dews to rove,[3]
With trembling eyes thy dreary steps to trace,
    Where thou and furies shared the baleful grove?

Wrapt in thy cloudy veil, the incestuous queen[4]
    Sighed the sad call her son and husband heard,
When once alone it broke the silent scene,
    And he the wretch of Thebes no more appeared.

O Fear! I know thee by my throbbing heart;
    Thy withering power inspired each mournful line;
Though gentle Pity claim her mingled part,
    Yet all the thunders of the scene are thine!

---

(1) *Epode.*—The three main divisions of the ancient Greek choral songs, in which lyric poetry originated, were called the strophe (or *turning*), the antistrophe (or *opposite turning*), and the epode (or *after-song*). These terms refer to the union of dancing, music, and poetry, which characterized the performance; thus the strophe denoted the turn from right to left, the antistrophe, that from left to right, and the epode, the cessation from dancing, while the singing was still going on in front of the spectators. These terms were subsequently retained, when their original meaning was lost, nearly in the sense of the word stanza, the strophe and antistrophe denoting the same kind of measure, and the epode a different one.

(2) *The bard.*—Æschylus, who was a warrior as well as a poet.

(3) *He, &c.*—Sophocles, who "left awhile," or ceased awhile to indulge in the softer themes which were congenial to him, and took in hand the terrible and revolting miseries of Œdipus, the "son and husband" referred to in the text.

(4) *Queen.*—Jocasta, Queen of Thebes.

ANTISTROPHE.

Thou who such weary lengths hast past,
Where wilt thou rest, mad nymph! at last?
Say, wilt thou shroud in haunted cell,
Where gloomy Rape and Murder dwell?
  Or in some hollowed seat,
    'Gainst which the big waves beat,
Hear drowning seaman's cries, in tempests brought?
Dark Power! with shuddering, meek, submissive thought,
Be mine to read the visions old
Which thy awakening bards have told:
And, lest[1] thou meet my blasted view,
Hold each strange tale devoutly true;
Ne'er be I found, by thee o'er-awed,
In that thrice-hallowed eve[2] abroad,
When ghosts, as cottage-maids believe,
Their pebbled beds permitted leave;
And goblins haunt, from fire, or fen,
Or mine, or flood, the walks of men!

  O thou, whose spirit[3] most possest
The sacred seat of Shakspere's breast!
By all that from thy prophet broke,
In thy divine emotions spoke;[4]
Hither again thy fury deal,
Teach me but once like him to feel:
His cypress wreath my meed decree,
And I, O Fear, will dwell with thee!

---

  (1) *And lest, &c.—i. e.* and that I may not incur thy severe displeasure. The entire force of the line is in the word "blasted," without which the sense would contradict what follows.

  (2) *Thrice-hallowed eve*—All-Hallows Eve— the 31st of October—a season consecrated of old, and even now in the rural districts, to superstitious observances and fears.

  (3) *Whose spirit, &c.*—In allusion to Shakspere's power in exciting the emotion of fear.

  (4) *In thy divine, &c.—i. e.* and by all that was spoken by him when powerfully moved by thee.

ON THE POETICAL CHARACTER.[1]

As once,[2]—if not with light regard
I read aright that gifted bard,
—Him whose school above the rest,
His loveliest elfin queen has blest!—
One, only one, unrivalled fair
Might hope the magic girdle wear,
At solemn turney hung on high,
The wish of each love-darting eye;
—Lo! to each other nymph, in turn, applied,
  As if, in air unseen, some hovering hand,
Some chaste and angel-friend to virgin fame,
  With whispered spell had burst the starting band,
It left unblest her loathed dishonoured side;
  Happier, hopeless fair, if never
  Her baffled hand, with vain endeavour,
Had touched that fatal zone to her denied!
Young Fancy thus—to me divinest name!—
  To whom, prepared and bathed in heaven,
  The cest of amplest power is given:
  To few the god-like gift assigns,
  To gird their blest prophetic loins,
And gaze her visions wild, and feel unmixed her flame!

The band[3] as fairy legends say,
Was wove on that creating day

---

(1) "Perhaps," remarks Hazlitt, "his 'Ode on the Poetical Character' is the best of all. A rich distilled perfume emanates from it, like the breath of genius; a golden cloud envelopes it."

(2) *As once, &c.*—The drift of this passage is, that as the magic girdle described by Spenser in the Faery Queene (see canto iv.) would only fit Florimel as one eminently conspicuous for her virtues, so, the cestus or "band" of Fancy, that is, the rich endowment of poetical inspiration, is destined only for a chosen few.

(3) *The band, &c.*—This is a passage of some difficulty, and the following is offered as a conjectural interpretation only:—The cestus of Fancy was woven one day, when the first poet, or the genius of Poetry, whose creative faculty may be said to have given life and animation to the tented sky, &c., having long been loved by Fancy, loved her in return, and enthroned her as his queen; and all the while the mystic powers were weaving her cestus, or in other words, aiding in the formation of the poetical character (the subject of the ode), music awoke around, the sun shed his glowing light, Wonder sat in listening ecstasy, Truth's piercing eyes gazed at the process, the mind's shadowy tribes of thoughts and conceptions fluttered over the scene, and celestial influences solemnised and sanctified the whole.

When he, who called with thought to birth[1]
Yon tented sky, this laughing earth,
And drest with springs and forests tall,
And poured the main engirting all,
Long by the loved enthusiast wooed,
Himself in some diviner mood,
Retiring, sat with her alone,
And placed her on his sapphire throne;
The whiles, the vaulted shrine around,
Seraphic wires were heard to sound,
Now sublimest triumph swelling,
Now on love and mercy dwelling;
And she, from out the veiling cloud,
Breathed her magic notes aloud;
And thou, thou rich-haired youth of morn,[2]
And all thy subject life was born!
The dangerous passions kept aloof,[3]
Far from the sainted growing woof:
But near it sat ecstatic Wonder,
Listening the deep applauding thunder;
And Truth, in sunny vest arrayed,
By whose the tarsel's[4] eyes were made;
All the shadowy tribes of Mind,
In braided dance their murmurs joined,
And all the bright uncounted Powers
Who feed on Heaven's ambrosial flowers.
—Where is the bard whose soul can now[5]
Its high presuming hopes avow?
Where he who thinks, with rapture blind,
This hallowed work for him designed?

High on some cliff,[6] to heaven up-piled,
Of rude access, of prospect wild,

(1) *Who called with thought, &c.*—i. e. by his creative thought or intellect, which represented the sky as "tented," the earth as "laughing," &c.

(2) *Rich-haired youth, &c.*—The sun.

(3) *The dangerous, &c.*—A fine conception, to denote the pure and elevated character of true poetry, living in a region above the influence of earth-born passions.

(4) *Tarsel*—the tercel or male hawk, whose eyes are so penetrating that they are said (somewhat fantastically) to be made like Truth's.

(5) *Now*—i. e. now that he sees how much is involved in the formation of the poetical character.

(6) *High on some cliff, &c.*—The conception and expression of the lines that follow place them in the highest order of English poetry. They are worthy of their subject, and would have done no discredit to Milton himself.

D D

Where, tangled round the jealous steep,
Strange shades o'erbrow the valleys deep,
And holy Genii guard the rock,
Its glooms embrown, its springs unlock,
 While on its rich ambitious head,
 An Eden, like his own,[1] lies spread,
I view that oak, the fancied glades among,
 By which as Milton lay, his evening ear,
From many a cloud that dropped ethereal dew,
 Nigh-sphered in heaven,[2] its native strains could hear;
On which that ancient trump he reached was hung:
 Thither oft, his glory greeting,
 From Waller's myrtle shades retreating,[3]
With many a vow from Hope's aspiring tongue
My trembling feet his guiding steps pursue;
 In vain—Such bliss to one alone,
 Of all the sons of soul, was known;
 And Heaven, and Fancy, kindred powers,
 Have now o'erturned the inspiring bowers,
Or curtained close such scene from every future view.

THE PASSIONS.[4]

AN ODE FOR MUSIC.

When Music, heavenly maid! was young,
While yet in early Greece she sung,

---

(1) *Like his own, &c.*—*i. e.* like that described by Milton in "Paradise Lost" (see p. 331).

(2) *Nigh-sphered, &c.*—*i. e.* his evening ear nigh-sphered, &c., or more definitely, Milton's spirit listening, as it were, in the calm of thought, would seem to be almost domiciled—"nigh-sphered"—in heaven, and hearing only its own *native* strains. Milton says of himself ("Paradise Lost," vii. 14)—

  "Into the heaven of heavens I have presumed,
   An earthly guest, and drawn empyreal air."

(3) *From Waller's myrtle shades, &c.*—Disdaining the effeminate muse of Waller.

(4) This has been, by some eminent judges, considered the finest lyric ode in our language. It is, indeed, difficult to exaggerate its merits, whether we regard the conception, the diction, or the apt management of the rhythm.

The Passions oft, to hear her shell,
Thronged around her magic cell;
Exulting, trembling, raging, fainting,
Possessed[1] beyond the Muse's painting;
By turns they felt the glowing mind
Disturbed,[2] delighted, raised, refined;
Till once, 'tis said, when all were fired,
Filled with fury, rapt,[3] inspired,
From the supporting myrtles round
They snatched her instruments of sound;
And as they oft had heard apart
Sweet lessons of her forceful art,
Each—for madness ruled the hour—
Would prove his own expressive power.

First FEAR his hand, its skill to try,
Amid the chords bewildered laid;
And back recoiled, he knew not why,
Even at the sound himself had made.

Next ANGER rushed; his eyes on fire
In lightnings owned his secret stings;
In one rude clash he struck the lyre,
And swept with hurried hand the strings.

With woeful[4] measures wan DESPAIR—
Low sullen sounds his grief beguiled;
A solemn, strange, and mingled air;
'Twas sad by fits, by starts 'twas wild.

But thou, O HOPE! with eyes so fair,
What was thy delighted measure?
Still it whispered promised pleasure,

---

(1) *Possessed, &c.*—i. e. more affected or inspired than can be described in verse.
(2) *Disturbed, &c.*—a beautiful line, describing the successive steps of the process by which music acts upon the mental tastes.
(3) *Rapt*—from the Latin *rap-ere*, to seize, carry off—hurried away by elevated feeling, in an ecstasy.
(4) *With woeful, &c.*—"It is observable," remarks Dr. Langhorne, "that though the measure is the same in which the musical efforts of Fear, Anger, and Despair are described, yet by the variation of the cadence, the character and operation of each is strongly expressed; this particularly of Despair, 'with woeful,' &c."

And bade the lovely scenes at distance[1] hail!
  Still would her touch the strain prolong;
  And from the rocks, the woods, the vale,
She called on Echo still through all the song;
  And where her sweetest theme she chose,
A soft responsive voice was heard at every close,
And Hope enchanted smiled, and waved her golden hair.
  And longer had she sung—but, with a frown,
    Revenge impatient rose;
He threw his blood-stained sword in thunder down,
    And, with a withering look,
    The war-denouncing trumpet took,
    And blew a blast so loud and dread,
Were ne'er prophetic sounds so full of woe!
    And, ever and anon he beat
    The doubling drum with furious heat;
  And though sometimes, each dreary pause between,
    Dejected Pity, at his side,
    Her soul-subduing voice applied,
  Yet still he kept his wild unaltered mien,
While each strained ball of sight seemed bursting from his head.

  Thy numbers, Jealousy, to nought were fixed;
    Sad proof of thy distressful state;
  Of differing themes the veering song was mixed,
And now it courted Love, now raving called on Hate.

    With eyes upraised, as one inspired,
    Pale Melancholy sat retired;
    And from her wild sequestered seat,
    In notes, by distance made more sweet,
  Poured through the mellow horn her pensive soul;
    And, dashing soft from rocks around,
    Bubbling runnels joined the sound;
  Through glades and glooms the mingled measure stole;

---

(1) *At distance, &c.*—There are many beauties in this description of Hope. She hails the lovely scenes *at a distance*. She *prolongs* the strain, a conception nearly equivalent to Pope's expression—"Hope springs eternal in the human breast." The introduction, too, of Echo as an associate of Hope is most tastefully devised and executed.

Or, o'er some haunted stream, with fond delay,
Round a holy calm diffusing,
Love of peace and lonely musing,
In hollow murmurs[1] died away.

But, oh! how altered was its[2] sprightlier tone,
When CHEERFULNESS,[3] a nymph of healthiest hue,
Her bow across her shoulder flung,
Her buskins gemmed with morning dew,
Blew an inspiring air, that dale and thicket rung,
The hunter's call, to Faun and Dryad known!
The oak-crowned sisters, and their chaste-eyed queen,
Satyrs and sylvan boys, were seen
Peeping from forth their alleys green;
Brown Exercise rejoiced to hear,
And Sport leaped up, and seized his beechen spear.

Last came Joy's[3] ecstatic trial:
He, with viny crown advancing,
First to the lively pipe his hand addressed;
But soon he saw the brisk, awakening viol,
Whose sweet entrancing voice he loved the best.
They would have thought who heard the strain,
They saw, in Tempe's vale, her native maids,
Amidst the festal-sounding shades,
To some unwearied minstrel dancing;
While, as his flying fingers kissed the strings,
Love framed with Mirth[3] a gay fantastic round;
Loose were her tresses seen, her zone unbound:
And he, amidst his frolic play,
As if he would the charming air repay,
Shook thousand odours from his dewy wings.

O Music! sphere-descended maid,
Friend of pleasure, Wisdom's aid,
Why, Goddess! why, to us denied,
Lay'st thou thy ancient lyre aside?

(1) *Hollow murmurs, &c.*—In several parts of this Ode, as here, the sound is a very apt "echo of the sense."

(2) *Its*—the horn's; the same instrument being introduced.

(3) *Cheerfulness, joy, mirth*—*Cheerfulness* is rather a habit, than a passion, of the mind; *Joy* is the outward revealing of inward happiness; *Mirth* is obstreperous joy.

As in that loved Athenian bower,
You learned an all-commanding power,
Thy mimic soul, O nymph endeared,
Can well recall what then it heard.
Where is thy native simple heart,
Devote to virtue, fancy, art?
Arise, as in that elder time,
Warm, energetic, chaste, sublime!
Thy wonders in that godlike age
Fill thy recording sister's[1] page—
'Tis said, and I believe the tale,
Thy humblest reed could more prevail,
Had more of strength, diviner rage,
Than all which charms this laggard age;
Even all[2] at once together found,
Cecilia's mingled world of sound—
Oh! bid our vain endeavours cease;
Revive the just designs of Greece;
Return in all thy simple state;
Confirm the tales[3] her sons relate!

YOUNG.

PRINCIPAL EVENTS OF HIS LIFE.—Edward Young—the poet of the "Night Thoughts"—was born in 1684, at Upham, a village near Winchester. At the renowned school of that city he received his early education, which was continued subsequently at New College, Oxford. His first profession was law, in which he graduated, but his success appearing doubtful, and his views undergoing a change, he, in 1727, took orders, and was appointed one of the royal chaplains. In 1731, he married Lady Elizabeth Lee, daughter of the Earl of Litchfield. The remainder of his life was spent in seclusion, and though his ambitious temperament fre-

---

(1) *Recording sister, &c.*—History.
(2) *Even all, &c.*—i. e. even when all the resources of the art are combined, as in the organ.
(3) *Confirm the tales, &c.*—i. e. prove to our own experience the wonderful influence attributed by the ancients to music.

quently led him to seek preferment in the Church, he never obtained it. He died in 1765.

PRINCIPAL WORKS.—Besides the "Night Thoughts," Dr. Young wrote a series of Satires in verse, entitled, "The Love of Fame, the Universal Passion," "The Last Day," "The Centaur not Fabulous," a prose satire, and some tragedies, of which "The Revenge" is the finest.

CHARACTERISTIC SPIRIT AND STYLE.—"The 'Night Thoughts' contain many splendid and happy conceptions, but their beauty is thickly marred by false wit and overlaboured antithesis: indeed, the whole ideas of the author seem to have been in a state of antithesis while he composed the poem. One portion of his fancy appears devoted to aggravate the picture of his desolate feelings; and the other half to contradict that picture by eccentric images and epigrammatic ingenuities. The reader most sensitive to his faults must, however, have felt that there is in him a spark of originality which is never long extinguished, however far it may be from vivifying the entire mass of his poetry. Many and exquisite are his touches of sublime expression, of profound reflection, and of striking imagery. It is recalling but a few of these to allude to his description, in the eighth book, of the man whose *thoughts are not of this world*, to his simile of the traveller, at the opening of the ninth book, to his spectre of the antediluvian world, and to some parts of his very unequal description of the conflagration; above all, to that noble and familiar image—

' When final Ruin fiercely drives
Her ploughshare o'er creation.' [1]

"It is true that he seldom, if ever, maintains a flight of poetry long free from oblique associations; but he has individual passages which philosophy might make her texts, and experience select for her mottoes."[2]

(1) This metaphor is borrowed by Burns in the poem "To a Daisy," see p. 78. The Scottish bard was a great admirer of Young.
(2) Campbell. "Specimens," &c., p. 467

EXTRACTS FROM THE "NIGHT THOUGHTS."

THE WONDROUS NATURE OF MAN.

THE bell strikes one.[1] We take no note of time
But from its loss: to give it then a tongue
Is wise in man. As if an angel spoke
I feel the solemn sound. If heard aright,
It is the knell of my departed hours.
Where are they? With the years beyond the Flood.
It is the signal that demands dispatch:
How much is to be done! My hopes and fears
Start up alarmed, and o'er life's narrow verge
Look down—On what? A fathomless abyss:
A dread eternity!—how surely mine!—
And can eternity belong to me,
Poor pensioner on the bounties of an hour?
　　How poor, how rich, how abject,[2] how august,
How complicate, how wonderful is man!
How passing wonder He who made him such!
Who centred in our make such strange extremes!
From different natures marvellously mixed,
Connexion exquisite of distant worlds!
Distinguished link in being's endless chain,
Midway from nothing to the Deity!
A beam ethereal, sullied and absorbed;[3]
Though sullied and dishonoured, still divine;
Dim miniature of greatness absolute!
An heir of glory! a frail child of dust!
Helpless immortal![4] insect infinite!

---

(1) *The bell strikes one—i. e.* one in the morning. This passage is extracted from "Night the First" of the poem, and aptly exemplifies its characteristic beauties and faults—the condensed thought, the poetical turn of phrase, as well as the overlaboured antithesis.

(2) *Abject, mean*—may be thus distinguished; *abject*—from the Latin *abjectus*, cast away—refers rather to the *circumstances*, and *mean*, to the *nature* of the individual; hence the former word is correctly employed here, the object of the writer being to show that man's nature is essentially noble.

(3) *Absorbed*—not reflected, dull and dim.

(4) *Helpless, immortal, &c.*—A manifest failure in expression, since there is no real antithesis between the first pair of words, and no distinct meaning in the second.

A worm! a god!—I tremble at myself,
And in myself am lost! At home a stranger,
Thought wanders up and down, surprised, aghast,
And wondering at her own.[1] How reason reels!
O what a miracle is man to man!
Triumphantly distressed! what joy! what dread!
Alternately transported and alarmed!
What can preserve my life, or what destroy?
An angel's arm can't snatch me from the grave;
Legions of angels can't confine me there.
  "Tis past conjecture; all things rise in proof:
While o'er my limbs Sleep's soft dominion spreads,
What though my soul fantastic measures trod
O'er fairy fields; or roamed along the gloom
Of pathless woods; or down the craggy steep
Hurled headlong, swam with pain the mantled pool,
Or scaled the cliff, or danced on hollow winds,
With antic shapes, wild natives of the brains?
Her ceaseless flight, though devious, speaks her nature
Of subtler essence than the trodden clod,
Active, aërial, towering, unconfined,
Unfettered with her gross companion's fall.
E'en silent night proclaims my soul immortal;
E'en silent night proclaims eternal day.
For human weal heaven husbands all events;
Dull sleep instructs, nor sport vain dreams in vain.
  Yet man, fool man! here buries all his thoughts;
Inters celestial hopes without one sigh.
Prisoner of earth, and pent beneath the moon,
Here pinions all his wishes; winged by heaven
To fly at infinite, and reach it there,
Where seraphs gather immortality
On life's fair tree, fast by the throne of God.
What golden joys ambrosial clustering glow
In his full beam, and ripen for the just,
Where momentary ages are no more!
When Time, and Pain, and Chance, and Death expire!
And is it in the flight of threescore years
To push eternity from human thought,

---

(1) *Wondering at her own*—What is our own is generally so familiar as to excite no surprise or wonder, but Thought being conceived of as a "stranger at home," may with consistency be said to be surprised even at her own.

And smother souls immortal in the dust?
A soul immortal, spending all her fires,
Wasting her strength in strenuous idleness,
Thrown into tumult, raptured or alarmed
At aught this scene can threaten or indulge,
Resembles ocean into tempest wrought,
To waft a feather, or to drown a fly.

PROCRASTINATION.

BE wise to-day; 'tis madness to defer:[1]
Next day the fatal precedent will plead;
Thus on, till wisdom is pushed out of life.
Procrastination is the thief of time;
Year after year it steals, till all are fled,
And to the mercies of a moment[2] leaves
The vast concerns of an eternal scene.
If not so frequent, would not this be strange?
That 'tis so frequent, this is stranger still.
  Of man's miraculous mistakes this bears
The palm—that all men are about to live,
For ever on the brink of being born.
All pay themselves the compliment to think
They one day shall not drivel; and their pride[3]
On this reversion takes up ready praise—
At least their own—their future selves applauds.
How excellent that life they ne'er will lead!
All promise is poor dilatory man,
And that through every stage. When young, indeed,
In full content we sometimes nobly rest
Unanxious for ourselves, and only wish,
As duteous sons, our fathers were more wise.
At thirty man suspects himself a fool;
Knows it at forty, and reforms his plan;
At fifty chides his infamous delay,

---

(1) *Defer, delay, procrastinate*—thus differ: to *delay* is to hold back in general; to *defer*, to put off for some specific purpose; to *procrastinate*, to put off till to-morrow, as a habit of the mind, and therefore culpably.

(2) *Moment*—i. e. the moment of death.

(3) *Their pride, &c.*—The construction here is somewhat abrupt and obscure, but the meaning seems to be that their pride, in the expectation of their one day becoming wise, compliments them with being so already—the present being at least their own, whatever the future may be—and thus they applaud their future selves.

Pushes his prudent purpose to resolve;
In all the magnanimity of thought
Resolves and re-resolves; then dies the same.
  And why? because he thinks himself immortal.
All men think all men mortal, but themselves;
Themselves,[1] when some alarming shock of Fate
Strikes through their wounded hearts the sudden dread;
But their hearts wounded, like the wounded air,
Soon close; where past the shaft no trace is found,
As from the wing no scar the sky retains,
The parted wave no furrow from the keel;
So dies in human hearts the thought of death.

THE MAN WHOSE THOUGHTS ARE NOT OF THIS WORLD.[2]

Some angel guide my pencil, while I draw—
What nothing less than angel can exceed—
A man on earth devoted to the skies;
Like ships in seas, while in, above the world.
  With aspect mild, and elevated eye,
Behold him seated on a mount serene,
Above the fogs of sense, and passion's storm;
All the black cares and tumults of this life,
Like harmless thunders, breaking at his feet,
Excite his pity, nor impair his peace.
Earth's genuine sons, the sceptered and the slave,
A mingled mob! a wandering herd! he sees,
Bewildered in the vale: in all unlike!
His full reverse in all! what higher praise?
What stronger demonstration of the right?
  The present all their care, the future his.
When public welfare calls, or private want,
They give to fame; his bounty he conceals.
Their virtues varnish Nature, his exalt.
Mankind's esteem they court, and he his own.
Theirs the wild chase of false felicities;
His the composed possession of the true.
Alike throughout is his consistent peace,

---

(1) *Themselves, &c.*—They think even themselves mortal when, &c.
(2) Young's peculiar style is finely displayed in this extract; the subject required strong contrasts of light and shade, and they are very strikingly introduced, especially in the passage commencing "He sees with other eyes," &c.

All of one colour, and an even thread;
While party coloured shreds of happiness,
With hideous gaps between, patch up for them
A madman's robe; each puff of Fortune blows
The tatters by, and shows their nakedness.
   He sees with other eyes than theirs; where they
Behold a sun, he spies a Deity.
What makes them only smile, makes him adore.
Where they see mountains, he but atoms sees;
An empire, in his balance, weighs a grain.
They things terrestrial worship as divine;
His hopes immortal blow them by as dust,
That dims his sight, and shortens his survey,
Which longs in infinite to lose all bound.
Titles and honours (if they prove his fate)
He lays aside to find his dignity;
No dignity they find in aught besides.
They triumph in externals, (which conceal
Man's real glory), proud of an eclipse;[1]
Himself too much he prizes to be proud,
And nothing thinks so great in man as man.
Too dear he holds his interest to neglect
Another's welfare, or his right invade;
Their interest, like a lion, lives on prey.
They kindle at the shadow of a wrong;
Wrong he sustains with temper, looks on Heaven,
Nor stoops to think his injurer his foe.
Nought but what wounds his virtue wounds his peace.
A covered heart their character defends;
A covered heart denies him half his praise.
Their no-joys end where his full feast begins:
His joys create, theirs murder, future bliss.
To triumph in existence, his alone;
And his alone, triumphantly to think
His true existence is not yet begun.
His glorious course[2] was, yesterday, complete:
Death, then, was welcome; yet life still is sweet.

---

(1) *Proud of an eclipse—i. e.* proud of that which eclipses or obscures them.

(2) *His glorious course, &c.—i. e.* even yesterday his course was complete, he was ready for death.

AKENSIDE.

PRINCIPAL EVENTS OF HIS LIFE.—Mark Akenside was born in 1721, at Newcastle-upon-Tyne. His father was a butcher, and being a member of the Presbyterian Church, seems to have desired to bring up his son as a minister of that communion. With this view, after receiving elementary instruction at a private school, he went at the age of eighteen to the University of Edinburgh. While resident here he decided on the profession of medicine, in preference to that of divinity, and having studied for three years, he went to Leyden, where he took his degree of M.D. On arriving in England, he settled at Northampton, whence he afterwards removed to Hampstead, and subsequently to London, but was never very successful as a physician. He died in 1770.

PRINCIPAL WORKS.—Besides his most distinguished work, "The Pleasures of Imagination," Akenside wrote many mediocre odes, and a finely conceived poem, entitled "Hymn to the Naiads," together with some very classical "Inscriptions."

CHARACTERISTIC SPIRIT AND STYLE.—"'The Pleasures of Imagination,' published, as it was, at the age of twenty-three, raised expectations that were not afterwards very amply satisfied. It has undoubtedly a just claim to very particular notice, as an example of great felicity of genius, and uncommon amplitude of acquisitions, of a young mind stored with images, and much exercised in combining and comparing them.

"The subject is well chosen, as it includes all images that can strike or please, and thus comprises every species of poetical delight. The only difficulty is in the choice of examples and illustrations, and it is not easy in such exuberance of matter to find the middle point between penury and satiety. The parts seem artificially disposed, with sufficient coherence, so that they cannot change their places without injury to the general design.

"His images are displayed with such luxuriance of expression, that they are hidden, like Butler's moon, by a *veil of light;* they are forms fantastically lost under superfluity of dress. *Pars minima est ipsa puella sui.* The words are multiplied till the sense is hardly perceived; attention deserts the mind and settles in the ear. The reader wanders through the gay diffusion, sometimes amazed, and sometimes delighted, but, after many turnings in the flowery labyrinth, comes out as he went in. He remarked little, and laid hold on nothing."[1]

"If his genius is to be estimated from this poem, it will be found to be lofty and elegant, chaste, correct, and classical; not marked with strong traits of originality, not ardent, not exuberant. His enthusiasm was rather of that kind which is kindled by reading and imbibing the spirit of authors, than by contemplating at first hand the works of nature. As a versifier, Akenside is allowed to stand amongst those who have given the most finished models of blank verse. His periods are long but harmonious, the cadence full of grace, and the measure is supported with uniform dignity; the muse professed the 'mien erect' and high commanding gait. We shall scarcely find a low or trivial expression introduced, a careless and unfinished line permitted to stand. His stateliness, however, is somewhat allied to stiffness. His verse is sometimes feeble, through too great a redundancy of ornament; and sometimes laboured into a degree of obscurity, from too anxious a desire of avoiding natural and simple expressions."[2]

EXTRACTS FROM "THE PLEASURES OF IMAGINATION."

GOD THE SOURCE OF EXCELLENCE.

From heaven my strains begin; from heaven descends
The flame of genius to the human breast,
And love, and beauty, and poetic joy,
And inspiration. Ere the radiant sun
Sprang from the east, or 'mid the vault of night
The moon suspended her serener lamp;
Ere mountains, woods, or streams, adorned the globe,
Or Wisdom taught the sons of men her lore,
Then lived the Almighty One; then deep retired
In his unfathomed essence, viewed the forms,[3]
The forms eternal, of created things:

---

(1) Dr. Johnson. "Lives of the Poets."
(2) Mrs. Barbauld. "Essay" prefixed to her edition of Akenside's Poems.
(3) *The forms, &c.*—The allusion here is to the notion that the idea or image of the universe dwelt in the divine mind from eternity, until at length his vital smile "unfolded it into being."

The radiant sun, the moon's nocturnal lamp,
The mountains, woods, and streams, the rolling globe,
And Wisdom's mien celestial. From the first
Of days on them his love divine he fixed,
His admiration, till, in time complete,
What he admired and loved his vital smile
Unfolded into being. Hence the breath
Of life informing[1] each organic frame,
Hence the green earth, and wild resounding waves,
Hence light and shade alternate, warmth and cold,
And clear autumnal skies and vernal showers,
And all the fair variety of things.

THE SOUL'S SYMPATHY WITH GREATNESS.[2]

Say, why was man so eminently raised
Amid the vast creation? why ordained
Through life and death to dart his piercing eye,
With thoughts beyond the limit of his frame,
But that the Omnipotent might send him forth,
In sight of mortal and immortal powers,
As on a boundless theatre, to run
The great career of justice, to exalt
His generous aim to all diviner deeds,
To chase each partial purpose from his breast,
And through the mists of passion and of sense,
And through the tossing tide of chance and pain,
To hold his course unfaltering, while the voice
Of Truth and Virtue up the steep ascent
Of Nature calls him to his high reward,
The applauding smile of Heaven? Else wherefore burns
In mortal bosoms this unquenched hope
That breathes from day to day sublimer things,
And mocks possession? Wherefore darts the mind,
With such resistless ardour to embrace
Majestic forms, impatient to be free;
Spurning the gross control of wilful might,
Proud of the strong contentions of her toils,
Proud to be daring? Who but rather turns
To heaven's broad fire his unconstrained view

---

(1) *Informing*—animating. (See note 3, p. 130).

(2) The main idea developed in these lines is avowedly borrowed from a passage in the treatise of Longinus, " De Sublimitate."

Than to the glimmering of a waxen flame?
Who that from Alpine heights[1] his labouring eye
Shoots round the wide horizon, to survey
Nilus or Ganges, rolling his bright wave
Through mountains, plains, through empires black with shade,
And continents of sand, will turn his gaze
To mark the windings of a scanty rill
That murmurs at his feet?[2] The high-born soul
Disdains to rest her heaven-aspiring wing
Beneath its native quarry.[3] Tired of earth,
And this diurnal scene, she springs aloft
Through fields of air, pursues the flying storm,
Rides on the volleyed lightning through the heavens,
Or, yoked with whirlwinds and the northern blast,
Sweeps the long track of day. Then high she soars
The blue profound, and, hovering round the sun,
Beholds him pouring the redundant[4] stream
Of light, beholds his unrelenting sway
Bend the reluctant planets to absolve
The fated rounds of time: thence far effused
She darts her swiftness up the long career
Of devious comets, through its burning signs
Exulting measures the perennial wheel
Of Nature; and looks back on all the stars,
Whose blended light as with a milky zone
Invests the orient. Now amazed she views
The empyreal waste, where happy spirits hold
Beyond this concave heaven their calm abode,
And fields of radiance, whose unfading light
Has travelled the profound six thousand years,
Nor yet arrived in sight of mortal things.
E'en on the barriers of the world untired
She meditates the eternal depth below,

---

(1) *Alpine heights*—Dr. Johnson censures the employment of the word "Alpine" here, in the sense of like the Alps, as "strained."

(2) The argument here is driven too far. We may easily and with pleasure turn from the vast to the minute, as Lord Byron does from the vision of "darkened Jura" to the "light drip of the suspended oar," and the chirping of the grasshopper (Childe Harold, iii. 86). And this comprehensiveness of mental grasp is, perhaps, one of the strongest points of the general argument here enforced.

(3) *Quarry*—the point aimed at. (See note 4, p. 40.)

(4) *Redundant*—probably in the sense of abundant, ample.

Till, half recoiling, down the headlong steep
She plunges, soon o'erwhelmed and swallowed up
In that immense of being. There her hopes
Rest at the fated goal: for, from the birth
Of mortal man, the sovereign Maker said,
That not in humble nor in brief delight,
Not in the fading echoes of Renown,
Power's purple robes, nor Pleasure's flowery lap,
The soul should find enjoyment; but, from these
Turning disdainful to an equal good,
Through all the ascent of things enlarge her view,
Till every bound at length should disappear,
And infinite perfection close the scene.

MORAL BEAUTY.

MIND, mind alone, (bear witness, earth and heaven!)
The living fountain in itself contains
Of beauteous and sublime: here, hand in hand,
Sit paramount the Graces; here, enthroned,
Celestial Venus, with divinest airs,
Invites the soul to never-fading joy.
Look, then, abroad through nature, to the range
Of planets, suns, and adamantine spheres,
Wheeling, unshaken, through the void immense;
And speak, O man![1] does this capacious scene
With half that kindling majesty dilate
Thy strong conception, as when Brutus rose
Refulgent from the stroke of Cæsar's fate,
Amid the crowd of patriots; and his arm
Aloft[2] extending, like eternal Jove,
When guilt brings down the thunder, called aloud
On Tully's name, and shook his crimson steel,

---

(1) *And speak, O man, &c.*—It is impossible to admit the propriety of this illustration, though we can scarcely fail to admire the skill with which it is introduced. Even without questioning the motives of Brutus and his confederates, the act was that of murder, and surely cannot be placed at the head of the instances of elevated virtue which the previous lines had prepared us to expect. The "crowd of patriots," moreover, if tried by any pure standard of principles, were but indifferent specimens of moral beauty. See some remarks on this subject in the notes appended by Mr. Long to his translation of Plutarch's life of Brutus.

(2) *His arm aloft, &c.*—This fact is related by Cicero himself in his second Philippic.

And bade the father of his country hail!
For, lo! the tyrant prostrate in the dust,
And Rome again is free! Is aught so fair,
In all the dewy landscapes of the spring,
In the bright eye of Hesper or the Morn,
In Nature's fairest forms, is aught so fair
As virtuous friendship? as the candid blush
Of him who strives[1] with fortune to be just?
The graceful tear that streams for others' woes?
Or the mild majesty of private life,
Where peace with ever-blooming olive crowns
The gate; where honour's liberal hands effuse
Unenvied treasures, and the snowy wings
Of innocence and love protect the scene?

ADVANTAGES OF A CULTIVATED TASTE.

Oh! blest of heaven, whom not the languid songs
Of Luxury, the syren! not the bribes
Of sordid Wealth, nor all the gaudy spoils
Of pageant Honour, can seduce to leave
Those ever-blooming sweets, which, from the store
Of nature, fair Imagination culls,
To charm the enlivened soul! What though not all
Of mortal offspring can attain the heights
Of envied life; though only few possess
Patrician treasures, or imperial state;
Yet nature's care, to all her children just,
With richer treasures, and an ampler state,
Endows at large whatever happy man
Will deign to use them. His the city's pomp,
The rural honours his: whate'er adorns
The princely dome, the column, and the arch,
The breathing marble, and the sculptured gold,
Beyond the proud possessor's narrow claim,
His tuneful breast enjoys. For him the Spring
Distils her dews, and from the silken gem
Its lucid leaves unfolds; for him the hand
Of Autumn tinges every fertile branch
With blooming gold, and blushes like the morn.

---

(1) *Of him who strives, &c.*—*i. e.* of him who struggles with adverse fortune, that he may still preserve an upright course.

Each passing hour sheds tribute from her wings:
And still new beauties meet his lonely walk,
And loves unfelt attract him. Not a breeze
Flies o'er the meadow, not a cloud imbibes
The setting sun's effulgence, not a strain
From all the tenants of the warbling shade
Ascends, but whence his bosom can partake
Fresh pleasure, unreproved: nor thence partakes
Fresh pleasure only, for the attentive mind,
By this harmonious action on her powers,
Becomes herself harmonious; wont so oft
In outward things to meditate the charm
Of sacred order, soon she seeks at home
To find a kindred order, to exert
Within herself this elegance of love,
This fair inspired delight: her tempered powers
Refine at length, and every passion wears
A chaster, milder, more attractive mien.
But if to ampler prospects, if to gaze
On Nature's form, where, negligent of all
These lesser graces, she assumes the port
Of that Eternal Majesty that weighed
The world's foundations, if to these the mind
Exalts her daring eye, then mightier far
Will be the change, and nobler. Would the forms
Of servile custom cramp her generous powers?
Would sordid policies, the barbarous growth
Of ignorance and rapine, bow her down
To tame pursuits, to indolence and fear?
Lo! she appeals to Nature, to the winds
And rolling waves, the sun's unwearied course,
The elements and seasons; all declare
For what the eternal Maker has ordained
The powers of man: we feel within ourselves
His energy divine; he tells the heart,
He meant, he made us to behold and love
What he beholds and loves, the general orb
Of life and being: to be great like him,
Beneficent and active. Thus the men
Whom nature's works can charm, with God himself
Hold converse; grow familiar, day by day,
With his conceptions; act upon his plan;
And form to his the relish of their souls.

GRAY.

Principal Events of his Life.—Thomas Gray was born in London, on the 20th of December, 1716. His father, like Milton's, was a money-scrivener, but, unlike Milton's, cared little for his son's education, which was carried on at Eton School, at the expense of his mother. On leaving Eton he entered at Peter House, Cambridge, where he resided three years. In the spring of 1739, he set out on a tour through France and Italy, in company with Horace Walpole. He has described the scenery and the incidents of his journey, in his elegant letters. After an absence of two years and a half, he returned to England in 1741, and again took up his abode at Cambridge, with a view to devote himself to the study of the law. This purpose, however, was not maintained, but he continued to reside the greater part of his remaining life at the University. In 1768, he was appointed Professor of Modern History, and on the 24th of July, 1771, he died of an attack of gout in the stomach. He was buried at Stoke Pogeis, in Buckinghamshire, by the side of his mother, whom he ever tenderly loved.

Principal Works.—Gray's works are few; consisting almost wholly of lyrical odes. The most admired are those, "On the Spring," "On a distant Prospect of Eton College," "To Adversity," "The Progress of Poetry," and "The Bard;" to which must be added the far-famed "Elegy written in a Country Churchyard." His letters too, from their elegance and classic style, take a high place in English literature.

Characteristic Spirit and Style.—"Antecedent to 'The Progress of Poetry' and to 'The Bard' no such lyrics had appeared. There is not an ode in the English language which is constructed, like these two compositions, with such power, such majesty, and such sweetness, with such proportioned pauses, and just cadences, with such regulated measures of the verse, with such master principles of lyrical art displayed and exemplified; and, at the same time, with such a concealment of the difficulty, which is lost in the uninterrupted flowing of the lines in each stanza, with such a musical magic, that every verse in it in succession dwells in the ear, and harmonizes with that which has gone before. If, indeed, the veil of classical reverence and of pardonable prejudice can be awhile removed, and if with honest unshrinking criticism we consider the subject as exemplified in Greece, and in Italy ancient and modern, and if we then weigh the merits of any single composition of Pindar, of Horace, of Dante, of Petrarch, or of any of their successors, it will fade before that excellence which encompasses, with an incommunicable brightness, 'The Bard' of Gray.

"It was from his ear, so exquisitely fine, and so musically formed; it was from the contemplation of the legitimate structure of a lyrical stanza, of the necessity of its regularity, and of the labour, and of the polish, which was required not only to perfect every verse, but every single expression to every verse; it was indeed from all these views combined, that Mr. Gray revolted from the vapid, vague, and unmeaning effusions of writers, who, refusing to submit to the indispensable laws of lyrical poetry, or from ignorance of them, called their own wildness, genius, and their contempt of rules, originality. He fixed his attention on all the most finished models of Greece, and of modern Italy, he seized and apportioned their specific and their diversified merits, united their spirit, improved upon their metre, and then, in conformity with his great preconceived idea, he gave at once a lyric poetry to every succeeding age, the law, the precept, and the example."[1]

"His moral spirit is as explicit as it is majestic; and deeply read as he was in Plato, he is never metaphysically perplexed. The fault of his meaning is to be latent, not indefinite or confused. When we give his beauties reperusal and attention they kindle and multiply to the view. The thread of association that conducts to his remote allusions, or that connects his abrupt transitions, ceases then to be invisible. His lyrical pieces are like paintings on glass, which must be placed in a strong light to give out the perfect radiance of their colouring."[2]

VERSIFICATION.—"Among the distinguishing excellences of the poetry of Gray, must be mentioned the peculiar harmony and variety of his versification. The attention of Gray, it must be observed, was not paid to that inferior part of the art of imitation in verse, the resemblance of sounds and motions, as those properties of things which can be imitated by words, and which is called representative versification; but to that more extended imitation produced by the interchange and position of different

---

(1) Mathias. "Observations on the Writings and on the Character of Mr. Gray," p. 71, &c.

(2) Campbell. "Specimens," &c., p. 505.

measures in his poetry; by the harmony and correspondence of the different parts; by the variety of melody in arrangement and succession; and by the movements of the metre, rather than the sound of the words."[1]

HYMN TO ADVERSITY.[2]

Daughter of Jove,[3] relentless power,
  Thou tamer of the human breast,
Whose iron scourge[4] and torturing hour,
  The bad affright, afflict the best!
Bound in thy adamantine chain,
The proud are taught to taste of pain,
And purple tyrants[5] vainly groan
With pangs unfelt before, unpitied, and alone.

When first thy sire to send on earth
  Virtue, his darling child, designed,
To thee he gave the heavenly birth,[6]
  And bade thee form her infant mind.
Stern, rugged nurse! thy rigid lore
With patience many a year she bore;
What sorrow was, thou bad'st her know,
And from her own, she learned to melt at others' woe.

---

(1) Mitford. "Essay on the Poetry of Gray," in his edition of Gray's Works, vol. ii. p. 15.

(2) The "sweet uses" of adversity (to employ Shakspere's phraseology) are displayed with admirable dignity, strength, and beauty, in the above poem.

(3) *Daughter of Jove*—This poetic parentage is originally due to Homer, and finely suggests the fundamental idea of the whole poem.

(4) *Iron scourge, &c.*—The phraseology here is borrowed from Milton's "Paradise Lost," ii. 90:—

    "When the scourge
Inexorably, and the torturing hour,
Calls us to penance."

(5) *Purple tyrants*—i. e. tyrants clad in purple robes—the classical insignia of kingly power. The expression is a translation of "*purpurei tyranni*," used by Horace, book i. ode 35.

(6) *Heavenly birth*—i.e. the child born in heaven. The conception of Adversity as the nurse of Virtue is very fine.

Scared at thy frown terrific, fly
   Self-pleasing Folly's idle brood,
Wild Laughter, Noise, and thoughtless Joy,
   And leave us leisure to be good.
Light they disperse, and with them go
The **summer** friend, the flattering foe!
By **vain** Prosperity received,
To her they vow their truth, and **are again believed.**

Wisdom,[1] **in** sable garb arrayed,
   Immersed in rapturous thought profound,
And Melancholy, silent maid,
   With leaden eye, that loves the ground,
Still on thy solemn steps attend;
Warm Charity, the general friend,
With Justice, to herself **severe,**
And Pity, **dropping soft** the sadly-pleasing tear.

Oh! gently on thy suppliant's head,
   Dread goddess, lay thy chastening[2] **hand!**
Not in thy Gorgon terrors[3] clad,
   Nor circled with the vengeful band,[4]
(As by the impious **thou** art seen),
With thundering voice, and threatening mien,
With screaming Horror's funeral cry,
Despair, and fell Disease, and ghastly Poverty.

Thy form benign, oh Goddess, **wear,**
   Thy milder influence impart;
Thy philosophic train[5] be there,
   To soften, **not to wound my** heart.

(1) *Wisdom, &c.*—This costume is **derived from Milton,** who, in "Il Penseroso," (see p. 311), speaks **of** Melancholy's face **as** "O'erlaid with black, staid Wisdom's hue," and of the "**sad leaden** downward **cast**" of her eyes.

(2) *Chastening*—*Chasten* **and** *punish* may be thus distinguished; we *chasten* an offender for his own good; we *punish* him for the good of society, and **to** satisfy the claims of justice.

(3) ***Gorgon*** *terrors*—" What single epithet," says Mr. Mitford, " what attribute **could the poet** have given to terror, which could have produced an effect equal **to** that of this image?" and hence he infers that the occasional insertion of classical allusions confers grace and beauty on a poem.

(4) **The** *vengeful band*—*i. e.* the Furies, who were represented in the **Greek mythology** as the ministers of divine wrath against crime.

(5) ***Thy*** *philosophic* **train**—*i. e.* the train of virtues which the **philosophic or** contemplative **mind may derive from adversity.**

The generous spark extinct revive,
Teach me to love, and to forgive,
Exact my own defects to scan,
What others are[1] to feel, and know myself a man.

THE PROGRESS OF POETRY.[2]

A PINDARIC ODE.

I. 1.

Awake, Æolian[3] lyre, awake,
And give to rapture all thy trembling strings.
  From Helicon's[4] harmonious springs
A thousand rills their mazy progress take:
The laughing flowers that round them blow,
Drink life and fragrance as they flow.
Now the rich stream of Music winds along,
Deep, majestic, smooth, and strong,
Through verdant vales, and Ceres' golden reign:
Now rolling down the steep amain,
Headlong, impetuous, see it pour!
The rocks and nodding groves rebellow to the roar.

---

(1) *What others are, &c.*—Sometimes erroneously printed "what others' are," that is, others' defects. The meaning is—teach me to feel what others are, and by this sympathy with men to become fully conscious that I also belong to the family of man.

(2) Dr. Johnson, in reference to this and the following ode, says slightingly, that at their first publication, "many were contented to be shown beauties that they could not see." The general estimate of these poems is, however, now very high, in spite of the obscurity of some particular parts. The writer has, indeed, in both poems, employed nearly all the resources of the poetic art, and frequently, with distinguished success.

(3) *Æolian*—Grecian or more especially Pindaric, which style the poet is about to imitate. Pindar speaks of his own poetry as an *Æolian strain*.

(4) *From Helicon's, &c.*—Poetry is here represented as a stream, sometimes quietly fertilising its shores, at other times rolling impetuously onward, a grand and awful spectacle; implying that poetry deals equally with the beautiful and the sublime.

I. 2.

Oh! Sovereign[1] of the willing soul,
Parent of sweet and solemn-breathing airs,
Enchanting shell! the sullen Cares
And frantic Passions hear thy soft control.
On Thracia's hills the Lord of War
Has curbed the fury of his car,
And dropt his thirsty lance, at thy command.
Perching on the sceptred hand
Of Jove, thy magic lulls the feathered king
With ruffled plumes and flagging wing:
Quenched in dark clouds of slumber lie
The terror of his beak, and lightning of his eye.

I. 3.

Thee the voice,[2] the dance, obey,
Tempered to thy warbled lay.
O'er Idalia's velvet green[3]
The rosy-crowned Loves are seen,
On Cytherea's day,
With antic Sports, and blue-eyed Pleasures,
Frisking light in frolic measures;
Now pursuing, now retreating,
   Now in circling troops they meet;
To brisk notes in cadence beating,
   Glance their many-twinkling feet.
Slow melting strains their Queen's approach declare:
   Where'er she turns, the Graces homage pay:
With arms sublime, that float upon the air,
   In gliding state she wins her easy way:
O'er her warm cheek, and rising bosom, move
The bloom of young desire, and purple[4] light of Love.

---

(1) *Oh! sovereign, &c.*—"Power of harmony to calm the turbulent sallies of the soul. The thoughts are borrowed from the first Pythian of Pindar."—*Gray.*

(2) *Thee the voice, &c.*—"Power of harmony to produce all the graces of motion in the body."—*Gray.*

(3) *Velvet green*—Dr Johnson lays down, in reference to these words, the following canon:—"An epithet or metaphor drawn from Nature ennobles Art; an epithet or metaphor drawn from Art degrades Nature." If, however, this rule be allowed to be generally correct, the exceptions to it are very numerous. The truth is, perhaps, that it is the *manner* in which epithets are introduced from either source that ennobles or degrades the subject, rather than any intrinsic superiority of Nature over Art. (See also note 2, p. 96.)

(4) *Purple*—i. e. in the classical sense, beautiful. (See note 2, p. 71.)

II. 1.

Man's feeble race[1] what ills await!
Labour and Penury, the racks of Pain,
Disease, and Sorrow's weeping train,
   And Death, sad refuge from the storms of Fate!
The fond complaint, my song, disprove,
And justify the laws of Jove.
Say, has he given in vain the heavenly Muse?
Night and all her sickly dews,
Her spectres wan, and birds of boding cry,
He gives to range the dreary sky;
Till[2] down the eastern cliffs afar
Hyperion's[3] march they spy, and glittering shafts of war.

II. 2.

In climes beyond[4] the solar road,
Where shaggy forms o'er ice-built mountains roam,
The Muse has broke the twilight gloom
   To cheer the shivering native's dull abode.
And oft, beneath the odorous shade
Of Chili's boundless forests laid,
She deigns to hear the savage youth repeat,
In loose numbers, wildly sweet,
Their feather-cinctured chiefs, and dusky loves.
Her track, where'er the goddess roves,
Glory pursues, and generous Shame,
The unconquerable Mind, and Freedom's holy flame.

II. 3.

Woods that wave[5] o'er Delphi's steep,
Isles that crown the Ægean deep,
   Fields, that cool Ilissus laves,
   Or where Meander's amber waves

---

(1) *Man's feeble race, &c.*—"To compensate the real and imaginary ills of life, the Muse was given to mankind by the same providence that sends the day, by its cheerful presence to dispel the gloom and terrors of the night."—*Gray.*

(2) *Till*—i. e. only until the sun appears, and then they vanish; and so poetry scatters cares and anxieties.

(3) *Hyperion*—"the one that goes or moves above," an epithet of the sun. The proper quantity is "Hyperīon."

(4) *In climes beyond, &c.*—"Extensive influence of poetic genius over the remotest and most uncivilized nations: its connection with liberty, and the virtues that naturally attend on it."—*Gray.*

(5) *Woods that wave, &c.*—"Progress of Poetry from Greece to Italy, and from Italy to England."—*Gray.*

In lingering labyrinths creep,
   How do your tuneful echoes languish,
   Mute, but to the voice of anguish!
Where each old poetic mountain
   Inspiration breathed around;
Every shade and hallowed fountain
   Murmured deep a solemn sound;
Till the sad Nine, in Greece's evil hour,
   Left their Parnassus for the Latian plains.
Alike they scorn[1] the pomp of tyrant Power,
   And coward Vice, that revels in her chains.
When Latium had her lofty spirit lost,
They sought, O Albion! next, thy sea-encircled coast.

III. 1.

Far from the sun and summer gale,
In thy green lap was nature's darling laid,
What time, where lucid Avon strayed,
   To him the mighty Mother did unveil
Her awful face: the dauntless child
Stretched forth his little arms, and smiled.
"This pencil take," she said, "whose colours clear
Richly paint the vernal year:
Thine too these golden keys, immortal boy!
This can unlock the gates of Joy;
Of Horror that, and thrilling Fears,[2]
Or ope the sacred source of sympathetic tears."

III. 2.

   Nor second he,[3] that rode sublime
Upon the seraph-wings of Ecstasy,

---

(1) *Alike they scorn, &c.*—Dr. Johnson says of this couplet, "His (Gray's) position is at least false: in the time of Dante and Petrarch, from whom we derive our first school of poetry, Italy was overrun by a tyrant power and 'coward vice,' nor was our state much better when we first borrowed the Italian arts." It is, however, probable that the author meant to attribute the "tyrant power" to the state of Greece, and the "coward vice" to that of Italy, and to assign them as the reasons for the Muses' abandonment of both.

(2) *Thrilling fears*—Compare the reference to Shakspere at the close of Collins' "Ode to Fear." (See p. 399.)

(3) *Nor second he, &c.*—This sublime eulogy on Milton must be pronounced in every respect worthy of its subject. The reference to the "living throne and sapphire blaze" is from Ezekiel i. 20, 26, 28. "This account," says Dr. Johnson, "of Milton's blindness, if we suppose it caused by study in the formation of his poem—a supposition surely allowable—is poetically true, and happily imagined."

The secrets of the abyss to spy.
 He passed the flaming bounds of place and time:
The living throne, the sapphire blaze,
Where angels tremble while they gaze,
He saw; but, blasted with excess of light,
Closed his eyes in endless night.
Behold, where Dryden's less presumptuous car,
Wide o'er the fields of glory bear
Two coursers[1] of ethereal race,
With necks in thunder clothed, and long-resounding pace.

III. 3.

Hark! his hands[2] the lyre explore!
Bright-eyed Fancy, hovering o'er,
Scatters from her pictured urn
Thoughts that[3] breathe, and words that burn:
But ah! 'tis heard no more—
 Oh! lyre divine, what daring spirit
Wakes thee now? Though he inherit
Nor the pride, nor ample pinion,
 That the Theban eagle[4] bare,
Sailing with supreme dominion,
 Through the azure deep of air:
Yet oft before[5] his infant eyes would run
 Such forms as glitter in the Muses' ray,
With orient hues, unborrowed of the sun:
 Yet shall he mount, and keep his distant way,
Beyond the limits of a vulgar fate,
Beneath the good how far!—but far above the great.

---

(1) *Two coursers, &c.*—This verse and the following, Gray himself informs us, "are meant to express the stately march and sounding energy of Dryden's rhymes." Dr. Johnson, however, remarks upon the passage—"The car of Dryden, with his 'two coursers,' has nothing in it peculiar; it is a car in which any other rider may be placed."

(2) *Hark! his hands, &c.*—In reference to Dryden, as the author of the Ode on St. Cecilia's Day.

(3) *Thoughts that, &c.*—i.e. thoughts that have a definite form and being, and words that kindle the feelings.

(4) *Theban eagle*—"Pindar compares himself to that bird, and his enemies to ravens, that croak and clamour in vain below, while it pursues its flight, regardless of their noise."—*Gray.*

(5) *Yet oft before, &c.*—Dugald Stewart has remarked, in his "Elements of the Philosophy of the Human Mind," p. 486, "that Gray, in describing the infantine reveries of poetical genius, has fixed with exquisite judgment on that class of our conceptions which are derived from *visible* objects."

THE BARD.

A PINDARIC ODE.[1]

I. 1.

"Ruin seize thee, ruthless King!
Confusion on thy banners wait!
Though fanned by Conquest's crimson wing,
They mock the air with idle state.
Helm nor hauberk's twisted mail,
Nor e'en thy virtues, tyrant, shall avail
To save thy secret soul from nightly fears,
From Cambria's curse, from Cambria's tears!"
Such were the sounds that o'er the crested pride
Of the first Edward scattered wild dismay,
As down the steep of Snowdon's shaggy side
He wound with toilsome march his long array.
Stout Gloster[2] stood aghast in speechless trance:
"To arms!" cried Mortimer,[3] and couched his quivering lance.

I. 2.

On a rock, whose haughty brow
Frowns o'er old Conway's foaming flood,
Robed in the sable garb of woe,
With haggard eyes the poet stood;
(Loose his beard and hoary hair
Streamed, like a meteor, to the troubled air),
And with a master's hand, and prophet's fire,
Struck the deep sorrows of his lyre:—
"Hark, how each giant-oak and desert cave,
Sighs to the torrent's awful voice beneath!
O'er thee, O king!"[4] their hundred arms they wave,
Revenge on thee in hoarser murmurs breathe;

---

(1) "This ode is founded on a tradition current in Wales, that Edward I., when he completed the conquest of that country, ordered all the bards that fell into his hands to be put to death."—*Gray.*

(2) *Gloster*—"Gilbert de Clare, surnamed the Red, Earl of Gloucester and Hertford, son-in-law to King Edward."—*Gray.*

(3) *Mortimer*—"Edmond de Mortimer, Lord of Wigmore."—*Gray.*

(4) *O'er thee, O king, &c.*—In this couplet the "hundred arms" must be referred to the "giant-oaks," and the "hoarser murmurs" to the "desert," or hollow caves above named.

Vocal no more, since Cambria's fatal day,
To high-born Hoel's[1] harp, or soft Llewellyn's lay.

I. 3.

"Cold is Cadwallo's tongue,
That hushed the stormy main:
Brave Urien sleeps upon his craggy bed:
Mountains, ye mourn in vain
Modred, whose magic song
Made huge Plinlimmon bow his cloud-topped head.
On dreary Arvon's[2] shore they lie,
Smeared with gore, and ghastly pale;
Far, far aloof[3] the affrighted ravens sail;
The famished eagle screams, and passes by.
Dear lost companions of my tuneful art,
Dear as the light that visits these sad eyes,
Dear as the ruddy drops[4] that warm my heart,
Ye died amidst your dying country's cries.—
No more I weep. They do not sleep.
On yonder cliffs, a grisly band,
I see them sit; they linger yet,
Avengers of their native land:
With me in dreadful harmony they join,
And weave with bloody hands the tissue of thy line.[5]

---

(1) *High-born Hoel, &c.*—Hoel, one of the famous bards of Wales, was the son of Owen Gwynedd, prince of North Wales, and Llewellyn was a prince of whom we are told that, though he "burnt like an outrageous fire" in battle, yet the songs that he composed and sang were mild and soft.

(2) *Arvon's shore*—"The shores of Carnarvonshire, opposite to the Isle of Anglesey."—*Gray.*

(3) *Far, far aloof, &c.*—These birds of prey do not venture to touch, or even approach anything so sacred as the corpses of the bards, though the eagle screams with hunger.

(4) *Dear as the ruddy drops, &c.*—Gray himself quotes the following lines from Shakspere, as the original of this expression:—

"As dear to me as are the ruddy drops
That visit my sad heart."—*Julius Cæsar*, Act ii. scene 2.

(5) *Tissue of thy line*—*i. e.* the web of fate, in which are pictured, as it were, the fortunes of thy descendants. This notion of weaving a web of destiny is directly borrowed from the Scandinavian mythology, though the thread which is spun by the Fates in the Greek mythology is closely connected with it. Dr. Johnson objects to the poet's "making weavers of slaughtered bards," inasmuch as in the original fable the operators are females.

II. 1.

"Weave the warp,[1] and weave the woof,
The winding-sheet of Edward's race.
Give ample room, and verge enough
The characters of hell to trace.
Mark the year,[2] and mark the night,
When Severn shall re-echo with affright
The shrieks of death, through Berkley's roofs that ring,
Shrieks of an agonizing king!
She-wolf of France,[3] with unrelenting fangs,
That tearest the bowels of thy mangled mate,
From thee be born,[4] who o'er thy country hangs,
The scourge of Heaven. What terrors round him wait!
Amazement[5] in his van with Flight combined,
And Sorrow's faded form, and Solitude behind.

II. 2.

"Mighty victor, mighty lord,
Low on his funeral[6] couch he lies!
No pitying heart, no eye, afford
A tear to grace his obsequies.
Is the sable warrior[7] fled?
Thy son is gone: he rests among the dead.
The swarm that in thy noon-tide beam were born?
Gone to salute the rising morn.[8]

---

(1) *Weave the warp*—Dr. Johnson also censures this expression as incorrect, "for," says he, "it is by crossing the woof with the warp that men weave the web or piece," but the learned doctor is himself wrong. The warp consists of the longitudinal, the woof of the latitudinal threads.

(2) *Mark the year, &c.*—The prophecy of the bard now begins by a reference to the cruel death of Edward II., in Berkley Castle.

(3) *She-wolf of France*—"Isabel of France, Edward II.'s adulterous queen."—*Gray.*

(4) *From thee be born, &c.*—In allusion to her son, Edward III., who proved a scourge to her native country.

(5) *Amazement, &c.*—In allusion to the victories which signalized the early part of his reign; the miseries of its close are indicated in the next line.

(6) *Low on his funeral couch, &c.*—"Death of that king, abandoned by his children, and even robbed in his last moments by his courtiers and his mistress."—*Gray.*

(7) *Sable warrior*—"Edward the Black Prince died some time before his father."—*Gray.*

(8) *Rising morn*—i. e. the early part of Richard II.'s reign.

Fair laughs[1] the morn, and soft the zephyr blows,
While, proudly riding o'er the azure realm,
In gallant trim the gilded vessel goes;
Youth on the prow, and Pleasure at the helm;
Regardless of the sweeping whirlwind's sway,
That, hushed in grim repose, expects his evening prey.

II. 3.

"Fill high[2] the sparkling bowl,
The rich repast prepare;
Reft of a crown he yet may share the feast;
Close by the regal chair
Fell Thirst and Famine scowl
A baleful smile upon their baffled guest.
Heard ye[3] the din of battle bray,
Lance to lance, and horse to horse?
Long years of havoc urge their destined course,
And through the kindred[4] squadrons mow their way.
Ye towers of Julius,[5] London's lasting shame,
With many a foul and midnight murder fed,
Revere[6] his consort's faith, his father's fame,
And spare the meek usurper's holy head.
Above, below, the rose of snow,
Twined with her blushing foe, we spread;
The bristled boar[7] in infant gore
Wallows beneath the thorny shade.
Now, brothers, bending o'er the accursed loom,
Stamp[8] we our vengeance deep, and ratify his doom.

(1) *Fair laughs, &c.*—This and the following lines embody one of the most perfect metaphors that was ever developed by poetic art. The diction and the measure—the tone and spirit of the whole—are most happily picturesque and beautiful.

(2) *Fill high, &c.*—In allusion to the profuse magnificence of Richard II.'s style of living, succeeded by his death from starvation in Pontefract Castle, Yorkshire.

(3) *Heard ye the din, &c.*—"Ruinous wars of York and Lancaster."—*Gray.*

(4) *Kindred*—because it was a civil war.

(5) *Ye towers of Julius, &c.*—"Henry VI., George Duke of Clarence, Edward V., Richard Duke of York, &c., believed to be murdered secretly in the Tower of London. The oldest part of that structure is vulgarly attributed to Julius Cæsar."—*Gray.*

(6) *Revere, &c.*—In allusion to Henry VI., his wife, Margaret of Anjou, and his father, Henry V.

(7) *The bristled boar, &c.*—"The silver boar was the badge of Richard III.; whence he was usually known in his own time by the name of 'The Boar.'"—*Gray.*

(8) *Stamp*—i. e. stamp or impress on the web.

III. 1.

"Edward, lo! to sudden fate
(Weave we the woof; the thread is spun)
Half of thy heart[1] we consecrate.
(The web is wove; the work is done.)—
Stay, oh stay! nor thus forlorn,
Leave me unblest, unpitied, here to mourn:
In yon bright track, that fires the western skies,
They melt, they vanish from my eyes.
But oh! what solemn scenes on Snowdon's height
Descending slow their glittering skirts unroll!
Visions of glory, spare my aching sight!
Ye unborn ages, crowd not on my soul!
No more[2] our long-lost Arthur we bewail:
All hail,[3] ye genuine kings, Britannia's issue, hail!

III. 2.

"Girt with many a baron bold,
Sublime their starry fronts they rear;
And gorgeous dames, and statesmen old
In bearded majesty appear.
In the midst a form divine!
Her eye proclaims her of the Briton-line;
Her lion-port, her awe-commanding face,
Attempered sweet to virgin grace.
What strings symphonious tremble in the air!
What strains of vocal transport round her play!
Hear from the grave, great Taliessin,[4] hear;
They breathe a soul to animate thy clay.
Bright rapture calls, and, soaring as she sings,
Waves in the eye of heaven her many-coloured wings.

(1) *Half of thy heart*—In allusion to his affectionate and high-minded wife, "Eleanor of Castile, who died a few years after the conquest of Wales."—*Gray.*

(2) *No more, &c.*—"It was the common belief of the Welsh nation that King Arthur was still alive in fairy-land, and would return again to rule over Britain."—*Gray.*

(3) *All hail, &c.*—"Both Merlin and Taliessin had prophesied that the Welsh should regain their sovereignty over this island; which seemed to be accomplished in the House of Tudor."—*Gray.*

(4) *Taliessin*—"Taliessin, chief of the bards, flourished in the sixth century. His works are still preserved, and his memory held in high veneration among his countrymen."—*Gray.*

III. 3.

"The verse adorn[1] again,
Fierce War, and faithful Love,
And Truth severe[2] by fairy Fiction dressed.
In buskined measures[3] move
Pale Grief, and pleasing Pain,
With Horror, tyrant of the throbbing breast.
A voice,[4] as of the cherub-choir,
Gales from blooming Eden bear;
And distant warblings[5] lessen on my ear,
That lost in long futurity expire.
Fond, impious man! think'st thou yon sanguine cloud,
Raised by the breath, has quenched the orb of day?
To-morrow he repairs the golden flood,
And warms the nations with redoubled ray.—
Enough for me: with joy I see
The different doom our fates assign.
Be thine despair, and sceptred care;
To triumph and to die are mine."
He spoke; and, headlong from the mountain's height,
Deep in the roaring tide he plunged to endless night.

GOLDSMITH.

PRINCIPAL EVENTS OF HIS LIFE.—Oliver Goldsmith was born in the year 1728, at Pallas, in the parish of Ferney, Longford, Ireland, or, as other authorities state, at Elphin, Roscommon. There was little promise, in his early years, of his subsequent literary, or any other eminence, nor did his studies at Trinity College, Dublin, distinguish him. On leaving college, he became

---

(1) *The verse adorn, &c.*—In allusion to Spenser, as appears plainly from the following line, from the beginning of the "Faerie Queene":—

"Fierce wars and faithful loves shall moralize my song."

(2) *Truth severe, &c.*—In allusion to the allegorical style and character of the "Faerie Queene," in which, to use Milton's words "more is meant than meets the ear."

(3) *In buskined measures, &c.*—Shakspere.

(4) *A voice, &c.*—Milton.

(5) *Distant warblings, &c.*—"The succession of poets after Milton's time."—*Gray.*

notorious only for idleness, **dissipation**, and imprudence, and **these** causes combined did much to frustrate the kind efforts that were made by his friends to settle him in the profession **of medicine.** He studied a short time at Leyden, and (probably) took a degree in medicine at Padua. Before returning to England, he travelled over a considerable part of the west of Europe on foot, subsisting, it is thought, on the casual contributions of strangers, in return for the exhibition of his skill in playing on the flute. When **at** length he arrived in London, "he found himself" (to use his own words), "without friends, recommendations, money, or impudence." He then tried various means of maintaining himself, but with little success, till at last, becoming acquainted with Dr. Johnson, that eminent man introduced him into the world of letters, and from this time the publication of his several works chronicles the principal events of his life. He died in the year 1774, and **was** buried in the Temple burying-ground, **London.**

PRINCIPAL **WORKS.**—"The **Vicar of Wakefield,"** t**he** poems entitled **"The Traveller,"** and **"The Deserted** Village," and the comedy **"She Stoops to Conquer,"** are considered Goldsmith's most important and original works.

CHARACTERISTIC SPIRIT AND **STYLE.**—"Goldsmith's poetry enjoys a calm **and steady** popularity. It inspires us, indeed, with no admiration **of daring** design, or of fertile invention; but **it** presents, within its narrow limits, a distinct and unbroken view **of** poetical delightfulness. His descriptions and sentiments have **the pure zest** of **nature. He is** refined without **false** delicacy, **and correct without insipidity.** Perhaps there is an intellectual com**posure in his manner which may,** in some passages, be **said to** approach **to the reserved and prosaic; but he unbends** from **this** graver strain **of reflection to tenderness, and even to** playfulness, with an ease and grace **almost exclusively his** own, and connects extensive views of **the** happiness and interests of society, with pictures of life that touch the heart by **their** familiarity. His language is certainly simple, **though** it **is not cast** in a rugged or careless mould. He is **no disciple of the** gaunt and famished **school** of simplicity. **Deliberately as he** wrote, he cannot be **accused** of wanting natural and **idiomatic** expression; but still it **is select** and refined expression. His whole manner has a still **depth of feeling and** reflection, **which** gives back the image of **nature unruffled and** minutely. He has no redundant thoughts or **false transports; but** seems, on every occasion, to have weighed **the impulse to which he** surrendered himself."[1]

(1) Campbell. "Specimens," &c., p. 525.

THE TRAVELLER;[1]

OR, A PROSPECT OF SOCIETY.

Remote, unfriended, melancholy, slow,[2]
Or by the lazy Scheldt, or wandering Po;
Or onward, where the rude Carinthian boor
Against the houseless stranger shuts the door;
Or where Campania's plain forsaken lies,
A weary waste expanding to the skies;
Where'er I roam, whatever realms to see,
My heart untravelled fondly turns to thee:
Still to my brother turns, with ceaseless pain,
And drags[3] at each remove a lengthening chain.

   Eternal blessings crown my earliest friend,
And round his dwelling guardian saints attend;
Blest be that spot, where cheerful guests retire
To pause from toil, and trim their evening fire;
Blest that abode, where want and pain repair,
And every stranger finds a ready chair;
Blest be those feasts with simple plenty crowned,
Where all the ruddy family around
Laugh at the jests or pranks that never fail,
Or sigh with pity at some mournful tale;
Or press the bashful stranger to his food,
And learn the luxury of doing good.

---

(1) This beautiful poem was partly written in Switzerland, and dedicated by the author to his brother, the Rev. Henry Goldsmith. In the dedication the writer thus describes the purpose of the poem:—"Without espousing," says he, "the cause of any party, I have attempted to moderate the rage of all; I have endeavoured to show that there may be equal happiness in states that are differently governed from our own; that every state has a particular principle of happiness, and this principle in each may be carried to a mischievous excess."

(2) *Slow*—With regard to this word, an amusing anecdote is found in Boswell's "Life of Johnson:"—"Chamier once asked him (Goldsmith) what he meant by *slow* (in the above passage)—'Did he mean tardiness of locomotion?' Goldsmith, who would say something, without consideration answered, 'Yes.' I (Johnson) was sitting by, and said, 'No, sir, you do not mean tardiness of locomotion; you mean that sluggishness of mind which comes upon a man in solitude.' Chamier believed then that I had written the line as much as if he had seen me write it."

(3) *And drags, &c.*—Goldsmith has the same idea in prose:—"Those ties that bind me to my native country and you are still unbroken; by every remove I only drag a greater length of chain."—*Citizen of the World*, vol. i. letter 3.

But me, not destined such delights to share,
My prime of life in wandering spent and care:
Impelled, with steps unceasing, to pursue
Some fleeting good, that mocks me with the view;
That, like the circle bounding earth and skies,
Allures from far, yet, as I follow, flies;
My fortune leads to traverse realms alone,
And find no spot of all the world my own.

E'en now, where Alpine solitudes ascend,
I sit me down a pensive hour to spend;
And, placed on high above the storm's career,
Look downward where a hundred realms appear;
Lakes, forests, cities, plains extending wide,
The pomp of kings, the shepherd's humbler pride.
 When thus creation's charms around combine,
Amidst the store, should thankless pride repine?
Say, should the philosophic mind disdain
That good which makes each humbler bosom vain?
Let school-taught pride dissemble all it can,
These little things are great to little man;
And wiser he, whose sympathetic mind
Exults in all the good of all mankind.
Ye glittering towns,[1] with wealth and splendour crowned;
Ye fields, where summer spreads profusion round;
Ye lakes, whose vessels catch the busy gale;
Ye bending swains, that dress the flowery vale;
For me your tributary stores combine:
Creation's heir, the world, the world is mine.

As some lone miser, visiting his store,
Bends at his treasure, counts, recounts it o'er;
Hoards after hoards his rising raptures fill,
Yet still he sighs, for hoards are wanting still;
Thus to my breast alternate passions rise,
Pleased with each good that Heaven to man supplies:
Yet oft a sigh prevails, and sorrows fall,
To see the hoard of human bliss so small;
And oft I wish, amidst the scene, to find
Some spot to real happiness consigned,
Where my worn soul, each wandering hope at rest,
May gather bliss to see my fellows blest.

(1) *Ye glittering towns, &c.*—This and the following lines are a beautiful specimen of what Campbell calls the "quiet enthusiasm" of our author.

But where to find that happiest spot below,
Who can direct, when all pretend to know?
The shuddering tenant of the frigid zone
Boldly proclaims that happiest spot his own;
Extols the treasures of his stormy seas,
And his long nights of revelry and ease:
The naked negro, panting at the line,
Boasts of his golden sands and palmy wine,
Basks in the glare, or stems the tepid wave,
And thanks his gods for all the good they gave.
Such is the patriot's boast, where'er he roam,
His first, best country, ever is, at home.
And yet, perhaps, if countries we compare,
And estimate the blessings which they share,
Though patriots flatter, still shall wisdom find
An equal portion dealt to all mankind;
As different good, by art or nature given,
To different nations makes their blessings even.

Nature, a mother kind alike to all,
Still grants her bliss at labour's earnest call;
With food as well the peasant is supplied
On Idra's cliffs as Arno's shelvy side;
And though the rocky crested summits frown,
These rocks, by custom, turn to beds of down.
From art more various are the blessings sent;
Wealth, commerce, honour, liberty, content.
Yet these each other's power so strong contest,
That either[1] seems destructive of the rest.

Where wealth and freedom reign, contentment fails;
And honour sinks[2] where commerce long prevails.
Hence every state, to one loved blessing prone,
Conforms and models life to that alone.
Each to the favourite happiness attends,
And spurns the plan that aims at other ends;
Till carried to excess in each domain,
This favourite good begets peculiar pain.

(1) *Either*—used here for "each."

(2) *Honour sinks, &c.*—If "commerce" be taken in its proper sense, it is not easy to see the truth of this position. There is surely nothing intrinsically dishonourable—but the contrary—in the pursuits of commerce; and if the wealth which commerce brings be sometimes unworthily employed, let the individual instances bear the blame they deserve.

But let us try these truths with closer eyes,
And trace them through the prospect as it lies:
Here for a while, my proper cares resigned,
Here let me sit in sorrow for mankind;
Like yon neglected shrub at random cast,
That shades the steep, and sighs at every blast.

Far to the right, where Apennine ascends,
Bright as the summer, Italy extends;
Its uplands sloping deck the mountain's side,
Woods over woods in gay theatric pride;[1]
While oft some temple's mouldering tops between
With venerable grandeur mark the scene.

Could Nature's bounty satisfy the breast,
The sons of Italy were surely blest.
Whatever fruits in different climes were found,
That proudly rise, or humbly court the ground;
Whatever blooms in torrid tracts appear,
Whose bright succession decks the varied year;
Whatever sweets salute the northern sky,
With vernal lives, that blossom but to die;
These here disporting own the kindred soil,
Nor ask luxuriance from the planter's toil;
While sea-born gales their gelid wings expand
To winnow fragrance round the smiling land.

But small the bliss that sense alone bestows,
And sensual bliss is all this nation knows.
In florid beauty groves and fields appear,
Man seems the only growth that dwindles here.
Contrasted faults through all his manners reign;
Though poor, luxurious; though submissive, vain;
Though grave, yet trifling; zealous, yet untrue;
And even in penance planning sins anew.
All evils here contaminate the mind,
That opulence departed leaves behind;
For wealth was theirs, not far removed the date,
When commerce proudly flourished through the state;[2]
At her command the palace learnt to rise,
Again the long-fallen column sought the skies;

---

(1) *Theatric pride*—i.e. like the benches of an ancient amphitheatre. Compare a passage in Milton (see p. 332).

(2) *State*—properly states—since at the period here designated the Italian commercial republics were sovereign and independent.

The canvas glowed beyond e'en nature warm,
The pregnant quarry teemed with human form.
Till, more unsteady than the southern gale,
Commerce on other shores displayed her sail;
While nought remained of all that riches gave,
But towns unmanned, and lords without a slave;
And late the nation found, with fruitless skill,
Its former strength was but plethoric ill.[1]

Yet still the loss of wealth is here supplied
By arts, the splendid wrecks of former pride;
From these the feeble heart and long-fallen mind
An easy compensation seem to find.
Here may be seen, in bloodless pomp arrayed,
The pasteboard triumph, and the cavalcade;
Processions formed for piety and love,
A mistress or a saint in every grove.
By sports like these are all their cares beguiled,
The sports of children satisfy the child:
Each nobler aim, represt by long control,
Now sinks at last, or feebly mans the soul;
While low delights, succeeding fast behind,
In happier meanness occupy the mind:
As in those domes, where Cæsars once bore sway,
Defaced by time, and tottering in decay,
There in the ruin, heedless of the dead,
The shelter-seeking peasant builds his shed;
And, wondering man could want the larger pile,
Exults, and owns his cottage with a smile.

My soul, turn from them! turn we to survey
Where rougher climes a nobler race display,
Where the bleak Swiss their stormy mansion tread,
And force a churlish soil for scanty bread.
No product here the barren hills afford,
But man and steel, the soldier and his sword;
No vernal blooms their torpid rocks array,
But winter, lingering, chills the lap of May;
No zephyr fondly sues the mountain's breast,
But meteors glare, and stormy glooms invest.

---

(1) *Its former strength, &c.*—Goldsmith elsewhere says—"In short, the state resembled one of those bodies bloated with disease, whose bulk is only a symptom of its wretchedness: their former opulence only rendered them more impotent."— *Citizen of the World*, vol. i. p. 98.

Yet still, even here, content can spread a charm,
Redress the clime, and all its rage disarm.
Though poor the peasant's hut, his feasts though small,
He sees his little lot the lot of all;
Sees no contiguous palace rear its head,
To shame the meanness of his humble shed;
No costly lord the sumptuous banquet deal,
To make him loath his vegetable meal;
But calm, and bred in ignorance and toil,
Each wish contracting, fits him to the soil.
Cheerful at morn, he wakes from short repose,
Breathes the keen air, and carols as he goes;
With patient angle trolls the finny deep,
Or drives his venturous ploughshare to the steep;
Or seeks the den where snow-tracks mark the way,
And drags the struggling savage into day.
At night returning, every labour sped,
He sits him down, the monarch of a shed;
Smiles by his cheerful fire, and round surveys
His children's looks, that brighten at the blaze;
While his loved partner, boastful of her hoard,
Displays her cleanly platter on the board:
And haply too some pilgrim, thither led,
With many a tale repays the nightly bed.

Thus every good his native wilds impart
Imprints the patriot passion on his heart;
And even those ills, that round his mansion rise,
Enhance the bliss his scanty fund supplies.
Dear is that shed to which his soul conforms,
And dear that hill which lifts him to the storms;
And as a child, when scaring sounds molest,
Clings close and closer to the mother's breast,
So the loud torrent, and the whirlwind's roar,
But bind him to his native mountains more.

Such are the charms to barren states assigned;
Their wants but few, their wishes all confined;
Yet let them only share the praises due,
If few their wants, their pleasures are but few;
For every want[1] that stimulates the breast
Becomes a source of pleasure when redrest.

---

(1) *For every want, &c.*—*i. e.* as there is a pleasure in the stimulus necessary for supplying our wants, if the wants are few, the pleasures are few also.

Whence from such lands each pleasing science flies,
That first excites desire, and then supplies;
Unknown to them, when sensual pleasures cloy,
To fill the languid pause with finer joy;
Unknown those powers that raise the soul to flame,
Catch every nerve, and vibrate through the frame.
Their level life is but a smouldering fire,
Unquenched by want, unfanned by strong desire;
Unfit for raptures, or, if raptures cheer
On some high festival of once a year,
In wild excess the vulgar breast takes fire,
Till, buried in debauch, the bliss expire.

But not their joys alone thus coarsely flow:
Their morals, like their pleasures, are but low;
For, as refinement stops, from sire to son,
Unaltered, unimproved, the manners run;
And love's and friendship's finely pointed dart
Fall blunted from each indurated heart.
Some sterner virtues o'er the mountain's breast
May sit, like falcons cowering on the nest;
But all the gentler morals, such as play
Through life's more cultured walks, and charm the way,
These, far dispersed, on timorous pinions fly,
To sport and flutter in a kinder sky.

To kinder skies, where gentler manners range,
I turn—and France displays her bright domain.
Gay, sprightly land of mirth and social ease,
Pleased with thyself, whom all the world can please;
How often have I led thy sportive choir,
With tuneless pipe,[1] beside the murmuring Loire!
Where shading elms along the margin grew,
And, freshened from the wave, the zephyr flew;
And haply, though my harsh touch faltering still,
But mocked all tune, and marred the dancer's skill,
Yet would the village praise my wondrous power,
And dance, forgetful of the noontide hour!
Alike all ages. Dames of ancient days
Have led their children through the mirthful maze,
And the gay grandsire, skilled in gestic lore,[2]
Has frisked beneath the burden of threescore.

---

(1) *Tuneless pipe, &c.*—See p. 435.
(2) *Gestic lore*—the art of movement or dancing.

So blest a life these thoughtless realms display,
Thus idly busy rolls their world away:
Theirs are those arts that mind to mind endear,
For honour forms the social temper here.
Honour, that praise which real merit gains,
Or even imaginary worth obtains,
Here passes current; paid from hand to hand,
It shifts in splendid traffic round the land:
From courts to camps, to cottages it strays,
And all are taught an avarice of praise;
They please,[1] are pleased, they give to get esteem,
Till, seeming blest, they grow to what they seem.
  But while this softer heart their bliss supplies,
It gives their follies also room to rise;
For praise too dearly loved, or warmly sought,
Enfeebles all eternal strength of thought.
And the weak soul, within itself unblest,
Leans for all pleasure on another's breast.
Hence ostentation here, with tawdry art,
Pants for the vulgar praise which fools impart;
Here vanity assumes her pert grimace,
And trims her robes of frieze with copper lace;
Here beggar pride defrauds her daily cheer,
To boast one splendid banquet once a year;
The mind still turns where shifting fashion draws,
Nor weighs the solid worth of self-applause.

  To men of other minds my fancy flies,
Embosomed in the deep where Holland lies.
Methinks her patient sons before me stand,
Where the broad ocean leans against the land,
And sedulous to stop the coming tide,
Lift the tall rampire's[2] artificial pride.
Onward, methinks, and diligently slow,
The firm connected bulwark seems to grow;
Spreads its long arms amidst the watery roar,
Scoops out an empire, and usurps the shore.

(1) *They please, &c.*—" There is perhaps no couplet in English rhyme more perspicuously condensed than those two lines of 'The Traveller,' in which he (Goldsmith) describes the [at] once flattering, vain, and happy character of the French—'They please,' &c."—*Campbell.*

(2) *Tall rampire's*—the famous dams built round the coast by the Dutch, to keep off the ocean.

While the pent ocean rising o'er the pile,
Sees an amphibious world beneath him smile;—
The slow canal, the yellow-blossomed vale,
The willow-tufted bank, the gliding sail,
The crowded mart, the cultivated plain,—
A new creation[1] rescued from his reign.
　　Thus, while around the wave-subjected soil
Impels the native to repeated toil,
Industrious habits in each bosom reign,
And industry begets a love of gain.
Hence all the good from opulence that springs,
With all those ills superfluous treasure brings,
Are here displayed. Their much-loved wealth imparts
Convenience, plenty, elegance, and arts;
But view them closer, craft and fraud appear,
Even liberty[2] itself is bartered here.
At gold's superior charms all freedom flies,
The needy sell it, and the rich man buys;
A land of tyrants, and a den of slaves,
Here wretches seek dishonourable graves,
And calmly bent, to servitude conform,
Dull as their lakes that slumber in the storm.
　　Heavens! how unlike their Belgic sires of old!
Rough, poor, content, ungovernably bold;
War in each breast, and freedom on each brow;
How much unlike the sons of Britain now!

　　Fired at the sound,[3] my genius spreads her wing,
And flies where Britain courts the western spring,
Where lawns extend that scorn Arcadian pride,
And brighter streams than famed Hydaspes glide;

---

(1) *A new creation*—"Holland seems to be a conquest upon the sea, and in a manner rescued from its bosom."—*Goldsmith's Animated Nature*, vol. i. p. 276.

(2) *Even liberty, &c.*—"Slavery was permitted in Holland; children were sold by their parents for a certain number of years."—*Mitford*.

(3) *Fired at the sound, &c.*—"We talked of Goldsmith's 'Traveller,' of which Dr. Johnson spoke highly; and while I was helping him on with his greatcoat, he repeatedly quoted from it the character of the British nation, which he did with such energy that the tears started in his eye."—*Boswell's Johnson*, p. 384, (Croker's edition, in one vol.)

There all around the gentlest breezes stray,
There gentle music melts on every spray;
Creation's mildest charms are there combined,
Extremes are only in the master's mind!
Stern o'er each bosom Reason holds her state,
With daring aims irregularly great;
Pride in their port, defiance in their eye,
I see the lords of humankind pass by;
Intent on high designs, a thoughtful band,
By forms unfashioned, fresh from Nature's hand;
Fierce in their native hardiness of soul,
True to imagined right, above control;
While even the peasant boasts these rights to scan,
And learns to venerate himself as man.

Thine, Freedom! thine the blessings pictured here;
Thine are those charms that dazzle and endear;
Too blest, indeed, were such without alloy;
But fostered even by freedom ills annoy:
That independence Britons prize too high,
Keeps man from man, and breaks the social tie;
The self-dependent lordlings stand alone,
All claims that bind and sweeten life unknown;
Here, by the bonds of nature feebly held,
Minds combat minds, repelling and repelled;
Ferments arise, imprisoned factions roar,
Repressed ambition struggles round her shore,
Till over-wrought, the general system feels
Its motion stop, or frenzy fire the wheels. * * *

Vain, very vain, my weary search to find
That bliss which only centres in the mind:
Why have I strayed, from pleasure and repose,
To seek a good each government bestows?
In every government, though terrors reign,
Though tyrant kings, or tyrant laws restrain,
How small,[1] of all that human hearts endure,
That part which laws or kings can cause or cure!
Still, to ourselves in every place consigned,
Our own felicity we make or find:
With secret course, which no loud storms annoy,
Glides the smooth current of domestic joy.

---

(1) *How small, &c.*—These concluding lines, with the exception of the last couplet but one, were written by Dr. Johnson.

The lifted axe, the agonizing wheel,
Luke's iron crown,[1] and Damiens' bed of steel,[2]
To men remote from power but rarely known,
Leave reason, faith, and conscience, all our own.

PICTURE OF A VILLAGE LIFE.[3]

Sweet Auburn![4] loveliest village of the plain,
Where health and plenty cheered the labouring swain;
Where smiling spring its earliest visit paid,
And parting summer's lingering blooms delayed;
Dear lovely bowers of innocence and ease,
Seats of my youth, when every sport could please;
How often have I loitered o'er thy green,
Where humble happiness endeared each scene!
How often have I paused on every charm,
The sheltered cot, the cultivated farm;
The never-failing brook, the busy mill,
The decent church that topped the neighbouring hill;
The hawthorn bush, with seats beneath the shade,
For talking age, and whispering lovers made!

---

(1) *Luke's iron crown*—"This appears to be a mistake. Luke and George Zeck, brothers, were both engaged in a desperate rebellion in Hungary, in 1514, and George suffered the torture of the red-hot crown of iron."—*Mitford*.

(2) *Damiens' bed of steel*—Damiens, a Frenchman, native of Artois, attempted to assassinate Louis XV., and was horribly put to death by being roasted alive in public, on a bed composed of red-hot bars of steel.

(3) The above extract contains the descriptive portions of the "Deserted Village," brought together into one view. The remainder of the poem is mainly political, and founded too on principles by no means universally allowed. The beauties of the "Deserted Village" need no recommendation, but the following sentence of Campbell's may be admitted:—"Fiction in poetry is not the reverse of truth, but her soft and enchanted resemblance; and this ideal beauty of nature has been seldom united with so much sober fidelity as in the groups and scenery of the 'Deserted Village.'"—*Specimens, &c.*, p. 526.

(4) *Auburn*—"Lissoy, near Ballymahon, where the poet's brother, the clergyman, had his living, claims the honour of being the spot from which the localities of the 'Deserted Village' are derived. The church which tops the neighbouring hill, the mill, and the brook, are still pointed out."—*Sir Walter Scott*.

How often have I blessed the coming day,
When toil remitting, lent its turn to play,
And all the village train, from labour free,
Led up their sports beneath the spreading tree;
While many a pastime circled in the shade,
The young contending as the old surveyed;
And many a gambol frolicked o'er the ground,
And sleights of art, and feats of strength went round,
And still, as each repeated pleasure tired,
Succeeding sports the mirthful band inspired;
The dancing pair that simply sought renown,
By holding out to tire each other down;
The swain, mistrustless of his smutted face,
While secret laughter tittered round the place;
The bashful virgin's sidelong looks of love,
The matron's glance that would those looks reprove—
These were thy charms, sweet village! sports like these,
With sweet succession, taught e'en toil to please.

   Sweet was the sound, when oft, at evening's close,
Up yonder hill the village murmur rose;
There as I passed, with careless steps and slow,
The mingling notes came softened from below:
The swain responsive as the milkmaid sung,
The sober herd that lowed to meet their young;
The noisy geese that gabbled o'er the pool,
The playful children just let loose from school;
The watch-dog's voice that bayed the whispering wind,
And the loud laugh that spoke the vacant mind;
These all in sweet confusion sought the shade,
And filled each pause the nightingale had made.

   Near yonder copse, where once the garden smiled,
And still where many a garden flower grows wild;
There, where a few torn shrubs the place disclose,
The village preacher's modest mansion rose.
A man he was to all the country dear,
And passing rich[1] with forty pounds a year.
Remote from towns he ran his godly race,
Nor e'er had changed, or wished to change, his place;
Unskilful he to fawn, or seek for power,
By doctrines fashioned to the varying hour;

---

(1) *Passing rich*—This was actually the stipend of the poet's brother, to whom reference has been already made. Mr. Todd thinks that Goldsmith, in delineating the above character, had Chaucer's "Persone" in his eye. (See p. 241.)

Far other aims his heart had learned to prize,
More bent to raise the wretched than to rise.
His house was known to all the vagrant train;
He chid their wanderings, but relieved their pain.
The long remembered beggar was his guest,
Whose beard descending swept his aged breast;
The ruined spendthrift, now no longer proud,
Claimed kindred there, and had his claims allowed;
The broken soldier, kindly bade to stay,
Sat by his fire, and talked the night away;
Wept o'er his wounds, or tales of sorrow done,
Shouldered his crutch, and showed how fields were won.
Pleased with his guests, the good man learned to glow,
And quite forgot their vices in their woe;
Careless their merits or their faults to scan,
His pity gave ere charity began.
 Thus to relieve the wretched was his pride,
And even his failings leaned to virtue's side;
But in his duty prompt at every call,
He watched and wept, he prayed and felt for all.
And as a bird each fond endearment tries,
To tempt her new-fledged offspring to the skies,
He tried each art, reproved each dull delay,
Allured to brighter worlds, and led the way.
 Beside the bed where parting life was laid,
And sorrow, guilt, and pain, by turns dismayed,
The reverend champion stood. At his control
Despair and anguish fled the struggling soul;
Comfort came down the trembling wretch to raise,
And his last faltering accents whispered praise.
 At church, with meek and unaffected grace,
His looks adorned the venerable place;
Truth from his lips prevailed with double sway,
And fools who came to scoff, remained to pray.
The service past, around the pious man,
With ready zeal, each honest rustic ran;
Ev'n children followed with endearing wile,
And plucked his gown, to share the good man's smile.
His ready smile a parent's warmth expressed,
Their welfare pleased him, and their cares distressed;
To them his heart, his love, his griefs were given,
But all his serious thoughts had rest in heaven:
As some tall cliff that lifts its awful form,
Swells from the vale, and midway leaves the storm,

Though round its breast the rolling clouds are spread,
Eternal sunshine settles on its head.

  Beside yon **straggling** fence that skirts the way,
With blossomed **furze** unprofitably gay,
There, in his noisy mansion, skilled to rule,
The village master taught his little school.
A man severe he was, and stern to view;
I knew him well, and every **truant** knew.
Well had the boding tremblers learned **to trace**
The day's disasters in his morning face;
Full well they laughed, with counterfeited glee,
At all his jokes, for many a joke had he;
Full well the busy whisper, circling round,
Conveyed the dismal tidings when he frowned:
Yet he was kind; **or,** if severe in aught,
The love he bore **to learning was in** fault.
The village **all declared how much he knew;**
'Twas certain he could write, and cipher too;
Lands he could measure, terms[1] **and** tides presage,
And even the story **ran that he** could gauge;
In arguing, too, the parson owned his skill,
For even though vanquished, he could argue still;
While words of learned length, and thundering sound
Amazed the gazing rustics ranged around;
And still they gazed, and still the wonder grew,
That one small head could carry all he knew.
But past is all his fame: the very spot
Where many a time he triumphed, is forgot.

  Near yonder thorn that lifts its head on high,
Where once the signpost caught the passing eye,
Low lies that house where nut-brown draughts inspired
Where grey-beard mirth and smiling toil retired;
Where village **statesmen** talked with looks **profound,**
And news much **older than** their ale **went round.**
Imagination fondly **stoops to trace**
The parlour splendours of **that festive** place;
The white-washed wall, the nicely-sanded floor,
The **varnished** clock that clicked behind the door;
The **chest,** contrived a double debt to pay,
A bed by night, a chest of drawers by day;

---

(1) *Terms*—*i. e.* **the** terms, movable feasts, &c., of the Calendar, which depend on mathematical calculations.

The pictures placed for ornament and use,
The Twelve Good Rules, the Royal Game of Goose;
The hearth, except when winter chilled the day,
With aspen boughs, and flowers, and fennel, gay;
While broken tea-cups, wisely kept for show,
Ranged o'er the chimney, glistened in a row.
  Yes! let the rich deride, the proud disdain
These simple blessings of the lowly train;
To me more dear, congenial to my heart,
One native charm, than all the gloss of art:
Spontaneous joys, where Nature has its play,
The soul adopts, and owns their first-born sway;
Lightly they frolic o'er the vacant mind,
Unenvied, unmolested, unconfined:
But the long pomp, the midnight masquerade,
With all the freaks of wanton wealth arrayed,
In these, ere triflers half their wish obtain,
The toiling pleasure sickens into pain;
And, even while fashion's brightest arts decoy,
The heart distrusting asks—if this be joy?

COWPER.

PRINCIPAL EVENTS OF HIS LIFE.—William Cowper was born in 1731, at Berkhampstead, in Hertfordshire. He received the latter part of his education at Westminster School, on leaving which he entered the office of a London solicitor. His progress, however, in the study of the law was inconsiderable, and was completely interrupted by the coming on of mental derangement. In 1765, he formed that congenial acquaintance with Mrs. Unwin and her family, which so soothed and comforted him during the remaining years of his life; and he accompanied them in their removal to Olney, in Buckinghamshire, in the year 1767. In this town he lived many years, and here he became an author for the first time, at the advanced age of fifty. He died on the 5th of April, 1800.

PRINCIPAL WORKS.—The most admired of Cowper's poems, independently of his numerous graceful and lively small pieces, are those entitled, "Truth," "Hope," "The Progress of Error," "Expostulation," "Conversation," and, above all, "The Task."

CHARACTERISTIC SPIRIT AND STYLE.—"The nature of Cowper's works makes us peculiarly identify the poet and the man in perusing them. As an individual, he was retired and weaned from the vanities of the world; and, as an original writer, he left the ambitious and luxuriant subjects of fiction and passion for those of real life and simple nature, and for the development of his own earnest feelings, in behalf of moral and religious truth. His language has such a masculine idiomatic strength, and his manner, whether he rises into grace or falls into negligence, has so much plain and familiar freedom, that we read no poetry with a deeper conviction of its sentiments having come from the author's heart, and of the enthusiasm, in whatever he describes, having been unfeigned and unexaggerated. He impresses us with the idea of a being whose fine spirit had been long enough in the mixed society of the world to be polished by its intercourse, and yet withdrawn so soon as to retain an unworldly degree of purity and simplicity. He was advanced in years before he became an author; but his compositions display a tenderness of feeling so youthfully preserved, and even a vein of humour so far from being extinguished by his ascetic habits, that we can scarcely regret his not having written them at an earlier period of life: for he blends the determination of age with an exquisite and ingenious sensibility; and though he sports very much with his subjects, yet, when he is in earnest, there is a gravity of long-felt conviction in his sentiments, which gives an uncommon ripeness of character to his poetry.

"It is due to Cowper to fix our regard on this unaffectedness and authenticity of his works, considered as representations of himself; because he forms a striking instance of genius writing the history of its own secluded feelings, reflections, and enjoyments, in a shape so interesting as to engage the imagination like a work of fiction. He has invented no character in fable, nor in the drama; but he has left a record of his own character, which forms not only an object of deep sympathy, but a subject for the study of human nature. His verse, it is true, considered as such a record, abounds with opposite traits of severity and gentleness, of playfulness and superstition, of solemnity and mirth, which appear almost anomalous; and there is undoubtedly sometimes an air of moody versatility in the extreme contrasts of his feelings. But looking to his poetry as an entire structure, it has a massive air of sincerity: it is founded in steadfast principles of belief; and, if we may prolong the architectural metaphor, though its arches may be sometimes gloomy, its tracery sportive, and its lights and shadows grotesquely crossed, yet altogether it still forms a vast, various, and interesting monument of the builder's mind.

[In "The Task"] "he leads us abroad into his daily walks; he exhibits the landscapes which he was accustomed to contemplate, and the trains of thought in which he habitually indulged. No attempt is made to interest us in legendary fictions, or historical recollections connected with the ground over which he expatiates; all is plainness and reality; but we instantly recognise the true poet in the clearness, sweetness, and fidelity of his scenic draughts; in his power of giving novelty to what is common; and in the high relish, the exquisite enjoyment of rural sights and sounds which he communicates to the spirit. 'His eyes drink the rivers with delight.'[1] He excites an idea that almost amounts to sensation, of the freshness and delight of a rural walk, even when he leads us to the wasteful common which,

> "'O'ergrown with fern, and rough
> With prickly gorse, that, shapeless and deform,
> And dangerous to the touch, has yet its bloom,
> And decks itself with ornaments of gold,
> Yields no unpleasing ramble; there the turf
> Smells fresh, and, rich in odoriferous herbs
> And fungous fruits of earth, regales the sense
> With luxury of unexpected sweets.'"[2]
>
> *The Task*, book i.

EXTRACTS FROM "THE TASK."

A LANDSCAPE.[3]

How oft, upon yon eminence,[4] our pace
Has slackened to a pause, and we have borne
The ruffling wind, scarce conscious that it blew,
While Admiration, feeding at the eye,

---

(1) An expression in one of his letters.
(2) Campbell. "Specimens," &c., p. 672.
(3) Campbell praises highly "the calm English character and familiar repose" of the above scene, which is, he adds, "in the finest manner of Cowper, and unites all his accustomed fidelity and distinctness, with a softness and delicacy which are not always to be found in his specimens of the picturesque."
(4) *Yon eminence*—The scenery here depicted is that of the neighbourhood of Olney, Buckinghamshire.

And still unsated, dwelt upon the scene.
Thence with what pleasure have we just discerned
The distant plough slow moving, and beside
His labouring team, that swerved not from the track,
The sturdy swain, diminished to a boy !¹
Here Ouse, slow winding through a level plain
Of spacious meads with cattle sprinkled o'er,
Conducts the eye along his sinuous course
Delighted. There, fast rooted in their bank,
Stand, never overlooked, our favourite elms,
That screen the herdsman's solitary hut;
While far beyond, and overthwart the stream,
That, as with molten glass, inlays the vale,
The sloping land recedes into the clouds;
Displaying on its varied side the grace
Of hedge-row beauties numberless, square tower,
Tall spire, from which the sound of cheerful bells
Just undulates upon the listening ear,
Groves, heaths, and smoking villages, remote.

RURAL SOUNDS.

Nor rural sights alone, but rural sounds,
Exhilarate the spirit, and restore
The tone of languid nature. Mighty winds,
That sweep the skirt of some far-spreading wood
Of ancient growth, make music not unlike
The dash of Ocean on his winding shore,
And lull the spirit while they fill the mind;
Unnumbered branches waving in the blast,
And all their leaves fast fluttering, all at once.
Nor less composure waits upon the roar
Of distant floods, or on the softer voice
Of neighbouring fountain, or of rills that slip
Through the cleft rock, and, chiming as they fall
Upon loose pebbles, lose themselves at length
In matted grass, that with a livelier green
Betrays the secret of their silent course.
Nature inanimate employs sweet sounds,

---

(1) *Diminished to a boy—*

" Yon tall anchoring bark,
Diminished to her cock ; her cock a buoy,
Almost too small for sight."—*King Lear*. (See p. 278.)

But animated nature sweeter still,
To soothe and satisfy the human ear.
Ten thousand warblers cheer the day, and one
The live-long night; nor these alone, whose notes
Nice-fingered art must emulate in vain,
But cawing rooks, and kites that swim sublime
In still-repeated circles, screaming loud,
The jay, the pie, and e'en the boding owl,
That hails the rising moon, have charms for me.
Sounds inharmonious in themselves and harsh,
Yet heard in scenes where peace for ever reigns,
And only there, please highly for their sake.

SLAVERY.[1]

Oh for a lodge in some vast wilderness,
Some boundless contiguity of shade,
Where rumour of oppression and deceit,
Of unsuccessful or successful war,
Might never reach me more. My ear is pained,
My soul is sick, with every day's report
Of wrong and outrage with which earth is filled.
There is no flesh in man's obdurate heart,
It does not feel for man; the natural bond
Of brotherhood is severed as the flax,
That falls asunder at the touch of fire.
He finds his fellow guilty of a skin
Not coloured like his own; and, having power
To enforce the wrong, for such a worthy cause
Dooms and devotes him as his lawful prey.
Lands intersected by a narrow frith
Abhor each other. Mountains interposed
Make enemies of nations, who had else,
Like kindred drops, been mingled into one.
Thus man devotes his brother, and destroys;
And, worse than all, and most to be deplored
As human nature's broadest, foulest blot,
Chains him, and tasks him, and exacts his sweat

---

(1) These lines were written at a time when the English colonies were cultivated by slaves—a state of things happily now at an end; but they so eloquently express the general principle, which is by no means obsolete, that they are inserted on that account.

With stripes, that Mercy, with a bleeding heart,
Weeps when she sees inflicted on a beast.
Then what is man? And what man, seeing this,
And having human feelings, does not blush,
And hang his head, to think himself a man?
I would not have a slave to till my ground,
To carry me, to fan me while I sleep,
And tremble when I wake, for all the wealth
That sinews bought and sold have ever earned.
No: dear as freedom is, and in my heart's
Just estimation prized above all price,
I had much rather be the slave myself,
And wear the bonds, than fasten them on him.
We have no slaves at home—then why abroad?
And they themselves, once ferried o'er the wave
That parts us, are emancipate and loosed.
Slaves cannot breathe in England; if their lungs
Receive our air, that moment they are free;
They touch our country, and their shackles fall.
That's noble, and bespeaks a nation proud
And jealous of the blessing. Spread it, then,
And let it circulate through every vein
Of all your empire; that, where Britain's power
Is felt, mankind may feel her mercy too.[1]

ADDRESS TO WINTER.

O Winter, ruler of the inverted year,
Thy scattered hair with sheet-like ashes filled,
Thy breath congealed upon thy lips, thy cheeks
Fringed with a beard made white with other snows
Than those of age, thy forehead wrapt in clouds,
A leafless branch thy sceptre and thy throne
A sliding car, indebted to no wheels,
But urged by storms along its slippery way,
I love thee, all unlovely as thou seemest,
And dreaded as thou art! Thou holdest the sun
A prisoner in the yet undawning east,
Shortening his journey between morn and noon,
And hurrying him, impatient of his stay,

---

[1] "Nothing can be farther from the stale commonplace and cuckooism of sentiment than the philanthropic eloquence of Cowper—he speaks 'like one having authority.'"—*Campbell.*

Down to the rosy west; but kindly still
Compensating his loss with added hours
Of social converse and instructive ease,
And gathering, at short notice, in one group
The family dispersed, and fixing thought,
Not less dispersed by daylight and its cares.
I crown thee king of intimate delights,[1]
Fire-side enjoyments, home-born happiness,
And all the comforts that the lowly roof
Of undisturbed retirement, and the hours
Of long uninterrupted evening, know.

THE WINTER WALK AT NOON.

There is in souls a sympathy with sounds;
And as the mind is pitched, the ear is pleased
With melting airs, or martial, brisk or grave;
Some chord, in unison with what we hear,
Is touched within us, and the heart replies.
How soft the music of those village bells,
Falling at intervals upon the ear
In cadence sweet; now dying all away,
Now pealing loud again, and louder still,
Clear and sonorous, as the gale comes on!
With easy force it opens all the cells
Where Memory slept. Wherever I have heard
A kindred melody, the scene recurs,
And with it all its pleasures and its pains.—
 The night was winter in his roughest mood;
The morning sharp and clear. But now, at noon,
Upon the southern side of the slant hills,
And where the woods fence off the northern blast,
The season smiles, resigning all its rage,
And has the warmth of May. The vault is blue
Without a cloud, and white without a speck
The dazzling splendour of the scene below.
Again the harmony comes o'er the vale;

---

(1) Referring to Cowper's felicitous description of "fire-side enjoyments," in this and other passages of "The Task," Campbell very gracefully says, that in perusing them, "we seem to recover a part of the forgotten value of existence, when we recognise the means of its blessedness, so widely dispersed and so cheaply attainable, and find them susceptible of description at once so enchanting and so faithful."

And through the trees I view the embattled tower,
Whence all the music. I again perceive
The soothing influence of the wafted strains,
And settle in soft musings as I tread
The walk, still verdant, under oak and elms,
Whose outspread branches over-arch the glade.
The roof, though movable through all its length
As the wind sways it, has yet well sufficed,
And, intercepting in their silent fall
The frequent flakes, has kept a path for me.
No noise is here, or none that hinders thought.
The redbreast warbles still, but is content
With slender notes, and more than half suppressed:
Pleased with his solitude, and flitting light
From spray to spray, where'er he rests he shakes
From many a twig the pendant drops of ice,
That tinkle in the withered leaves below.
Stillness, accompanied with sounds so soft,
Charms more than silence. Meditation here
May think down hours to moments. Here the heart
May give a useful lesson to the head,
And Learning wiser grow without his books.
Knowledge and wisdom,[1] far from being one,
Have ofttimes no connection; knowledge dwells
In heads replete with thoughts of other men;
Wisdom in minds attentive to their own.
Knowledge, a rude unprofitable mass,
The mere materials with which wisdom builds,
Till smoothed and squared, and fitted to its place,
Does but encumber whom it seems to enrich.
Knowledge is proud that he has learned so much;
Wisdom is humble that he knows no more.

THE MILLENNIUM.[2]

O SCENES surpassing fable, and yet true—
Scenes of accomplished bliss! which who can see,

---

(1) *Knowledge and wisdom, &c.*—See p. 232.
(2) "We doubt," says the Rev. Thomas Dale, in his "Life of Cowper," "whether anything in the whole range of English poetry, the 'Messiah' of Pope itself not excepted, can afford any parallel to the exquisite grouping of prophetic imagery in that splendid passage which describes the millennial glory of the Church, commencing

"'O scenes surpassing fable,' &c."

Though but in distant prospect, and not feel
His soul refreshed with foretaste of the joy?
Rivers of gladness water all the earth,
And clothe all climes with beauty; the reproach
Of barrenness is past. The fruitful field
Laughs with abundance, and the land, once lean,
Or fertile only in its own disgrace,
Exults to see its thistly curse repealed.
The various seasons woven into one,
And that one season an eternal spring,
The garden fears no blight, and needs no fence,
For there is none to covet, all are full.
The lion, and the libbard, and the bear,
Graze with the fearless flocks; all bask at noon
Together, or all gambol in the shade
Of the same grove, and drink one common stream:
Antipathies are none. No foe to man
Lurks in the serpent now: the mother sees,
And smiles to see her infant's playful hand
Stretched forth to dally with the crested worm,
To stroke his azure neck, or to receive
The lambent homage of his arrowy tongue.
All creatures worship man, and all mankind
One Lord, one Father. Error has no place;
That creeping pestilence is driven away;
The breath of heaven has chased it. In the heart
No passion touches a discordant string;
But all is harmony and love. Disease
Is not: the pure and uncontaminated blood
Holds its due course, nor fears the frost of age.
One song employs all nations: and all cry,
"Worthy the Lamb, for he was slain for us!"
The dwellers in the vales and on the rocks
Shout to each other, and the mountain tops
From distant mountains catch the flying joy;
Till, nation after nation taught the strain,
Earth rolls the rapturous Hosanna round.
Behold the measure of the promise filled;
See Salem built, the labour of a God!
Bright as a sun the sacred city shines;
All kingdoms and all princes of the earth
Flock to that light; the glory of all lands
Flows into her; unbounded is her joy,
And endless her increase. Thy rams are there,

Nebaioth,[1] and the flocks of **Kedar**[1] there:
The looms of Ormus and the mines of Ind,
And Saba's spicy **groves, pay tribute** there.
Praise is in all her **gates, upon her walls**
And in her streets, and in her spacious courts,
Is heard salvation. Eastern Java there
Kneels with the native of the farthest west;
And Ethiopia spreads abroad the hand,
And worships. Her **report has travelled forth**
Into all lands; **from** every clime **they come**
To see thy beauty, and to share thy **joy,**
O Sion! an assembly such as earth
Saw never, such as Heaven stoops down to see.

BURNS.

PRINCIPAL EVENTS OF HIS LIFE.—Robert Burns was born January 25th, 1759, in a clay-built cottage, raised by his father's **own** hands, on the banks of the Doon, in the district of Kyle, Ayrshire. At the age of six he **was sent** to school, and appears to have been a diligent little student. At an early age he assisted his father in his farming business, continuing his education at intervals. When about twenty, he composed several of the poems which afterwards distinguished his name. After various domestic trials, when **on the** point of leaving England **for** Jamaica, where **he had got a** situation, the publication **of** his poems awakened **so much interest** in their **author, that** he abandoned his purpose, **and after an unsuccessful** experiment in farming, obtained an **appointment in the Excise.** He died at Dumfries, in the year 1796.

PRINCIPAL WORKS.—Amongst many brief, but beautiful poems, it is difficult to particularize the principal; but perhaps those entitled "Tam o' Shanter," "The Cotter's Saturday Night," "To a Mountain Daisy," "The **Twa Dogs," "To** Mary in Heaven," **may be** designated the best.

---

(1) "*Nebaioth and Kedar*—the sons of Ishmael, and progenitors of the Arabs, in the prophetic Scriptures here alluded **to** [see Isaiah lx., throughout] may be reasonably considered as representatives of the Gentiles at large."

CHARACTERISTIC SPIRIT AND STYLE.—"The excellence of Burns is indeed among the rarest, whether in poetry or prose; but at the same time, it is plain and easily recognised—it is his sincerity—his indisputable air of truth. Here are no fabulous woes or joys; no hollow fantastic sentimentalities; no wiredrawn refinings, either in thought or feeling; the passion that is traced before us has glowed in a living heart; the opinion he utters has risen in his own understanding, and been a light to his own steps. He does not write from heresay, but from sight and experience; they are the scenes that he has lived and laboured amongst that he describes; those scenes, rude and humble as they are, have kindled beautiful emotions in his soul—noble thoughts and definite resolves—and he speaks forth what is in him, not from any outward call of vanity or interest, but because his heart is too full to be silent. He speaks it too with such modulation as he can, and though but in homely rustic jingle, it is his own, and genuine. This is the grand secret for finding readers and retaining them: let him who would move and convince others, be first moved and convinced himself. But, independently of this essential gift of true poetic feeling, there is a certain rugged, sterling worth pervades whatever Burns has written. A virtue, as of green fields and mountain breezes, dwells in his poetry—it is redolent of natural life, and of hardy, natural men. There is a decisive strength in him, and yet frequently a sweet native gracefulness. He is tender, and he is vehement; yet without constraint or visible effort. He melts the heart, or inflames it with a power which seems habitual and familiar to him. He has a consonance in his bosom for every note of human feeling; the high and the low—the sad and the ludicrous—the mournful and the joyful are welcome in their turns, to his all-conceiving spirit. And then, with what a prompt and eager force he grasps his subject, be it what it may! How he fixes, *as it were*, the full image of the matter in his eye, full and clear in every lineament, and catches the real type and essence of it, among a thousand incidents and superficial circumstances—no one of which misleads him! No poet, of any age or nation, is more graphic than Burns. The characteristic features disclose themselves to him at a glance. Three lines from his hand and we have a likeness!"[1]

(1) Thomas Carlyle. "Miscellanies," vol. L.

THE COTTER'S SATURDAY NIGHT.[1]

November chill blaws loud wi' angry sugh;[2]
    The shortening winter-day is near a close;
The miry beasts retreating frae the pleugh;
    The blackening trains o' craws to their repose;
The toil-worn Cotter frae his labour goes,
    This night his weekly moil is at an end,
Collects his spades, his mattocks, and his hoes,
    Hoping the morn in ease and rest to spend,
And weary, o'er the moor, his course does hameward bend.

At length his lonely cot appears in view,
    Beneath the shelter of an aged tree;
The expectant wee-things, toddlin', stacher[3] thro'
    To meet their dad, wi' flichterin'[4] noise an' glee.
His wee bit ingle,[5] blinkin' bonnily,
    His clean hearth-stane, his thriftie wifie's smile,
The lisping infant prattling on his knee,
    Does a' his weary carking cares beguile,
An' makes him quite forget his labour an' his toil.

Belyve[6] the elder bairns come drapping in,
    At service out amang the farmers roun';
Some ca'[7] the pleugh, some herd, some tentie[8] rin,
    A cannie errand to a neebor town:
Their eldest hope, their Jenny, woman grown,
    In youthfu' bloom, love sparkling in her e'e,
Comes hame, perhaps, to shew a braw new gown,
    Or deposite her sair-worn penny-fee,
To help her parents dear, if they in hardship be.

---

(1) "'The Cotter's Saturday Night' is tender and moral, solemn and devotional, and rises at length into a strain of grandeur and sublimity which modern poetry has not surpassed. The noble sentiments of patriotism with which it concludes, correspond with the rest of the poem. In no age or country have the pastoral muses breathed such elevated accents, if the 'Messiah' of Pope be excepted, which is indeed a pastoral in form only."—*Dr. Corrie.*

"The Cotter, in the 'Saturday Night,' is an exact copy of my father in his manners, his family devotion, and exhortations; yet the other parts of the description do not apply to our family. None of us were ever 'at service out amang the farmers round.'"—*Gilbert Burns* (brother of the author).

(2) *Sugh*—whistling sound. (3) *Stacher*—stagger. (4) *Flichterin'*—fluttering. (5) *Wee bit ingle*—little fire or fire-place. (6) *Belyve*—by-and-by. (7) *Ca'*—drive. (8) *Tentie*—carefully, heedfully.

Wi' joy unfeigned, brothers and sisters meet,
   An' each for others' weelfare kindly spiers;[1]
The social hours, swift-winged, unnoticed fleet;
   Each tells the uncos[2] that he sees or hears:
The parents, partial, eye their hopeful years;
   Anticipation forward points the view.
The mither, wi' her needle an' her shears,
   Gars[3] auld claes look amaist as weel's the new;—
The father mixes a' wi' admonition due.

Their master's an' their mistress's command,
   The younkers a' are warnéd to obey;
An' mind their labours wi' an eydent[4] hand,
   An' ne'er, tho' out o' sight, to jauk[5] or play;
"An' O! be sure to fear the Lord alway!
   An' mind your duty, duly, morn an' night!
Lest in temptation's path ye gang astray,
   Implore His counsel, an' assisting might;
They never sought in vain, that sought the Lord aright!

But hark! a rap comes gently to the door:
   Jenny, wha kens the meaning o' the same,
Tells how a neebor lad cam o'er the moor,
   To do some errands, and convoy her hame.
The wily mother sees the conscious flame
   Sparkle in Jenny's e'e, and flush her cheek;
Wi' heart-struck anxious care, inquires his name,
   While Jenny hafflins[6] is afraid to speak;
Weel pleased the mother hears it's nae wild worthless rake.

Wi' kindly welcome Jenny brings him ben;[7]
   A strappan youth: he taks the mother's eye;
Blythe Jenny sees the visit's no ill-ta'en;
   The father cracks o' horses, pleughs, and kye.[8]
The youngster's artless heart o'erflows wi' joy,
   But blate and laithfu',[9] scarce can weel behave;
The mother, wi' a woman's wiles, can spy,
   What maks the youth sae bashfu' and sae grave;
Weel pleased to think her bairn's respected like the lave.[10]

---

(1) *Spiers*—inquires. (2) *Uncos*—uncommon things, news. (3) *Gars*—makes. (4) *Eydent*—diligent. (5) *Jauk*—trifle. (6) *Hafflins*—partly, half. (7) *Ben*—in. (8) *Kye*—cows. (9) *Blate and laithfu'*—bashful and sheepish. (10) *The lave*—the rest, others.

But now the supper crowns their simple board,
    The halesome parritch, chief o' Scotia's food:
The soupe their only hawkie[1] does afford,
    That 'yont the hallan[2] snugly chows her cood:
The dame brings forth, in complimental mood,
    To **grace the** lad, her well-hained kebbuck,[3] fell;
An' **aft he's** prest, an' aft he ca's it guid;
    The frugal wifie, garrulous, **will** tell,
How 'twas a **towmond**[4] auld, sin' lint was i' the bell.[5]

The **cheerfu'** supper **done,** wi' serious face,
    They, **round** the ingle, form a circle wide;
The sire turns o'er, wi' patriarchal grace,
    The big ha'-bible, ance his father's pride:
His bonnet reverently is laid aside,
    His lyart haffets[6] wearing thin an' **bare;**
Those strains that **once did sweet in Zion glide,**
    He wales[7] a portion with **judicious care;**
And "Let us worship God!" he says, with solemn air.

They chant their artless notes in simple guise;
    They tune their hearts, **by far the** noblest aim;
Perhaps "Dundee's" wild warbling measures rise,
    Or plaintive "Martyrs," worthy of the name;
Or noble "Elgin" beets[8] **the** heaven-ward flame,
    The sweetest far of **Scotia's** holy lays:
Compared with these, **Italian** trills are tame:
    The tickled **ears no heart-felt raptures raise;**
Nae **unison hae they with our Creator's praise.**

The priest-like father reads the sacred page,
    How Abram was the friend **of God** on high;
Or, Moses **bade eternal warfare** wage
    With **Amalek's** ungracious progeny:
Or how **the** royal Bard did groaning lie
    Beneath the stroke of Heaven's avenging **ire;**
Or Job's pathetic plaint, and wailing cry;
    Or rapt Isaiah's wild, seraphic fire;
Or other **holy Seers** that **tune the sacred lyre.**

---

(1) *Hawkie*—cow.   (2) *Hallan*—cottage-wall.   (3) *Weel-hained kebbuck*—well-kept **cheese.**   (4) *Towmond*—**twelvemonth.**   (5) *Sin' lint, &c.*—Since flax was in the flower.   (6) *Lyart haffets*—grey temples.   (7) *Wales*—chooses.   (8) *Beets*—adds fuel to.

Perhaps the Christian volume is the theme,
  How guiltless blood for guilty man was shed;
How He, who bore in heaven the second name,
  Had not on earth whereon to lay his head:
How his first followers and servants sped;
  The precepts sage they wrote to many a land:
How he, who lone in Patmos banished,
  Saw in the sun a mighty angel stand;
And heard great Babylon's doom pronounced by Heaven's command.

Then kneeling down, to Heaven's Eternal King,
  The saint, the father, and the husband, prays:
Hope " springs exulting on triumphant wing,"[1]
  That thus they all shall meet in future days:
There ever bask in uncreated rays,
  No more to sigh, or shed the bitter tear,
Together hymning their Creator's praise,
  In such society, yet still more dear;
While circling time moves round in an eternal sphere.

Compared with this, how poor Religion's pride,
  In all the pomp of method and of art,
When men display to congregations wide
  Devotion's ev'ry grace, except the heart!
The Power, incensed, the pageant will desert,
  The pompous strain, the sacerdotal stole;
But haply, in some cottage far apart,
  May hear, well-pleased, the language of the soul;
And in his Book of Life the inmates poor enroll.

Then hameward all take off their several way;
  The youngling cottagers retire to rest:
The parent-pair their secret homage pay,
  And proffer up to Heaven the warm request
That He, who stills the raven's clamorous nest,
  And decks the lily fair in flowery pride,
Would, in the way His wisdom sees the best,
  For them, and for their little ones, provide;
But, chiefly, in their hearts, with grace divine preside.

(1) A line from Pope's " Windsor Forest."

From scenes like these, old Scotia's grandeur springs,
    That makes her loved at home, revered abroad:
Princes and lords are but the breath of kings,
    "An honest man's the noblest work of God:"
And certes,[1] in fair virtue's heavenly road,
    The cottage leaves the palace far behind:
What is a lordling's pomp?—a cumbrous load,
    Disguising oft the wretch of human kind,
Studied in arts of hell, in wickedness refined!

O Scotia! my dear, my native soil!
    For whom my warmest wish to heaven is sent!
Long may thy hardy sons of rustic toil
    Be blest with health, and peace, and sweet content!
And, oh may Heaven their simple lives prevent
    From Luxury's contagion, weak and vile!
Then howe'er crowns and coronets be rent,
    A virtuous populace may rise the while;
And stand a wall of fire around their much loved isle.

O Thou! who poured the patriotic tide
    That streamed through Wallace's undaunted heart;
Who dared to nobly stem tyrannic pride,
    Or nobly die, the second glorious part,
(The patriot's God peculiarly thou art,
    His friend, inspirer, guardian, and reward!)
Oh never, never, Scotia's realms desert;
    But still the patriot, and the patriot bard,
In bright succession raise, her ornament and guard!

VERSES LEFT AT A FRIEND'S HOUSE.

O thou dread Power, who reign'st above,
    I know thou wilt me hear,
When for this scene of peace and love
    I make my prayer sincere.

(1) *Certes*—certainly.

The hoary sire—the mortal stroke,
    Long, long, be pleased to spare!
To bless his little filial flock,
    And show what good men are.

She, who her lovely offspring eyes
    With tender hopes and fears,
Oh, bless her with a mother's joys,
    But spare a mother's tears!

Their hope, their stay, their darling youth,
    In manhood's dawning blush;
Bless him, thou God of love and truth,
    Up to a parent's wish!

The beauteous, seraph sister-band,
    With earnest tears I pray,—
Thou know'st the snares on ev'ry hand,
    Guide thou their steps alway!

When soon or late they reach that coast,
    O'er life's rough ocean driven,
May they rejoice, no wanderer lost,
    A family in Heaven!

APPENDIX.

Note A. (*See page* 2.)

It is possible that the "resentment" spoken of in the third stanza was intended to indicate the anger of the Romans against the Druids. The meaning then would be—we are silent because the Romans have cruelly imposed silence upon us. We learn from Tacitus [Annales xiv. 30] that the Druids had just before, by their imprecations and threats, caused a temporary panic in the Roman army, and that in consequence their groves had been cut down, and a garrison placed over them. This fact gives some colour to the interpretation here hazarded; and which has been suggested by a literary friend of the editor.

Note B. (*See page* 5.)

To avoid the tautology in the commencement of this poem, some unknown author has thus altered, with doubtful advantage, the original reading:—

> "The lofty pillars of the sky,
> And spacious concave raised on high,
> Spangled with stars," &c.

Also—

> "The unwearied sun, from day to day,
> Pours knowledge in his golden ray."

Note C. (*See page* 7.)

The opinion that exact knowledge increases rather than diminishes the pleasure of imagination, is thus expressed by Akenside:—

> "Nor ever yet
> The melting rainbow's vernal tinctured hues
> To me have shone so pleasing as when first
> The hand of science pointed out the path
> In which the sunbeams, gleaming from the west,
> Fall on the watery cloud, whose darksome veil
> Involves the orient."

Note D. (*See page* 8.)

The expression, "the world's grey fathers," seems to have been borrowed from an old poem by Henry Vaughan, a writer of the seventeenth century, who thus addresses the rainbow:—

> "How bright wert thou when Shem's admiring eye
> Thy burnished flaming arch did first descry;
> When Zerah, Nahor, Haran, Abram, Lot,
> The youthful *world's grey fathers*, in one knot,
> Did with intentive looks watch every hour
> For thy new light, and trembled at each shower!"

LONDON: PRINTED BY
SPOTTISWOODE AND CO., NEW-STREET SQUARE
AND PARLIAMENT STREET

April 1874.

A LIST
OF
School and Juvenile Books
PUBLISHED BY
LOCKWOOD & CO.
7 STATIONERS'-HALL COURT, LUDGATE HILL, E.C.

WORKS BY JOSEPH PAYNE,
Vice-President of the Council of the College of Preceptors, &c.

PAYNE'S SELECT POETRY for CHILDREN, with brief Explanatory Notes, arranged for the use of Schools and Families. *Eighteenth Edition*, with fine Steel Frontispiece. 18mo. new and elegant cloth binding, 2s. 6d.; gilt edges, 3s.

*** The present edition has been carefully revised and considerably enlarged, by the insertion of several poems by living authors, for which permission has been most kindly given to the Editor.

PAYNE'S STUDIES in ENGLISH POETRY; with short Biographical Sketches, and Notes Explanatory and Critical, intended as a Text-Book for the Higher Classes of Schools. *Sixth Edition*, revised. Post 8vo. in new and elegant cloth binding, 5s.

'The selection is both extensive and varied, including many of the choicest specimens of English poetry.'—*Eclectic Review.*

PAYNE'S STUDIES in ENGLISH PROSE. Specimens of the Language in its various stages; with Notes Explanatory and Critical. By JOSEPH PAYNE, Vice-President of the Council of the College of Preceptors, Author of 'Select Poetry for Children' &c. Post 8vo. in new and elegant cloth binding, 5s.

'"Studies in English Prose" admirably accomplishes the object aimed at by its Editor, which is to furnish, in the form of specimens, a continuous and systematic view of the development of the English language. It is a rare collection of literary gems, and it is difficult to imagine a more useful manual.'—*Scotsman.*

'An unique attempt, so far as we are aware, to give specimens of the English language from the period previous to the Norman Conquest down to quite modern times. The design, which we think a good one, has been well executed. The selected passages are worthy to represent the style and opinions of their respective authors.'—*John Bull.*

DR. FALCK LEBAHN'S GERMAN SCHOOL BOOKS.

'As an educational writer in the German tongue, Dr. Lebahn stands alone; none other has made even a distant approach to him.'—BRITISH STANDARD.

LEBAHN'S GERMAN LANGUAGE in ONE VOLUME. *Seventh Edition*, containing a Practical Grammar; Undine, a Tale; aud a Vocabulary of 4,500 Words, synonymous in English and German. Crown 8vo. cloth, 8s. With KEY, 10s. 6d. KEY separate, 2s. 6d.

'Had we to recommence the study of German, of all the German grammars which we have examined—and they are not a few—we should unhesitatingly say, Falck Lebahn's is the book for us.'—*Educational Times.*

LEBAHN'S FIRST GERMAN COURSE. *Fourth Edition.* Crown 8vo. 2s. 6d. cloth.

'It is hardly possible to have a simpler or better book for beginners in German.'—*Athenæum.*

LEBAHN'S FIRST GERMAN READER. *Fifth Edition.* Crown 8vo. 3s. 6d. cloth.

'An admirable book for beginners, which indeed may be used without a master.'—*Leader.*

LEBAHN'S EDITION of SCHMID'S HENRY von EICHENFELS. With Vocabulary and Familiar Dialogues. *Seventh Edition.* Crown 8vo. 3s. 6d. cloth.

'Excellently adapted to assist self-exercise.'—*Spectator.*

LEBAHN'S EXERCISES in GERMAN. Crown 8vo. 3s. 6d. cloth. A Key to the same, 2s. 6d. cloth.

LEBAHN'S SELF-INSTRUCTOR in GERMAN. Crown 8vo. 3s. 6d. cloth.

LEBAHN'S GERMAN CLASSICS; with Notes and Complete Vocabularies. Crown 8vo. cloth, 3s. 6d. each:—
EGMONT. A Tragedy in Five Acts, by GOETHE.
WILHELM TELL. A Drama, in Five Acts, by SCHILLER.
GOETZ VON BERLICHINGEN. A Drama, by GOETHE.
PAGENSTREICHE, a Page's Frolics. A Comedy, by KOTZEBUE.
EMILIA GALOTTI. A Tragedy, in Five Acts, by LESSING.
UNDINE. A Tale, by FOUQUE.
SELECTIONS from the GERMAN POETS.

'With such aids, a student will find no difficulty in these masterpieces.'—*Athenæum.*

LEBAHN'S (Mrs.) LITTLE SCHOLAR'S FIRST STEP in the GERMAN LANGUAGE. 18mo. cloth. 1s.

LEBAHN'S (Mrs.) LITTLE SCHOLAR'S FIRST STEP in GERMAN READING. 18mo. cloth, 1s.

DR. DE FIVAS' FRENCH SCHOOL BOOKS.

Attention is respectfully invited to the following eminently useful Series of French Class Books, which have enjoyed an unprecedented popularity, and are in use at most of the Colleges and Schools throughout the United Kingdom and the Colonies.

DE FIVAS' NEW GRAMMAR of FRENCH GRAMMARS; comprising the substance of all the most approved French Grammars extant, but more especially of the standard work 'La Grammaire des Grammaires,' sanctioned by the French Academy and the University of Paris. By Dr. V. DE FIVAS, M.A., F.E.I.S., Member of the Grammatical Society of Paris, &c. &c. *Thirty-seventh Edition*, strongly bound, 3s. 6d.—A KEY to the same, 3s. 6d.

'This French Grammar has for a long time been recognised as the best we have in England, and it seems to be rapidly superseding most others.' —*Educational Times, Oct.* 1870.

DE FIVAS' NEW GUIDE to MODERN FRENCH CONVERSATION; or, the Student and Tourist's French Vade-Mecum. *Twenty-fourth Edition*, 18mo. half-bound, 2s. 6d.

'The very best work of the kind with which we are acquainted. The work is also valuable as exhibiting throughout in a peculiarly distinct manner the correct pronunciation of the French language.'—*Edinburgh Advertiser.*

DE FIVAS, BEAUTÉS des ÉCRIVAINS FRANÇAIS, ANCIENS et MODERNES. *Quatorzième Edition*, augmentée de Notes Historiques, Geographiques, Philosophiques, Littéraires, Grammaticales, &c., 12mo. bound, 3s. 6d.

'An elegant volume, containing a selection of pieces in both prose and verse, which, while it furnishes a convenient reading book for the student of the French language, at the same time affords a pleasing and interesting view of French literature.'—*Observer.*

DE FIVAS, INTRODUCTION à la LANGUE FRANÇAISE; ou, Fables et Contes Choisis; Anecdotes Instructives, Faits Mémorables, &c. Avec un Dictionnaire de tous les Mots traduits en Anglais. *Twenty-third Edition*, 12mo. bound, 2s. 6d.

'Incomparably superior to former works in use as introductions.'— *Guardian.*

DE FIVAS, Le TRÉSOR NATIONAL; or, Guide to the Translation of English into French at Sight. *Fifth Edition*, 12mo. bound, 2s. 6d.—A KEY to the same, 12mo. 2s.

M'HENRY'S SPANISH COURSE.

M'HENRY'S NEW and IMPROVED SPANISH GRAMMAR. Containing the Elements of the Language and the Rules of Etymology and Syntax Exemplified; with Notes and Appendix, consisting of Dialogues, Select Poetry, Commercial Correspondence, Vocabulary, &c. Designed for every class of Learners, especially for such as are their own Instructors. *New Edition*, revised and corrected by ALFRED ELWES. 12mo. bound, 6s.

'Justice compels us to say that this is the most complete Spanish Grammar for the use of Englishmen extant. It fully performs the promises in the title-page.'—*British Neptune.*

M'HENRY'S EXERCISES on the ETYMOLOGY, SYNTAX, IDIOMS, &c. of the SPANISH LANGUAGE. *New Edition*, revised by ALFRED ELWES. 12mo. bound, 3s. *** KEY to the EXERCISES, revised and corrected by ALFRED ELWES. Price 4s. bound.

'Unquestionably the best book of Spanish Exercises which has hitherto been published.'—*Gentleman's Magazine.*

M'HENRY'S SYNONYMS of the SPANISH LANGUAGE EXPLAINED. 12mo. bound, 4s.

'Anxious to render the work as interesting as possible, the Author has expended considerable time and labour in making a selection of characteristic extracts from the most approved writers, which, while they serve to exemplify or elucidate the particular synonyms under consideration, may at the same time recommend themselves to the learner by their intrinsic value.'—*Extract from the Preface.*

RAGONOT'S VOCABULAIRE SYMBOLIQUE.

A SYMBOLIC FRENCH and ENGLISH VOCABULARY, for Students of every age in all classes; in which the most Useful and Common Words are taught by Illustrations. By L. C. RAGONOT, Professor of the French Language. *Ninth Edition*, with upwards of 850 Woodcuts and 9 full-page Copper-plates. 4to. cloth, 5s.

Ragonot's Symbolisches Englisch-Deutsches Wörterbuch.

THE SYMBOLIC ANGLO-GERMAN VOCABULARY, adapted from RAGONOT'S 'Vocabulaire Symbolique Anglo-Français.' Edited by FALCK LEBAHN, Ph. Dr. With 850 Woodcuts and 8 full-page Lithographic Plates. Demy 8vo. cloth, 6s.

CIVIL SERVICE HANDBOOKS.

Indispensable for Candidates for Examinations.

THE CIVIL SERVICE GEOGRAPHY, General and Political. By the late L. M. D. SPENCE. Revised by THOMAS GRAY, of the Board of Trade. *Fourth Edition*, Woodcuts and Six Maps, fcp. 2s. 6d. cloth.

'A thoroughly reliable as well as a most ingenious compendium of geography.'—*Civil Service Gazette.*

THE CIVIL SERVICE HISTORY OF ENGLAND: being a Fact Book of English History. By F. A. WHITE, B.A. *Second Edition*, revised by H. A. DOBSON, of the Board of Trade, with four Maps, 2s. 6d. cloth.

'We do not remember to have seen anything of the kind so compendious, complete, accurate, and convenient for use.'—*Athenæum.*

THE CIVIL SERVICE BOOK-KEEPING; or, **Book-keeping no Mystery.** Its Principles Popularly Explained, **and the Theory** of Double Entry Analysed. By an EXPERIENCED **BOOK-KEEPER.** *Second Edition*, fcp. 2s. cloth.

'It is clear and concise, and exactly such a text-book as students require.'—*Quarterly Journal of Education.*

THE CIVIL SERVICE ORTHOGRAPHY: a Handy Book of English Spelling, with Rules and Exercises. By E. S. H. B., fcp. 2s. 6d. cloth.

☞ *Of 1,972 rejections of candidates for the Civil Service during five years, all except 106 were for deficiency in spelling or arithmetic.*

'A very handy, carefully written, and complete little book.'—*Pall Mall Gazette.*

THE CIVIL SERVICE CHRONOLOGY OF HISTORY, ART, LITERATURE, and PROGRESS, from the Creation to the Conclusion of the Franco-German War. The continuation by W. D. HAMILTON, F.S.A., of H.M. Public Record Office, fcp. 3s. 6d. cloth.

'Accurate, wide, and thorough. Most useful to those who are reading up for examinations.'—*English Churchman.*

THE CIVIL SERVICE ENGLISH GRAMMAR: being Notes on the History and Grammar of the English Language. By W. T. YATES, Head Master, Windermere Grammar School, fcp. 2s. cloth.

'We cannot call to mind any single work which would render so much assistance as is offered here to the student preparing to undergo examination in Grammar and Language.'—*The School Board Chronicle.*

THE CIVIL SERVICE HANDBOOK of ENGLISH LITERATURE. By H. A. DOBSON, **Board** of Trade, Editor of the 'Civil Service History of England,' &c., fcp. 2s. 6d. cloth.

THE CIVIL SERVICE FIRST FRENCH BOOK: being a Practical First Course of French Grammar, with Exercises combined, for the use of Civil Service Candidates, Classes, and Private Students. By ACHILLE MOTTEAU, fcp. 2s. cloth.

SCHOOL AND JUVENILE BOOKS

FOR NURSERY OR MATERNAL TUITION.

ENGLISH.

CHICKSEED WITHOUT CHICKWEED: being very Easy and Entertaining Lessons for Little Children. New Edition, with Frontispiece. 12mo. cloth, 1s.
*** *A book for every mother.*

COBWEBS to CATCH FLIES; or, Dialogues in short sentences, adapted for Children from the age of three to eight years. Part I. Easy Lessons; Part II. Short Stories. Cloth, 2s. complete. *** The Parts separately, 1s. each.

THE FIRST or MOTHER'S DICTIONARY. By Mrs. JAMESON. *Tenth Edition.* 18mo. cloth, 2s. 6d.
*** *Words unsuited for children are omitted, and the definitions given adapted to the infant capacity.*

SCHOOL-ROOM LYRICS. A selection of 143 poems for youthful Readers, compiled and edited by ANNE KNIGHT. New Edition. 18mo. cloth, 1s.

FRENCH.

LA BAGATELLE; intended to introduce Children of five or six years old to some knowledge of the French Language. Revised by Madame N. L. New and improved Edition, with entirely new cuts. 18mo. bound, 2s. 6d.

BARBAULD, LEÇONS pour des ENFANTS de l'Âge de Deux Ans jusqu'à Cinq. Traduites de l'Anglais de Mme. BARBAULD par M. PASQUIER. Suivies des HYMNES en PROSE pour les ENFANTS, traduites de l'Anglais de Mme. BARBAULD par M. CLÉMENCE. Nouvelle Edition, le tout revu par CLOTILDE NORRIS. Avec un Vocabulaire complet Français-Anglais. 18mo. cloth, 2s.

BARBAULD, HYMNES EN PROSE, pour les Enfants, traduites de l'Anglaise par M. Clémence. 18mo. limp, 1s.

GERMAN.

THE LITTLE SCHOLAR'S FIRST STEP in the GERMAN LANGUAGE. By Mrs. FALCK LEBAHN. 18mo. cloth, 1s.

THE LITTLE SCHOLAR'S FIRST STEP in GERMAN READING. Containing Fifty Short Moral Tales from CHRISTOPH VON SCHMID, with Notes and Vocabulary. By Mrs. FALCK LEBAHN. 18mo. cloth, 1s.

PUBLISHED BY LOCKWOOD & CO.   7

EVENTS to be REMEMBERED in the HISTORY of ENGLAND. A Series of Interesting Narratives of the most Remarkable Occurrences in each Reign. By CHARLES SELBY. *Twenty-sixth Edition*, 12mo. fine paper, with 9 beautiful Illustrations by Anelay, 3s. 6d. cloth elegant, gilt edges.

A SCHOOL EDITION, without the Illustrations, cloth, 2s. 6d.

⁎ *Great care has been taken to render this book unobjectionable to the most fastidious, by excluding everything that could not be read aloud in schools and families, and by abstinence from all party spirit, alike in politics as in religion.*

THE HISTORICAL FINGER-POST: a Handy Book of Terms, Phrases, Epithets, Cognomens, Allusions, &c. in connection with Universal History. By EDWARD SHELTON, Assistant Editor of 'The Dictionary of Daily Wants,' &c. *Cheaper Edition*, 1 vol. crown 8vo. cloth, 2s. 6d.

TOMKINS' POETRY.—POETRY for SCHOOLS and FAMILIES; or, the Beauties of English Poetry. Selected for the Use of Youth. By E. TOMKINS. *Twenty-second Edition*, with considerable Additions and fine Steel Frontispiece. Fcp. 8vo. cloth, 2s. 6d.; gilt edges, 3s.

THE ART of EXTEMPORE SPEAKING: Hints for the Pulpit, the Senate, and the Bar. By M. BAUTAIN, Vicar-General and Professor at the Sorbonne, &c. Translated from the French. *Fifth Edition*, fcp. cloth, 3s. 6d.

WHEN to DOUBLE YOUR CONSONANTS. See the WRITER'S ENCHIRIDION, a List of all the Verbs that Double their Consonants on taking ED, EST, ING, &c. By J. S. SCARLETT. 18mo. cloth limp, 1s.

MIND YOUR H's and TAKE CARE of YOUR R's. Exercises for Acquiring the Use and Correcting the Abuse of the Letter H; with Additional Exercises on the Letter R. By CHAS. WM. SMITH, Author of 'Clerical Elocution,' &c. Fcp. cloth limp, 1s.

THE YOUNG REPORTER: a Practical Guide to the Art and the Profession of Shorthand Writing, with a Dictionary of Latin Quotations, &c. Fcp. cloth, 1s.

SCHOOL AND JUVENILE BOOKS

THINGS NOT GENERALLY KNOWN FAMILIARLY EXPLAINED. By JOHN TIMBS. *New Edition*, in 4 double volumes (VOL. I. General Information; VOL. II. Curiosities of Science; VOL. III. Curiosities of History, and Popular Errors Explained; VOL. IV. Notable Things, and Things to be Remembered), either cloth elegant or strongly half-bound, gilt backs, 20s.

'A remarkably pleasant and instructive book; a book to take a bite of now and then, and always with a relish; as full of information as a pomegranate is full of seed.'—*Punch*.

⁎ *The above are sold separately, price 5s. each, and in Single Volumes as follows:—*

GENERAL INFORMATION. 2 vols. 2s. 6d. each, cloth.
CURIOSITIES of SCIENCE. 2 vols. 2s. 6d. each, cloth.
CURIOSITIES of HISTORY; POPULAR ERRORS EXPLAINED. 2 vols. 2s. 6d. each, cloth.
NOTABLE THINGS; THINGS TO BE REMEMBERED. 2 vols. 2s. 6d. each, cloth.

TRUTHS ILLUSTRATED BY GREAT AUTHORS; A Dictionary of nearly Four Thousand Aids to Reflection, Quotations of Maxims, Metaphors, Counsels, Cautions, Proverbs, Aphorisms, &c. &c. In Prose and Verse. Compiled from the Great Writers of all Ages and Countries. Fourteenth Edition, fcp. 8vo. cloth, gilt edges, pp. 568, 5s.

'The quotations are perfect gems; their selection evinces sound judgment and an excellent taste.'—*Dispatch*.

'We accept the treasure with profound gratitude—it should find its way to every home.'—*Era*.

THE FABLES of BABRIUS: Translated into English Verse, from the Text of Sir G. CORNEWALL LEWIS, by the Rev. JAMES DAVIES, Lincoln College, Oxford. Fcp. cloth antique, 6s.

'"Who was Babrius?" The reply may not improbably startle the reader. Babrius was the real original Æsop.'—*Daily News*.

THE POCKET ENGLISH CLASSICS. 32mo. neatly printed, bound in cloth, lettered, price 6d. each:—

The Vicar of Wakefield	Scott's Lady of the Lake
Goldsmith's Poetical Works	Scott's Lay of the Last Minstrel
Falconer's Shipwreck	Walton's Angler, 2 Parts, 1s.
Rasselas	Elizabeth; or, the Exiles
Sterne's Sentimental Journey	Cowper's Task
Locke on the Understanding	Pope's Essay and Blair's Grave
Thomson's Seasons	Gray and Collins
Inchbald's Nature and Art	Gay's Fables
Bloomfield's Farmer's Boy	Paul and Virginia

THE LAWGIVER OF THE PLAYGROUND.

THE BOY'S OWN BOOK: a Complete Encyclopædia of Sports and Pastimes, Athletic, Scientific, and Recreative. *A New and greatly enlarged Edition*, including the Newest Games and Amusements; with more than 600 Illustrations (many of them quite new), 10 Vignette Titles printed in Gold, and over 700 pages. Handsomely bound in cloth, 8s. 6d.; or in French morocco, gilt edges, 12s.

PRINCIPAL CONTENTS.

MINOR SPORTS: Games with Marbles—with Tops—with Balls—Indian Ball Game—Sports of Agility and Speed—Miscellaneous Outdoor Sports—Indoor Sports—Sports with Toys.

DRAWING-ROOM GAMES: Minor Games—Shadow Pantomimes—Bouts Rimés—Definitions—Forfeits—Acting Charades—Acting Proverbs—Tableaux Vivants, &c.

ATHLETIC SPORTS: Cricket—Golf—Football—Croquet—Troco—Hockey—Rackets and Fives—Tennis and Pallone—Quoits, Bowls, Skittles, &c.—Aunt Sally—Fencing—Broadsword and Single-stick—Archery—Riding—Driving—Gymnastics—Boxing and Wrestling, &c.

AQUATIC SPORTS: Angling, Sea Fishing—Swimming—Rowing—Canoeing—Sailing—Skating—Sliding—Curling, &c.

THE NATURALIST: Singing Birds—Talking Birds—Poultry-Yard—Pigeons—Rabbits—Guinea-pigs—Dogs—Cats—Squirrels—White Mice—Silkworms—Bees—Aquarium, &c.

SCIENTIFIC RECREATIONS Arithmetical Amusements—Magnetism—Electricity—Galvanism and Electro-Magnetism—Chemistry—Fireworks—Aërostatic Amusements—Acoustics and Pneumatics—Optics—The Microscope—The Telescope—Photography, &c.

GAMES OF SKILL: Chess—Draughts—Backgammon—Dominoes—Solitaire—Bagatelle—Billiards—Minor Games, &c.

LEGERDEMAIN, &c.: Simple Deceptions and Easy Tricks—Tricks with Money—with Cards—Feats requiring Special Apparatus or Confederacy—Paradoxes and Puzzles, &c.

APPENDIX: **The** *Young Velocipedist—The American National Game, Base Ball—La Crosse, the Canadian Game.*

'Not one amongst its rivals—not half-a-dozen of them rolled into one—can match our old favourite.... It is still peerless!... More truly than ever the lawgiver of the playground.'—*Sun*.

'"The Boy's Own Book" has had many imitators, but they have been but puny counterfeits, and the new edition just issued may bid defiance to them all. Brought up to the present day, it is "itself alone" THE *book for boys*.'—*Bailey's Magazine of Sports*.

'"The Boy's Own Book" is still *the* book which English lads take most delight in, and read with the greatest interest. It stands alone, and is likely to stand alone for many generations to come, as the young Briton's treasury of pleasant, instructive, and entertaining knowledge.'—*Civil Service Gazette*.

SCHOOL AND JUVENILE BOOKS

'MANY HAPPY RETURNS of the DAY!' A Birthday Book for Boys and Girls. By CHARLES and MARY COWDEN CLARKE, Authors of the 'Concordance to Shakspeare,' &c. *Second Edition.* Profusely illustrated by the Brothers DALZIEL and others. Post 8vo. with illuminated cloth binding, gilt edges, 6s.

'Mr. and Mrs. Clarke have here invited all our "big little people" to a grand conversazione. Who will not desire to partake of the enjoyment offered by such hosts?'—*Athenæum.*

'A very charming little book. . . . . The volume does not contain a chapter from which something may not be learnt, and as we had every right to expect, from the names upon its title-page, it evinces a vast amount of elegant and discursive reading. We can strongly and conscientiously recommend it to those parents and friends who, in making a present, consult not only the gratification, but also the benefit of the recipients, who will, we feel assured, at any season, on receiving it, mentally wish themselves "Many Happy Returns of the Day!"'—*Literary Gazette.*

'An unobjectionable child's book is the rarest of all books. "Many Happy Returns of the Day!" is not only this, but may rely, without shrinking, upon its positive excellences for a long and deserved popularity.'—*Westminster Review.*

MERRY TALES for LITTLE FOLK. Edited by Madame DE CHATELAIN. Illustrated with more than Two Hundred Pictures. Cloth gilt, price 3s. 6d.; gilt edges, 4s. Containing—

The House that Jack Built—Little Bo-Peep—The Old Woman and her Eggs—Old Mother Goose—Cock Robin—Old Mother Hubbard—Henny Penny—The Three Bears—The Ugly Little Duck—The White Cat—The Charmed Fawn—The Eleven Wild Swans—The Blue Bird—Little Maia—Jack the Giant Killer—Jack and the Bean Stalk—Sir Guy of Warwick—Tom Hickathrift—Bold Robin Hood—Tom Thumb—Puss in Boots—Little Red Riding-Hood—Little Dame Crump—Little Goody Two Shoes—The Sleeping Beauty in the Wood—The Fairy One with Golden Locks—Beauty and the Beast—Cinderella—Princess Rosetta—The Elves of the Fairy Forest—The Elfin Plough—The Nine Mountains—Johnny and Lisbeth—The Little Fisher Boy—Hans in Luck—The Giant and the Brave Little Tailor—Peter the Goatherd—Red Jacket; or, The Nose Tree—The Three Golden Hairs—The Jew in the Bramble Bush.

'A charming collection of favourite stories.'—*Athenæum.*

'A comfortable, pretty and charmingly illustrated volume, which ought to be placed in every nursery by Act of Parliament.'—*Aunt Judy's Magazine.*

'All good uncles and aunts—all dear grandfathers and grandmothers—as you wish to contribute to the happiness of the little darlings who love you, take with you, on your next visit, these "Merry Tales for Little Folk."'—*Lady's Own Paper.*

PUBLISHED BY LOCKWOOD & CO.   11

THE BOY'S HOME BOOK of SPORTS, GAMES, EXERCISES and PURSUITS. By Writers of 'THE BOY'S OWN MAGAZINE.' Beautifully printed on toned paper, with Two Hundred Engravings, and Coloured Frontispiece and Title. Cloth elegant, gilt edges, 2s. 6d.

CONTENTS: In-door Games—The Playground—Football—Hockey—Golf—Croquet—Cricket—Skittles—Quoits—Bowles—Running and Walking—Gymnastics—Fencing—Archery—Angling—Swimming—Rowing—Skating—Riding—Driving—Chess—Draughts—Dominoes—Singing and Talking Birds—The Poultry Yard—Rabbits—Dogs—Bees—Silkworms—Gold and Silver Fish, &c. &c.

'It is a charming little volume, especially suited for holiday times, and full of information healthful to mind and body.'—*Civil Service Gazette.*

THE WAY to WIN: a Story of Adventure, Afloat and Ashore. By CHARLES A. BEACH, Author of 'Lost Lenore,' 'Ran Away from Home,' &c. With full-page Engravings, cloth elegant, 3s. 6d.

'A delightful work to read, with a good moral.'—*Rock.*

'We have seldom read a book which has pleased us more than this. The subject matter is extremely interesting, the moral running through it is excellent, the style in which it is written is at once manly and simple, and the work, as a whole, is eminently instructive.'—*Civil Service Gazette.*

CAST AWAY on the AUCKLAND ISLES; a Narrative of the Wreck of the 'Grafton,' and of the Escape of the Crew, after Twenty Months' Suffering. From the Private Journals of Captain THOMAS MUSGRAVE. Edited by JOHN J. SHILLINGLAW, F.R.G.S. Post 8vo. with Portrait and Sketch Map, 3s. 6d.

The *Times'* Correspondent says that Captain Musgrave's Diary is almost as interesting as Daniel Defoe, besides being, as the children say, "all true."'

'A more interesting book of travels and privation has not appeared since "Robinson Crusoe;" and it has this advantage over the work of fiction, that it is a fact.'—*Observer.*

'Captain Musgrave has added another name to the muster-roll of those who prosper by self-help. He fully deserves a place in Mr. Smiles's volume.'—*Saturday Review.*

A MANUAL of SWIMMING; including Bathing, Plunging, Diving, Floating, Scientific Swimming, and Training; with a Chapter on Drowning, Rescuing, &c. By CHARLES STEEDMAN, several years Champion Swimmer of Victoria. With Thirty-one Illustrations. Fcp. cloth, 3s. 6d.

'The most complete work of the kind we have seen, and we have every confidence in recommending it.'—*Educational Times.*

SCHOOL AND JUVENILE BOOKS

SCHOOL-DAYS of EMINENT MEN. Containing School and College Lives of the most celebrated British Authors, Poets, and Philosophers; Inventors and Discoverers; Divines, Heroes, Statesmen, &c. By JOHN TIMBS. *Second Edition.* Frontispiece by John Gilbert, 13 views of public schools, and 20 Portraits by Harvey. Fcp. price 3s. 6d. cloth.

'A book to interest all boys, but more especially those of Westminster, Eton, Harrow, Rugby, and Winchester; for of these, as of many other schools of high repute, the accounts are full and interesting.'—*Notes and Queries.*

'A most amusing volume, and will be a most acceptable present to any schoolboy ambitious of figuring in a future edition as one of England's "Eminent Men."'—*Gentleman's Magazine.*

STORIES of INVENTORS and DISCOVERERS in SCIENCE and the USEFUL ARTS. By JOHN TIMBS. *Second Edition.* Many illustrations, price 3s. 6d. cloth.

'Another interesting and well-collected book, ranging from Archimedes and Roger Bacon to the Stephensons.'—*Athenæum.*

'These stories by Mr. Timbs are as marvellous as the "Arabian Nights' Entertainments," and are wrought into a volume of great interest and worth.'—*Atlas.*

BEST EDITION OF LAMB'S TALES FROM SHAKESPEARE.

TALES from SHAKESPEARE. Designed for the Use of Young Persons. By CHARLES and MARY LAMB. 15th Edition, with Steel Portrait and Twenty beautiful full-page engravings, by HARVEY. Fcp. 8vo. extra cloth gilt, price 3s. 6d.; gilt edges, 4s.

COMPANION VOLUME TO LAMB'S TALES.

TALES from CHAUCER, in PROSE. With a Memorial of the Poet. Designed chiefly for the Use of Young Persons. By CHARLES COWDEN CLARKE, Author of 'The Riches of Chaucer,' 'Shakespeare Characters,' &c. New and revised Edition, with Twelve full-page engravings Fcp. 8vo. extra cloth gilt, price 3s. 6d.; gilt edges, 4s.

'For intelligent young folk a pleasanter, and at the same time more profitable gift, it would be hard to desire, than the Prose "Tales from Chaucer."'—*Daily Telegraph.*

'Mr. Clarke has done that for Chaucer which Charles and Mary Lamb did for Shakespeare. The quaint old Stories, with their digressions and entanglements and disfigurements, have been taken in hand by him, and are here presented thoroughly purged from their impurities, and newly dressed.'—*City Press.*

PUBLISHED BY LOCKWOOD & CO.

RIDDLES in RHYME: a Book of Enigmas, Charades, Conundrums, &c., with Answers. Edited by EDMUND SYER FULCHER. In cloth extra, gilt edges, 2s. 6d.

DOUBLE ACROSTICS. By various Authors. Edited by K. L. *Second Edition*, revised and enlarged. In cloth extra, gilt edges, price 2s. 6d.

DO YOU GIVE IT UP? A Collection of the most amusing Conundrums, Riddles, &c. of the Day, with Answers. *Second Edition*. In cloth limp, lettered, price 1s.

BEETON'S BOOK of ANECDOTE, WIT, and HUMOUR: being a Collection of Wise and Witty Things in Prose and Verse: together with a Selection of Curious Epitaphs. *Fourth Edition*, in coloured wrapper, price 1s.

BEETON'S BOOK of JOKES and JESTS; or, Good Things Said and Sung. *Second Edition*, in coloured wrapper, price 1s.

GOOD THINGS for RAILWAY READERS. One Thousand Anecdotes, original and selected. By the Editor of 'The Railway Anecdote Book.' Large type, crown 8vo. with Frontispiece, price 2s. 6d.

'A capital collection, and will certainly become a favourite with all railway readers.'—*Reader*.
'Fresh, racy, and original.'—*John Bull*.

THE LAWS and BYE-LAWS of GOOD SOCIETY: a Code of Modern Etiquette. 32mo. neatly bound, price 6d.

THE ART of DRESSING WELL: a Book of Hints on the Choice of Colours to suit the Complexion and the Hair; with the Theory and Practice of the Art of Dress, &c. 32mo. neatly bound, price 6d.

'Two pretty little volumes for those who have the privilege of entering into society, but are unacquainted with its forms.'—*Sunday Times*.
'These little books are superior to those usually published on similar subjects; they are gems in their way.'—*Civil Service Gazette*.

A TRAP to CATCH a SUNBEAM. Fortieth Edition, price 9*d*. cloth ; or in coloured wrapper, 6*d*.

> '*Aide toi, et le ciel l'aidera*, is the moral of this pleasant and interesting story, to which we assign in this Gazette a place immediately after Charles Dickens, as its due, for many passages not unworthy of him, and for a general scheme quite in unison with his best feelings towards the lowly and depressed.'—*Literary Gazette*.

Also, by the same Author, each cloth lettered, price 9*d*. ; *or in Coloured Wrapper,* 6*d*. :—

MARRIED and SETTLED.
'COMING HOME;' a New Tale for all Readers.
OLD JOLLIFFE ; not a Goblin Story.
The SEQUEL to OLD JOLLIFFE.
The HOUSE on the ROCK.
'ONLY ;' a Tale for Young and Old.
The CLOUD with the SILVER LINING.
The STAR in the DESERT.
AMY'S KITCHEN, a VILLAGE ROMANCE.
'A MERRY CHRISTMAS.'

SUNBEAM STORIES. A selection of the Tales by the Author of 'A Trap to Catch a Sunbeam,' &c. Illustrated by Absolon and Anelay. FIRST SERIES. Contents :—A Trap to Catch a Sunbeam—Old Jolliffe—The Sequel to Old Jolliffe—The Star in the Desert—'Only'—'A Merry Christmas.' Fcp. cloth elegant, 3*s*. 6*d*.

Uniform with the above :—

SUNBEAM STORIES. SECOND SERIES. Illustrated by Absolon and Anelay. Contents :—The Cloud with the Silver Lining—Coming Home—Amy's Kitchen—The House on the Rock. Fcp. cloth elegant, 3*s*. 6*d*.

SUNBEAM STORIES. THIRD SERIES. Illustrated by James Godwin, &c. Contents :—The Dream Chintz—Sibert's Wold ; or, Cross Purposes. Fcp. cloth elegant, 3*s*. 6*d*.

SUNBEAM STORIES. FOURTH SERIES. Contents :—Minnie's Love, and the New Tale, Married and Settled. Illustrated with four full-page Engravings. Fcp. cloth elegant, 3*s*. 6*d*.

THE BIBLE OPENED for CHILDREN. In Two Series. Comprising numerous Stories from the Old and New Testament. By MARY BRADFORD. Illustrated with Twelve full-page Engravings by DALZIEL Brothers. Small crown 8vo. cloth, price 2s. 6d.

'The stories of the lives and adventures of Scriptural characters are herein simply told, and all those parents who feel the impossibility of giving children of tender years the Bible to read, may overcome the difficulty they have in conveying to their minds the facts of the sacred narrative by consulting this neat little volume, which is adequately illustrated by the famous Dalziels.'—*Weekly Dispatch.*

'The writer of this book has made a successful attempt to relate several of the principle narratives embodied in the Old and New Testaments, in simple language, and in an easy style, suited to the comprehension of young children, who are thereby led to gain a more intimate acquaintance with the principal events in Bible history than they would if they had read them for the first time in the Bible itself.'—*Bookseller.*

LITTLE SUNSHINE: a Tale to be Read to very Young Children. By the Author of 'A Trap to Catch a Sunbeam.' In square 16mo. coloured borders, engraved Frontispiece and Vignette, fancy boards, price 2s.

'Just the thing to rivet the attention of children.'—*Stamford Mercury.*

'Printed in the sumptuous manner that children like best.'—*Bradford Observer.*

'As pleasing a child's book as we recollect seeing.'—*Plymouth Herald.*

SIDNEY GREY: a Tale of School Life. By the Author of 'Mia and Charlie.' *Second Edition*, with 6 beautiful Illustrations. Fcp. cloth, 3s. 6d.

SIBERT'S WOLD; or, Cross Purposes. A Tale. By the Author of 'A Trap to Catch a Sunbeam,' &c. &c. *Third Edition*, cloth limp, 2s.

THE DREAM CHINTZ. By the Author of 'A Trap to Catch a Sunbeam,' &c. With Illustrations by JAMES GODWIN. *Second Edition*, in appropriate fancy cover, cloth, 2s. 6d.

'We take leave of this little book with unfeigned regret. Its whole spirit and tendency is to purify, strengthen, console: to make us contented with our lot; to lead us never to doubt Almighty mercy, nor to relax in our own proper exertions; to be kind and charitable to our fellow-creatures, and to despise none, since none are created in vain; to hope, believe, love here, as we desire hereafter to meet again the loved ones who have gone before into "the beautiful country."'—*Literary Gazette.*

BOHN'S MINIATURE LIBRARY.

A Series of elegantly-printed Pocket Volumes, each containing a fine Steel Frontispiece or Portrait, and bound in best red cloth, gilt back and sides.

BARBAULD and AIKIN'S EVENINGS at HOME. 2s. 6d.

BOURRIENNE'S MEMOIRS of NAPOLEON. 3s. 6d.

BYRON'S POETICAL WORKS, with Life by H. LYTTON BULWER. 3s. 6d.

BUNYAN'S PILGRIM'S PROGRESS, with a Life and Notes. Frontispiece, and 25 full-size Woodcuts. 3s. 6d.

CHEEVER'S LECTURES on BUNYAN'S PILGRIM'S PROGRESS, and the Life and Times of Bunyan. 2s. 6d.

COLERIDGE'S SELECT POETICAL WORKS. 2s.

COWPER'S POETICAL WORKS, with all the Copyright Poems, and a Short Life by SOUTHEY. 3s. 6d.

DRYDEN'S POETICAL WORKS. 3s. 6d.

ENCYCLOPÆDIA of MANNERS and ETIQUETTE, comprising Chesterfield's Advice, &c. 2s.

HEBER'S (Bp.), HEMANS' (Mrs.), and RADCLIFFE'S (Ann) POETICAL WORKS. 3 Vols. in 1. 2s. 6d.

HERRICK'S POETICAL WORKS. 2s. 6d.

MILTON'S POETICAL WORKS, Complete. With Life by Dr. STEBBING. 3s. 6d.

OSSIAN'S POEMS. Translated by MACPHERSON. 2s. 6d.

POPE'S HOMER'S ILIAD, with Notes and Index. 3s.

SCOTT'S POETICAL WORKS. 3s. 6d.

STURM'S REFLECTIONS on the WORKS of GOD. 3s.

THOMSON'S SEASONS, with his CASTLE of INDOLENCE. With 4 fine Woodcuts by HARVEY. 2s.

VATHEK and the AMBER WITCH. 2s. 6d.

Spottiswoode & Co., Printers, New-street Square, London.

www.ingramcontent.com/pod-product-compliance
Lightning Source LLC
Chambersburg PA
CBHW021419300426
44114CB00010B/559